D1452057

THE BOOK OF DISCIPLINE
OF
THE UNITED METHODIST CHURCH

"The Book Editor, the Secretary of the General Conference, the Publisher of The United Methodist Church and the Committee on Correlation and Editorial Revision shall be charged with editing the *Book of Discipline*. . . . The editors, in the exercise of their judgment, shall have the authority to make changes in wording as may be necessary to harmonize legislation without changing its substance. The editors, in consultation with the Judicial Council, shall also have authority to delete provisions of the *Book of Discipline* that have been ruled unconstitutional by the Judicial Council."
—Plan of Organization and Rules of Order of the General Conference, 2016

See Judicial Council Decision 96, which declares the *Discipline* to be a book of law.

Errata can be found at Cokesbury.com, word search for *Errata*.

L. Fitzgerald Reist
Secretary of the General Conference

Brian K. Milford
President and Publisher
Book Editor of The United Methodist Church

Brian O. Sigmon
Managing Editor

The Committee on Correlation and Editorial Revision
Naomi G. Bartle, Co-chair
Robert Burkhart, Co-chair
Maidstone Mulenga, Secretary
Melissa Drake
Paul Fleck
Karen Ristine
Dianne Wilkinson
Brian Williams

Alternates:
Susan Hunn
Beth Rambikur

THE BOOK OF DISCIPLINE
OF
THE UNITED
METHODIST CHURCH

2016

The United Methodist Publishing House
Nashville, Tennessee

ISBN 978-1-501-83321-2

USB Flash Drive (with *Book of Resolutions*) ISBN 978-1-501-83328-1
2-PACK Discipline and Resolutions ISBN 978-1-501-83327-4
Discipline eBook ISBN 978-1-501-83322-9
Korean Edition ISBN 978-1-501-83331-1
Spanish Edition ISBN 978-1-501-83329-8

16 17 18 19 20 21 22 23 24 25—10 9 8 7 6 5 4 3 2 1

PRINTED IN THE UNITED STATES OF AMERICA

EPISCOPAL GREETINGS

To all people and pastors of United Methodism:
"Grace and peace to you from God our Father and the Lord
Jesus Christ."

—1 Corinthians 1:3

The Book of Discipline of The United Methodist Church is the
product of over two hundred years of the General Conferences of
the denominations that now form The United Methodist Church.

The *Discipline* as the instrument for setting forth the laws,
plan, polity, and process by which United Methodists govern
themselves remains constant. Each General Conference amends,
perfects, clarifies, and adds its own contribution to the *Discipline*.
We do not see the *Discipline* as sacrosanct or infallible, but we do
consider it a document suitable to our heritage and an expression of a future with hope. It is the most current statement of how
United Methodists agree to live their lives together and "maintain
the unity of the Spirit in the bond of peace." It reflects our understanding of the church and articulates the mission of The United
Methodist Church: To make disciples of Jesus Christ for the transformation of the world. The *Discipline* defines what is expected
of its laity and clergy as they seek to be effective witnesses in the
world as a part of the whole body of Christ.

This book of covenant sets forth the theological grounding of
The United Methodist Church in biblical faith and affirms that
we go forward as "loyal heirs to all that [is] best in the Christian past." It makes clear that The United Methodist Church is an
inclusive society without regard to ethnic origin, economic condition, gender, age, or the disabilities of its constituents. It asserts
that all who are baptized and confirmed are ministers of Jesus

Christ. It affirms the conciliar principle and connectionalism as distinctive marks of United Methodist ecclesiology, makes clear the global character of the Church's mission, and declares interdependence with other Christian bodies both in spirit and cooperation. It affirms with John Wesley that solitary religion is invalid and that Christ lays claim upon the whole life of those who accept him as Lord and Savior.

We therefore commend this *Discipline* to all in our constituency and to friends beyond our bounds who would seek to understand what it means to be a United Methodist. Communication is essential for understanding what the Church is and does. We expect the *Discipline* to be found in libraries of local churches, colleges, universities, and seminaries, as well as in the homes of ordained, diaconal, and licensed ministers and lay members of The United Methodist Church. We pray that it will enable all persons to celebrate God's grace, exalt the meaning of faithful discipleship, align with the mission, and inspire on the part of many a deeper desire to be more effective witnesses for the head of the church, even Jesus Christ our Lord.

The Council of Bishops
Bruce R. Ough, President
Kenneth H. Carter, President-Designate
Cynthia Fierro Harvey, Secretary

CONTENTS

Note: The basic unit in *The Book of Discipline* is the paragraph (¶) rather than page, chapter, or section. The paragraphs are numbered consecutively within each chapter or section, but many numbers are skipped between parts, chapters, and sections in order to allow for future enactments and to fit with the following plan:

PART I
THE CONSTITUTION
¶¶ 1–61

CONTENTS

PART II
GENERAL BOOK OF DISCIPLINE
¶ 101

PART III
DOCTRINAL STANDARDS
AND OUR THEOLOGICAL TASK
¶¶ 102–105

PART IV
THE MINISTRY OF ALL CHRISTIANS
¶¶ 120–143

CONTENTS

Chapter Two
THE MINISTRY OF THE ORDAINED

CONTENTS

Chapter Five
ADMINISTRATIVE ORDER

Chapter Six
CHURCH PROPERTY

CONTENTS

Chapter Seven
JUDICIAL ADMINISTRATION

UNITED METHODIST BISHOPS

A List Compiled for The Book of Discipline
by the Council of Bishops

NAME	ELECTED	NAME	ELECTED
Thomas Coke	1784	David Edwards	1849
Francis Asbury	1784	Henry Bidleman Bascom	1850
Richard Whatcoat	1800	Levi Scott	1852
Phillip William Otterbein	1800	Matthew Simpson	1852
Martin Boehm	1800	Osman Cleander Baker	1852
Jacob Albright	1807	Edward Raymond Ames	1852
William M'Kendree	1808	Lewis Davis	1853
Christian Newcomer	1813	George Foster Pierce	1854
Enoch George	1816	John Early	1854
Robert Richford Roberts	1816	Hubbard Hinde	
Andrew Zeller	1817	Kavanaugh	1854
Joseph Hoffman	1821	Francis Burns	1858
Joshua Soule	1824	William W. Orwig	1859
Elijah Hedding	1824	Jacob Markwood	1861
Henry Kumler Sr.	1825	Daniel Shuck	1861
John Emory	1832	John Jacob Esher	1863
James Osgood Andrew	1832	Davis Wasgatt Clark	1864
Samuel Heistand	1833	Edward Thomson	1864
William Brown	1833	Calvin Kingsley	1864
Beverly Waugh	1836	Jonathan Weaver	1865
Thomas Asbury Morris	1836	William May Wightman	1866
Jacob Erb	1837	Enoch Mather Marvin	1866
John Seybert	1839	David Seth Doggett	1866
Henry Kumler Jr.	1841	Holland Nimmons	
John Coons	1841	McTyeire	1866
Joseph Long	1843	John Wright Roberts	1866
Leonidas Lent Hamline	1844	John Dickson	1869
Edmund Storer Janes	1844	John Christian Keener	1870
John Russel	1845	Reuben Yeakel	1871
Jacob John Glossbrenner	1845	Thomas Bowman	1872
William Hanby	1845	William Logan Harris	1872
William Capers	1846	Randolph Sinks Foster	1872
Robert Paine	1846	Isaac William Wiley	1872

1

NAME	ELECTED	NAME	ELECTED
Stephen Mason Merrill	1872	Wesley Matthias Stanford	1891
Edward Gayer Andrews	1872	Christian S. Haman	1891
Gilbert Haven	1872	Sylvanus C. Breyfogel	1891
Jesse Truesdell Peck	1872	William Horn	1891
Rudolph Dubs	1875	Job S. Mills	1893
Thomas Bowman	1875	Charles Cardwell	
Milton Wright	1877	McCabe	1896
Nicholas Castle	1877	Joseph Crane Hartzell	1896
Henry White Warren	1880	Earl Cranston	1896
Cyrus David Foss	1880	Warren Akin Candler	1898
John Fletcher Hurst	1880	Henry Clay Morrison	1898
Erastus Otis Haven	1880	David Hastings Moore	1900
Ezekiel Boring Kephart	1881	John William Hamilton	1900
Alpheus Waters Wilson	1882	Edwin Wallace Parker	1900
Linus Parker	1882	Francis Wesley Warne	1900
John Cowper Granbery	1882	George Martin Mathews	1902
Robert Kennon		Alexander Coke Smith	1902
Hargrove	1882	Elijah Embree Hoss	1902
William Xavier Ninde	1884	Henry Burns Hartzler	1902
John Morgan Walden	1884	William Franklin Heil	1902
Willard Francis		Joseph Flintoft Berry	1904
Mallalieu	1884	Henry Spellmeyer	1904
Charles Henry Fowler	1884	William Fraser	
William Taylor	1884	McDowell	1904
Daniel Kumler		James Whitford	
Flickinger	1885	Bashford	1904
William Wallace Duncan	1886	William Burt	1904
Charles Betts Galloway	1886	Luther Barton Wilson	1904
Eugene Russell Hendrix	1886	Thomas Benjamin Neely	1904
Joseph Stanton Key	1886	Isaiah Benjamin Scott	1904
John Heyl Vincent	1888	William Fitzjames	
James Newbury		Oldham	1904
FitzGerald	1888	John Edward Robinson	1904
Isaac Wilson Joyce	1888	Merriman Colbert Harris	1904
John Philip Newman	1888	William Marion Weekley	1905
Daniel Ayres Goodsell	1888	William Melvin Bell	1905
James Mills Thoburn	1888	Thomas Coke Carter	1905
James W. Hott	1889	John James Tigert III	1906
Atticus Greene Haygood	1890	Seth Ward	1906
Oscar Penn Fitzgerald	1890	James Atkins	1906

NAME	ELECTED	NAME	ELECTED
Samuel P. Spreng	1907	Adna Wright Leonard	1916
William Franklin Anderson	1908	Matthew Simpson Hughes	1916
John Louis Nuelsen	1908	Charles Bayard Mitchell	1916
William Alfred Quayle	1908	Franklin Elmer Ellsworth Hamilton	1916
Charles William Smith	1908		
Wilson Seeley Lewis	1908	Alexander Priestly Camphor	1916
Edwin Holt Hughes	1908	Eben Samuel Johnson	1916
Robert McIntyre	1908	William H. Washinger	1917
Frank Milton Bristol	1908	John Monroe Moore	1918
Collins Denny	1910	William Fletcher McMurry	1918
John Carlisle Kilgo	1910		
William Belton Murrah	1910	Urban Valentine Williams Darlington	1918
Walter Russell Lambuth	1910		
Richard Green Waterhouse	1910	Horace Mellard DuBose	1918
Edwin DuBose Mouzon	1910	William Newman Ainsworth	1918
James Henry McCoy	1910		
William Hargrave Fouke	1910	James Cannon, Jr.	1918
Uriah Frantz Swengel	1910	Matthew T. Maze	1918
Homer Clyde Stuntz	1912	Lauress John Birney	1920
William Orville Shepard	1912	Frederick Bohn Fisher	1920
Theodore Sommers Henderson	1912	Charles Edward Locke	1920
		Ernest Lynn Waldorf	1920
Naphtali Luccock	1912	Edgar Blake	1920
Francis John McConnell	1912	Ernest Gladstone Richardson	1920
Frederick DeLand Leete	1912		
Richard Joseph Cooke	1912	Charles Wesley Burns	1920
Wilbur Patterson Thirkield	1912	Harry Lester Smith	1920
		George Harvey Bickley	1920
John Wesley Robinson	1912	Frederick Thomas Keeney	1920
William Perry Eveland	1912		
Henry Harness Fout	1913	Charles Larew Mead	1920
Cyrus Jeffries Kephart	1913	Anton Bast	1920
Alfred Taylor Howard	1913	Robert Elijah Jones	1920
Gottlieb Heinmiller	1915	Matthew Wesley Clair	1920
Lawrence Hoover Seager	1915	Arthur R. Clippinger	1921
		William Benjamin Beauchamp	1922
Herbert Welch	1916		
Thomas Nicholson	1916	James Edward Dickey	1922

NAME	ELECTED	NAME	ELECTED
Samuel Ross Hay	1922	John McKendree Springer	1936
Hoyt McWhorter Dobbs	1922	F. H. Otto Melle	1936
Hiram Abiff Boaz	1922	Ralph Ansel Ward	1937
John Francis Dunlap	1922	Victor Otterbein Weidler	1938
George Amos Miller	1924	Ivan Lee Holt	1938
Titus Lowe	1924	William Walter Peele	1938
George Richmond Grose	1924	Clare Purcell	1938
Brenton Thoburn Badley	1924	Charles Claude Selecman	1938
Wallace Elias Brown	1924	John Lloyd Decell	1938
Arthur Biggs Statton	1925	William Clyde Martin	1938
John S. Stamm	1926	William Turner Watkins	1938
Samuel J. Umbreit	1926	James Henry Straughn	1939
Raymond J. Wade	1928	John Calvin Broomfield	1939
James Chamberlain Baker	1928	William Alfred Carroll Hughes	1940
Edwin Ferdinand Lee	1928	Lorenzo Houston King	1940
Grant D. Batdorf	1929	Bruce Richard Baxter	1940
Ira David Warner	1929	Shot Kumar Mondol	1940
John W. Gowdy	1930	Clement Daniel Rockey	1941
Chih Ping Wang	1930	Enrique Carlos Balloch	1941
Arthur James Moore	1930	Z. T. Kaung	1941
Paul Bentley Kern	1930	Wen Yuan Chen	1941
Angie Frank Smith	1930	George Carleton Lacy	1941
George Edward Epp	1930	Fred L. Dennis	1941
Joshwant Rao Chitamber	1930	Dionisio Deista Alejandro	1944
Juan Ermete Gattinoni	1932	Fred Pierce Corson	1944
Junius Ralph Magee	1932	Walter Earl Ledden	1944
Ralph Spaulding Cushman	1932	Lewis Oliver Hartman	1944
Elmer Wesley Praetorius	1934	Newell Snow Booth	1944
Charles H. Stauffacher	1934	Willis Jefferson King	1944
Jarrell Waskom Pickett	1935	Robert Nathaniel Brooks	1944
Roberto Valenzuela Elphick	1936	Edward Wendall Kelly	1944
Wilbur Emery Hammaker	1936	William Angie Smith	1944
Charles Wesley Flint	1936	Paul Elliott Martin	1944
Garfield Bromley Oxnam	1936	Costen Jordan Harrell	1944
Alexander Preston Shaw	1936	Paul Neff Garber	1944

NAME	ELECTED	NAME	ELECTED
Charles Wesley Brashares	1944	Alsie Raymond Grant	1952
Schuyler Edward Garth	1944	Julio Manuel Sabanes	1952
Arthur Frederick Wesley	1944	Friedrich Wunderlich	1953
John Abdus Subhan	1945	Odd Arthur Hagen	1953
John Balmer Showers	1945	Ferdinand Sigg	1954
August Theodor Arvidson	1946	Reuben Herbert Mueller	1954
Johann Wilhelm Ernst Sommer	1946	Harold Rickel Heininger	1954
John Wesley Edward Bowen	1948	Lyle Lynden Baughman	1954
Lloyd Christ Wicke	1948	Prince Albert Taylor Jr.	1956
John Wesley Lord	1948	Eugene Maxwell Frank	1956
Dana Dawson	1948	Nolan Bailey Harmon	1956
Marvin Augustus Franklin	1948	Bachman Gladstone Hodge	1956
Roy Hunter Short	1948	Hobart Baumann Amstutz	1956
Richard Campbell Raines	1948	Ralph Edward Dodge	1956
Marshall Russell Reed	1948	Mangal Singh	1956
Harry Clifford Northcott	1948	Gabriel Sundaram	1956
Hazen Graff Werner	1948	Paul E. V. Shannon	1957
Glenn Randall Phillips	1948	John Gordon Howard	1957
Gerald Hamilton Kennedy	1948	Hermann Walter Kaebnick	1958
Donald Harvey Tippett	1948	W. Maynard Sparks	1958
Jose Labarrete Valencia	1948	Paul Murray Herrick	1958
Sante Uberto Barbieri	1949	Bowman Foster Stockwell	1960
Raymond Leroy Archer	1950	Fred Garrigus Holloway	1960
David Thomas Gregory	1950	William Vernon Middleton	1960
Frederick Buckley Newell	1952	William Ralph Ward Jr.	1960
Edgar Amos Love	1952	James Kenneth Mathews	1960
Matthew Walker Clair	1952	Oliver Eugene Slater	1960
John Warren Branscomb	1952	William Kenneth Pope	1960
Henry Bascom Watts	1952	Paul Vernon Galloway	1960
D. Stanley Coors	1952	Aubrey Grey Walton	1960
Edwin Edgar Voigt	1952	Kenneth Wilford Copeland	1960
Francis Gerald Ensley	1952	Everett Walter Palmer	1960
		Ralph Taylor Alton	1960
		Edwin Ronald Garrison	1960

NAME	ELECTED	NAME	ELECTED
Torney Otto Nall Jr.	1960	Roy Calvin Nichols	1968
Charles Franklin Golden	1960	Arthur James Armstrong	1968
Noah Watson Moore Jr.	1960	William Ragsdale	
Marquis LaFayette		Cannon	1968
Harris	1960	Abel Tendekayi	
James Walton Henley	1960	Muzorewa	1968
Walter Clark Gum	1960	Cornelio M. Ferrer	1968
Paul Hardin Jr.	1960	Paul Locke A.	
John Owen Smith	1960	Granadosin	1968
Paul William Milhouse	1960	Joseph R. Lance	1968
Pedro Ricardo Zottele	1962	Ram Dutt Joshi	1968
James Samuel Thomas	1964	Eric Algernon Mitchell	1969
William McFerrin Stowe	1964	Federico Jose Pagura	1969
Walter Kenneth		Armin E. Härtel	1970
Goodson	1964	Ole Edvard Borgen	1970
Dwight Ellsworth Loder	1964	Finis Alonzo	
Robert Marvin Stuart	1964	Crutchfield Jr.	1972
Edward Julian		Joseph Hughes Yeakel	1972
Pendergrass Jr.	1964	Robert E. Goodrich Jr.	1972
Thomas Marion Pryor	1964	Carl Julian Sanders	1972
Homer Ellis Finger Jr.	1964	Ernest T. Dixon Jr.	1972
Earl Gladstone Hunt Jr.	1964	Don Wendell Holter	1972
Francis Enmer Kearns	1964	Wayne K. Clymer	1972
Lance Webb	1964	Joel Duncan McDavid	1972
Escrivao Anglaze		Edward Gonzalez	
Zunguze	1964	Carroll	1972
Robert Fielden Lundy	1964	Jesse Robert DeWitt	1972
Harry Peter Andreassen	1964	James Mase Ault	1972
John Wesley Shungu	1964	John B. Warman	1972
Alfred Jacob Shaw	1965	Mack B. Stokes	1972
Prabhakar Christopher		Jack Marvin Tuell	1972
Benjamin Balaram	1965	Melvin E. Wheatley Jr.	1972
Stephen Trowen Nagbe	1965	Edward Lewis Tullis	1972
Franz Werner Schäfer	1966	Frank Lewis Robertson	1972
Benjamin I. Guansing	1967	Wilbur Wong Yan Choy	1972
Lineunt Scott Allen	1967	Robert McGrady	
Paul Arthur Washburn	1968	Blackburn	1972
Carl Ernst Sommer	1968	Emilio J. M. de Carvalho	1972
David Frederick Wertz	1968	Fama Onema	1972
Alsie Henry Carleton	1968	Mamidi Elia Peter	1972

NAME	ELECTED	NAME	ELECTED
Bennie de Quency Warner	1973	Felton Edwin May	1984
J. Kenneth Shamblin	1976	Ernest A. Fitzgerald	1984
Alonzo Monk Bryan	1976	R. Kern Eutsler	1984
Kenneth William Hicks	1976	J. Woodrow Hearn	1984
James Chess Lovern	1976	Walter L. Underwood	1984
Leroy Charles Hodapp	1976	Richard B. Wilke	1984
Edsel Albert Ammons	1976	J. Lloyd Knox	1984
C. Dale White	1976	Neil L. Irons	1984
Ngoy Kimba Wakadilo	1976	Roy Isao Sano	1984
Almeida Penicela	1976	Lewis Bevel Jones III	1984
LaVerne D. Mercado	1976	Forrest C. Stith	1984
Hermann Ludwig Sticher	1977	Ernest W. Newman	1984
Shantu Kumar A. Parmar	1979	Woodie W. White	1984
Thomas Syla Bangura	1979	Robert Crawley Morgan	1984
John Alfred Ndoricimpa	1980	David J. Lawson	1984
William Talbot Handy Jr.	1980	Elias Gabriel Galvan	1984
John Wesley Hardt	1980	Rueben Philip Job	1984
Benjamin Ray Oliphint	1980	Leontine T. Kelly	1984
Louis Wesley Schowengerdt	1980	Judith Craig	1984
Melvin George Talbert	1980	Rüdiger Rainer Minor	1986
Paul Andrews Duffey	1980	Jose Castro Gamboa Jr.	1986
Edwin Charles Boulton	1980	Thomas Barber Stockton	1988
John William Russell	1980	Harold Hasbrouck Hughes Jr.	1988
Fitz Herbert Skeete	1980	Richard Carl Looney	1988
George Willis Bashore	1980	Robert Hitchcock Spain	1988
Roy Clyde Clark	1980	Susan Murch Morrison	1988
William Boyd Grove	1980	R. Sheldon Duecker	1988
Emerson Stephen Colaw	1980	Joseph Benjamin Bethea	1988
Marjorie Swank Matthews	1980	William B. Oden	1988
Carlton Printess Minnick Jr.	1980	Bruce P. Blake	1988
Calvin Dale McConnell	1980	Charles Wilbourne Hancock	1988
Kainda Katembo	1980	Clay Foster Lee Jr.	1988
Emerito P. Nacpil	1980	Sharon A. Brown Christopher	1988
Arthur Flumo Kulah	1980	Dan E. Solomon	1988
		William B. Lewis	1988
		William W. Dew Jr.	1988

7

NAME	ELECTED	NAME	ELECTED
Moises Domingos Fernandes	1988	C. Joseph Sprague	1996
Joao Somane Machado	1988	Peter D. Weaver	1996
Walter Klaiber	1989	Jonathan D. Keaton	1996
Heinrich Bolleter	1989	Ray W. Chamberlain, Jr.	1996
Hans Växby	1989	John L. Hopkins	1996
Alfred Lloyd Norris	1992	Michael J. Coyner	1996
Joe Allen Wilson	1992	Edward W. Paup	1996
Robert Eugene Fannin	1992	Ntambo Nkulu Ntanda	1996
Amelia Ann B. Sherer	1992	Larry M. Goodpaster	2000
Albert Frederick Mutti	1992	Rhymes H. Moncure Jr.	2000
Raymond Harold Owen	1992	Beverly J. Shamana	2000
Joel Neftali Martinez	1992	Violet L. Fisher	2000
Donald Arthur Ott	1992	Gregory Vaughn Palmer	2000
Kenneth Lee Carder	1992	William W. Hutchinson	2000
Hae Jong Kim	1992	B. Michael Watson	2000
William Wesley Morris	1992	D. Max Whitfield	2000
Marshall LeRoy Meadors Jr.	1992	Benjamin Roy Chamness	2000
Charles Wesley Jordan	1992	Linda Lee	2000
Sharon Zimmerman Rader	1992	James R. King	2000
S. Clifton Ives	1992	Bruce R. Ough	2000
Mary Ann Swenson	1992	Warner H. Brown Jr.	2000
Done Peter Dabale	1992	José Quipungo	2000
Joseph Humper	1992	Gaspar Joao Domingos	2000
Christopher Jokomo	1992	Leo A. Soriano	2000
Daniel C. Arichea Jr.	1994	Benjamin A. Justo	2000
Benjamin Gutierrez	1994	John G. Innis	2000
G. Lindsey Davis	1996	Øystein Olsen	2001
Joseph E. Pennel Jr.	1996	Timothy W. Whitaker	2001
Charlene Payne Kammerer	1996	Solito K. Toquero	2001
Alfred Johnson	1996	Marcus Matthews	2004
Cornelius L. Henderson	1996	Sudarshana Devadhar	2004
Susan Wolfe Hassinger	1996	Jeremiah J. Park	2004
J. Lawrence McCleskey	1996	Hope Morgan Ward	2004
Ernest S. Lyght	1996	William H. Willimon	2004
Janice Riggle Huie	1996	James E. Swanson Sr	2004
Marion M. Edwards	1996	Hee-Soo Jung	2004
		Robert E. Hayes Jr	2004
		Alfred W. Gwinn Jr	2004
		John R. Schol	2004

NAME	ELECTED	NAME	ELECTED
Richard J. Wills Jr	2004	Christian Alsted	2009
Robert C. Schnase	2004	L. Jonathan Holston	2012
Deborah L. Kiesey	2004	Kenneth H. Carter	2012
Jane Allen Middleton	2004	Sandra Lynn Steiner Ball	2012
Thomas J. Bickerton	2004	William T. McAlilly	2012
Scott J. Jones	2004	Deborah Wallace-Padgett	2012
Charles N. Crutchfield	2004	Martin McLee	2012
Robert T. Hoshibata	2004	Young Jin Cho	2012
Mary Virginia Taylor	2004	Cynthia Fierro Harvey	2012
Sally Dyck	2004	Mark J. Webb	2012
Minerva G. Carcaño	2004	Gary E. Mueller	2012
Eben K. Nhiwatiwa	2004	Michael McKee	2012
Hans Växby	2005	Gabriel Yemba Unda	2012
David K. Yemba	2005	John Wesley Yohanna	2012
Rosemarie J. Wenner	2005	Eduard Khegay	2012
Benjamin Boni	2005	Pedro M. Torio, Jr.	2012
Patrick Ph. Streiff	2005	Ciriaco Q. Francisco	2012
Daniel A. Wandabula	2006	Sharma Lewis	2016
Kefas K. Mavula	2007	David Graves	2016
Paul Lee Leeland	2008	Leonard Fairley	2016
Wilbert Earl Bledsoe	2008	Lawson Bryan	2016
Peggy A. Johnson	2008	Sue Haupert-Johnson	2016
John Michael Lowry	2008	Cynthia Moore-KoiKoi	2016
Julius Calvin Trimble	2008	Tracy Smith Malone	2016
Grant J. Hagiya	2008	Frank Beard	2016
James E. Dorff	2008	David Bard	2016
Elaine J. W. Stanovsky	2008	LaTrelle Easterling	2016
Joaquina Filipe Nhanala	2008	Ruben Saenz	2016
Rodolfo Alfonso Juan	2008	Laurie Haller	2016
Lito Cabacungan Tangonan	2008	James Nunn	2016
John Kpahun Yambasu	2008	Robert Farr	2016
		Karen Oliveto	2016

A BRIEF HISTORY OF THE UNITED METHODIST CHURCH

Ecclesial Heritage

The history of The United Methodist Church includes God's self-revelation and action in history through the call of Abraham, the Hebrew exodus from Egypt, and especially the incarnation, life, death, and resurrection of God's Word Jesus Christ, and the outpouring of the Holy Spirit at Pentecost. The United Methodist Church shares this history with the whole church, as contained in the canonical Scriptures.

In the early 1500s, various reform movements emerged in Western Europe that created forms of western Christianity not in communion with the Roman Catholic pope. These became known as Protestantism. They emphasized a return to the sources of faith: that is, God's action in salvation and Scripture as the authority for doctrine and practice. Different contexts and visions produced Lutheran, Reformed, Anabaptist, and Anglican Protestantism, all of which influenced the traditions that came together in United Methodism.

During the late 1600s, a renewal movement, often referred to as Pietism, emerged in Europe. Broadly conceived, the movement emphasized the Christian experience of new birth, sanctification, the possibility of societal transformation, and small groups. The movement affected most confessions including Lutheran, Reformed, Anglican, and Anabaptist. Expressions of this movement included the philanthropic and mission work of August Hermann Franke in Germany, the growth of Moravianism under the leadership of Ludwig von Zinzendorf, the Religious Societies Movement begun by Anthony Horneck in England, as well as Reformed and more radical groups.

John and Charles Wesley and the Evangelical Revival in England

All Wesleyan and Methodist Christians are connected to the lives and ministries of John Wesley (1703-1791) and his brother, Charles (1707-1788). Both John and Charles were Church of England priests who volunteered as missionaries to the colony of Georgia, arriving in March, 1736. Their mission was far from an unqualified success, and both returned to England disillusioned and discouraged, Charles in December, 1736, and John in February, 1738.

The Wesley brothers had transforming religious experiences in May, 1738, under the influence of Moravian missionaries. John's experience on May 24 of that year at a Moravian meeting on Aldersgate Street, London, has a prominent place in the Church's memory. Shortly thereafter, both brothers began preaching a message of new birth and sanctification in Anglican religious societies and outdoors to whomever would listen. They also established missional and philanthropic enterprises to promote social change.

The goal of this movement was to "reform the nation, particularly the church; and to spread scriptural holiness over the land." Over time a pattern of organization and discipline emerged. It included a set of General Rules, societies made up of class meetings (small groups in which members of Methodist societies watched over one another), and band meetings (smaller confessional groups divided by gender), all connected by traveling lay preachers.

Beginnings in America, 1760-1816

Methodism in America began without authorization or support from England, as lay Methodists immigrated to America. Among its earliest leaders were Robert Strawbridge, an immigrant farmer who organized work in Maryland and Virginia around 1760; Philip Embury and his cousin Barbara Heck, who began work in New York in 1766; and Captain Thomas Webb, whose labors were instrumental in Methodist beginnings in Philadelphia in 1767. The first Methodist societies included active participation by people of European and African descent.

To strengthen the Methodist work in the colonies, John Wesley sent two lay preachers, Richard Boardman and Joseph Pilmore, to America in 1769. Two years later, Richard Wright and Francis Asbury were dispatched to undergird the growing American Methodist societies. Asbury became the most important figure in early American Methodism. His energetic devotion to the principles of Wesleyan theology, ministry, and organization shaped Methodism in America in ways unmatched by any other individual.

The first conference of Methodist preachers in the colonies was held in Philadelphia in 1773. The ten who attended pledged allegiance to Wesley's leadership and agreed that, as laypeople, they would not administer the sacraments. Methodists would receive the sacraments of baptism and the Lord's Supper at a local Anglican parish church. They emphasized strong discipline among the societies and preachers. A system of regular conferences was inaugurated, similar to those Wesley had instituted in England to conduct the business of the Methodist movement.

The American Revolution profoundly impacted Methodism. John Wesley's loyalty to the king and his writings against the revolutionary cause did not enhance the image of Methodism among many who supported independence. Furthermore, a number of Methodist preachers refused to bear arms to aid the patriots.

When independence from England was won, Wesley recognized that changes were necessary for American Methodism to thrive. He sent Thomas Coke to America to superintend the work with Asbury. Coke brought with him a prayer book entitled *The Sunday Service of the Methodists in North America*, prepared by Wesley and incorporating his revision of the Church of England's Thirty-Nine Articles of Religion. Richard Whatcoat and Thomas Vasey, whom Wesley had ordained, accompanied Coke. Wesley's ordinations set a precedent that ultimately permitted Methodists in America to become an independent church.

In December 1784, the famous Christmas Conference of preachers was held in Baltimore at Lovely Lane Chapel. Most of the American preachers attended, probably including African Americans, Harry Hosier and Richard Allen. At this gathering the movement became organized as The Methodist Episcopal Church in America. In the following years The Methodist Episcopal Church published its first *Discipline* (1785), adopted a quadrennial General Conference, the first of which was held in 1792, and drafted a Constitution (1808). It also established a publishing house and became a proponent of revivalism and the camp meeting.

Two other churches were forming in America, which, in their earliest years were composed almost entirely of German-speaking people. The first was founded by Philip William Otterbein (1726-1813) and Martin Boehm (1725-1812). Otterbein, a German Reformed pastor, and Boehm, a Mennonite, preached an evangelical message similar to the Methodists. In 1800, their followers formally organized the Church of the United Brethren in Christ, which included a similar organization of traveling preachers. Otterbein attended the Christmas Conference and participated in Asbury's ordination.

A second church, The Evangelical Association, was begun by Jacob Albright (1759-1808). Albright, a Lutheran farmer and tile-maker in eastern Pennsylvania, was converted by the United Brethren and nurtured in a Methodist class meeting. He later established his own connection of preachers, better to reach fellow German-speakers. The Evangelical Association was officially organized in 1803.

Early attempts at merging these churches failed. By the time of Asbury's death in March 1816, Otterbein, Boehm, and Albright had also died. The churches they nurtured had survived and were beginning to expand numerically and geographically. The German churches united in 1946 as The Evangelical United Brethren Church, which in turn joined with The Methodist Church in 1968 to form The United Methodist Church.

Revival and Growth, 1817-1843

The Second Great Awakening was the dominant religious development among Protestants in America during the first half of the nineteenth century. Through revivals and camp meetings, sinners experienced conversion. Circuit-riding preachers and lay pastors knit them into a connection. This style of Christian faith and discipline was very agreeable to Methodists, United Brethren, and Evangelicals who favored its emphasis on the experiential. The memberships of these churches increased dramatically, as did the number of preachers serving them.

Preachers and laity were expected to be seriously committed to both the faith and mission. Preachers were to possess a sound conversion and divine calling, as well as to demonstrate gifts and skills for fruitful ministry. The financial benefits were meager. The general membership's commitment was exhibited in their willingness to submit to the discipline of their churches. Methodists, for example, were strictly guided by the General Rules adopted at the Christmas Conference of 1784 and still included in United Methodism's *Book of Discipline*. They were urged to avoid evil, do good, and use the means of grace supplied by God. Those who did not adhere to the *Discipline* were to be removed from membership.

The structure of Methodist, United Brethren, and Evangelical Association churches allowed them to function in ways to support, consolidate, and expand their ministries. Local classes could spring up wherever a few women and men were gathered under the direction of a class leader. The itinerant preacher, who had a circuit of appointments under his care, visited regularly. This system served the diverse needs of city, town, or frontier outpost. The churches could go to the people wherever they settled. Annual conferences under episcopal leadership provided the mechanism for admitting and ordaining clergy, appointing itinerant preachers to their churches, and supplying them with mutual support. General Conferences, meeting quadrennially, proved sufficient to set the main course for the church, including the creation of the *Discipline* by which it was governed.

The Methodist Book Concern, organized in 1789, was the first church publishing house in America. The Evangelical Association and United Brethren also authorized the formation of publishing agencies in the early nineteenth century. From these presses came a succession of hymnals, *Disciplines*, newspapers, tracts, and magazines. Profits were usually designated for the support and welfare of retired and indigent preachers and their families.

The founding period was not without serious problems, especially for the Methodists. Conflict between Methodism's structure and values and American cultural norms (especially over episcopacy, race, and slavery) sometimes led to schism. In 1792, James O'Kelly founded the Republican Methodists to reduce the authority of bishops. Richard Allen (1760-1831), an emancipated slave and Methodist preacher who was mistreated because of his race, left the church and in 1816 organized The African Methodist Episcopal Church. For similar reasons, The African Methodist Episcopal Zion Church was begun in 1821. In 1830, about 5,000 preachers and laypeople left the denomination because it would not grant representation to the laity or permit the election of presiding elders (district superintendents). This new body was called The Methodist Protestant Church, which in 1939 united with The Methodist Episcopal Church and The Methodist Episcopal Church, South, to become The Methodist Church. In 1843, abolitionist preachers Orange Scott and Luther Lee formed the Wesleyan Methodist Church over Methodism's weakening prohibition against slaveholding.

Even with these tensions, Methodism spread to new cultures and overseas. African American Methodist preacher, John Stewart, began an unauthorized mission to the Wyandot Indians in Ohio in 1815, which was adopted by the Ohio Conference in 1819. Another African American preacher, Daniel Coker, who had been ordained by Asbury and participated in the organizing conference of the African Methodist Episcopal Church, was among the eighty-eight emigrants who sailed to Africa in 1820, assisted by the American Colonization Society. While still at sea he organized a church. The group landed in what is today Liberia. Missionary work in Africa was carried out mainly by lay people until 1833, when Melville Beveridge Cox became the first missionary of the Methodist Episcopal Church appointed to Liberia.

Other institutions also developed. By 1841, Methodists, Evangelicals, and United Brethren had all begun denominational missionary societies. Sunday schools were encouraged in every place where they could be started and maintained. Interest in education was also evident in the establishment of secondary schools and colleges. By 1845, each had instituted courses of study for their preachers to ensure that they had a basic knowledge of the Bible, theology, and pastoral ministry.

Division in America and Expansion Overseas, 1844-1860

John Wesley had been an ardent opponent of slavery. In 1789, the General Rules were officially adopted by American Methodism. A rule forbidding participation in slavery, which had not been deemed necessary in England, was included. But as Methodism expanded, that prohibition was relaxed or not enforced where slavery was legal. Because membership spanned regions, classes, and races, contention over slavery ultimately split Methodism into separate northern and southern churches.

At the 1844 General Conference, pro-slavery and anti-slavery factions clashed over episcopacy, race, and slavery. Their most serious conflict concerned one of the church's five bishops, James O. Andrew, who had acquired slaves through marriage. After acrimonious debate, the General Conference voted to suspend Bishop

Andrew from the exercise of his office so long as he could not, or would not, free his slaves. A few days later, dissidents drafted a Plan of Separation, which permitted the annual conferences in slaveholding states to separate from The Methodist Episcopal Church in order to organize their own ecclesiastical structure. The Plan of Separation was adopted and the groundwork laid for the creation of The Methodist Episcopal Church, South.

Delegates from the southern states met in Louisville, Kentucky, in May 1845, to organize their new church. Their first General Conference was held the following year in Petersburg, Virginia, where a *Discipline* and hymnbook were adopted. The Methodist Protestant Church was also affected by the slavery controversy, splitting in 1858 and reuniting in 1877. The United Brethren and The Evangelical Association, being concentrated in northern states, were able to avoid the passionate struggle that fractured The Methodist Episcopal Church.

Despite conflict and division in America, Methodism continued to expand overseas. In 1847, Judson D. Collins, Moses C. White, and his wife Jane Isabel Altwater landed in Fuzhou, China, under the auspices of the Missionary Society of the Methodist Episcopal Church. Despite a slow beginning, the Missionary Society gained valuable lessons that enabled Robert S. Maclay to enter Japan in 1873. In 1885, William B. Scranton, his mother Mary F. Scranton, and Henry G. Appenzeller began work in Korea. American Methodists also set their sights on South Asia. In 1856, William Butler landed in Kolkata with his wife, Clementina Rowe Butler (one of the future founders of Woman's Foreign Missionary Society), and two of their children.

European Methodism also began, as migrants, sailors, soldiers, and others who encountered Methodism outside of Europe shared the message back home. Ludwig Jacoby joined the Methodists after immigrating to Cincinnati in 1838. He returned to Germany in 1849 and began gathering a church in Bremen. The Evangelical Association, with ethnic and linguistic links to Germany, sent Conrad Link as its first official missionary to Germany in 1850. Norwegian seaman Ole Peter Petersen, after hearing Methodists in Charleston, South Carolina, in 1845, preached to Norwegians and Danes in America and Norway in 1849. The first congregation in Denmark was established by Christian Willerup in 1856.

The Civil War to World War I, 1860-1913

Bitterness between northern and southern Methodists had intensified in the years leading to Abraham Lincoln's election in 1860 and then through the carnage of the Civil War. Each church claimed divine sanction for its region and prayed fervently for God's will to be accomplished in victory for its side.

The Civil War devastated The Methodist Episcopal Church, South. Its churches lay in ruins or were seriously damaged. Many of its clergy were killed or wounded, and its educational, publishing, and missionary programs were disrupted. African American membership declined significantly during and after the war. In 1870, the General Conference voted to transfer all remaining African Americans to a new church. The Colored Methodist Episcopal Church (now The Christian Methodist Episcopal Church) resulted. The Methodist Episcopal Church, Methodist Protestants, United Brethren, and Evangelicals also lost preachers and members but did not suffer the same economic loss as southern Methodism.

The period from the Civil War to World War I saw growth in membership for all branches of Methodism, Evangelicals, and United Brethren. The value of church property increased dramatically, Sunday schools were strengthened through increased training of teachers, and publishing houses maintained ambitious programs to furnish members with literature. Higher educational standards for the clergy were cultivated, and theological seminaries were founded. The period was also marked by theological developments and controversies. The holiness movement, which emphasized a Christian's experience of entire sanctification, together with the rise of liberal theology and the Social Gospel Movement, were sources of conflict.

Rural and poorer segments of the church, especially those associated with the holiness movement, were skeptical of prestige and affluence. A Methodist preacher, Benjamin Titus Roberts, had formed the Free Methodist Church in 1860 to oppose worldliness, especially the grand middle class churches in cities financed by renting pews. In 1895, the Pentecostal Church of the Nazarene (now the Nazarene Church) was formed under the encouragement of Phineas Bresee, a Methodist Episcopal preacher, presiding elder, and delegate to the General Conferences of 1872 and 1892. The goal for the new denomination, founded in 1894, was to have churches furnished to welcome the poor where holiness was preached.

Two other issues that caused substantial debate in the churches during this period were lay representation and the role of women. Methodist Protestants had granted the laity representation from the time they organized in 1830. The clergy in The Methodist Episcopal Church, The Methodist Episcopal Church, South, The Evangelical Association, and the Church of the United Brethren in Christ were much slower in permitting laity an official voice. It was not until 1932 that the last of these churches allowed lay representation.

Even more contentious was the question of women's ordination and eligibility for lay offices and representation in the church. Women had been ordained in holiness denominations as early as the 1860s, and the United Brethren General Conference approved ordination for women in 1889. However, The Methodist Episcopal Church and The Methodist Episcopal Church, South, did not ordain women until well after their reunion in 1939.[1] The Evangelical Association never ordained women. Lay representation for women was also resisted. Women were not admitted as delegates to the General Conferences of The Methodist Protestant Church until 1892, the United Brethren until 1893, The Methodist Episcopal Church until 1904, and The Methodist Episcopal Church, South, until 1922.

Mission work continued to rise on the agendas of the churches. Women formed missionary societies beginning in 1869 to educate, recruit, and raise funds for these endeavors. Missionaries like Isabella Thoburn, Susan Bauernfeind, and Harriett Brittan, and administrators like Bell Harris Bennett and Lucy Rider Meyer, motivated thousands of church women to support home and foreign missions.

Domestic mission programs sought to Christianize the city. Home missionaries established schools for former slaves and their children. In 1871, the southern Methodist church ordained Alejo Hernandez, making him the first Hispanic preacher ordained in Methodism, although Benigno Cardenas had preached in Spanish in Santa Fe, New Mexico, as early as 1853. Significant Methodist ministries among Asian Americans were instituted during this period, especially among Chinese and Japanese immigrants. A Japanese layman, Kanichi Miyama, was ordained in California in 1887.

---

1. The Methodist Episcopal Church ordained women as "local elders" starting in 1924. However, The Methodist Church (1939) did not grant full clergy rights to women until 1956.

Methodism continued to expand in Asia, Europe, Africa, and Latin America. From 1870 to 1875 Methodist missionaries embarked on revival campaigns in India south of the Ganges River under the leadership of James M. Thoburn, and the famous holiness evangelist William Taylor. These efforts gave birth to the South India Conference in 1876. Thoburn also began work in Southeast Asia when he opened mission work in Rangoon, Burma (Myanmar), in 1879. In 1885, he led the establishment of Methodist work in Singapore, which later expanded into the Malaya Peninsular and Sarawak to become the Malaysia Annual Conference in 1902. The conference also sent the first Methodist pastor to Indonesia in 1905. Methodism reached the Philippines when Thoburn organized work in Manila in 1899, which quickly grew to become the Philippine Islands Annual Conference in 1908.

At the Methodist Episcopal General Conference of 1884, a petition from the Liberia Conference was presented, asking for a resident bishop in Africa. William Taylor was elected to the episcopacy as missionary bishop to Africa. Taylor went with two specific assignments: overseeing Liberia and expanding missions on the African continent. Between May 20 and September 10, 1885, the Methodist Episcopal Church founded five strategic points to start their work in Angola. In 1886, the bishop and his party entered the Lower Congo. Taylor also visited the king of Portugal in 1886 and received permission to do mission work in Portuguese East Africa (Mozambique). Taylor established self-supporting churches in southern Liberia, Sierra Leone, Angola, in what is today Mozambique, and in Zaire. In 1896, Joseph Crane Hartzell was elected Bishop for Africa, and by 1897 the Methodist Episcopal Church reached Rhodesia (Zimbabwe). During this period, annual conferences other than those in the United States were organized regionally into what was termed central conferences.

The War Years of the Early 20ᵗʰ Century, 1914-1945

In the years prior to World War I, the Methodist Episcopal Church demonstrated its concern for social issues by adopting a Social Creed at its 1908 General Conference. Social problems were also a spur in the movement toward ecumenism and interchurch cooperation. Each of the denominations now included in The United Methodist Church became active in the Federal Council of Churches, the first major ecumenical venture among American Protestants. There was also much sympathy in the churches for negotiation and arbitration as an alternative to international armed conflict. Many church members and clergy openly professed pacifism. When the United Sates officially entered the war in 1917, pacifism faded as American patriotism was identified with the war effort.

After the war, the churches returned their energies to social change. One of their perennial concerns was temperance, and they were quick to recognize it among their highest priorities. They published and distributed large amounts of temperance literature. Members pledged that they would abstain from alcoholic beverages.

There was significant theological ferment during this period. Biblical fundamentalists and neo-orthodox theologians questioned liberal Protestant theology and accused it of undermining the very essence of the Christian message. Since each of these theological parties—fundamentalist, neo-orthodox, and liberal—was well represented among the forerunners of United Methodism, heated doctrinal disputes were present in these churches.

Despite internal theological strife, the churches continued to cooperate with other denominations and acted to heal earlier schisms. A division that had occurred in The Evangelical Association in 1894 was repaired in 1922, when two factions united as The Evangelical Church.

A numerically larger union took place among three Methodist bodies—The Methodist Episcopal Church, The Methodist Protestant Church, and The Methodist Episcopal Church, South. Representatives of these churches began meeting in 1916 to forge a plan of union. By the 1930s, their proposal included partitioning the united church into six administrative units called jurisdictions. Five of these were geographical; the sixth, the Central Jurisdiction, was racial, including African American churches and annual conferences wherever they were geographically located in the United States. African American Methodists and some others were troubled by this prospect and opposed the plan. The majority of Methodist Protestants favored the union, even though it meant episcopal government, which they had not had since their church was organized in 1830. Following overwhelming approvals at the General Conferences and annual conferences of the three churches, they were united in April, 1939, into The Methodist Church. At the time of its formation, the new church included 7.7 million members.

Conflict in Europe was heating up again. Although Methodists, Evangelicals, and United Brethren each had published strong statements condemning war and advocating peaceful reconciliation among the nations, once again the strength of their positions was largely lost with American involvement in the hostilities of World War II.

Quest for Unity, 1945-1968

As the war ended, the churches actively worked to secure world peace and order. Many laity, pastors, bishops, and church agencies supported the establishment of a world organization to serve as a forum for the resolution of international social, economic, and political problems. In April 1945, their labors contributed to the founding of the United Nations.

During this era, there were at least three other important matters that occupied the attention of the churches that now compose United Methodism. First, they maintained their concern for ecumenism and church union. On November 16, 1946, in Johnstown, Pennsylvania, The Evangelical Church and The United Brethren Church were united into The Evangelical United Brethren Church following twenty years of negotiation. At the time of union, the new church included about 700,000 members.

The Methodist Church was also interested in closer ties with other Methodist and Wesleyan bodies. In 1951, it participated in the formation of the World Methodist Council, successor to the Ecumenical Methodist Conferences that began in 1881. Methodists and the Evangelical United Brethren became active members of the World Council of Churches, founded in 1948, and the National Council of Churches, founded in 1950. The two churches also cooperated with seven other Protestant denominations in forming the Consultation of Church Union in 1960.

Second, the churches demonstrated growing uneasiness with the problem of racism in both the nation and the church. Many Methodists were especially disturbed by the manner in which racial segregation was built into the fabric of their denominational structure. The Central Jurisdiction was a constant reminder of racial discrimination. Proposals to eliminate the Central Jurisdiction were introduced at General Conferences from 1956 to 1966. Finally, plans to abolish the Central Jurisdiction were agreed upon with the contemplated union with the Evangelical United Brethren in 1968, although a few African American annual conferences continued for a short time thereafter.

Third, the churches debated women's ordination. The issue was critical in the creation of The Evangelical United Brethren Church. The Evangelical Church had never ordained women. The United Brethren had ordained women since 1889. In order to facilitate the union of these two churches, the United Brethren accepted the Evangelical practice, and women's ordination was stopped. Methodists debated the issue for several years after their unification in 1939. The Methodist Church began ordaining women in 1956. In that same year, women were granted full clergy rights and could be elected as members in full connection to an annual conference.

United Methodism as a World Church, 1968-

In 1968, The Evangelical United Brethren and The Methodist Church united. Full clergy status for women was included in the plan of union. Since then, an increasing number of women have been admitted to the ordained ministry, appointed to the district superintendency, elected to positions of denominational leadership, and consecrated as bishops. In 1980, Marjorie Matthews was the first woman elected to the Church's episcopacy.

When The United Methodist Church was created in 1968, it had approximately 11 million members, making it one of the largest Protestant churches in the world. Since then the church has become increasingly aware of itself as a world church with membership and conferences in Africa, Asia, Europe, and the United States. While worldwide membership in The United Methodist Church has grown since 1968, membership in Europe and the United States has declined, offset by significant growth in Africa and Asia. In Africa, The United Methodist Church has expanded episcopal areas to include East Africa, Sierra Leone, Cote d'Ivoire, East Congo, Zimbabwe, Mozambique, and South Africa.

Changes in worship style, the rise of the charismatic movement, the growth of nondenominationalism, and the emergence of megachurches have all challenged the church as it entered its third century. Most trying, The United Methodist Church has had to negotiate cultural shifts with regard to gender and sexuality, especially in the United States and Europe. Conflicts over homosexuality, marriage, and abortion have continued uninterrupted nearly since the formation of the denomination. These debates have opened up large domestic, international, and ecumenical rifts over the church's doctrine and discipline.

The United Methodist Church continues to represent the confluence of three streams of tradition: Methodism, the Church of the United Brethren in Christ, and The Evangelical Association. With other churches that are also members of the body of Christ, it humbly and gratefully offers up its praise to God through Jesus Christ and the Holy Spirit for creating and sustaining grace. It seeks further grace as it ministers to the world.

Part I

THE CONSTITUTION

PREAMBLE

The church is a community of all true believers under the Lordship of Christ. It is the redeemed and redeeming fellowship in which the Word of God is preached by persons divinely called, and the sacraments are duly administered according to Christ's own appointment. Under the discipline of the Holy Spirit the church seeks to provide for the maintenance of worship, the edification of believers, and the redemption of the world.

The church of Jesus Christ exists in and for the world, and its very dividedness is a hindrance to its mission in that world.

The prayers and intentions of The United Methodist Church and its predecessors, The Methodist Church and The Evangelical United Brethren Church, have been and are for obedience to the will of our Lord that his people be one, in humility for the present brokenness of the Church and in gratitude that opportunities for reunion have been given.

Therefore, The United Methodist Church has adopted and amended the following Constitution.[1]

DIVISION ONE—GENERAL

¶ 1. *Article I. Declaration of Union*—The Evangelical United Brethren Church and The Methodist Church have been united into

---

1. The Constitution was adopted in Chicago, Illinois, on Nov. 11, 1966, by the General Conferences of The Evangelical United Brethren Church and The Methodist Church and thereafter by the requisite vote in the annual conferences of the two churches. The Plan of Union was made effective by the Uniting Conference in Dallas, Texas, on April 23, 1968. Preamble amended 2000.

one Church. The United Methodist Church, as thus constituted, is, and shall be, the successor of the two uniting churches.[2]

¶ 2. *Article II. Name*—The name of the Church shall be The United Methodist Church. The name of the Church may be translated freely into languages other than English as the General Conference may determine.

¶ 3. *Article III. Articles of Religion and the Confession of Faith*— The Articles of Religion and the Confession of Faith of The United Methodist Church are those held by The Methodist Church and The Evangelical United Brethren Church, respectively, at the time of their uniting.[3]

¶ 4. *Article IV. Inclusiveness of the Church*—The United Methodist Church is a part of the church universal, which is one Body in Christ. The United Methodist Church acknowledges that all persons are of sacred worth. All persons without regard to race, color, national origin, status,[4] or economic condition, shall be eligible to attend its worship services, participate in its programs, receive the sacraments, upon baptism be admitted as baptized members, and upon taking vows declaring the Christian faith, become professing members in any local church in the connection.[5] In The United Methodist Church no conference or other organizational unit of the Church shall be structured so as to exclude any member or any constituent body of the Church because of race, color, national origin, status or economic condition.[6]

¶ 5. *Article V. Racial Justice*—The United Methodist Church proclaims the value of each person as a unique child of God and commits itself to the healing and wholeness of all persons. The United Methodist Church recognizes that the sin of racism has been destructive to its unity throughout its history. Racism continues to cause painful division and marginalization. The United Methodist Church shall confront and seek to eliminate racism, whether in organizations or in individuals, in every facet of its life and in society at large. The United Methodist Church shall work collaboratively with others to address concerns that threaten the cause of racial justice at all times and in all places.[7]

---

2. Amended 1984, 2000.
3. Amended 2000.
4. Amended 1992.
5. Amended 2000.
6. See Judicial Council Decisions 242, 246, 340, 351, 362, 377, 398, 594, 601, and Decisions 4 and 5, Interim Judicial Council.
7. Amended 2000.

¶ **6.** *Article VI.* *Ecumenical Relations*—As part of the church universal, The United Methodist Church believes that the Lord of the church is calling Christians everywhere to strive toward unity; and therefore it will pray, seek, and work for unity at all levels of church life: through world relationships with other Methodist churches and united churches related to The Methodist Church or The Evangelical United Brethren Church, through councils of churches, and through plans of union and covenantal relationships[8] with churches of Methodist or other denominational traditions.

¶ **7.** *Article VII.* *Title to Properties*—Titles to properties formerly held by[9] The Evangelical United Brethren Church and The Methodist Church shall be held and administered in accordance with the *Book of Discipline*.[10] Nothing in the Plan of Union at any time after the union is to be construed so as to require any local church or any other property owner of the former The Evangelical United Brethren Church or the former The Methodist Church to alienate or in any way change the title to property contained in its deed or deeds at the time of union and lapse of time.

DIVISION TWO—ORGANIZATION

Section I. Conferences

¶ **8.** *Article I.*—There shall be a General Conference for the entire Church with such powers, duties, and privileges as are hereinafter set forth.

¶ **9.** *Article II.*—There shall be jurisdictional conferences for the Church in the United States of America, with such powers, duties, and privileges as are hereinafter set forth,[11] provided that in The United Methodist Church there shall be no jurisdictional or central conference based on any ground other than geographical and regional division.

¶ **10.** *Article III.*—There shall be central conferences for the Church outside the United States of America and, if necessary, provisional central conferences, all with such powers, duties, and privileges as are hereinafter set forth.

---

8. Amended 1996.
9. Amended 2000.
10. Amended 1984.
11. See Judicial Council Decision 128.

¶ 11. *Article IV.*—There shall be annual conferences as the fundamental bodies of the Church and, if necessary, provisional annual conferences, with such powers, duties, and privileges as are hereinafter set forth.

¶ 12. *Article V.*—There shall be a charge conference for each church or charge with such powers, duties, and privileges as are hereinafter set forth.[12]

Section II. General Conference

¶ 13. *Article I.*—1. The General Conference shall be composed of not less than 600 nor more than 1,000 delegates, one half of whom shall be clergy and one half lay members, to be elected by the annual conferences. The missionary conferences shall be considered as annual conferences for the purpose of this article.[13]

2. Delegates shall be elected in a fair and open process by the annual conferences. Delegates may be elected by other autonomous Methodist churches if and when the General Conference shall approve concordats with such other autonomous Methodist churches for the mutual election and seating of delegates in each other's legislative conferences.[14]

3. In the case of The Methodist Church in Great Britain, mother church of Methodism, provision shall be made for The United Methodist Church to send two delegates annually to the British Methodist Conference, and The Methodist Church in Great Britain to send four delegates quadrennially to The United Methodist General Conference, the delegates of both conferences having vote and being evenly divided between clergy and laity.[15]

¶ 14. *Article II.*—The General Conference shall meet once in four years at such time and in such place as shall be determined by the General Conference or by its duly authorized committees. The change in the preceding sentence shall become effective at the close of General Conference in 2016.

A special session of the General Conference, possessing the authority and exercising all the powers of the General Conference, may be called by the Council of Bishops, or in such other manner as the General Conference may from time to time prescribe, to meet at such time and in such place as may be stated in the call.

---

12. See Judicial Council Decision 516.
13. Amended 1976.
14. See Judicial Council Decisions 435 and 592.
15. Amended 1996.

Such special session of the General Conference shall be composed of the delegates to the preceding General Conference or their lawful successors, except that when a particular annual conference or missionary conference[16] shall prefer to have a new election it may do so.[17] The purpose of such special session shall be stated in the call, and only such business shall be transacted as is in harmony with the purpose stated in such call unless the General Conference by a two-thirds vote shall determine that other business may be transacted.[18]

¶ 15. *Article III.*—The General Conference shall fix the ratio of representation in the General, jurisdictional, and central conferences from the annual conferences, missionary conferences,[19] and the provisional annual conferences, computed on a two-factor basis: (1) the number of clergy members of the annual conference and the missionary conference,[20] and (2) the number of professing[21] members in the annual conference and the missionary conference,[22] provided that each annual conference, missionary conference,[23] or provisional annual conference shall be entitled to at least one clergy and one lay delegate in the General Conference and also in the jurisdictional or central conference.[24]

¶ 16. *Article IV.*—The General Conference shall have full legislative power over all matters distinctively connectional, and in the exercise of this power shall have authority as follows:[25]

1. To define and fix the conditions, privileges, and duties of Church membership, which shall in every case be without reference to race, gender, or status.[26]

2. To define and fix the powers and duties of elders, deacons, supply preachers, local preachers, exhorters, deaconesses, and home missioners.[27]

3. To define and fix the powers and duties of annual conferences, provisional annual conferences, missionary conferences and

---

16. Amended 1976.
17. See Judicial Council Decisions 221, 226, 228, 238, 302.
18. See Judicial Council Decision 227.
19. Amended 1976.
20. Amended 1976.
21. Amended 2000.
22. Amended 1976.
23. Amended 1976.
24. See Judicial Council Decision 403.
25. See Judicial Council Decisions 96, 232, 236, 318, 325, 544.
26. See Judicial Council Decision 558.
27. See Judicial Council Decisions 58, 313.

missions, and of central conferences, district conferences, charge conferences, and congregational meetings.[28]

4. To provide for the organization, promotion, and administration of the work of the Church outside the United States of America.[29]

5. To define and fix the powers, duties, and privileges of the episcopacy, to adopt a plan for the support of the bishops, to provide a uniform rule for their retirement, and to provide for the discontinuance of a bishop because of inefficiency or unacceptability.[30]

6. To provide and revise the hymnal and ritual of the Church and to regulate all matters relating to the form and mode of worship, subject to the limitations of the first and second Restrictive Rules.[31]

7. To provide a judicial system and a method of judicial procedure for the Church, except as herein otherwise prescribed.

8. To initiate and to direct all connectional enterprises of the Church and to provide boards for their promotion and administration.[32]

9. To determine and provide for raising and distributing funds necessary to carry on the work of the Church.[33]

10. To fix a uniform basis upon which bishops shall be elected by the jurisdictional conferences and to determine the number of bishops that may be elected by central conferences.[34]

11. To select its presiding officers from the bishops, through a committee, provided that the bishops shall select from their own number the presiding officer of the opening session.[35]

12. To change the number and the boundaries of jurisdictional conferences upon the consent of a majority of the annual conferences in each jurisdictional conference involved.[36]

13. To establish such commissions for the general work of the Church as may be deemed advisable.

---

28. See Judicial Council Decision 411.
29. See Judicial Council Decision 182; amended 1976.
30. See Judicial Council Decisions 35, 114, 312, 365, 413.
31. See Judicial Council Decision 694.
32. See Judicial Council Decisions 214, 364, 411, 1210.
33. See Judicial Council Decisions 30, 1208.
34. See Judicial Council Decisions 598, 735.
35. See Judicial Council Decision 126.
36. See Judicial Council Decisions 55, 56, 215.

14. To secure the rights and privileges of membership in all agencies, programs, and institutions in The United Methodist Church regardless of race, gender, or status.[37]

15. To allow the annual conferences to utilize structures unique to their mission, other mandated structures notwithstanding.[38]

16. To enact such other legislation as may be necessary, subject to the limitations and restrictions of the Constitution of the Church.[39]

Section III. Restrictive Rules

¶ **17.** *Article I.*—The General Conference shall not revoke, alter, or change our Articles of Religion or establish any new standards or rules of doctrine contrary to our present existing and established standards of doctrine.[40]

¶ **18.** *Article II.*—The General Conference shall not revoke, alter, or change our Confession of Faith.

¶ **19.** *Article III.*—The General Conference shall not change or alter any part or rule of our government so as to do away with episcopacy or destroy the plan of our itinerant general superintendency.

¶ **20.** *Article IV.*—The General Conference shall not do away with the privileges of our clergy of right to trial by a committee and of an appeal; neither shall it do away with the privileges of our members of right to trial before the church, or by a committee, and of an appeal.[41]

¶ **21.** *Article V.*—The General Conference shall not revoke or change the General Rules of Our United Societies.[42]

¶ **22.** *Article VI.*—The General Conference shall not appropriate the net income of the publishing houses, the book concerns, or the Chartered Fund to any purpose other than for the benefit of retired or disabled preachers, their spouses, widows, or widowers, and children or other beneficiaries of the ministerial pension systems.[43]

---

37. See Decisions 4, 5, Interim Judicial Council; Judicial Council Decisions 427, 433, 442, 451, 540, 558, 567, 588, 594, 601.
38. See Judicial Council Decision 825; amended 1996.
39. See Judicial Council Decisions 215, 1220.
40. See Judicial Council Decisions 86, 142, 243, 358, 847, 871.
41. See Judicial Council Decisions 351, 522, 557, 595, 982.
42. See Judicial Council Decisions 358, 468, 847, 871.
43. See Judicial Council Decisions 322, 330.

Section IV. Jurisdictional Conferences

¶ 23. *Article I.*—The jurisdictional conferences shall be composed of as many representatives from the annual conferences and missionary conferences[44] as shall be determined by a uniform basis established by the General Conference, provided that no jurisdictional conference shall have fewer than 100 delegates. The missionary conferences shall be considered as annual conferences for the purpose of this article.[45]

¶ 24. *Article II.*—All jurisdictional conferences shall have the same status and the same privileges of action within the limits fixed by the Constitution. The ratio of representation of the annual conferences and missionary conferences[46] in the General Conference shall be the same for all jurisdictional conferences.

¶ 25. *Article III.*—The General Conferences shall fix the basis of representation in the jurisdictional conferences, provided that the jurisdictional conferences shall be composed of an equal number of clergy and lay delegates to be elected by the annual conferences, the missionary conferences[47] and the provisional annual conferences.

¶ 26. *Article IV.*—Each jurisdictional conference shall meet at the time determined by the Council of Bishops or its delegated committee, each jurisdictional conference convening on the same date as the others and at a place selected by the jurisdictional committee on entertainment, appointed by its College of Bishops unless such a committee has been appointed by the preceding jurisdictional conference.

¶ 27. *Article V.*—The jurisdictional conferences shall have the following powers and duties and such others as may be conferred by the General Conferences:

1. To promote the evangelistic, educational, missionary, and benevolent interests of the Church and to provide for interests and institutions within their boundaries.[48]

2. To elect bishops and to cooperate in carrying out such plans for their support as may be determined by the General Conference.[49]

---

44. Amended 1976.
45. Amended 1976.
46. Amended 1976.
47. Amended 1976.
48. See Judicial Council Decision 67.
49. See Judicial Council Decision 1208.

3. To establish and constitute jurisdictional conference boards as auxiliary to the general boards of the Church as the need may appear and to choose their representatives on the general boards in such manner as the General Conference may determine.

4. To determine the boundaries of their annual conferences, provided that there shall be no annual conference with a membership of fewer than fifty clergy in full connection, except by the consent of the General Conference.

5. To make rules and regulations for the administration of the work of the Church within the jurisdiction, subject to such powers as have been or shall be vested in the General Conference.[50]

6. To appoint a committee on appeals to hear and determine the appeal of a traveling preacher of that jurisdiction from the decision of a trial committee.

Section V. Central Conferences

¶ **28.** *Article I.*—There shall be central conferences for the work of the Church outside the United States of America[51] with such duties, powers, and privileges as are hereinafter set forth. The number and boundaries of the central conferences shall be determined by the Uniting Conference. Subsequently the General Conference shall have authority to change the number and boundaries of central conferences. The central conferences shall have the duties, powers, and privileges hereinafter set forth.

¶ **29.** *Article II.*—The central conferences shall be composed of as many delegates as shall be determined by a basis established by the General Conference. The delegates shall be clergy and lay in equal numbers.[52]

¶ **30.** *Article III.*—The central conferences shall meet within the year succeeding the meeting of the General Conference at such times and places as shall have been determined by the preceding respective central conferences or by commissions appointed by them or by the General Conference. The date and place of the first meeting succeeding the Uniting Conference shall be fixed by the bishops of the respective central conferences, or in such manner as shall be determined by the General Conference.

---

50. See Judicial Council Decision 1208.
51. Amended 1976.
52. Amended 1992.

¶ 31. *Article IV*.—The central conferences shall have the following powers and duties and such others as may be conferred by the General Conference:

1. To promote the evangelistic, educational, missionary, social-concern, and benevolent interests and institutions of the Church within their own boundaries.

2. To elect the bishops for the respective central conferences in number as may be determined from time to time, upon a basis fixed by the General Conference, and to cooperate in carrying out such plans for the support of their bishops as may be determined by the General Conference.[53]

3. To establish and constitute such central conference boards as may be required and to elect their administrative officers.[54]

4. To determine the boundaries of the annual conferences within their respective areas.

5. To make such rules and regulations for the administration of the work within their boundaries including such changes and adaptations of the General *Discipline* as the conditions in the respective areas may require, subject to the powers that have been or shall be vested in the General Conference.[55]

6. To appoint a judicial court to determine legal questions arising on the rules, regulations, and such revised, adapted, or new sections of the central conference *Discipline* enacted by the central conference.

7. To appoint a committee on appeals to hear and determine the appeal of a traveling preacher of that central conference from the decision of a committee on trial.[56]

Section VI. Annual Conferences

¶ 32. *Article I*.—The annual conference shall be composed of clergy and lay members. The clergy membership shall consist of deacons and elders in full connection, provisional members, associate members, and local pastors under appointment. The lay membership shall consist of professing[57] lay members elected by each charge, the diaconal ministers, the active deaconesses, and home missioners under episcopal appointment within the bounds

---

53. See Judicial Council Decision 370.
54. See Judicial Council Decision 69.
55. See Judicial Council Decisions 142, 147, 313.
56. See Judicial Council Decision 595.
57. Amended 2000.

of the annual conference,[58] the conference president of United Methodist Women, the conference president of United Methodist Men, the conference lay leader, district lay leaders, the conference director of Lay Servant Ministries, conference secretary of Global Ministries (if lay), the president or equivalent officer of the conference young adult organization, the president of the conference youth organization, the chair of the annual conference college student organization,[59] and one young person between the ages of twelve (12) and seventeen (17) and one young person between the ages of eighteen (18) and thirty (30)[60] from each district to be selected in such a manner as may be determined by the annual conference.[61] In the annual conferences of the central conferences, the four-year participation and the two-year membership requirements may be waived by the annual conference for young persons under thirty (30)[62] years of age. Such persons must be professing[63] members of The United Methodist Church and active participants at the time of election.[64] Each charge served by more than one clergy shall be entitled to as many lay members as there are clergy members. The lay members shall have been for the two years next preceding their election members of The United Methodist Church[65] and shall have been active participants in The United Methodist Church for at least four years next preceding their election.[66]

If the lay membership should number less than the clergy members of the annual conference, the annual conference shall, by its own formula, provide for the election of additional lay members to equalize lay and clergy membership of the annual conference.[67]

¶ 33. *Article II.*—The annual conference is the basic body in the Church and as such shall have reserved to it the right to vote on all constitutional amendments, on the election of clergy and lay delegates to the General and the jurisdictional or central conferences, on all matters relating to the character and conference

---

58. Amended 1996.
59. Amended 1996.
60. Amended 2000.
61. Amended 1968, 1970, 1980, 1984.
62. Amended 2000.
63. Amended 2000.
64. Amended 1988.
65. Amended 1972, 1976.
66. Amended 1976.
67. See Judicial Council Decisions 24, 113, 129, 349, 378, 479, 495, 511, 553, 561, 1212; and Decision 7, Interim Judicial Council.

relations of its clergy members, and on the ordination of clergy and such other rights as have not been delegated to the General Conference under the Constitution, with the exception that the lay members may not vote on matters of ordination, character, and conference relations of clergy except that the lay members of the conference board of ordained ministry and the committee on investigation may vote on matters of ordination, character, and conference relations of clergy, with the further exception that lay members of the district committee on ordained ministry be full participating members of the district committee on ordained ministry with vote.[68] It shall discharge such duties and exercise such powers as the General Conference under the Constitution may determine.[69]

¶ 34. *Article III.*—The annual conference shall elect clergy and lay delegates to the General Conference and to its jurisdictional or central conference in the manner provided in this section, Articles IV and V.[70] The persons first elected up to the number determined by the ratio for representation in the General Conference shall be representatives in that body. Additional delegates shall be elected to complete the number determined by the ratio for representation in the jurisdictional or central conference, who, together with those first elected as above, shall be delegates in the jurisdictional or central conference. The additional delegates to the jurisdictional or central conference shall in the order of their election be the reserve delegates to the General Conference.[71] The annual conference shall also elect reserve clergy and lay delegates to the jurisdictional or central conference as it may deem desirable. These reserve clergy and lay delegates to the jurisdictional or central conferences may act as reserve delegates to the General Conference when it is evident that not enough reserve delegates are in attendance at the General Conference.[72]

¶ 35. *Article IV.*—The clergy delegates to the General Conference and to the jurisdictional or central conference shall be elected from[73] the clergy members in full connection and shall be elected by the clergy members of the annual conference or provisional

---

68. Amended 1996.
69. See Judicial Council Decisions 78, 79, 132, 405, 406, 524, 532, 534, 552, 584, 690, 742, 782, 862.
70. See Judicial Council Decisions 435, 592.
71. See Judicial Council Decision 352.
72. Amended 1992.
73. Amended 1996.

annual conference who are deacons and elders in full connection, associate members, and those provisional members who have completed all of their educational requirements and local pastors who have completed course of study or an M. Div. degree and have served a minimum of two consecutive years under appointment immediately preceding the election.[74]

¶ 36. *Article V.*—The lay delegates to the General and jurisdictional or central conferences shall be elected by the lay members of the annual conference or provisional annual conference without regard to age, provided such delegates[75] shall have been professing[76] members of The United Methodist Church for at least two years next preceding their election, and shall have been active participants in The United Methodist Church for at least four years next preceding their election,[77] and are members thereof within the annual conference electing them at the time of holding the General and jurisdictional or central conferences.[78]

Section VII. Boundaries

¶ 37. *Article I.*—The United Methodist Church shall have jurisdictional conferences made up as follows:

Northeastern—Bermuda,[79] Connecticut, Delaware, District of Columbia, Maine, Maryland, Massachusetts, New Hampshire, New Jersey, New York, Pennsylvania, Rhode Island, Vermont, the Virgin Islands,[80] West Virginia.

Southeastern—Alabama, Florida, Georgia, Kentucky, Mississippi, North Carolina, South Carolina, Tennessee, Virginia.

North Central—Illinois, Indiana, Iowa, Michigan, Minnesota, North Dakota, Ohio, South Dakota, Wisconsin.

South Central—Arkansas, Kansas, Louisiana, Missouri, Nebraska, New Mexico, Oklahoma, Texas.

Western—Alaska, Arizona, California, Colorado, Hawaii, Idaho, Montana, Nevada, Oregon, Utah, Washington, and Wyoming and the territory of the United States in the Pacific region.[81]

---

74. See Judicial Council Decision 1181. Amended 2008.
75. Amended 1972.
76. Amended 2000.
77. Amended 1976.
78. See Judicial Council Decisions 403, 887.
79. Amended 2008.
80. Amended 1980.
81. Amended 1980.

¶ **38.** *Article II.*—The work of the Church outside the United States of America[82] may be formed into central conferences, the number and boundaries of which shall be determined by the Uniting Conference, the General Conference having authority subsequently to make changes in the number and boundaries.

¶ **39.** *Article III.*—Changes in the number, names, and boundaries of the jurisdictional conferences may be effected by the General Conference upon the consent of a majority of the annual conferences of each of the jurisdictional conferences involved.[83]

¶ **40.** *Article IV.*—The number, names, and boundaries of the annual conferences and episcopal areas shall be determined by the jurisdictional conferences in the United States of America[84] and by the central conferences outside the United States of America according to the provisions under the respective powers and pursuant to the respective structures[85] of the jurisdictional and the central conferences. The authority of jurisdictional and central conferences provided herein is not circumscribed or limited by the authority provided to the College of Bishops to arrange a plan of episcopal supervision.[86]

¶ **41.** *Article V. Transfer of Local Churches*—1. A local church may be transferred from one annual conference to another in which it is geographically located upon approval by a two-thirds vote of those present and voting in each of the following:

a) the charge conference;

b) the congregational meeting of the local church;

c) each of the two annual conferences involved.

The vote shall be certified by the secretaries of the specified conferences or meetings to the bishops having supervision of the annual conferences involved, and upon their announcement of the required majorities the transfer shall immediately be effective.

2. The vote on approval of transfer shall be taken by each annual conference at its first session after the matter is submitted to it.

3. Transfers under the provisions of this article shall not be governed or restricted by other provisions of this Constitution relating to changes of boundaries of conferences.

---

82. Amended 1972.
83. See Judicial Council Decisions 55, 56, 85, 215.
84. Amended 1992.
85. Amended 1992.
86. See Judicial Council Decision 1180.

Section VIII. District Conferences

¶ **42.** *Article I.*—There may be organized in an annual conference, district conferences composed of such persons and invested with such powers as the General Conference may determine.

Section IX. Charge Conferences

¶ **43.** *Article I.*—There shall be organized in each charge a charge conference composed of such persons and invested with such powers as the General Conference shall provide.

¶ **44.** *Article II. Election of Church Officers*—Unless the General Conference shall order otherwise, the officers of the church or churches constituting a charge shall be elected by the charge conference or by the professing[87] members of said church or churches at a meeting called for that purpose, as may be arranged by the charge conference, unless the election is otherwise required by local church charters or state or provincial law.

DIVISION THREE—EPISCOPAL SUPERVISION

¶ **45.** *Article I.*—There shall be a continuance of an episcopacy in The United Methodist Church of like plan, powers, privileges, and duties as now exist in The Methodist Church and in The Evangelical United Brethren Church in all those matters in which they agree and may be considered identical; and the differences between these historic episcopacies are deemed to be reconciled and harmonized by and in this Plan of Union and Constitution of The United Methodist Church and actions taken pursuant thereto so that a unified superintendency and episcopacy is hereby created and established of, in, and by those who now are and shall be bishops of The United Methodist Church; and the said episcopacy shall further have such powers, privileges, and duties as are herein set forth.[88]

¶ **46.** *Article II.*—The bishops shall be elected by the respective jurisdictional and central conferences and consecrated in the historic manner at such time and place as may be fixed by the General Conference for those elected by the jurisdictions and by each central conference for those elected by such central conference.[89]

---

87. Amended 2000.
88. See Judicial Council Decisions 4, 114, 127, 363, 1208.
89. See Judicial Council Decisions 21, 127.

¶ **47. *Article III.***—There shall be a Council of Bishops composed of all the bishops of The United Methodist Church. The council shall meet at least once a year and plan for the general oversight and promotion of the temporal and spiritual interests of the entire Church and for carrying into effect the rules, regulations, and responsibilities prescribed and enjoined by the General Conference and in accord with the provisions set forth in this Plan of Union.[90]

¶ **48. *Article IV.***—The bishops of each jurisdictional and central conference shall constitute a College of Bishops, and such College of Bishops shall arrange the plan of episcopal supervision of the annual conferences, missionary[91] conferences, and missions within their respective territories.[92]

¶ **49. *Article V.***—The bishops shall have residential and presidential supervision in the jurisdictional or central conferences[93] in which they are elected or to which they are transferred. Bishops may be transferred from one jurisdiction to another jurisdiction for presidential and residential supervision under the following conditions: (1) The transfer of bishops may be on either of two bases: (*a*) a jurisdiction that receives a bishop by transfer from another jurisdiction may transfer to that jurisdiction or to a third jurisdiction one of its own bishops eligible for transfer, so that the number transferred in by each jurisdiction shall be balanced by the number transferred out; or (*b*) a jurisdiction may receive a bishop from another jurisdiction and not transfer out a member of its own College of Bishops. (2) No bishop shall be transferred unless that bishop shall have specifically consented. (3) No bishop shall be eligible for transfer unless the bishop shall have served one quadrennium in the jurisdiction that elected the bishop to the episcopacy. (4) All such transfers shall require the approval by a majority vote of the members present and voting of the jurisdictional committees on episcopacy of the jurisdictions that are involved.[94] After the above procedures have been followed, the transferring bishop shall become a member of the receiving College of Bishops and shall be subject to residential assignment by that jurisdictional conference.

---

90. See Judicial Council Decision 424.
91. Amended 1976.
92. See Judicial Council Decisions 517, 735.
93. Amended 1980.
94. Amended 1992.

A bishop may be assigned by the Council of Bishops for presidential service or other temporary service in another jurisdiction than that which elected the bishop, provided that the request is made by a majority of the bishops in the jurisdiction of the proposed service.

In the case of an emergency in any jurisdiction or central conference through the death or disability of a bishop or other cause, the Council of Bishops may assign a bishop from another jurisdiction or central conference to the work of the said jurisdiction or central conference, with the consent of a majority of the bishops of that jurisdiction or central conference.

¶ **50.** *Article VI.*—The bishops, both active and retired, of The Evangelical United Brethren Church and of The Methodist Church at the time union is consummated shall be bishops of The United Methodist Church.

The bishops of The Methodist Church elected by the jurisdictions, the active bishops of The Evangelical United Brethren Church at the time of union, and bishops elected by the jurisdictions of The United Methodist Church shall have life tenure. Each bishop elected by a central conference of The Methodist Church shall have such tenure as the central conference electing him shall have determined.[95]

The jurisdictional conference shall elect a standing committee on episcopacy to consist of one clergy and one lay delegate from each annual conference, on nomination of the annual conference delegation. The committee shall review the work of the bishops, pass on their character and official administration, and report to the jurisdictional conference its findings for such action as the conference may deem appropriate within its constitutional warrant of power. The committee shall recommend the assignments of the bishops to their respective residences for final action by the jurisdictional conference.

¶ **51.** *Article VII.*—A bishop presiding over an annual, central, or jurisdictional conference shall decide all questions of law coming before the bishop in the regular business of a session,[96] provided that such questions be presented in writing and that the decisions be recorded in the journal of the conference.

Such an episcopal decision shall not be authoritative except for the pending case until it shall have been passed upon by the

---

95. See Judicial Council Decisions 4, 303, 361, 709.
96. See Judicial Council Decision 33.

Judicial Council. All decisions of law made by each bishop shall be reported in writing annually, with a syllabus of the same, to the Judicial Council, which shall affirm, modify, or reverse them.[97]

¶ **52.** *Article VIII.*—The bishops of the several jurisdictional and central conferences shall preside in the sessions of their respective conferences.[98]

¶ **53.** *Article IX.*—In each annual conference there shall be one or more district superintendents who shall assist the bishop in the administration of the annual conference and shall have such responsibilities and term of office as the General Conference may determine.[99]

¶ **54.** *Article X.*—The bishops shall appoint, after consultation with the district superintendents, ministers to the charges; and they shall have such responsibilities and authorities as the General Conference shall prescribe.[100]

DIVISION FOUR—THE JUDICIARY

¶ **55.** *Article I.*—There shall be a Judicial Council. The General Conference shall determine the number and qualifications of its members, their terms of office, and the method of election and the filling of vacancies.

¶ **56.** *Article II.*—The Judicial Council shall have authority:

1. To determine the constitutionality of any act of the General Conference upon an appeal of a majority of the Council of Bishops or one-fifth of the members of the General Conference and to determine the constitutionality of any act of a jurisdictional or central conference upon an appeal of a majority of the bishops of that jurisdictional or central conference or upon the appeal of one-fifth of the members of that jurisdictional or central conference.

2. To hear and determine any appeal from a bishop's decision on a question of law made in the annual conference when said appeal has been made by one-fifth of that conference present and voting.

3. To pass upon decisions of law made by bishops in annual conferences.

4. To hear and determine the legality of any action taken therein by any General Conference board or jurisdictional or central

---

97. See Judicial Council Decision 763.
98. See Judicial Council Decisions 395, 1194, 1195, 1196.
99. See Judicial Council Decisions 368, 398.
100. See Judicial Council Decision 1307.

conference board or body, upon appeal by one-third of the members thereof, or upon request of the Council of Bishops or a majority of the bishops of a jurisdictional or a central conference.

5. To have such other duties and powers as may be conferred upon it by the General Conference.

6. To provide its own methods of organization and procedure.

¶ **57.** *Article III.*—All decisions of the Judicial Council shall be final. When the Judicial Council shall declare unconstitutional any act of the General Conference then in session, that decision shall be reported back to that General Conference immediately.

¶ **58.** *Article IV.*—The General Conference shall establish for the Church a judicial system that shall guarantee to our clergy a right to trial by a committee and an appeal, and to our members a right to trial before the Church, or by a committee, and an appeal.[101]

DIVISION FIVE—AMENDMENTS

¶ **59.** *Article I.*—Amendments to the Constitution shall be made upon a two-thirds majority of the General Conference present and voting and a two-thirds affirmative vote of the aggregate number of members of the several annual conferences present and voting, except in the case of the first and second Restrictive Rules, which shall require a three-fourths majority of all the members of the annual conferences present and voting. The vote, after being completed, shall be canvassed by the Council of Bishops, and the amendment voted upon shall become effective upon their announcement of its having received the required majority.[102]

In the event that the General Conference adopts an amendment to the Constitution, the General Conference may immediately adopt enabling legislation for such amendment which shall be contingent on ratification of the amendment by the required two-thirds affirmative vote of the aggregate number of members of the several annual conferences present and voting, and effective once the Council of Bishops, operating as a canvasser of votes, announces that the amendment has been passed. In the same manner, an annual conference may approve legislation in anticipation of such a change in the *Discipline* and/or Constitution

---

101. See Judicial Council Decision 522.

102. See Judicial Council Decisions 154, 243, 244, 349, 483, 884, 961; amended 1976.

that would likewise become effective upon the effective date of said disciplinary change or Constitutional Amendment.

¶ **60.** *Article II.*—Amendments to the Constitution may originate in either the General Conference or the annual conferences.

¶ **61.** *Article III.*—A jurisdictional or central conference[103] may by a majority vote propose changes in the Constitution of the Church, and such proposed changes shall be submitted to the next General Conference. If the General Conference adopts the measure by a two-thirds vote, it shall be submitted to the annual conferences according to the provision for amendments.

---

103. Amended 1980.

Part II

GENERAL BOOK OF DISCIPLINE

¶ **101.** The *General Book of Discipline* reflects our Wesleyan way of serving Christ through doctrine and disciplined Christian life. We are a worldwide denomination united by doctrine, discipline, and mission through our connectional covenant. The *General Book of Discipline* expresses that unity. Each central conference may make changes and adaptations to the *General Book of Discipline* to more fruitfully accomplish our mission in various contexts. However, some portions of the *General Book of Discipline* are not subject to adaptation. The following parts and paragraphs are not subject to change or adaptation except by action of the General Conference. The Standing Committee on Central Conference Matters has primary responsibility for proposing to General Conference revisions to this paragraph.

Parts I -V
  I. Constitution ¶¶ 1-61
  II. General Book of Discipline ¶ 101
  III. Doctrinal Standards and Our Theological Task ¶¶ 102-105
  IV. The Ministry of All Christians ¶¶ 120-143
  V. Social Principles Preface, Preamble, and ¶¶ 160-166

The Standing Committee on Central Conference Matters, in consultation with the Committee on Faith and Order, will bring legislation to the 2020 General Conference to change the structure of the *General Book of Discipline* to include a *Part VI, General Organization and Administration* not subject to change or adaptation by central conferences, and a *Part VII, Additional Organization and Administration*, adaptable by central conferences according to ¶ 31.5. The content of Part VI of the 2016 *Book of Discipline* will be included in either Part VI or Part VII of the *General Book of Discipline*. For the work on Part VI, Chapter 2 (The Ministry of the Ordained) and Chapter 3 (The Superintendency) of the 2016 *Book of Discipline*, the Standing Committee on Central Conference Matters will work in consultation with the Commission for the Study of Ministry, and for Part VI, Chapter 5 (Administrative Order) of the 2016 *Book of Discipline*, the Standing Committee on Central Conference Matters will work in consultation with the Connectional Table.

The Commission on the General Conference is directed to set aside adequate time in the first three days of the 2020 General Conference for plenary consideration and action on *Part VI, General Administration and Organization*, submitted by the Standing Committee on Central Conference Matters. Subsequent changes to Part VI shall be reviewed by the Standing Committee on Central Conference Matters for submission to General Conference.[1]

---

1. See Judicial Council Decision 1272.

Part III

DOCTRINAL STANDARDS AND OUR THEOLOGICAL TASK[1]

¶ 102. SECTION 1—OUR DOCTRINAL HERITAGE

United Methodists profess the historic Christian faith in God, incarnate in Jesus Christ for our salvation and ever at work in human history in the Holy Spirit. Living in a covenant of grace under the Lordship of Jesus Christ, we participate in the first fruits of God's coming reign and pray in hope for its full realization on earth as in heaven.

Our heritage in doctrine and our present theological task focus upon a renewed grasp of the sovereignty of God and of God's love in Christ amid the continuing crises of human existence.

Our forebears in the faith reaffirmed the ancient Christian message as found in the apostolic witness even as they applied it anew in their own circumstances.

Their preaching and teaching were grounded in Scripture, informed by Christian tradition, enlivened in experience, and tested by reason.

Their labors inspire and inform our attempts to convey the saving gospel to our world with its needs and aspirations.

Our Common Heritage as Christians

United Methodists share a common heritage with Christians of every age and nation. This heritage is grounded in the apostolic

---

1. The Judicial Council ruled in 1972 that all sections of Part III except ¶ 104 were "legislative enactments and neither part of the Constitution nor under the Restrictive Rules" (see Judicial Council Decision 358).

47

witness to Jesus Christ as Savior and Lord, which is the source and measure of all valid Christian teaching.

Faced with diverse interpretations of the apostolic message, leaders of the early church sought to specify the core of Christian belief in order to ensure the soundness of Christian teaching.

The determination of the canon of Christian Scripture and the adoption of ecumenical creeds such as the formulations of Nicaea and Chalcedon were of central importance to this consensual process. Such creeds helped preserve the integrity of the church's witness, set boundaries for acceptable Christian doctrine, and proclaimed the basic elements of the enduring Christian message. These statements of faith, along with the Apostles' Creed, contain the most prominent features of our ecumenical heritage.

The Protestant reformers of the sixteenth and seventeenth centuries devised new confessional statements that reiterated classical Christian teaching in an attempt to recover the authentic biblical witness. These documents affirmed the primacy of Scripture and provided formal doctrinal standards through their statements of essential beliefs on matters such as the way of salvation, the Christian life, and the nature of the church.

Many distinctively Protestant teachings were transmitted into United Methodist understandings through doctrinal formulations such as the Articles of Religion of the Church of England and the Heidelberg Catechism of the Reformed tradition.

Various doctrinal statements in the form of creeds, confessions of belief, and articles of faith were officially adopted by churches as standards of Christian teaching. Notwithstanding their importance, these formal doctrinal standards by no means exhausted authoritative Christian teaching.

The standards themselves initially emerged from a much wider body of Christian thought and practice, and their fuller significance unfolded in the writings of the church's teachers. Some writings have proved simply to be dated benchmarks in the story of the church's continuing maturation.

By contrast, some sermons, treatises, liturgies, and hymns have gained considerable practical authority in the life and thought of the church by virtue of their wide and continuing acceptance as faithful expositions of Christian teaching. Nonetheless, the basic measure of authenticity in doctrinal standards, whether formally established or received by tradition, has been their fidelity to the apostolic faith grounded in Scripture and evidenced in the life of the church through the centuries.

Basic Christian Affirmations

With Christians of other communions we confess belief in the triune God—Father, Son, and Holy Spirit. This confession embraces the biblical witness to God's activity in creation, encompasses God's gracious self-involvement in the dramas of history, and anticipates the consummation of God's reign.

The created order is designed for the well-being of all creatures and as the place of human dwelling in covenant with God. As sinful creatures, however, we have broken that covenant, become estranged from God, wounded ourselves and one another, and wreaked havoc throughout the natural order. We stand in need of redemption.

We hold in common with all Christians a faith in the mystery of salvation in and through Jesus Christ. At the heart of the gospel of salvation is God's incarnation in Jesus of Nazareth. Scripture witnesses to the redeeming love of God in Jesus' life and teachings, his atoning death, his resurrection, his sovereign presence in history, his triumph over the powers of evil and death, and his promised return. Because God truly loves us in spite of our willful sin, God judges us, summons us to repentance, pardons us, receives us by that grace given to us in Jesus Christ, and gives us hope of life eternal.

We share the Christian belief that God's redemptive love is realized in human life by the activity of the Holy Spirit, both in personal experience and in the community of believers. This community is the church, which the Spirit has brought into existence for the healing of the nations.

Through faith in Jesus Christ we are forgiven, reconciled to God, and transformed as people of the new covenant.

"Life in the Spirit" involves diligent use of the means of grace such as praying, fasting, attending upon the sacraments, and inward searching in solitude. It also encompasses the communal life of the church in worship, mission, evangelism, service, and social witness.

We understand ourselves to be part of Christ's universal church when by adoration, proclamation, and service we become conformed to Christ. We are initiated and incorporated into this community of faith by baptism, receiving the promise of the Spirit that re-creates and transforms us. Through the regular celebration of Holy Communion, we participate in the risen presence of Jesus Christ and are thereby nourished for faithful discipleship.

We pray and work for the coming of God's realm and reign to the world and rejoice in the promise of everlasting life that overcomes death and the forces of evil.

With other Christians we recognize that the reign of God is both a present and future reality. The church is called to be that place where the first signs of the reign of God are identified and acknowledged in the world. Wherever persons are being made new creatures in Christ, wherever the insights and resources of the gospel are brought to bear on the life of the world, God's reign is already effective in its healing and renewing power.

We also look to the end time in which God's work will be fulfilled. This prospect gives us hope in our present actions as individuals and as the Church. This expectation saves us from resignation and motivates our continuing witness and service.

We share with many Christian communions a recognition of the authority of Scripture in matters of faith, the confession that our justification as sinners is by grace through faith, and the sober realization that the church is in need of continual reformation and renewal.

We affirm the general ministry of all baptized Christians who share responsibility for building up the church and reaching out in mission and service to the world.

With other Christians, we declare the essential oneness of the church in Christ Jesus. This rich heritage of shared Christian belief finds expression in our hymnody and liturgies. Our unity is affirmed in the historic creeds as we confess one holy, catholic, and apostolic church. It is also experienced in joint ventures of ministry and in various forms of ecumenical cooperation.

Nourished by common roots of this shared Christian heritage, the branches of Christ's church have developed diverse traditions that enlarge our store of shared understandings. Our avowed ecumenical commitment as United Methodists is to gather our own doctrinal emphases into the larger Christian unity, there to be made more meaningful in a richer whole.

If we are to offer our best gifts to the common Christian treasury, we must make a deliberate effort as a church to strive for critical self-understanding. It is as Christians involved in ecumenical partnership that we embrace and examine our distinctive heritage.

Our Distinctive Heritage as United Methodists

The underlying energy of the Wesleyan theological heritage stems from an emphasis upon practical divinity, the implementation of genuine Christianity in the lives of believers.

Methodism did not arise in response to a specific doctrinal dispute, though there was no lack of theological controversy. Early Methodists claimed to preach the scriptural doctrines of the Church of England as contained in the Articles of Religion, the Homilies, and the *Book of Common Prayer*.

Their task was not to reformulate doctrine. Their tasks were to summon people to experience the justifying and sanctifying grace of God and encourage people to grow in the knowledge and love of God through the personal and corporate disciplines of the Christian life.

The thrust of the Wesleyan movement and of the United Brethren and Evangelical Association was "to reform the nation, particularly the Church, and to spread scriptural holiness over the land."

Wesley's orientation toward the practical is evident in his focus upon the "scripture way of salvation." He considered doctrinal matters primarily in terms of their significance for Christian discipleship.

The Wesleyan emphasis upon the Christian life—faith and love put into practice—has been the hallmark of those traditions now incorporated into The United Methodist Church. The distinctive shape of the Wesleyan theological heritage can be seen in a constellation of doctrinal emphases that display the creating, redeeming, and sanctifying activity of God.

Distinctive Wesleyan Emphases

Although Wesley shared with many other Christians a belief in grace, justification, assurance, and sanctification, he combined them in a powerful manner to create distinctive emphases for living the full Christian life. The Evangelical United Brethren tradition, particularly as expressed by Phillip William Otterbein from a Reformed background, gave similar distinctive emphases.

Grace pervades our understanding of Christian faith and life. By grace we mean the undeserved, unmerited, and loving action of God in human existence through the ever-present Holy Spirit. While the grace of God is undivided, it precedes salvation as "prevenient grace," continues in "justifying grace," and is brought to fruition in "sanctifying grace."

We assert that God's grace is manifest in all creation even though suffering, violence, and evil are everywhere present. The goodness of creation is fulfilled in human beings, who are called to covenant partnership with God. God has endowed us with dignity and freedom and has summoned us to responsibility for our lives and the life of the world.

In God's self-revelation, Jesus Christ, we see the splendor of our true humanity. Even our sin, with its destructive consequences for all creation, does not alter God's intention for us—holiness and happiness of heart. Nor does it diminish our accountability for the way we live.

Despite our brokenness, we remain creatures brought into being by a just and merciful God. The restoration of God's image in our lives requires divine grace to renew our fallen nature.

Prevenient Grace—We acknowledge God's prevenient grace, the divine love that surrounds all humanity and precedes any and all of our conscious impulses. This grace prompts our first wish to please God, our first glimmer of understanding concerning God's will, and our "first slight transient conviction" of having sinned against God.

God's grace also awakens in us an earnest longing for deliverance from sin and death and moves us toward repentance and faith.

Justification and Assurance—We believe God reaches out to the repentant believer in justifying grace with accepting and pardoning love. Wesleyan theology stresses that a decisive change in the human heart can and does occur under the prompting of grace and the guidance of the Holy Spirit.

In justification we are, through faith, forgiven our sin and restored to God's favor. This righting of relationships by God through Christ calls forth our faith and trust as we experience regeneration, by which we are made new creatures in Christ.

This process of justification and new birth is often referred to as conversion. Such a change may be sudden and dramatic, or gradual and cumulative. It marks a new beginning, yet it is part of an ongoing process. Christian experience as personal transformation always expresses itself as faith working by love.

Our Wesleyan theology also embraces the scriptural promise that we can expect to receive assurance of our present salvation as the Spirit "bears witness with our spirit that we are children of God."

Sanctification and Perfection—We hold that the wonder of God's acceptance and pardon does not end God's saving work, which continues to nurture our growth in grace. Through the power of the Holy Spirit, we are enabled to increase in the knowledge and love of God and in love for our neighbor.

New birth is the first step in this process of sanctification. Sanctifying grace draws us toward the gift of Christian perfection, which Wesley described as a heart "habitually filled with the love of God and neighbor" and as "having the mind of Christ and walking as he walked."

This gracious gift of God's power and love, the hope and expectation of the faithful, is neither warranted by our efforts nor limited by our frailties.

Faith and Good Works—We see God's grace and human activity working together in the relationship of faith and good works. God's grace calls forth human response and discipline.

Faith is the only response essential for salvation. However, the General Rules remind us that salvation evidences itself in good works. For Wesley, even repentance should be accompanied by "fruits meet for repentance," or works of piety and mercy.

Both faith and good works belong within an all-encompassing theology of grace, since they stem from God's gracious love "shed abroad in our hearts by the Holy Spirit."

Mission and Service—We insist that personal salvation always involves Christian mission and service to the world. By joining heart and hand, we assert that personal religion, evangelical witness, and Christian social action are reciprocal and mutually reinforcing.

Scriptural holiness entails more than personal piety; love of God is always linked with love of neighbor, a passion for justice and renewal in the life of the world.

The General Rules represent one traditional expression of the intrinsic relationship between Christian life and thought as understood within the Wesleyan tradition. Theology is the servant of piety, which in turn is the ground of social conscience and the impetus for social action and global interaction, always in the empowering context of the reign of God.

Nurture and Mission of the Church—Finally, we emphasize the nurturing and serving function of Christian fellowship in the

Church. The personal experience of faith is nourished by the worshiping community.

For Wesley there is no religion but social religion, no holiness but social holiness. The communal forms of faith in the Wesleyan tradition not only promote personal growth; they also equip and mobilize us for mission and service to the world.

The outreach of the church springs from the working of the Spirit. As United Methodists, we respond to that working through a connectional polity based upon mutual responsiveness and accountability. Connectional ties bind us together in faith and service in our global witness, enabling faith to become active in love and intensifying our desire for peace and justice in the world.

Doctrine and Discipline in the Christian Life

No motif in the Wesleyan tradition has been more constant than the link between Christian doctrine and Christian living. Methodists have always been strictly enjoined to maintain the unity of faith and good works through the means of grace, as seen in John Wesley's *Nature, Design, and General Rules of the United Societies* (1743). The coherence of faith with ministries of love forms the discipline of Wesleyan spirituality and Christian discipleship.

The General Rules were originally designed for members of Methodist societies who participated in the sacramental life of the Church of England. The terms of membership in these societies were simple: "a desire to flee from the wrath to come and to be saved from their sins."

Wesley insisted, however, that evangelical faith should manifest itself in evangelical living. He spelled out this expectation in the three-part formula of the Rules:

"It is therefore expected of all who continue therein that they should continue to evidence their desire of salvation,

"First: By doing no harm, by avoiding evil of every kind . . . ;

"Secondly: By . . . doing good of every possible sort, and, as far as possible, to all . . . ;

"Thirdly: By attending upon all the ordinances of God" (see ¶ 104).

Wesley's illustrative cases under each of these three rules show how the Christian conscience might move from general principles to specific actions. Their explicit combination highlights the spiritual spring of moral action.

Wesley rejected undue reliance upon these rules. Discipline was not church law; it was a way of discipleship. Wesley insisted that true religion is "the knowledge of God in Christ Jesus," "the life which is hid with Christ in God," and "the righteousness that [the true believer] thirsts after."

General Rules and Social Principles

Upon such evangelical premises, Methodists in every age have sought to exercise their responsibility for the moral and spiritual quality of society. In asserting the connection between doctrine and ethics, the General Rules provide an early signal of Methodist social consciousness.

The Social Principles (¶¶ 160-166) provide our most recent official summary of stated convictions that seek to apply the Christian vision of righteousness to social, economic, and political issues. Our historic opposition to evils such as smuggling, inhumane prison conditions, slavery, drunkenness, and child labor was founded upon a vivid sense of God's wrath against human injustice and wastage.

Our struggles for human dignity and social reform have been a response to God's demand for love, mercy, and justice in the light of the Kingdom. We proclaim no *personal gospel* that fails to express itself in relevant social concerns; we proclaim no *social gospel* that does not include the personal transformation of sinners.

It is our conviction that the good news of the Kingdom must judge, redeem, and reform the sinful social structures of our time.

The *Book of Discipline* and the General Rules convey the expectation of discipline within the experience of individuals and the life of the Church. Such discipline assumes accountability to the community of faith by those who claim that community's support.

Support without accountability promotes moral weakness; accountability without support is a form of cruelty.

A church that rushes to punishment is not open to God's mercy, but a church lacking the courage to act decisively on personal and social issues loses its claim to moral authority. The church exercises its discipline as a community through which God continues to "reconcile the world to himself."

Conclusion

These distinctive emphases of United Methodists provide the basis for "practical divinity," the experiential realization of the gospel of Jesus Christ in the lives of Christian people. These emphases have been preserved not so much through formal doctrinal declarations as through the vital movement of faith and practice as seen in converted lives and within the disciplined life of the Church.

Devising formal definitions of doctrine has been less pressing for United Methodists than summoning people to faith and nurturing them in the knowledge and love of God. The core of Wesleyan doctrine that informed our past rightly belongs to our common heritage as Christians and remains a prime component within our continuing theological task.

¶ 103. SECTION 2—OUR DOCTRINAL HISTORY

The pioneers in the traditions that flowed together into The United Methodist Church understood themselves as standing in the central stream of Christian spirituality and doctrine, loyal heirs of the authentic Christian tradition. In John Wesley's words, theirs was "the old religion, the religion of the Bible, the religion . . . of the whole church in the purest ages." Their gospel was grounded in the biblical message of God's self-giving love revealed in Jesus Christ.

Wesley's portrayal of the spiritual pilgrimage in terms of "the scripture way of salvation" provided their model for experiential Christianity. They assumed and insisted upon the integrity of basic Christian truth and emphasized its practical application in the lives of believers.

This perspective is apparent in the Wesleyan understanding of "catholic spirit." While it is true that United Methodists are fixed upon certain religious affirmations, grounded in the gospel and confirmed in their experience, they also recognize the right of Christians to disagree on matters such as forms of worship, structures of church government, modes of baptism, or theological explorations. They believe such differences do not break the bond of fellowship that ties Christians together in Jesus Christ. Wesley's familiar dictum was, "As to all opinions which do not strike at the root of Christianity, we think and let think."

But, even as they were fully committed to the principles of religious toleration and theological diversity, they were equally confident that there is a "marrow" of Christian truth that can be identified and that must be conserved. This living core, as they believed, stands revealed in Scripture, illumined by tradition, vivified in personal and corporate experience, and confirmed by reason. They were very much aware, of course, that God's eternal Word never has been, nor can be, exhaustively expressed in any single form of words.

They were also prepared, as a matter of course, to reaffirm the ancient creeds and confessions as valid summaries of Christian truth. But they were careful not to set them apart as absolute standards for doctrinal truth and error.

Beyond the essentials of vital religion, United Methodists respect the diversity of opinions held by conscientious persons of faith. Wesley followed a time-tested approach: "In essentials, unity; in non-essentials, liberty; and in all things, charity."

The spirit of charity takes into consideration the limits of human understanding. "To be ignorant of many things and to be mistaken in some," Wesley observed, "is the necessary condition of humanity." The crucial matter in religion is steadfast love for God and neighbor, empowered by the redeeming and sanctifying work of the Holy Spirit.

The Wesleyan "Standards" in Great Britain

In this spirit, the British Methodists under the Wesleys never reduced their theology to a confessional formula as a doctrinal test. Methodism was a movement within the Church of England, and John Wesley constantly maintained that he taught the scriptural doctrines contained in the Thirty-Nine Articles, the Homilies, and the *Book of Common Prayer* of his national church. The Bible, of course, constituted for him the final authority in all doctrinal matters.

As the movement grew, Wesley provided his people with published sermons and a Bible commentary for their doctrinal instruction. His *Sermons on Several Occasions* (1746-60) set forth those doctrines which, he said, "I embrace and teach as the essentials of true religion." In 1755, he published *Explanatory Notes Upon the New Testament* as a guide for Methodist biblical exegesis and doctrinal interpretation.

As occasional controversies arose, the need for a standard measure of Methodist preaching became evident. In 1763, Wesley produced a "Model Deed" for Methodist properties, which stipulated that the trustees for each preaching house were responsible for ensuring that the preachers in their pulpits "preach no other doctrine than is contained in Mr. Wesley's *Notes Upon the New Testament* and four volumes of *Sermons*."

These writings, then, contained the standard exposition of Methodist teaching. They provide a model and measure for adequate preaching in the Wesleyan tradition. The primary norm for Wesley's writings was Scripture, as illumined by historic traditions and vital faith. Wesley put forth no summary of biblical revelation for the British Methodists because the Thirty-Nine Articles of the Church of England were already available.

The Wesley brothers also composed hymns that were rich in doctrinal and experiential content. The hymns, especially those of Charles Wesley, not only are among the best-loved within Methodism but also are major resources for doctrinal instruction.

Furthermore, John Wesley specified various disciplines and rules, such as the General Rules, to implement in personal and communal life the practical divinity he proclaimed.

In addition to these writings, Wesley established the conference to instruct and supervise the Methodist preachers. He produced Minutes to ensure their fidelity to the doctrines and disciplines of the Methodist movement. These writings and structures filled out the Wesleyan understanding of the church and the Christian life.

Doctrinal Standards in American Methodism

As long as the American colonies were primarily under British control, the Methodists could continue as part of the sacramental community of the Church of England. The early conferences, under the leadership of British preachers, declared their allegiance to the Wesleyan principles of organization and doctrine. They stipulated that the Minutes of the British and American conferences, along with the *Sermons* and *Notes* of Wesley, contained their basic doctrine and discipline.

After the formal recognition of American independence in 1783, Wesley realized that the Methodists in America were free of English control, religious as well as civil, and should become an independent Methodist church. Wesley then furnished the American Methodists with a liturgy (*The Sunday Service of the Methodists in North America*) and a doctrinal statement (*The Articles of Religion*). The *Sunday Service* was Wesley's abridgment of the *Book of*

Common Prayer; the Articles of Religion were his revision of the Thirty-Nine Articles.

The American Methodist preachers, gathered at Baltimore in December 1784, adopted the Sunday Service and the Articles of Religion as part of their actions in forming the new Methodist Episcopal Church. This "Christmas Conference" also accepted a hymnbook that Wesley had prepared (1784) and adopted a slightly modified version of the General Rules as a statement of the Church's nature and discipline. The conference spent most of its time adapting the British "Large Minutes" to American conditions. Subsequent editions of this document came to be known as the *Doctrines and Discipline of the Methodist Episcopal Church* (the *Book of Discipline*).

The shift from "movement" to "church" had changed the function of doctrinal norms within American Methodism. Rather than prescribing doctrinal emphases for preaching within a movement, the Articles outlined basic norms for Christian belief within a church, following the traditional Anglican fashion.

The preface to the first separate publication of the Articles states, "These are the doctrines taught among the people called Methodists. Nor is there any doctrine whatever, generally received among that people, contrary to the articles now before you."

American Methodists were not required to subscribe to the Articles after the Anglican manner, but they were accountable (under threat of trial) for keeping their proclamation of the gospel within the boundaries outlined therein. For generations, the *Doctrines and Discipline* cited only the Articles as the basis for testing correct doctrine in the newly formed church: The charge of doctrinal irregularity against preachers or members was for "disseminating doctrines contrary to our Articles of Religion." In this manner, the church protected its doctrinal integrity against the heresies that were prevalent at the time—Socinianism, Arianism, and Pelagianism (see Articles I, II, and IX).

The Articles of Religion, however, did not guarantee adequate Methodist preaching; they lacked several Wesleyan emphases, such as assurance and Christian perfection. Wesley's *Sermons* and *Notes,* therefore, continued to function as the traditional standard exposition of distinctive Methodist teaching.

The General Conference of 1808, which provided the first Constitution of The Methodist Episcopal Church, established the Articles of Religion as the Church's explicit doctrinal standards. The first Restrictive Rule of the Constitution prohibited any change, alteration, or addition to the Articles themselves, and it stipulated that no new standards or rules of doctrine could be adopted that were contrary to the "present existing and established standards of doctrine."

Within the Wesleyan tradition, then as now, the *Sermons* and *Notes* furnished models of doctrinal exposition. Other documents have also served American Methodism as vital expressions of Methodist teaching and preaching. Lists of recommended doctrinal resources vary from generation to generation but generally acknowledge the importance of the hymnbook, the ecumenical creeds, and the General Rules. Lists of such writings in the early nineteenth century usually included John Fletcher's *Checks Against Antinomianism* and Richard Watson's *Theological Institutes*.

The doctrinal emphases of these statements were carried forward by the weight of tradition rather than the force of law. They became part of the heritage of American Methodism to the degree that they remained useful to continuing generations.

During the great frontier revivals of the nineteenth century, the influence of European theological traditions waned in America. Preaching focused on "Christian experience," understood chiefly as "saving faith in Christ." Among the Methodists there was a consistent stress on free will, infant baptism, and informal worship, which led to protracted controversies with the Presbyterians, Baptists, and Episcopalians, respectively.

Methodist interest in formal doctrinal standards remained secondary to evangelism, nurture, and mission. The Wesleyan hymnody served in practice as the most important single means of communicating and preserving the doctrinal substance of the gospel.

By the end of the nineteenth century, Methodist theology in America had become decidedly eclectic, with less specific attention paid to its Wesleyan sources.

The force of the Articles of Religion underwent several shifts. For a time, the first Restrictive Rule was exempted from the process of constitutional amendment, thus allowing no consideration of change in doctrinal standards. Mention of the Articles of Religion was included in the membership vows of The Methodist Episcopal Church, South.

At the beginning of the twentieth century, however, the waning force of doctrinal discipline and the decreasing influence of

the Wesleyan theological heritage among the American Methodists, along with minor but significant changes in the wording of
the *Book of Discipline* regarding doctrinal standards, led to a steady
dilution of the force of the Articles of Religion as the Church's
constitutional standards of doctrine.

During this same period, theologians and church leaders began
to explore ways of expressing the gospel that were in keeping
with developing intellectual currents. These leaders also began to
rethink the historical social compassion of the Wesleyan tradition
in the midst of the emerging industrial, urban civilization. They
deepened our awareness of the systemic nature of evil and the
urgency to proclaim the gospel promise of social redemption.
Consequently, theologies supportive of the social gospel found
fertile soil within the Methodist traditions.

These years were times of theological and ethical controversy
within Methodism as new patterns of thought clashed with the
more familiar themes and styles of the previous two centuries.

In recent decades there has been a strong recovery of interest
in Wesley and in the more classic traditions of Christian thought.
This recovery has been part of a broad resurgence of Reformation
theology and practice in Europe and America, renewing the historical legacy of Protestantism in the context of the modern world.
These trends have been reinforced in North America by the reaffirmation of evangelical piety.

The ecumenical movement has brought new appreciation
for the unity as well as the richness and diversity of the church
catholic.

Currents of theology have developed out of Black people's
struggle for freedom, the movement for the full equality of
women in church and society, and the quest for liberation and
for indigenous forms of Christian existence in churches around
the world.

The challenge to United Methodists is to discern the various
strands of these vital movements of faith that are coherent, faithful understandings of the gospel and the Christian mission for
our times.

The task of defining the scope of our Wesleyan tradition in
the context of the contemporary world includes much more
than formally reaffirming or redefining standards of doctrine,
although these tasks may also be involved. The heart of our task
is to reclaim and renew the distinctive United Methodist doctrinal

heritage, which rightly belongs to our common heritage as Christians, for the life and mission of the whole church today.

Doctrinal Traditions in The Evangelical Church and The United Brethren Church

The unfolding of doctrinal concerns among Jacob Albright's Evangelical Association and Phillip William Otterbein's United Brethren in Christ roughly parallels Methodist developments. Differences emerged largely from differing ecclesiastical traditions brought from Germany and Holland, together with the modified Calvinism of the Heidelberg Catechism.

In the German-speaking communities of America, Albright and Otterbein considered evangelism more important than theological speculation. Although they were not doctrinally indifferent, they stressed conversion, "justification by faith confirmed by a sensible assurance thereof," Christian nurture, the priesthood of all believers in a shared ministry of Christian witness and service, and entire sanctification as the goal of Christian life.

As with Wesley, their primary source and norm for Christian teaching was Scripture. Otterbein enjoined his followers "to be careful to preach no other doctrine than what is plainly laid down in the Bible." Each new member was asked "to confess that he received the Bible as the Word of God." Ordinands were required to affirm without reserve the plenary authority of Scripture.

Matched with these affirmations was the conviction that converted Christians are enabled by the Holy Spirit to read Scripture with a special Christian consciousness. They prized this principle as the supreme guide in biblical interpretation.

Jacob Albright was directed by the conference of 1807 to prepare a list of Articles of Religion. He died before he could attempt the task.

George Miller then assumed the responsibility. He recommended to the conference of 1809 the adoption of the German translation of the Methodist Articles of Religion, with the addition of a new one, "Of the Last Judgment." The recommendation was adopted. This action affirms a conscious choice of the Methodist Articles as normative. The added article was from the Augsburg Confession, on a theme omitted in the Anglican Articles.

In 1816, the original twenty-six Articles were reduced to twenty-one by omitting five polemical articles aimed at Roman

Catholics, Anabaptists, and sixteenth-century sectaries. This act of deletion reflected a conciliatory spirit in a time of bitter controversy.

In 1839, a few slight changes were made in the text of 1816. It was then stipulated that "the Articles of Faith . . . should be constitutionally unchangeable among us."

In the 1870s, a proposal to revise the Articles touched off a flurry of debate, but the conference of 1875 decisively rejected the proposal.

In later action the twenty-one Articles were reduced to nineteen by combining several, but without omitting any of their original content.

These nineteen were brought intact into the Evangelical United Brethren union of 1946.

Among the United Brethren in Christ, a summary of normative teaching was formulated in 1813 by Christian Newcomer and Christopher Grosch, colleagues of Otterbein. Its first three paragraphs follow the order of the Apostles' Creed. Paragraphs four and five affirm the primacy of Scripture and the universal proclamation of "the biblical doctrine . . . of man's fall in Adam and his deliverance through Jesus Christ." An added section commends "the ordinances of baptism and the remembrance of the Lord" and approves foot washing as optional.

The first General Conference of the United Brethren in Christ (1815) adopted a slight revision of this earlier statement as the denomination's Confession of Faith. A further revision was made in 1841, with the stipulation that there be no further changes: "No rule or ordinance shall at any time be passed to change or do away with the Confession of Faith as it now stands." Even so, agitation for change continued.

In 1885, a church commission was appointed to "prepare such a form of belief and such amended fundamental rules for the government of this church in the future as will, in their judgment, be best adapted to secure its growth and efficiency in the work of evangelizing the world."

The resulting proposal for a new Confession of Faith and Constitution was submitted to the general membership of the Church, the first such referendum on a Confession of Faith in United Brethren history, and was then placed before the General Conference of 1889. Both the general membership and the conference approved the Confession by preponderant majorities. It was thereupon enacted by episcopal "proclamation." However, this action was protested by a minority as a violation of the Restrictive Rule of 1841 and became a basic cause for a consequent schism, resulting in the formation of The United Brethren Church (Old Constitution).

The Confession of Faith of 1889 was more comprehensive than any of its antecedents, with articles on depravity, justification, regeneration and adoption, sanctification, the Christian Sabbath, and the future state. The article on sanctification, though brief, is significant in its reflection of the doctrine of holiness of the Heidelberg Catechism. The 1889 Confession was brought by the United Brethren into the union with the Evangelicals in 1946.

The Evangelical United Brethren Confession of Faith

The *Discipline* of the new Evangelical United Brethren Church (1946) contained both the Evangelical Articles and the United Brethren Confession. Twelve years later the General Conference of the united church authorized its board of bishops to prepare a new Confession of Faith.

A new Confession, with sixteen articles, of a somewhat more modern character than any of its antecedents, was presented to the General Conference of 1962 and adopted without amendment. The Evangelical article, "Entire Sanctification and Christian Perfection," is reflected in this confession as a distinctive emphasis. The Confession of Faith replaced both former Articles and Confession and was brought over intact into the *Discipline* of The United Methodist Church (1968).

Doctrinal Standards in The United Methodist Church

In the Plan of Union for The United Methodist Church, the preface to the Methodist Articles of Religion and the Evangelical United Brethren Confession of Faith explains that both were accepted as doctrinal standards for the new church. Additionally, it stated that although the language of the first Restrictive Rule never has been formally defined, Wesley's *Sermons* and *Notes* were understood specifically to be included in our present existing and established standards of doctrine. It also stated that the Articles, the Confession, and the Wesleyan "standards" were "thus deemed congruent if not identical in their doctrinal perspectives and not in conflict." This declaration was accepted by subsequent rulings of the Judicial Council.[2]

The Constitution of The United Methodist Church, in its Restrictive Rules (see ¶¶ 17-22), protects both the Articles of Religion and the Confession of Faith as doctrinal standards that shall not be revoked, altered, or changed. The process of creating new "standards or rules of doctrine" thus continues to be restricted, requiring either that they be declared "not contrary to" the present standards or that they go through the difficult process of constitutional amendment.

The United Methodist Church stands continually in need of doctrinal reinvigoration for the sake of authentic renewal, fruitful evangelism, and ecumenical dialogue. In this light, the recovery and updating of our distinctive doctrinal heritage—catholic, evangelical, and reformed—is essential.

This task calls for the repossession of our traditions as well as the promotion of theological inquiry both within the denomination and in our ecumenical efforts. All are invited to share in this endeavor to stimulate an active interest in doctrinal understanding in order to claim our legacy and to shape that legacy for the Church we aspire to be.

¶ 104. SECTION 3—OUR DOCTRINAL STANDARDS AND GENERAL RULES

THE ARTICLES OF RELIGION OF THE METHODIST CHURCH[3]

[Bibliographical Note: The Articles of Religion are here reprinted from the *Discipline* of 1808 (when the first Restrictive Rule took effect), collated against Wesley's original text in *The Sunday Service of the Methodists* (1784). To these are added two Articles: "Of Sanctification" and "Of the Duty of Christians to the Civil Authority," which are legislative enactments and not integral parts of the document as protected by the Constitution (see Judicial Council Decisions 41, 176).]

Article I—Of Faith in the Holy Trinity

There is but one living and true God, everlasting, without body or parts, of infinite power, wisdom, and goodness; the maker

---

2. See Judicial Council Decision 358.
3. Protected by Restrictive Rule 1 (¶ 17).

and preserver of all things, both visible and invisible. And in unity of this Godhead there are three persons, of one substance, power, and eternity—the Father, the Son, and the Holy Ghost.

Article II—Of the Word, or Son of God, Who Was Made Very Man

The Son, who is the Word of the Father, the very and eternal God, of one substance with the Father, took man's nature in the womb of the blessed Virgin; so that two whole and perfect natures, that is to say, the Godhead and Manhood, were joined together in one person, never to be divided; whereof is one Christ, very God and very Man, who truly suffered, was crucified, dead, and buried, to reconcile his Father to us, and to be a sacrifice, not only for original guilt, but also for actual sins of men.

Article III—Of the Resurrection of Christ

Christ did truly rise again from the dead, and took again his body, with all things appertaining to the perfection of man's nature, wherewith he ascended into heaven, and there sitteth until he return to judge all men at the last day.

Article IV—Of the Holy Ghost

The Holy Ghost, proceeding from the Father and the Son, is of one substance, majesty, and glory with the Father and the Son, very and eternal God.

Article V—Of the Sufficiency of the Holy Scriptures for Salvation

The Holy Scripture containeth all things necessary to salvation; so that whatsoever is not read therein, nor may be proved thereby, is not to be required of any man that it should be believed as an article of faith, or be thought requisite or necessary to salvation. In the name of the Holy Scripture we do understand those canonical books of the Old and New Testament of whose authority was never any doubt in the church. The names of the canonical books are:

Genesis, Exodus, Leviticus, Numbers, Deuteronomy, Joshua, Judges, Ruth, The First Book of Samuel, The Second Book of Samuel, The First Book of Kings, The Second Book of Kings, The First Book of Chronicles, The Second Book of Chronicles, The Book of

Ezra, The Book of Nehemiah, The Book of Esther, The Book of Job, The Psalms, The Proverbs, Ecclesiastes or the Preacher, Cantica or Songs of Solomon, Four Prophets the Greater, Twelve Prophets the Less.

All the books of the New Testament, as they are commonly received, we do receive and account canonical.

Article VI—Of the Old Testament

The Old Testament is not contrary to the New; for both in the Old and New Testament everlasting life is offered to mankind by Christ, who is the only Mediator between God and man, being both God and Man. Wherefore they are not to be heard who feign that the old fathers did look only for transitory promises. Although the law given from God by Moses as touching ceremonies and rites doth not bind Christians, nor ought the civil precepts thereof of necessity be received in any commonwealth; yet notwithstanding, no Christian whatsoever is free from the obedience of the commandments which are called moral.

Article VII—Of Original or Birth Sin

Original sin standeth not in the following of Adam (as the Pelagians do vainly talk), but it is the corruption of the nature of every man, that naturally is engendered of the offspring of Adam, whereby man is very far gone from original righteousness, and of his own nature inclined to evil, and that continually.

Article VIII—Of Free Will

The condition of man after the fall of Adam is such that he cannot turn and prepare himself, by his own natural strength and works, to faith, and calling upon God; wherefore we have no power to do good works, pleasant and acceptable to God, without the grace of God by Christ preventing us, that we may have a good will, and working with us, when we have that good will.

Article IX—Of the Justification of Man

We are accounted righteous before God only for the merit of our Lord and Saviour Jesus Christ, by faith, and not for our own works or deservings. Wherefore, that we are justified by faith, only, is a most wholesome doctrine, and very full of comfort.

Article X—Of Good Works

Although good works, which are the fruits of faith, and follow after justification, cannot put away our sins, and endure the severity of God's judgment; yet are they pleasing and acceptable to God in Christ, and spring out of a true and lively faith, insomuch that by them a lively faith may be as evidently known as a tree is discerned by its fruit.

Article XI—Of Works of Supererogation

Voluntary works—besides, over and above God's commandments—which they call works of supererogation, cannot be taught without arrogancy and impiety. For by them men do declare that they do not only render unto God as much as they are bound to do, but that they do more for his sake than of bounden duty is required; whereas Christ saith plainly: When you have done all that is commanded you, say, We are unprofitable servants.

Article XII—Of Sin After Justification

Not every sin willingly committed after justification is the sin against the Holy Ghost, and unpardonable. Wherefore, the grant of repentance is not to be denied to such as fall into sin after justification. After we have received the Holy Ghost, we may depart from grace given, and fall into sin, and, by the grace of God, rise again and amend our lives. And therefore they are to be condemned who say they can no more sin as long as they live here; or deny the place of forgiveness to such as truly repent.

Article XIII—Of the Church

The visible church of Christ is a congregation of faithful men in which the pure Word of God is preached, and the Sacraments duly administered according to Christ's ordinance, in all those things that of necessity are requisite to the same.

Article XIV—Of Purgatory[4]

The Romish doctrine concerning purgatory, pardon, worshiping, and adoration, as well of images as of relics, and also invoca-

---

4. For the contemporary interpretation of this and similar articles (i.e., Articles XIV, XV, XVI, XVIII, XIX, XX, and XXI) in consonance with our best ecumenical insights and judgment, see "Resolution of Intent: With a View to Unity" (*The Book of Resolutions*, 2016, Resolution Number 3144).

tion of saints, is a fond thing, vainly invented, and grounded upon no warrant of Scripture, but repugnant to the Word of God.

Article XV—Of Speaking in the Congregation in Such a Tongue as the People Understand

It is a thing plainly repugnant to the Word of God, and the custom of the primitive church, to have public prayer in the church, or to minister the Sacraments, in a tongue not understood by the people.

Article XVI—Of the Sacraments

Sacraments ordained of Christ are not only badges or tokens of Christian men's profession, but rather they are certain signs of grace, and God's good will toward us, by which he doth work invisibly in us, and doth not only quicken, but also strengthen and confirm, our faith in him.

There are two Sacraments ordained of Christ our Lord in the Gospel; that is to say, Baptism and the Supper of the Lord.

Those five commonly called sacraments, that is to say, confirmation, penance, orders, matrimony, and extreme unction, are not to be counted for Sacraments of the Gospel; being such as have partly grown out of the *corrupt* following of the apostles, and partly are states of life allowed in the Scriptures, but yet have not the like nature of Baptism and the Lord's Supper, because they have not any visible sign or ceremony ordained of God.

The Sacraments were not ordained of Christ to be gazed upon, or to be carried about; but that we should duly use them. And in such only as worthily receive the same, they have a wholesome effect or operation; but they that receive them unworthily, purchase to themselves condemnation, as St. Paul saith.

Article XVII—Of Baptism

Baptism is not only a sign of profession and mark of difference whereby Christians are distinguished from others that are not baptized; but it is also a sign of regeneration or the new birth. The Baptism of young children is to be retained in the Church.[5]

---

5. See Judicial Council Decision 142.

Article XVIII—Of the Lord's Supper

The Supper of the Lord is not only a sign of the love that Christians ought to have among themselves one to another, but rather is a sacrament of our redemption by Christ's death; insomuch that, to such as rightly, worthily, and with faith receive the same, the bread which we break is a partaking of the body of Christ; and likewise the cup of blessing is a partaking of the blood of Christ.

Transubstantiation, or the change of the substance of bread and wine in the Supper of our Lord, cannot be proved by Holy Writ, but is repugnant to the plain words of Scripture, overthroweth the nature of a sacrament, and hath given occasion to many superstitions.

The body of Christ is given, taken, and eaten in the Supper, only after a heavenly and spiritual manner. And the means whereby the body of Christ is received and eaten in the Supper is faith.

The Sacrament of the Lord's Supper was not by Christ's ordinance reserved, carried about, lifted up, or worshiped.

Article XIX—Of Both Kinds

The cup of the Lord is not to be denied to the lay people; for both the parts of the Lord's Supper, by Christ's ordinance and commandment, ought to be administered to all Christians alike.

Article XX—Of the One Oblation of Christ, Finished upon the Cross

The offering of Christ, once made, is that perfect redemption, propitiation, and satisfaction for all the sins of the whole world, both original and actual; and there is none other satisfaction for sin but that alone. Wherefore the sacrifice of masses, in the which it is commonly said that the priest doth offer Christ for the quick and the dead, to have remission of pain or guilt, is a blasphemous fable and dangerous deceit.

Article XXI—Of the Marriage of Ministers

The ministers of Christ are not commanded by God's law either to vow the estate of single life, or to abstain from marriage; therefore it is lawful for them, as for all other Christians, to marry at their own discretion, as they shall judge the same to serve best to godliness.

Article XXII—Of the Rites and Ceremonies of Churches

It is not necessary that rites and ceremonies should in all places be the same, or exactly alike; for they have been always different, and may be changed according to the diversity of countries, times, and men's manners, so that nothing be ordained against God's Word. Whosoever, through his private judgment, willingly and purposely doth openly break the rites and ceremonies of the church to which he belongs, which are not repugnant to the Word of God, and are ordained and approved by common authority, ought to be rebuked openly, that others may fear to do the like, as one that offendeth against the common order of the church, and woundeth the consciences of weak brethren.

Every particular church may ordain, change, or abolish rites and ceremonies, so that all things may be done to edification.

Article XXIII—Of the Rulers of the United States of America

The President, the Congress, the general assemblies, the governors, and the councils of state, *as the delegates of the people,* are the rulers of the United States of America, according to the division of power made to them by the Constitution of the United States and by the constitutions of their respective states. And the said states are a sovereign and independent nation, and ought not to be subject to any foreign jurisdiction.

Article XXIV—Of Christian Men's Goods

The riches and goods of Christians are not common as touching the right, title, and possession of the same, as some do falsely boast. Notwithstanding, every man ought, of such things as he possesseth, liberally to give alms to the poor, according to his ability.

Article XXV—Of a Christian Man's Oath

As we confess that vain and rash swearing is forbidden Christian men by our Lord Jesus Christ and James his apostle, so we judge that the Christian religion doth not prohibit, but that a man may swear when the magistrate requireth, in a cause of faith and charity, so it be done according to the prophet's teaching, in justice, judgment, and truth.

[The following Article from the Methodist Protestant *Discipline* is placed here by the Uniting Conference (1939). It was not one of the Articles of Religion voted upon by the three churches.]

Of Sanctification

Sanctification is that renewal of our fallen nature by the Holy Ghost, received through faith in Jesus Christ, whose blood of atonement cleanseth from all sin; whereby we are not only delivered from the guilt of sin, but are washed from its pollution, saved from its power, and are enabled, through grace, to love God with all our hearts and to walk in his holy commandments blameless.

[The following provision was adopted by the Uniting Conference (1939). This statement seeks to interpret to our churches in foreign lands Article XXIII of the Articles of Religion. It is a legislative enactment but is not a part of the Constitution. (See Judicial Council Decisions 41, 176, and Decision 6, Interim Judicial Council.)]

Of the Duty of Christians to the Civil Authority

It is the duty of all Christians, and especially of all Christian ministers, to observe and obey the laws and commands of the governing or supreme authority of the country of which they are citizens or subjects or in which they reside, and to use all laudable means to encourage and enjoin obedience to the powers that be.

THE CONFESSION OF FAITH
OF THE EVANGELICAL UNITED BRETHREN CHURCH[6]

[Bibliographical Note: The text of the Confession of Faith is identical to that of its original in *The Discipline of The Evangelical United Brethren Church* (1963).]

Article I—God

We believe in the one true, holy and living God, Eternal Spirit, who is Creator, Sovereign and Preserver of all things visible and invisible. He is infinite in power, wisdom, justice, goodness and love, and rules with gracious regard for the well-being and salvation of men, to the glory of his name. We believe the one God reveals himself as the Trinity: Father, Son and Holy Spirit, distinct but inseparable, eternally one in essence and power.

---

6. Protected by Restrictive Rule 2 (¶ 18).

Article II—Jesus Christ

We believe in Jesus Christ, truly God and truly man, in whom the divine and human natures are perfectly and inseparably united. He is the eternal Word made flesh, the only begotten Son of the Father, born of the Virgin Mary by the power of the Holy Spirit. As ministering Servant he lived, suffered and died on the cross. He was buried, rose from the dead and ascended into heaven to be with the Father, from whence he shall return. He is eternal Savior and Mediator, who intercedes for us, and by him all men will be judged.

Article III—The Holy Spirit

We believe in the Holy Spirit who proceeds from and is one in being with the Father and the Son. He convinces the world of sin, of righteousness and of judgment. He leads men through faithful response to the gospel into the fellowship of the Church. He comforts, sustains and empowers the faithful and guides them into all truth.

Article IV—The Holy Bible

We believe the Holy Bible, Old and New Testaments, reveals the Word of God so far as it is necessary for our salvation. It is to be received through the Holy Spirit as the true rule and guide for faith and practice. Whatever is not revealed in or established by the Holy Scriptures is not to be made an article of faith nor is it to be taught as essential to salvation.

Article V—The Church

We believe the Christian Church is the community of all true believers under the Lordship of Christ. We believe it is one, holy, apostolic and catholic. It is the redemptive fellowship in which the Word of God is preached by men divinely called, and the sacraments are duly administered according to Christ's own appointment. Under the discipline of the Holy Spirit the Church exists for the maintenance of worship, the edification of believers and the redemption of the world.

Article VI—The Sacraments

We believe the Sacraments, ordained by Christ, are symbols and pledges of the Christian's profession and of God's love toward us. They are means of grace by which God works invisibly in us, quickening, strengthening and confirming our faith in him. Two Sacraments are ordained by Christ our Lord, namely Baptism and the Lord's Supper.

We believe Baptism signifies entrance into the household of faith, and is a symbol of repentance and inner cleansing from sin, a representation of the new birth in Christ Jesus and a mark of Christian discipleship.

We believe children are under the atonement of Christ and as heirs of the Kingdom of God are acceptable subjects for Christian Baptism. Children of believing parents through Baptism become the special responsibility of the Church. They should be nurtured and led to personal acceptance of Christ, and by profession of faith confirm their Baptism.

We believe the Lord's Supper is a representation of our redemption, a memorial of the sufferings and death of Christ, and a token of love and union which Christians have with Christ and with one another. Those who rightly, worthily and in faith eat the broken bread and drink the blessed cup partake of the body and blood of Christ in a spiritual manner until he comes.

Article VII—Sin and Free Will

We believe man is fallen from righteousness and, apart from the grace of our Lord Jesus Christ, is destitute of holiness and inclined to evil. Except a man be born again, he cannot see the Kingdom of God. In his own strength, without divine grace, man cannot do good works pleasing and acceptable to God. We believe, however, man influenced and empowered by the Holy Spirit is responsible in freedom to exercise his will for good.

Article VIII—Reconciliation Through Christ

We believe God was in Christ reconciling the world to himself. The offering Christ freely made on the cross is the perfect and sufficient sacrifice for the sins of the whole world, redeeming man from all sin, so that no other satisfaction is required.

Article IX—Justification and Regeneration

We believe we are never accounted righteous before God through our works or merit, but that penitent sinners are justified or accounted righteous before God only by faith in our Lord Jesus Christ.

We believe regeneration is the renewal of man in righteousness through Jesus Christ, by the power of the Holy Spirit, whereby we are made partakers of the divine nature and experience newness of life. By this new birth the believer becomes reconciled to God and is enabled to serve him with the will and the affections.

We believe, although we have experienced regeneration, it is possible to depart from grace and fall into sin; and we may even then, by the grace of God, be renewed in righteousness.

Article X—Good Works

We believe good works are the necessary fruits of faith and follow regeneration but they do not have the virtue to remove our sins or to avert divine judgment. We believe good works, pleasing and acceptable to God in Christ, spring from a true and living faith, for through and by them faith is made evident.

Article XI—Sanctification and Christian Perfection

We believe sanctification is the work of God's grace through the Word and the Spirit, by which those who have been born again are cleansed from sin in their thoughts, words and acts, and are enabled to live in accordance with God's will, and to strive for holiness without which no one will see the Lord.

Entire sanctification is a state of perfect love, righteousness and true holiness which every regenerate believer may obtain by being delivered from the power of sin, by loving God with all the heart, soul, mind and strength, and by loving one's neighbor as one's self. Through faith in Jesus Christ this gracious gift may be received in this life both gradually and instantaneously, and should be sought earnestly by every child of God.

We believe this experience does not deliver us from the infirmities, ignorance, and mistakes common to man, nor from the possibilities of further sin. The Christian must continue on guard against spiritual pride and seek to gain victory over every temptation to sin. He must respond wholly to the will of God so that sin will lose its power over him; and the world, the flesh, and the devil are put under his feet. Thus he rules over these enemies with watchfulness through the power of the Holy Spirit.

Article XII—The Judgment and the Future State

We believe all men stand under the righteous judgment of Jesus Christ, both now and in the last day. We believe in the resurrection of the dead; the righteous to life eternal and the wicked to endless condemnation.

Article XIII—Public Worship

We believe divine worship is the duty and privilege of man who, in the presence of God, bows in adoration, humility and dedication. We believe divine worship is essential to the life of the Church, and that the assembling of the people of God for such worship is necessary to Christian fellowship and spiritual growth.

We believe the order of public worship need not be the same in all places but may be modified by the church according to circumstances and the needs of men. It should be in a language and form understood by the people, consistent with the Holy Scriptures to the edification of all, and in accordance with the order and *Discipline* of the Church.

Article XIV—The Lord's Day

We believe the Lord's Day is divinely ordained for private and public worship, for rest from unnecessary work, and should be devoted to spiritual improvement, Christian fellowship and service. It is commemorative of our Lord's resurrection and is an emblem of our eternal rest. It is essential to the permanence and growth of the Christian Church, and important to the welfare of the civil community.

Article XV—The Christian and Property

We believe God is the owner of all things and that the individual holding of property is lawful and is a sacred trust under God. Private property is to be used for the manifestation of Christian love and liberality, and to support the Church's mission in the world. All forms of property, whether private, corporate or public, are to be held in solemn trust and used responsibly for human good under the sovereignty of God.

Article XVI—Civil Government

We believe civil government derives its just powers from the sovereign God. As Christians we recognize the governments under whose protection we reside and believe such governments should be based on, and be responsible for, the recognition of human rights under God. We believe war and bloodshed are contrary to the gospel and spirit of Christ. We believe it is the duty of Christian citizens to give moral strength and purpose to their respective governments through sober, righteous and godly living.

THE STANDARD SERMONS OF WESLEY

[Bibliographical Note: The Wesleyan "standards" have been reprinted frequently. The critical edition of Wesley's *Sermons* is included in *The Works of John Wesley*, vols. 1-4 (Nashville: Abingdon Press, 1984-87).]

THE EXPLANATORY NOTES UPON THE NEW TESTAMENT

[Bibliographical Note: *The Explanatory Notes Upon the New Testament* (1755) is currently in print (Schmul Publishing Company's 1975 edition) and is forthcoming as vols. 5-6 of *The Works of John Wesley*.]

THE GENERAL RULES OF THE METHODIST CHURCH[7]

[Bibliographical Note: The General Rules are printed here in the text of 1808 (when the fifth Restrictive Rule took effect), as subsequently amended by constitutional actions in 1848 and 1868.]

The Nature, Design, and General Rules of Our United Societies

In the latter end of the year 1739 eight or ten persons came to Mr. Wesley, in London, who appeared to be deeply convinced of sin, and earnestly groaning for redemption. They desired, as did two or three more the next day, that he would spend some time with them in prayer, and advise them how to flee from the wrath to come, which they saw continually hanging over their heads. That he might have more time for this great work, he appointed a day when they might all come together, which from thenceforward they did every week, namely, on Thursday in the evening. To these, and as many more as desired to join with them

---

7. Protected by Restrictive Rule 5 (¶ 21).

(for their number increased daily), he gave those advices from time to time which he judged most needful for them, and they always concluded their meeting with prayer suited to their several necessities.

This was the rise of the **United Society,** first in Europe, and then in America. Such a society is no other than "a company of men having the *form* and seeking the *power* of godliness, united in order to pray together, to receive the word of exhortation, and to watch over one another in love, that they may help each other to work out their salvation."

That it may the more easily be discerned whether they are indeed working out their own salvation, each society is divided into smaller companies, called **classes,** according to their respective places of abode. There are about twelve persons in a class, one of whom is styled the **leader.** It is his duty:

1. To see each person in his class once a week at least, in order: (1) to inquire how their souls prosper; (2) to advise, reprove, comfort or exhort, as occasion may require; (3) to receive what they are willing to give toward the relief of the preachers, church, and poor.

2. To meet the ministers and the stewards of the society once a week, in order: (1) to inform the minister of any that are sick, or of any that walk disorderly and will not be reproved; (2) to pay the stewards what they have received of their several classes in the week preceding.

There is only one condition previously required of those who desire admission into these societies: "a desire to flee from the wrath to come, and to be saved from their sins." But wherever this is really fixed in the soul it will be shown by its fruits.

It is therefore expected of all who continue therein that they should continue to evidence their desire of salvation,

First: By doing no harm, by avoiding evil of every kind, especially that which is most generally practiced, such as:

The taking of the name of God in vain.

The profaning the day of the Lord, either by doing ordinary work therein or by buying or selling.

Drunkenness: buying or selling spirituous liquors, or drinking them, unless in cases of extreme necessity.

Slaveholding; buying or selling slaves.

Fighting, quarreling, brawling, brother going to law with brother; returning evil for evil, or railing for railing; the using many words in buying or selling.

The buying or selling goods that have not paid the duty.

The giving or taking things on usury—i.e., unlawful interest.

Uncharitable or unprofitable conversation; particularly speaking evil of magistrates or of ministers.

Doing to others as we would not they should do unto us.

Doing what we know is not for the glory of God, as:

The putting on of gold and costly apparel.

The taking such diversions as cannot be used in the name of the Lord Jesus.

The singing those songs, or reading those books, which do not tend to the knowledge or love of God.

Softness and needless self-indulgence.

Laying up treasure upon earth.

Borrowing without a probability of paying; or taking up goods without a probability of paying for them.

It is expected of all who continue in these societies that they should continue to evidence their desire of salvation,

Secondly: By doing good; by being in every kind merciful after their power; as they have opportunity, doing good of every possible sort, and, as far as possible, to all men:

To their bodies, of the ability which God giveth, by giving food to the hungry, by clothing the naked, by visiting or helping them that are sick or in prison.

To their souls, by instructing, reproving, or exhorting all we have any intercourse with; trampling under foot that enthusiastic doctrine that "we are not to do good unless *our hearts be free to it.*"

By doing good, especially to them that are of the household of faith or groaning so to be; employing them preferably to others; buying one of another, helping each other in business, and so much the more because the world will love its own and them only.

By all possible diligence and frugality, that the gospel be not blamed.

By running with patience the race which is set before them, denying themselves, and taking up their cross daily; submitting to bear the reproach of Christ, to be as the filth and offscouring of the world; and looking that men should say all manner of evil of them *falsely,* for the Lord's sake.

It is expected of all who desire to continue in these societies that they should continue to evidence their desire of salvation,

Thirdly: By attending upon all the ordinances of God; such are:

The public worship of God.
The ministry of the Word, either read or expounded.
The Supper of the Lord.
Family and private prayer.
Searching the Scriptures.
Fasting or abstinence.

These are the General Rules of our societies; all of which we are taught of God to observe, even in his written Word, which is the only rule, and the sufficient rule, both of our faith and practice. And all these we know his Spirit writes on truly awakened hearts. If there be any among us who observe them not, who habitually break any of them, let it be known unto them who watch over that soul as they who must give an account. We will admonish him of the error of his ways. We will bear with him for a season. But then, if he repent not, he hath no more place among us. We have delivered our own souls.

¶ 105. SECTION 4—OUR THEOLOGICAL TASK

Theology is our effort to reflect upon God's gracious action in our lives. In response to the love of Christ, we desire to be drawn into a deeper relationship with "faith's pioneer and perfecter." Our theological explorations seek to give expression to the mysterious reality of God's presence, peace, and power in the world. By so doing, we attempt to articulate more clearly our understanding of the divine-human encounter and are thereby more fully prepared to participate in God's work in the world.

The theological task, though related to the Church's doctrinal expressions, serves a different function. Our doctrinal affirmations assist us in the discernment of Christian truth in ever-changing contexts. Our theological task includes the testing, renewal, elaboration, and application of our doctrinal perspective in carrying out our calling "to spread scriptural holiness over these lands."

While the Church considers its doctrinal affirmations a central feature of its identity and restricts official changes to a constitutional process, the Church encourages serious reflection across the theological spectrum.

As United Methodists, we are called to identify the needs both of individuals and of society and to address those needs out of the resources of Christian faith in a way that is clear, convincing, and effective. Theology serves the Church by interpreting the world's needs and challenges to the Church and by interpreting the gospel to the world.

The Nature of Our Theological Task

Our theological task is both critical and constructive. It is *critical* in that we test various expressions of faith by asking: Are they true? Appropriate? Clear? Cogent? Credible? Are they based on love? Do they provide the Church and its members with a witness that is faithful to the gospel as reflected in our living heritage and that is authentic and convincing in the light of human experience and the present state of human knowledge?

Our theological task is *constructive* in that every generation must appropriate creatively the wisdom of the past and seek God in their midst in order to think afresh about God, revelation, sin, redemption, worship, the church, freedom, justice, moral responsibility, and other significant theological concerns. Our summons is to understand and receive the gospel promises in our troubled and uncertain times.

Our theological task is both individual and communal. It is a feature in the ministry of *individual* Christians. It requires the participation of all who are in our Church, lay and ordained, because the mission of the Church is to be carried out by everyone who is called to discipleship. To be persons of faith is to hunger to understand the truth given to us in Jesus Christ.

Theological inquiry is by no means a casual undertaking. It requires sustained disciplines of study, reflection, and prayer.

Yet the discernment of "plain truth for plain people" is not limited to theological specialists. Scholars have their role to play in assisting the people of God to fulfill this calling, but all Christians are called to theological reflection.

Our theological task is *communal.* It unfolds in conversations open to the experiences, insights, and traditions of all constituencies that make up United Methodism.

This dialogue belongs to the life of every congregation. It is fostered by laity and clergy, by the bishops, by the boards, agencies, and theological schools of the Church.

Conferences speak and act for United Methodists in their official decisions at appropriate levels. Our conciliar and representative forms of decision-making do not release United Methodists as individuals from the responsibility to develop sound theological judgment.

Our theological task is contextual and incarnational. It is grounded upon God's supreme mode of self-revelation—the incarnation in Jesus Christ. God's eternal Word comes to us in flesh and blood in a given time and place, and in full identification with humanity. Therefore, theological reflection is energized by our incarnational involvement in the daily life of the Church and the world, as we participate in God's liberating and saving action.

Our theological task is essentially practical. It informs the individual's daily decisions and serves the Church's life and work. While highly theoretical constructions of Christian thought make important contributions to theological understanding, we finally measure the truth of such statements in relation to their practical significance. Our interest is to incorporate the promises and demands of the gospel into our daily lives.

Theological inquiry can clarify our thinking about what we are to say and do. It presses us to pay attention to the world around us.

Realities of intense human suffering, threats to the survival of life, and challenges to human dignity confront us afresh with fundamental theological issues: the nature and purposes of God, the relations of human beings to one another, the nature of human freedom and responsibility, and the care and proper use of all creation.

Theological Guidelines: Sources and Criteria

As United Methodists, we have an obligation to bear a faithful Christian witness to Jesus Christ, the living reality at the center of the Church's life and witness. To fulfill this obligation, we reflect critically on our biblical and theological inheritance, striving to express faithfully the witness we make in our own time.

Two considerations are central to this endeavor: the sources from which we derive our theological affirmations and the criteria by which we assess the adequacy of our understanding and witness.

Wesley believed that the living core of the Christian faith was revealed in Scripture, illumined by tradition, vivified in personal experience, and confirmed by reason.

Scripture is primary, revealing the Word of God "so far as it is necessary for our salvation." Therefore, our theological task, in both its critical and constructive aspects, focuses on disciplined study of the Bible.

To aid his study of the Bible and deepen his understanding of faith, Wesley drew on Christian tradition, in particular the Patristic writings, the ecumenical creeds, the teachings of the Reformers, and the literature of contemporary spirituality.

Thus, tradition provides both a source and a measure of authentic Christian witness, though its authority derives from its faithfulness to the biblical message.

The Christian witness, even when grounded in Scripture and mediated by tradition, is ineffectual unless understood and appropriated by the individual. To become our witness, it must make sense in terms of our own reason and experience.

For Wesley, a cogent account of the Christian faith required the use of reason, both to understand Scripture and to relate the biblical message to wider fields of knowledge. He looked for confirmations of the biblical witness in human experience, especially the experiences of regeneration and sanctification, but also in the "common sense" knowledge of everyday experience.

The interaction of these sources and criteria in Wesley's own theology furnishes a guide for our continuing theological task as United Methodists. In that task Scripture, as the constitutive witness to the wellsprings of our faith, occupies a place of primary authority among these theological sources.

In practice, theological reflection may also find its point of departure in tradition, experience, or rational analysis. What matters most is that all four guidelines be brought to bear in faithful, serious, theological consideration. Insights arising from serious study of the Scriptures and tradition enrich contemporary experience. Imaginative and critical thought enables us to understand better the Bible and our common Christian history.

Scripture

United Methodists share with other Christians the conviction that Scripture is the primary source and criterion for Christian doctrine. Through Scripture the living Christ meets us in the experience of redeeming grace. We are convinced that Jesus Christ is the living Word of God in our midst whom we trust in life and death.The biblical authors, illumined by the Holy Spirit, bear witness that in Christ the world is reconciled to God. The Bible bears authentic testimony to God's self-disclosure in the life, death, and resurrection of Jesus Christ as well as in God's work of creation, in the pilgrimage of Israel, and in the Holy Spirit's ongoing activity in human history.

As we open our minds and hearts to the Word of God through the words of human beings inspired by the Holy Spirit, faith is born and nourished, our understanding is deepened, and the possibilities for transforming the world become apparent to us.

The Bible is sacred canon for Christian people, formally acknowledged as such by historic ecumenical councils of the church. Our doctrinal standards identify as canonical thirty-nine books of the Old Testament and the twenty-seven books of the New Testament.

Our standards affirm the Bible as the source of all that is "necessary" and "sufficient" unto salvation (Articles of Religion) and "is to be received through the Holy Spirit as the true rule and guide for faith and practice" (Confession of Faith).

We properly read Scripture within the believing community, informed by the tradition of that community.

We interpret individual texts in light of their place in the Bible as a whole.

We are aided by scholarly inquiry and personal insight, under the guidance of the Holy Spirit. As we work with each text, we take into account what we have been able to learn about the original context and intention of that text. In this understanding we draw upon the careful historical, literary, and textual studies of recent years, which have enriched our understanding of the Bible.

Through this faithful reading of Scripture, we may come to know the truth of the biblical message in its bearing on our own lives and the life of the world. Thus, the Bible serves both as a source of our faith and as the basic criterion by which the truth and fidelity of any interpretation of faith is measured.

While we acknowledge the primacy of Scripture in theological reflection, our attempts to grasp its meaning always involve tradition, experience, and reason. Like Scripture, these may become creative vehicles of the Holy Spirit as they function within the Church. They quicken our faith, open our eyes to the wonder of God's love, and clarify our understanding.

The Wesleyan heritage, reflecting its origins in the catholic and reformed ethos of English Christianity, directs us to a self-conscious use of these three sources in interpreting Scripture and in formulating faith statements based on the biblical witness.

These sources are, along with Scripture, indispensable to our theological task.

The close relationship of tradition, experience, and reason appears in the Bible itself. Scripture witnesses to a variety of diverse traditions, some of which reflect tensions in interpretation within the early Judeo-Christian heritage. However, these traditions are woven together in the Bible in a manner that expresses the fundamental unity of God's revelation as received and experienced by people in the diversity of their own lives.

The developing communities of faith judged them, therefore, to be an authoritative witness to that revelation. In recognizing the interrelationship and inseparability of the four basic resources for theological understanding, we are following a model that is present in the biblical text itself.

Tradition

The theological task does not start anew in each age or each person. Christianity does not leap from New Testament times to the present as though nothing were to be learned from that great cloud of witnesses in between. For centuries Christians have sought to interpret the truth of the gospel for their time.

In these attempts, tradition, understood both in terms of process and form, has played an important role. The passing on and receiving of the gospel among persons, regions, and generations constitutes a dynamic element of Christian history. The formulations and practices that grew out of specific circumstances constitute the legacy of the corporate experience of earlier Christian communities.

These traditions are found in many cultures around the globe. But the history of Christianity includes a mixture of ignorance, misguided zeal, and sin. Scripture remains the norm by which all traditions are judged.

The story of the church reflects the most basic sense of tradition, the continuing activity of God's Spirit transforming human life. Tradition is the history of that continuing environment of grace in and by which all Christians live, God's self-giving love in Jesus Christ. As such, tradition transcends the story of particular traditions.

In this deeper sense of tradition, all Christians share a common history. Within that history, Christian tradition precedes Scripture, and yet Scripture comes to be the focal expression of the tradition.

As United Methodists, we pursue our theological task in openness to the richness of both the form and power of tradition.

The multiplicity of traditions furnishes a richly varied source for theological reflection and construction. For United Methodists, certain strands of tradition have special importance as the historic foundation of our doctrinal heritage and the distinctive expressions of our communal existence.

We are now challenged by traditions from around the world that accent dimensions of Christian understanding that grow out of the sufferings and victories of the downtrodden. These traditions help us rediscover the biblical witness to God's special commitment to the poor, the disabled, the imprisoned, the oppressed, the outcast. In these persons we encounter the living presence of Jesus Christ.

These traditions underscore the equality of all persons in Jesus Christ. They display the capacity of the gospel to free us to embrace the diversity of human cultures and appreciate their values. They reinforce our traditional understanding of the inseparability of personal salvation and social justice. They deepen our commitment to global peace.

A critical appreciation of these traditions can compel us to think about God in new ways, enlarge our vision of shalom, and enhance our confidence in God's provident love.

Tradition acts as a measure of validity and propriety for a community's faith insofar as it represents a consensus of faith. The various traditions that presently make claims upon us may contain conflicting images and insights of truth and validity. We examine such conflicts in light of Scripture, reflecting critically upon the doctrinal stance of our Church.

It is by the discerning use of our standards and in openness to emerging forms of Christian identity that we attempt to maintain fidelity to the apostolic faith.

At the same time, we continue to draw on the broader Christian tradition as an expression of the history of divine grace within which Christians are able to recognize and welcome one another in love.

Experience

In our theological task, we follow Wesley's practice of examining experience, both individual and corporate, for confirmations of the realities of God's grace attested in Scripture.

Our experience interacts with Scripture. We read Scripture in light of the conditions and events that help shape who we are, and we interpret our experience in terms of Scripture.

All religious experience affects all human experience; all human experience affects our understanding of religious experience.

On the personal level, experience is to the individual as tradition is to the church: It is the personal appropriation of God's forgiving and empowering grace. Experience authenticates in our own lives the truths revealed in Scripture and illumined in tradition, enabling us to claim the Christian witness as our own.

Wesley described faith and its assurance as "a sure trust and confidence" in the mercy of God through our Lord Jesus Christ, and a steadfast hope of all good things to be received at God's hand. Such assurance is God's gracious gift through the witness of the Holy Spirit.

This "new life in Christ" is what we as United Methodists mean when we speak of "Christian experience." Christian experience gives us new eyes to see the living truth in Scripture. It confirms the biblical message for our present. It illumines our understanding of God and creation and motivates us to make sensitive moral judgments.

Although profoundly personal, Christian experience is also corporate; our theological task is informed by the experience of the church and by the common experiences of all humanity. In our attempts to understand the biblical message, we recognize that God's gift of liberating love embraces the whole of creation.

Some facets of human experience tax our theological understanding. Many of God's people live in terror, hunger, loneliness, and degradation. Everyday experiences of birth and death, of growth and life in the created world, and an awareness of wider social relations also belong to serious theological reflection.

A new awareness of such experiences can inform our appropriation of scriptural truths and sharpen our appreciation of the good news of the kingdom of God.

As a source for theological reflection, experience, like tradition, is richly varied, challenging our efforts to put into words the totality of the promises of the gospel. We interpret experience in the light of scriptural norms, just as our experience informs our reading of the biblical message. In this respect, Scripture remains central in our efforts to be faithful in making our Christian witness.

Reason

Although we recognize that God's revelation and our experiences of God's grace continually surpass the scope of human language and reason, we also believe that any disciplined theological work calls for the careful use of reason.

By reason we read and interpret Scripture.

By reason we determine whether our Christian witness is clear.

By reason we ask questions of faith and seek to understand God's action and will.

By reason we organize the understandings that compose our witness and render them internally coherent.

By reason we test the congruence of our witness to the biblical testimony and to the traditions that mediate that testimony to us.

By reason we relate our witness to the full range of human knowledge, experience, and service.

Since all truth is from God, efforts to discern the connections between revelation and reason, faith and science, grace and nature, are useful endeavors in developing credible and communicable doctrine. We seek nothing less than a total view of reality that is decisively informed by the promises and imperatives of the Christian gospel, though we know well that such an attempt will always be marred by the limits and distortions characteristic of human knowledge.

Nevertheless, by our quest for reasoned understandings of Christian faith we seek to grasp, express, and live out the gospel in a way that will commend itself to thoughtful persons who are seeking to know and follow God's ways.

In theological reflection, the resources of tradition, experience, and reason are integral to our study of Scripture without displacing Scripture's primacy for faith and practice. These four sources—each making distinctive contributions, yet all finally working together—guide our quest as United Methodists for a vital and appropriate Christian witness.

The Present Challenge to Theology in the Church

In addition to historic tensions and conflicts that still require resolution, new issues continually arise that summon us to fresh theological inquiry. Daily we are presented with an array of concerns that challenge our proclamation of God's reign over all of human existence.

Of crucial importance are concerns generated by great human struggles for dignity, liberation, and fulfillment—aspirations that are inherent elements in God's design for creation. These concerns are borne by theologies that express the heart cries of the downtrodden and the aroused indignation of the compassionate.

The perils of nuclear destruction, terrorism, war, poverty, violence, and injustice confront us. Injustices linked to race, gender, class, and age are widespread in our times. Misuse of natural resources and disregard for the fragile balances in our environment contradict our calling to care for God's creation. Secularism pervades high-technology civilizations, hindering human awareness of the spiritual depths of existence.

We seek an authentic Christian response to these realities that the healing and redeeming work of God might be present in our words and deeds. Too often, theology is used to support practices that are unjust. We look for answers that are in harmony with the gospel and do not claim exemption from critical assessment.

A rich quality of our Church, especially as it has developed in the last century, is its global character. We are a Church with a distinctive theological heritage, but that heritage is lived out in a global community, resulting in understandings of our faith enriched by indigenous experiences and manners of expression.

We affirm the contributions that United Methodists of varying ethnic, language, cultural, and national groups make to one another and to our Church as a whole. We celebrate our shared commitment to clear theological understanding and vital missional expression.

United Methodists as a diverse people continue to strive for consensus in understanding the gospel. In our diversity, we are held together by a shared inheritance and a common desire to participate in the creative and redemptive activity of God.

Our task is to articulate our vision in a way that will draw us together as a people in mission.

In the name of Jesus Christ we are called to work within our diversity while exercising patience and forbearance with one another. Such patience stems neither from indifference toward truth nor from an indulgent tolerance of error but from an awareness that we know only in part and that none of us is able to search the mysteries of God except by the Spirit of God. We proceed with our theological task, trusting that the Spirit will grant us wisdom to continue our journey with the whole people of God.

Ecumenical Commitment

Christian unity is founded on the theological understanding that through faith in Jesus Christ we are made members-in-common of the one body of Christ. Christian unity is not an option; it is a gift to be received and expressed.

United Methodists respond to the theological, biblical, and practical mandates for Christian unity by firmly committing ourselves to the cause of Christian unity at local, national, and world levels. We invest ourselves in many ways by which mutual recognition of churches, of members, and of ministries may lead us to sharing in Holy Communion with all of God's people.

Knowing that denominational loyalty is always subsumed in our life in the church of Jesus Christ, we welcome and celebrate the rich experience of United Methodist leadership in church councils and consultations, in multilateral and bilateral dialogues, as well as in other forms of ecumenical convergence that have led to the healing of churches and nations.

We see the Holy Spirit at work in making the unity among us more visible.

Concurrently, we have entered into serious interfaith encounters and explorations between Christians and adherents of other living faiths of the world. Scripture calls us to be both neighbors and witnesses to all peoples. Such encounters require us to reflect anew on our faith and to seek guidance for our witness among neighbors of other faiths. We then rediscover that the God who has acted in Jesus Christ for the salvation of the whole world is also the Creator of all humankind, the One who is "over all, through all, and in all" (Ephesians 4:6).

As people bound together on one planet, we see the need for a self-critical view of our own tradition and accurate appreciation of other traditions. In these encounters, our aim is not to reduce doctrinal differences to some lowest common denominator of religious agreement, but to raise all such relationships to the highest possible level of human fellowship and understanding.

We labor together with the help of God toward the salvation, health, and peace of all people. In respectful conversations and in practical cooperation, we confess our Christian faith and strive to display the manner in which Jesus Christ is the life and hope of the world.

Conclusion

Doctrine arises out of the life of the Church—its faith, its worship, its discipline, its conflicts, its challenges from the world it would serve.

Evangelism, nurture, and mission require a constant effort to integrate authentic experience, rational thought, and purposeful action with theological integrity.

A convincing witness to our Lord and Savior Jesus Christ can contribute to the renewal of our faith, bring persons to that faith, and strengthen the Church as an agent of healing and reconciliation.

This witness, however, cannot fully describe or encompass the mystery of God. Though we experience the wonder of God's grace at work with us and among us, and though we know the joy of the present signs of God's kingdom, each new step makes us more aware of the ultimate mystery of God, from which arises a heart of wonder and an attitude of humility. Yet we trust that we can know more fully what is essential for our participation in God's saving work in the world, and we are confident in the ultimate unfolding of God's justice and mercy.

In this spirit we take up our theological task. We endeavor through the power of the Holy Spirit to understand the love of God given in Jesus Christ. We seek to spread this love abroad. As we see more clearly who we have been, as we understand more fully the needs of the world, as we draw more effectively upon our theological heritage, we will become better equipped to fulfill our calling as the people of God.

> Now to God
> who by the power at work within us
> is able to do far more abundantly
> than all that we ask or think,
> to God be glory in the church
> and in Christ Jesus to all generations,
> for ever and ever. Amen.
> —Ephesians 3:20-21 (based on RSV)

Part IV

THE MINISTRY OF ALL CHRISTIANS

THE MISSION AND MINISTRY OF THE CHURCH

Section I. The Churches

¶ **120.** *The Mission*—The mission of the Church is to make disciples of Jesus Christ for the transformation of the world. Local churches and extension ministries of the Church provide the most significant arenas through which disciple-making occurs.

¶ **121.** *Rationale for Our Mission*—The mission of the Church is to make disciples of Jesus Christ for the transformation of the world by proclaiming the good news of God's grace and by exemplifying Jesus' command to love God and neighbor, thus seeking the fulfillment of God's reign and realm in the world. The fulfillment of God's reign and realm in the world is the vision Scripture holds before us. The United Methodist Church affirms that Jesus Christ is the Son of God, the Savior of the world, and the Lord of all. As we make disciples, we respect persons of all religious faiths and we defend religious freedom for all persons. Jesus' words in Matthew provide the Church with our mission: "Therefore, go and make disciples of all nations, baptizing them in the name of the Father and of the Son and of the Holy Spirit, teaching them to obey everything that I've commanded you" (28:19-20), and *"You must love the Lord your God with all your heart, with all your being, and with all your mind. . . .You must love your neighbor as you love yourself"* (22:37, 39).

This mission is our grace-filled response to the Reign of God in the world announced by Jesus. God's grace is active everywhere, at all times, carrying out this purpose as revealed in the Bible. It is *expressed* in God's covenant with Abraham and Sarah, in the Exodus of Israel from Egypt, and in the ministry of the prophets. It is fully *embodied* in the life, death, and resurrection of Jesus Christ. It is *experienced* in the ongoing creation of a new people by the Holy Spirit.

John Wesley, Phillip Otterbein, Jacob Albright, and our other spiritual forebears understood this mission in this way. Whenever United Methodism has had a clear sense of mission, God has used our Church to save persons, heal relationships, transform social structures, and spread scriptural holiness, thereby changing the world. In order to be truly alive, we embrace Jesus' mandate to love God and to love our neighbor and to make disciples of all peoples.

¶ **122.** *The Process for Carrying Out Our Mission*—We make disciples as we:

—proclaim the gospel, seek, welcome and gather persons into the body of Christ;

—lead persons to commit their lives to God through baptism by water and the spirit and profession of faith in Jesus Christ;

—nurture persons in Christian living through worship, the sacraments, spiritual disciplines, and other means of grace, such as Wesley's Christian conferencing;

—send persons into the world to live lovingly and justly as servants of Christ by healing the sick, feeding the hungry, caring for the stranger, freeing the oppressed, being and becoming a compassionate, caring presence, and working to develop social structures that are consistent with the gospel; and

—continue the mission of seeking, welcoming and gathering persons into the community of the body of Christ.

¶ **123.** *The Global Nature of Our Mission*—The Church seeks to fulfill its global mission through the Spirit-given servant ministries of all Christians, both lay and clergy. Faithfulness and effectiveness demand that all ministries in the Church be shaped by the mission of making disciples of Jesus Christ.

¶ **124.** *Our Mission in the World*—God's self-revelation in the life, death, and resurrection of Jesus Christ summons the Church to ministry in the world through witness by word and deed in light of the Church's mission. The visible church of Christ as a faithful community of persons affirms the worth of all humanity and the value of interrelationship in all of God's creation.

In the midst of a sinful world, through the grace of God, we are brought to repentance and faith in Jesus Christ. We become aware of the presence and life-giving power of God's Holy Spirit. We live in confident expectation of the ultimate fulfillment of God's purpose.

We are called together for worship and fellowship and for the upbuilding of the Christian community. We advocate and work for the unity of the Christian church. We call all persons into discipleship under the Lordship of Jesus Christ.

As servants of Christ we are sent into the world to engage in the struggle for justice and reconciliation. We seek to reveal the love of God for men, women, and children of all ethnic, racial, cultural, and national backgrounds and to demonstrate the healing power of the gospel with those who suffer.

¶ 125. United Methodists throughout the world are bound together in a connectional covenant in which we support and hold each other accountable for faithful discipleship and mission. Integrally holding connectional unity and local freedom, we seek to proclaim and embody the gospel in ways responsible to our specific cultural and social context while maintaining "a vital web of interactive relationships" (¶ 132). At the same time, we desire to affirm and celebrate our relationships, covenants, and partnership with autonomous, affiliated autonomous, affiliated united covenanting, and concordat churches (¶¶ 570-574) as well as other partners in the Wesleyan and ecumenical Christian families. Our worldwide connectional relationship is one of the ways we carry out our missional calling beyond national and regional boundaries. For our connectionalism to become a living practice, we need to carry the worldwide nature of The United Methodist Church deep into the life and mission of our local congregations. Only when we commit ourselves to interdependent worldwide partnerships in prayer, mission, and worship can connectionalism as the Wesleyan ecclesial vision be fully embodied. Guided by the Holy Spirit, United Methodist churches throughout the world are called afresh into a covenant of mutual commitment based on shared mission, equity, and hospitality.

In covenant with God and with each other:

We affirm our unity in Christ, and take faithful steps to live more fully into what it means to be a worldwide church in mission for the transformation of the world.

We commit ourselves to crossing boundaries of language, culture, and social or economic status. We commit ourselves to be in ministry with all people, as we, in faithfulness to the gospel, seek to grow in mutual love and trust.

We participate in God's mission as partners in ministry, recognizing that our God-given gifts, experiences, and resources are of equal value, whether spiritual, financial, or missional.

We commit ourselves to full equity and accountability in our relationships, structures, and responsibilities for the denomination.

We enter afresh into a relationship of mutuality, creating a new sense of community and joyously living out our worldwide connection in our mission to make disciples of Jesus Christ for the transformation of the world.

A Companion Litany to Our Covenant for the Worldwide United Methodist Church

Leader: In covenant with God and each other, we affirm our unity in Christ.

People: We will take faithful steps to live as a worldwide church in our mission to make disciples of Jesus Christ for the transformation of the world.

Leader: In covenant with God and each other, we commit ourselves to be in ministry with all people.

People: In faithfulness to the gospel, we will cross boundaries of language, culture, social or economic status as we grow in mutual love and trust.

Leader: In covenant with God and each other, we participate in God's mission as partners in ministry.

People: We share our God-given gifts, experiences, and resources recognizing that they are of equal value, whether spiritual, financial, or missional.

Leader: In covenant with God and each other, we commit ourselves to full equality.

People: We uphold equity and accountability in our relationships, structures, and responsibilities for the denomination.

Leader: In covenant with God and each other, we enter afresh into a relationship of mutuality.

People: With God's grace, we joyfully live out our worldwide connection in our mission to make disciples of Jesus Christ for the transformation of the world.

Section II. The Ministry of All Christians

¶ **126.** *The Heart of Christian Ministry*—The heart of Christian ministry is Christ's ministry of outreaching love. Christian ministry is the expression of the mind and mission of Christ by a community of Christians that demonstrates a common life of gratitude and devotion, witness and service, celebration and discipleship. All Christians are called through their baptism to this ministry of servanthood in the world to the glory of God and for human fulfillment. The forms of this ministry are diverse in locale, in interest, and in denominational accent, yet always catholic in spirit and outreach.

¶ **127.** *The Ministry of the Laity*—The ministry of the laity flows from a commitment to Christ's outreaching love. Lay members of The United Methodist Church are, by history and calling, active advocates of the gospel of Jesus Christ. Every layperson is called to carry out the Great Commission (Matthew 28:18-20); every layperson is called to be missional. The witness of the laity, their Christ-like examples of everyday living as well as the sharing of their own faith experiences of the gospel, is the primary evangelistic ministry through which all people will come to know Christ and The United Methodist Church will fulfill its mission.

¶ **128.** *The Ministry of the Community*—The church as the community of the new covenant has participated in Christ's ministry of grace across the years and around the world. It stretches out to human needs wherever love and service may convey God's love and ours. The outreach of such ministries knows no limits. Beyond the diverse forms of ministry is this ultimate concern: that all persons will be brought into a saving relationship with God through Jesus Christ and be renewed after the image of their creator (Colossians 3:10). This means that all Christians are called to minister wherever Christ would have them serve and witness in deeds and words that heal and free.

¶ **129.** *Ministry as Gift and Task*—This ministry of all Christians in Christ's name and spirit is both a gift and a task. The gift is God's unmerited grace; the task is unstinting service. Entrance into the church is acknowledged in baptism and may include persons of all ages. In baptism, water is administered in the name of the triune God (specified in the ritual as Father, Son, and Holy Spirit) by an authorized person, and the Holy Spirit is invoked with the laying on of hands, ordinarily in the presence of the congregation. In this sacrament the church claims God's promise and the seal of the Spirit (Ephesians 1:13). Baptism is followed by nurture and the consequent awareness by the baptized of the claim to ministry in Christ placed upon their lives by the church. Such a ministry is confirmed by the church when the pledges of baptism are accepted through profession of faith, and renewed for life and mission. Entrance into and acceptance of ministry begin in a local church, but the impulse to minister always moves one beyond the congregation toward the whole human community. God's gifts are richly diverse for a variety of services; yet all have dignity and worth.

¶ **130.** *Faithful Ministry*—The people of God, who are the church made visible in the world, must convince the world of the reality of the gospel or leave it unconvinced. There can be no evasion or delegation of this responsibility; the church is either faithful as a witnessing and serving community, or it loses its vitality and its impact on an unbelieving world.

¶ **131.** *The Unity of Ministry in Christ*—There is but one ministry in Christ, but there are diverse gifts and evidences of God's grace in the body of Christ (Ephesians 4:4-16). The ministry of all Christians is complementary. No ministry is subservient to another. All United Methodists are summoned and sent by Christ to live and work together in mutual interdependence and to be guided by the Spirit into the truth that frees and the love that reconciles

¶ **132.** *The Journey of a Connectional People*—Connectionalism in the United Methodist tradition is multi-leveled, global in scope, and local in thrust. Our connectionalism is not merely a linking of one charge conference to another. It is rather a vital web of interactive relationships.

We are connected by sharing a common tradition of faith, including Our Doctrinal Standards and General Rules (¶ 104); by sharing together a constitutional polity, including a leadership of general superintendency; by sharing a common mission, which we seek to carry out by working together in and through conferences that reflect the inclusive and missional character of our fellowship; by sharing a common ethos that characterizes our distinctive way of doing things.

Section III. Servant Ministry and Servant Leadership

¶ **133.** *Mission as Active Expectancy*—The ministry of all Christians consists of service for the mission of God in the world.

The mission of God is best expressed in the prayer that Jesus taught his first disciples: Thy kingdom come; thy will be done, on earth as in heaven. All Christians, therefore, are to live in active expectancy: faithful in service of God and their neighbor; faithful in waiting for the fulfillment of God's universal love, justice, and peace on earth as in heaven.

Pending this time of fulfillment, the ministry of all Christians is shaped by the teachings of Jesus. The handing on of these teachings is entrusted to leaders who are gifted and called by God to appointed offices in the church: some apostles, some prophets, some evangelists, and some pastors and teachers. "His purpose was to equip God's people for the work of serving and building up the body of Christ" (Ephesians 4:11-12). For these persons to lead the church effectively, they must embody the teachings of Jesus in servant ministries and servant leadership. Through these ministries and leadership, congregations of the church are faithfully engaged in the forming of Christian disciples and vitally involved in the mission of God in the world.

¶ **134.** *Calling and Gifts of Leadership*—The United Methodist Church has traditionally recognized these gifts and callings in the ordained offices of elder and deacon. The United Methodist tradition has recognized that laypersons as well as ordained persons are gifted and called by God to lead the Church. The servant leadership of these persons is essential to the mission and ministry of congregations. They help to form Christian disciples in covenant community within the local congregation through spiritual formation and guidance for Christian living in the world.

Section IV. Servant Ministry

¶ **135.** *Christian Discipleship*—The ministry of all Christians consists of privilege and obligation. The privilege is a relationship with God that is deeply spiritual. The obligation is to respond to God's call to holy living in the world. In the United Methodist tradition these two dimensions of Christian discipleship are wholly interdependent.

¶ **136.** *Our Relationship with God: Privilege*—Christians experience growth and transition in their spiritual life just as in their physical and emotional lives. While this growth is always a work of grace, it does not occur uniformly. Spiritual growth in Christ is a dynamic process marked by awakening, birth, growth, and maturation. This process requires careful and intentional nurture for the disciple to reach perfection in the Christian life. There are stages of spiritual growth and transition: Christian beginnings; Christian birth; Christian growth; and Christian maturity. These require careful and intentional nurture for the disciple to come to maturity in the Christian life and to engage fully in the ministry of all Christians.

¶ **137.** *Our Relationship with Christ in the World: Obligation*— The ministry of all Christians in the United Methodist tradition has always been energized by deep religious experience, with emphasis on how ministry relates to our obligation to Jesus Christ. The early Methodists developed a way of life that fostered reliability, and their methodical discipleship is best expressed in the General Rules that John Wesley first published in 1743, which remain in *The United Methodist Book of Discipline*, pages 77-80.

Section V. Servant Leadership

¶ **138.** *Leadership Privileges and Responsibilities*—Within The United Methodist Church, there are those called to servant leadership, lay and ordained. Such callings are evidenced by special gifts, evidence of God's grace, and promise of usefulness. God's call to servant leadership is inward as it comes to the individual and outward through the discernment and validation of the Church. The privilege of servant leadership in the Church is the call to share in the preparation of congregations and the whole Church for the mission of God in the world. The obligation of servant leadership is the forming of Christian disciples in the covenant community of the congregation. This involves discerning and nurturing the spiritual relationship with God that is the privilege of all servant ministers. It also involves instructing and guiding Christian disciples in their witness to Jesus Christ in the world through acts of worship, devotion, compassion, and justice under the guidance of the Holy Spirit. John Wesley described this as "watching over one another in love."

¶ **139.** *Ordained Ministry*—Ordained ministers are called by God to a lifetime of servant leadership in specialized ministries among the people of God. Ordained ministers are called to interpret to the Church the needs, concerns, and hopes of the world and the promise of God for creation. Within these specialized ministries, deacons are called to ministries of Word, Service (¶ 328), Compassion, and Justice and elders are called to ministries of Service, Word, Sacrament, and Order (¶ 332). Through these distinctive functions ordained ministers devote themselves wholly to the work of the Church and to the upbuilding of the ministry of all Christians. They do this through the careful study of Scripture and its faithful interpretation; through effective proclamation of the gospel and responsible administration of the sacraments; through diligent pastoral leadership of their congregations for fruitful discipleship; and by following the guidance of the Holy Spirit in witnessing beyond the congregation in the local community and to the ends of the earth. The ordained ministry is defined by its faithful commitment to servant leadership following the example of Jesus Christ, by its passion for the hallowing of life, and by its concern to link all local ministries with the widest boundaries of the Christian community.

Section VI. Called to Inclusiveness

¶ 140. We recognize that God made all creation and saw that it was good. As a diverse people of God who bring special gifts and evidences of God's grace to the unity of the Church and to society, we are called to be faithful to the example of Jesus' ministry to all persons.

Inclusiveness means openness, acceptance, and support that enables all persons to participate in the life of the Church, the community, and the world; therefore, inclusiveness denies every semblance of discrimination. The services of worship of every local church of The United Methodist Church shall be open to all persons.

The mark of an inclusive society is one in which all persons are open, welcoming, fully accepting, and supporting of all other persons, enabling them to participate fully in the life of the church, the community, and the world. A further mark of inclusiveness is the setting of church activities in facilities accessible to persons with disabilities.

In The United Methodist Church inclusiveness means the freedom for the total involvement of all persons who meet the requirements of The United Methodist *Book of Discipline* in the membership and leadership of the Church at any level and in every place. In the spirit of this declaration, United Methodist seminaries will begin or continue to improve access to facilities, to information and communication, and to appropriate support services and accommodations as delineated by The United Nations Standard Rules on the Equalization of Opportunities for Persons with Disabilities and applicable World Council of Churches guidelines.

Section VII. The Fulfillment of Ministry Through The United Methodist Church

¶ **141.** *The Church*—Affirming the spiritual dimensions of the ministry of all Christians, as proclaimed in ¶¶ 120-143 of this *Book of Discipline*, it is recognized that this ministry exists in the secular world and that civil authorities may seek legal definition predicated on the nature of The United Methodist Church in seeking fulfillment of this ministry. Accordingly, it is appropriate that the meaning of "The United Methodist Church," "the general Church," "the entire Church," and "the Church" as used in the *Book of Discipline* should now be stated consistently with the traditional self-understanding of United Methodists as to the meaning of these words.

These terms refer to the overall denomination and connectional relation and identity of its many local churches, the various conferences and their respective councils, boards, and agencies, and other Church units, which collectively constitute the religious system known as United Methodism. Under the Constitution and disciplinary procedures set forth in this *Book of Discipline*, "The United Methodist Church" as a denominational whole is not an entity, nor does it possess legal capacities and attributes. It does not and cannot hold title to property, nor does it have any officer, agent, employee, office, or location. Conferences, councils, boards, agencies, local churches, and other units bearing the name "United Methodist" are, for the most part, legal entities capable of suing and being sued and possessed of legal capacities.

¶ **142.** *Definition of Clergy*—Clergy in The United Methodist Church are individuals who serve as commissioned ministers, deacons, elders, and local pastors (full- and part-time), who hold membership in an annual conference, and who are commissioned, ordained, or licensed.

¶ **143.** *Employment Status of Clergy*—Ministry in the Christian church is derived from the ministry of Christ (¶ 301). Jesus makes it clear to us that he is a shepherd and not a hireling (John 10:11-15). Similarly, United Methodist clergy appointed to local churches are not employees of the local church, the district, or the annual conference. It is recognized that for certain limited purposes such as taxation, benefits, and insurance, governments and other entities may classify clergy as employees. Such classifications are not to be construed as affecting or defining United Methodist polity, including the historic covenants that bind annual conferences, clergy, and congregations, episcopal appointive powers and procedures, or other principles set forth in the Constitution or the *Book of Discipline* (see e.g., ¶¶ 301; 328-329; 333-334; 338; 340). In addition, any such classifications should be accepted, if at all, only for limited purposes, as set forth above, and with the full recognition and acknowledgment that it is the responsibility of the clergy to be God's servants.

Part V
SOCIAL PRINCIPLES

PREFACE

The United Methodist Church has a long history of concern for social justice. Its members have often taken forthright positions on controversial issues involving Christian principles. Early Methodists expressed their opposition to the slave trade, to smuggling, and to the cruel treatment of prisoners.

A social creed was adopted by The Methodist Episcopal Church (North) in 1908. Within the next decade similar statements were adopted by The Methodist Episcopal Church, South, and by The Methodist Protestant Church. The Evangelical United Brethren Church adopted a statement of social principles in 1946 at the time of the uniting of the United Brethren and The Evangelical Church. In 1972, four years after the uniting in 1968 of The Methodist Church and The Evangelical United Brethren Church, the General Conference of The United Methodist Church adopted a new statement of Social Principles, which was revised in 1976 (and by each successive General Conference).

The Social Principles, while not to be considered church law,[1] are a prayerful and thoughtful effort on the part of the General Conference to speak to the human issues in the contemporary world from a sound biblical and theological foundation as historically demonstrated in United Methodist traditions. They are a call to faithfulness and are intended to be instructive and persuasive in the best of the prophetic spirit. The Social Principles are a call

---

1. See Judicial Council Decisions 833, 1254.

to all members of The United Methodist Church to a prayerful, studied dialogue of faith and practice. (See ¶ 509.)

PREAMBLE

We, the people called United Methodists, affirm our faith in God our Creator and Father, in Jesus Christ our Savior, and in the Holy Spirit, our Guide and Guard.

We acknowledge our complete dependence upon God in birth, in life, in death, and in life eternal. Secure in God's love, we affirm the goodness of life and confess our many sins against God's will for us as we find it in Jesus Christ. We have not always been faithful stewards of all that has been committed to us by God the Creator. We have been reluctant followers of Jesus Christ in his mission to bring all persons into a community of love. Though called by the Holy Spirit to become new creatures in Christ, we have resisted the further call to become the people of God in our dealings with each other and the earth on which we live.

We affirm our unity in Jesus Christ while acknowledging differences in applying our faith in different cultural contexts as we live out the gospel. We stand united in declaring our faith that God's grace is available to all, that nothing can separate us from the love of God in Christ Jesus.

Grateful for God's forgiving love, in which we live and by which we are judged, and affirming our belief in the inestimable worth of each individual, we renew our commitment to become faithful witnesses to the gospel, not alone to the ends of earth, but also to the depths of our common life and work.

¶ 160.   I. THE NATURAL WORLD

All creation is the Lord's, and we are responsible for the ways in which we use and abuse it. Water, air, soil, minerals, energy resources, plants, animal life, and space are to be valued and conserved because they are God's creation and not solely because they are useful to human beings. God has granted us stewardship of creation. We should meet these stewardship duties through acts of loving care and respect. Economic, political, social, and technological developments have increased our human numbers, and lengthened and enriched our lives. However, these developments have led to regional defoliation, dramatic extinction of species, massive human suffering, overpopulation, and misuse and overconsumption of natural and nonrenewable resources, particularly by industrialized societies. This continued course of action jeopardizes the natural heritage that God has entrusted to all generations. Therefore, let us recognize the responsibility of the church and its members to place a high priority on changes in economic, political, social, and technological lifestyles to support a more ecologically equitable and sustainable world leading to a higher quality of life for all of God's creation.

A) Water, Air, Soil, Minerals, Plants—We support and encourage social policies that serve to reduce and control the creation of industrial byproducts and waste; facilitate the safe processing and disposal of toxic and nuclear waste and move toward the elimination of both; encourage reduction of municipal waste; provide for appropriate recycling and disposal of municipal waste; and assist the cleanup of polluted air, water, and soil. We call for the preservation of old-growth forests and other irreplaceable natural treasures, as well as preservation of endangered plant species. We support measures designed to maintain and restore natural ecosystems. We support policies that develop alternatives to chemicals used for growing, processing, and preserving food, and we strongly urge adequate research into their effects upon God's creation prior to utilization. We urge development of international agreements concerning equitable utilization of the world's resources for human benefit so long as the integrity of the earth is maintained. We are deeply concerned about the privatization of water resources, the bottling of water to be sold as a commodity for profit, and the resources that go into packaging bottled water. We urge all municipalities and other governmental organizations to develop processes for determining sustainability of water resources and to determine the environmental, economic, and social consequences of privatization of water resources prior to the licensing and approval thereof.

B) Energy Resources Utilization—The whole earth is God's good creation and as such has inherent value. We are aware that the current utilization of energy resources threatens this creation at its very foundation. As members of The United Methodist Church we are committed to approaching creation, energy production, and especially creation's resources in a responsible, careful and economic way. We call upon all to take measures to save energy. Everybody should adapt his or her lifestyle to the average consumption of energy that respects the limits of the planet earth.

We encourage persons to limit CO_2 emissions toward the goal of one tonne per person annually. We strongly advocate for the priority of the development of renewable energies. The deposits of carbon, oil, and gas resources are limited and their continuous utilization accelerates global warming. The use of nuclear power is no solution for avoiding CO_2 emissions. Nuclear power plants are vulnerable, unsafe, and potential health risks. A safe, permanent storage of nuclear waste cannot be guaranteed. It is therefore not responsible to future generations to operate them. The production of agricultural fuels and the use of biomass plants rank lower than the provision of safe food supplies and the continued existence for small farming businesses.

C) *Animal Life*—We support regulations that protect and conserve the life and health of animals, including those ensuring the humane treatment of pets, domesticated animals, animals used in research, wildlife, and the painless slaughtering of meat animals, fish, and fowl. We recognize unmanaged and managed commercial, multinational, and corporate exploitation of wildlife and the destruction of the ecosystems on which they depend threatens the balance of natural systems, compromises biodiversity, reduces resilience, and threatens ecosystem services. We encourage commitment to effective implementation of national and international governmental and business regulations and guidelines for the conservation of all animal species with particular support to safeguard those threatened with extinction.

D) *Global Climate Stewardship*—We acknowledge the global impact of humanity's disregard for God's creation. Rampant industrialization and the corresponding increase in the use of fossil fuels have led to a buildup of pollutants in the earth's atmosphere. These "greenhouse gas" emissions threaten to alter dramatically the earth's climate for generations to come with severe environmental, economic, and social implications. The adverse impacts of global climate change disproportionately affect individuals and nations least responsible for the emissions. We therefore support efforts of all governments to require mandatory reductions in greenhouse gas emissions and call on individuals, congregations, businesses, industries, and communities to reduce their emissions.

E) *Space*—The universe, known and unknown, is the creation of God and is due the respect we are called to give the earth. We therefore reject any nation's efforts to weaponized space and urge that all nations pursue the peaceful and collaborative development of space technologies and of outer space itself.

F) *Science and Technology*—We recognize science as a legitimate interpretation of God's natural world. We affirm the validity of the claims of science in describing the natural world and in determining what is scientific. We preclude science from making authoritative claims about theological issues and theology from making authoritative claims about scientific issues. We find that science's descriptions of cosmological, geological, and biological evolution are not in conflict with theology. We recognize medical, technical, and scientific technologies as legitimate uses of God's natural world when such use enhances human life and enables all of God's children to develop their God-given creative potential without violating our ethical convictions about the relationship of humanity to the natural world. We reexamine our ethical convictions as our understanding of the natural world increases. We find that as science expands human understanding of the natural world, our understanding of the mysteries of God's creation and word are enhanced.

In acknowledging the important roles of science and technology, however, we also believe that theological understandings of human experience are crucial to a full understanding of the place of humanity in the universe. Science and theology are complementary rather than mutually incompatible. We therefore encourage dialogue between the scientific and theological communities and seek the kind of participation that will enable humanity to sustain life on earth and, by God's grace, increase the quality of our common lives together.

G) *Food Safety*—We support policies that protect the food supply and that ensure the public's right to know the content of the foods they are eating. We call for rigorous inspections and controls on the biological safety of all foodstuffs intended for human consumption. We urge independent testing for chemical residues in food, and the removal from the market of foods contaminated with potentially hazardous levels of pesticides, herbicides, or fungicides; drug residues from animal antibiotics, steroids, or hormones; contaminants due to pollution that are carried by air, soil, or water from incinerator plants or other industrial operations. We call for clear labeling of all processed, genetically created, or genetically altered foods, with premarket safety testing required. We oppose weakening the standards for organic foods. We call for policies that encourage and support a gradual transition to sustainable and organic agriculture.

H) Food Justice—We support policies that increase access to quality food, particularly for those with the fewest resources. We affirm local, sustainable, and small-scale agriculture opportunities that allow communities to feed themselves. We decry policies that make food inaccessible to the communities where it is grown and the farmworkers involved in its growth.

¶ 161.   II. THE NURTURING COMMUNITY

The community provides the potential for nurturing human beings into the fullness of their humanity. We believe we have a responsibility to innovate, sponsor, and evaluate new forms of community that will encourage development of the fullest potential in individuals. Primary for us is the gospel understanding that all persons are important—because they are human beings created by God and loved through and by Jesus Christ and not because they have merited significance. We therefore support social climates in which human communities are maintained and strengthened for the sake of all persons and their growth. We also encourage all individuals to be sensitive to others by using appropriate language when referring to all persons. Language of a derogatory nature (with regard to race, nationality, ethnic background, gender, sexuality, and physical differences) does not reflect value for one another and contradicts the gospel of Jesus Christ.

A) Culture and Identity—We believe that our primary identity is as children of God. With that identity comes societal and cultural constructions that have both positive and negative impacts on humanity and the Church. Cultural identity evolves through our history, traditions, and experiences. The Church seeks to fully embrace and nurture cultural formation and competency as a means to be fully one body, expressed in multiple ways. Each of us has multiple identities of equal value that intersect to form our complete self. We affirm that no identity or culture has more legitimacy than any other. We call the Church to challenge any hierarchy of cultures or identities. Through relationships within and among cultures we are called to and have the responsibility for learning from each other, showing mutual respect for our differences and similarities as we experience the diversity of perspectives and viewpoints.

B) The Family—We believe the family to be the basic human community through which persons are nurtured and sustained in mutual love, responsibility, respect, and fidelity. We affirm the importance of loving parents for all children. We also understand the family as encompassing a wider range of options than that of the two-generational unit of parents and children (the nuclear family). We affirm shared responsibility for parenting where there are two parents and encourage social, economic, and religious efforts to maintain and strengthen relationships within families in order that every member may be assisted toward complete personhood.

C) Marriage—We affirm the sanctity of the marriage covenant that is expressed in love, mutual support, personal commitment, and shared fidelity between a man and a woman. We believe that God's blessing rests upon such marriage, whether or not there are children of the union. We reject social norms that assume different standards for women than for men in marriage. We support laws in civil society that define marriage as the union of one man and one woman.[2]

D) Divorce—God's plan is for lifelong, faithful marriage. The church must be on the forefront of premarital, marital, and post-marital counseling in order to create and preserve healthy relationships. However, when a married couple is estranged beyond reconciliation, even after thoughtful consideration and counsel, divorce is a regrettable alternative in the midst of brokenness. We grieve over the devastating emotional, spiritual, and economic consequences of divorce for all involved, understanding that women and especially children are disproportionately impacted by such burdens. As the Church we are concerned about high divorce rates. It is recommended that methods of mediation be used to minimize the adversarial nature and fault-finding that are often part of our current judicial processes, encouraging reconciliation wherever possible. We also support efforts by governments to reform divorce laws and other aspects of family law in order to address negative trends such as high divorce rates.

Although divorce publicly declares that a marriage no longer exists, other covenantal relationships resulting from the marriage remain, such as the nurture and support of children and extended family ties. We urge respectful negotiations in deciding the custody

---

2. See Judicial Council Decision 694.

of minor children and support the consideration of either or both parents for this responsibility in that custody not be reduced to financial support, control, or manipulation and retaliation. The welfare of each child is the most important consideration.

Divorce does not preclude a new marriage. We encourage an intentional commitment of the Church and society to minister compassionately to those in the process of divorce, as well as members of divorced and remarried families, in a community of faith where God's grace is shared by all.

E) Single Persons—We affirm the integrity of single persons, and we reject all social practices that discriminate or social attitudes that are prejudicial against persons because they are single. This also includes single parents, and we recognize the extra responsibilities involved.

F) Women and Men—We affirm with Scripture the common humanity of male and female, both having equal worth in the eyes of God. We reject the erroneous notion that one gender is superior to another, that one gender must strive against another, and that members of one gender may receive love, power, and esteem only at the expense of another. We especially reject the idea that God made individuals as incomplete fragments, made whole only in union with another. We call upon women and men alike to share power and control, to learn to give freely and to receive freely, to be complete and to respect the wholeness of others. We seek for every individual opportunities and freedom to love and be loved, to seek and receive justice, and to practice ethical self-determination. We understand our gender diversity to be a gift from God, intended to add to the rich variety of human experience and perspective; and we guard against attitudes and traditions that would use this good gift to leave members of one sex more vulnerable in relationships than members of another.

G) Human Sexuality—We affirm that sexuality is God's good gift to all persons. We call everyone to responsible stewardship of this sacred gift.

Although all persons are sexual beings whether or not they are married, sexual relations are affirmed only with the covenant of monogamous, heterosexual marriage.

We deplore all forms of the commercialization, abuse, and exploitation of sex. We call for strict global enforcement of laws prohibiting the sexual exploitation of children and for adequate protection, guidance, and counseling for abused children. All per-

sons, regardless of age, gender, marital status, or sexual orientation, are entitled to have their human and civil rights ensured and
to be protected against violence. The Church should support the
family in providing age-appropriate education regarding sexuality to children, youth, and adults.

We affirm that all persons are individuals of sacred worth,
created in the image of God. All persons need the ministry of the
Church in their struggles for human fulfillment, as well as the
spiritual and emotional care of a fellowship that enables reconciling relationships with God, with others, and with self. The United
Methodist Church does not condone the practice of homosexuality and considers this practice incompatible with Christian teaching. We affirm that God's grace is available to all. We will seek
to live together in Christian community, welcoming, forgiving,
and loving one another, as Christ has loved and accepted us. We
implore families and churches not to reject or condemn lesbian
and gay members and friends. We commit ourselves to be in ministry for and with all persons.[3]

H) Family Violence and Abuse—We recognize that family violence and abuse in all its forms—verbal, psychological, physical,
sexual—is detrimental to the covenant of the human community.
We encourage the Church to provide a safe environment, counsel,
and support for the victim and to work with the abuser to understand the root causes and forms of abuse and to overcome such
behaviors. Regardless of the cause or the abuse, both the victim
and the abuser need the love of the Church. While we deplore the
actions of the abuser, we affirm that person to be in need of God's
redeeming love.

I) Sexual Abuse—Violent, disrespectful, or abusive sexual
expressions do not confirm sexuality as God's good gift. We
reject all sexual expressions that damage the humanity God has
given us as birthright, and we affirm only that sexual expression that enhances that same humanity. We believe that sexual
relations where one or both partners are exploitative, abusive, or
promiscuous are beyond the parameters of acceptable Christian
behavior and are ultimately destructive to individuals, families,
and the social order. We deplore all forms of the commercialization
and exploitation of sex, with their consequent cheapening and
degradation of human personality. To lose freedom and be sold

---

3. See Judicial Council Decision 702.

by someone else for sexual purposes is a form of slavery, and we denounce such business and support the abused and their right to freedom.

We call for strict global enforcement of laws prohibiting the sexual exploitation or use of children by adults and encourage efforts to hold perpetrators legally and financially responsible. We call for the establishment of adequate protective services, guidance, and counseling opportunities for children thus abused.

J) Sexual Harassment—We believe human sexuality is God's good gift. One abuse of this good gift is sexual harassment. We define sexual harassment as any unwanted sexual comment, advance, or demand, either verbal or physical, that is reasonably perceived by the recipient as demeaning, intimidating, or coercive. Sexual harassment must be understood as an exploitation of a power relationship rather than as an exclusively sexual issue. Sexual harassment includes, but is not limited to, the creation of a hostile or abusive working environment resulting from discrimination on the basis of gender. Contrary to the nurturing community, sexual harassment creates improper, coercive, and abusive conditions wherever it occurs in society. Sexual harassment undermines the social goal of equal opportunity and the climate of mutual respect between men and women. Unwanted sexual attention is wrong and discriminatory. Sexual harassment interferes with the moral mission of the Church.

K) Abortion—The beginning of life and the ending of life are the God-given boundaries of human existence. While individuals have always had some degree of control over when they would die, they now have the awesome power to determine when and even whether new individuals will be born. Our belief in the sanctity of unborn human life makes us reluctant to approve abortion.

But we are equally bound to respect the sacredness of the life and well-being of the mother and the unborn child.

We recognize tragic conflicts of life with life that may justify abortion, and in such cases we support the legal option of abortion under proper medical procedures by certified medical providers. We support parental, guardian, or other responsible adult notification and consent before abortions can be performed on girls who have not yet reached the age of legal adulthood. We cannot affirm abortion as an acceptable means of birth control, and we unconditionally reject it as a means of gender selection or eugenics (see Resolution 3184).

We oppose the use of late-term abortion known as dilation and extraction (partial-birth abortion) and call for the end of this practice except when the physical life of the mother is in danger and no other medical procedure is available, or in the case of severe fetal anomalies incompatible with life. This procedure shall be performed only by certified medical providers. Before providing their services, abortion providers should be required to offer women the option of anesthesia.

We call all Christians to a searching and prayerful inquiry into the sorts of conditions that may cause them to consider abortion. We entrust God to provide guidance, wisdom, and discernment to those facing an unintended pregnancy.

The Church shall offer ministries to reduce unintended pregnancies. We commit our Church to continue to provide nurturing ministries to those who terminate a pregnancy, to those in the midst of a crisis pregnancy, and to those who give birth.

We mourn and are committed to promoting the diminishment of high abortion rates. The Church shall encourage ministries to reduce unintended pregnancies such as comprehensive, age-appropriate sexuality education, advocacy in regard to contraception, and support of initiatives that enhance the quality of life for all women and girls around the globe.

Young adult women disproportionately face situations in which they feel that they have no choice due to financial, educational, relational, or other circumstances beyond their control. The Church and its local congregations and campus ministries should be in the forefront of supporting existing ministries and developing new ministries that help such women in their com- munities. They should also support those crisis pregnancy centers and pregnancy resource centers that compassionately help women explore all options related to unplanned pregnancy. We particularly encourage the Church, the government, and social service agencies to support and facilitate the option of adoption. (See ¶ 161M.) We affirm and encourage the Church to assist the ministry of crisis pregnancy centers and pregnancy resource centers that compassionately help women find feasible alternatives to abortion.

Governmental laws and regulations do not provide all the guidance required by the informed Christian conscience. Therefore, a decision concerning abortion should be made only after thoughtful and prayerful consideration by the parties involved, with medical, family, pastoral, and other appropriate counsel.

L) Ministry With Those Who Have Experienced an Abortion—We urge local pastors to become informed about the symptoms and behaviors associated with post-abortion stress. We commit our Church to continue to provide nurturing ministries to those who terminate a pregnancy, to those in the midst of a crisis pregnancy, and to those who give birth. We further encourage local churches to make available contact information for counseling agencies that offer programs to address post-abortion stress for all seeking help.

M) Adoption—Children are a gift from God to be welcomed and received. We recognize that some circumstances of birth make the rearing of a child difficult. We affirm and support the birth parent(s) whose choice it is to allow the child to be adopted. We recognize the agony, strength, and courage of the birth parent(s) who choose(s) in hope, love, and prayer to offer the child for adoption. In addition, we also recognize the anxiety, strength, and courage of those who choose in hope, love, and prayer to be able to care for a child. We affirm and support the adoptive parent(s)' desire to rear an adopted child as they would a biological child. When circumstances warrant adoption, we support the use of proper legal procedures. When appropriate and possible, we encourage open adoption so that a child may know all information and people related to them, both medically and relationally. We support and encourage greater awareness and education to promote adoption of a wide variety of children through foster care, international adoption, and domestic adoption. We commend the birth parent(s), the receiving parent(s), and the child to the care of the Church, that grief might be shared, joy might be celebrated, and the child might be nurtured in a community of Christian love.

N) Faithful Care for Dying Persons—While we applaud medical science for efforts to prevent disease and illness and for advances in treatment that extend the meaningful life of human beings, we recognize that every mortal life will ultimately end in death. Death is never a sign that God has abandoned us, no matter what the circumstances of the death might be. As Christians we must always be prepared to surrender the gift of mortal life and claim the gift of eternal life through the death and resurrection of Jesus Christ. Care for dying persons is part of our stewardship of the divine gift of life when cure is no longer possible. We encourage the use of medical technologies to provide palliative care at the end of life when life-sustaining treatments no longer support the goals of life, and when they have reached their limits. There is no moral or religious obligation to use these when they impose undue burdens or only extend the process of dying. Dying persons and their families are free to discontinue treatments when they cease to be of benefit to the patient.

We recognize the agonizing personal and moral decisions faced by the dying, their physicians, their families, their friends, and their faith community. We urge that decisions faced by the dying be made with thoughtful and prayerful consideration by the parties involved, with medical, pastoral, and other appropriate counsel. We further urge that all persons discuss with their families, their physicians, and their pastoral counselors, their wishes for care at the end of life and provide advance directives for such care when they are not able to make these decisions for themselves. Even when one accepts the inevitability of death, the Church and society must continue to provide faithful care, including pain relief, companionship, support, and spiritual nurture for the dying person in the hard work of preparing for death. We encourage and support the concept of hospice care whenever possible at the end of life. Faithful care does not end at death but continues during bereavement as we care for grieving families. We reject euthanasia and any pressure upon the dying to end their lives. God has continued love and purpose for all persons, regardless of health. We affirm laws and policies that protect the rights and dignity of the dying.

O) Suicide—We believe that suicide is not the way a human life should end. Often suicide is the result of untreated depression, or untreated pain and suffering. The Church has an obligation to see that all persons have access to needed pastoral and medical care and therapy in those circumstances that lead to loss of self-worth, suicidal despair, and/or the desire to seek physician-assisted suicide. We encourage the Church to provide education to address the biblical, theological, social, and ethical issues related to death and dying, including suicide. United Methodist theological seminary courses should also focus on issues of death and dying, including suicide.

A Christian perspective on suicide begins with an affirmation of faith that nothing, including suicide, separates us from the love of God (Romans 8:38-39). Therefore, we deplore the condemnation of people who complete suicide, and we consider unjust the stigma that so often falls on surviving family and friends.

We encourage pastors and faith communities to address this issue through preaching and teaching. We urge pastors and faith communities to provide pastoral care to those at risk, survivors, and their families, and to those families who have lost loved ones to suicide, seeking always to remove the oppressive stigma around suicide. The Church opposes assisted suicide and euthanasia.

P) *Sexual Assault*—Sexual assault is wrong. We affirm the right of all people to live free from such assaults, encourage efforts of law enforcement to prosecute such crimes, and condemn rape in any form. It does not matter where the person is, what the person is wearing, whether or not he or she is intoxicated, if he or she is flirtatious, what is the victim's gender, or any other circumstance.

Q) *Pornography*—Scripture teaches that humans are created in God's image and that we are accountable to God through right relationship. Sexual images can celebrate the goodness of human sexuality through positive depiction in art, literature, and education. We deplore, however, images that distort this goodness and injure healthy sexual relationships.

We oppose all forms of pornography and consider its use a form of sexual misconduct. Pornography is sexually explicit material that portrays violence, abuse, coercion, domination, humiliation, or degradation for the purpose of sexual arousal. Pornography sexually exploits and objectifies both women and men. Any sexually explicit material that depicts children is abhorrent and victimizes children. Pornography can ruin lives, careers, and relationships.

We grieve the pervasiveness of Internet pornography, including among Christians, and especially its impact on young people and marriages.

The Church is called to transformation and healing for all persons adversely affected by pornography. Congregations should send a clear message of opposition to pornography and commitment to safe environments for everyone. We encourage strategies to eradicate pornography, to support victims, and to provide open and transparent conversation and education around sexuality and sexual ethics. We also believe that people can be rehabilitated and should have the opportunity to receive treatment; therefore, churches should seek ways to offer support and care for addressing issues of addiction. Further, all churches are encouraged to review and update appropriate child, youth, and adult protection policies to reflect The United Methodist Church's position that the use of pornography is a form of sexual misconduct. By encouraging education, prevention, and pathways to recovery for all affected by pornography, we live out our Wesleyan understanding of grace and healing.

R) *Bullying*—Bullying is a growing problem in parts of the connection. It is a contributing factor in suicide and in the violence we see in some cultures today. We affirm the right of all people, regardless of gender, socioeconomic status, race, religion, disability, age, physical appearance, sexual orientation and gender identity, to be free of unwanted aggressive behavior and harmful control tactics.

As the Church, we can play a pivotal role in ending this problem. We urge churches to seek opportunities to be trained in responding to the needs of those who have been bullied, to those who perpetrate bullying, and to support those in authority who may witness or be called to intervene on behalf of those who have been bullied. Churches are urged to connect with community associations and schools in this outreach.

We encourage churches to adopt a policy of zero tolerance for bullying, including cyberbullying, within their spheres of influence; stand with persons being bullied; and take a leadership role in working with the schools and community to prevent bullying.

¶ 162.   III. THE SOCIAL COMMUNITY

The rights and privileges a society bestows upon or withholds from those who comprise it indicate the relative esteem in which that society holds particular persons and groups of persons. We affirm all persons as equally valuable in the sight of God. We therefore work toward societies in which each person's value is recognized, maintained, and strengthened. We support the basic rights of all persons to equal access to housing, education, communication, employment, medical care, legal redress for grievances, and physical protection. We deplore acts of hate or violence against groups or persons based on race, color, national origin, ethnicity, age, gender, disability, status, economic condition, sexual orientation, gender identity, or religious affiliation. Our respect for the inherent dignity of all persons leads us to call for the recognition, protection, and implementation of the principles of *The Universal Declaration of Human Rights* so that communities and individuals may claim and enjoy their universal, indivisible, and inalienable rights.

A) Rights of Racial and Ethnic Persons—Racism is the combination of the power to dominate by one race over other races and a value system that assumes that the dominant race is innately superior to the others. Racism includes both personal and institutional racism. Personal racism is manifested through the individual expressions, attitudes, and/or behaviors that accept the assumptions of a racist value system and that maintain the benefits of this system. Institutional racism is the established social pattern that supports implicitly or explicitly the racist value system. Racism, manifested as sin, plagues and hinders our relationship with Christ, inasmuch as it is antithetical to the gospel itself. In many cultures white persons are granted unearned privileges and benefits that are denied to persons of color. We oppose the creation of a racial hierarchy in any culture. Racism breeds racial discrimination. We define racial discrimination as the disparate treatment and lack of full access and equity in resources, opportunities, and participation in the Church and in society based on race or ethnicity.

Therefore, we recognize racism as sin and affirm the ultimate and temporal worth of all persons. We rejoice in the gifts that particular ethnic histories and cultures bring to our total life. We commit as the Church to move beyond symbolic expressions and representative models that do not challenge unjust systems of power and access.

We commend and encourage the self-awareness of all racial and ethnic groups and oppressed people that leads them to demand their just and equal rights as members of society. We assert the obligation of society and people within the society to implement compensatory programs that redress long-standing, systemic social deprivation of racial and ethnic persons. We further assert the right of members of historically underrepresented racial and ethnic persons to equal and equitable opportunities in employment and promotion; to education and training of the highest quality; to nondiscrimination in voting, access to public accommodations, and housing purchase or rental; to credit, financial loans, venture capital, and insurance policies; to positions of leadership and power in all elements of our life together; and to full participation in the Church and society. We support affirmative action as one method of addressing the inequalities and discriminatory practices within the Church and society.

B) Rights of Religious Minorities—Religious persecution has been common in the history of civilization. We urge policies and practices that ensure the right of every religious group to exercise its faith free from legal, political, or economic restrictions. We condemn all overt and covert forms of religious intolerance, being especially sensitive to their expression in media stereotyping. We assert the right of all religions and their adherents to freedom from legal, economic, and social discrimination.

C) *Rights of Children*—Once considered the property of their parents, children are now acknowledged to be full human beings in their own right, but beings to whom adults and society in general have special obligations. Thus, we support the development of school systems and innovative methods of education designed to assist every child toward complete fulfillment as an individual person of worth. All children have the right to quality education, including full sex education appropriate to their stage of development that utilizes the best educational techniques and insights. Christian parents and guardians and the Church have the responsibility to ensure that children receive sex education consistent with Christian morality, including faithfulness in marriage and abstinence in singleness. Moreover, children have the rights to food, shelter, clothing, health care, and emotional well-being as do adults, and these rights we affirm as theirs regardless of actions or inactions of their parents or guardians. In particular, children must be protected from economic, physical, emotional, and sexual exploitation and abuse.

D) *Rights of Young People*—Our society is characterized by a large population of young people who frequently find full participation in society difficult. Therefore, we urge development of policies that encourage inclusion of young people in decision-making processes and that eliminate discrimination and exploitation. Creative and appropriate employment opportunities should be legally and socially available for young people.

E) *Rights of the Aging*—In a society that places primary emphasis upon youth, those growing old in years are frequently isolated from the mainstream of social existence. We support social policies that integrate the aging into the life of the total community, including sufficient incomes, increased and nondiscriminatory employment opportunities, educational and service opportunities, and adequate medical care and housing within existing communities. We urge social policies and programs, with emphasis on the unique concerns of older women and ethnic persons, that ensure to the aging the respect and dignity that is their right as senior members of the human community. Further, we urge increased consideration for adequate pension systems by employers, with provisions for the surviving spouse.

F) Rights of Women—We affirm women and men to be equal in every aspect of their common life. We therefore urge that every effort be made to eliminate sex-role stereotypes in activity and portrayal of family life and in all aspects of voluntary and compensatory participation in the Church and society. We affirm the right of women to equal treatment in employment, responsibility, promotion, and compensation. We affirm the importance of women in decision-making positions at all levels of Church and society and urge such bodies to guarantee their presence through policies of employment and recruitment. We support affirmative action as one method of addressing the inequalities and discriminatory practices within our Church and society. We urge employers of persons in dual career families, both in the Church and society, to apply proper consideration of both parties when relocation is considered. We affirm the right of women to live free from violence and abuse and urge governments to enact policies that protect women against all forms of violence and discrimination in any sector of society.

G) Rights of Men—Because we affirm women and men to be equal in every aspect of their common life, we also affirm the rights of men. We affirm equal opportunities in employment, responsibility, and promotion. Men should not be ignored or lose opportunities or influence because they are men.

We recognize that men are also victims of domestic violence and abuse. We encourage communities to offer the same policies and protection as provided for women in similar situations. We affirm the right of men to live free from violence and abuse and urge governments to enact policies that protect men against all forms of violence and discrimination in any sector of society.

We recognize that men's role in raising children is in equal importance to women's and call for equal rights as women in opportunities for parental leave. When parents divorce, men often have less contact with their children. We call for equal access to child-custody, but emphasize that the best interest of the child always is the most important.

H) Rights of Immigrants—We recognize, embrace, and affirm all persons, regardless of country of origin, as members of the family of God. We affirm the right of all persons to equal opportunities for employment, access to housing, health care, education, and freedom from social discrimination. We urge the Church and society to recognize the gifts, contributions, and struggles of those who are immigrants and to advocate for justice for all. We oppose immigration policies that separate family members from each other or that include detention of families with children, and we call on local churches to be in ministry with immigrant families.

I) Rights of Persons With Disabilities—We recognize and affirm the full humanity and personhood of all individuals with mental, physical, developmental, neurological, and psychological conditions or disabilities as full members of the family of God. We also affirm their rightful place in both the Church and society. We affirm the responsibility of the Church and society to be in ministry with children, youth, and adults with mental, physical, developmental, and/or psychological and neurological conditions or disabilities whose particular needs in the areas of mobility, communication, intellectual comprehension, or personal relationships might make more challenging their participation or that of their families in the life of the Church and the community. We urge the Church and society to recognize and receive the gifts of persons with disabilities to enable them to be full participants in the community of faith. We call the Church and society to be sensitive to, and advocate for, programs of rehabilitation, services, employment, education, appropriate housing, and transportation. We call on the Church and society to protect the civil rights of persons with all types and kinds of disabilities.

J) Equal Rights Regardless of Sexual Orientation—Certain basic human rights and civil liberties are due all persons. We are committed to supporting those rights and liberties for all persons, regardless of sexual orientation. We see a clear issue of simple justice in protecting the rightful claims where people have shared material resources, pensions, guardian relationships, mutual powers of attorney, and other such lawful claims typically attendant to contractual relationships that involve shared contributions, responsibilities, and liabilities, and equal protection before the law. Moreover, we support efforts to stop violence and other forms of coercion against all persons, regardless of sexual orientation.

K) Population—Since the growing worldwide population is increasingly straining the world's supply of food, minerals, and water and sharpening international tensions, the reduction of the rate of consumption of resources by the affluent and the reduction of current world population growth rates have become impera-tive. People have the duty to consider the impact on the total world community of their decisions regarding childbearing and should have access to information and appropriate means to limit their fertility, including voluntary sterilization. We affirm that programs to achieve a stabilized population should be placed in a context of total economic and social development, including an equitable use and control of resources; improvement in the sta-tus of women in all cultures; a human level of economic security, health care, and literacy for all. We oppose any policy of forced abortion or forced sterilization.

L) Alcohol and Other Drugs—We affirm our long-standing support of abstinence from alcohol as a faithful witness to God's liberating and redeeming love for persons. We support abstinence from the use of any illegal drugs. Since the use of illegal drugs, as well as illegal and problematic use of alcohol, is a major factor in crime, disease, death, and family dysfunction, we support edu-cational programs as well as other prevention strategies encour-aging abstinence from illegal drug use and, with regard to those who choose to consume alcoholic beverages, judicious use with deliberate and intentional restraint, with Scripture as a guide.

Millions of living human beings are testimony to the benefi-cial consequences of therapeutic drug use, and millions of others are testimony to the detrimental consequences of drug misuse. We encourage wise policies relating to the availability of potentially beneficial or potentially damaging prescription and over-the-coun-ter drugs; we urge that complete information about their use and misuse be readily available to both doctor and patient. We support the strict administration of laws regulating the sale and distribution of alcohol and controlled substances. We support regulations that protect society from users of drugs of any kind, including alcohol, where it can be shown that a clear and present social danger exists. Drug-dependent persons and their family members, including those who are assessed or diagnosed as dependent on alcohol, are individuals of infinite human worth deserving of treatment, rehabilitation, and ongoing life-changing recovery. Misuse or abuse may also require intervention, in order to prevent progres-sion into dependence. Because of the frequent interrelationship between alcohol abuse and mental illness, we call upon legislators and health care providers to make available appropriate mental illness treatment and rehabilitation for drug-dependent persons.

We commit ourselves to assisting those who suffer from abuse or dependence, and their families, in finding freedom through Jesus Christ and in finding good opportunities for treatment, for ongoing counseling, and for reintegration into society.

M) Tobacco—We affirm our historic tradition of high standards of personal discipline and social responsibility. In light of the overwhelming evidence that tobacco smoking and the use of smokeless tobacco are hazardous to the health of persons of all ages, we recommend total abstinence from the use of tobacco. We urge that our educational and communication resources be utilized to support and encourage such abstinence. Further, we recognize the harmful effects of passive smoke and support the restriction of smoking in public areas and workplaces.

N) Medical Experimentation—Physical and mental health has been greatly enhanced through discoveries by medical science. It is imperative, however, that governments and the medical profession carefully enforce the requirements of the prevailing medical research standard, maintaining rigid controls in testing new technologies and drugs utilizing human beings. The standard requires that those engaged in research shall use human beings as research subjects only after obtaining full, rational, and uncoerced consent.

O) Genetic Technology—The responsibility of humankind to God's creation challenges us to deal carefully with and examine the possibilities of genetic research and technology in a conscientious, careful, and responsible way. We welcome the use of genetic technology for meeting fundamental human needs for health and a safe environment. We oppose the cloning of humans and the genetic manipulation of the gender of an unborn child.

Because of the effects of genetic technologies on all life, we call for effective guidelines and public accountability to safeguard against any action that might lead to abuse of these technologies, including political or military ends. We recognize that cautious, well-intended use of genetic technologies may sometimes lead to unanticipated harmful consequences. The risks of genetic technology that can hardly be calculated when breeding animals and plants and the negative ecological and social impacts on agriculture make the use of this technology doubtful. We approve modern methods of breeding that respect the existence of the natural borders of species.

Human gene therapies that produce changes that cannot be passed to offspring (somatic therapy) should be limited to the alleviation of suffering caused by disease. Genetic therapies for eugenic choices or that produce waste embryos are deplored. Genetic data of individuals and their families should be kept secret and held in strict confidence unless confidentiality is waived by the individual or by his or her family, or unless the collection and use of genetic identification data is supported by an appropriate court order. Because its long-term effects are uncertain, we oppose genetic therapy that results in changes that can be passed to offspring (germ-line therapy). All the genetic procedures must be accompanied by independent, ethically oriented measures of testing, approval, and control.

P) Rural Life—We support the right of persons and families to live and prosper as farmers, farm workers, merchants, professionals, and others outside of the cities and metropolitan centers. We believe our culture is impoverished and our people deprived of a meaningful way of life when rural and small-town living becomes difficult or impossible. We recognize that the improvement of this way of life may sometimes necessitate the use of some lands for nonagricultural purposes. We oppose the indiscriminate diversion of agricultural land for nonagricultural uses when nonagricultural land is available. Further, we encourage the preservation of appropriate lands for agriculture and open space uses through thoughtful land use programs. We support governmental and private programs designed to benefit the resident farmer rather than the factory farm and programs that encourage industry to locate in nonurban areas.

We further recognize that increased mobility and technology have brought a mixture of people, religions, and philosophies to rural communities that were once homogeneous. While often this is seen as a threat to or loss of community life, we understand it as an opportunity to uphold the biblical call to community for all persons. Therefore, we encourage rural communities and individuals to maintain a strong connection to the earth and to be open to: offering mutual belonging, caring, healing, and growth; sharing and celebrating cooperative leadership and diverse gifts; supporting mutual trust; and affirming individuals as unique persons of worth, and thus to practice shalom.

Q) Sustainable Agriculture—A prerequisite for meeting the nutritional needs of the world's population is an agricultural system that uses sustainable methods, respects ecosystems, and promotes a livelihood for people that work the land.

We support a sustainable agricultural system that will maintain and support the natural fertility of agricultural soil, promote the diversity of flora and fauna, and adapt to regional conditions and structures—a system where agricultural animals are treated humanely and where their living conditions are as close to natural systems as possible. We aspire to an effective agricultural system where plant, livestock, and poultry production maintains the natural ecological cycles, conserves energy, and reduces chemical input to a minimum.

Sustainable agriculture requires a global evaluation of the impact of agriculture on food and raw material production, the preservation of animal breeds and plant varieties, and the preservation and development of the cultivated landscape.

World trade of agricultural products needs to be based on fair trade and prices, based on the costs of sustainable production methods, and must consider the real costs of ecological damage. The needed technological and biological developments are those that support sustainability and consider ecological consequences.

R) *Urban-Suburban Life*—Urban-suburban living has become a dominant style of life for more and more persons. For many it furnishes economic, educational, social, and cultural opportunities. For others, it has brought alienation, poverty, and depersonalization. We in the Church have an opportunity and responsibility to help shape the future of urban-suburban life. Massive programs of renewal and social planning are needed to bring a greater degree of humanization into urban-suburban lifestyles. We must judge all programs, including economic and community development, new towns, and urban renewal, by the extent to which they protect and enhance human values, permit personal and political involvement, and make possible neighborhoods open to persons of all races, ages, and income levels. We affirm the efforts of all developers who place human values at the heart of their planning. We must help shape urban-suburban development so that it provides for the human need to identify with and find meaning in smaller social communities. At the same time, such smaller communities must be encouraged to assume responsibilities for the total urban-suburban community instead of isolating themselves from it.

S) *Media Violence and Christian Values*—In our society, the media plays an important role. It influences people all over the world. Content, representations, pictures, scenes, however, are often in a stark contrast to human and Christian values. We express disdain of dehumanizing portrayals, sensationalized through mass media "entertainment" and "news." These practices degrade humankind and violate the teachings of Christ and the Bible.

United Methodists, along with those of other faith groups, must be made aware that the mass media often undermine the truths of Christianity by promoting permissive lifestyles and detailing acts of graphic violence. Instead of encouraging, motivating, and inspiring its audiences to adopt lifestyles based on the sanctity of life, the entertainment industry often advocates the opposite, painting a cynical picture of violence, abuse, greed, profanity, and a constant denigration of the family. The media must be held accountable for the part they play in the decline of values we observe in society today. Many in the media remain aloof to the issue, claiming to reflect rather than to influence society. For the sake of our human family, Christians must work together to halt this erosion of moral and ethical values in the world community. We oppose any kind of sexist image as well as those that glorify violence. We reject the implicit message that conflicts can be resolved and just peace can be established by violence. Within the bounds of the freedom of speech and the freedom of the press, the media are responsible for respecting human rights. In support of these matters, we work together with all people of good will.

T) Information Communication Technology—Because effective personal communication is key to being a responsible and empowered member of society, and because of the power afforded by information communication technologies to shape society and enable individuals to participate more fully, we believe that access to these technologies is a basic right.

Information communication technologies provide us with information, entertainment, and a voice in society. They can be used to enhance our quality of life and provide us with a means to interact with each other, our government, and people and cultures all over the world. Most information about world events comes to us by broadcast, cable, print media, and the Internet. Concentrating the control of media to large commercial interests limits our choices and often provides a distorted view of human values. Therefore, we support the regulation of media communication technologies to ensure a variety of independent information sources and provide for the public good.

Personal communication technologies such as the Internet allow persons to communicate with each other and access vast information resources that can have commercial, cultural, political, and personal value. While the Internet can be used to nurture minds and spirits of children and adults, it is in danger of being overrun with commercial interests and is used by some to distribute inappropriate and illegal material. Therefore, the Internet must be managed responsibly in order to maximize its benefits while minimizing its risks, especially for children. Denying access in today's world to basic information communication technologies like the Internet due to their cost or availability, limits people's participation in their government and society. We support the goal of universal access to telephone and Internet services at an affordable price.

U) *Persons Living With HIV and AIDS*—Persons diagnosed as positive for Human Immune Virus (HIV) and with Acquired Immune Deficiency Syndrome (AIDS) often face rejection from their families and friends and various communities in which they work and interact. In addition, they are often faced with a lack of adequate health care, especially toward the end of life.

All individuals living with HIV and AIDS should be treated with dignity and respect.

We affirm the responsibility of the Church to minister to and with these individuals and their families regardless of how the disease was contracted. We support their rights to employment, appropriate medical care, full participation in public education, and full participation in the Church.

We urge the Church to be actively involved in the prevention of the spread of AIDS by providing educational opportunities to the congregation and the community. The Church should be available to provide counseling to the affected individuals and their families.

V) *Right to Health Care*—Health is a condition of physical, mental, social, and spiritual well-being. John 10:10b says, "I came so that they could have life—indeed, so that they could live life to the fullest." Stewardship of health is the responsibility of each person to whom health has been entrusted. Creating the personal, environmental, and social conditions in which health can thrive is a joint responsibility—public and private. We encourage individuals to pursue a healthy lifestyle and affirm the importance of preventive health care, health education, environmental and

occupational safety, good nutrition, and secure housing in achieving health. Health care is a basic human right.

Providing the care needed to maintain health, prevent disease, and restore health after injury or illness is a responsibility
each person owes others and government owes to all, a responsibility government ignores at its peril. In Ezekiel 34:4a, God points
out the failures of the leadership of Israel to care for the weak:
"You don't strengthen the weak, heal the sick, bind up the injured,
bring back the strays, or seek out the lost." As a result all suffer.
Like police and fire protection, health care is best funded through
the government's ability to tax each person equitably and directly
fund the provider entities. Countries facing a public health crisis
such as HIV/AIDS must have access to generic medicines and to
patented medicines. We affirm the right of men and women to
have access to comprehensive reproductive health/family planning information and services that will serve as a means to prevent unplanned pregnancies, reduce abortions, and prevent the
spread of HIV/AIDS. The right to health care includes care for
persons with brain diseases, neurological conditions, or physical
disabilities, who must be afforded the same access to health care
as all other persons in our communities. It is unjust to construct
or perpetuate barriers to physical or mental wholeness or full participation in community.

We believe it is a governmental responsibility to provide all
citizens with health care.

We encourage hospitals, physicians, and medical clinics to
provide access to primary health care to all people regardless of
their health-care coverage or ability to pay for treatment.

W) Organ Transplantation and Donation—We believe that organ
transplantation and organ donation are acts of charity, *agape* love,
and self-sacrifice. We recognize the life-giving benefits of organ
and other tissue donation and encourage all people of faith to
become organ and tissue donors as a part of their love and ministry to others in need. We urge that it be done in an environment of
respect for deceased and living donors and for the benefit of the
recipients, and following protocols that carefully prevent abuse to
donors and their families.

X) Mental Health—The World Health Organization defines
mental health as "a state of well-being in which the individual
realizes his or her own abilities, can cope with the normal stresses
of life, can work productively and fruitfully, and is able to make

a contribution to his or her community." Unfortunately, mental health eludes many in our world resulting in considerable distress, stigma, and isolation. Mental illness troubles our relationships because it can affect the way we process information, relate to others, and choose actions. Consequently, mental illnesses often are feared in ways that other illnesses are not. Nevertheless, we know that regardless of our illness we remain created in the image of God (Genesis 1:27) and that nothing can separate us from the love of God (Romans 8:38-39).

No person deserves to be stigmatized because of mental illness. Those with mental illness are no more violent than other persons are. Rather, they are much more likely to be victims of violence or preyed on by others. When stigma happens within the church, mentally ill persons and their families are further victimized. Persons with mental illness and their families have a right to be treated with respect on the basis of common humanity and accurate information. They also have a right and responsibility to obtain care appropriate to their condition. The United Methodist Church pledges to foster policies that promote compassion, advocate for access to care, and eradicate stigma within the Church and in communities.

¶ 163.　IV. THE ECONOMIC COMMUNITY

We claim all economic systems to be under the judgment of God no less than other facets of the created order. Therefore, we recognize the responsibility of governments to develop and implement sound fiscal and monetary policies that provide for the economic life of individuals and corporate entities and that ensure full employment and adequate incomes with a minimum of inflation. We believe private and public economic enterprises are responsible for the social costs of doing business, such as employment and environmental pollution, and that they should be held accountable for these costs. We support measures that would reduce the concentration of wealth in the hands of a few. We further support efforts to revise tax structures and to eliminate governmental support programs that now benefit the wealthy at the expense of other persons.

A) Property—We believe private ownership of property is a trusteeship under God, both in those societies where it is encouraged and where it is discouraged, but is limited by the overriding needs of society. We believe that Christian faith denies to any person or group of persons exclusive and arbitrary control of any other part of the created universe. Socially and culturally conditioned ownership of property is, therefore, to be considered a responsibility to God. We believe, therefore, governments have the responsibility, in the pursuit of justice and order under law, to provide procedures that protect the rights of the whole society as well as those of private ownership.

B) Collective Bargaining—We support the right of all public and private employees and employers to organize for collective bargaining into unions and other groups of their own choosing. Further, we support the right of both parties to protection in so doing and their responsibility to bargain in good faith within the framework of the public interest. In order that the rights of all members of the society may be maintained and promoted, we support innovative bargaining procedures that include representatives of the public interest in negotiation and settlement of labor-management contracts, including some that may lead to forms of judicial resolution of issues. We reject the use of violence by either party during collective bargaining or any labor/management disagreement. We likewise reject the permanent replacement of a worker who engages in a lawful strike.

C) Work and Leisure—Every person has the right to a job at a living wage. Where the private sector cannot or does not provide jobs for all who seek and need them, it is the responsibility of government to provide for the creation of such jobs. We support social measures that ensure the physical and mental safety of workers, that provide for the equitable division of products and services, and that encourage an increasing freedom in the way individuals may use their leisure time. We recognize the opportunity leisure provides for creative contributions to society and encourage methods that allow workers additional blocks of discretionary time. We support educational, cultural, and recreational outlets that enhance the use of such time. We believe that persons come before profits. We deplore the selfish spirit that often pervades our economic life. We support policies that encourage the sharing of ideas in the workplace, cooperative and collective work arrangements. We support rights of workers to refuse to work in situations that endanger health and/or life without jeopardy to their jobs. We support policies that would reverse the increasing concentration of business and industry into monopolies.

D) Consumption—Consumers should exercise their economic power to encourage the manufacture of goods that are necessary and beneficial to humanity while avoiding the desecration of the environment in either production or consumption. Consumers should avoid purchasing products made in conditions where workers are being exploited because of their age, gender, or economic status.

And while the limited options available to consumers make this extremely difficult to accomplish, buying "Fair Trade Certified" products is one sure way consumers can use their purchasing power to make a contribution to the common good. The International Standards of Fair Trade are based on ensuring livable wages for small farmers and their families, working with democratically run farming cooperatives, buying direct so that the benefits and profits from trade actually reach the farmers and their communities, providing vitally important advance credit, and encouraging ecologically sustainable farming practices. Consumers should not only seek out companies whose product lines reflect a strong commitment to these standards, but should also encourage expanded corporate participation in the Fair Trade market.

Consumers should evaluate their consumption of goods and services in the light of the need for enhanced quality of life rather than unlimited production of material goods. We call upon consumers, including local congregations and Church-related institutions, to organize to achieve these goals and to express dissatisfaction with harmful economic, social, or ecological practices through such appropriate methods as boycott, letter writing, corporate resolution, and advertisement.

E) Poverty—In spite of general affluence in the industrialized nations, the majority of persons in the world live in poverty. In order to provide basic needs such as food, clothing, shelter, education, health care, and other necessities, ways must be found to share more equitably the resources of the world. Increasing technology, when accompanied by exploitative economic practices, impoverishes many persons and makes poverty self-perpetuating. Poverty due to natural catastrophes and environmental changes is growing and needs attention and support. Conflicts and war impoverish the population on all sides, and an important way to support the poor will be to work for peaceful solutions.

As a church, we are called to support the poor and challenge the rich. To begin to alleviate poverty, we support such policies as:

adequate income maintenance, quality education, decent housing, job training, meaningful employment opportunities, adequate medical and hospital care, humanization and radical revisions of welfare programs, work for peace in conflict areas and efforts to protect creation's integrity. Since low wages are often a cause of poverty, employers should pay their employees a wage that does not require them to depend upon government subsidies such as food stamps or welfare for their livelihood.

Because we recognize that the long-term reduction of poverty must move beyond services to and employment for the poor, which can be taken away, we emphasize measures that build and maintain the wealth of poor people, including asset-building strategies such as individual development savings accounts, micro-enterprise development programs, progams enabling home ownership, and financial management training and counseling. We call upon churches to develop these and other ministries that promote asset-building among the poor. We are especially mindful of the Global South, where investment and micro-enterprise are especially needed. We urge support for policies that will encourage equitable economic growth in the Global South and around the world, providing a just opportunity for all.

Poverty most often has systemic causes, and therefore we do not hold poor people morally responsible for their economic state.

F) Foreign Workers—For centuries people have moved across borders in search of work. In our global world this is still a relevant and increasing form of immigration. Improved wages, better working conditions, and jobs available are reasons for immigration due to work opportunities. Workers from other countries are in many societies an important resource to fill the society's need of workers. But foreign workers too often meet exploitation, absence of protecting laws, and unreasonable wages and working conditions.

We call upon governments and all employers to ensure for foreign workers the same economic, educational, and social benefits enjoyed by other citizens.

Foreign workers also need a religious fellowship, and we call for the churches to include these in their care and fellowships and to support them in their efforts for better conditions.

G) Gambling—Gambling is a menace to society, deadly to the best interests of moral, social, economic, and spiritual life, destructive of good government and good stewardship. As an act of faith and concern, Christians should abstain from gambling and should strive to minister to those victimized by the practice. Where gambling has become addictive, the Church will encourage such individuals to receive therapeutic assistance so that the individual's energies may be redirected into positive and constructive ends. The Church acknowledges the dichotomy that can occur when opposing gambling while supporting American Indian tribal sovereignty and self-determination. Therefore, the Church's role is to create sacred space to allow for dialogue and education that will promote a holistic understanding of the American Indians' historic quest for survival. The Church's prophetic call is to promote standards of justice and advocacy that would make it unnecessary and undesirable to resort to commercial gambling—including public lotteries, casinos, raffles, Internet gambling, gambling with an emerging wireless technology, and other games of chance—as a recreation, as an escape, or as a means of producing public revenue or funds for support of charities or government.

H) Family Farms—The value of family farms has long been affirmed as a significant foundation for free and democratic societies. In recent years, the survival of independent farmers worldwide has been threatened by various factors, including the increasing concentration of all phases of agriculture into the hands of a limited number of transnational corporations. The concentration of the food supply for the many into the hands of the few raises global questions of justice that cry out for vigilance and action.

We call upon the agribusiness sector to conduct itself with respect for human rights primarily in the responsible stewardship of daily bread for the world, and secondarily in responsible corporate citizenship that respects the rights of all farmers, small and large, to receive a fair return for honest labor. We advocate for the rights of people to possess property and to earn a living by tilling the soil.

We call upon governments to revise support programs that disproportionately benefit wealthier agricultural producers, so that more support can be given to programs that benefit medium- and smaller-sized farming operations, including programs that build rural processing, storage, distribution, and other agricultural infrastructure; which link local farmers to local schools; and which promote other community food security measures.

We call upon our churches to do all in their power to speak prophetically to the matters of food supply and the people who grow the food for the world and to develop ministries that build food security in local communities.

I) Corporate Responsibility—Corporations are responsible not only to their stockholders, but also to other stakeholders: their workers, suppliers, vendors, customers, the communities in which they do business, and for the earth, which supports them. We support the public's right to know what impact corporations have in these various arenas, so that people can make informed choices about which corporations to support.

We applaud corporations that voluntarily comply with standards that promote human well-being and protect the environment.

J) Finance—Financial institutions serve a vital role in society. They must guard, however, against abusive and deceptive lending practices that take advantage of the neediest among us for the gain of the richest. Banking regulations must prevent the collection of usurious interest that keeps people in cycles of debt. Personal-credit-issuing institutions must operate with responsibility and clarity that allow all parties to understand the full terms of agreements.

K) Trade and Investment—We affirm the importance of international trade and investment in an interdependent world. Trade and investment should be based on rules that support the dignity of the human person, a clean environment and our common humanity. Trade agreements must include mechanisms to enforce labor rights and human rights as well as environmental standards. Broad-based citizen advocacy and participation in trade negotiations must be ensured through democratic mechanisms of consultation and participation.

L) Graft and Corruption—God's good creation, the fullness of its bounty, and the loving, nurturing relationships that bind all together are intended by God to be enjoyed in freedom and responsible stewardship. To revere God's creation is a sacred trust that enables us to fashion just, equitable, sustainable relationships and communities. The strength, stability, security, and progress of such relationships and communities depend on the integrity of their social, economic, political, and cultural processes, institutions, and stakeholders. Graft, referring to unfair or illegal means of acquiring money, gain, or advantage, especially by abusing one's position in politics, business, and social institutions, transgresses human dignity and violates human rights. Corruption, referring to dishonest and undue exploitation of power for personal gain, subverts God's intention for the fullness of life and creation. Graft and corruption tangle the social thread of communities, erode the moral fiber of human relationships, and sully the reputation of social institutions. Legislative and judicial mechanisms, including a strong, just criminal justice system, must deal with graft and corruption at every level of society. Good, just political governance characterized by transparency, accountability, and integrity is crucial to the eradication of graft and corruption. Societies that are graft-ridden and plagued with corruption are needful of God's pardoning love and redeeming grace.

M) Public Indebtedness—The huge budget deficits produced by years of overspending by governments around the world is of great concern. We acknowledge that for a limited time in a nation's history governmental deficits are sometimes necessary. However, long periods of excessive overspending by governments have produced huge deficits and significant economic challenges for many nations. Such wanton carelessness cannot continue. Therefore, we call upon all governments to reduce budget deficits and to live within their means. We ask the governments and institutions that lend money to reduce significantly the interest rates on the money borrowed. We ask that public officials, when making financial adjustments, remember first and foremost obligations that promote the well-being of society such as the funding of schools and other opportunities that foster the growth of the individual, as well as agencies that care for the poor, the elderly, the disabled, and the disenfranchised.

We recognize that, if deficits are not brought under control, future generations will be shackled with a burden of public indebtedness that will force societies to live under the specter of coerced repayments, rising inflation, mass unemployment, and despair. Thus, this is not just a financial issue, but an issue of justice for those who are yet to be born. Wise stewardship is needed today to provide for future generations. We call on church leadership throughout the connection to encourage public officials to reduce public indebtedness and to begin the process toward balanced and fair budgets.

¶ 164.　　V. THE POLITICAL COMMUNITY

While our allegiance to God takes precedence over our allegiance to any state, we acknowledge the vital function of government as a principal vehicle for the ordering of society. Because we know ourselves to be responsible to God for social and political life, we declare the following relative to governments:

A) Basic Freedoms and Human Rights—We hold governments responsible for the protection of the rights of the people to free and fair elections and to the freedoms of speech, religion, assembly, communications media, and petition for redress of grievances without fear of reprisal; to the right to privacy; and to the guarantee of the rights to adequate food, clothing, shelter, education, and health care. Blockades and embargoes that seek to impede the flow or free commerce of food and medicines are practices that cause pain and suffering, malnutrition, or starvation with all its detrimental consequences to innocent and noncombatant civilian populations, especially children. We reject these as instruments of domestic and foreign policy regardless of political or ideological views. The form and the leaders of all governments should be determined by exercise of the right to vote guaranteed to all adult citizens. We also strongly reject domestic surveillance and intimidation of political opponents by governments in power and all other misuses of elective or appointive offices. The use of detention and imprisonment for the harassment and elimination of political opponents or other dissidents violates fundamental human rights. Furthermore, the mistreatment or torture, and other cruel, inhumane, and degrading treatment or punishment of persons by governments for any purpose violates Christian teaching and must be condemned and/or opposed by Christians and churches wherever and whenever it occurs.

The Church regards the institution of slavery, the practice and commission of genocide, war crimes, crimes against humanity, and aggression as infamous and atrocious evils. Such evils are destructive of humanity, promote impunity, and therefore must be unconditionally prohibited by all governments and shall never be tolerated by the Church.

B) Political Responsibility—The strength of a political system depends upon the full and willing participation of its citizens. The church should continually exert a strong ethical influence upon the state, supporting policies and programs deemed to be just and opposing policies and programs that are unjust.

C) *Church and State Relations*—The United Methodist Church has for many years supported the separation of church and state. In some parts of the world this separation has guaranteed the diversity of religious expressions and the freedom to worship God according to each person's conscience. Separation of church and state means no organic union of the two, but it does permit interaction. The state should not use its authority to promote particular religious beliefs (including atheism), nor should it require prayer or worship in the public schools, but it should leave students free to practice their own religious convictions. We believe that the state should not attempt to control the church, nor should the church seek to dominate the state. The rightful and vital separation of church and state, which has served the cause of religious liberty, should not be misconstrued as the abolition of all religious expression from public life.

D) *Freedom of Information*—Citizens of all countries should have access to all essential information regarding their government and its policies. Illegal and unconscionable activities directed against persons or groups by their own governments must not be justified or kept secret, even under the guise of national security.

E) *Education*—We believe that every person has the right to education. We also believe that the responsibility for education of the young rests with the family, faith communities, and the government. In society, this function can best be fulfilled through public policies that ensure access for all persons to free public elementary and secondary schools and to post-secondary schools of their choice. Persons should not be precluded by financial barriers from access to church-related and other independent institutions of higher education. We affirm the right of public and independent colleges and universities to exist, and we endorse public policies that ensure access and choice and that do not create unconstitutional entanglements between church and state. We believe that colleges and universities are to ensure that academic freedom is protected for all members of the academic community and a learning environment is fostered that allows for a free exchange of ideas. We affirm the joining of reason and faith; therefore, we urge colleges and universities to guard the expression of religious life on campus.

F) *Civil Obedience and Civil Disobedience*—Governments and laws should be servants of God and of human beings. Citizens have a duty to abide by laws duly adopted by orderly and just process of government. But governments, no less than individuals, are subject to the judgment of God. Therefore, we recognize the right of individuals to dissent when acting under the constraint of conscience and, after having exhausted all legal recourse, to resist or disobey laws that they deem to be unjust or that are discriminately enforced. Even then, respect for law should be shown by refraining from violence and by being willing to accept the costs of disobedience. We do not encourage or condone any form of violent protest as a legitimate exercise of free speech or civil disobedience. We offer our prayers for those in rightful authority who serve the public, and we support their efforts to afford justice and equal opportunity for all people. We assert the duty of churches to support those who suffer because of their stands of conscience represented by nonviolent beliefs or acts. We urge governments to ensure civil rights, as defined by the International Covenant on Civil and Political Rights, to persons in legal jeopardy because of those nonviolent acts.

G) The Death Penalty—We believe the death penalty denies the power of Christ to redeem, restore, and transform all human beings. The United Methodist Church is deeply concerned about crime throughout the world and the value of any life taken by a murder or homicide. We believe all human life is sacred and created by God and therefore, we must see all human life as significant and valuable. When governments implement the death penalty (capital punishment), then the life of the convicted person is devalued and all possibility of change in that person's life ends. We believe in the resurrection of Jesus Christ and that the possibility of reconciliation with Christ comes through repentance. This gift of reconciliation is offered to all individuals without exception and gives all life new dignity and sacredness. For this reason, we oppose the death penalty (capital punishment) and urge its elimination from all criminal codes.

H) Criminal and Restorative Justice—To protect all persons from encroachment upon their personal and property rights, governments have established mechanisms of law enforcement and courts. A wide array of sentencing options serves to express community outrage, incapacitate dangerous offenders, deter crime, and offer opportunities for rehabilitation. We support governmental measures designed to reduce and eliminate crime that are consistent with respect for the basic freedom of persons.

We reject all misuse of these mechanisms, including their use for the purpose of revenge or for persecuting or intimidating those whose race, appearance, lifestyle, economic condition, or beliefs differ from those in authority. We reject all careless, callous, or discriminatory enforcement of law that withholds justice from persons with disabilities and all those who do not speak the language of the country in which they are in contact with the law enforcement. We further support measures designed to remove the social conditions that lead to crime, and we encourage continued positive interaction between law enforcement officials and members of the community at large.

In the love of Christ, who came to save those who are lost and vulnerable, we urge the creation of a genuinely new system for the care and restoration of victims, offenders, criminal justice officials, and the community as a whole. Restorative justice grows out of biblical authority, which emphasizes a right relationship with God, self, and community. When such relationships are violated or broken through crime, opportunities are created to make things right.

Most criminal justice systems around the world are retributive. These retributive justice systems profess to hold the offender accountable to the state and use punishment as the equalizing tool for accountability. In contrast, restorative justice seeks to hold the offender accountable to the victimized person, and to the disrupted community. Through God's transforming power, restorative justice seeks to repair the damage, right the wrong, and bring healing to all involved, including the victim, the offender, the families, and the community. The Church is transformed when it responds to the claims of discipleship by becoming an agent of healing and systemic change.

I) Military Service—We deplore war and urge the peaceful settlement of all disputes among nations. From the beginning, the Christian conscience has struggled with the harsh realities of violence and war, for these evils clearly frustrate God's loving purposes for humankind. We yearn for the day when there will be no more war and people will live together in peace and justice. Some of us believe that war, and other acts of violence, are never acceptable to Christians. We also acknowledge that many Christians believe that, when peaceful alternatives have failed, the force of arms may regretfully be preferable to unchecked aggression, tyranny, and genocide. We honor the witness of pacifists who will not allow us to become complacent about war and violence. We also respect those who support the use of force, but only in extreme situations and only when the need is clear beyond reasonable doubt, and through appropriate international organizations. We urge the establishment of the rule of law in international affairs as a means of elimination of war, violence, and coercion in these affairs.

We reject national policies of enforced military service as incompatible with the gospel. We acknowledge the agonizing tension created by the demand for military service by national governments. We urge all young adults to seek the counsel of the Church as they reach a conscientious decision concerning the nature of their responsibility as citizens. Pastors are called upon to be available for counseling with all young adults who face conscription or who are considering voluntary enlistment in the armed forces, including those who conscientiously refuse to cooperate with a system of conscription.

We support and extend the ministry of the Church to those persons who conscientiously oppose all war, or any particular war, and who therefore refuse to serve in the armed forces or to cooperate with systems of military conscription. We also support and extend the Church's ministry to all persons. This includes those who conscientiously choose to serve in the armed forces or to accept alternative service. When persons choose to serve in the armed forces, we support their right to adequate care for injuries suffered, and advocate for sufficient resources to meet their physical and mental health needs, both during and after their service. We are aware that we can become guilty both by military action and by conscientious objection, and that we all are dependent on God's forgiveness.

¶ 165.   VI. THE WORLD COMMUNITY

God's world is one world. The unity now being thrust upon us by technological revolution has far outrun our moral and spiritual capacity to achieve a stable world. The enforced unity of humanity, increasingly evident on all levels of life, presents the Church as well as all people with problems that will not wait for answers: injustice, war, exploitation, privilege, population, international ecological crisis, proliferation of arsenals of nuclear weapons, development of transnational business organizations that operate beyond the effective control of any governmental structure, and the increase of tyranny in all its forms. This generation must find viable answers to these and related questions if humanity is to continue on this earth. We commit ourselves as a Church to the achievement of a world community that is a fellowship of persons who honestly love one another. We pledge ourselves to seek the meaning of the gospel in all issues that divide people and threaten the growth of world community.

A) *Nations and Cultures*—As individuals are affirmed by God in their diversity, so are nations and cultures. We recognize that no nation or culture is absolutely just and right in its treatment of its own people, nor is any nation totally without regard for the welfare of its citizens. The Church must regard nations as accountable for unjust treatment of their citizens and others living within their borders. While recognizing valid differences in culture and political philosophy, we stand for justice and peace in every nation.

B) *National Power and Responsibility*—Some nations possess more military and economic power than do others. Upon the powerful rests responsibility to exercise their wealth and influence with restraint. We will promote restorative justice strategies to support positive social change and peace building. We affirm the right and duty of people of all nations to determine their own destiny. We urge the major political powers to use their nonviolent power to maximize the political, social, and economic self-determination of other nations rather than to further their own special interests. We applaud international efforts to develop a more just international economic order in which the limited resources of the earth will be used to the maximum benefit of all nations and peoples. We urge Christians in every society to encourage the governments under which they live and the economic entities within their societies to aid and work for the development of more just economic orders.

C) *War and Peace*—We believe war is incompatible with the teachings and example of Christ. We therefore reject war as an instrument of national foreign policy. We oppose unilateral first/ preemptive strike actions and strategies on the part of any government. As disciples of Christ, we are called to love our enemies, seek justice, and serve as reconcilers of conflict. We insist that the first moral duty of all nations is to work together to resolve by peaceful means every dispute that arises between or among them. We advocate the extension and strengthening of international treaties and institutions that provide a framework within the rule of law for responding to aggression, terrorism, and genocide. We believe that human values must outweigh military claims as governments determine their priorities; that the militarization of society must be challenged and stopped; that the manufacture, sale, and deployment of armaments must be reduced and controlled; and that the production, possession, or use of nuclear weapons be condemned. Consequently, we endorse general and complete disarmament under strict and effective international control.

D) Justice and Law—Persons and groups must feel secure in their life and right to live within a society if order is to be achieved and maintained by law. We denounce as immoral an ordering of life that perpetuates injustice and impedes the pursuit of peace. Peoples and nations feel secure in the world community when law, order, and human rights are respected and upheld.

Believing that international justice requires the participation of all peoples and nations, we endorse the United Nations, its related bodies, the International Court of Justice, and the International Criminal Court as the best instruments now in existence to achieve a world of justice and law. We commend the efforts of all people in all countries who pursue world peace through law. We endorse international aid and cooperation on all matters of need and conflict. We urge acceptance for membership in the United Nations of all nations who wish such membership and who accept United Nations responsibility. We urge the United Nations to take a more aggressive role in the development of international arbitration of disputes and actual conflicts among nations by developing binding third-party arbitration. Bilateral or multilateral efforts outside of the United Nations should work in concert with, and not contrary to, its purposes. We reaffirm our historic concern for the world as our parish and seek for all persons and peoples full and equal membership in a truly world community.

¶ 166.   VII. OUR SOCIAL CREED

We believe in God, Creator of the world; and in Jesus Christ, the Redeemer of creation. We believe in the Holy Spirit, through whom we acknowledge God's gifts, and we repent of our sin in misusing these gifts to idolatrous ends.

We affirm the natural world as God's handiwork and dedicate ourselves to its preservation, enhancement, and faithful use by humankind.

We joyfully receive for ourselves and others the blessings of community, sexuality, marriage, and the family.

We commit ourselves to the rights of men, women, children, youth, young adults, the aging, and people with disabilities; to improvement of the quality of life; and to the rights and dignity of all persons.

We believe in the right and duty of persons to work for the glory of God and the good of themselves and others and in the protection of their welfare in so doing; in the rights to property as a trust from God, collective bargaining, and responsible consumption; and in the elimination of economic and social distress.

We dedicate ourselves to peace throughout the world, to the rule of justice and law among nations, and to individual freedom for all people of the world.

We believe in the present and final triumph of God's Word in human affairs and gladly accept our commission to manifest the life of the gospel in the world. Amen.

(It is recommended that this statement of Social Principles be continually available to United Methodist Christians and that it be emphasized regularly in every congregation. It is further recommended that "Our Social Creed" be frequently used in Sunday worship.)

A COMPANION LITANY TO OUR SOCIAL CREED

God in the Spirit revealed in Jesus Christ,
calls us by grace
> *to be renewed in the image of our Creator,*
> *that we may be one*
> *in divine love for the world.*

Today is the day
God cares for the integrity of creation,
> wills the healing and wholeness of all life,
> weeps at the plunder of earth's goodness.

And so shall we.

Today is the day
God embraces all hues of humanity,
> delights in diversity and difference,
> favors solidarity transforming strangers into friends.

And so shall we.

Today is the day
God cries with the masses of starving people,
> despises growing disparity between rich and poor,
> demands justice for workers in the marketplace.

And so shall we.

Today is the day
God deplores violence in our homes and streets,
> rebukes the world's warring madness,
> humbles the powerful and lifts up the lowly.

And so shall we.

Today is the day
God calls for nations and peoples to live in peace,
> celebrates where justice and mercy embrace,
> exults when the wolf grazes with the lamb.

And so shall we.

Today is the day
God brings good news to the poor,
> *proclaims release to the captives,*
> *gives sight to the blind, and*
> *sets the oppressed free.*

And so shall we.

Part VI

ORGANIZATION
AND ADMINISTRATION

Chapter One
THE LOCAL CHURCH

Section I. The Church and Pastoral Charge

¶ **201.** *Definition of a Local Church*—The local church provides the most significant arena through which disciple-making occurs. It is a community of true believers under the Lordship of Christ. It is the redemptive fellowship in which the Word of God is preached by persons divinely called and the sacraments are duly administered according to Christ's own appointment. Under the discipline of the Holy Spirit, the church exists for the maintenance of worship, the edification of believers, and the redemption of the world.

¶ **202.** *The Function of the Local Church*—The church of Jesus Christ exists in and for the world. It is primarily at the level of the charge consisting of one or more local churches that the church encounters the world. The local church is a strategic base from which Christians move out to the structures of society. The function of the local church, under the guidance of the Holy Spirit, is to help people to accept and confess Jesus Christ as Lord and Savior and to live their daily lives in light of their relationship with God. Therefore, the local church is to minister to persons in the community where the church is located, to provide appropriate training and nurture to all, to cooperate in ministry with other local churches, to defend God's creation and live as an ecologically responsible community, and to participate in the worldwide mission of the church, as minimal expectations of an authentic church.

¶ **203.** *Relation to the Wider Church*—The local church is a connectional society of persons who have been baptized, have professed their faith in Christ, and have assumed the vows of membership in The United Methodist Church. They gather in fellowship to hear the Word of God, receive the sacraments, praise and worship the triune God, and carry forward the work that Christ has committed to his church. Such a society of believers, being within The United Methodist Church and subject to its *Discipline,* is also an inherent part of the church universal, which is composed of all who accept Jesus Christ as Lord and Savior, and which in the Apostles' Creed we declare to be the holy catholic church.

¶ **204.** *Care of Members*—Each local church shall have a definite evangelistic, nurture, and witness responsibility for its members and the surrounding area and a missional outreach responsibility to the local and global community. It shall be responsible for ministering to all its members, wherever they live, and for persons who choose it as their church.

¶ **205.** *Definition of a Pastoral Charge*—1. A pastoral charge shall consist of one or more churches that are organized under and subject to the *Discipline* of The United Methodist Church, with a charge conference, and to which an ordained or licensed minister is or may be duly appointed or appointable as pastor in charge or co-pastor. Where co-pastors are appointed, the bishop may designate for administrative purposes one as pastor in charge.[1]

2. A pastoral charge of two or more churches may be designated a circuit or a cooperative parish.

3. A pastoral charge may be designated by the bishop and cabinet as a "teaching parish" when either a local church with a pastor or a cooperative parish with a director is available to serve as a counseling elder for a provisional, local, or student pastor appointed or assigned to the teaching parish. A teaching parish shall have a demonstrable commitment to a cooperative or team ministry style and the training of pastors.

---

1. See Judicial Council Decisions 113, 319.

4. When a pastoral charge is not able to be served by an ordained or licensed minister, the bishop, upon recommendation of the cabinet, may assign a qualified and trained layperson, lay minister or lay missioner to do the work of ministry in that charge. The layperson is accountable to the district superintendent or another ordained or licensed minister appointed to oversee the charge, who will make provision for sacramental ministry. Upon the bishop's assignment, the layperson will be assigned an additional clergyperson as a guide to provide support in the assignment. If the assignment is to continue longer than one year, within that year the layperson will begin the process of becoming either a certified lay minister or a certified candidate, thus coming under the care of the District Committee on Ministry. The layperson assigned is also accountable to the policies and procedures of the annual conference where assigned.

Section II. Cooperative Parish

¶ **206.** 1. Local churches, with the guidance of the Holy Spirit, may enhance their witness to one another and to the world by showing forth the love of Jesus Christ through forms of mutual cooperation.

2. Annual conferences shall implement a process of cooperative parish development through which cooperative parish ministries are initiated and developed in both urban and town-and-country situations. Where cooperative parish ministries already exist in an annual conference, the conference shall direct the appropriate conference boards and agencies to develop strategies designed to make use of cooperative ministries as means of creating greater effectiveness in the nurture, outreach, and witness ministries of urban, suburban, and town-and-country situations; and the annual conference shall prepare and adopt a formal written policy concerning cooperative parish ministries, including a plan for financial support. Parish development is an intentional plan of enabling congregations, church-related agencies, and pastors in a defined geographic area to develop a relationship of trust and mutuality that results in coordinated church programs and ministry, supported by appropriate organizational structures and policy. A superintendent or director of parish development may be appointed to work with the cabinet(s) in the implementation of these ministries in a conference or an area. In addition, district superintendents shall submit recommendations annually

regarding those churches in their districts that would benefit from being included in a cooperative ministry.

3. Cooperative ministries may be expressed in one or more of the forms contained in the following categories.

a) Beginning and Exploratory Forms: *1. Cluster Groups*—a group of churches located in the same geographic area with a loosely knit organization that allows the participating congregations and pastoral charges to engage in cooperative programs in varying degrees. A district may be divided into cluster groups for administrative purposes. *2. Probe Staff*—composed of the pastors and other staff assigned to a geographic area to explore possibilities for cooperation and developing strategies for improving ministry. *3. Group Ministry*—a loosely organized group of two or more pastoral charges in which pastors are appointed or assigned to charges. The pastors and/or lay council representing all churches may designate a coordinator.

b) Structured Forms: *1. Multiple Charge Parishes*—intentionally organized group of two or more pastoral charges in which each church continues to relate to its charge conference on the organizational level and also participates in a parish-wide council. The pastors are appointed or assigned to the charges and also to the parish, and a director or coordinator is appointed or assigned by the bishop.[2] *2. Larger Parish*—a number of congregations working together using a parish-wide council and other committees and work groups, as the parish may determine which provides representation on boards and committees from all churches; guided by a constitution or covenant and served by a staff appointed or assigned by the bishop and involving a director. *3. Blended Ministry*—the merging of the organizations and memberships of churches spread throughout a defined geographical area into one congregation that intentionally develops two or more worship/program centers, and for which there is one charge conference and one set of committees and other groups, guided by a covenant and served by a staff and a director appointed or assigned to the parish by the bishop.

c) Specialized Forms: *1. Enlarged Charge*—two or more congregations, usually on the same charge and of relatively equal size that work as a unit with the leadership of one or more pastors. There may be a charge council and appropriate committees.

---

2. See Judicial Council Decision 556.

2. *Extended or Shared Ministry*—a larger membership church sharing ministry with a smaller membership church, usually served by the pastor(s) of the larger church. 3. *Cooperative Ecumenical Parish*—two or more local churches of different Christian traditions including a United Methodist congregation, working together. Either of the above forms may be utilized. 4. *Shared Facilities*—two or more congregations, one of which shall be United Methodist, sharing a building, office equipment, etc., such as congregations which use different languages or which are of different racial/ethnic/cultural groups. The congregations may enter into a covenant that ensures representation and preserves the autonomy of each congregation on such bodies as church councils, boards of trustees and other committees and work groups. The congregations may negotiate a financial agreement about the use of the facility in order to provide appropriate financial support.

4. Each general board and agency shall arrange for its directors and staff to be trained in cooperative ministry concepts better to provide support resources for annual conferences and local churches.

5. Bishops, district superintendents, conference staff, and other leaders shall become familiar through training with the benefits of cooperative ministries. They shall provide leadership and training opportunities for pastors and local church leaders as to the value of cooperative ministries in moving toward excellence in nurture, outreach, and witness ministries. They are to explore and develop meaningful ministries to persons in congregations, communities, and the global community.

6. Cabinets shall give priority in the appointment process to appointing directors and clergy staff of cooperative ministries, especially cooperative parish ministries, who have been trained in cooperative ministry concepts and who have demonstrated effective ministries of nurture, outreach, and witness. The cabinet shall develop and implement strategies designed to enable and equip pastors presently appointed to cooperative parish ministries to provide effective ministries of nurture, outreach, and witness.

7. Annual conferences and cabinets are urged to assist in the development and strengthening of cooperative ministries by pursuing funding assistance from general Church, annual conference, and other sources for each cooperative ministry, including cooperative parish ministries.

Section III. Ecumenical Shared Ministries

¶ **207.** Local churches, with the guidance of the Holy Spirit, may respond to opportunities for ecumenical resource sharing in their communities by creating ecumenical shared ministries, working with local congregations of other Christian churches to enhance ministry, make wise stewardship of limited resources, and live out the ecumenical spirit in creative ways responsive to the needs of God's peoples as well as to opportunities for expanded mission and ministry.

¶ **208.** *Definition*—Ecumenical shared ministries are ecumenical congregations formed by a local United Methodist church and one or more local congregations of other Christian traditions. Forms of ecumenical shared ministries include: *(a)* a federated church, in which one congregation is related to two or more denominations, with persons choosing to hold membership in one or the other of the denominations; *(b)* a union church, in which a congregation with one unified membership roll is related to two or more denominations; *(c)* a merged church, in which two or more congregations of different denominations form one congregation that relates to only one of the constituent denominations; *(d)* a yoked parish, in which congregations of different denominations share a pastor.

¶ **209.** *Covenanting*—Congregations entering into an ecumenical shared ministry shall develop a clear covenant of mission, set of bylaws, or articles of agreement that address financial and property matters, church membership, denominational askings and apportionments, committee structure and election procedures, terms and provisions of the pastorate, reporting procedures, relationship with the parent denominations, and matters related to amending or dissolving the agreement. Ministries shall notify the district superintendent of any amending of the covenant agreement and shall consult with the district superintendent prior to dissolving the covenant agreement. In the formation of an ecumenical shared ministry, ¶¶ 243 and 247.1-.2 shall be followed in its organization. In an interdenominational local church merger, ¶¶ 2547 and 2548 shall be followed. In the case of federated and union churches, ¶ 2548 shall be followed.

¶ **210.** *Connectional Responsibilities*—Cabinets, conference staff and other leaders shall be expected to work with ecumenical shared ministries at their inception as well as in maintaining avenues of vital relationship and connection to The United Methodist

Church, while recognizing that such avenues must also be maintained with the denominational partners in ministry.

¶ **211.** *Cabinet Priority*—Cabinets shall be urged to give priority in the appointment process to the providing of ecumenical shared ministries with pastoral leaders who have demonstrated commitment to ecumenism and who exhibit a clear appreciation for a variety of denominational expressions and polities.

Section IV. Churches in Transitional Communities

¶ **212.** Since many of the communities in which the local church is located are experiencing transition, special attention must be given to forms of ministry required in such communities. The local church is required to respond to the changes that are occurring in its surrounding community and to organize its mission and ministry accordingly.

1. When the communities where the church is located experience transition especially identified as economic and/or ethnic, the local church shall engage in deliberate analysis of the community change and alter its program to meet the needs and cultural patterns of the new residents. The local church shall make every effort to remain in the community and develop effective ministries to those who are newcomers, whether of a cultural, economic, or ethnic group different from the original or present members.

2. In communities in transition, the local church shall be regarded as a principal base of mission from which unjust structures of society shall be confronted, evangelization shall occur, and a principal witness to the changing community, including ministry with the poor, shall be realized.

3. It is recommended that decisions concerning ministry in transitional communities be made after thorough consultation has taken place between structures and agencies in the connection.

4. It is recommended that the commitment of resources in terms of money and personnel to ministries in transitional communities be of sufficient longevity to allow for experimentation, evaluation, and mid-course corrections to ensure an adequate effort in ministry in those situations. Evaluations shall involve those on the local level as well as those at the funding level.

5. The ministry of the local church in transitional areas may be enhanced by review and possible development of some form of cooperative ministry.

6. Every effort should be made to educate the congregation on the changes in the surrounding community. The local church has always been called to "minister to persons in the community where the church is located" (¶ 202), so in times of transition the membership should understand that the Church's mission is to serve their surrounding community.

¶ **213.** *A Process for Assessment of Local Church Potential*—Since every congregation is located in a community in some type of transition, every local church is encouraged to study their congregation's potential. Upon the request of the congregation the district superintendent shall appoint a study task force to assist in an extensive study of the past, present, and potential ministry of that local church. Alternatively, the district superintendent may appoint such a task force when the future viability of the congregation is in question or whenever he or she deems it necessary for other reasons. The task force shall be composed of an equal number of lay and clergypersons and shall include persons from that congregation.

1. This study shall include, but not be limited to: *a)* unique missional opportunities and needs of the community; *b)* present ministries of the congregation; *c)* number of leaders and style of leadership; *d)* growth potential of the surrounding community; *e)* fiscal and facilities needs; *f)* distance from other United Methodist churches; *g)* number and size of churches of other denominations in the community; *h)* other items that may impact the church's ability to fulfill the mission of the Church as stated in Chapter One, Section I.

2. The findings shall be published and presented to the congregation with recommendations as to how best to fulfill the local church's call to ministry and to optimize the stewardship of the ministry resources available. The recommendations shall explore options for serving the community with nurture, outreach, and witness ministries as an organized church (¶¶ 201-204) or cooperative parish ministries (¶ 206) or ecumenical shared ministries (¶ 207); or give special attention to redevelopment, relocation, or discontinuance. Those invited to the presentation shall include: the members of the congregation, the pastor(s), the district superintendent, and members of the district board of church location and building (¶ 2519).

3. *a)* The members of the local church shall consider the recommendations and develop goals and a ministry action plan

in response to the recommendations. The district superintendent shall report the results of the study and the congregation's response to the cabinet, with recommendations for the allocation of conference staff, resourcing, financial support, or other resources needed to undergird the congregation's efforts to reach its recommended potential. Such annual conference support shall be committed no longer than three years. b) For any church that has been through this process, the district superintendent may convene a special session of the conference to take action concerning the ministry recommendations. In addition to the local church charge conference membership, the members of the District Board of Church Location and Building will be present with voice only.

Section V. Church Membership

¶ **214.** *Eligibility*—The United Methodist Church is a part of the holy catholic (universal) church, as we confess in the Apostles' Creed. In the church, Jesus Christ is proclaimed and professed as Lord and Savior. All people may attend its worship services, participate in its programs, receive the sacraments and become members in any local church in the connection (¶ 4). In the case of persons whose disabilities prevent them from reciting the vows, their legal guardian[s], themselves members in full covenant relationship with God and the Church, the community of faith, may recite the appropriate vows on their behalf.

¶ **215.** *Definition of Membership*—The membership of a local United Methodist church shall include all people who have been baptized and all people who have professed their faith.

1. The baptized membership of a local United Methodist church shall include all baptized people who have received Christian baptism in the local congregation or elsewhere, or whose membership has been transferred to the local United Methodist church subsequent to baptism in some other congregation.

2. The professing membership of a local United Methodist church shall include all baptized people who have come into membership by profession of faith through appropriate services of the baptismal covenant in the ritual or by transfer from other churches.

3. For statistical purposes, church membership is equated to the number of people listed on the roll of professing members.

4. All baptized or professing members of any local United Methodist church are members of the worldwide United Methodist connection and members of the church universal.

THE MEANING OF MEMBERSHIP

¶ 216. 1. Christ constitutes the church as his body by the power of the Holy Spirit (1 Corinthians 12:13, 27). The church draws new people into itself as it seeks to remain faithful to its commission to proclaim and exemplify the gospel. Baptism is the sacrament of initiation and incorporation into the body of Christ. After baptism, the church provides the nurture that makes possible a comprehensive and lifelong process of growing in grace. Becoming a professing member requires the answer of faith of the baptized person made visible in a service of profession of Christian faith and confirmation using the vows of the baptismal covenant.

a) Baptized infants and children are to be instructed and nurtured in the meaning of the faith, the rights and responsibilities of their baptism, and spiritual and moral formation using materials approved by The United Methodist Church. Using the services of the baptismal covenant, youth will profess their faith, commit themselves to a life of discipleship, and be confirmed. Confirmation is both a human act of commitment and the gracious action of the Holy Spirit strengthening and empowering discipleship.

b) Youth and adults who have not been baptized and who are seeking to be saved from their sins and profess Jesus Christ as their Lord and Savior are proper candidates for baptism in The United Methodist Church. It shall be the duty of the congregation, led by the pastor, to instruct them in the meaning of baptism, in the meaning of the Christian faith, and in the history, organization, and teachings of The United Methodist Church, using materials approved by The United Methodist Church for that purpose. After the completion of the period of nurture and instruction, the sponsor(s) and pastor shall bring the candidates before the congregation and administer the services of Baptismal Covenant, in which people are baptized, confirmed, and received into the Church.

2. *a)* Formation in the baptismal covenant and in the call to ministry in daily life is a lifelong process and is carried on through all the activities that have educational value. The pastor gives specific leadership that prepares youth for their profession of faith and commitment to discipleship and for the Holy Spirit's action confirming them in their faith and empowering their discipleship. This preparation focuses attention upon the meaning of discipleship and the need for members to be in mission in all of life's relationships.

b) There are many occasions as people mature in the faith when the Holy Spirit's confirming action may be celebrated, such as in the reaffirmation of the baptismal covenant or other services related to life passages. Unlike baptism, which is a once-made covenant and can only be reaffirmed and not repeated, confirmation is a dynamic action of the Holy Spirit that can be repeated.

3. Preparation for the experience of profession of faith and confirmation shall be provided for all people, including adults. Youth who are completing the sixth grade shall normally be the youngest people recruited for such preparation. When younger people, of their own volition, seek enrollment in preparation for profession of faith and confirmation, such preparation shall be at the discretion of the pastor.

¶ **217.** When persons unite as professing members with a local United Methodist church, they profess their faith in God, the Father Almighty, maker of heaven and earth; in Jesus Christ his only Son; and in the Holy Spirit. Thus, they make known their desire to live their daily lives as disciples of Jesus Christ. They covenant together with God and with the members of the local church to keep the vows which are a part of the order of confirmation and reception into the Church:

1. To renounce the spiritual forces of wickedness, reject the evil powers of the world, and repent of their sin;

2. To accept the freedom and power God gives them to resist evil, injustice, and oppression;

3. To confess Jesus Christ as Savior, put their whole trust in his grace, and promise to serve him as their Lord;

4. To remain faithful members of Christ's holy church and serve as Christ's representatives in the world;

5. To be loyal to Christ through The United Methodist Church and do all in their power to strengthen its ministries;

6. To faithfully participate in its ministries by their prayers, their presence, their gifts, their service, and their witness;

7. To receive and profess the Christian faith as contained in the Scriptures of the Old and New Testaments.

¶ **218.** *Growth in Faithful Discipleship*—Faithful membership in the local church is essential for personal growth and for developing a deeper commitment to the will and grace of God. As members involve themselves in private and public prayer, worship, the sacraments, study, Christian action, systematic giving, and holy discipline, they grow in their appreciation of Christ, understanding of God at work in history and the natural order, and an understanding of themselves.

¶ **219.** *Mutual Responsibility*—Faithful discipleship includes the obligation to participate in the corporate life of the congregation with fellow members of the body of Christ. A member is bound in sacred covenant to shoulder the burdens, share the risks, and celebrate the joys of fellow members. A Christian is called to speak the truth in love, always ready to confront conflict in the spirit of forgiveness and reconciliation.

¶ **220.** *The Call to Ministry of All the Baptized*—All members of Christ's universal church are called to share in the ministry which is committed to the whole church of Jesus Christ. Therefore, each member of The United Methodist Church is to be a servant of Christ on mission in the local and worldwide community. This servanthood is performed in family life, daily work, recreation and social activities, responsible citizenship, the stewardship of property and accumulated resources, the issues of corporate life, and all attitudes toward other persons. Participation in disciplined groups such as covenant discipleship groups or class meetings is an expected part of personal mission involvement. Each member is called upon to be a witness for Christ in the world, a light and leaven in society, and a reconciler in a culture of conflict. Each member is to identify with the agony and suffering of the world and to radiate and exemplify the Christ of hope. The standards of attitude and conduct set forth in the Social Principles (Part V) shall be considered as an essential resource for guiding each member of the Church in being a servant of Christ on mission.

¶ **221.** *Accountability*—1. All members are to be held accountable for faithfulness to their covenant of baptism.

2. If a baptized member neglects faithfulness and discipline in terms of the baptismal covenant, every means of encouraging that member to return and of nurturing him or her to assume the vows of professing membership should be made.

3. If a professing member should be accused of violating the covenant and failing to keep the vows as stated in ¶ 217, then it shall be the responsibility of the local church, working through its pastor and its agencies, to minister to that member in compliance with the provisions of ¶ 228 in an effort to enable the member to faithfully perform the vows and covenant of membership.

4. In the event that those efforts fail, then the professing member and the local church may agree to voluntary mediation

in which the parties are assisted by a trained, neutral third-party mediator, mediation team, and/or their district superintendent in reaching a settlement or agreement satisfactory to all parties.

5. In the further event that those efforts fail to effect reconciliation and reaffirmation of the vows and covenant of ¶ 217 by the professing member, then the professing members of the church may pursue the procedures set forth in ¶¶ 2702.3, 2706.5, and 2714.

ADMISSION INTO THE CHURCH

¶ 222. *Non-Local Church Settings*—Duly appointed clergy of The United Methodist Church, while serving as chaplain of any organization, institution, or military unit, as an extension minister, or as a campus minister, or while otherwise present where a local church is not available, may receive a person into the membership of The United Methodist Church under the conditions of ¶ 216 or ¶ 217. Where possible, before the sacrament of baptism or vows of profession of faith are administered, such appointed minister shall consult with the pastor of the local church (should one be nearby) on the choice of the person concerned; and upon agreement by the pastor, a statement verifying that such sacrament was administered or that such vows were made shall be issued. The pastor thereof on receiving such statement shall duly enroll that person as a baptized or professing member.

¶ 223. *General Church Membership Roll*—When a person is baptized or professes his or her Christian faith and is received into the Church by a duly appointed campus minister, a chaplain endorsed by the Board of Higher Education and Ministry or other duly appointed clergy of The United Methodist Church, while serving as a chaplain of any organization, institution, or military unit, or as an extension minister, or while otherwise present where a local church is not available, and said person has no local church to which the membership and records may be sent, the clergy shall send the name, address (if there is one), and related facts to the General Board of Higher Education for recording on the General Church Membership Roll. It is desirable that as soon as possible such people be transferred from the General Church Membership Roll to the membership record of the local United Methodist church of their choice. The name of any professing member who has been on the General Church Membership Roll for more than eight years and for whom a current mailing address cannot be obtained shall be removed from the General Church Membership Roll.

¶ **224.** *Outside of Congregational Settings*—Any candidate for church membership who for good reason is unable to appear before the congregation may, at the discretion of the pastor, be received elsewhere in accordance with the Ritual of The United Methodist Church. In any such case lay members should be present to represent the congregation. Names of such persons shall be placed on the church roll, and announcement of their reception shall be made to the congregation.

¶ **225.** *Transfer from Other Denominations*—A member in good standing in any Christian denomination who has been baptized and who desires to unite with The United Methodist Church shall be received as either a baptized or a professing member. Such a person may be received as a baptized member by a proper certificate of transfer from that person's former church or some certification of Christian baptism and as a professing member upon taking vows declaring the Christian faith through appropriate services of the baptismal covenant in our ritual (see ¶¶ 214-217). In baptism water is administered in the name of the triune God by an authorized person. The pastor will report to the sending church the date of reception of such a member. It is recommended that instruction in the faith, work, and polity of the Church be provided for all such persons. Persons received from churches that do not issue certificates of transfer or letters of recommendation shall be listed as "Received From Other Denominations."

¶ **226.** *Care of Children and Youth*—1. Because the redeeming love of God revealed in Jesus Christ extends to all persons, and because Jesus explicitly included the children in his kingdom, the pastor of each charge shall earnestly exhort all Christian parents or guardians to present their children to the Lord in baptism at an early age. Before baptism is administered, the pastor shall diligently instruct the parents or guardians regarding the meaning of this sacrament and the vows that they assume. It is expected of parents or guardians who present their children for baptism that they shall use all diligence in bringing them up in conformity to the Word of God and in the fellowship of the Church and to encourage them to participate in preparation for their profession of faith and confirmation at the appropriate time. At least one parent or guardian shall be a member of a Christian church; or sponsor(s) or godparent(s) who are members shall renew their own baptismal vows. They shall be admonished of this obligation and be earnestly exhorted to faithfulness therein. At the time of baptism they shall be informed that the Church, with its Christian education program, will aid them in the Christian nurture of their children.

2. *a)* The pastor of the church shall, at the time of administering the sacrament of baptism, furnish the parent(s), guardian(s), sponsor(s), or godparent(s) of the child who is baptized with a certificate of baptism, which shall also clearly state that the child is now a baptized member in The United Methodist Church.

b) The pastor shall be responsible for seeing that the membership secretary adds the full name of the baptized child to the membership record.

c) When the baptized child lives in a community not served by the pastor who administers the sacrament of baptism, the pastor shall ensure this is not a private event (that the body of Christ beyond the immediate family is present in accordance with ¶ 224 of the *Book of Discipline*), and is responsible for contacting in advance (where possible) and reporting the baptism to a pastor and/or district superintendent who serves in the area where the baptized child lives. The pastor administering the sacrament shall then be responsible for reporting in writing to that pastor or district superintendent the child's name to be entered on the record of a church in that location.

d) A pastor of a church who receives notification of a baptism administered elsewhere shall be responsible for entering the required information on that church's record and for notifying the pastor who administered the baptism that the child has been received by transfer. When the pastor of the church in which the child is baptized receives written confirmation that the child's name has been entered on the membership record of another church, a notation may be made on the record of the church where the sacrament was administered that the child has been transferred to another church.

e) The pastor shall, at the time of administering the sacrament of baptism and at other appropriate times, admonish members of the congregation of their responsibility for the Christian nurture of the child.

3. The pastor or membership secretary shall regularly review the membership record to identify those who have not become professing members, for purposes of nurturing them toward

profession of faith. The number of people so identified shall be reported annually, or at such other times as may be requested, to the charge conference or the annual conference. The congregation has ongoing responsibility to nurture baptized children, youth, and adults in the life of discipleship.

4. It shall be the duty of the pastor, the parent(s), guardian(s), sponsor(s), or godparent(s), the officers and teachers of the church school, the local church scouting coordinator, and all members of the congregation to provide training for the children of the Church throughout their childhood that will lead to a personal commitment to Jesus Christ as Lord and Savior and to an understanding of the Christian faith and the meaning of baptism. Building on the preparation that youth have received throughout their childhood, the pastor shall, at least annually, organize them into classes to the end that they may profess their faith and be confirmed (¶ 216). This instruction shall be based on materials produced by The United Methodist Church or on other resources that present the mission, history, doctrine, and beliefs of The United Methodist Church for this purpose. When youth so prepared shall give evidence of their own Christian faith, and understanding of the meaning and practice of membership, they may be received as professing members. The God and Me and God and Family portions of the Program of Religious Activities with Youth (P.R.A.Y.) program may be available to elementary children as an additional resource (¶ 256.4).

5. Youth who are members of the Church have all rights and responsibilities of membership within the baptismal covenant. (See ¶ 256.3.) It is strongly recommended that each local church offer for all senior high youth continuing instruction in the meaning of the Christian life and discipleship. It is further recommended that this course, taught by or under the guidance of the pastor, or other staff or layperson, emphasize the doctrines of The United Methodist Church and the nature and mission of the Church, leading to continued growth in the knowledge, grace, and service of our Lord Jesus Christ. The Program of Religious Activities with Youth (P.R.A.Y.) program may be available to all youth, with the God and Church portion providing study of The United Methodist Church, and the God and Life program challenging the youth to integrate their faith into their daily life (¶ 256.4) It shall be the responsibility of the pastor to participate in the growth process through interaction and ministry with youth.

AFFILIATE AND ASSOCIATE MEMBERSHIP

¶ **227.** A professing member of The United Methodist Church, of an affiliated autonomous Methodist or united church, or of a Methodist church that has a concordat agreement with The United Methodist Church, who resides for an extended period in a city or community at a distance from the member's home church, may on request be enrolled as an affiliate member of a United Methodist church located in the vicinity of the temporary residence. The home pastor shall be notified of the affiliate membership. Such membership shall entitle the person to the fellowship of that church, to its pastoral care and oversight, and to participation in its activities, including the holding of office; except such as would allow one to vote in a United Methodist body other than the local church. However, that person shall be counted and reported as a professing member of the home church only. A member of another denomination may become an associate member under the same conditions, but may not become a voting member of the church council.[3] This relationship may be terminated at the discretion of the United Methodist church in which the affiliate or associate membership is held whenever the affiliate or associate member shall move from the vicinity of the United Methodist church in which the affiliate or associate membership is held.

CARE OF MEMBERS

¶ **228.** 1. The local church shall endeavor to enlist each member in activities for spiritual growth and in participation in the services and ministries of the Church and its organizations. It shall be the duty of the pastor and of the members of the church council by regular visitation, care, and spiritual oversight to provide necessary activities and opportunities for spiritual growth through individual and family worship and individual and group study to connect faith and daily living, and continually to aid the members to keep their vows to uphold the Church by attendance, prayers, gifts, service, and witness. The Church has a moral and spiritual obligation to nurture its nonparticipating and indifferent members and to lead them into an active church relationship.

2. *Care of Members—a)* The pastor in cooperation with the church council may arrange the membership in groups—with a

---

3. See Judicial Council Decision 372.

leader for each group—designed to involve the membership of the Church in its ministry to the community. These groups shall be of such size, usually not larger than eight or ten families, as to be convenient and effective for service. Such groups may be especially helpful in evangelistic outreach by contacting newcomers and unreached persons, by visitation, by mobilizing neighbors to meet social issues in the community, by responding to personal and family crises, by holding prayer meetings in the homes, by distributing Christian literature, and by other means. Nonresident members should constitute a special group to be served by correspondence. The groups shall be formed and the leaders appointed by the church council upon recommendation of the pastor.

b) While primary responsibility and initiative rests with each professing member to faithfully perform the vows of the baptismal covenant that have been solemnly assumed, if the member should be neglectful of that responsibility, these procedures shall be followed:

(1) If a professing member residing in the community is negligent of the vows or is regularly absent from the worship of the church without valid reason, the pastor and the membership secretary shall report that member's name to the church council, which shall do all in its power to reenlist the member in the active fellowship of the church. It shall visit the member and make clear that, while the member's name is on the roll of a particular local church, one is a member of The United Methodist Church as a whole, and that, since the member is not attending the church where enrolled, the member is requested to do one of four things: *(a)* reaffirm the baptismal vows and return to living in the community of the baptismal covenant in the church where the member's name is recorded, *(b)* request transfer to another United Methodist church where the member will return to living in the community of the baptismal covenant (see ¶ 239), *(c)* arrange transfer to a particular church of another denomination (see ¶ 240), or *(d)* request withdrawal. If the member does not comply with any of the available alternatives over a period of two years, the member's name may be removed. (See § (4) below.)

(2) If a professing member whose address is known is residing outside the community and is not participating in the worship or activity of the church, the directives to encourage a transfer of the member shall be followed each year until that

member joins another church or requests in writing that the name be removed from the roll of professing members; provided, however, that if after two years the council has not been able to relate that member to the church at the new place of residence, the name may be removed from the roll of members by the procedure of § (4) below.

(3) If the address of a professing member is no longer known to the pastor, the membership secretary and the evangelism ministry group chairperson shall make every effort to locate the member. If the member can be located, the directives of either § (1) or § (2) above shall be followed, but if after two years of such efforts the address is still unknown, the member's name may be removed from the roll of members by the procedure of § (4) below.

(4) If the directives of §§ (1), (2), or (3) above have been followed for the specified number of years without success, the member's name may be removed as a professing member by vote of the charge conference on recommendation of the pastor and the evangelism ministry chairperson, each name being considered individually, provided that the member's name shall have been entered in the minutes of the annual charge conference for two consecutive years. On the membership record there shall be entered after the name: "Removed by Charge Conference Action"; and if the action is on the basis of § (3), there shall be added: "Reason: Address Unknown." The record shall be retained in order that upon reaffirmation of the baptismal covenant the person may be restored as a member. Should a transfer of membership be requested, the pastor may, after consultation with the person, issue the certificate of transfer.

(5) A written complaint or grievance may be filed against a professing member by serving the complaint or grievance on the professing member, the pastor of the professing member, and the district superintendent of the professing member.

(6) The pastor and district superintendent of the accused professing member shall attempt a just resolution process similar to the supervisory response in ¶ 362.1(b, c) with the professing member's district superintendent or designee leading the process.

(7) If the procedures of ¶ 362.1(b, c) do not result in resolution of the matter and if the conduct alleged in the complaint or grievance, if true, would be a chargeable offense found in ¶ 2702.3, then the procedures of ¶ 2701 and following paragraphs

are to be followed unless the accused professing member agrees to use the procedure described in ¶ 228.2b (8) below.

(8) If the procedures of ¶ 362.1(*b*, *c*) do not result in resolution of the matter and if the conduct alleged in the complaint or grievance, if true, would not be a chargeable offense found in ¶ 2702.3, then a group of four persons: the pastor of the accused professing member, the lay leader of the accused professing member's church, the district lay leader, and the district superintendent, ex officio, without vote but with voice, where the accused professing member's church is located, shall hear information from the accused professing member and the complainant or grievant and shall determine an unappealable resolution of the matter.

(9) When a professing member is charged with an offense and wishes to forego trial, the charge conference may permit the member to withdraw (¶ 2719.3). In this case, the notation "Withdrawn under charges" shall be entered alongside the member's name on the record, along with the date.

(10) Recognizing that the Church has a continuing moral and spiritual obligation to nurture all persons, it is recommended that a list of names thus removed shall be maintained. It shall then become the responsibility of the church council to provide for the review of this list at least once a year. (See also ¶ 234.) After the review has been made, it is recommended that the pastor and/or the commission on evangelism contact those whose names appear on this list, either in person or by other means, in the most effective and practical manner. The names and addresses of those who have moved outside the local church's area should be sent to local churches in their new communities that those churches may visit and minister to them.

c) The pastor, along with other adult workers with youth and young adults in the local church and beyond (¶ 634.4c[4]), shall disseminate information about United Methodist-related Campus Ministry to college/university students or potential college/university students who are baptized members, professing members, or other constituents of the congregation. They shall also nurture, counsel, and guide young people as they explore United Methodist and non-United Methodist colleges and universities and non-college vocation options in light of their faith.

¶ **229.** *Transfer from Discontinued Local Churches*—If a local church is discontinued, the district superintendent shall select another United Methodist church and transfer its members thereto, or to such other churches as the members may select. (See ¶ 2549.2.)

MEMBERSHIP RECORDS AND REPORTS

¶ **230.** *Membership Records*—1. Each local church shall accurately maintain a membership record for each baptized or professing member including:

a) the person's name, date of birth, address, place of birth, date of baptism, officiating pastor, and sponsors;

b) date of confirmation/profession of faith, officiating pastor, and sponsors;

c) if transferred from another church, date of reception, sending church, and receiving pastor;

d) if transferred to another church, date of transfer, receiving church, and address of receiving church;

e) date of removal or withdrawal and reason;

f) date of restoration of professing membership and officiating pastor;

g) date of death, date and place of funeral/memorial, place of burial, and officiating pastor.

2. Annually, names of professing members to be removed by charge conference action shall be reported to the charge conference (¶ 228.2.b.4).

3. Constituency Roll, containing the names and addresses of such persons as are not members of the church concerned, including unbaptized children, youth, and adults whose names are not on the membership record, and other nonmembers for whom the local church has pastoral responsibility.

4. Affiliate Membership Roll (¶ 227).

5. Associate Membership Roll (¶ 227).

6. In the case of a union or federated church with another denomination, the governing body of such a church may report an equal share of the total membership to each judicatory, and such membership shall be published in the minutes of each church, with a note to the effect that the report is that of a union or federated church, and with an indication of the total actual membership.

¶ **231.** *Annual Membership Report and Audit*—The pastor shall report to the charge conference annually the names of persons received into the membership of the church or churches of the pastoral charge and the names of persons removed since the last charge conference, indicating how each was received or removed. The church council shall appoint a committee to audit the membership record, submitting the report annually to the charge conference.

¶ **232.** *Annual Report of Members Attending Colleges and Universities*—The pastor shall report annually the names and contact information for professing and baptized members attending colleges and universities to the district superintendent, the chairperson of the Conference Board of Higher Education and Campus Ministry by one month before the start of the school term and to the charge conference. The Conference Board of Higher Education and Campus Ministry has the responsibility to share the information with the appropriate UM-related campus ministries.

¶ **233.** *Permanent Records*—The basic membership records in each local church shall consist of: a permanent church register and a card index, a loose-leaf book, or a membership record on an electronic information system (see ¶ 245). All baptism, membership, marriage, and funeral records are the property of the local church and cannot be sold. If the church is discontinued, these records are placed in the care of the Conference Commission on Archives and History.

1. The permanent church register shall be kept on either paper-based or electronic media. If it is on a paper medium, it shall be a volume of durable material prepared by The United Methodist Publishing House. The format and content of the record forms contained in it and the manner of its binding shall be as approved by a committee designated by the General Council on Finance and Administration (see ¶ 807.14). If on a paper medium, the names shall be recorded chronologically as each person is received into the fellowship of that church and without reference to alphabetical order. The names shall be numbered in regular numerical order, and the number of each shall appear on the corresponding card, page, or record in the card index, loose-leaf book, or electronic information system membership record. If it is on an electronic medium, it will not be necessary to maintain a chronological number. The number that is assigned automatically by the computer system is sufficient for this purpose. However, the electronic medium shall meet the following criteria:

a) It shall contain all of the information required by the General Council on Finance and Administration.

b) Conversion of the information from paper records to an electronic medium shall be followed by a complete audit to ensure the accuracy of the converted records.

c) Off-site storage and electronic backup shall be maintained.

2. The card index, loose-leaf book, or electronic system membership record shall be kept on a form approved by the General Council on Finance and Administration or, in the case of electronically maintained records, shall contain the same information as required in the approved form with the exception of the sequential number. This record of membership shall be filed in alphabetical order and shall show the number appearing opposite each name on the permanent register. The pastor shall report annually to the annual conference the total professing membership of the local church as shown on the membership records.

3. When an electronic information system is used for record keeping, printout copies of the membership records and backup electronic media shall be retained in a secure off-site place (see ¶ 245).

¶ **234.** *Membership Secretary*—The charge conference shall name a membership secretary who, under the direction of the pastor, shall keep accurate records of the membership (see ¶ 230) and shall report at least annually to the church council.

CHANGES IN CHURCH MEMBERSHIP OR LOCAL CHURCH MEMBERSHIP

¶ **235.** Members whose names are removed from professing member status for cause (see ¶ 2714), or who have been transferred, have died, or have withdrawn shall be so noted on the membership record. It shall be the duty of the pastor of the charge or of the membership secretary to keep an accurate record of such changes and reasons and to report them to the charge conference annually.

¶ **236.** *Members Who Move*—If a member of a United Methodist church shall move to another community so far removed from the home church that the member cannot participate regularly in its worship and activity, this member shall be encouraged to transfer membership to a United Methodist church in the community of the newly established residence. As soon as the pastor is reliably informed of this change of residence, actual or contemplated, it shall be the pastor's duty and obligation to assist the member to become established in the fellowship of a church in the community of the future home and to send to a United Methodist pastor in such community, or to the district superintendent, a letter of notification, giving the latest known address of the person or persons concerned and requesting local pastoral oversight.

¶ **237.** *Lay Missionaries in Non-United Methodist Churches*— Laypersons in service outside the United States under the General Board of Global Ministries and assigned to churches other than United Methodist may accept all the rights and privileges, including associate membership, offered them by a local church in their place of residence without impairing their relationship to their home local church.

¶ **238.** *Members Residing at a Distance*—When a pastor discovers a member of The United Methodist Church residing in the community whose membership is in a church so far removed from the place of residence that the member cannot participate regularly in its worship and activity, it shall be the duty and obligation of the pastor to give pastoral oversight to such person and to encourage transfer of membership to a United Methodist church in the community where the member resides.

¶ **239.** *Transfer to Other United Methodist Churches*—When a pastor receives a request for a transfer of membership from the pastor of another United Methodist church or a district superintendent, that pastor shall send the proper certificate directly to the pastor of the United Methodist church to which the member is transferring, or if there is no pastor, to the district superintendent. On receipt of such a certificate of transfer, the pastor or district superintendent shall enroll the name of the person so transferring after public reception in a regular service of worship, or if circumstances demand, public announcement in such a service. The pastor of the church issuing the certificate shall then be notified, whereupon said pastor shall remove the member from the roll.

Certificates of transfer shall be accompanied by two official forms. A "Notice of Transfer of Membership" is to be sent to the member by the pastor who transfers the membership. An "Acknowledgment of Transfer of Membership" is to be sent to the former pastor by the pastor who receives the transferred member.

In case the transfer is not made effective, the pastor shall return the certificate to the pastor of the sending church.

¶ **240.** *Transfer to Other Denominations*—A pastor, upon receiving a request from a member to transfer to a church of another denomination, or upon receiving such request from a pastor or duly authorized official of another denomination, shall (with the approval of the member) issue a certificate of transfer and, upon receiving confirmation of the member's reception into another congregation, shall properly record the transfer of such person on the membership record of the local church. For the transfer of a member of The United Methodist Church to a church of another denomination, an official "Transfer of Membership to Another Denomination" form shall be used.

¶ **241.** *Withdrawal Without Notice*—If a pastor is informed that a member has without notice united with a church of another denomination, the pastor shall make diligent inquiry and, if the report is confirmed, shall enter "Withdrawn" after the person's name on the membership roll and shall report the same to the next charge conference.

¶ **242.** *Restoration of Professing Membership*—1. A person whose name has been removed from professing membership by withdrawal, or action by charge conference, or trial court (¶ 2714), may ask to be restored to membership in the local church.

2. A person whose membership was recorded as having been withdrawn after becoming a member of another denomination may, when that denomination will not transfer membership, be restored to professing membership by reaffirmation of the baptismal vows.

3. A person who has withdrawn at his or her own written request may return to the church and, upon reaffirmation of the baptismal vows, become a professing member.

4. A person whose name was removed by charge conference action may return to the church and, at his or her request, be restored to professing membership in the local church through reaffirmation of the baptismal vows.

5. A person who withdrew under charges or was removed by trial court (¶ 2714) may ask to return to the church. Upon evidence of a renewed life, approval of the charge conference, and reaffirmation of the baptismal vows, the person may be restored to professing membership.

Section VI. Organization and Administration

¶ **243.** *Primary Tasks*—The local church shall be organized so that it can pursue its primary task and mission in the context of its own community—reaching out and receiving with joy all who will respond; encouraging people in their relationship with God and inviting them to commitment to God's love in Jesus Christ; providing opportunities for them to seek strengthening and growth in spiritual formation; and supporting them to live lovingly and justly in the power of the Holy Spirit as faithful disciples.

In carrying out its primary task, it shall be organized so that adequate provision is made for these basic responsibilities: (1) planning and implementing a program of nurture, outreach, and witness for persons and families within and without the congregation; (2) providing for effective pastoral and lay leadership; (3) providing for financial support, physical facilities, and the legal obligations of the church; (4) utilizing the appropriate relationships and resources of the district and annual conference; (5) providing for the proper creation, maintenance, and disposition of documentary record material of the local church; and (6) seeking inclusiveness in all aspects of its life.

¶ **244.** *Organization*—The basic organizational plan for the local church shall include provision for the following units: a charge conference, a church council, a committee on pastor-parish relations, a board of trustees, a committee on finance, a committee on nominations and leadership development, and such other elected leaders, commissions, councils, committees, and task forces as the charge conference may determine. Every local church shall develop a plan for organizing its administrative and programmatic responsibilities. Each local congregation shall provide a comprehensive program of nurture, outreach, and witness, along with leadership training, and the planning and administration of the congregation's organizational and temporal life, in accordance with the mission of The United Methodist Church (see ¶¶ 120-124).

1. The church council and all other administrative and programmatic structures of the local church shall be amenable to the charge conference (see ¶ 246). The church council shall function as the executive agency of the charge conference.

2. Alternative plans may be developed in accordance with the provisions of ¶ 247.2. Such alternatives include: nurture, out-

reach, and witness ministries; administrative council; or administrative board/council on ministries.

3. Members of the church council or alternative structure shall be persons of genuine Christian character who love the church, are morally disciplined, are committed to the mandate of inclusiveness in the life of the church, are loyal to the ethical standards of The United Methodist Church set forth in the Social Principles, and are competent to administer its affairs. It shall include youth and young adult members chosen according to the same standards as adults. All persons with vote shall be members of the local church, except where central conference legislation provides otherwise. The pastor shall be the administrative officer and, as such, shall be an ex officio member of all conferences, boards, councils, commissions, committees, and task forces, unless otherwise restricted by the *Discipline*.[4]

¶ 245. *Information Technology*—Each local church, as it creates or maintains computerized information and data, is strongly encouraged to confer with its annual conference for recommendations and guidelines as it relates to information technology.

THE CHARGE CONFERENCE

Members of the charge conference shall be persons of genuine Christian character who love the Church, are morally disciplined, are committed to the mandate of inclusiveness in the life of the Church, are loyal to the ethical standards of The United Methodist Church set forth in the Social Principles, and are competent to administer its affairs. It shall include youth members chosen according to the same standards as adults. All shall be professing members of the local church, except where central conference legislation provides otherwise. The pastor shall be the administrative officer, and as such shall be an ex officio member of all conferences, boards, councils, commissions, committees, and task forces, unless restricted by the *Discipline*.

¶ 246. *General Provisions*—1. Within the pastoral charge the basic unit in the connectional system of The United Methodist Church is the charge conference. The charge conference shall therefore be organized from the church or churches in every pastoral charge as set forth in the Constitution (¶ 43). It shall meet

---

4. See Judicial Council Decisions 469, 500.

annually for the purposes set forth in ¶ 247. It may meet at other times as indicated in § 7 below.

2. The membership of the charge conference shall be all members of the church council or other appropriate body, together with retired ordained ministers and retired diaconal ministers who elect to hold their membership in said charge conference and any others as may be designated in the *Discipline*. If more than one church is on the pastoral charge, all members of each church council shall be members of the charge conference.

3. The charge conference may make provision for recognition of the faithful service of members of the church council by electing them honorary members. An honorary member shall be entitled to all the privileges of a member, except the right to vote.

4. The district superintendent shall fix the time of meetings of the charge conference. The charge conference shall determine the place of meeting.

5. The district superintendent shall preside at the meetings of the charge conference or may designate an elder to preside.

6. The members present and voting at any duly announced meeting shall constitute a quorum.

7. Special sessions may be called by the district superintendent after consultation with the pastor of the charge, or by the pastor with the written consent of the district superintendent. The purpose of such special session shall be stated in the call, and only such business shall be transacted as is in harmony with the purposes stated in the call. Any such special session may be convened as a church conference in accordance with ¶ 248.

8. Notice of time and place of a regular or special session of the charge conference shall be given at least ten days in advance by two or more of the following (except as local laws may otherwise provide): from the pulpit of the church, in its weekly bulletin, in a local church publication, or by mail.

9. A charge conference shall be conducted in the language of the majority, with adequate provision being made for translation.

10. A joint charge conference for two or more pastoral charges may be held at the same time and place, as the district superintendent may determine.

¶ **247.** *Powers and Duties*—1. The charge conference shall be the connecting link between the local church and the general Church and shall have general oversight of the church council(s).

2. The charge conference, the district superintendent, and the pastor, when a pastor has been appointed (see ¶ 205.4), shall organize and administer the pastoral charge and churches according to the policies and plans herein set forth. When the membership size, program scope, mission resources, or other circumstances so require, the charge conference may, in consultation with and upon the approval of the district superintendent, modify the organizational plans, provided that the provisions of ¶ 243 are observed. Such other circumstances may include, but not be limited to, alternative models for the conception of a local church, such as coffee house ministries, mall ministries, outdoor ministries, retirement home ministries, restaurant ministries, and other emergent ways in which people can gather in God's name to be the church.

3. The primary responsibilities of the charge conference in the annual meeting shall be to review and evaluate the total mission and ministry of the church (¶¶ 120-124), receive reports, and adopt objectives and goals recommended by the church council that are in keeping with the objectives of The United Methodist Church.

4. The charge conference recording secretary shall keep an accurate record of the proceedings and shall be the custodian of all records and reports and, with the presiding officer, shall sign the minutes. A copy of the minutes shall be provided for the district superintendent, and a permanent copy shall be retained for church files. When there is only one local church on a charge, the secretary of the church council shall be the secretary of the charge conference. When there is more than one church on a charge, one of the secretaries of the church councils shall be elected by the charge conference to serve as its secretary.

5. *a)* It is strongly recommended that the charge conference elect a church historian in order to preserve the history of each local church. The responsibilities of the historian are to keep the historical records up to date; serve as chairperson of the committee on records and history, if any; cooperate with the annual conference commission on archives and history; provide an annual report on the care of church records and historical materials to the charge conference; and also provide, with the pastor and the committee on records and history, if any, for the preservation of all local church records and historical materials no longer in current use. Records and historical materials include all documents, minutes, journals, diaries, reports, letters, pamphlets, papers,

manuscripts, maps, photographs, books, audiovisuals, sound recordings, magnetic or other tapes, or any other documentary material, regardless of form or characteristics, made or received pursuant to any provisions of the *Discipline* in connection with the transaction of church business by any local church of The United Methodist Church or any of its constituent predecessors. The church historian may be a member of the church council. This person may also hold another elected position on the council.

b) There may be a local church committee on records and history, chaired by the church historian, to assist in fulfilling these responsibilities.

6. Each charge is encouraged to be inclusive in the make-up of the council so that all segments of the congregation are represented.

7. The charge conference may establish a limit to the consecutive terms of office for any or all of the elected or appointed officers of the local church, except where otherwise mandated. It is recommended that no officer serve more than three consecutive years in the same office.

8. The charge conference shall examine and recommend to the district committee on ordained ministry, faithfully adhering to the provisions of ¶ 310.1e, candidates for licensed or ordained ministry who have been professing members in good standing of The United Methodist Church for at least one year; whose gifts, evidence of God's grace, and call to the ministry clearly establish them as candidates; and who have met the educational requirements. It is out of the faith and witness of the congregation that men and women respond to God's call to licensed or ordained ministry. Every local church should intentionally nurture candidates for licensed or ordained ministry, providing for spiritual and financial support, as well as supporting the Ministerial Education Fund, for their education and formation as servant leaders for the ministry of the whole people of God.

9. The charge conference shall examine and recommend, faithfully adhering to the provisions of ¶ 313, renewal of candidacy of candidates for the ordained ministry.

10. The charge conference shall examine and recommend to the responsible Church agency any candidates for Church-related vocations.

11. The charge conference shall inquire annually into the gifts, labors, and usefulness of the lay servants and certified lay ministers related to the charge and recommend to the district

and/or conference committee on Lay Servant Ministries those persons who have met the standards set forth for a local church lay servant and/or for certified lay servant and certified lay minister (¶¶ 266-269).

12. The charge conference shall receive reports annually on all local church organized Volunteers In Mission (UMVIM) teams, and the total number of local church participants in any UMVIM team, and shall forward the combined report to the annual conference and the general Church through the regular annual local church statistical report.

13. The charge conference shall in consultation with the district superintendent set the compensation of the pastor and other staff appointed by the bishop.[5]

14. As soon as practicable after the session of annual conference, each district superintendent or designated agent shall notify each local church in the district what amounts have been apportioned to it for World Service, conference benevolences and other general Church, jurisdictional, and annual conference funds. In the event that the conference uses an apportionment formula whereby the local church contributes a specified percentage of its current income and/or expenses, the specified percentage may be used in lieu of an actual dollar amount. In preparation for and at the charge conference, it shall be the responsibility of the district superintendent, the pastor, and the lay member(s) of the annual conference and/or the church lay leader(s) to interpret to each charge conference the importance of these apportioned funds, explaining the causes supported by each of them and their place in the total program of the Church. The World Service Fund is basic in the financial program of The United Methodist Church. World Service on apportionment represents the minimum needs for the mission and ministry of the Church. Conference benevolences represent the minimum needs for mission and ministry in the annual conference. Payment in full of these apportionments by local churches is the first benevolent responsibility of the church (¶ 812).[6]

15. The charge conference shall receive and act on the annual report from the pastor concerning the membership. (See ¶ 231.)

16. The charge conference shall receive a report on the names and addresses of college students to send to the United Methodist campus ministers and chaplains.

---

5. See Judicial Council Decisions 213, 252, 461, 1014, 1123.
6. See Judicial Council Decision 1054.

17. In those instances where there are two or more churches on a pastoral charge, the charge conference may provide for a charge or parish council, a chargewide or parish treasurer, and such other officers, commissions, committees, and task groups as necessary to carry on the work of the charge.

18. In those instances where there are two or more churches on a pastoral charge, the charge conference may elect a chargewide or parish committee on nominations and leadership development, a chargewide or parish committee on pastor-parish relations, a chargewide or parish committee on finance, and a chargewide or parish board of trustees in such instances where property is held in common by two or more churches of the charge. All churches of the charge shall be represented on such chargewide or parish committees or boards. Chargewide or parish organization shall be consistent with disciplinary provisions for the local church.

19. In instances of multiple church charges, the charge conference shall provide for an equitable distribution of parsonage maintenance and upkeep expense or adequate housing allowance (if annual conference policy permits) among the several churches.

20. The charge conference shall promote awareness of and concurrence with the Doctrinal Standards and General Rules of The United Methodist Church, and with policies relative to Socially Responsible Investments (¶ 717), the Social Principles (¶¶ 160-166), and *The Book of Resolutions of The United Methodist Church*.

21. If any charge conference initiates, joins, monitors, or terminates a boycott, the guidelines in *The Book of Resolutions,* 2012, should be followed. The General Conference is the only body that can initiate, empower, or join a boycott in the name of The United Methodist Church.

22. When authorized by the district superintendent and the district board of church location and building, the charge conference may provide for the sponsoring of satellite congregations.

23. The charge conference shall have such other duties and responsibilities as the General, jurisdictional, or annual conference may duly commit to it.

¶ **248.** *The Church Conference*—To encourage broader participation by members of the church, the charge conference may be convened as the church conference, extending the vote to all professing members of the local church present at such meetings. The church conference shall be authorized by the district superinten-

dent. It may be called at the discretion of the district superintendent or following a written request to the district superintendent
by one of the following: the pastor, the church council, or 10 percent of the professing membership of the local church. In any case
a copy of the request shall be given to the pastor. Additional regulations governing the call and conduct of the charge conference as
set forth in ¶¶ 246-247 shall apply also to the church conference. A
joint church conference for two or more churches may be held at
the same time and place as the district superintendent may determine. A church conference shall be conducted in the language of
the majority with adequate provision being made for translation.
(For church local conference see ¶ 2527.)

¶ **249.** *Election of Leaders*—The charge conference, or church
conference authorized by the district superintendent, shall
elect upon recommendation by the committee on nominations
and leadership development of each local church on the pastoral charge, or by nomination from the floor and by vote of each
such local church, at least the following leaders for the four basic
responsibilities (¶ 244):

1. Chairperson of the church council.

2. The committee on nominations and leadership development.

3. The committee on pastor-parish relations and its chairperson.

4. A chairperson and additional members of the committee
on finance; the financial secretary and the church treasurer(s) if
not paid employees of the local church; and the trustees as provided in ¶¶ 2526-2528, unless otherwise required by state law.

5. The lay member(s) of the annual conference and lay
leader(s).

6. A recording secretary (see ¶ 247.4).

7. Special attention shall be given to the inclusion of women,
men, youth, young adults, persons over sixty-five years of age,
persons with disabilities, and racial and ethnic persons.

8. All local church offices and all chairs of organizations
within the local church may be shared between two persons, with
the following exceptions: trustee, officers of the board of trustees,
treasurer, lay member of annual conference, member and chairperson of the committee on staff- or pastor-parish relations. When
two persons jointly hold a position that entails membership on
the church council, both may be members of it.

¶ 250. *Removal of Officers and Filling of Vacancies*—If a leader or officer who has been elected by the charge conference is unable or unwilling to perform the duties reasonably expected of such a leader or officer, the district superintendent may call a special session of the charge conference in accordance with ¶ 246.7. The purpose of such special session shall be stated as "Consideration for the removal of person(s) from office and the election of person(s) to fill vacancy(ies)." The committee on nominations and leadership development (¶¶ 258.1, 247.18) shall meet as soon as possible after the special session of the charge conference has been announced and shall propose person(s) who may be elected if vacancy(ies) occur at the charge conference. If the charge conference votes to remove a person or persons from office, the vacancy(ies) shall be filled in the manner prescribed for elections in accordance with ¶ 249. When a local church trustee is under consideration for removal and the pastoral charge consists of two or more churches, a church local conference shall be called instead of a charge conference, in accordance with ¶ 2526.

¶ 251. *Duties of Leaders and Members*—1. Out of the professing membership of each local church (¶ 128), there shall be elected by the charge conference a lay leader who shall function as the primary lay representative of the laity in that local church and shall have the following responsibilities:

a) fostering awareness of the role of laity both within the congregation and through their ministries in the home, workplace, community, and world, and finding ways within the community of faith to recognize all these ministries;

b) meeting regularly with the pastor to discuss the state of the church and the needs for ministry;

c) membership in the charge conference and the church council, the committee on finance, the committee on nominations and leadership development, and the committee on pastor-parish relations or staff-parish relations, where, along with the pastor, the lay leader shall serve as an interpreter of the actions and programs of the annual conference and the general Church (to be better equipped to comply with this responsibility, it is recommended that a lay leader also serve as a lay member of annual conference);

d) continuing involvement in study and training opportunities to develop a growing understanding of the Church's reason for existence and the types of ministry that will most effectively fulfill the Church's mission;

e) assisting in advising the church council of opportunities available and the needs expressed for a more effective ministry of the church through its laity in the community;

f) informing the laity of training opportunities provided by the annual conference. Where possible, the lay leader shall attend training opportunities in order to strengthen his or her work. The lay leader is urged to become a certified lay servant

In instances where more than one church is on a charge, the charge conference shall elect additional lay leaders so that there will be one lay leader in each church. Associate lay leaders may be elected to work with the lay leader in any local church.

2. The lay member(s) of the annual conference and alternates shall be elected annually or quadrennially as the annual conference directs. If the charge's lay representative to the annual conference shall cease to be a member of the charge or shall for any reason fail to serve, an alternate member in the order of election shall serve in place.

Both the lay members and the alternates shall have been professing members in good standing of The United Methodist Church for at least two years and shall have been active participants for at least four years next preceding their election (see ¶ 32), except in a newly organized church, which shall have the privilege of representation at the annual conference session.[7] No local pastor shall be eligible as a lay member or alternate.[8] United Methodist churches that become part of an ecumenical shared ministry shall not be deprived of their right of representation by a lay member in the annual conference. The lay member(s) of the annual conference, along with the pastor, shall serve as an interpreter of the actions of the annual conference session. These persons shall report to the local church council on actions of the annual conference as soon as possible, but not later than three months after the close of the conference.

3. The church council chairperson shall be elected by the charge conference annually and shall have the following responsibilities:

a) leading the council in fulfilling its responsibilities (see ¶ 249);

b) preparing and communicating the agenda of the council meetings in consultation with the pastor(s), lay leader, and other appropriate persons;

---

7. See Judicial Council Decisions 170, 305, 342, 469, 495.
8. See Judicial Council Decision 328.

c) reviewing and assigning responsibility for the implementation of actions taken by the council;

d) communicating with members of the council and others as appropriate to permit informed action at council meetings;

e) coordinating the various activities of the council;

f) providing the initiative and leadership for the council as it does the planning, establishing of objectives and goals, and evaluating;

g) participating in leadership training programs as offered by the annual conference and/or district.

The church council chairperson shall be entitled to attend meetings of all boards and committees of the church unless specifically limited by the *Book of Discipline*. The chairperson is encouraged to attend annual conference.

THE CHURCH COUNCIL

¶ **252.** 1. *Purpose*—The church council shall provide for planning and implementing a program of nurture, outreach, witness, and resources in the local church. It shall also provide for the administration of its organization and temporal life. It shall envision, plan, implement, and annually evaluate the mission and ministry of the church. The church council shall be amenable to and function as the administrative agency of the charge conference (¶ 244).

2. *Mission and Ministry*—Nurture, outreach, and witness ministries and their accompanying responsibilities include:

a) The nurturing ministries of the congregation shall give attention to but not be limited to education, worship, Christian formation, membership care, small groups, and stewardship. Attention must be given to the needs of individuals and families of all ages.

b) The outreach ministries of the church shall give attention to local and larger community ministries of compassion, justice, and advocacy. These ministries include church and society, global ministries, higher education and campus ministry, health and welfare, Christian unity and interreligious concerns, religion and race, and the status and role of women.

c) The witness ministries of the church shall give attention to developing and strengthening evangelistic efforts of sharing of personal and congregational stories of Christian experience, faith, and service; communications; Lay Servant Ministries; and other means that give expressions of witness for Jesus Christ.

d) The leadership development and resourcing ministries shall give attention to the ongoing preparation and development of lay and clergy leaders for the ministry of the church (¶ 258.1).

e) The nurture, outreach, and witness ministries and their accompanying responsibilities shall include consideration of (i) the election of a prayer coordinator to promote prayer and mobilize the local church to pray, (ii) establishing a prayer room or designated place for prayer and prayer resources, and (iii) encouraging intentional prayer for the pastoral leadership of the local church.

3. *Meetings*—*a)* The council shall meet at least quarterly. The chairperson or the pastor may call special meetings.

b) In order for the council to give adequate consideration to the missional purpose of the local church, it is recommended that the first agenda item at each meeting be related to its ministries of nurture, outreach, and witness. The administrative and supportive responsibilities of the church will then be given attention. It is recommended that the council use a consensus/discernment model of decision-making.

4. *Other Responsibilities*—It will also be the responsibility of the church council to:

a) review the membership of the local church;

b) fill interim vacancies occurring among the lay officers of the church between sessions of the annual charge conference;

c) establish the budget on recommendation of the committee on finance and ensure adequate provision for the financial needs of the church;

d) recommend to the charge conference the salary and other remuneration of the pastor(s) and staff members after receiving recommendations from the committee on pastor-parish relations (staff-parish relations);

e) review the recommendation of the committee on pastor-parish relations regarding provision of adequate housing for the pastor(s), and report the same to the charge conference for approval. Housing provisions shall comply with the annual conference housing policy and parsonage standards. Housing shall not be considered as part of compensation or remuneration except to the extent provided for in denominational pension and benefit plans.

5. *Membership*—The charge conference will determine the size of the church council. Members of the church council shall be involved in the mission and ministry of the congregation as defined in ¶ 252.2. The membership of the council may consist of as few as eleven persons or as many as the charge conference deems appropriate. The council shall include persons who represent the program ministries of the church as outlined in ¶ 243. The membership shall include but not be limited to the following:

a) the chairperson of the church council;

b) the lay leader;

c) the chairperson and/or a representative of the pastor-parish relations committee;

d) the chairperson and/or a representative of the committee on finance;

e) the chairperson and/or a representative of the board of trustees;

f) the church treasurer;

g) a lay member to annual conference;

h) the president and/or a representative of the United Methodist Men;

i) the president and/or a representative of the United Methodist Women;

j) a young adult representative

k a representative of the United Methodist Youth;

l) the pastor(s).

6. *Quorum*—The members present and voting at any duly announced meeting shall constitute a quorum.

SPECIALIZED MINISTRIES

¶ **253.** *Age-Level, Family, and Specialized-Ministries Coordinators* (see also ¶ 252)—The charge conference may elect annually a coordinator of children's ministries, a coordinator of youth ministries, a coordinator of adult ministries, and a coordinator of family ministries. Where young adult and specific age-level ministries would be enhanced, coordinators of young adult and/or older adult ministries may be elected. Where camps and retreats are part of faith formation across the age span, a coordinator of camp and retreat ministries may be elected. Where there are civic youth-serving agencies or scouting ministry units present there may be elected a scouting coordinator. Where needs for specialized areas of ministry arise (for example, single adults or persons with addictions, mental illness or disabilities), coordinators of these areas of ministry may be elected.

¶ 254. *Other Ministry Group Coordinators*—In order to fulfill the mission of the local church, the charge conference may elect annually a coordinator or ministry group chairperson for any or all of these areas: Christian unity and interreligious relationships, church and society, community volunteers, education, evangelism, higher education and campus ministry, missions, prayer advocacy, religion and race, status and role of women, earth advocacy, stewardship, worship, advocacy for persons with special needs, and church media resources. Every local United Methodist church may have a campus ministry coordinator, who may have membership on the church council. A primary responsibility of the campus ministry coordinator shall be to report the names and contact information (i.e., addresses, phone numbers, and e-mail addresses) of all college students from their local church each semester to the appropriate United Methodist campus ministry, such as the Wesley Foundation. The campus ministry coordinator shall be encouraged to contact every college student from their church each semester by letter, e-mail, or phone and encourage the student's active participation in United Methodist student ministry. The campus ministry coordinator in every church shall also promote financial and other support of United Methodist campus ministries, such as the Wesley Foundations, within their local church.

Where desirable, the charge conference may combine coordinators' or ministry group chairpersons' assignments. Each coordinator or ministry group chairperson, if elected, shall work with the church council (or other appropriate body), pastor(s), and other church leaders to address the needs and opportunities of the particular area, utilizing all appropriate resources and relationships of the district, annual conference, and/or general church.

¶ 255. *Church-School Superintendent and Small-Group Coordinator*—The charge conference may elect: (1) a superintendent of the church school or Sunday school, and/or a coordinator of small-group ministries, who shall be responsible for helping to organize and supervise the total program for nurturing faith, building Christian community, and equipping people of all ages for ministry in daily life through small groups in the church; (2) a health-and-welfare ministries coordinator, who shall assist the local church and its people in being involved in direct service to persons in need; and (3) a communications coordinator, who shall assist the local church and its members with communication tasks by making available ideas, resources, and skills.

¶ **256.** *Program Ministries*—The ministries of the local church are offered so that people encounter God's redeeming love for the world and respond by participating in God's action in the world. To achieve this ministry, people need to be involved in a variety of small-group settings. Some will be formed by the church council. Others will emerge with the approval of this body. Another type is historical, expressing itself in organizational structures that are related to counterparts in annual conferences and the general Church. These are referred to as program ministries and are related to the church council.

1. *The Church School and Small-Group Ministries*—In each local church there shall be a variety of small-group ministries, including the church school, for supporting the formation of Christian disciples focused on the transformation of the world. These small groups may concentrate on teaching and learning, fellowship, support, community ministries, and accountability. Members of small groups will build their knowledge of the Bible, the Christian faith, The United Methodist Church, and the societal context in which the church finds itself. In addition, small groups, including the church school, shall provide people with opportunities for practicing skills for faithful discipleship, including but not limited to worship, faith sharing, the creation of new faith communities, spiritual discernment, Bible study, theological reflection, prayer, community building, service with the poor and marginalized, and advocacy for peace and justice. Local churches or charges are strongly encouraged to develop policies and procedures to provide for the safety of the infants, children, youth, and vulnerable adults entrusted to their care.

a) The Church School—In each local church there shall be a church school for the purpose of accomplishing the church's educational ministry.

The church school is challenged to create communities in which people of all ages experience God's active presence in their lives; foster healthy, nonviolent relationships within the congregation and community; testify to the reconciling love of God through Christ; and live out their faith in the world as witnesses to the coming reign of God.

b) Accountable Discipleship—Historically class leaders provided lay pastoral leadership, and classes and class meetings were the basic structural means of Christian spiritual formation in the early Methodist societies.

Class leaders may be commissioned and classes may be organized within the local congregation for the purpose of forming persons as faithful disciples of Jesus Christ through mutual accountability and support for witnessing to him in the world and for following his teachings through acts of compassion, justice, worship, and devotion under the guidance of the Holy Spirit. (See ¶ 104, "The Nature, Design, and General Rules of Our United Societies" [page 77], and ¶ 1117.)

c) Mission and Ministry Groups—Christian discipleship is patterned after the servanthood of Jesus, who cared for the sick, fed the hungry, and befriended the outcast. People may participate in small groups in order to serve the needs of the poor and marginalized, advocate for social justice, and demonstrate their faith in all their relationships and whatever setting they find themselves in.

d) Support Groups—Where needed, the local church may organize small groups to support particular needs of congregation and community members, including but not limited to care and prayer groups, divorce recovery, grief recovery, parenting groups, and support for people who are suffering from chronic illness, including persons with mental illnesses and their families.

2. *Children's Ministries*—Children's ministries—for, with, and by children—include all ministries involving children within the life of the congregational community, including but not limited to Sunday school, vacation Bible school, nursery ministries, children's choir and music ministries, fellowship groups, support groups, short-term study groups, children's worship experiences, mission education experiences, intergenerational activities, and all weekday programs for children of all ages.

a) If there is a coordinator of children's ministries, the coordinator shall be responsible for assuring that children are considered and included within the life of the congregation. The coordinator will lead the children's council, when organized, and will work closely with clergy and other program-related staff. The coordinator will vision, plan, and advocate for children, particularly in the areas of faith development, safety, and discipleship. The coordinator will work with other leaders in the congregation to assure that policies and procedures are in place to help keep all children and the adults who care for and work with them safe. These policies and procedures include such things as background checks, having at least two adults per group, and cardiopulmonary resuscitation and first-aid training. The coordinator will also advocate for mission education for children, including The United Methodist Children's Fund for Christian Mission.

b) If there is a children's council, it shall be responsible for planning, visioning, and advocating for children within the congregation, the community, and the world. The council will set policies and procedures related to children, oversee the planning of short-term experiences, consider children's ministry needs within the whole of the congregation's ministries, and communicate with parents and the congregation. The children's council will work closely with the coordinator of children's ministries and church staff responsible for ministry with children, including children's choirs and weekday ministries. The children's council is accountable to the group responsible for the local church's educational ministry.

c) Weekday Ministry Board—The term weekday ministry applies to any regularly planned ministry for children. When appropriate, one or more weekday ministry boards may be organized to oversee the weekday ministry programs of the congregation. The board's membership should be mostly professing members of the congregation, with parent, church staff, and weekday ministry staff representatives. The board will set policies consistent with the congregation's policies, state mandates, and sound business practices. The board will guide weekday ministries as appropriate opportunities for faith development, mission outreach, Christian education, evangelism, and safety. They will advocate for inclusion of children from various socioeconomic, cultural, and racial/ethnic backgrounds. Weekday ministry board(s) accountability should be placed within the local church organizational structure with consideration to the group responsible for the congregation's education ministry.

3. Young People's Ministries—The term young people is inclusive of all persons from approximately twelve through thirty years of age in the United States and thirty-five in the central conferences. The term encompasses both youth and young-adult ministries and allows for age flexibility given the different age definitions for young people in various cultures around the

world. The term *youth ministry* is an inclusive title, encompassing all the concerns of the Church and all activities by, with, and for youth. The youth ministry of The United Methodist Church shall include all persons from approximately twelve through eighteen years of age in the United States and up to twenty-four in the central conferences, taking into account the grouping of youth in the public schools, who are currently or potentially associated with the church or any of its activities. Youth who are professing members of the church have all rights and responsibilities of church membership except voting on matters prohibited by state law (see ¶ 226.5). The term *young-adult ministry* is an inclusive title, encompassing all the concerns of the Church and all activities by, with, and for young adults. The young-adult ministry of The United Methodist Church shall include all persons from approximately eighteen through thirty in the United States and twenty-four through thirty-five in the central conferences who are currently or potentially associated with the church or any of its activities. Young adults who are professing members of the church have all rights and responsibilities of church membership.

a) The coordinator/staff for youth ministries and the youth leadership team, when organized, shall be responsible for recommending to the church council activities, program emphases, and settings for youth. The coordinator/staff and the leadership team shall use available resources and means to inform youth concerning the Youth Service Fund and shall cultivate its support, provided that prior to this cultivation or as a part of it, the youth shall have been challenged to assume their financial responsibilities in connection with the total program and budget of the local church.

b) The local church may organize settings for ministries with young people as appropriate in their ministry context.

c) In each charge conference where there are at least five youth, there may be a youth leadership team.

(1) The leadership team shall be made up of no less than one-half youth. Nominations for members of the leadership team (both youth and adults) may come from the youth group (or related structure). The nominations will then be sent to the committee on nominations and leadership development for approval and then to the charge conference for approval.

The council shall be composed of:

(a) The coordinator/staff for youth ministries

and other related leaders as ex officio members with voice but not vote.

(b) Any youth serving on a district, conference, jurisdictional, or general Church board or agency.

(c) Any adult serving on a district, conference, jurisdictional, or general Church organization on youth ministry.

(2) There shall be co-chairs with one adult and one youth to lead the meetings. Other officers may be a mix of adults and youth depending on the skills, gifts, and needs of the leadership team.

(3) The leadership team shall meet at least semiannually. It may meet additionally at the request of the pastor, coordinator/staff for youth ministries or any member of the committee.

Responsibilities:

(a) To assist the coordinator/staff for youth ministry and other related leaders in planning and developing activities, program emphases, and settings for youth in the local church.

(b) To develop a program budget for their youth ministry

(c) To assist the coordinator/staff for youth ministry in finding and encouraging qualified adults and interns to work with youth in the local church.

(d) To develop a covenant for all adult volunteer youth workers.

(e) To encourage and facilitate the furthering of education for the coordinator/staff for youth ministries and others in leadership with youth.

(f) To be informed of and follow the conference child safety policies, procedures, and requirements to be followed by the local church.

(g) To encourage and educate youth on possible careers in professional ministry and how to consider any vocational calling and opportunity to serve.

(h) To be a resource for other churches interested in starting or revitalizing youth ministry within their own local churches.

(i) To further educate youth and adults on The United Methodist Church as a connectional church by encouraging and supporting the participation of youth and adults in district, annual, jurisdictional, and central conferences, and other general Church ministries.

(*j*) To promote and educate persons about the Youth Service Fund.

(*k*) To promote the camping and retreat ministries within the local church.

(*l*) To promote, introduce, and encourage youth and young adults to become active in United Methodist campus ministry when they attend a college or university.

(*m*) To empower youth to be full participants and active leaders in The United Methodist Church.

(*n*) To consult with the pastor/staff parish relations committee in: 1) developing written job descriptions; 2) nominating; 3) evaluating the job performance of the coordinator/staff for youth ministries and any other volunteer and paid staff related to youth ministry in the local church.

(*m*) It is strongly recommended that the council develop a program budget for their ministry.

d) The coordinator/staff for young-adult ministries and the young adult leadership team, when organized, shall be responsible for recommending to the church council the activities, program emphases, and settings for young adults, gather the names and addresses of all college students to send to the campus minister or chaplain of the college or university the students are attending, encourage college students to participate in United Methodist campus ministry, and recommend opportunities for the congregation to support and participate with annual conference campus ministries and annual conference-related colleges and universities.

4. Scouting ministry through civic youth-serving agencies offer another setting for ministry to children, youth, their leaders, and their families. The Programs of Religious Activities with Youth (P.R.A.Y.) award program is available to all appropriate age-level participants of the local church education program including the church school, youth ministry, and scouting ministry.

a) Each local church may have a local church scouting coordinator (or the central conferences equivalent) who shall relate to the church council, the superintendent of the church school, the coordinator of children's ministries, the coordinator of youth ministries, and all the various youth-serving agency structures. The local church scouting coordinator (or the central conferences equivalent) may relate to the district scouting coordinator and annual conference scouting coordinator who are resource and training advisors. All churches shall be encouraged to have a signed partnership agreement with all the units of these agencies which are part of their ministry.

5. *United Methodist Women*—In every local church there shall be an organized unit of United Methodist Women. The following is the authorized constitution:

Article 1. Name—The name of this organization shall be United Methodist Women.

Article 2. Relationships—The unit of United Methodist Women in the local church is directly related to the district and conference and national organizations of United Methodist Women.

Article 3. Purpose—The organized unit of United Methodist Women shall be a community of women whose purpose is to know God and to experience freedom as whole persons through Jesus Christ; to develop a creative, supportive fellowship; and to expand concepts of mission through participation in the global ministries of the Church.

Article 4. Membership—Membership shall be open to any woman who indicates her desire to belong and to participate in the global mission of the Church through United Methodist Women. The pastor(s) shall be an ex officio member of the local unit and of its executive committee.

Article 5. Officers and Committees—The local unit shall elect a president, a vice president, a secretary, a treasurer, and a committee on nominations. Additional officers and committees shall be elected or appointed as needed, in accordance with the plans of the United Methodist Women's national organization as set forth in the bylaws for the local unit of United Methodist Women.

Article 6. Funds—a) The organized unit of United Methodist Women shall secure funds for the fulfillment of its purpose.

b) All funds from whatever source secured by the unit of United Methodist Women belong to the organization and shall be disbursed only in accordance with its constitution and by its order.

c) The total budget secured and administered by the organized unit in the local church shall include: (1) pledges and other money for the programs and responsibilities of the United Methodist Women's national organization to be directed through regular channels of finance of United Methodist Women; and (2) funds to be used in mission locally, which shall include amounts for administration and membership development.

d) The organized unit in the local church shall make an annual pledge to the total budget of the district or conference organization of United Methodist Women.

e) All undesignated funds channeled to the United Methodist Women's national organization shall be appropriated by the organization.

Article 7. Meetings—The organized unit in the local church shall hold such meetings for implementing the purpose and transacting its business as the unit itself shall decide.

Article 8. Relationship in the Local Church—The organized unit of United Methodist Women shall encourage all women to participate in the total life and work of the Church and shall support them in assuming positions of responsibility and leadership.

Article 9. Amendments—Proposed amendments to this constitution may be sent to the recording secretary of the United Methodist Women's national organization before the last annual meeting of the organization in the quadrennium.

Note: For a description of the United Methodist Women's national organization and its subsidiary organizations, see ¶¶ 1901-1912.

6. *United Methodist Men*—Each church or charge shall have an organized unit of United Methodist Men chartered and annually renewed through the General Commission on United Methodist Men. Other organized men's ministry groups in a local United Methodist Church shall annually report to the charge conference and be resourced through the General Commission on United Methodist Men. All local church men's organizations shall provide a dedicated ministry for building men spiritually and involving men in the total ministry of the Church (¶ 2302).

a) Local church resource material for supporting effective men's ministries shall be provided by the district, conference, and jurisdictional organizations of United Methodist Men and the General Commission on United Methodist Men (¶ 2302).

b) United Methodist Men exists to declare the centrality of Christ in every man's life. Men's ministry leads to the spiritual growth of men and effective discipleship. This purpose is served as men are called to model the servant leadership of Jesus Christ.

c) Individual and group strategies form the foundation of United Methodist Men ministry.

(1) Enhance Evangelism, Mission, and Spiritual Life (EMS), as men become servant leaders.

(2) Advocate programs that train men within local churches to promote specific ministries including prayer, missions, stewardship, and civic/youth-serving ministries.

(3) Forge pastoral partnerships by men committed to the effective support and service of clergy and local congregations.

(4) Enhance organizational strength through effective leadership, resources, membership growth, and financial accountability.

(5) Assist men in their ever-changing relationships, roles, and responsibilities in the family setting, workplace, and society.

(6) Understand the organization, doctrines, and beliefs of The United Methodist Church.

(7) Fulfill the membership vows through the commitment to prayer, presence, gifts, service, and witness in congregational life.

(8) Fulfill the Great Commission with and through The United Methodist Church as one part of the body of Christ.

d) Men seeking membership in a local unit of United Methodist Men will be asked to subscribe to the major strategies listed in § *c* above and to these personal objectives:

(1) To engage daily in Bible study and prayer.

(2) To bear witness to Christ's way in daily work and in all personal contacts through words and actions.

(3) To engage in Christian service.

e) United Methodist Men may be organized in one or more components within a local church as needed. Multiple local churches may also form a single unit of United Methodist Men according to their needs.

f) Membership shall be open to any man who indicates his desire to belong and to participate in the ministry of the church through United Methodist Men.

g) The appointed clergy of the local church or charge shall be ex officio member(s) of the unit and its executive committee

h) The organized unit of United Methodist Men shall secure funds for the fulfillment of its purpose. All funds from whatever source secured by the United Methodist Men's unit belong to the organization and shall be disbursed only in accordance with its constitution and/or by-laws and by its order.

(1) United Methodist Men's unit may have their own bank accounts.

(2) The UM Men's unit shall have an annual financial audit.

7. *Supplemental Ministries*—In view of the fact that the needs of women and men are complex, dynamic, and unique in every congregation, local churches are encouraged to develop a variety of supplemental ministry programs for women and men, in addition to United Methodist Women and United Methodist Men.

¶ **257.** *Other Age-Level Councils*—Where the size of the church and the extent of the program indicate the need, the work of the church council (or other appropriate body) may be facilitated by one or more age-level councils and/or a family council, or such other means as fit the needs of the congregation. The membership of these councils shall be elected by the church council (or other appropriate body).

ADMINISTRATIVE COMMITTEES

¶ **258.** 1. There shall be elected annually, by the charge conference in each local church, a committee on nominations and leadership development that is composed of professing members of the local church. The charge of this committee is to identify, develop, deploy, evaluate, and monitor Christian spiritual leadership for the local congregation. Members of the committee shall engage in and be attentive to developing and enhancing their own Christian spiritual life in light of the mission of the Church (Part VI, Chapter One, Section 1).

In conducting its work, the committee shall engage in biblical and theological reflections on the mission of the church, the primary task, and ministries of the local church. It shall provide a means of identifying the spiritual gifts and abilities of the membership. The committee shall work with the church council, or alternative administrative bodies, to determine the diverse ministry tasks of the congregation and the skills needed for leadership.

a) The committee on nominations and leadership development shall serve throughout the year to guide the church council, or alternative structure, on matters regarding the leadership (other than employed staff) of the congregation so as to focus on mission and ministry as the context for service; guide the development and training of spiritual leaders; recruit, nurture, and support spiritual leaders; and assist the church council, or alternative structure, in assessing the changing leadership needs.

b) The committee shall recommend to the charge conference, at its annual session, the names of people to serve as officers and leaders of designated ministries of the church council, or alternative administrative body required for the work of the church and as the law of the church requires or as the charge conference deems necessary to its work.

c) This committee is to be composed of not more than nine persons, in addition to the pastor and the lay leader. At least one young adult elected by the charge conference shall serve as a member of the committee. One or more members elected by the charge conference may be youth. The pastor shall be the chairperson. A layperson elected by the committee on nominations and leadership development shall serve as the vice chairperson of the committee.

d) In order to secure experience and stability, the membership shall be divided into three classes, one of which shall be elected each year for a three-year term. To begin the process of rotation where such has not been in place, in the first year, one class shall be elected for one year, one class for two years, and one class for three years. Each year's new class, and vacancies at the time of charge conference, shall be elected from nominees, from the floor of the charge conference, and/or through the recommendation of the committee on nominations and leadership development. Retiring members of the committee shall not succeed themselves. Only one person from an immediate family residing in the same household shall serve on the committee. When vacancies occur during the year, nominees shall be elected by the church council, or alternative church structure, with the permission of the district superintendent.

e) In the identification and selection process, care shall be given that the leadership of ministries reflects inclusivity and diversity.

2. There shall be elected annually by the charge conference in each local church a committee on pastor-parish relations who are professing members of the local church or charge or associate members (¶ 227), except in cases where central conference legislation or local law provides otherwise. People serving on this committee must be engaged in and attentive to their Christian spiritual development so as to give proper leadership in the responsibilities with which the committee is entrusted.

In conducting its work, the committee shall identify and clarify its values for ministry. It shall engage in biblical and theological reflections on the mission of the church, the primary task, and ministries of the local church.

The committee shall reflect biblically and theologically on the role and work of the pastor(s) and staff as they carry out their leadership responsibilities. The committee shall assist the pastor(s) and staff in assessing their gifts, maintaining health holistically and work-life balance, and setting priorities for leadership and service. It is the responsibility of the committee to communicate with the committee on nominations and leadership development and/or the church council when there is a need for other leaders or for employed staff to perform in areas where utilization of the gifts of the pastor(s) and staff proves an inappropriate stewardship of time.

a) The committee shall be composed of not fewer than five nor more than nine persons representative of the total charge. One of the members shall be a young adult and one member may be a youth. In addition, the lay leader and a lay member of the annual conference shall be members. No staff member or immediate family member of a pastor or staff member may serve on the committee. Only one person from an immediate family residing in the same household shall serve on the committee.

b) In order to secure experience and stability, the membership shall be divided into three classes, one of which shall be elected each year for a three-year term. The lay member of the annual conference and the lay leader are exempt from the three-year term. To begin the process of rotation where such a process has not been in place, on the first year one class shall be elected for one year, one class for two years, and one class for three years. Members of the committee shall be able to succeed themselves for one three-year term. When vacancies occur during the year, nominees shall be elected at the church council (or alternative church structure).

c) In those charges where there is more than one church, the committee shall include at least one representative and the lay leader from each local church.

d) The committees on pastor-parish relations of charges that are in cooperative parish ministries shall meet together to consider the professional leadership needs of the cooperative parish ministry as a whole.

e) The committee shall meet at least quarterly. It shall meet additionally at the request of the bishop, the district superintendent, the pastor, any other person accountable to the committee, or the chairperson of the committee. The committee shall meet only with the knowledge of the pastor and/or the district superintendent. The pastor shall be present at each meeting of the committee on pastor-parish relations or staff-parish relations except where he or she voluntarily excuses himself or herself.

The committee may meet with the district superintendent without the pastor or appointed staff under consideration being present. However, the pastor or appointed staff under consideration shall be notified prior to such meeting with the district superintendent and be brought into consultation immediately thereafter.

The committee shall meet in closed session, and information shared in the committee shall be confidential.

f) In the event that only one congregation on a charge containing more than one church has concerns it wishes to share, its member(s) in the committee may meet separately with the pastor or any other person accountable to the committee or the district superintendent, but only with the knowledge of the pastor and/or district superintendent.

g) The duties of the committee shall include the following:

(1) To encourage, strengthen, nurture, support, and respect the pastor(s) and staff and their family(s).

(2) To promote unity in the church(es).

(3) To confer with and counsel the pastor(s) and staff on the matters pertaining to the effectiveness of ministry; relationships with the congregation; the pastor's health and self-care, conditions that may impede the effectiveness of ministry; and to interpret the nature and function of the ministry.

(4) To confer with, consult, and counsel the pastor(s) and staff on matters pertaining to priorities in the use of gifts, skills, and time and priorities for the demands and effectiveness of the mission and ministry of the congregation.

(5) To provide evaluation at least annually for the use of the pastor(s) and staff in an ongoing effective ministry and for identifying continuing educational needs and plans.

(6) To communicate and interpret to the congregation the nature and function of ministry in The United Methodist Church regarding open itinerancy, the preparation for ordained ministry, and the Ministerial Education Fund.

(7) To develop and approve written job descriptions and titles for associate pastors and other staff members in cooperation with the senior pastor. The term *associate pastor* is used as a general term to indicate any pastoral appointment in a local church other than the pastor in charge (see ¶ 339). Committees shall be encouraged to develop specific titles for associate pastors that reflect the job descriptions and expectations.

(8) To consult with the pastor and staff concerning continuing education, work-life balance, dimensions of personal health and wellness, and spiritual renewal, to arrange with the church council for the necessary time and financial assistance for the attendance of the pastor and/or staff at such continuing education, self-care, and spiritual renewal events as may serve their professional and spiritual growth, and to encourage staff members to seek professional certification in their fields of specialization.

(9) To enlist, interview, evaluate, review, and recommend annually to the charge conference lay preachers and persons for candidacy for ordained ministry (see ¶¶ 247.8 and 310), and to enlist and refer to the General Board of Global Ministries persons for candidacy for missionary service, recognizing that The United Methodist Church affirms the biblical and theological support of persons regardless of gender, race, ethnic origin, or disabilities for these ministries. Neither the pastor nor any member of the committee on pastor-parish relations shall be present during the consideration of a candidacy application or renewal for a member of their immediate family. The committee shall provide to the charge conference a list of students from the charge who are preparing for ordained ministry, diaconal ministry, and/or missionary service, and shall maintain contact with these students, supplying the charge conference with a progress report on each student.

(10) To interpret preparation for ordained ministry and the Ministerial Education Fund to the congregation.

(11) To confer with the pastor and/or other appointed members of the staff if it should become evident that the best interests of the charge and pastor(s) will be served by a change of pastor(s). The committee shall cooperate with the pastor(s), the district superintendent, and the bishop in securing clergy leadership. Its relationship to the district superintendent and the bishop shall be advisory only.[9] (See ¶¶ 425-428.)

---

9. See Judicial Council Decision 701.

(12) To recommend to the church council, after consultation with the pastor, the professional and other staff positions (whether employee or contract) needed to carry out the work of the church or charge. The committee and the pastor shall recommend to the church council a written statement of policy and procedures regarding the process for hiring, contracting, evaluating, promoting, retiring, and dismissing staff personnel who are not subject to episcopal appointment as ordained clergy. Until such a policy has been adopted, the committee and the pastor shall have the authority to hire, contract, evaluate, promote, retire, and dismiss nonappointed personnel. When persons are hired or contracted, consideration shall be given to the training qualifications and certification standards set forth by the general Church agency to which such positions are related. The committee shall further recommend to the church council a provision for adequate health and life insurance and severance pay for all lay employees. In addition, the committee shall recommend that the church council provide, effective on and after January 1, 2006, 100 percent vested pension benefits of at least 3 percent of compensation for lay employees of the local church who work at least 1040 hours per year, are at least 21 years of age, and have at least one year of permanent service. The church council shall have authority to provide such pension benefits through either a denominational pension program administered by the General Board of Pension and Health Benefits or another pension program administered by another pension provider.

(13) To recommend to the charge conference, when the size of the employed staff of the charge makes it desirable, the establishment of a personnel committee. This committee shall be composed of such members of the committee on pastor-parish relations as it may designate and such additional members as the charge conference may determine.

(14) To educate the church community on the value of diversity of selection in clergy and lay staff and develop a commitment to same.

(15) Members of the committee on pastor-parish relations (or staff-parish relations) shall keep themselves informed of personnel matters in relationship to the Church's policy, professional standards, liability issues, and civil law. They are responsible for communicating and interpreting such matters to staff. Committee members should make themselves available for educational and training opportunities provided by the conference,

district, and/or other arenas that will enable them to be effective in their work.

(16) To consult on matters pertaining to pulpit supply, proposals for compensation, travel expense, vacation, health and life insurance, pension, housing (which may be a church-owned parsonage or housing allowance in lieu of parsonage if in compliance with the policy of the annual conference), and other practical matters affecting the work and families of the pastor and staff, and to make annual recommendations regarding such matters to the church council, reporting budget items to the committee on finance. The parsonage is to be mutually respected by the pastor's family as the property of the church and by the church as a place of privacy for the pastor's family. The committee will follow up to assure timely resolution of parsonage problems affecting the health of the pastor or pastor's family. The chairperson of the committee on pastor-parish relations, the chairperson of the board of trustees, and the pastor shall make an annual review of the church-owned parsonage to assure proper maintenance and to give immediate resolution to parsonage issues affecting the family's health and well-being.

(17) To encourage, monitor, and support clergy and lay staff pursuit of health and wholeness.

3. There shall be a board of trustees, whose membership and duties are detailed in ¶¶ 2525-2551.

4. There shall be a committee on finance, elected annually by the charge conference upon recommendation by the committee on nominations and leadership development or from the floor, composed of the chairperson; the pastor(s); a lay member of the annual conference; the chairperson of the church council; the chairperson or representative of the committee on pastor-parish relations; a representative of the trustees to be selected by the trustees; the chairperson of the ministry group on stewardship; the lay leader; the financial secretary; the treasurer; the church business administrator; and other members to be added as the charge conference may determine. It is recommended that the chairperson of the committee on finance shall be a member of the church council. The financial secretary, treasurer, and church business administrator, if paid employees, shall be members without vote.

The positions of treasurer and financial secretary should not be combined and held by one person, and the persons holding these two positions should not be immediate family members.

No immediate family members of any appointed clergy may
serve as treasurer, finance chair, financial secretary, counter, or
serve in any paid or unpaid position under the responsibilities
of the committee on finance, as described herein. These restrictions would apply only to the church or charge where the clergy
serves.

The committee on finance shall give stewardship of financial
resources as their priority throughout the year. It may delegate
the responsibility to either a sub-group or task force that would
plan, strategize, and implement ways to generate more resources
for mission and ministries of local churches and beyond. It is
strongly recommended that the committee on finance, in collaboration with the church council, find creative ways to turn their
congregations into tithing congregations with an attitude of gen-
erosity. All financial askings to be included in the annual budget
of the local church shall be submitted to the committee on finance.
The committee on finance shall compile annually a complete budget for the local church and submit it to the church council for
review and adoption. The committee on finance shall be charged
with responsibility for developing and implementing plans that
will raise sufficient income to meet the budget adopted by the
church council. It shall administer the funds received according
to instructions from the church council.

The committee shall carry out the church council's directions
in guiding the treasurer(s) and financial secretary.

  a) The committee shall designate at least two persons not
of the immediate family residing in the same household to count
the offering. They shall work under the supervision of the financial secretary. A record of all funds received shall be given to the
financial secretary and treasurer. Funds received shall be deposited promptly in accordance with the procedures established
by the committee on finance. The financial secretary shall keep
records of the contributions and payments.

  b) The church treasurer(s) shall disburse all money contributed to causes represented in the local church budget, and
such other funds and contributions as the church council may
determine. The treasurer(s) shall remit each month to the conference treasurer all World Service and conference benevolence
funds then on hand. Contributions to benevolence shall not
be used for any cause other than that to which they have been
given. The church treasurer shall make regular and detailed

reports on funds received and expended to the committee on finance and the church council.[10] The treasurer(s) shall be adequately bonded.

c) The committee on finance shall establish written financial policies to document the internal controls of the local church. The written financial policies should be reviewed for adequacy and effectiveness annually by the committee on finance and submitted as a report to the charge conference annually.

d) The committee shall make provision for an annual audit of the financial statements of the local church and all its organizations and accounts. The committee shall make a full and complete report to the annual charge conference. A local church audit is defined as an independent evaluation of the financial reports and records and the internal controls of the local church by a qualified person or persons.

The audit shall be conducted for the purpose of reasonably verifying the reliability of financial reporting, determining whether assets are being safeguarded, and determining compliance with local law, local church policies and procedures, and the *Book of Discipline*.

The audit may include: 1) a review of the cash and investment reconciliations; 2) interviews with the treasurer, financial secretary, pastor(s), finance committee chair, business manager, those who count offerings, church secretary, etc., with inquiries regarding compliance with existing written financial policies and procedures; 3) a review of journal entries and authorized check signers for each checking and investment account; and 4) other procedures requested by the committee on finance.

The audit shall be performed by an audit committee composed of persons unrelated to the persons listed in 2. above or by an independent certified public accountant (CPA), accounting firm, or equivalent.

e) The committee shall recommend to the church council proper depositories for the church's funds. Funds received shall be deposited promptly in the name of the local church.

f) Contributions designated for specific causes and objects shall be promptly forwarded according to the intent of the donor and shall not be used for any other purpose.[11]

---

10. See Judicial Council Decisions 63, 320, 539.
11. See Judicial Council Decision 976.

g) After the budget of the local church has been approved, additional appropriations or changes in the budget must be approved by the church council.

h) The committee shall prepare annually a report to the church council of all designated funds that are separate from the current expense budget.

5. The church council may appoint such other committees as it deems advisable, including: committee on communications, committee on records and history, committee on health and welfare, and committee on memorial gifts.

Section VII. The Method of Organizing a New Church

¶ **259.** 1. A new local church or mission congregation shall be established only with the consent of the bishop in charge and the cabinet and with due consideration of the conference entity assigned the responsibility for congregational development. The bishop shall designate the district within whose bounds the church or mission congregation shall be organized. The district superintendent of that district, or his or her designee, shall be the agent in charge of the project and shall recommend to the district board of church location and building (¶ 2519) the method of organization, and whether a specific site shall be selected or an area of organization be designated. The district superintendent shall avail him/herself of existing demographic, lifestyle and ethnographic information in the process of establishing a new congregation and its location, or shall recommend to the board of trustees of a selected local church that they share their facility with the proposed congregation. If there is a city or district missionary organization, or if funds for the project are anticipated from a conference organization, those bodies shall also be asked to approve the method of organization and location for a new congregation.

a) A mission congregation may be designated when any of the following conditions exist: 1) Membership opportunities and resources are limited and not likely to result in a chartered congregation for an extended period of time. 2) A strategic demographic, cultural, or language opportunity for serving a limited population is present. 3) It is expected that long-term sustaining funding from sources outside the congregation will be necessary to enable the congregation to exist, and the assumption of full connectional support items by the congregation is unlikely.

4) It is probable that the annual conference will need to provide long-term administrative guidance, including attention to the distinctive property needs of the congregation. When any of these conditions exist, the cabinet, in consultation with the congregational development area of the annual conference, may designate an entity a mission congregation. The mission congregation may be organized in the same manner and have the same rights and powers as any local church.

2. The bishop may appoint a pastor to launch a new local church, or with the bishop's approval the district superintendent may authorize a local church or group of local churches to launch a new church by gathering interested people in small groups for Bible study, outreach, community building, and worship at a site in an area approved by the district board of church location and building.

3. A pastor of The United Methodist Church, while serving as the pastor of a new church prior to the convening of a constituting conference (¶ 259.7), may receive a person into the membership of The United Methodist Church under the conditions of ¶ 217. When a person is received as either a baptized or a professing member, the pastor shall send the name, address, and related facts to the annual conference secretary for recording on a general membership roll. These names shall be transferred as soon as possible to the roll of the new church, when constituted, or to another church upon the member's request. If the new church is being sponsored by an existing church, membership may be recorded on the roll of that church.

4. Each annual conference or its equivalent may determine the minimum number of members and other criteria required for the organization of a local United Methodist church.

5. When the number of people interested in being charter members of the new church reaches the number necessary as set by the conference to charter a new church, the district superintendent shall call the interested people to meet at an appointed time for the purpose of organizing them into a chartered (organized) local church, or may by written authorization designate an elder in the district to call such a meeting. The district superintendent or the designated elder shall preside and shall appoint a secretary to keep a record of the meeting. Following a time of worship, opportunity shall be given to those in attendance to present themselves for membership.

6. People desiring to become professing members by transfer or on profession of their faith in Christ shall also be given opportunity to present themselves for membership. Any who have not been baptized shall receive the sacrament of baptism, profess their faith and be received as members. Other baptized people are to be received as baptized members.

7. Those who will be members of the constituting church conference shall be those received into the professing membership.

8. The constituting church conference shall then be called to order by the district superintendent or by an elder whom the superintendent designates (see ¶ 246.5). A committee on nominations, elected on nominations from the floor as the conference may determine, shall nominate members of the proposed church council. The chairperson of the committee on nominations shall be the appointed pastor (see ¶ 258.1c). When the members have been chosen, the district superintendent or the designated elder shall declare the church properly constituted.

9. The district superintendent or an elder whom the superintendent designates shall then adjourn the constituting church conference and call to order the charge conference of the pastoral charge. The membership of the charge conference shall be those newly elected, and any others entitled to membership. The charge conference shall then elect such officers of the church as the *Discipline* requires, including trustees of church property, and shall organize its structure as provided in the *Discipline*. When such officers have been duly elected and such structure put in place, the church is duly organized, and from this point its work shall proceed as described in the *Discipline*, provided that when a newly organized church is attached to a circuit, the charge conference shall not be held until such time as representatives from all the churches of the charge can be properly assembled for that purpose.

10. The charge conference may take action, at its discretion, authorizing and directing the newly elected trustees to incorporate the newly organized church in accordance with local laws and the provisions of the *Discipline*.

Section VIII. Transfer of a Local Church

¶ 260. A local church may be transferred from one annual conference to another in which it is geographically located by a two-thirds vote of the professing members who are present and voting in each of the following: (1) the charge conference, (2) a congregational meeting of the local church, and (3) each of the two annual conferences involved. Upon announcement of the required majorities by the bishop or bishops involved, the transfer shall immediately be effective. The votes required may originate in the local church or either of the annual conferences involved and shall be effective regardless of the order in which taken. In each case a two-thirds vote of those present and voting shall remain effective unless and until rescinded prior to the completion of the transfer by a vote of a majority of those present and voting.

Section IX. Protection of Rights of Congregations

¶ **261.** Nothing in the Plan and Basis of Union at any time after the union is to be construed so as to require any local church of the former Church of the United Brethren in Christ, or of the former The Evangelical Church, or of the former The Evangelical United Brethren Church, or of the former The Methodist Church to alienate or in any way to change the title to property contained in its deed or deeds at the time of union; and lapse of time or usage shall not affect said title or control.

Section X. Special Sundays

¶ **262.** The special Sundays in The United Methodist Church intended to illustrate the nature and calling of the church are celebrated annually. The special Sundays are placed on the calendar to make clear the calling of the church as the people of God and to give persons the opportunity to contribute offerings to special programs.

Six churchwide special Sundays provide for churchwide offerings to express our commitment: Human Relations Day, UMCOR Sunday, World Communion Sunday, United Methodist Student Day, Peace with Justice Sunday, and Native American Ministries Sunday. Five special Sundays are without offering: Heritage Sunday, Laity Sunday, Organ and Tissue Donor Sunday, Men's Ministry Sunday, and Women's Ministry Sunday. Five churchwide Sundays—Christian Education, Golden Cross, Disability Awareness, Rural Life, and Volunteers in Mission Awareness provide opportunities for annual conference offerings.

The special Sundays approved by General Conference shall be the only Sundays of churchwide emphasis. The program calendar of the denomination shall include only the special Sundays approved by General Conference, special Sundays approved by ecumenical agencies to which The United Methodist Church officially relates, and the days and seasons of the Christian Year.

Because the central conferences represent a diversity of history and heritages, they shall not be required to observe all of the special days listed below. The central conferences are authorized to observe other special days appropriate to their unique history and heritages.

GENERAL PROVISIONS REGARDING CHURCHWIDE SPECIAL SUNDAYS WITH OFFERINGS

¶ **263.** Six churchwide special Sundays with offerings shall be celebrated in each United Methodist Church.

Purpose—General Conference shall determine the purpose of the churchwide offerings upon recommendation of the General Council on Finance and Administration, after consultation with the Council of Bishops and the Connectional Table. The purpose of these offerings shall remain constant for the quadrennium, and the net receipts shall be distributed on ratio to the administering agencies by the treasurer of the General Council on Finance and Administration (see ¶ 824.7 and ¶ 805.6). The General Commission on Communication shall promote these offerings in cooperation with the agencies responsible for the administration of these funds. (See ¶ 1806.12.) Each offering shall be promptly remitted in full by the local church treasurer to the annual conference treasurer, who shall transmit the funds in full, except where noted differently below, to the General Council on Finance and Administration within thirty days of receipt in the office of the annual conference treasurer.

1. *Human Relations Day*—Historically, Human Relations Day has been celebrated with an offering on the Sunday before the observance of Martin Luther King Jr.'s birthday. Congregations are to observe Human Relations Day on this date or another date appropriate to the local church. This Sunday occurs during Epiphany, the season of manifesting God's light to the world. Human Relations Day calls the Church to recognize the right of all God's children in realizing their potential as human beings in relationship with each other. The purpose of the day is to further the development of better human relations.

In connection with Human Relations Day the General Commission on Communication shall conduct a churchwide appeal. Net receipts, after payment of promotional expenses, shall be allocated on ratio by the treasurer of the General Council on Finance and Administration, to the administering agencies:

a) *Community Developers Program:* 57 percent (General Board of Global Ministries);

b) *United Methodist Voluntary Services Program:* 33 percent (General Board of Global Ministries) and;

c) *Youth Offender Rehabilitation Program:* 10 percent (General Board of Church and Society).

2. *UMCOR Sunday*—Historically, UMCOR Sunday[12] has been celebrated with an offering on the Fourth Sunday in Lent. Congregations are to observe UMCOR Sunday on this date or on another date appropriate to the local church. Lent is the season of repentance, self-examination, and awareness of the hurts of the peoples of the world. UMCOR Sunday calls the Church to share the goodness of life with those who hurt. In connection with UMCOR Sunday, the General Commission on Communication shall conduct a churchwide appeal. The observance shall be under the general supervision of the United Methodist Committee on Relief, General Board of Global Ministries. Net receipts, after payment of promotional expenses, shall be remitted by the treasurer of the General Council on Finance and Administration to the General Board of Global Ministries.

3. *World Communion Sunday*—Historically, World Communion Sunday has been celebrated with an offering on the first Sunday of October. Congregations are to observe World Communion Sunday on this date or on another date appropriate to the local church. World Communion Sunday calls the church to be the catholic inclusive church. In connection with World Communion Sunday the General Commission on Communication shall conduct a churchwide appeal. The observance shall be under the general supervision of the General Board of Global Ministries and the General Board of Higher Education and Ministry. Each local church shall be requested to remit as provided in ¶ 824.8 all of the communion offering received on World Communion Sunday and such portion of the communion offering received at other observances of the sacrament of the Lord's Supper as the local church may designate.

Net receipts, after payment of promotional expenses, shall be divided on ratio by the treasurer of the General Council on Finance and Administration to the administering agencies:

---

12. One Great Hour of Sharing is now called UMCOR Sunday in The United Methodist Church. See General Conference 2016 Calendar Item 53 (*DCA* page 2101).

a) World Communion Scholarships: 50 percent (General Board of Global Ministries), with at least one half of the annual amount for ministries beyond the United States;

b) Ethnic Scholarship Program: 35 percent (General Board of Higher Education and Ministry); and

c) Ethnic In-Service Training Program: 15 percent (General Board of Higher Education and Ministry).

4. *United Methodist Student Day*—Historically, United Methodist Student Day has been celebrated with an offering on the last Sunday in November. Congregations are to observe United Methodist Student Day on this date or on another date appropriate to the local church. United Methodist Student Day calls the Church to support students as they prepare for life in uniting faith with knowledge. The offering supports United Methodist scholarships and the United Methodist Student Loan Fund. In connection with United Methodist Student Day, the General Commission on Communication shall conduct a churchwide appeal. The observance shall be under the general supervision of the General Board of Higher Education and Ministry. Net receipts, after payment of promotional expenses, shall be remitted by the treasurer of the General Council on Finance and Administration to the administering agency.

5. *Peace with Justice Sunday*—Historically, Peace with Justice Sunday has been celebrated with an offering on the First Sunday After Pentecost. Congregations are to observe Peace with Justice Sunday on this date or on another date appropriate to the local church. Pentecost celebrates the outpouring of the Holy Spirit calling for God's shalom. Peace with Justice witnesses to God's demand for a faithful, just, disarmed, and secure world. In connection with Peace with Justice Sunday, the General Commission on Communication shall conduct a churchwide appeal. The observance shall be under the general supervision of the General Board of Church and Society.

a) The annual conference treasurer shall retain 50 percent of the receipts for Peace with Justice ministries in the annual conference, to be administered by the annual conference board of church and society or an equivalent structure.

b) The annual conference treasurer shall remit the remaining 50 percent of the receipts to the General Council on Finance and Administration. Net receipts, after payment of promotional expenses, shall be distributed by the treasurer of the

General Council on Finance and Administration to the administering agency for Peace with Justice ministries.

6. *Native American Ministries Sunday*—Historically, Native American Ministries Sunday has been celebrated with an offering on the Third Sunday of Easter. United States congregations are to observe Native American Ministries Sunday on this date or on another date appropriate to the local church. This Sunday serves to remind the Church of the gifts and contributions made by Native Americans to our society. In connection with Native American Ministries Sunday, the General Commission on Communication shall conduct a churchwide appeal. The observance shall be under the general supervision of the General Board of Global Ministries and the General Board of Higher Education and Ministry.

a) The annual conference treasurer shall retain 50 percent of the receipts to develop and strengthen Native American ministries within the annual conference, to be administered by the annual conference committee on Native American ministry.

Should there be no Native American ministries within the annual conference, the annual conference treasurer shall remit this 50 percent to the General Council on Finance and Administration.

b) The annual conference treasurer shall report gross receipts and remit the remaining 50 or 100 percent of the receipts as applicable to the General Council on Finance and Administration.

c) Net receipts, after payment of promotional expenses, shall be distributed by the treasurer of the General Council on Finance and Administration to the administering agencies: (1) Scholarships for Native Americans attending United Methodist schools of theology and schools of theology approved by the University Senate of The United Methodist Church: 50 percent (General Board of Higher Education and Ministry). (2) Strengthen, develop and equip Native American rural, urban, and reservation congregations, ministries, and communities: 50 percent (General Board of Global Ministries) : 50 percent (General Board of Global Ministries).

General Provisions Regarding
Special Sundays Without Churchwide Offerings

¶ **264.** Five special Sundays without churchwide offering shall be approved by General Conference upon recommendation of the Connectional Table after consultation with the Council of

Bishops. The program functions assigned to the general agencies are carried out by the respective agencies through normal programmatic channels. Special Sundays are not needed for these program functions to be implemented.

1. *Heritage Sunday*—Heritage Sunday shall be observed on Aldersgate Day (May 24), or the Sunday preceding that date (see Historical Statement, page 12). The day provides an opportunity for reflection on heritage, celebration of where the Church has been, how it understands itself as it shapes us today, and the meaning of Christian conferencing. Heritage Sunday calls the Church to remember the past by committing itself to the continuing call of God. The observance of Heritage Sunday shall be under the general supervision of the General Commission on Archives and History. Any general agency of the Church which desires to recommend a theme for a given year for this Sunday may do so one year prior to the observance for which the recommendation is made. This recommendation is to be made to the General Commission on Archives and History, and the decision of the annual theme of this Sunday shall be made by the voting members of the General Commission on Archives and History.

2. *Laity Sunday*—Laity Sunday shall be observed annually, preferably on the third Sunday in October. Laity Sunday calls the Church to celebrate the ministry of all lay Christians, as their lives are empowered for ministry by the Holy Spirit. The observance of Laity Sunday shall be under the general supervision of the General Board of Discipleship. The Association of Annual Conference Lay Leaders will recommend themes for an entire quadrennium to the General Board of Discipleship two years before the beginning of a new quadrennium.

3. *Organ and Tissue Donor Sunday*—Organ and Tissue Donor Sunday shall be observed annually, preferably on the second Sunday in November since the date is close to Thanksgiving and is viewed as a time to come together around the issues of life and Thanksgiving. Congregations are encouraged to support Organ and Tissue Donor Sunday by including the topic in their worship services. The General Board of Church and Society will have responsibility for the supervision and promotion of the observance of this special Sunday. Worship resource materials are available at all of the not-for-profit donor programs in the United States.

4. *Men's Ministry Sunday*—Men's Ministry Sunday may be observed annually on a Sunday designated by the local congre-

gation. The day is to celebrate the men's ministry within and beyond the local church. This includes: organized (chartered or unchartered) units of United Methodist Men; male Emmaus reunion communities; work teams; prayer groups; Bible studies; study and enrichment groups; and other places and organizations where men of The United Methodist Church join together for fellowship, nurture, spiritual development, witness, and outreach. Resources for this observance shall be provided by the General Commission on United Methodist Men.

5. *Women's Ministry Sunday*—Women's Ministry Sunday may be observed annually on a Sunday designated by the local congregation. The day is designed to celebrate a variety of women's ministries, women's history and the contribution of women within and beyond the local church. This includes, but is not limited to, organized (chartered or unchartered) units of United Methodist Women; women Emmaus communities; work teams; prayer groups; Bible studies; study and enrichment groups; MOPS groups; and other places and organizations where women of The United Methodist Church join together for fellowship, nurture, spiritual development, witness, and outreach. Resources for this observance may be available through a variety of organizations or may be developed through the local church depending on the groups that choose to participate.

¶ **265.** *Approved Sundays for Annual Conference Observance*— Five special Sundays approved by General Conference provide opportunities for annual conference offerings. Local church treasurers shall remit the receipts of the following five offerings to the annual conference treasurer, and receipts will be acknowledged in accordance with the procedure of the annual conference. Local churches shall report the amount of the offering in the manner indicated in the local church report to the annual conference.

1. *Christian Education Sunday*—Christian Education Sunday shall be observed on a date determined by the annual conference. It calls the Church as the people of God to be open to growth and learning as disciples of Jesus Christ. If the annual conference so directs, an offering may be received for Christian education within the annual conference. The observance of Christian Education Sunday shall be under the general supervision of the General Board of Discipleship.

2. *Golden Cross Sunday*—Golden Cross Sunday shall be observed annually on a date determined by the annual confer-

ence. If the annual conference so directs, an offering may be
received for health and welfare ministries in the annual conference. The observance of Golden Cross Sunday shall be under the
general supervision of the General Board of Global Ministries.

3. *Rural Life Sunday*—Rural Life Sunday shall be observed
on a date to be determined by the annual conference. Rural Life
Sunday shall call the Church to celebrate the rural heritage of The
United Methodist Church, to recognize the ongoing crisis occurring in rural areas of the nation and the world today, and to affirm
the interdependence of rural and urban communities. The observance of Rural Life Sunday shall be under the general supervision
of the General Board of Global Ministries. Anyone who desires
to recommend a Rural Life Sunday theme for a given year may
do so one year before the observance for which the recommendation is made. Recommendations are to be made to the General
Board of Global Ministries, and the voting members of the board
shall determine the annual theme of this Sunday. If the annual
conference so directs, an offering may be received to strengthen
the nurture, outreach, and witness of congregations in town and
rural areas.

4. *Disability Awareness Sunday*—Disability Awareness Sunday shall be observed annually on a date to be determined by the
annual conference. Disability Awareness Sunday calls the Church
to celebrate the gifts and graces of persons with disabilities and
calls the Church and society to full inclusion of persons with disabilities in the community. If the annual conference so directs,
an offering may be received and the funds used by the annual
conference to promote the creation of architectural and attitudi-
nal accessibility in local churches. The observance of Disability
Awareness Sunday shall be under the general supervision of the
General Board of Global Ministries.

5. *Volunteers in Mission Awareness Sunday*—Volunteers in
Mission (UMVIM) Awareness Sunday shall be observed annually
on a date to be determined by the annual conference. UMVIM
Awareness Sunday calls the Church to celebrate those who have
served in short-term missions and the work of UMVIM throughout the world. If the annual conference so directs, an offering
may be received and used by the annual conference volunteers in
mission program. The observance of UMVIM Awareness Sunday
shall be under the general supervision of General Board of Global
Ministries Mission Volunteers.

Annual conferences may determine other special Sundays with or without offering. Special Sundays with offering shall be approved by the annual conference upon recommendation of the conference council on ministries in consultation with the conference council on finance and administration. Special Sundays without offering shall be approved by the conference upon recommendation of the conference council on ministries. Local church treasurers shall remit the receipts of all annual conference special Sundays with offering to the conference treasurer, and receipts will be acknowledged in accordance with procedures of the annual conference. Local churches shall report the amount of the offering in the manner indicated in the Local Church Report to the annual conference.

Section XI. Lay Servant Ministries

¶ **266.** *Certified Lay Servant*—1. A certified lay servant is a professing member of a local church or charge, or a baptized participant of a recognized United Methodist collegiate ministry or other United Methodist ministry setting, who desires to serve the Church and who knows and is committed to Scripture and the doctrine, heritage, organization, and life of The United Methodist Church and who has received specific training to witness to the Christian faith through spoken communication, to lead within a church and community, and to provide caring ministry.

2. The certified lay servant serves the local church or charge (or beyond the local church or charge) in ways in which his or her witness, leadership, and service inspires others to a deeper commitment to Christ and more effective discipleship. The certified lay servant, through continued study and training, should prepare to undertake one or more of the following functions, giving primary attention to service within the local church or charge, United Methodist collegiate ministry, or other United Methodist ministry setting:

a) Provide leadership, assistance, and support to the program emphases of the church or other United Methodist ministry.

b) Lead meetings for prayer, training, study, and discussion when requested by the pastor, district superintendent, or committee on Lay Servant Ministries.

c) Conduct, or assist in conducting, services of worship, preach the Word, or give addresses when requested by the pastor, district superintendent, or committee on Lay Servant Ministries.

d) Work with appropriate committees and teams which provide congregational and community leadership or foster caring ministries.

e) Assist in the distribution of the elements of Holy Communion upon request by a pastor.

f) Teach the Scriptures, doctrine, organization, and ministries of The United Methodist Church.

3. One may be recognized as a certified lay servant by the district or conference committee on Lay Servant Ministries after he or she has:

a) Obtained recommendation from the pastor and the church council or charge conference of the local church or other United Methodist ministry in which he or she holds membership.

b) Completed the Lay Servant Ministries BASIC course.

c) Completed a Lay Servant Ministries advanced course.

d) Applied to and had qualifications reviewed by the district committee on Lay Servant Ministries, or equivalent structure (See ¶ 668.3).

4. Recognition as a certified lay servant may be renewed annually by the district committee on Lay Servant Ministries, or equivalent structure, after the certified lay servant has:

a) Submitted an annual report and renewal application to the charge conference or church council and to the district committee on Lay Servant Ministries, or equivalent structure, giving evidence of satisfactory performance as a certified lay servant.

b) Obtained recommendation for renewal from the pastor and the church council or charge conference of the local church or other United Methodist ministry in which he or she holds membership.

c) Completed a Lay Servant Ministries advanced course in the last three years.

5. A certified lay servant may transfer certification to another district or conference upon receipt of a letter from the previous district's committee on Lay Servant Ministries, or equivalent structure, confirming current certification and the completion date of the most recent advanced course taken. Further renewal is in accordance with ¶ 266.4.

6. It is recommended that a service of commitment be held for persons recognized as certified lay servants.

7. Lay Servant Ministries courses shall be those recommended by the General Board of Discipleship or alternative

advanced courses approved by the conference committee on Lay Servant Ministries. Courses should be inclusive of language and cultural groups as relevant to the context. Lay Servant Ministries courses are open to all, whether or not a participant desires recognition as a certified lay servant.

8. A certified lay servant is a volunteer but an honorarium for pulpit supply is appropriate.

¶ **267.** *Certified Lay Speaker*—1. A certified lay speaker is a certified lay servant (or equivalent as defined by his or her central conference) whose call has been affirmed by the conference committee on Lay Servant Ministries or equivalent structure to serve the church in pulpit supply in accordance and compliance with ¶ 341.1.

2. The certified lay speaker serves by preaching the Word when requested by the pastor, district superintendent, or committee on Lay Servant Ministries, in accordance and compliance with ¶ 341.1.

3. One may be certified as a lay speaker after he or she has:

a) Been certified as a lay servant (or equivalent as defined by his or her central conference).

b) Obtained recommendation from the pastor and the church council or charge conference of the local church in which he or she holds membership.

c) Completed a track of study including courses on leading worship, leading prayer, discovering spiritual gifts, preaching, United Methodist heritage and polity, and/or other courses as determined by the conference committee on Lay Servant Ministries or equivalent structure.

d) Interviewed with and obtained recommendation from the district committee on Lay Servant Ministries, or equivalent structure, to be submitted to the conference committee on Lay Servant Ministries, or equivalent structure, for approval and certification.

4. Recognition as a certified lay speaker may be renewed annually by the conference committee on Lay Servant Ministries, or equivalent structure, after the certified lay speaker has:

a) Submitted an annual report and renewal application to the charge conference or church council and to the district committee on Lay Servant Ministries, or equivalent structure, giving evidence of satisfactory performance as a certified lay speaker.

b) Obtained recommendation for continued recognition as a certified lay speaker from the pastor and the church council or charge conference of the local church or other United Methodist ministry in which he or she holds membership.

c) Completed a Lay Servant Ministries advanced course in the last three years.

d) In the last three years, interviewed with and obtained recommendation for renewal as a certified lay speaker from the district committee on Lay Servant Ministries, or equivalent structure, and the approval of the conference committee on Lay Servant Ministries, or equivalent structure for recertification.

5. A certified lay speaker may transfer certification to another district or conference upon receipt of a letter from the previous district's committee on Lay Servant Ministries, or equivalent structure, confirming current certification and the completion date of the most recent advanced course taken. Further renewal is in accordance with ¶ 267.4.

6. A certified lay speaker is a volunteer but an honorarium is appropriate.

¶ **268.** *Certified Lay Minister*—1. A certified lay minister is a certified lay servant, certified lay missioner, or equivalent as defined by his or her central conference, who is called and equipped to conduct public worship, care for the congregation, assist in program leadership, develop new and existing faith communities, preach the Word, lead small groups, or establish community outreach ministries as part of a ministry team with the supervision and support of a clergyperson. A certified lay minister is assigned by a district superintendent in accordance with ¶ 419.2.

2. The certified lay minister serves to enhance the quality of ministry much like a class leader did in early Methodism through service in the local church, circuit or cooperative parish, or by expanding team ministry in other churches and charges. As with lay ministry in early Methodism, the certified lay minister uses his or her spiritual gifts as evidence of God's grace.

3. One may be recognized by the conference committee on lay servant ministries, or equivalent structure, as a certified lay minister after he or she has:

a) been certified as a lay servant, lay missioner, or equivalent as defined by his or her central conference;

b) obtained written recommendation from the pastor

and the church council or charge conference of the local church in which he or she holds membership;

c) completed a track of study for certified lay ministers relevant to the candidate's assignment as defined by the General Board of Discipleship, or the National Plan for Hispanic/Latino Ministry in collaboration with the General Board of Discipleship, and the conference committee on Lay Servant Ministries or equivalent structure;

d) received a letter of recommendation from his or her district superintendent;

e) had all requirements for certification, including appropriate screening and assessment as defined by the annual conference, reviewed by the conference committee on Lay Servant Ministries, or equivalent structure, for referral to the district committee on ordained ministry for examination of persons who have applied in writing to be certified lay ministers and to make recommendation for certification (see ¶ 666.10). After the district committee on ordained ministry interviews the candidate, the district committee on ordained ministry will make a recommendation to the conference committee on Lay Servant Ministries for final certification by that committee.

4. Recognition as a certified lay minister may be renewed every two years by the conference committee on Lay Servant Ministries, or equivalent structure, after the certified lay minister has:

a) submitted an annual report to the charge conference or church council where membership is held and to the conference committee on Lay Servant Ministries, or equivalent structure, giving evidence of satisfactory performance as a certified lay minister;

b) obtained a ministry review by the committee on pastor-parish relations, church council, or charge conference from the congregation of which he or she is a member, or when under assignment, from the committee on pastor-parish relations, charge conference, or supervisory board of the ministry setting in which he or she is assigned;

c) completed a Lay Servant Ministries advanced course or approved continuing education event, as defined by the conference committee on Lay Servant Ministries or equivalent structure in the last two years;

d) obtained recommendation for recertification from the district superintendent;

e) had all requirements for recertification reviewed by the conference committee on Lay Servant Ministries, or equivalent structure, for referral to the district committee on ordained ministry for examination of persons who have applied in writing to be renewed as certified lay ministers and to make recommendations for recertification (see ¶ 666.10). After the district committee on ordained ministry interviews the certified lay minister, the district committee on ordained ministry will make a recommendation to the conference committee on Lay Servant Ministries for final recertification by that committee.

5. A certified lay minister may transfer certification to another district or conference upon receipt of a letter from the previous conference committee on Lay Servant Ministries, or equivalent structure, confirming current certification and the completion date of the most recent advanced course taken. Further renewal is in accordance with ¶ 268.4.

6. A certified lay minister is not eligible for support by equitable compensation funds or pension funds that are provided for clergy. If a certified lay minister is a lay staff member of a church, circuit or cooperative parish, the local congregation is encouraged to provide compensation and withhold taxes appropriate to a layperson.

¶ **269.** *Lay Missioner*—Lay missioners are committed laypersons, mostly volunteers, who are willing to be trained and to work together as a ministry team with their pastor-mentor, in order to develop and lead faith communities, establish community ministries, develop church school extension programs, and engage in congregational development with and into the local community. Lay missioners are formed according to, and follow the guidelines established by, the National Committee of the National Plan for Hispanic/Latino Ministry, working in conjunction with the annual conference. They are certified jointly by their annual conference and the National Plan for Hispanic/Latino Ministry. The ministry team is supported by and accountable to the local congregation, district or annual conference entity that assigns it to its mission. The concept of the lay missioner is based theologically on the ministry of the laity, in order to complement the work of the pastor.[13]

---

13. See Judicial Council Decision 693.

A certified lay missioner shall be equivalent to a certified lay servant in the processes of certification as a lay minister (¶ 268.3-6); and the Module I-Module II formational sequence and Module IIIs for continuing education of the National Plan for Hispanic/Latino Ministry shall be equivalent to the track of study for certified lay ministers relevant to the candidate's assignment, and the advanced course or approved continuing education events described therein.

Chapter Two

THE MINISTRY OF THE ORDAINED

Section I. The Meaning of Ordination and Conference Membership

¶ 301. 1. Ministry in the Christian church is derived from the ministry of Christ, who calls all persons to receive God's gift of salvation and follow in the way of love and service. All Christian ministry is grounded in the covenant of baptism by which we are initiated into the body of Christ and called into a life of discipleship. The sacraments of baptism and Holy Communion ground the ministry of the whole church. They are celebrated in the Christian community as means of grace. Thus, the whole church receives and accepts this call, and all Christians participate in this continuing ministry (see ¶¶ 120-140).

2. Within the church community, there are persons whose gifts, evidence of God's grace, and promise of future usefulness are affirmed by the community, and who respond to God's call by offering themselves in leadership as set-apart ministers, ordained and licensed (¶ 302). Individuals discern God's call as they relate with God and their communities, and the Church guides and confirms those callings. Calls—and the discernment and confirmation of them—are gifts of the Holy Spirit.

¶ 302. *Ordination and Apostolic Ministry*—The pattern for this response to the call is provided in the development of the early church. The apostles led in prayer, teaching and preaching, ordered the spiritual and temporal life of the community, established leadership for the ministry of service, and provided for the proclamation of the gospel to new persons and in new places. The early church, through the laying on of hands, set apart persons with responsibility to preach, to teach, to administer the sacraments, to nurture, to heal, to gather the community in worship, and to send them forth in witness. The church also set apart other persons to care for the physical needs of others, reflecting the concerns for the people of the world. In the New Testament (Acts 6), we see the apostles identifying and authorizing persons to a ministry of service. These functions, though set apart, were never separate from the ministry of the whole people of God. Paul states (Ephesians 4:1-12) that different gifts and ministries are given to all persons. The Wesleyan tradition has, from the beginning, encouraged a culture of call and a community of discernment, which affirms and supports the ministry of all Christians and identifies and authorizes persons into ministries of the ordained.

¶ **303.** *Purpose of Ordination*—1. Ordination to this ministry is a gift from God to the church. In ordination, the church affirms and continues the apostolic ministry through persons empowered by the Holy Spirit. As such, those who are ordained make a commitment to conscious living of the whole gospel and to the proclamation of that gospel to the end that the world may be saved.

2. Ordination is fulfilled in leadership of the people of God through ministries of Service, Word, Sacrament, Order, Compassion, and Justice. The Church's ministry of service is a primary representation of God's love. Those who respond to God's call to lead in service, word, compassion, and justice and equip others for this ministry through teaching, proclamation, and worship and who assist elders in the administration of the sacraments are ordained as deacons. Those whose leadership in service includes preaching and teaching the Word of God, administration of the sacraments, ordering the Church for its mission and service, and administration of the discipline of the Church are ordained as elders.

3. Ordained persons exercise their ministry in covenant with all Christians, especially with those whom they lead and serve in ministry. They also live in covenant of mutual care and accountability with all those who share their ordination, especially in The United Methodist Church, with the ordained who are members of the same annual conference and part of the same Order. The covenant of ordained ministry is a lifetime commitment, and those who enter into it dedicate their whole lives to the personal and spiritual disciplines it requires.

4. The effectiveness of the Church in mission depends on these covenantal commitments to the ministry of all Christians and the ordained ministry of the Church. Through ordination and through other offices of pastoral leadership, the Church provides for the continuation of Christ's ministry, which has been committed to the church as a whole. Without creative use of the diverse gifts of the entire body of Christ, the ministry of the church is less effective. Without responsible leadership, the focus, direction, and continuity of that ministry is diminished. It is out of the faith and witness of the congregation that men and women respond to God's call to ordained ministry. Every local church should intentionally nurture candidates for ordained ministry and provide

spiritual and financial support for their education as servant leaders for the ministry of the whole people of God.

5. In keeping with ancient Christian teaching and our Wesleyan tradition, we affirm that ordination for the same, or equivalent order, is not repeatable.

¶ **304.** *Qualifications for Ordination*—1. Those whom the Church ordains shall be conscious of God's call to ordained ministry, and their call shall be acknowledged and authenticated by the Church. God's call has many manifestations, and the Church cannot structure a single test of authenticity. Nevertheless, the experience of the Church and the needs of its ministry require certain qualities of faith, life, and practice from those who seek ordination as deacons and elders. In order that The United Methodist Church may be assured that those persons who present themselves as candidates for ordained ministry are truly called of God, the Church expects persons seeking ordination to:

a) Have a personal faith in Christ and be committed to Christ as Savior and Lord.

b) Nurture and cultivate spiritual disciplines and patterns of holiness.

c) Teach and model generous Christian giving with a focus on tithing as God's standard of giving

d) Acknowledge a call by God to give themselves completely to ordained ministry following Jesus' pattern of love and service.

e) Communicate persuasively the Christian faith in both oral and written form.

f) Make a commitment to lead the whole Church in loving service to humankind.

g) Give evidence of God's gifts for ordained ministry, evidence of God's grace in their lives, and promise of future usefulness in the mission of the Church.

h) Be persons in whom the community can place trust and confidence.

i) Accept that Scripture contains all things necessary for salvation through faith in God through Jesus Christ; be competent in the disciplines of Scripture, theology, church history, and Church polity; possess the skills essential to the practice of ordained ministry; and lead in making disciples for Jesus Christ.

j) Be accountable to The United Methodist Church, accept its Doctrinal Standards and *Discipline* and authority, accept the supervision of those appointed to this ministry, and be prepared to live in the covenant of its ordained ministers.

2. For the sake of the mission of Jesus Christ in the world and the most effective witness to the Christian gospel, and in consideration of the influence of an ordained minister on the lives of other persons both within and outside the Church, the Church expects those who seek ordination to make a complete dedication of themselves to the highest ideals of the Christian life. To this end, they agree to exercise responsible self-control by personal habits conducive to bodily health, mental and emotional maturity, integrity in all personal relationships, fidelity in marriage and celibacy in singleness, social responsibility, and growth in grace and in the knowledge and love of God.

3. While persons set apart by the Church for ordained ministry are subject to all the frailties of the human condition and the pressures of society, they are required to maintain the highest standards of holy living in the world. The practice of homosexuality is incompatible with Christian teaching. Therefore self-avowed practicing homosexuals[1] are not to be certified as candidates, ordained as ministers, or appointed to serve in The United Methodist Church.[2]

4. The United Methodist Church entrusts those persons who are in the ordained ministry with primary responsibility for maintaining standards of education and preparation for ordination. Having been originally recommended by a charge conference or equivalent body (¶ 310.1e) and by authorization of the ordained members in full connection with the annual conference, according to the procedures set out in the *Book of Discipline* for the examination and approval of candidates for ordination, persons are elected to membership in the annual conference and ordained by the bishop.

5. In all votes regarding license, ordination, or conference membership, the requirements set forth herein are minimum requirements. Each person voting is expected to vote prayerfully based on personal judgment of the applicant's gifts, evidence of God's grace, and promise of future usefulness for the mission of the Church.

---

1. *"Self-avowed practicing homosexual"* is understood to mean that a person openly acknowledges to a bishop, district superintendent, district committee of ordained ministry, Board of Ordained Ministry, or clergy session that the person is a practicing homosexual. See Judicial Council Decisions 702, 708, 722, 725, 764, 844, 984, 1020.

2. See Judicial Council Decisions 984, 985, 1027, 1028

Section II. Clergy Orders in The United Methodist Church

¶ **305.** *Orders in Relation to the Ministry of All Christians*—Baptism is God's gift of unmerited grace through the Holy Spirit. It is an incorporation into Christ which marks the entrance of each person into the church and its ministry (Romans 6:3, 4, 18).

The New Testament witness to Jesus Christ makes clear that the primary form of his ministry in God's name is that of service, *diakonia,* in the world. Very early in its history, the church came to understand that all of its members were commissioned in baptism to ministries of love, justice, and service within local congregations and the larger communities in which they lived; all who follow Jesus have a share in the ministry of Jesus, who came not to be served, but to serve. There is thus a general ministry of all baptized Christians (see ¶¶ 126-137).

Within the people of God, some persons are called to the ministry of deacon. The words deacon, deaconess, and diaconate all spring from a common Greek root—*diakonos,* or "servant," and *diakonia,* or "service." Very early in its history the church, as an act of worship and praise of God, instituted an order of ordained ministers to personify or focus the servanthood to which all Christians are called. These people were named *deacons.* This ministry exemplifies and leads the Church in the servanthood every Christian is called to live both in the church and the world. Those called to the ministry of deacon are called to witness to the Word in their words and actions, and to embody and lead the community's service in the world for the sake of enacting God's compassion and justice.

Within the people of God, other persons are called to the ministry of elder. The elders carry on the historic work of the *presbyteros* in the life of the Church. Beginning in some of the very early Christian communities, the *presbyteros* assisted the bishop in leading the gathered community in the celebration of sacraments and the guidance and care of its communal life. Those called to the ministry of elder are called to bear authority and responsibility to preach and teach the Word, to administer the sacraments, and to order the life of the church so it can be faithful in making disciples of Jesus Christ for the transformation of the world.

¶ **306.** *Order of Deacons and Order of Elders*—There shall be in each annual conference an Order of Deacons and an Order of Elders. All persons ordained as clergy in The United Methodist Church upon election to full membership in the annual conference shall be members of and participate in an order appropriate to their election. An order is a covenant community within the church to mutually support, care for, and hold accountable its members for the sake of the life and mission of the church. These orders, separately or together, seek to respond to the spiritual hunger among clergy for a fulfilling sense of vocation, for support among peers during this stressful time of change in the Church, and for a deepening relationship with God.

¶ **307.** *Purpose of an Order*—The specific and limited function of each order is to: (1) provide for regular gatherings of ordained deacons and ordained elders for continuing formation in relationship to Jesus Christ through such experiences as Bible study, study of issues facing the church and society, and theological exploration in vocational identity and leadership; (2) assist in plans for individual study and retreat experiences; (3) develop a bond of unity and common commitment to the mission and ministry of The United Methodist Church and the annual conference; (4) enable the creation of relationships that allow mutual support and trust; and (5) hold accountable all members of the order in the fulfilling of these purposes. All of the functions of the order(s) shall be fulfilled in cooperation and coordination with the Board of Ordained Ministry and do not replace the normal supervisory processes, the processes of evaluation for ordained ministers, or the responsibilities of the Board of Ordained Ministry, the cabinet, or the clergy session.

¶ **308.** *Organization of an Order*—The bishop shall convene and provide continuing spiritual leadership for the order, with the support and assistance of the Board of Ordained Ministry. Necessary financial support shall be provided by the annual conference through the budget of the board. The board may also use other appropriate funding sources for this purpose. The board shall nominate from within the order's membership and the order shall elect quadrennially a chairperson of the order who, in cooperation with and under the guidance of the bishop, will provide continuing leadership for the order. The chairperson will be responsible for implementation of plans and activities of the order and will represent the order to the conference Board of Ordained Ministry. The chairperson will serve as a member of the board's executive committee. Activities of the order and proposals for funding shall be regularly reported to the board.

¶ **309.** *Membership in an Order*—1. Persons shall become members of the Order of Deacons or Order of Elders following their election to full membership in the annual conference. Acceptance of the status of full membership will constitute a commitment to regular participation in the life of the order.

2. *Changing Orders*—Upon recommendation of the Board of Ordained Ministry and vote of the clergy members in full connection in an annual conference, elders may be received as deacons in full connection, and deacons in full connection may be received as elders, provided they are in good standing and have:

    a) informed the bishop and district superintendent of their intention,

    b) applied in writing to the Board of Ordained Ministry,

    c) articulated to the Board of Ordained Ministry their call to the ministry of the deacon or the elder,

    d) completed all academic and other requirements for admission to the order for which they are applying, ¶ 324, ¶ 330, ¶ 335, and

    e) completed at least two years, and no more than eight years, under appointment while licensed for the ministry of the order to which they are transitioning.

3. Such persons shall retain their credentials and full membership in the annual conference through the transition period from one order to the other. When ordained to the order to which they are transitioning, they shall surrender to the conference secretary the credentials of the order from which they are leaving.

Section III. Candidacy for Licensed and Ordained Ministry

¶ 310. *Candidacy and Certification for Licensed and Ordained Ministry*—The licensed or ordained ministry is recognized by The United Methodist Church as a called-out and set-apart ministry. Therefore, it is appropriate that those persons who present themselves as candidates for licensed or ordained ministry be examined regarding the authenticity of their call by God to set-apart ministry.

Persons, upon hearing and heeding the call to servant leadership through licensed or ordained ministry, shall contact a clergyperson in their local church, another clergy, or the district superintendent of the district in which they participate in a United Methodist ministry setting to inquire about the process of candidacy. Persons are encouraged to use resources recommended by the General Board of Higher Education and Ministry, such as *The Christian as Minister* and the *Ministry Inquiry Process*.

1. Those beginning candidacy for licensed or ordained ministry:

a) shall be a professing member in good standing of The United Methodist Church or a baptized participant of a recognized United Methodist campus ministry or other United Methodist ministry setting for a minimum of one (1) year;

b) shall write to the district superintendent requesting admission to the candidacy process and the assignment of a candidacy mentor. Include a statement of call. Request registration through the district superintendent with the General Board of Higher Education and Ministry;

c) after registration by the district superintendent with the General Board of Higher Education and Ministry, mentor and candidate will study the resources adopted by the conference Board of Ordained Ministry;

d) shall write their statement of call. The candidate will consult with the pastor or equivalent in a ministry setting specified by the district committee on ordained ministry to request a meeting of the pastor-parish relations committee or equivalent body specified by the district committee on ordained ministry to consider the statement of call and to be interviewed in light of Wesley's historic questions;

(1) Do they know God as pardoning God? Have they the love of God abiding in them? Do they desire nothing but God? Are they holy in all manner of conversation?

(2) Have they gifts, as well as evidence of God's grace, for the work? Have they a clear, sound understanding; a right judgment in the things of God; a just conception of salvation by faith? Do they speak justly, readily, clearly?

(3) Have they fruit? Have any been truly convinced of sin and converted to God, and are believers edified by their service?

As long as these marks occur in them, we believe they are called of God to serve. These we receive as sufficient proof that they are moved by the Holy Spirit.

e) after approval of the candidate by the pastor-parish relations committee or equivalent body specified by the district committee on ordained ministry, shall meet with a charge conference or body specified by the district committee on ordained ministry called to recommend the candidate to the district committee on ordained ministry. Approval of the candidate must be by two-thirds written ballot, and the candidate shall have been graduated from an accredited high school or received a certificate of equivalency.

2. Candidates seeking to become certified for licensed or ordained ministry shall:

a) request to meet with the district committee on ordained ministry. In preparation for meeting with the district committee on ordained ministry, consult with the mentor to provide the following written information, in addition to the material written for ¶ 310.1*d*: (i) the most formative experience of their Christian life; (ii) God's call to licensed or ordained ministry and role of the church in their call; (iii) their beliefs as a Christian; (iv) their gifts for ministry; (v) their present understanding of their call to ministry as elder, deacon, or licensed ministry; and (vi) their support system;

b) complete and release required psychological reports, criminal background and credit checks. They shall submit, on a form provided by the conference Board of Ordained Ministry:

(1) a notarized statement detailing any convictions for felony or misdemeanor or written accusations of sexual misconduct or child abuse; or

(2) a notarized statement certifying that this candidate has neither been accused in writing nor convicted of a felony, misdemeanor, any incident of sexual misconduct, or child abuse.

The district committee on ordained ministry through the Board of Ordained Ministry shall seek ways to consider cultural and ethnic/racial realities and language translations as candidates meet these requirements, including interviews, psychological assessments, criminal background, and credit checks.

c) provide other information as the district committee may require for determining gifts, evidence of God's grace, fruit, and demonstration of the call to licensed or ordained ministry;

d) agree for the sake of the mission of Jesus Christ in the world and the most effective witness of the gospel, and in consideration of their influence as clergy, to make a complete dedication of themselves to the highest ideals of the Christian life as set forth in ¶¶ 103-105; 160-166. To this end they shall agree to exercise responsible self-control by personal habits conducive to bodily health, mental and emotional maturity, fidelity in marriage and celibacy in singleness, social responsibility, and growth in grace and the knowledge and love of God.[3] The local church is encouraged to assist candidates with the expenses of candidacy;

    e) be voted on by individual written ballot by the committee members present. A three-fourths majority vote of the committee members present is required for certification (¶ 666.6); and

    f) upon vote of certification, be encouraged by the district committee on ordained ministry to attend a United Methodist seminary.

    3. In special circumstances, the district committee on ordained ministry may authorize other United Methodist ministry settings to serve in the role of the local church for the purpose of recommending candidacy and specify the persons or bodies that will serve in the roles of pastor, pastor parish-relations committee, and charge conference.

---

3. In adopting the statements in ¶¶ 304.2 and 310.2d on the moral and social responsibility of ordained ministers, the General Conference seeks to elevate the standards by calling for a more thoroughgoing moral commitment by the candidate and for a more careful and thorough examination of candidates by district committees and boards of the ministry. The legislation in no way implies that the use of tobacco is a morally indifferent question. In the light of the developing evidence against the use of tobacco, the burden of proof would be upon all users to show that their use of it is consistent with the highest ideals of the Christian life. Similarly, regarding beverage alcohol, the burden of proof would be upon users to show that their action is consistent with the ideals of excellence of mind, purity of body, and responsible social behavior.

Therefore, the changes here do not relax the traditional view concerning the use of tobacco and beverage alcohol by ordained ministers in The United Methodist Church. Rather they call for higher standards of self-discipline and habit formation in all personal and social relationships. They call for dimensions of moral commitment that go far beyond any specific practices which might be listed. (See Judicial Council Decision 318.)

The General Conference, in response to expressions throughout the Church regarding homosexuality and ordination, reaffirms the present language of the *Discipline* regarding the character and commitment of persons seeking ordination and affirms its high standards.

For more than 200 years candidates for ordination have been asked Wesley's Questions, including " . . . Have they a clear, sound understanding; a right judgment in the things of God; a just conception of salvation by faith? . . ." (¶ 310). All candidates agree to make a complete dedication of themselves to the highest ideals of the Christian life and to this end agree "to exercise responsible self-control, by personal habits conducive to bodily health, mental and emotional maturity, integrity in all personal relationships, fidelity in marriage and celibacy in singleness, social responsibility, and growth in grace and the knowledge and love of God" (¶ 304.2).

The character and commitment of candidates for the ordained ministry is described or examined in six places in the *Book of Discipline* (¶¶ 304, 310.2, 324, 330, 333, and 335). These say in part: "Only those shall be elected to full membership who are of unquestionable moral character and genuine piety, sound in the fundamental doctrines of Christianity, and faithful in the discharge of their duties" (¶ 333).

¶ **311.** *Appointment of Certified Candidates*—A certified candidate is eligible for appointment as a local pastor upon completion of License for Pastoral Ministry (¶ 315). Those appointed as local pastors are clergy members of the annual conference (¶ 602.1) and are no longer listed as certified candidates. They do not continue with candidacy mentors but are assigned a clergy mentor (¶ 348.4).

¶ **312.** *Orientation to Ministry*—An orientation to ministry is required for all candidates for licensed and ordained ministry. Attendance at the orientation and becoming a certified candidate may be sequential or concurrent. This common ministry preparation experience is for the purpose of building collegiality and understanding among the varieties of set-apart ministry (deacons, elders, local pastors).

The statement on ordination (¶ 304.2) states: *"The Church expects those who seek ordination to make a complete dedication of themselves to the highest ideals of the Christian life . . . [and to] agree to exercise responsible self-control by personal habits. . . ."*

There are eight crucial steps in the examination of candidates. They are:

(1) The self-examination of the individual seeking ordination as he or she responds to God's call in personal commitment to Christ and his church.

(2) The decision of the committee on pastor-parish relations, which makes the first recommendation to the charge conference when a member seeks to become a candidate for ordained ministry.

(3) The decision of the charge conference, which must recommend the candidate.

(4) The decision of the district committee on ordained ministry, which must recommend the candidate to the conference Board of Ordained Ministry and, where applicable, the decision of the district conference.

(5) The decision of the Board of Ordained Ministry, which must recommend deacon's ordination and provisional membership. See Judicial Council Decisions 513, 536, 542.

(6) The decision of the clergy members of the annual conference, who must elect candidates to provisional membership.

(7) The recommendation of the Board of Ordained Ministry for deacon's or elder's ordination and full membership.

(8) The election to deacon's or elder's ordination and full membership by the clergy members of the annual conference.

All clergy members of the annual conference are accountable as to character and effectiveness to the annual conference throughout their entire ministry.

The General Conference has made it clear in the "Doctrinal Standards and Our Theological Task" (Part III of the *Discipline*) that Scripture, tradition, experience, and reason are our guidelines. "United Methodists share with other Christians the conviction that Scripture is the primary source and criterion for Christian doctrine."

In the Social Principles, the General Conference has said that we "do not condone the practice of homosexuality and consider this practice incompatible with Christian teaching." Furthermore, the Principles state that "we affirm the sanctity of the marriage covenant that is expressed in love, mutual support, personal commitment, and shared fidelity between a man and a woman. We believe that God's blessing rests upon such marriage, whether or not there are children of the union.

1. The orientation shall be held in each annual conference and is the responsibility of the conference Board of Ordained Ministry.

2. Collegiality in ministry and commonalities and distinctions among the categories of ministry (deacon, elder, local pastor) will be emphasized to facilitate understanding and appreciation of the gifts contributed through team ministry, and the practice of set-apart ministry within the United Methodist connection will be articulated.

3. Guidelines will be made available from the General Board of Higher Education and Ministry, Division of Ordained Ministry.

¶ 313. *Continuation of Candidacy*—The progress of candidates shall be reviewed annually by the district committee on ordained ministry which shall interview the candidate annually and may then continue the candidacy when the following conditions have been met satisfactorily:[4]

1. The candidate has received the annual recommendation of his or her charge conference or equivalent body as specified by the district committee on ordained ministry (see ¶ 310.3).

2. The candidate is making satisfactory progress in his or her studies. A candidate preparing for ordained ministry who is enrolled as a student in a school, college, university, or school of theology recognized by the University Senate shall present annually to the district committee on ordained ministry an official transcript from the school the person is attending and provide a report as to whether his or her local church is supporting him or her spiritually and financially (see ¶ 247.8).

The transcript shall be considered by the district committee on ordained ministry as part of the evidence of his or her progress. The report of local church financial support may be used by the district superintendent to express gratitude for this support or

---

We reject social norms that assume different standards for women than for men in marriage." Also, "we affirm the integrity of single persons, and we reject all social practices that discriminate or social attitudes that are prejudicial against persons because they are single."

The General Conference affirms the wisdom of our heritage expressed in the disciplinary provisions relating to the character and commitment of ordained ministers. The United Methodist Church has moved away from prohibitions of specific acts, for such prohibitions can be endless. We affirm our trust in the covenant community and the process by which we ordain ministers.

In our covenant we are called to trust one another as we recommend, examine, and elect candidates for the ordained ministry and conference membership. *See* Judicial Council Decision 480.

4. See Judicial Council Decision 1263.

encourage a local congregation to improve its basic care for those it recommends.

3. The candidate continues to evidence gifts, fruits and God's grace for the work of ministry.

4. A person who is a certified candidate or who is in the candidacy process may have her or his status or studies accepted by another district committee in the same or another annual conference.

5. A certified candidate may be continued as a candidate for no more than twelve years following certification (¶ 324.1).

¶ **314.** *Discontinuance and Reinstatement of Certified Candidates—*1. *Discontinuance of a Certified Candidate—*Certified candidates may be discontinued on their own request, upon severing their relationship with The United Methodist Church, or upon action to discontinue by the district committee on ordained ministry. The district committee on ordained ministry shall file with the conference Board of Ordained Ministry a permanent record of the circumstances relating to the discontinuance of the certified candidate.

2. *Reinstatement of Certified Candidate's Status—*Certified candidates whose status has been discontinued by a district committee on ordained ministry of an annual conference of The United Methodist Church shall only be reinstated by the district committee of the district in which they were discontinued. When approved by the district committee on ordained ministry, their certified candidate's credentials shall be reissued and they shall be eligible to continue the process.

Section IV. License for Pastoral Ministry

¶ **315.** *License for Pastoral Ministry—*All persons not ordained as elders who are appointed to preach and conduct divine worship and perform the duties of a pastor shall have a license for pastoral ministry. The Board of Ordained Ministry (¶ 635.2*h*) may recommend to the clergy session of the annual conference the licensing of those persons who are:

1. Provisional elders commissioned by the annual conference, or

2. Local pastors who have completed the following:

    a) The conditions for candidacy certification in ¶¶ 310.1-2;

    b) The Orientation to Ministry;

c) The studies for the license as a local pastor as prescribed and supervised by the Division of Ordained Ministry or one-third of their work for a Master of Divinity degree at a school of theology listed by the University Senate;

d) Been examined and recommended by a three-fourths majority vote of the district committee on ordained ministry (¶ 666.9); or

3. Associate members of the annual conference

4. Deacons in full connection, seeking to qualify for ordination as an elder; or

5. Licensed or ordained clergy from other denominations who have training equivalent to the studies for license as a local pastor prescribed by the Division of Ordained Ministry, but do not meet the educational requirements for provisional membership in the annual conference.

6. In every case, those who are licensed shall have:

a) Released the required psychological reports, criminal background and credit checks, and reports of sexual misconduct and/or child abuse. They shall submit, on a form provided by the conference Board of Ordained Ministry:

(1) a notarized statement detailing any convictions for felony or misdemeanor or written accusations of sexual misconduct or child abuse; or

(2) a notarized statement certifying that the candidate has not been convicted of a felony or misdemeanor, or accused in writing of sexual misconduct or child abuse.

b) Been approved by a three-fourths majority vote of the Board of Ordained Ministry (¶ 635.2*h*);

c) Provided the board with a satisfactory certificate of good health on a prescribed form from a physician approved by that board.

d) Received approval by a three-fourths majority vote of the clergy session.

¶ **316.** *Responsibilities and Duties of Those Licensed for Pastoral Ministry*—1. Provisional elders approved annually by the Board of Ordained Ministry and local pastors approved annually by the district committee on ordained ministry may be licensed by the bishop to perform all the duties of a pastor (¶ 340), including the sacraments of baptism and Holy Communion as well as the service of marriage (where state laws allow),[5] burial, confirmation,

---

5. See Judicial Council Decision 694.

and membership reception, within and while appointed to a particular charge or extension ministry. For the purposes of these paragraphs the charge or extension ministry will be defined as "people within or related to the community or ministry setting being served." Those licensed for pastoral ministry may be appointed to extension ministry settings when approved by the bishop and the Board of Ordained Ministry.

2. Such authorization granted by the license may be renewed annually by the district committee or the Board of Ordained Ministry.

3. The license shall remain valid only so long as the appointment continues and shall be recertified by the bishop when assignments change between sessions of the annual conference.[6]

4. A local pastor shall be under the supervision of a district superintendent and shall be assigned a clergy mentor while in the Course of Study or in seminary (¶ 348).

5. Local pastors shall be amenable to the clergy session of the annual conference in the performance of their pastoral duties and shall attend the sessions of the annual conference.

6. The membership of local pastors under full-time and part-time appointment is in the annual conference where they shall have the right to vote on all matters except constitutional amendments, election of delegates to General, jurisdictional, or central conferences, and matters of ordination, character, and conference relations of clergy. Local pastors who have completed Course of Study or a Master of Divinity degree and have served a minimum of two consecutive years under appointment before the election may vote to elect clergy delegates to General and jurisdictional or central conferences.[7]

7. All local pastors shall receive written communication about decisions made regarding their relationship with the annual conference

8. Local pastors who have completed the Course of Study may upon retirement annually request from the District Committee of Ordained Ministry and the bishop a license to continue to serve in the local church where they hold membership for the purpose of providing sacramental rites of baptism and Holy Communion, at the request of the appointed pastor.

---

6. See Judicial Council Decision 112.
7. See Judicial Council Decision 1181 and ¶ 35.

¶ **317.** *Interim License as Local Pastor*—Between sessions of the annual conference, persons who have completed the conditions for licensing listed above may be granted interim license as a local pastor upon recommendation of the cabinet, the district committee on ordained ministry, and executive committee of the conference Board of Ordained Ministry, and may be appointed by the bishop.

¶ **318.** *Categories of Local Pastor*—Upon satisfactory completion of the requirements of ¶ 315, the district committee on ordained ministry shall certify the completion of the prescribed studies to the candidates and the Board of Ordained Ministry, and they shall be listed in the journal as eligible to be appointed as local pastors. Award of the license shall not be made until an appointment to a pastoral charge is made in accordance with ¶ 337. In recommending to the annual conference those who have met the requirements to serve as local pastors for the ensuing year, the Board of Ordained Ministry shall classify them in three categories with educational and other requirements of their category. Any person who fails to meet these requirements shall be discontinued as a local pastor. The categories shall be defined as follows:

1. *Full-Time Local Pastors*—Those eligible to be appointed full-time local pastors are persons *(a)* who may devote their entire time to the church in the charge to which they are appointed and its outreach in ministry and mission to the community; *(b)* who receive in cash support per annum from all Church sources a sum equal to or larger than the minimum base compensation established by the annual conference for full-time local pastors; *(c)* who, unless they have completed the Course of Study or other approved theological education, shall (i) complete four courses per year in a Course of Study school, or (ii) shall have made progress in the correspondence curriculum prescribed by the General Board of Higher Education and Ministry (¶ 1421.3*d*), or (iii) be enrolled as a pre-theological or theological student in a college, university, or school of theology approved by the University Senate; *(d)* who, when they have completed the Course of Study or a Master of Divinity degree from a seminary listed by the University Senate, are involved in continuing education (¶ 350); *(e)* who shall not be enrolled as a full-time student in any school.

2. *Part-Time Local Pastors*—Those eligible to be appointed as part-time local pastors are persons *(a)* who have met the provi-

sions of ¶ 315; *(b)* who do not devote their entire time to the charge to which they are appointed; or *(c)* do not receive in cash support per annum from all Church sources a sum equal to or larger than the minimum base compensation established by the annual conference for full-time local pastors; and *(d)* who, unless they have completed the Course of Study or other approved theological education, shall (i) complete two courses per year in a Course of Study school, or (ii) have made progress in the correspondence curriculum prescribed by the General Board of Higher Education and Ministry, or (iii) be enrolled as a pre-theological or theological student in a college, university, or school of theology approved by the University Senate.

Part-time local pastors may be appointed to small membership churches that are grouped together in a charge under the supervision of a mentor.

3. *Students Appointed as Local Pastors*—Students enrolled as pre-theological or theological students in a college, university, or school of theology listed by the University Senate *(a)* who have met the provisions of ¶ 315, and *(b)* who shall make appropriate progress in their educational program as determined by the Board of Ordained Ministry may be appointed as part-time or full-time local pastors in a conference other than the conference in which they are certified candidates. *(c)* Students who are appointed as local pastors continue to relate to the district committee on ordained ministry in the conference in which they are certified candidates and shall be responsible to them for the continuation of their certified candidacy.

4. Upon recommendation of the Board of Ordained Ministry, the clergy members in full connection may vote approval annually for students of other denominations enrolled in a school of theology listed by the University Senate to serve as local pastors for the ensuing year under the direction of the district superintendent, provided that they shall indicate to the satisfaction of the Board of Ordained Ministry their agreement to support and maintain the doctrine and polity of The United Methodist Church while under appointment.

5. Local pastors may serve on any board, commission, or committee with voice and vote, except on matters of clergy character, qualifications, status, and ordination. However, local pastors who have completed the Course of Study may serve on the district committee on ordained ministry with voice and vote.

Local pastors who have completed the Course of Study may serve on the Board of Ordained Ministry with voice and vote.

¶ **319.** *Continuance as a Local Pastor*—1. Persons licensed as local pastors who are not provisional members shall continue in college, in a program of theological education at an approved seminary, or in the Course of Study.

2. Upon completing each year's education and other qualifications, a local pastor who is not a provisional member may be recommended for continuance by the district committee on ordained ministry. The clergy members in full connection of the annual conference may approve continuance of a local pastor after reference to and recommendation by its Board of Ordained Ministry.[8]

3. A full-time local pastor shall complete the Course of Study curriculum within eight years and a part-time local pastor within twelve, unless a family situation or other circumstance precludes the local pastor's opportunity to meet said requirements. The local pastor may be granted an annual extension beyond the prescribed limit upon a three-fourths vote of the district committee on ordained ministry, recommendation by the conference Board of Ordained Ministry, and the vote of the clergy members in full connection.[9]

4. A local pastor may choose to remain in a local relationship with the annual conference upon having completed the Course of Study.

5. None of the provisions in this legislation shall be interpreted to change or limit authorizations to local pastors ordained as deacon and elder prior to 1996.[10]

¶ **320.** *Exiting, Reinstatement, and Retirement of Local Pastors Who Are Not Provisional Members*—1. *Discontinuance of Local Pastor*—Whenever a local pastor retires or is no longer approved for appointment by the annual conference as required in ¶ 318, whenever any local pastor severs relationship with The United Methodist Church, whenever the appointment of a local pastor is discontinued by the bishop, or whenever the district committee on ordained ministry does not recommend continuation of license, license and credentials shall be surrendered to the district superintendent for deposit with the secretary of the conference.

---

8. See Judicial Council Decision 1076.
9. See Judicial Council Decisions 436, 439.
10. See Judicial Council Decisions 436, 439.

After consultation with the pastor, the former local pastor shall designate the local church in which membership shall be held. The Board of Ordained Ministry shall file with the resident bishop a permanent record of the circumstances relating to the discontinuance of local pastor status as required in ¶ 635.3d.

2. *Withdrawal Under Complaints and Charges*—When a local pastor is accused of an offense under ¶ 2702 and desires to withdraw from the Church, the procedures described in ¶ 2719.2 shall apply.

3. *Trial of Local Pastor*—When a local pastor is accused of an offense under ¶ 2702, the procedures described in ¶¶ 2703-2713 shall apply.[11]

4. *Reinstatement of Local Pastor Status*—Local pastors whose approved status has been discontinued from an annual conference of The United Methodist Church or one of its legal predecessors may be reinstated only by the annual conference that previously approved them, its legal successor, or the annual conference of which the major portion of their former conference is a part, only upon recommendation by the district committee on ordained ministry from which their license was discontinued, the Board of Ordained Ministry, and the cabinet. Persons seeking reinstatement shall provide evidence that they have been members of a local United Methodist church for at least one year prior to their request for reinstatement. The district committee shall require a recommendation from the charge conference where his or her membership is currently held. When approved by the clergy members in full connection as provided in ¶ 337, their license and credentials shall be restored, and they shall be eligible for appointment as pastors of a charge. They shall complete current studies and meet requirements as provided in ¶¶ 315, 318.

Whenever persons whose approval as local pastors has been discontinued by an annual conference are being considered for appointment or temporary employment in another annual conference, the Board of Ordained Ministry where these persons are being considered shall obtain from the Board of Ordained Ministry of the conference where approval has been discontinued verification of their qualifications and information about the circumstances relating to the termination of their approval as local pastors.

---

11. See Judicial Council Decision 982.

5. *Retirement of Local Pastor*—A local pastor who has made satisfactory progress in the Course of Study as specified in ¶ 318.1 or .2 may be recognized as a retired local pastor. Retirement provisions for local pastors shall be the same as those for clergy members in ¶ 358.1, .2, .4, with pensions payable in accordance with ¶ 1506.5*a*. Retired local pastors may attend annual conference sessions with voice but not vote. A retired local pastor may be appointed by the bishop to a charge and licensed upon recommendation by the district committee on ordained ministry without creating additional claim upon the conference minimum compensation nor further pension credit.

Section V. Associate Membership

¶ **321.** *Eligibility and Rights of Associate Members*—Associate members of an annual conference are in the itinerant ministry of the Church and are available on a continuing basis for appointment by the bishop. They offer themselves without reserve to be appointed (and to serve as their superiors in office shall direct). They shall be amenable to the annual conference in the performance of their ministry and shall be granted the same security of appointment as provisional members and members in full connection.[12]

1. Associate members shall have a right to vote in the annual conference on all matters except the following: *(a)* constitutional amendments; *(b)* all matters of ordination, character, and conference relations of clergy.

2. Associate members may serve on any board, commission, or committee of an annual conference. They shall not be eligible for election as delegates to the General or jurisdictional or central conferences.

3. Associate members shall be subject to the provisions governing sabbatical leave, leave of absence, location, retirement, minimum salary, and pension.

¶ **322.** *Requirements for Election as Associate Members*—1. Local pastors may be elected to associate membership by a three-fourths majority vote of the clergy session, when they have met the following conditions. They shall have: (1) been recommended to the clergy session based on a three-fourths majority vote of the conference Board of Ordained Ministry; (2) reached age forty; (3) served

---

12. See Judicial Council Decision 1226.

four years as full-time local pastors; (4) completed the Course of Study in addition to the studies for license as a local pastor, up to one half of which may be taken by correspondence or online/distance learning courses, or received a Master of Divinity degree that includes the basic graduate theological studies from a school of theology listed by the University Senate; (5) completed a minimum of sixty semester hours toward the Bachelor of Arts or an equivalent degree in a college or university recognized by the University Senate; (6) been recommended by a three-fourths majority vote by the district committee on ordained ministry and the Board of Ordained Ministry; (7) declared their willingness to accept continuing full-time appointment; (8) satisfied the board regarding their physical, mental, and emotional health (the annual conference shall require psychological reports, criminal background and credit checks, and reports of sexual misconduct and/or child abuse to provide additional information on the candidate's fitness for the ministry); (9) for the sake of the mission of Jesus Christ in the world and the most effective witness to the Christian gospel, and in consideration of his/her influence as a clergy member of the annual conference, be willing to make a complete dedication of himself/herself to the highest ideals of the Christian life; and to this end agree to exercise responsible self-control by personal habits conducive to bodily health, mental and emotional maturity, fidelity in marriage and celibacy in singleness, social responsibility, and growth in grace and the knowledge and love of God; and (10) prepared at least one written sermon on a biblical passage specified by the Board of Ordained Ministry and given satisfactory answers in a written doctrinal examination administered by the Board of Ordained Ministry. (Consideration shall be given to the questions listed in ¶ 324.9.)

2. Upon recommendation of the Board of Ordained Ministry, an annual conference may equate part-time service to the requirement of full-time service. Such equivalence is to be determined in light of the years of service involved, the quality of that service, the maturity of the applicant, and other relevant factors.[13]

3. Associate members may retire under the provisions of ¶ 357 of the *Discipline*. They shall retain their license for pastoral ministry for service in the local church and maintain their relationship as retired clergy members of the annual conference.

---

13. See Judicial Council Decisions 343, 572, 1181.

4. Associate members may be received as provisional members in the annual conference under conditions as set forth in ¶ 324.6 upon receiving a three-fourths majority vote of the clergy members of the conference in full connection, present and voting.

¶ **323.** *Fellowship of Local Pastors and Associate Members*—Each annual conference shall organize a Fellowship of Local Pastors and Associate Members. All licensed local pastors and associate members shall be members of and participate in the Fellowship. The Fellowship will provide mutual support for its members for the sake of the life and mission of the church.

1. The specific and limited function is to:

a) provide for regular gatherings of local pastors and associate members for continuing formation in relationship to Jesus Christ through such experiences as Bible study, study of issues facing the church and society, and theological exploration in vocational identity and leadership;

b) encourage local pastors and associate members in continued study beyond the Course of Study and Advanced Course of Study;

c) develop a bond of unity and common commitment to the mission and ministry of The United Methodist Church and the annual conference; and

d) enable the creation of relationships that allow mutual support and trust.

2. The bishop shall convene the fellowship and the Board of Ordained Ministry shall coordinate its life and work. Necessary financial support shall be provided by the annual conference through the budget of the board. The board shall nominate from within the Fellowship membership and the Fellowship shall elect quadrennially a chairperson of the Fellowship during a gathered meeting of the annual session of the Fellowship conference who, in cooperation with and under the guidance of the bishop, will provide continuing leadership for the Fellowship. The elected Fellowship chairperson, full-time or part-time, shall be a member of the Board of Ordained Ministry and its executive committee as specified in ¶ 635.1*a*.

Activity of the Fellowship will be reported regularly to the Board of Ordained Ministry.

Section VI. Provisional Membership

¶ **324.** *Qualifications for Election to Provisional Membership*—A person shall be eligible for election to provisional membership in the annual conference by a three-fourths majority vote of the clergy session on recommendation of its Board of Ordained Ministry after meeting the following qualifications.[14]

1. *Candidacy Requirement:* Each candidate shall have been a certified candidate for at least one year. Those appointed as local pastors are clergy members of the annual conference and are no longer certified candidates (¶ 311).

2. *Service Requirement:* Each candidate shall have demonstrated his or her gifts for ministries of service and leadership to the satisfaction of the district committee on ordained ministry as a condition for provisional membership.

3. *Undergraduate Requirement:* A candidate for provisional membership shall have completed a bachelor's degree from a college or university recognized by the University Senate. Exceptions to the undergraduate degree requirements may be made in consultation with the General Board of Higher Education and Ministry in some instances, for missional purposes, for persons who have a minimum of sixty semester hours of Bachelor of Arts credit and:

a) have been prevented from pursuit of the normal course of baccalaureate education,

b) are members of a group whose cultural practices and training enhance insight and skills for effective ministry not available through conventional formal education, or

c) have graduated with a bachelor's degree or its equivalent from a college not recognized by the University Senate and have completed one half of the studies of the Master of Divinity or equivalent first professional degree in a school of theology listed by the University Senate.

4. *Graduate Requirement:*

a) Candidates for deacon or elder shall have completed a minimum of one-half of the 27 semester hours of basic graduate theological studies in the Christian faith. These courses may be included within or in addition to a seminary degree. These basic graduate theological studies must include courses in Old Testament; New Testament; theology; church history; mission of the church in the world; evangelism; worship/liturgy; and United Methodist doctrine, polity and history.

b) a candidate for ordination as an elder shall have completed one half of the studies toward a Master of Divinity degree

---

14. See Judicial Council Decision 318.

or its equivalent, including one half of the basic graduate theological studies from a seminary listed by the University Senate.

   c) a candidate for ordination as a deacon shall have:

   (1) completed one half of the studies of a master's degree from a United Methodist seminary or one listed by the University Senate, or

   (2) received a master's degree in the area of the specialized ministry in which the candidate will serve

   (3) completed one half of the basic graduate theological studies, in a context which will provide formation as a United Methodist deacon in full connection within a cohesive program developed by the seminary and approved by the General Board of Higher Education and Ministry, documented by a record of completion from that school.

   5. In some instances a candidate who is pursuing ordination to serve as deacon in full connection may fulfill the academic requirements through the following professional certification alternate route:

   a) shall have reached thirty-five years of age at the time to become a certified candidate;

   b) completed a bachelor's degree, received professional certification or license in the area of ministry in which the candidate will serve, have completed a minimum of eight semester hours of graduate credit or equivalent quarter hours in the area of specialization, and have been recommended by the conference Board of Ordained Ministry;

   c) have completed a minimum of one half of the twenty-seven semester hours of the basic graduate theological studies of the Christian faith including the areas of: Old Testament; New Testament; theology; church history; mission of the church in the world; evangelism; worship/liturgy; and United Methodist doctrine, polity, and history, in a context which will provide a cohesive program and formation as a United Methodist deacon in full connection within a cohesive program developed by the seminary and approved by the General Board of Higher Education and Ministry, documented by a record of completion from that school.

   6. Local pastors may fulfill the requirements for provisional membership as elders when they have:

   a) completed four years of full-time service or the equivalent;

b) satisfied all requirements of Sections 1-3 and 7-14 of this paragraph;

c) completed the Course of Study. Course of Study requirements may be fulfilled as determined by the General Board of Higher Education and Ministry (¶ 1421.3*d*) by:

1. Completion of Course of Study, of which no more than one-half may be taken by correspondence or Internet; up to one-half of Course of Study may be online courses; and

2. Completion of an equivalent program of study embedded in an undergraduate degree at a UM-related college or university.

d) completed an Advanced Course of Study consisting of thirty-two semester hours of graduate theological study offered by a seminary recognized by the University Senate or its equivalent as determined by the General Board of Higher Education and Ministry. The Advanced Course of Study shall include the basic graduate theological studies (¶ 324.4*a*).[15]

7. The Board of Ordained Ministry shall require an official transcript of credits from each school before recognizing any of the applicant's educational claims. In case of doubt, the board may submit a transcript to the General Board of Higher Education and Ministry.

8. Each candidate shall present a satisfactory certificate of good health by a physician on the prescribed form. Disabilities are not to be construed as unfavorable health factors when a person with disability is capable of meeting the professional standards and is able to render effective service as a provisional member.

9. Each candidate shall respond to a written and oral doctrinal examination administered by the conference Board of Ordained Ministry. The examination shall cover the following:

a) Describe your personal experience of God and the understanding of God you derive from biblical, theological, and historical sources.

b) What is your understanding of evil as it exists in the world?

c) What is your understanding of humanity, and the human need for divine grace?

d) How do you interpret the statement Jesus Christ is Lord?

---

15. See Judicial Council Decisions 823, 1077.

e) What is your conception of the activity of the Holy Spirit in personal faith, in the community of believers, and in responsible living in the world?

f) What is your understanding of the kingdom of God; the Resurrection; eternal life?

g) How do you intend to affirm, teach, and apply Part III of the *Discipline* (Doctrinal Standards and Our Theological Task) in your work in the ministry to which you have been called?

h) The United Methodist Church holds that the living core of the Christian faith was revealed in Scripture, illumined by tradition, vivified in personal experience, and confirmed by reason. What is your understanding of this theological position of the Church?

i) Describe the nature and mission of the Church. What are its primary tasks today?

j) Discuss your understanding of the primary characteristics of United Methodist polity.

k) Explain your understanding of the distinctive vocations of the Order of Elders and the Order of Deacons. How do you perceive yourself, your gifts, your motives, your role, and your commitment as a provisional deacon or provisional elder in The United Methodist Church?

l) Describe your understanding of *diakonia*, the servant ministry of the church, and the servant ministry of the provisional member.

m) What is the meaning of ordination in the context of the general ministry of the Church?

n) Describe your understanding of an inclusive church and ministry.

o) You have agreed as a candidate for the sake of the mission of Jesus Christ in the world and the most effective witness of the gospel, and in consideration of their influence as ministers, to make a complete dedication of yourself to the highest ideals of the Christian life, and to this end agree to exercise responsible self-control by personal habits conducive to bodily health, mental and emotional maturity, integrity in all personal relationships, fidelity in marriage and celibacy in singleness, social responsibility, and growth in grace and the knowledge and love of God. What is your understanding of this agreement?

p) Explain the role and significance of the sacraments in the ministry to which you have been called.

10. Each candidate shall have been recommended in writing to the conference Board of Ordained Ministry, based on a three-fourths majority vote of the district committee on ordained ministry.

11. Each candidate shall have a personal interview with the conference Board of Ordained Ministry to complete his or her candidacy.

12. Each candidate shall submit on a form provided by the Board of Ordained Ministry a notarized statement detailing any convictions for felony, or misdemeanor, or written accusations and its disposition of sexual misconduct or child abuse; or certifying that this candidate has not been convicted of a felony or misdemeanor or accused in writing of sexual misconduct or child abuse. The candidate also shall release required psychological reports, criminal background, credit checks and reports of child abuse.

13. Each candidate shall file with the board a written, concise, autobiographical statement (in duplicate on a prescribed form) regarding age, health, family status, Christian experience, call to ministry, educational record, formative Christian experiences, and plans for service in the Church.

14. Each candidate shall have been recommended in writing to the clergy session based on at least a three-fourths majority vote of the conference Board of Ordained Ministry.

¶ 325. *Commissioning*—Commissioning is the act of the church that publicly acknowledges God's call and the response, talents, gifts, and training of the candidate. The church invokes the Holy Spirit as the candidate is commissioned to be a faithful servant leader among the people, to lead the church in service, to proclaim the Word of God and to equip others for ministry.

Through commissioning, the church sends persons in leadership and service in the name of Jesus Christ and marks their entrance into a time of provisional membership as they prepare for ordination. Commissioned ministers are provisional clergy members of the annual conference and are accountable to the bishop and the clergy session for the conduct of their ministry.

During the residency program the clergy session discerns their fitness for ordination and their effectiveness in ministry. After fulfilling all candidacy requirements and upon recommendation of the conference Board of Ordained Ministry, the clergy session shall vote on the provisional membership and commissioning of the candidates. The bishop and secretary of the conference shall provide credentials as a provisional member and a commissioned minister in the annual conference.

The period of commissioned ministry is concluded when the provisional members are received as full members of the annual conference and ordained as either deacon or elder, or a decision is made not to proceed toward ordination and provisional membership is ended.

¶ **326.** *Service of Provisional Members*—All persons who are provisional members shall be appointed by a bishop (¶ 425) and serve as a provisional member of the annual conference for a minimum of two years following the completion of education requirements for full connection. During the provisional period, arrangements shall be offered by the Board of Ordained Ministry for all provisional members to be involved in a residency curriculum that extends theological education by using covenant groups and mentoring to support the practice and work of their ministry as servant leaders, to contemplate the grounding of ordained ministry, and to understand covenant ministry in the life of the conference. Provisional members may be appointed to attend school, to extension ministry, or in appointments beyond the local church. Wherever they are appointed, the service of provisional members shall be evaluated by the district superintendent and the Board of Ordained Ministry in terms of the provisional member's ability to express and give leadership in servant ministry.

1. Provisional members planning to give their lives as deacons in full connection shall be in ministries of Word, Service, Compassion, and Justice in the local church or in an approved appointment beyond the local church. A provisional member preparing for ordination as a deacon shall be licensed for the practice of ministry during provisional membership to perform the duties of the ministry of the deacon as stated in ¶ 328 and be granted support as stated in ¶ 331.10. Such authorization granted by the license may be renewed annually by the clergy session upon recommendation of the Board of Ordained Ministry.

2. Provisional members planning to give their lives as elders in full connection shall be in ministries of Word, Sacrament, Order, and Service in the local church or in an approved extension ministry. A provisional member preparing for ordination as an elder shall be licensed for pastoral ministry (¶ 315). Such authorization granted by the license may be renewed annually by the clergy session upon recommendation of the Board of Ordained Ministry.

3. Provisional members who are serving in extension ministries, enrolled in graduate degree programs, or appointments beyond the local church shall be accountable to the district superintendent and the Board of Ordained Ministry for the conduct of ministry, and for demonstrating their effectiveness in the ministry of the order to which they seek to be ordained. In all cases, they will also demonstrate their effectiveness in servant leadership in the local church to the satisfaction of the Board of Ordained Ministry.

4. Provisional members seeking to change their ordination track shall:

a) Write to the Board of Ordained Ministry and inform the district superintendent and bishop of their intention.

b) Interview with the Board of Ordained Ministry to articulate and clarify their call.

c) Fulfill academic and service requirements.

Upon the recommendation of the Board of Ordained Ministry and by vote of the clergy session the person may be received into full connection with the annual conference and be ordained into the order to which they are transitioning.

¶ **327.** *Eligibility and Rights of Provisional Membership*—Provisional members are on trial in preparation for membership in full connection in the annual conference as deacons or elders. They are on probation as to character, servant leadership, and effectiveness in ministry. The annual conference, through the clergy session, has jurisdiction over provisional members. Annually, the Board of Ordained Ministry shall review and evaluate their relationship and make recommendation to the clergy members in full connection regarding their continuance. No member shall be continued on provisional membership beyond the eighth regular session following their admission to provisional membership.

1. Provisional members who are preparing for deacon's or elder's orders may be ordained deacons or elders when they qualify for membership in full connection in the annual conference.

2. Provisional members shall have the right to vote in the annual conference on all matters except the following:

a) constitutional amendments;

b) all matters of ordination, character, and conference relations of clergy. Provisional clergy members who have completed all of their educational requirements may vote to elect clergy delegates to General and jurisdictional or central conferences.[16]

---

16. See Judicial Council Decision 1181 and ¶ 35.

3. Provisional members may serve on any board, commission, or committee of the annual conference except the Board of Ordained Ministry (¶ 635.1). They shall not be eligible for election as delegates to the General, central, or jurisdictional conferences.

4. Provisional members shall be amenable to the annual conference in the performance of their ministry and are subject to the provisions of the *Book of Discipline* in the performance of their duties. They shall be supervised by the district superintendent under whom they are appointed. They shall also be assigned a deacon or elder as mentor by the Board of Ordained Ministry. Provisional members preparing to become elders shall be eligible for appointment by meeting disciplinary provisions (¶ 315).

5. Provisional members in appointments beyond the local church shall relate themselves to the district superintendent in the area where their work is done. The district superintendent shall give them supervision and report annually to their Board of Ordained Ministry.

6. *Discontinuance from Provisional Membership*—Provisional members may request discontinuance of this relationship or may be discontinued by the clergy session upon recommendation of the Board of Ordained Ministry. When provisional members in good standing withdraw to unite with another denomination or to terminate their membership in The United Methodist Church, their action shall be considered a request for discontinuance of their relationship and their credentials shall be surrendered to a district superintendent. In the case of discontinuation without consent, prior to any final recommendation, a provisional member will be advised of the right to a fair process hearing before the committee on conference relations of the Board of Ordained Ministry. A report of the action will be made to the full board for final action. The provisions of fair process (¶ 361.2) shall be observed and there shall be a review by the administrative review committee under ¶ 636 prior to hearing by the annual conference. When this relationship is discontinued, they shall no longer be permitted to exercise ministerial functions and shall return their credentials to the district superintendent for deposit with the secretary of the conference, and their membership shall be transferred by the district superintendent to the local church they designate after consultation with the pastor. The Board of Ordained Ministry shall file with the resident bishop and the secretary of the conference a permanent record of the circumstances relating to discontinuance

as a provisional member as required in ¶ 635.3*d*. After discontinuance, provisional members may be classified and approved as local pastors in accordance with the provision of ¶ 316.

7. Provisional members may not be retired under the provisions of ¶ 357. Provisional members who have reached the mandatory retirement age shall be automatically discontinued. Provisional elders may be classified as retired local pastors under the provisions of ¶ 320.5.

Section VII. The Ordained Deacon in Full Connection

¶ **328.** *The Ministry of a Deacon*—From among the baptized, deacons are called by God to a lifetime of servant leadership, authorized by the Church, and ordained by a bishop. From the earliest days of the church, deacons were called and set apart for the ministry of Love, Justice, and Service and for connecting the church with the most needy, neglected, and marginalized among the children of God. This ministry grows out of the Wesleyan passion for social holiness and ministry among the poor. It is the deacons, in both person and function, whose distinctive ministry is to embody, articulate, and lead the whole people of God in its servant ministry. Deacons fulfill servant ministry in the world and lead the Church in relating the gathered life of Christians to their ministries in the world, interrelating worship in the gathered community with service to God in the world. Deacons give leadership in the Church's life: in teaching and proclaiming the Word; in contributing to worship, in assisting the elders in administering the sacraments of baptism and Holy Communion, or in presiding at the celebration of the sacraments when contextually appropriate and duly authorized; in forming and nurturing disciples; in conducting marriages and burying the dead; in embodying the church's mission to the world; and in leading congregations in interpreting the needs, concerns, and hopes of the world. For the sake of extending the mission and ministry of the church and offering the means of grace to the world, the resident bishop of the annual conference in which the deacon is appointed may authorize the deacon to preside at the celebration of the sacraments. Presiding at the celebration of the sacraments involves taking responsibility to lead the gathered community in celebrating baptism and Holy Communion. As members of the Order of Deacons, all deacons are in covenant with all other deacons in the annual conference and shall participate in the life of their order.

Deacons lead the congregation in its servant ministry and equip and support all baptized Christians in their ministry. The distinct ministry of the deacon has evolved in United Methodism over many years—the continuing work of the deaconess, the home missionary, and the diaconal minister. The Church, recognizing the gifts and impact of all predecessor embodiments of the diaconate and providing for the continuation of the office of deaconess, affirms that this distinctiveness is made visible and central to the Church's life and ministry through ordination and that the ministry of the deacon is a faithful response of the mission of the Church meeting the emerging needs of the future. Deacons are accountable to the annual conference and the bishop for the fulfillment of their call to servant leadership.

¶ **329.** *Ministry, Authority, and Responsibilities of Deacons in Full Connection*—1. Deacons are persons called by God, authorized by the Church, and ordained by a bishop to a lifetime ministry of Word, Service, Compassion, and Justice, to both the community and the congregation in a ministry that connects the two. Deacons exemplify Christian discipleship and create opportunities for others to enter into discipleship. The work of deacons is a work of justice, serving with compassion as they seek to serve those on the margins of society. In the congregation, the ministry of the deacon is to teach and to form disciples, and to lead worship together with other ordained and laypersons.

2. The deacon in full connection shall have the rights of voice and vote in the annual conference where membership is held; shall be eligible to serve as clergy on boards, commissions, or committees of the annual conference and hold office on the same; and shall be eligible for election as a clergy delegate to the General, central, or jurisdictional conference. The deacon in full connection shall attend all the sessions of the annual conference and share with elders in full connection responsibility for all matters of ordination, character, and conference relations of clergy (¶ 334.1).

3. As members of the Order of Deacons, all deacons in full connection are in covenant with all other such deacons in the annual conference and shall participate in the life of their order.

¶ **330.** *Requirements for Ordination as Deacon and Admission to Full Connection*—Provisional members who are applying for admission into full connection and who have been provisional members for at least two years following the completion of the educational requirements for ordination as a deacon specified in .3 below may be admitted into membership in full connection in an annual conference by three-fourths majority vote of the clergy members in full connection of the annual conference, upon recommendation by three-fourths majority vote of the Board of Ordained Ministry, after they have qualified as follows:

1. They shall have served under episcopal appointment in a ministry of service for at least two full annual conference years. Upon recommendation of the Board of Ordained Ministry, the annual conference may equate less than full-time or nonsalaried service as meeting this qualification. Such equivalence is to be determined in light of the years of service involved, the quality of that service, the maturity of the applicant, and other relevant factors determined by the board. Supervision is to be: *(a)* by the district superintendent, and *(b)* by the Board of Ordained Ministry. The applicant's service must be evaluated by the Board of Ordained Ministry as effective according to written guidelines developed by the board and adopted by the clergy members in full connection. Laypersons directly involved in the applicant's servant ministry shall be involved by the board in the annual evaluation.

2. They shall have been previously elected as a provisional member.

3. They shall have met the following educational requirements: *(a)* graduation with a Bachelor of Arts or equivalent degree from a college or university listed by the University Senate or its equivalent as determined by the General Board of Higher Education and Ministry; *(b)* graduation with a Master of Divinity degree or a master's degree from a graduate theological school recognized by the University Senate, or a master's degree in an area of specialized ministry; *(c)* or are candidates over the age of 35 with professional certification or license in their area of ministry including a minimum of eight semester hours of graduate academic credit. Educational requirements in every case shall include the completion of the basic graduate theological studies of the Christian faith, as outlined in ¶ 324.4*a*.

4. The candidate shall have (1) satisfied the board regarding physical, mental, and emotional health; (2) prepared and preached at least one written sermon on a biblical passage specified by the Board of Ordained Ministry or another act of proclamation of the Word appropriate to the candidate's ministry setting;

(3) presented a detailed plan and outline for teaching a Bible study; (4) presented a project that demonstrates fruitfulness in carrying out the church's mission of "Making Disciples of Jesus Christ for the Transformation of the World"; (5) responded to a written or oral doctrinal examination administered by the Board of Ordained Ministry. The candidate shall demonstrate the ability to communicate clearly in both oral and written form.

The candidate's reflections and the board's response shall be informed by the insights and guidelines of Part III of the *Book of Discipline*. The examination shall also focus upon the covenantal relationship of the applicant to God, to the Church, and to the Order of Deacons, as well as the understanding of *diakonia*, servant leadership, and the interrelatedness of the Church and the world. The applicant shall be able to articulate the call of God to the Order of Deacons and to relate that call to leadership within the ministry of all Christians, through the setting of their service, the local church, and the annual conference.

5. The following questions are guidelines for the preparation of the examination:

　　a) Theology

　　　　(1) Give examples of how the practice of ministry has affected your experience and understanding of:

　　　　　　(*a*) God

　　　　　　(*b*) Humanity

　　　　　　(*c*) The need for divine grace

　　　　　　(*d*) The Lordship of Jesus Christ

　　　　　　(*e*) The work of the Holy Spirit

　　　　　　(*f*) The meaning and significance of the sacraments

　　　　　　(*g*) The kingdom of God

　　　　　　(*h*) Resurrection and eternal life

　　　　(2) How do you understand the following traditional evangelical doctrines: (*a*) repentance; (*b*) justification; (*c*) regeneration; (*d*) sanctification? What are the marks of the Christian life?

　　　　(3) How has the practice of ministry informed your understanding of the nature and mission of the Church? What are its primary challenges today?

　　　　(4) The United Methodist Church holds that Scripture, tradition, experience, and reason are sources and norms for belief and practice, but that the Bible is primary among them. What is your understanding of this theological position of the

Church, and how has your practice of ministry been affected by this understanding?

      b) Vocation

         (1) How has the experience of ministry shaped your understanding of your vocation as an ordained deacon?

      c) The Practice of Ministry

         (1) Do you offer yourself to be appointed by the bishop to a service ministry?

         (2) Describe and evaluate your personal gifts for ministry and how they have resulted in fruitful ministry. What would be your areas of strength and areas in which you need to be strengthened in order to be more fruitful in ministry?

         (3) For the sake of the mission of Jesus Christ in the world and the most effective witness to the Christian gospel, and in consideration of your influence as an ordained minister, are you willing to make a complete dedication of yourself to the highest ideals of the Christian life; and to this end will you agree to exercise responsible self-control by personal habits conducive to physical health, intentional intellectual development, fidelity in marriage and celibacy in singleness, integrity in all personal relationships, social responsibility, and growth in grace and the knowledge of the love of God?[17]

         (4) Provide evidence of your willingness to relate yourself in ministry to all persons without regard to race, color, ethnicity, national origin, social status, gender, sexual orientation, age, economic condition, or disability.

         (5) Will you regard all pastoral conversations of a confessional nature as a trust between the person concerned and God?

         (6) Provide evidence of experience in peace and justice ministries.

      d) *Historic Examination for Admission into Full Connection and Ordination as Deacon*—The bishop as chief pastor shall engage those seeking to be admitted in serious self-searching and prayer to prepare them for their examination before the conference. At the time of the examination, the bishop shall also explain to the conference the historic nature of the following questions and seek to interpret their spirit and intent. The questions are these and any others which may be thought necessary:

---

17. See Judicial Council Decision 542.

(1) Have you faith in Christ?

(2) Are you going on to perfection?

(3) Do you expect to be made perfect in love in this life?

(4) Are you earnestly striving after perfection in love?

(5) Are you resolved to devote yourself wholly to God and God's work?

(6) Do you know the General Rules of our Church?

(7) Will you keep the General Rules of our Church?

(8) Have you studied the doctrines of The United Methodist Church?

(9) After full examination do you believe that our doctrines are in harmony with the Holy Scriptures?

(10) Have you studied our form of Church discipline and polity?

(11) Do you approve our Church government and polity?

(12) Will you support and maintain them?

(13) Will you exercise the ministry of compassion?

(14) Will you diligently instruct the children in every place?

(15) Will you visit from house to house?

(16) Will you recommend fasting or abstinence, both by precept and example?

(17) Are you determined to employ all your time in the work of God?

(18) Are you in debt so as to embarrass you in your work?

(19) Will you observe the following directions?

(a) Be diligent. Never be unemployed. Never be triflingly employed. Never trifle away time; neither spend any more time at any one place than is strictly necessary.

(b) Be punctual. Do everything exactly at the time. And do not mend our rules, but keep them; not for wrath, but for conscience' sake.

6. A provisional member of the annual conference who has completed the requirements for deacon's orders and admission into full membership shall be eligible for election to full membership and ordination as deacon by a bishop. Following election, the bishop and secretary of the conference shall provide a certificate

of full membership in the annual conference, and following ordination, a certificate of ordination.

7. A deacon shall be ordained by a bishop by the laying on of hands, employing the Order of Service for the Ordination of Deacons (see ¶ 415.6). The bishops shall be assisted by other deacons and may include laity designated by the bishop representing the Church community. Judicatory leaders from full communion partners and other communions may participate in the ordination service and may join the ordaining bishop in laying hands on the head of the candidate, while participating deacons and laity may lay hands on the back or shoulders of the candidate.

Section VIII. Appointments of Deacons and Provisional Deacons to Various Ministries

¶ 331. *Appointment of Deacons and Provisional Deacons to Various Ministries*—1. Deacons and provisional deacons may be appointed to serve in the following settings:

a) Agencies and settings beyond the local church, including ecumenical agencies, that extend the witness and service of Christ's love and justice in the world and connect the church with the most needy, neglected, and marginalized;

b) United Methodist Church-related agencies, schools, colleges, theological schools, and within the connectional structures of The United Methodist Church;

c) A local congregation, charge, or cooperative parish, leading in the congregation's mission to the world and equipping all Christians to fulfill their own calls to Christian service;

d) As students in research doctoral programs that may lead to appointments in academic settings as instructors or professors in colleges, universities, and theological schools affiliated with The United Methodist Church;

e) As instructors or professors or administrators in colleges, universities, and theological schools affiliated with The United Methodist Church.

2. Deacons and provisional deacons may be appointed to attend school.

3. Deacons and provisional deacons shall be appointed to settings that allow fulfillment of their call and where supervision is provided with goals, evaluation, and accountability acceptable to the bishop, the cabinet and the Board of Ordained Ministry.

4. *Deacons and Provisional Deacons Appointed Beyond the Local Church.*

a) Deacons and provisional deacons may be appointed to settings not connected to either The United Methodist Church or ecumenical agencies when the appointment is approved by the bishop and the Board of Ordained Ministry as a ministry beyond the local church that is a witness and service of Christ's love and justice in the world. Those seeking such an appointment shall submit a written statement to the bishop and the Board of Ordained Ministry, describing in detail the proposed setting for their ministry, sharing a sense of calling to that ministry and their gifts and evidence of God's grace for it, and expressing how the proposed ministry is an intentional fulfillment of their ordination vows. This statement shall also include a detailed description of the accountability structures related to the proposed ministry setting.

b) Deacons or provisional deacons who are appointed beyond the local church may pursue endorsement by the General Board of Higher Education and Ministry. The General Board of Higher Education and Ministry shall annually request the deacon or provisional deacon's bishop in the conference of membership to verify the appropriate employment of persons under its endorsement and request the bishop to reappoint.

c) Deacons and provisional deacons are amenable to the annual conference of which they are members and insofar as possible should maintain close working relationship with and effective participation in the work of their annual conference, assuming whatever responsibilities they are qualified and requested to assume. When deacons or provisional deacons are appointed to a setting beyond the local church outside of the conference where they hold membership, the appointment shall be made by the bishop of the conference where membership is held in consultation with the bishop of the area in which the appointment is located.

d) Deacons and provisional deacons appointed to settings beyond the local church shall submit annually to the bishop, the district superintendent, and the Board of Ordained Ministry, a written report on the official form developed for the Church by the General Council on Finance and Administration for use by the annual conference.

Deacons and provisional deacons appointed to settings outside the annual conference in which they hold membership shall also furnish a copy of their report to the bishop of the area in which the appointment is located.

e) The General Board of Higher Education and Ministry, Division of Ordained Ministry, in order to assist the Boards of Ordained Ministry and cabinets, will provide guidelines for validating the appropriateness of appointment settings beyond the local church and will be available for consultation with bishops, cabinets, and Boards of Ordained Ministry.

5. When deacons and provisional deacons serve in an agency or setting beyond the local church, the bishop, after consultation with the deacon or provisional deacon and the pastor in charge, shall appoint the deacon or provisional deacon to a local congregation where they will take missional responsibility for leading other Christians into ministries of service. In this ministry the deacons and provisional deacons shall be accountable to the pastor in charge, the charge conference, and other bodies that coordinate the ministry of the local church. In those instances where the appointment is in another episcopal area, the appointment to a local church shall be made in consultation with the bishop of that area.

6. The appointment of deacons and provisional deacons shall be made by the bishop.

a) It may be initiated by the bishop or the district superintendent, the individual deacon or provisional deacon, or the agency requesting the service of the deacon or provisional deacon.

b) It shall be clarified by a written statement of intentionality of servant leadership in order to establish a clear distinction between the work to which all Christians are called and the work for which deacons and provisional deacons are appropriately prepared and authorized.

c) If the bishop and cabinet consider an appointment not to be in the best interest of the Church, the bishop may choose not to make the appointment. In such event, the bishop shall consult with the deacon or provisional deacon and the Board of Ordained Ministry. The deacon or provisional deacon shall then seek another appointment, request a leave of absence or transitional leave, or relinquish his or her certificate of conference membership for deposit with the conference secretary, or be terminated by disciplinary procedures. The procedures for fair process in administrative hearings (¶ 361.2) shall be followed in any involuntary termination procedure.

d) Deacons and provisional deacons at their own request or with their consent may be appointed to a nonsalaried position. Such missional appointments will serve to express the Church's concern for social holiness, for ministry among the poor, and for advancing emerging needs of the future. In such cases, the bishop will carefully review plans for expressing this appointed ministry and will consult with the deacon or provisional deacon about the well-being and financial security of his or her family.

7. At the request of the deacon or provisional deacon and with the consent of the bishop and cabinet where conference membership is held, the deacon or provisional deacon may receive a less than full-time appointment under the following conditions:

a) The deacon or provisional deacon shall present a written request to the bishop, district superintendent, and the conference Board of Ordained Ministry, giving a rationale for the request at least ninety days prior to the annual conference at which the appointment is to be made.

b) Reappointment to less than full-time service shall be requested annually of the bishop by the deacon or provisional deacon.

c) The bishop may make an interim appointment to less than full-time service upon request of a deacon or provisional deacon, with the recommendation of the executive committee of the conference Board of Ordained Ministry.

8. Deacons and provisional deacons, with the approval of their bishop and the judicatory authorities of the other denomination may receive an appointment to another denomination while retaining their home conference membership. The appointment may be made in response to exceptional missional needs.

9. *Charge Conference Membership of Deacons and Provisional Deacons.*

a) Deacons and provisional deacons who are appointed to a local congregation, charge, or cooperative parish, shall be members of that charge conference.

b) Deacons and provisional deacons who are appointed to settings beyond the local church shall, after consultation and with the written consent of the pastor in charge, and the district superintendent designate a charge conference within the bounds of the annual conference in which they shall hold membership and to which they shall submit an annual report. Deacons and provisional deacons serving in appointments outside the conference in which they hold membership shall, after consultation and with the written consent of the pastor in charge, also establish an affiliate relationship with a charge conference in the annual conference in which the appointment is located.

10. *Support for Deacons and Provisional Deacons Appointed by a Bishop.*

a) Deacons and provisional deacons shall receive their support under the policies and agreements of the setting to which they are appointed.

b) Deacons who are appointed to a local congregation, charge, or cooperative parish, shall receive a salary from the local church, charge, or cooperative parish (¶ 625.2) not less than the minimum established by the equitable compensation policy of the annual conference for elders. Provisional deacons who are appointed to a local congregation, charge, or cooperative parish shall receive a salary from the local church, charge, or cooperative parish (¶ 625.2, .4) not less than the minimum established for provisional elders. When deacons or provisional deacons are appointed to less than full-time ministry in a local congregation, charge, or cooperative parish, they shall receive a salary that is no less than the minimum salary for elders or provisional elders, prorated in one-quarter time increments (see ¶ 331.6*d*).

c) Deacons and provisional deacons shall participate in the denominational pension and benefit plans and programs. They shall participate in the health benefit and supplemental programs of the annual conference subject to the provisions and standards of those programs as established by the annual conference when health benefit coverage is not provided from another source.

d) The above (§ 10 [*a-c*]) does not apply to a deacon or provisional deacon appointed by a bishop to a nonsalaried position (§ 6 [*d*]).

e) Since deacons and provisional deacons are not guaranteed a place of employment in the Church, special attention shall be given to termination procedures that allow time for seeking another service appointment. Notification of dismissal shall provide for a ninety-day period prior to final termination of the appointment except for causes as listed in ¶ 2702. Deacons or provisional deacons shall not be dismissed from a local church appointment without prior consultation between the deacon or provisional deacon and the staff-parish relations committee, nor without the full knowledge of the overseeing district superinten- dent and the presiding bishop.

Section IX. The Ordained Elder in Full Connection

¶ 332. *Ministry of an Elder*—Elders are ordained ministers who, by God's grace, have completed their formal preparation and have been commissioned and served as a provisional mem- ber, have been found by the Church to be of sound learning, of Christian character, possessing the necessary gifts and evidence of God's grace, and whose call by God to ordination has been con- firmed by the Church. Elders are ordained to a lifetime ministry of Word, Sacrament, Order, and Service. By the authority given in their ordination, they are authorized to preach and teach the Word of God, to provide pastoral care and counsel, to administer the sacraments of baptism and Holy Communion, and to order the life of the Church for service in mission and ministry. The servant leadership of the elder, in both parish and extension ministries, is expressed by leading the people of God in worship and prayer, by leading persons to faith in Jesus Christ, by exercising pastoral supervision, and by ordering the Church in mission in the world.

As members of the Order of Elders, all elders are in covenant with all other elders in the annual conference and shall participate in the life of their order.

¶ 333. *Elders in Full Connection*—1. Elders in full connection with an annual conference by virtue of their election and ordina- tion are bound in special covenant with all the ordained elders of the annual conference. In the keeping of this covenant they perform the ministerial duties and maintain the ministerial stan- dards established by those in the covenant. They offer themselves without reserve to be appointed and to serve, after consultation, as the appointive authority may determine.[18] They live with all other ordained ministers in mutual trust and concern and seek with them the sanctification of the fellowship. By entering into the covenant, they accept and subject themselves to the process of clergy discipline, including serving on committees on investi- gation, trial courts, or appellate committees. Only those shall be elected to full membership who are of unquestionable moral char-

---

18. See Judicial Council Decision 492.

acter and genuine piety, sound in the fundamental doctrines of Christianity, and faithful in the discharge of their duties.[19]

2. A provisional member of the annual conference who has completed the requirements for elder's orders and admission into full membership shall be eligible for election to full membership and ordination as elder by a bishop. Following election, the bishop and secretary of the conference shall provide a certificate of full membership in the annual conference, and following ordination, a certificate of ordination.

3. An elder shall be ordained by a bishop by the laying on of hands, employing the Order of Service for the Ordination of Elders (see ¶ 415.6). The bishop shall be assisted by other elders and may include laity designated by the bishop representing the Church community. Judicatory leaders from full communion partners may participate in the ordination service and may join the ordaining bishop in laying hands on the head of the candidate, while participating elders and laity may lay hands on the back or shoulders of the candidate.

¶ 334. *Ministry, Authority, and Responsibilities of an Elder in Full Connection*—An elder in full connection is authorized to give spiritual and temporal servant leadership in the Church in the following manner:

1. Elders in full connection shall have the right to vote on all matters in the annual conference except in the election of lay delegates to the General and jurisdictional or central conferences (¶ 602.1a) and shall share with deacons in full connection responsibility for all matters of ordination, character, and conference relations of clergy. This responsibility shall not be limited by the recommendation or lack of recommendation by the Board of Ordained Ministry, notwithstanding provisions which grant to the Board of Ordained Ministry the right of recommendation.[20] They shall be eligible to hold office in the annual conference and to be elected delegates to the General and jurisdictional or central conferences under the provision of the Constitution (¶ 35, Article IV). Every effective elder in full connection who is in good standing shall be continued under appointment by the bishop provided that if the elder is appointed to serve in an affiliated relationship in a missionary conference (¶ 586) and that appointment is terminated by the bishop who presides in the missionary conference,

---

19. See Judicial Council Decisions 406, 534.
20. See Judicial Council Decision 690.

then the responsibility for meeting this obligation rests with the bishop of the conference of which the elder is a member.[21]

2. There are professional responsibilities (¶ 340) that elders are expected to fulfill and that represent a fundamental part of their accountability and a primary basis of their continued eligibility for annual appointment. These shall include:

     a) Continuing availability for appointment.[22]

     b) Annual participation in a process of evaluation with committees on pastor-parish relations or comparable authority as well as annual participation in a process of evaluation with the district superintendent or comparable authority.

     c) Evidence of continuing effectiveness reflected in annual evaluations by the pastor-parish relations committee and by the district superintendent or comparable authorities

     d) Growth in professional competence and effectiveness through continuing education and formation. The Board of Ordained Ministry may set the minimum standards and specific guidelines for continuing education and formation for conference members;

     e) Willingness to assume supervisory and mentoring responsibilities within the connection.

3. When an elder's effectiveness is in question, the bishop shall complete the following procedure:

     a) Identify the concerns. These can include an elder's failed professional responsibilities or vocational ineffectiveness.

     b) Hold supervisory conversations with the elder that identifies the concerns and designs, collaboratively with the elder, a corrective plan of action.

     c) Upon evaluation, determine that the plan of action has not been carried out or produced fruit that gives a realistic expectation of future effectiveness.

4. If an elder fails to demonstrate vocational competence or effectiveness (¶ 340) as defined by the annual conference through the Board of Ordained Ministry and cabinet, then the bishop may begin the administrative location process as outlined in ¶ 359.

5. Clergy who are retired, on medical leave, or on sabbatical leave may at their own initiative apply to the conference Board of Ordained Ministry for affiliate membership in the annual conference where they reside. By a two-thirds vote of the executive

---

21. See Judicial Council Decisions 462, 492, 534, 555.
22. See Judicial Council Decision 492.

session, such clergy may be received with rights and privileges, including service on conference boards, agencies, task forces, and committees, with voice but without vote. Voting membership shall be retained in the clergy member's home annual conference for the duration of affiliate member relationship. Such persons may serve on the board, agency, task force, or committee of only one annual conference at any one time.

¶ **335.** *Requirements for Admission to Full Connection and Ordination as Elder*—Provisional members who are candidates for full connection and ordination as elders and have been provisional members for at least two years may be admitted into membership in full connection in an annual conference and approved for elder's ordination by three-fourths majority vote of the clergy members in full connection of the annual conference, upon recommendation by three-fourths majority vote of the Board of Ordained Ministry,[23] after they have qualified as follows. They shall have: (1) served full-time under episcopal appointment for at least two full annual conference years following the completion of the educational requirements specified in (3)(*b*) on the next page. Years of service in any ministry setting requiring the regular proclamation of the word, the administration of the sacraments, and the short or long-term ordering of the life of the community of faith may count toward the fulfillment of this requirement. Such ministry settings may include campus ministry, college and university chaplaincy, hospital and prison chaplaincy, military chaplaincy, overseas/mission work, and other ministries so recognized by the Division of Ordained Ministry of the General Board of Higher Education and Ministry. Upon recommendation of the Board of Ordained Ministry, an annual conference may equate less than full-time to the requirement of full-time service.[24]

Such equivalence is to be determined in light of the years of service involved, the quality of that service, the maturity of the applicant, and other relevant factors. Supervision is to be (*a*) personally assumed or delegated by the district superintendent, and (*b*) assumed by a mentor assigned by the Board of Ordained Ministry. Their service shall be evaluated by the Board of Ordained Ministry as effective according to written guidelines developed by the board and adopted by the clergy members in full connection.[25]

---

23. See Judicial Council Decisions 157, 344, 1199.
24. See Judicial Council Decision 440.
25. See Judicial Council Decisions 555, 719.

In rare cases, the Board of Ordained Ministry may, by a two-thirds vote, approve years of service in an autonomous Methodist church as meeting this requirement if adequate supervision has been provided; (2) been previously elected as provisional members; (3) met the following educational requirements: *(a)* graduation with a Bachelor of Arts or equivalent degree from a college or university listed by the University Senate, or demonstrated competency equivalence through a process designed in consultation with the General Board of Higher Education and Ministry; *(b)* graduation with a Master of Divinity degree from a school of theology listed by the University Senate, or its equivalent as determined by the General Board of Higher Education and Ministry; or *(c)* met the education requirements of ¶ 324.6 for local pastors; *(d)* educational requirements in every case shall include completion of the basic graduate theological studies of the Christian faith as outlined in ¶ 324.4*a*; (4) satisfied the board regarding physical, mental, and emotional health; (5) prepared and preached at least one written sermon on a biblical passage specified by the Board of Ordained Ministry; (6) presented a detailed plan and outline for teaching a Bible study; (7) presented a project that demonstrates fruitfulness in carrying out the church's mission of "Making Disciples of Jesus Christ for the Transformation of the World"; (8) responded to a written or oral doctrinal examination administered by the Board of Ordained Ministry. The candidate should demonstrate the ability to communicate clearly in both oral and written form. The candidate's reflections and the board's response should be informed by the insights and guidelines of Part III of the *Discipline*. The following questions are guidelines for the preparation of the examination:

    a) Theology.

        (1) Give examples of how the practice of ministry has affected your experience and understanding of:

        (a) God
        (b) Humanity
        (c) The need for divine grace
        (d) The Lordship of Jesus Christ
        (e) The work of the Holy Spirit
        (f) The meaning and significance of the sacraments
        (g) The kingdom of God
        (h) Resurrection and eternal life

(2) How do you understand the following traditional evangelical doctrines: *(a)* repentance; *(b)* justification; *(c)* regeneration; *(d)* sanctification? What are the marks of the Christian life?

(3) How has the practice of ministry informed your understanding of the nature and mission of the Church? What are its primary challenges today?

(4) The United Methodist Church holds that Scripture, tradition, experience, and reason are sources and norms for belief and practice, but that the Bible is primary among them. What is your understanding of this theological position of the Church, and how has your practice of ministry been affected by this understanding?

b) Vocation

(1) How has the experience of ministry shaped your understanding of your vocation as an ordained elder?

c) The Practice of Ministry

(1) How has the practice of ministry affected your understanding of the expectations and obligations of the itinerant system? Do you offer yourself without reserve to be appointed and to serve as the appointive authority may determine?

(2) Describe and evaluate your personal gifts for ministry and how they have resulted in fruitful ministry. What would be your areas of strength and areas in which you need to be strengthened in order to be more fruitful in ministry?

(3) For the sake of the mission of Jesus Christ in the world and the most effective witness to the Christian gospel and in consideration of your influence as an ordained minister, are you willing to make a complete dedication of yourself to the highest ideals of the Christian life; and to this end will you agree to exercise responsible self-control by personal habits conducive to physical health, intentional intellectual development, fidelity in marriage and celibacy in singleness, integrity in all personal relationships, social responsibility, and growth in grace and the knowledge and love of God?[26]

(4) Provide evidence of your willingness to relate yourself in ministry with all persons without regard to race, color, ethnicity, national origin, social status, gender, sexual orientation, age, economic condition, or disability.

(5) Will you regard all pastoral conversations of a confessional nature as a trust between the person concerned and God?

---

26. See Judicial Council Decision 542.

(6) Provide evidence of experience in peace and justice ministries.

ADMISSION AND CONTINUANCE OF FULL MEMBERSHIP
IN THE ANNUAL CONFERENCE

¶ 336. *Historic Examination for Admission into Full Connection—* The bishop as chief pastor shall engage those seeking to be admitted in serious self-searching and prayer to prepare them for their examination before the conference. At the time of the examination the bishop shall also explain to the conference the historic nature of the following questions and seek to interpret their spirit and intent. The questions are these and any others that may be thought necessary:

1. Have you faith in Christ?
2. Are you going on to perfection?
3. Do you expect to be made perfect in love in this life?
4. Are you earnestly striving after it?
5. Are you resolved to devote yourself wholly to God and his work?
6. Do you know the General Rules of our Church?
7. Will you keep them?
8. Have you studied the doctrines of The United Methodist Church?
9. After full examination, do you believe that our doctrines are in harmony with the Holy Scriptures?
10. Will you preach and maintain them?
11. Have you studied our form of Church discipline and polity?
12. Do you approve our Church government and polity?
13. Will you support and maintain them?
14. Will you diligently instruct the children in every place?
15. Will you visit from house to house?
16. Will you recommend fasting or abstinence, both by precept and example?
17. Are you determined to employ all your time in the work of God?
18. Are you in debt so as to embarrass you in your work?
19. Will you observe the following directions?

   a) Be diligent. Never be unemployed. Never be triflingly employed. Never trifle away time; neither spend any more time at any one place than is strictly necessary.

b) Be punctual. Do everything exactly at the time. And do not mend our rules, but keep them; not for wrath, but for conscience' sake.[27]

Section X. Appointments to Various Ministries

¶ **337.** *General Provisions*-1. All elders in full connection who are in good standing in an annual conference shall be continued under appointment by the bishop unless they are granted a sabbatical leave, a medical leave (¶ 356), family leave, a leave of absence, retirement, or have failed to meet the requirements for continued eligibility (¶ 334.2, .3), provided that if the elder is appointed to serve in an affiliated relationship in a missionary conference (¶ 586.4*b*) and that appointment is terminated by the bishop who presides in the missionary conference, then the responsibility for meeting this obligation rests with the bishop of the conference of which the elder is a member.[28]

2. In addition to ordained elders, persons who have been granted a license for pastoral ministry and who have been approved by vote of the clergy members in full connection may be appointed to local churches as pastors in charge under certain conditions, which are specified in ¶¶ 315-318.[29] All clergy members and licensed local pastors to be appointed shall assume a lifestyle consistent with Christian teaching as set forth in the Social Principles.

3. Elders, associate members, provisional elders, and persons licensed for pastoral ministry may be appointed to ministry settings that extend the ministry of The United Methodist Church and the witness and service of Christ's love and justice in the world. They shall be given the same moral and spiritual support by the annual conference as are persons in appointments to pastoral charges. Their effectiveness shall be evaluated in the context of the specific setting in which their ministry is performed. Such ministry settings shall include teaching, pastoral care and counseling, chaplaincy, campus ministry, social services, and other ministries so recognized by the conference Board of Ordained Ministry and approved by the bishop.

---

27. These are the questions that every Methodist preacher from the beginning has been required to answer upon becoming a full member of an annual conference. These questions were formulated by John Wesley and have been little changed throughout the years.

28. See Judicial Council Decisions 380, 462, 492, 524, 702, 985, 1226.

29. See Judicial Council Decision 1226.

a) Full connection and provisional member elders, associate members, and persons licensed for pastoral ministry may be appointed to Extension Ministries serving in ministries of pastoral care in specialized settings. See ¶¶ 326, 343-344 for specific information about Extension Ministries.

b) Elders may be appointed to extension ministries that include appointments as students in research doctoral programs that may lead to appointments in academic settings as instructors or professors in colleges, universities, and theological schools affiliated with The United Methodist Church. Elders may also be appointed to extension ministries, including service as instructors or professors or administrators in colleges, universities, and theological schools affiliated with The United Methodist Church.

c) All persons in such appointments should:

(1) be appointed to a setting that provides an appropriate support and accountability structure;

(2) continue to be accountable to the annual conference for the practice of their ministry;

(3) provide an annual report, including a narrative of their ministry, evidence of continuing education, and evidence of an annual evaluation in their setting;

(4) maintain a relationship with a charge conference.

¶ **338.** *The Itinerant System*—The itinerant system is the accepted method of The United Methodist Church by which ordained elders, provisional elders, and associate members are appointed by the bishop to fields of labor.[30] All ordained elders, provisional elders, and associate members shall accept and abide by these appointments.[31] Bishops and cabinets shall commit to and support open itineracy and the protection of the prophetic pulpit and diversity. Persons appointed to multiple-staff ministries, either in a single parish or in a cluster or larger parish, shall have personal and professional access to the bishop and cabinet, the committee on pastor-parish relations, as well as to the pastor in charge. The nature of the appointment process is specified in ¶¶ 425-429.

1. Full-time service shall be the norm for ordained elders, provisional elders, and associate members in the annual conference. Full-time service shall mean that the person's entire vocational time, as defined by the district superintendent in consul-

---

30. See Judicial Council Decision 713.
31. See Judicial Council Decision 492.

tation with the pastor and the committee on pastor-parish relations, is devoted to the work of ministry in the field of labor to
which one is appointed by the bishop.

2. *Less Than Full-Time Service*—On occasion, less than full-
time service is requested by or required of an elder, provisional
elder, or associate member. A clergy member may be appointed
in one-quarter, one-half, or three-quarter time increments by the
bishop to less than full-time service without loss of essential rights
or membership in the annual conference. Division of Ordained
Ministry-endorsed appointments beyond the local church may be
for less than full-time service.

a) Appointment to less than full-time service is not a
guarantee, but may be made by the bishop under the following
circumstances:

(1) *Limited Itinerary*—Less than full-time service may
be granted—but is not guaranteed—when the elder, provisional
elder, or associate member has declared in writing that itinerancy
is limited due to temporary constraints. The clergy member shall
present that written declaration to the bishop and the chairperson
of the Board of Ordained Ministry prior to the annual conference
session at which the appointment is made.

(2) *Self-Initiated*—The elder, provisional elder, or
associate member seeking less than full-time service shall present
a written request to the bishop and the chairperson of the Board
of Ordained Ministry at least 90 days prior to the annual conference session at which the appointment is made. Exceptions to the
90-day deadline shall be approved by the cabinet and the executive committee of the Board of Ordained Ministry.

(3) *Bishop-Initiated*—For missional purposes, the
bishop may appoint an elder, provisional elder, or an associate
member to less than full-time service. The clergyperson shall be
notified at least 90 days prior to final termination of the current
appointment. Special attention shall be given to ensure that the
values of open itinerancy are preserved.

b) Provisions for Less Than Full-time Appointment

(1) Following appropriate consultation, as established in ¶¶ 338 and 425-429, and upon joint recommendation of
the cabinet and the Board of Ordained Ministry, the less than full-
time category shall be confirmed by a two-thirds vote of the clergy
members in full connection of the annual conference.

(2) Reappointment to less than full-time service shall be approved annually by the bishop and cabinet and shall not be granted for more than a total of eight years, except by a three-fourths vote of the clergy members in full connection of the annual conference.

(3) Elders, provisional elders, and associate members who receive appointment at less than full-time service remain within the itineracy and, as such, remain available, upon consultation with the bishop and cabinet, for appointment to full-time service. A written request to return to full-time appointment shall be made to the bishop and cabinet at least six months prior to the annual conference session at which the appointment is to be made.

(4) The bishop may make *ad interim* appointments at less than full-time service upon request of the elder, provisional elder, or associate member following consultation as specified in ¶¶ 424-428 and upon recommendation of the cabinet and executive committee of the Board of Ordained Ministry, the same to be acted upon by the next regular session of the annual conference.[32]

3. Interim appointments may be made to charges that have special transitional needs.

a) Interim clergy may serve outside the annual conference where membership is held under the provision of ¶ 346.1, with approval and consent of the bishops involved.

b) Interim appointments will be for a specified length of time, established in advance following consultation with the district superintendent, the pastor-parish relations committee, and the interim pastor.

4. Associate members, provisional members, or full members may be appointed to attend any school, college, or theological seminary listed by the University Senate, or participate in a program of clinical pastoral education in a setting accredited by the Association for Clinical Pastoral Education or another accrediting agency approved by the General Board of Higher Education and Ministry.

¶ **339.** *Definition of a Pastor*—A pastor is an ordained elder, probationary deacon (according to 1992 *Book of Discipline*), associate member, provisional elder, or local pastor approved by vote of the clergy session and may be appointed by the bishop to be in

---

32. See Judicial Council Decision 579.

charge of a station, circuit, cooperative parish, extension ministry, ecumenical shared ministry,[33] or to a church of another denomination, or on the staff of one such appointment.

¶ **340.** *Responsibilities and Duties of Elders and Licensed Pastors*—1. The responsibilities of elders are derived from the authority given in ordination. Elders have a fourfold ministry of Word, Sacrament, Order, and Service and thus serve in the local church and in extension ministries in witness and service of Christ's love and justice. Elders are authorized to preach and teach the Word, to provide pastoral care and counsel, to administer the sacraments, and to order the life of the church for service in mission and ministry as pastors, superintendents, and bishops.

2. Licensed pastors share with the elders the responsibilities and duties of a pastor for this fourfold ministry, within the context of their appointment.

a) *Word and ecclesial acts:*

(1) To preach the Word of God, lead in worship, read and teach the Scriptures, and engage the people in study and witness.

(*a*) To ensure faithful transmission of the Christian faith.

(*b*) To lead people in discipleship and evangelistic outreach that others might come to know Christ and to follow him.

(2) To counsel persons with personal, ethical, or spiritual struggles.

(3) To perform the ecclesial acts of marriage and burial.

(*a*) To perform the marriage ceremony after due counsel with the parties involved and in accordance with the laws of the state and the rules of The United Methodist Church. The decision to perform the ceremony shall be the right and responsibility of the pastor.

---

33. *Ecumenical shared ministries* are ecumenical congregations formed by a local United Methodist church and one or more local congregations of other Christian traditions. Forms of ecumenical shared ministries include: (a) a federated congregation, in which one congregation is related to two denominations, with persons holding membership in one or the other of the denominations; (b) a union congregation, in which a congregation with one unified membership roll is related to two denominations; (c) a merged congregation, in which two or more congregations of different denominations form one congregation which relates to only one of the constituent denominations; and (d) a yoked parish, in which a United Methodist congregation is yoked with one or more congregations of other denominations.

(*b*) To conduct funeral and memorial services and provide care and grief counseling.

(4) To visit in the homes of the church and the community, especially among the sick, aged, imprisoned, and others in need.

(5) To maintain all confidences inviolate, including confessional confidences except in the cases of suspected child abuse or neglect, or in cases where mandatory reporting is required by civil law.

b) Sacrament:

(1) To administer the sacraments of baptism and the Supper of the Lord according to Christ's ordinance.

(*a*) To prepare the parents and sponsors before baptizing infants or children, and instruct them concerning the significance of baptism and their responsibilities for the Christian training of the baptized child.

(*b*) To encourage reaffirmation of the baptismal covenant and renewal of baptismal vows at different stages of life.

(*c*) To encourage people baptized in infancy or early childhood to make their profession of faith, after instruction, so that they might become professing members of the church.

(*d*) To explain the meaning of the Lord's Supper and to encourage regular participation as a means of grace to grow in faith and holiness.

(*e*) To select and train deacons and lay members to serve the consecrated communion elements.

(2) To encourage the private and congregational use of the other means of grace.

c) Order:

(1) To be the administrative officer of the local church and to assure that the organizational concerns of the congregation are adequately provided for.

(*a*) To give pastoral support, guidance, and training to the lay leadership, equipping them to fulfill the ministry to which they are called.

(*b*) To give oversight to the educational program of the church and encourage the use of United Methodist literature and media.

(*c*) To be responsible for organizational faithfulness, goal setting, planning and evaluation.

(*d*) To search out and counsel men and women for the ministry of deacons, elders, local pastors, and other church-related ministries.

(2) To administer the temporal affairs of the church in their appointment, the annual conference, and the general Church.

(*a*) To administer the provisions of the *Discipline*.

(*b*) To give an account of their pastoral ministries to the charge and annual conference according to the prescribed forms.

(*c*) To provide leadership for the funding ministry of the congregation. To ensure membership care including compliance with charitable giving documentation requirements and to provide appropriate pastoral care, the pastor, in cooperation with the financial secretary, shall have access to and responsibility for professional stewardship of congregational giving records.

(*d*) To model and promote faithful financial stewardship and to encourage giving as a spiritual discipline by teaching the biblical principles of giving.

(*e*) To lead the congregation in the fulfillment of its mission through full and faithful payment of all apportioned ministerial support, administrative, and benevolent funds.

(*f*) To care for all church records and local church financial obligations, and certify the accuracy of all financial, membership, and any other reports submitted by the local church to the annual conference for use in apportioning costs back to the church.

(3) To participate in denominational and conference programs and training opportunities.

(*a*) To seek out opportunities for cooperative ministries with other United Methodist pastors and churches.

(*b*) To be willing to assume supervisory responsibilities within the connection.

(4) To lead the congregation in racial and ethnic inclusiveness.

d) Service:

(1) To embody the teachings of Jesus in servant ministries and servant leadership.

(2) To give diligent pastoral leadership in ordering the life of the congregation for discipleship in the world.

(3) To build the body of Christ as a caring and giving community, extending the ministry of Christ to the world.

(4) To participate in community, ecumenical, and interreligious concerns and to encourage the people to become so involved and to pray and labor for the unity of the Christian community.

¶ **341.** *Unauthorized Conduct*—1. Pastors shall first obtain the written consent of the district superintendent before engaging for an evangelist any person who is not a general evangelist (¶¶ 630.3f, 1112.7), a clergy member of an annual conference, a local pastor, or a certified lay servant in good standing in The United Methodist Church.

2. No pastor shall discontinue services in a local church between sessions of the annual conference without the consent of the charge conference and the district superintendent.

3. No pastor shall arbitrarily organize a pastoral charge. (See ¶ 259 for the method of organizing a local church.)

4. No pastor shall hold a religious service within the bounds of a pastoral charge other than the one to which appointed without the consent of the pastor of the charge, or the district superintendent. No pastor shall hold a religious service within the bounds of a pastoral charge or establish a ministry to a college or university campus served by The United Methodist Church without the consent of the pastor of the charge, or campus minister or chaplain serving the charge, or the district superintendent. If that pastor does not refrain from such conduct, he or she shall then be liable to the provisions of ¶ 362.1 and ¶ 2702.

5. All clergy of The United Methodist Church are charged to maintain all confidences inviolate, including confessional confidences, except in the cases of suspected child abuse or neglect or in cases where mandatory reporting is required by civil law.[34]

6. Ceremonies that celebrate homosexual unions shall not be conducted by our ministers and shall not be conducted in our churches.[35]

7. No pastor shall re-baptize. The practice of re-baptism does not conform with God's action in baptism and is not consistent with Wesleyan tradition and the historic teaching of the church. Therefore, the pastor should counsel any person seeking re-baptism to participate in a rite of reaffirmation of baptismal vows.

---

34. See Judicial Council Decision 936.
35. See Judicial Council Decision 1115.

¶ **342.** *Support for Elders in Full Connection Appointed to Pastoral Charges*—To strengthen the effectiveness of the connectional system, assumption of the obligations of the itinerant ministry required upon admission to the traveling connection places upon the Church a counter obligation to provide adequate support for the entire ministry of the Church (¶ 620). The Church shall provide, and the ordained minister is entitled to receive, not less than the equitable compensation established by the annual conference for clergy members according to provisions of ¶ 625.3.[36]

1. *Support for Elders in Full Connection Appointed to Pastoral Charges Who Render Full-Time Service*—Each elder in full connection of an annual conference who is in good standing and who is appointed to full-time service under the provision of ¶ 338.1 shall have a claim upon the conference Equitable Compensation Fund and a right to receive not less than base compensation established by the annual conference for persons in full-time service.[37]

2. *Support for Ordained Elders Appointed to Pastoral Charges Who Render Less than Full-Time Service*—Each elder in full connection who is in good standing and who is appointed by the bishop to less than full-time service under the provisions of ¶ 338.2 shall have a claim upon the conference Equitable Compensation Fund in one-quarter increments according to the guidelines established by the annual conference commission on equitable compensation.

3. Notwithstanding anything herein to the contrary, the benefits provided to ordained ministers, in addition to the cash compensation, under the benefit programs administered by the General Board of Pension and Health Benefits may be different for ordained ministers serving full-time as pastors to local charges and for ordained ministers serving other types of appointments.

4. No pastor shall be entitled to any claim for unpaid base compensation against any church or charge served after pastoral connection with the church or charge has ceased.

Section XI. Appointments to Extension Ministries

¶ **343.** *Appointments Extending the Ministry of The United Methodist Church*—1. Elders in effective relationship may be appointed to serve in ministry settings beyond the local United Methodist church in the witness and service of Christ's love and justice.

---

36. See Judicial Council Decisions 968, 988.
37. See Judicial Council Decisions 579, 587, 968, 1038.

Persons in these appointments remain within the itineracy and shall be accountable to the annual conference. They shall be given the same moral and spiritual support by it as are persons in appointments to pastoral charges.[38] Their effectiveness shall be evaluated in the context of the specific setting in which their ministry is performed.

2. The institution or agency desiring to employ an ordained minister shall, when feasible, through its appropriate official, consult the ordained minister's bishop and secure approval before completing any agreement to employ the ordained minister. If the institution or agency is located in another area, the bishop of that area shall also be consulted.

3. Elders desiring an appointment extending the ministry of The United Methodist Church or change of appointment shall consult with their bishop and/or district superintendent prior to any interviews relative to such an appointment.

¶ **344.** *Provisions for Appointment to Extension Ministries*— Elders and associate members in appointments extending the ministry of the local United Methodist church are full participants in the itinerant system. Therefore, a conference member in an appointment beyond the local United Methodist church must be willing upon consultation to receive an appointment in a pastoral charge. When either the conference member or the annual conference requests appointment to a pastoral charge, the request shall be made in writing to or from the bishop, the cabinet, and the Board of Ordained Ministry. Such a request should be made at least six months prior to annual conference. In both instances, consultation shall give due regard to the individual's special training, experience, skills, and leadership potential.

1. *Categories of Appointment*—In order to establish a clear distinction between the work to which all Christians are called and the tasks for which clergy are appropriately prepared and authorized, the following categories are established for appointments of elders and associate members within the itineracy and those licensed for pastoral ministry of The United Methodist Church.

a) Appointments within the connectional structures of United Methodism:

(1) Appointments for which the annual conference provides for pension contributions to the Ministerial Pension Plan,

---

38. See Judicial Council Decisions 321, 325.

amended and restated effective January 1, 2007, as the Clergy Retirement Security Program, such as district superintendents, staff members of conference councils and boards, treasurers, bishops' assistants, superintendents or directors of parish development, general evangelists, and campus ministers. Only elders in full connection may be appointed district superintendents;

(2) Appointments to a general agency for which the general agency provides pension contributions through December 31, 2006, to the Ministerial Pension Plan and, effective January 1, 2007, to the Retirement Security Program for General Agencies of The United Methodist Church, amended and restated effective January 1, 2010, as the Retirement Plan for General Agencies;

(3) Appointments to a United Methodist institution or other ministry, such as superintendents or directors of parish development, general evangelists, campus ministers, missionaries, faculty and administrators of United Methodist schools of theology or other educational institutions approved by the University Senate; and

(4) Appointments to an ecumenical agency.

b) Appointments to extension ministries of elders in full connection, associate members, and those licensed for pastoral ministry under endorsement by the General Board of Higher Education and Ministry and other ministry settings which the bishop and conference Board of Ordained Ministry may designate.[39] The board shall annually verify the appropriate employment of persons under its endorsement and request their reappointment.

c) Elders, associate members, and those licensed for pastoral ministry in service under the General Board of Global Ministries may be appointed to the ministries listed in *a)* and *b)* above. They may be assigned to service either in annual conferences or central conferences, or with affiliated autonomous churches, independent churches, churches resulting from the union of Methodist Churches and other communions, mission institutions, or in other denominational or ecumenical ministries. They may accept such rights and privileges, including affiliate membership, as may be offered them by central conferences or by other churches to which they are assigned without impairing their relationship to their home annual conference. If appointment is to a missionary conference, the terms of the appointment shall be as provided in ¶ 586.4.

---

39. See Judicial Council Decisions 321, 325, 329.

d) Elders, associate members, and those licensed for pastoral ministry may receive appointments beyond the ministry usually extended through the local United Methodist church and other institutions listed above in *a)* and *b)*[40] when considered by the bishop and the annual conference Board of Ordained Ministry to be a true extension of the Christian ministry of the Church. They may be appointed to pastoral ministry in other Christian denominations at the request of appropriate judicatory officers of that denomination. These ministries shall be initiated in missional response to the needs of persons in special circumstances and unique situations and shall reflect the commitment of the clergy to intentional fulfillment of their ordination vows to Word, Sacrament, Order, and Service. These appointments may involve clergy with expertise from other vocations. Conference members in such appointments retain conference membership, and the annual conference may choose to extend financial support and benefits for its clergy by vote of the annual conference. (See ¶ 625.3, .5.)

Conference members who serve as staff members of ecumenical agencies or as pastors of non-United Methodist congregations may also be considered as holding an extension ministry, provided their position is approved by the bishop and the conference Board of Ordained Ministry. They shall remain accountable to their vows as members of their annual conference.

The General Board of Higher Education and Ministry, in order to assist boards of ordained ministry, will provide standards and consultation to assist in validating the appropriateness of special ministry settings. In addition, it will provide advocacy for persons serving in settings approved under this paragraph and shall encourage the development of emerging ministries that extend the ministry of the Church into the world.

Those seeking such an appointment shall submit a written statement to the cabinet, and the Board of Ordained Ministry, describing in detail the proposed setting for their ministry, sharing a sense of calling to that ministry and their gifts and evidence of God's grace for it, and expressing the intentional fulfillment of their ordination vows. This material will be submitted not later than 120 days before desired appointment to the proposed setting. On recommendation of the cabinet and the Board of Ordained Ministry, such positions are to be confirmed by a two-thirds vote of the clergy members of the annual conference.

---

40. See Judicial Council Decisions 380, 877.

The bishop may make *ad interim* appointments in this category after consultation with the cabinet and executive committee of the Board of Ordained Ministry, the position to be formally acted upon by the next session of the annual conference.

2. *Relation to the Annual Conference—a) Accountability to the Annual Conference*—All clergy in extension ministries are amenable to the annual conference of which they are members and insofar as possible should maintain close working relationship with and effective participation in the work of their annual conference, assuming whatever responsibilities they are qualified and requested to assume.

All clergy under appointment in extension ministries shall submit annually to the bishop, the district superintendent, and the Board of Ordained Ministry a written report on the official form developed for the Church by the General Council on Finance and Administration for use by the annual conference. This report shall serve as the basis for the evaluation of these clergy in light of the missional needs of the Church and the fulfillment of their licensing or ordination to be minister of Service, Word, Sacrament, and Order. All clergy formally evaluated by the institutions in which they serve will provide, instead of an evaluation, a narrative report reflecting their ministry. All clergy serving in appointments outside the conference in which they hold membership shall furnish a copy of their report also to the bishop of the area in which they serve. Annual conferences shall review the qualifications of persons in extension ministry status and integrate them into the ongoing work of the annual conference.

b) Responsibility of the Annual Conference—The bishop, representatives of the cabinet, and an endorsed representative from extension ministries within the Board of Ordained Ministry shall provide an opportunity to meet annually with clergy in extension ministries who perform their ministry within the bounds of annual conference, both of that annual conference and those who hold membership elsewhere. The bishop shall convene the meeting, which is to be planned by the cabinet and the Board of Ordained Ministry. The purpose of this meeting is to gain understanding of one another's role and function in ministry; to report to other ordained ministers appointed to extension ministries and discuss with them matters concerning the overall approach to ministry in the episcopal area; to interpret the role and function of extension ministries to the larger church through the offices of the bishop and his or her representatives; to nurture the development of various ministries as significant in assisting the mission of the Church; and to discuss specific programs and services that the bishop and his or her representatives may initiate, in which the various ordained ministers serving in appointments beyond the local church may be qualified as consultants and supervisors. Using the appropriate resources and personnel of the annual conference, the bishop shall provide for an annual visit to the ministry setting of all persons under appointment in extension ministries assigned within the geographical bounds of the annual conference and shall provide a report of the visit to the bishop of persons from other annual conferences.

3. *Relation to the Local Church—a)* All clergy appointed in extension ministries shall establish membership in a charge conference in their home annual conference in consultation with the pastor in charge and with approval of the district superintendent and the bishop. They shall submit to their home charge conference an annual report of pastoral duties and the fulfillment of their licensing or ordination through their special appointment, including ministerial activities in the charge where they have an affiliate membership relation and in other units of the Church at large, as well as continuing formation experiences completed and anticipated. This report may be the one submitted to the bishop, district superintendent, and Board of Ordained Ministry (¶ 344.2a). District superintendents, because of the nature of their work and the relationship defined in ¶¶ 424.3, 362.1a, and 661, shall not be required to have a charge conference affiliation.

All conference members who are elders in full connection, including those in extension ministries, shall be available and on call to administer the sacraments of baptism and the Lord's Supper as required by the *Discipline* (¶ 340.2b) and requested by the district superintendent of the district in which the appointment is held.

*b) Affiliate Relation to a Local Church—*All clergy under appointment to extension ministries and serving outside of the geographical bounds of their home annual conference shall promptly notify the bishop of the area in which they reside of their names, addresses, and the annual conferences in which their credentials are held. They shall be affiliate members without vote of a charge conference either within the district where they carry out the primary work of their appointment or within the district where they reside. Persons serving outside the geographic bounds of any annual conference are exempt from this requirement. The selection of the charge conference shall be made after consultation between the person in extension ministry and the pastor of the local United Methodist church.

These clergy under appointment in extension ministries and serving outside the geographical boundaries of their home annual conference shall submit to the charge conference of which they are affiliate members a copy of the report submitted to their home charge conference and/or an oral report concerning their ministry and the fulfillment of their licensing or ordination. The district superintendent shall be responsible for the notification to these ministers concerning the time and place of the charge conference.

4. *Affiliate Relation to Annual Conference*—Ordained clergy appointed to extension ministries or appointments beyond the local church outside the boundary of their annual conference may at their own initiative apply to the Board of Ordained Ministry for affiliate membership in the annual conference in which their appointment is located or in which they reside. By a two-thirds vote of the clergy session, such clergy may be received with rights and privileges, including service on conference boards, agencies, task forces, and committees, with voice and vote but with voice and without vote in the annual conference session. Voting membership shall be retained in the appointee's home annual conference for the duration of affiliate member relationship. Nomination to general Church boards and agencies and election as delegates to General and jurisdictional conferences shall originate in the appointee's home annual conference. Such persons may serve on the board, agency, task force, or committee of only one annual conference at any one time.[41]

5. *General Provisions*—*a)* These appointments shall be made only to positions related to adequate accountability structures, according to guidelines established by the Board of Ordained Ministry and cabinet in the annual conferences in which membership is held.

b) For information regarding pensions, the conference will continue to list the source of annuity claim for each of its clergy.

c) All conference secretaries shall submit to the editors of the General Minutes a list of such appointments beyond the local

---

41. See Judicial Council Decision 554.

church made in their annual conferences, and there shall be published in the General Minutes a list of ordained ministers in the Church serving in the major categories under these appointments.

d) All clergy appointed to extension ministries shall attend the annual conference in which membership is held.

e) Individual participation in Armed Forces Reserve or National Guard units and part-time employment with the Veteran's Administration shall be reflected in annual conference journals.

PROVISIONS FOR APPOINTMENTS
TO ECUMENICAL SHARED MINISTRIES

¶ **345.** United Methodist clergy members in full connection may be appointed annually to churches of other Christian denominations or to ecumenical shared ministries. Persons in these appointments remain in the itinerancy and shall be accountable to the annual conference. Their effectiveness shall be evaluated in the context of the specific setting in which their ministry is performed. (See ¶ 344.1*d*.)

Section XII. Clergy From Other Annual Conferences, Other Methodist and Christian Denominations

¶ **346.** *Provisions for Clergy From Outside the Annual Conference*—Ordained clergy or provisional members from other annual conferences and Christian denominations may receive an appointment in the annual conference in the following manner:

1. *Ordained Clergy or Provisional Members From Other Annual Conferences and Other Methodist Denominations*—With approval and consent of the bishops or other judicatory authorities involved, ordained clergy or provisional members of other annual conferences or other Methodist churches may receive appointments in the annual or missionary conference while retaining their home conference membership or denominational affiliation. Appointments are to be made by the resident bishop of the conference in which the clergy person is to serve. If appointment is to a missionary conference, the terms of the appointment shall be as provided in ¶ 586.4. Otherwise upon the recommendation of the Board of Ordained Ministry, clergy in such appointments may be granted voice but not vote in the annual conference to which they are appointed. Their membership on conference boards and agencies is restricted to the conference of which they are a member. They

shall be compensated no less than the equitable salary provisions of the annual conference in which they serve and participate in the pension and insurance programs of that annual conference. Such appointments are renewable annually. Furthermore, it shall be the responsibility of the board of pensions of the annual conference in which the appointment is received to enroll such clergy in the Clergy Retirement Security Program or any successor retirement plan and the Comprehensive Protection Plan or any successor welfare plan (see ¶ 1506.17).[42]

2. *Elders or Ordained Clergy From Other Denominations*—On recommendation of the Board of Ordained Ministry, the clergy members in full connection may approve annually clergy in good standing in other Christian denominations to serve appointments or ecumenical ministries within the bounds of the annual conference while retaining their denominational affiliation, provided they present suitable credentials, give assurance of their Christian faith and experience, and release required psychological reports, criminal background and credit checks, and reports of sexual misconduct and/or child abuse. They shall submit, on a form provided by the conference Board of Ordained Ministry: a notarized statement detailing any convictions for felony or misdemeanor or written accusations of sexual misconduct or child abuse; or a notarized statement certifying that the candidate has not been convicted of a felony or misdemeanor, or accused in writing of sexual misconduct or child abuse. They shall give evidence of their agreement with and willingness to support and maintain United Methodist doctrine, discipline, and polity. Their ordination credentials shall be examined by the bishop and the Board of Ordained Ministry and, upon its recommendation, may be recognized as valid elders in The United Methodist Church while they are under appointment. When the Board of Ordained Ministry certifies that their credentials are at least equal to those of United Methodist elders, they may be accorded the right to vote in the annual conference on all matters except the following: *(a)* constitutional amendments; *(b)* election of delegates to the General and jurisdictional or central conferences; *(c)* all matters of ordination, character, and conference relations of ministers. They may serve on any board, commission, or committee of an annual conference, except the Board of Ordained Ministry and the board of trustees

---

42. See Judicial Council Decision 554.

(¶¶ 635.1, 2512.1). They shall not be eligible for election as delegates to the General, jurisdictional, or central conferences. They shall also be subject to the provisions governing sabbatical leave, leave of absence, location, retirement, minimum salary, and pension. They shall not have security of appointment.[43]

3. Between conference sessions, the Board of Ordained Ministry may approve them for appointment pending the recognition of their orders. The bishop may make *ad interim* recognition of valid ordination after consultation with the cabinet and executive committee of the Board of Ordained Ministry, pending recognition by the vote of the clergy members in full connection. In every case, prior examination shall be made of the ordained minister's understanding, acceptance, and willingness to support and maintain United Methodist doctrine, discipline, and polity.[44]

¶ 347. *Transfers*—1. *From Other Annual Conferences*—Ordained clergy or provisional members from other annual conferences of The United Methodist Church may be received by transfer into provisional or full membership with the consent of the bishops involved. Recommendation by the executive committee of the Board of Ordained Ministry and approval of the clergy session shall take place prior to the transfer.

2. *From Other Methodist Denominations—a)* Ordained elders or ordained clergy from other Methodist churches may be received by transfer into provisional or full conference membership or as local pastors, with the consent of the bishops or other authorities involved, without going through the process required for ministers from other denominations. The General Board of Higher Education and Ministry shall establish a list of denominations that meet this definition. Prior consultation with the chairperson or executive committee of the Board of Ordained Ministry shall be held in order to determine that the minister meets the standards for conference membership established by the *Discipline* and the annual conference. A psychological report, criminal background and credit check, and reports of sexual misconduct and/or child abuse shall be required. They shall submit, on a form provided by the conference Board of Ordained Ministry:

(1) a notarized statement detailing any convictions for felony or misdemeanor or written accusations of sexual misconduct or child abuse; or

---

43. See Judicial Council Decision 16.
44. See Judicial Council Decision 444.

(2) a notarized statement certifying that this candidate has not been convicted of a felony or misdemeanor, or accused in writing of sexual misconduct or child abuse.

b) Ordained elders or ordained clergy being transferred from other Methodist churches shall meet the educational requirements of The United Methodist Church, or the equivalent approved by the General Board of Higher Education and Ministry.

c) The General Board of Higher Education and Ministry shall certify the satisfaction of educational requirements for conference membership and, in cases where additional education is required, shall develop an educational program in consultation with the Board of Ordained Ministry.

3. *From Other Denominations—a)* On recommendation of the Board of Ordained Ministry, the clergy members in full connection may recognize the orders of ordained clergy from other denominations and receive them as provisional members or local pastors. They shall present their credentials for examination by the bishop and Board of Ordained Ministry and give assurance of their Christian faith and experience. They shall give evidence of their agreement with and willingness to support and maintain United Methodist doctrine, discipline, and polity and present a satisfactory certificate of good health on the prescribed form from a physician approved by the Board of Ordained Ministry. The Board of Ordained Ministry, in consultation with the General Board of Higher Education and Ministry, shall determine whether they meet the educational requirements for conference membership. A psychological report, criminal background and credit check, and reports of sexual misconduct and/or child abuse shall be required. They shall submit, on a form provided by the conference Board of Ordained Ministry:

(1) a notarized statement detailing any convictions for felony or misdemeanor or written accusations of sexual misconduct of child abuse; or

(2) a notarized statement certifying that the candidate has not been convicted of a felony or misdemeanor, or accused in writing of sexual misconduct or child abuse.

b) Ordained elders or ordained clergy from other Christian denominations shall serve as provisional members for at least two years and complete all the requirements of ¶ 335, including courses in United Methodist history, doctrine, and polity, before being admitted into full conference membership.

c) Following the provisional member's election to full conference membership as a deacon or elder as provided in ¶ 326, the bishop and secretary of the conference shall provide a certificate of full membership in the annual conference.

4. The Board of Ordained Ministry of an annual conference is required to ascertain from an ordained clergyperson seeking admission into its membership on credentials from another denomination whether or not membership in the effective relation was previously held in an annual conference of The United Methodist Church or one of its legal predecessors, and if so, when and under what circumstances the ordained minister's connection with such annual conference was severed.

5. Ordained clergy seeking admission into an annual conference on credentials from another denomination who have previously withdrawn from membership in the effective relation in an annual conference of The United Methodist Church or one of its legal predecessors shall not be admitted or readmitted without the consent of the annual conference from which they withdrew or its legal successor, or the annual conference of which the major portion of their former conference is a part, such consent to be granted upon recommendation of its Board of Ordained Ministry.

6. After the orders of an ordained minister of another church shall have been duly recognized, and the minister has been approved for full membership, the certificates of ordination by said church shall be returned to the minister with the following inscription written plainly on the back:

These orders are recognized by the _____ *Annual Conference of The United Methodist Church, this* _____ *day of* _____, _____ *[year].*

_____, *President*

_____, *Secretary*

The ordained minister also will be furnished with a certificate of recognition of orders signed by the bishop.

Section XIII. Mentoring and Mentors

¶ **348.** *Mentors*—1. Mentors shall be recommended by the cabinet, selected, trained and held accountable by the Board of Ordained Ministry. There are two categories of mentor, each with distinct functions and responsibilities as follows:

a) Candidacy mentors are clergy in full connection, associate members, or local pastors who have completed the Course of Study trained to provide counsel and guidance related to the candidacy process. Candidates will be assigned to a candidacy mentoring group, wherever possible, or to a candidacy mentor by the district committee on ordained ministry in consultation with the vocational discernment coordinator (wherever named) and the district superintendent (¶ 310). Candidates will be assigned to a candidacy mentor or mentoring groups to meet with until they begin serving as a local pastor or provisional member.

b) Clergy mentors are clergy in full connection, associate members, full-time, or part-time local pastors who have completed the Course of Study trained to provide ongoing oversight and counsel with local pastors and with provisional members. Local pastors will be assigned a clergy mentor by the district committee on ordained ministry in consultation with the district superintendent. Provisional members will be assigned a clergy mentor in full connection by the conference Board of Ordained Ministry in consultation with the district superintendent. A candidacy mentor may continue with the same person if trained to serve as a clergy mentor.

2. Mentoring occurs within a relationship where the mentor takes responsibility for creating a safe place for reflection and growth. An effective mentor has a mature faith, models effective ministry, and possesses the necessary skill to help individuals discern their call in ministry. Mentoring is a part of the preparation and growth for inquirers and candidates for ordained ministry, local pastors and provisional members of an annual conference. Mentoring is distinct from the evaluative and supervisory process that is a part of preparation for ministry.

3. Local pastors and provisional members will be assigned to a clergy mentoring group, wherever possible, or to a clergy mentor by the Board of Ordained Ministry. Persons transferring from other denominations will also be assigned a clergy mentor (¶ 347.3*b*).

4. Clergy mentoring begins when a person receives an appointment as a local pastor or as a provisional member.

It is expected that all annual conferences will make available and encourage the use of spiritual guides, life coaches, pastoral counselors or vocational mentors for all clergy, separate from the superintendent, and that clergy will utilize these kinds of support as a standard practice of ministry throughout the clergy career, and in all assignments or appointments.

Section XIV. Evaluation for Continuing Formation for Full Members and Local Pastors

¶ **349.** *Evaluation*—Evaluation is a continuous process for formation in servant ministry and servant leadership that must take place in a spirit of understanding and acceptance. Evaluation serves as a process for clergy to assess their effectiveness in ministry and to discern God's call to continue in ordained ministry.

1. For clergy serving local churches, the district superintendent, in consultation with the pastor-parish relations committee, will evaluate annually each clergy's effectiveness for ministry (¶¶ 334.2*c*, 419, 635.2*o*, *r*), using criteria, processes, and training developed by the cabinet and the Board of Ordained Ministry. The clergy in local churches shall participate annually in an evaluation with the committee on pastor-parish relations to enhance an ongoing effective ministry and to identify continuing education needs and plans (¶ 258.2*g*[5]), using criteria, processes, and training developed by the Board of Ordained Ministry and the cabinet. The process of evaluation shall include self-assessment and appropriate metrics, and the General Board of Higher Education and Ministry will offer models to guide cabinets and Boards of Ordained Ministry in the evaluation process.

2. Deacons in appointments beyond the local church and elders and local pastors in appointments to extension ministries will undergo annual evaluation by their immediate supervisors, engage in annual self-evaluation, and include copies of these evaluations in the annual report submitted to their bishop, district superintendent, and the Board of Ordained Ministry (¶ 344.2*a*). They shall have an annual conversation with their district superintendent about their ministry.

3. Every clergyperson shall also engage in a six-month process of personal and professional assessment and development every eight years. The process will be designed and implemented by the cabinet and Board of Ordained Ministry for each annual conference in consultation with the Chairs of the Orders of Deacons and Elders and Fellowship of Local Pastors and Associate Members. The process shall include both a formal review and an in-depth renewal opportunity, such as a retreat or series of coaching and mentoring sessions.

a) The formal review shall include a self-evaluation, metrics appropriate to the ministry settings to which clergy are appointed, observations of trends from the previous eight years, and reviews or interviews with people close to the ministry of the clergy being reviewed.

b) The in-depth renewal opportunity shall be designed by the cabinet and Board of Ordained Ministry in a form appropriate to the conference. The renewal opportunities shall include a combination of elements, such as: time apart for prayer and reflection, reflection with a covenant group, meetings with a coach, celebration of ministry milestones, and discernment of future ministry challenges and opportunities. When deemed important to help in the evaluation process, psychological assessments may be requested by the cabinet or Board of Ordained Ministry.

c) The district superintendent shall review the portfolio and provide the initial report of the eighth year review of effectiveness. When recommended by the district superintendent, a meeting with the bishop and members of the cabinet may be held.

d) Each annual conference shall develop and initiate a plan for such assessment by January 1, 2020.

¶ **350.** *Continuing Education and Spiritual Growth*—1. Throughout their careers, clergy shall engage in continuing education for ministry, professional development, and spiritual formation and growth in order to lead the church in fulfilling the mission of making disciples for Jesus Christ. This shall include carefully developed personal programs of study augmented periodically by involvement in organized educational and spiritual growth activities. These practices embody the Wesleyan emphasis on life-long growth in faith, fostered by personal spiritual practices and participation in covenant communities. Each annual conference, through the chairs of the Clergy Orders and Fellowship or other leaders designated by the bishop, shall provide spiritual enrichment opportunities and covenant groups for deacons, elders, and local pastors.

2. A clergy member's continuing education and spiritual growth program shall include professional formation leaves at least one week each year and may include at least one month during one year of every quadrennium. Such leaves shall not be considered as part of the ministers' vacations and shall be planned in consultation with their charges or other agencies to which they

are appointed as well as the bishop, district superintendent, and annual conference continuing education committee.

3. A clergy member may request a formational and spiritual growth leave of up to six months while continuing to hold an appointment in the local church. Such leaves are available to clergy members who have held full-time appointments for at least six years. Such a leave shall be with the approval of the committee on pastor-parish relations, the church council, and the district superintendent. Annual conferences are encouraged to assist with pulpit supply and other temporary support for such leaves.

4. Financial arrangements for continuing education as part of one's professional development, formation, and spiritual growth shall be negotiated in the following manner: *(a)* for elders and local pastors it shall be done in consultation with the district superintendent and the committee on pastor-parish relations; *(b)* for deacons, with an appropriate supervisory body; *(c)* for district superintendents, with the district committee on superintendency; *(d)* for conference staff, with the appropriate supervisory body; *(e)* for others in extension ministries or appointments beyond the local church, with the appropriate persons in their agency.

5. Clergy shall be asked by the district superintendent in the charge conference to report on their programs of continuing education, formation, and spiritual growth for the past year and plans for the year to come. The district superintendent shall also ask the local church to describe its provision for time and financial support of continuing education for ministry, professional development, formation and spiritual growth for the pastors, diaconal ministers and deacons serving their primary appointment in that local church.

6. Clergy in extension ministries and appointments beyond the local church shall give evidence of their continuing formation and spiritual growth program and future plans in their annual reports (¶ 344.2*a*).

¶ 351. *Sabbatical Leave*—A sabbatical leave should be allowed for a program of study or travel approved by the conference Board of Ordained Ministry. Associate members or clergy members in full connection who have been serving in a full-time appointment for six consecutive years, or in a less than full-time appointment equivalent to six consecutive full-time years, from the time of their reception into full or associate membership may be granted a sabbatical leave for up to one year. Whenever possible, the compensation level of the last appointment served before the leave should be maintained in the appointment made at the termination of the leave. The appointment to sabbatical leave is to be made by the bishop holding the conference, upon the vote of the annual conference after recommendation by the Board of Ordained Ministry. Associate members and clergy members in full connection shall submit a written request for a sabbatical leave, including plans for study or travel, to the Board of Ordained Ministry, with copies to the bishop and district superintendent, ordinarily six months before the opening session of the annual conference. To be eligible for an additional sabbatical leave, associate members and clergy members in full connection shall have served six consecutive years under full-time appointment, or in a less than full-time appointment equivalent to six consecutive full-time years, following the previous sabbatical leave.[45] After consultation and with the written consent of the pastor in charge, and with the approval of the district superintendent, clergy members granted sabbatical leave shall designate a charge conference within the bounds of the annual conference in which they shall hold membership and to which they shall submit an annual report.

Section XV. Changes of Conference Relationship

¶ **352.** *Provision for Change in Conference Relationship*—When a change in conference relationship is deemed necessary or desirable by a provisional or associate member, clergy in full connection, district superintendent or bishop, whether for a short or long term, the person(s) requesting the change shall make written request to their Board of Ordained Ministry stating the reasons for the requested change of relationship. In addition, the Board of Ordained Ministry may request personal interviews with the provisional or associate members and members in full connection named in the requested change, except where personal appearance results in undue hardship.[46] Clergy appointed to a general agency of The United Methodist Church shall be covered by the policies of the agency in relation to family leave, maternity or paternity leave, and medical leave.

---

45. See Judicial Council Decision 473.
46. See Judicial Council Decisions 524, 530.

¶ 353. *Voluntary Leave of Absence*

1. Provisional, associate, or members in full connection of the annual conference who for sufficient reason choose to temporarily take leave from their ministerial appointment may request in writing with a copy to the bishop and their district superintendent a voluntary leave through the Board of Ordained Ministry. This leave is granted or renewed by vote of the clergy members in full connection upon recommendation by the Board of Ordained Ministry.

2. A voluntary leave of absence may be taken for a variety of reasons:

a) Personal Leave—A relationship that is granted to clergy who self-determine for personal reasons that they are temporarily unable or unwilling to continue in a ministry appointment.

b) Family Leave—A relationship that is granted to clergy who, because of an immediate family member's need for full-time care, are temporarily unable to continue in a ministry appointment.

c) Transitional Leave—A leave granted for up to twelve months with approval of the bishop and the Board of Ordained Ministry executive committee to provisional and associate members and full clergy members in good standing who are temporarily between appointments.

A transitional leave of absence may be granted for the following reasons:

(1) A provisional or full member deacon needs to seek and secure an appointable primary position—compensated or nonsalaried.

(2) A provisional or full member elder, or an associate member needs to transition from an extension ministry to another appointment, or from a local church appointment to an extension ministry appointment.

During transitional leave, the clergyperson shall provide quarterly substantiation of his or her effort to obtain such an appointable position to the bishop and to the Board of Ordained Ministry executive committee.[47]

3. Written request for a voluntary leave of absence, with the exception of transitional leave, should be made at least ninety days prior to the annual conference session giving specific reasons for the request.[48] Representatives of the annual conference Board of Ordained Ministry may interview the clergy member to

---

47. See Jurisdictional Council Decisions 450, 459, 508, 1226.
48. See Judicial Council Decision 782.

determine sufficient cause. Personal leave and family leave shall be approved annually upon written request of the clergy member and personal or family leave shall not be granted for more than five years in succession, except by a two-thirds vote of the clergy members in full connection.[49] Transitional leave shall not be renewed beyond a twelve-month period. Voluntary leave shall be counted as a part of the eight-year limit for provisional members (¶ 327).[50]

4. Between sessions of the annual conference, voluntary leave of absence may be granted or terminated by the executive committee of the Board of Ordained Ministry after consultation with and approval by the bishop and district superintendents. This interim action shall be subject to the approval of the clergy session of the annual conference at its next session.[51]

5. Should there be active complaints or charges, a request for voluntary leave of absence shall not be permitted until those complaints or charges have been resolved.

6. Clergy on voluntary leave of absence shall have no claim on the conference funds. Notwithstanding the foregoing, where the conference has made certain elections under applicable benefit plans that require continued participation by clergy on voluntary leaves of absence, the clergy shall continue to participate in such plans. They may participate in the conference health program through their own contributions, if applicable. However, in exceptional circumstances, on recommendation of the bishop and district superintendents, salary and/or other benefits, subject to the terms of the applicable benefit plans, may be granted to a clergy member, if applicable, by vote of the clergy session of members in full connection with the annual conference. In an interim between sessions of the annual conference, by vote of the bishop, cabinet, and executive committee of the Board of Ordained Ministry, salary and/or benefits, subject to the terms of the applicable benefit plans, may be granted, if applicable.

7. Clergypersons on voluntary leave shall be eligible for membership on annual conference committees, commissions, or boards. They may vote for other clergy delegates to General or jurisdictional conferences and may be elected to serve as delegates themselves.[52]

---

49. See Judicial Council Decision 689.
50. See Judicial Council Decision 1216.
51. See Judicial Council Decision 689.
52. See Judicial Council Decision 473.

8. After consultation and with the written consent of the pastor in charge, and with the approval of the district superintendent and the staff-parish relations committee of a local church, clergy members shall designate a charge conference within the bounds of the annual conference to which they shall relate and submit an annual report. They shall report all marriages performed, baptisms administered, funerals conducted and other ministerial activities to the charge conference, pastor in charge, and Board of Ordained Ministry. The exercise of this ministry shall be limited to the charge conference in which their membership is held and with the written permission of the pastor in charge unless special permission is granted by the bishop of the conference where membership is held. With the permission of the bishop of the conference where membership is held, under the supervision of the district superintendent, the clergy member may preach, teach, perform marriages, and, if holding sacramental privileges, administer the sacraments outside of the charge where membership is held.[53]

9. Those on voluntary leave of absence shall be held amenable to the annual conference for their conduct and the performance of their ministry. In case of failure to report to the Board of Ordained Ministry, the provisions for administrative location (¶ 359) may be invoked.

10. Clergy members on voluntary leave of absence may, with the permission of the bishop and with the approval of the United Methodist Endorsing Agency, continue to hold an existing reserve commission as an armed forces chaplain, but may not voluntarily serve on extended active duty.

11. When an end to voluntary leave of absence is requested, except for transitional leave, it shall be by written request at least six months prior to the session of annual conference. The Board of Ordained Ministry shall review the circumstances surrounding the granting of the leave for the purpose of determining whether those circumstances have been alleviated or resolved. When the board has determined that the circumstances of the voluntary leave have not been alleviated or resolved and the request is denied, the board will inform the person of the remaining options, which include: a) remaining on voluntary leave of absence; b) taking honorable location; c) being recommended to the bishop and district superintendents to be placed on involuntary leave,

---

53. See Judicial Council Decision 581.

administrative location, or involuntary retirement, using the fair process of ¶ 361.2; or *d*) such other action as deemed appropriate.

12. When clergy members on voluntary leave of absence do not request an annual extension of the leave of absence during the five-year period or do not indicate willingness to receive an appointment at the end of the five-year period, following documented efforts to make contact with the clergyperson, the provisions of administrative location (¶ 359) may be invoked.

¶ **354.** *Involuntary Leave of Absence*

1. The bishop and the district superintendents may request an involuntary leave of absence without the consent of the provisional, associate, or full member. They shall give to the clergy member and the Board of Ordained Ministry in writing specific reasons for the request. The fair process for administrative hearings as set forth in ¶ 361.2 shall be followed in any involuntary leave of absence procedure.

2. An involuntary leave may be requested by the bishop and the district superintendent. The request shall be referred to the Board of Ordained Ministry and follow procedures for a fair process hearing as set forth in ¶ 361.2 when:

a) A written and signed complaint is not resolved through the supervisory (¶ 362.1*b*, *c*), complaint (¶ 362.1*e*), or trial process within 90 days, or clearly cannot be resolved within 90 days.

b) Action pursuant to ¶ 363 (Involuntary Status Change) is required to address allegations of incompetence, ineffectiveness, or inability to perform ministerial duties.[54]

3. Should there be complaints or charges pending at the time of a request for involuntary leave of absence, they should be placed in the personnel file of the clergyperson. All subsequent actions concerning such entries should be duly noted and placed in the file.[55]

4. Involuntary leave of absence shall be approved by two-thirds vote of the clergy session of members in full connection with the annual conference.[56] Involuntary leave shall be approved annually upon written request of the district superintendents and shall not be approved for more than three years in succession.

5. Between sessions of the annual conference, the bishop and cabinet may request that an involuntary leave of absence be granted

---

54. See Judicial Council Decisions 524, 530, 689, 721, 1010.
55. See Judicial Council Decisions 524, 530.
56. See Judicial Council Decision 782.

or terminated (¶ 363), by the executive committee of the Board of Ordained Ministry. This interim action shall be subject to the approval of the clergy session of members in full connection with the annual conference at its next session.

6. Clergy on involuntary leave shall have no claim on the annual conference funds. The annual conference assumes no financial responsibility for salary, pension, or other benefits for clergy on involuntary leave of absence. Notwithstanding the foregoing, where the conference has made certain elections under applicable benefit plans that require continued participation by clergy on involuntary leaves of absence, the clergy shall continue to participate in such plans. They may participate in the conference health plan through their own contributions, if applicable. In exceptional circumstances, with the recommendation of the bishop and cabinet, salary and/or other benefits, subject to the terms of the applicable benefit plans, may be granted by vote of the clergy session of the annual conference. Between sessions of the annual conference, in unusual circumstances, the bishop and cabinet may recommend and the executive committee of the Board of Ordained Ministry may approve funding of pensions and other benefits, subject to the terms of the applicable benefit plans, pending approval by the annual conference.

7. Clergy placed on involuntary leave shall designate a charge conference within the bounds of the annual conference. Ministerial service shall be limited to that charge and shall only be provided with the written consent of the pastor in charge and with the approval of the district superintendent, bishop, and pastor/staff parish relations committee.[57]

8. Clergy on involuntary leave shall not participate in the boards and agencies of the annual conference, be delegates to General and jurisdictional conferences, or vote on other clergy delegates.

9. When an end to the involuntary leave of absence is requested by the bishop and district superintendents, it shall be by written request at least six months prior to the session of annual conference. The Board of Ordained Ministry shall review the circumstances surrounding the granting of the relationship for the purpose of determining whether the conditions of the leave have been met. If the board determines that the conditions of the involuntary leave have not been resolved, it may continue invol-

---

57. See Judicial Council Decision 524.

untary leave of absence for up to the three-year limit or it shall pursue administrative location (see §2 above).

10. If the district superintendents and bishop do not intend to appoint a person after three (3) years on involuntary leave, they shall notify both the Board of Ordained Ministry and the clergyperson at least six months prior to the session of the annual conference and pursue administrative location or initiate the complaint process, if it has not already been initiated.

11. The administrative review committee (¶ 636) shall ensure that the disciplinary procedures for involuntary leave of absence were properly followed. The entire process leading to the recommendation for involuntary leave of absence and its resolution shall be reviewed by the administrative review committee, and it shall report its findings to the clergy session of members in full connection with the annual conference.

¶ 355. *Maternity or Paternity Leave*—Maternity or paternity leave, not to exceed one-fourth of a year, will be available and shall be granted by the bishop and the cabinet, and the executive committee of the Board of Ordained Ministry to any local pastor, provisional member, associate member, or clergy member in full connection who so requests it at the birth or arrival of a child into the home for purposes of adoption.

1. Persons desiring maternity or paternity leave should file their request with the committee on pastor-parish relations after consulting with the district superintendent at least ninety days prior to its beginning to allow adequate pastoral care for the churches involved to be developed.

2. During the leave, the clergy member's annual conference relations will remain unchanged, and the health and welfare benefit plans will remain in force.

3. A maternity or paternity leave of up to one-quarter of a year will be considered as an uninterrupted appointment for pension purposes.

4. Compensation will be maintained for no less than the first eight weeks of leave.

5. During the leave time, pastoral responsibility for the church or churches involved will be handled through consultation with the committee on pastor-parish relations of the local church(es) and the district superintendent.

6. Special arrangements shall be made for district superintendents, bishops, and those under special appointment.

¶ **356.** *Medical Leave Due to Medical and Disabling Conditions That Prevent Performance of Ministerial Duties*—1. When clergy who are members of an annual conference (¶ 369) are unable to perform their ministerial duties because of medical and disabling conditions, upon recommendations of the conference Board of Ordained Ministry and the conference board of pensions, and by a majority vote of the executive session of clergy members in full connection with the annual conference who are present and voting, they may be granted annual medical leave without losing their relationship to the annual conference; provided, however, that such leave may be granted or renewed upon reasonable and appropriate investigation of the case by the joint committee on clergy medical leave of the annual conference, or the party responsible for managing clergy medical leaves in accordance with the annual conference's policies, which will report its findings to the conference Board of Ordained Ministry and the conference board of pensions. This relationship may be initiated by the clergy member or cabinet with or without the consent of the clergy member through the Board of Ordained Ministry. When medical leave is given without the clergy member's consent, reasonable accommodation shall be offered whenever possible. When a clergy member is granted medical leave by the annual conference, if the medical evidence has not yet met the standards for the receipt of benefits as set forth in the Comprehensive Protection Plan, section 5.04, the conference board of pensions may authorize payment of the benefits in the amount that would otherwise be payable from the Comprehensive Protection Plan. The payments shall be made by the General Board of Pension and Health Benefits as a charge to the annual conference granting the medical leave. If payments from the Comprehensive Protection Plan are subsequently approved, the annual conference will be reimbursed for benefits already paid, not to exceed the amount otherwise payable from the Comprehensive Protection Plan. Each medical leave granted by the annual conference shall be recorded in the conference minutes.

2. When clergy who are members of an annual conference are unable to perform their ministerial duties between sessions of the annual conference on account of medical conditions, with the approval of a majority of the district superintendents, after consultation with the executive committee of the conference Board of Ordained Ministry and the executive committee of the conference

board of pensions, a medical leave may be granted by the bishop for the remainder of the conference year; provided, however, that such leave may be granted upon reasonable and appropriate investigation of the case including accommodation provisions by the joint committee on clergy medical leave of the annual conference, or the party responsible for managing clergy medical leaves in accordance with the annual conference's policies, which will report its findings to the conference Board of Ordained Ministry and the conference board of pensions. When a clergy member is granted medical leave by the bishop, if the medical evidence has not yet met the standards for receipt of benefits as set forth in the Comprehensive Protection Plan, section 5.04, the conference board of pensions may authorize payment of the benefits in the amount that would otherwise be payable from the Comprehensive Protection Plan. The payments shall be made by the General Board of Pension and Health Benefits as a charge to the annual conference granting the medical leave. If payments from the Comprehensive Protection Plan are subsequently approved, the annual conference will be reimbursed for benefits already paid, not to exceed the amount otherwise payable from the Comprehensive Protection Plan.

3. When clergy members on medical leave provide medical evidence that they have recovered sufficiently to resume ministerial duties, or are able to return through reasonable accommodation, in consultation with the appointive cabinet, upon recommendation of the joint committee on clergy medical leave or the conference relations committee, and with the approval of the executive committee of the conference Board of Ordained Ministry, they may receive an appointment from a bishop between sessions of the annual conference, thereby terminating the medical leave. Such appointment shall be reported immediately by the cabinet to the conference board of pensions and to the General Board of Pension and Health Benefits. Such termination of leave, together with the effective date, shall also be recorded in the minutes of the annual conference at its next regular session.[58]

4. A person under consideration for medical leave shall have the right to appear before the joint committee on clergy medical leave or to designate someone to meet with the committee on his or her behalf. In the event of unresolved issues, a person will be

---

58. See Judicial Council Decision 1012.

ensured of fair process per the guidelines for administrative hearings in ¶ 361.2.

5. Any person eligible to receive an appointment from a bishop and able to perform ministerial duties may not be placed on involuntary medical leave solely because of a medical condition. All reasonable accommodations should be made to enable qualified clergy with disabilities to serve in ministry settings compatible with their gifts and graces. (See 2016 *Book of Resolutions,* 3002.)

¶ **357.** *Retirement*—Retired clergy members are those who have been placed in the retired relation either at their own request or by action of the clergy session upon recommendation of the Board of Ordained Ministry.[59] (See ¶¶ 1506-1509 and the Ministerial Pension Plan, amended and restated effective January 1, 2007, as the Clergy Retirement Security Program, for pension information.) Requests for retirement shall be stated in writing to the bishop, cabinet, and Board of Ordained Ministry at least one hundred twenty days prior to the date on which retirement is to be effective unless waived by the bishop and cabinet. The Board of Ordained Ministry shall provide guidance and counsel to the retiring member and family as they begin a new relationship in the local church.[60]

1. *Mandatory Retirement*—Every clergy member of an annual conference who will have attained age seventy-two on or before July 1 in the year in which the conference is held shall automatically be retired.[61]

2. *Voluntary Retirement—a) With Twenty Years of Service*—Any clergy members of the annual conference who have completed twenty years or more of service under appointment as ordained ministers or as local pastors with pension credit for service before 1982 or with full participation in the Comprehensive Protection Plan since 1981 prior to the opening date of the session of the conference may request the annual conference to place them in the retired relation with the privilege of receiving their pensions for the number of approved years served in the annual conference or conferences and such other benefits as the final annual conference may provide, payment to begin the first of any month after the ordained minister attains age sixty-two.[62] If pension begins prior

---

59. See Judicial Council Decisions 87, 88, 531.
60. See Judicial Council Decision 995.
61. See Judicial Council Decisions 7, 165, 413, 578.
62. See Judicial Council Decision 717.

to the age at which retirement under ¶ 357.2c could have occurred, then the actuarial reduction provisions of the Clergy Retirement Security Program shall apply.

b) With Thirty Years of Service or at Age Sixty-two—At their own request and by vote of the clergy members in full connection, any clergy members who will have attained age sixty-two on or before July 1 in the year in which the session of the annual conference is held or will have completed thirty years of service under appointment as an ordained minister, or a local pastor with pension credit for service before 1982 or with full participation in the Comprehensive Protection Plan since 1981, as of the conference session may be placed in the retired relation with an annuity claim for an actuarially reduced pension.[63]

c) With Forty Years of Service or at Age Sixty-five—At their own request and by vote of the clergy members in full connection, any clergy members who will have attained age sixty-five on or before July 1 in the year in which the session of the conference is held or will have completed forty years of service under appointment as an ordained minister, or as a local pastor with pension credit for service before 1982 or with full participation in the Comprehensive Protection Plan since 1981, as of the conference session may be placed in the retired relation with the privilege of making an annuity claim.[64]

d) The dates specified in ¶ 357.1 and .2a-c notwithstanding, between sessions of the annual conference any member who attains the age and/or number of years of service specified in those sections may, upon the member's own request and with the approval of the bishop, cabinet, and executive committee of the Board of Ordained Ministry, be granted the retired relation *ad interim*, with applicable annuity claim, subject to the approval of the clergy members in full connection at the next annual conference session.

e) The annual conference, at its discretion, upon joint recommendation of the Board of Ordained Ministry and the conference board of pensions, may designate any time within the ensuing conference year as the effective date of retirement of a clergy member who is placed in the retired relation under the provisions of § 2b or § 2c above.[65]

---

63. See Judicial Council Decision 428.
64. See Judicial Council Decision 379.
65. See Judicial Council Decision 769.

3. *Involuntary Retirement*—By a two-thirds vote of those present and voting, the clergy members in full connection may place any clergy members in the retired relation with or without their consent and irrespective of their age if such relation is recommended by the Board of Ordained Ministry and the cabinet.[66] The procedures for fair process in administrative hearings shall be followed in any involuntary retirement procedure. The cabinet may recommend to the Board of Ordained ministry the involuntary retirement of the clergy member, or the Board of Ordained Ministry may make the recommendation upon its own motion. Written notice of the intended action shall be given to such member by the Board of Ordained Ministry at least 180 days prior to annual conference. Written notice also should be given to the chairperson of the administrative review committee.

The administrative review committee (¶ 636) shall ensure that the disciplinary procedures for involuntary retirement were properly followed. The entire process leading to the recommendation for involuntary retirement shall be reviewed by the administrative review committee, and it shall report its findings to the clergy session of members in full connection of the annual conference. Any clergy member who is placed in the retired relationship under this subparagraph shall be entitled to the privilege of receiving his or her pension for the number of approved years served in the annual conference or conferences and such other benefits as the final annual conference may provide, payment to begin the first of any month after the ordained minister attains age sixty-two. If pension begins prior to the age at which retirement under ¶ 357.2c could have occurred, then the actuarial reduction provisions of the Clergy Retirement Security Program shall apply.

4. *Preretirement Counseling*—The Board of Ordained Ministry in cooperation with the conference board of pensions shall offer to all clergy members anticipating retirement preconsultation at least five years prior to the date of anticipated retirement (¶ 635.2o). The purpose of the consultation will be to assist the clergy and spouses to plan and to prepare for the adjustments associated with retirement as well as providing guidance and counsel for their return to a new relationship in the local church. In preretirement counseling the Board of Ordained Ministry and the conference board of pensions may relate to the annual confer-

---

66. See Judicial Council Decisions 522, 769.

ence association of retired ministers or similar organization where it exists. The boards shall take initiative in assisting retirees to establish such organizations.

5. *Charge Conference Membership—a)* All retired clergy members who are not appointed as pastors of a charge, after consultation with the pastor and the district superintendent, shall have a seat in the charge conference and all the privileges of membership in the church where they elect to hold such membership except as set forth in the *Discipline*. They shall report to the charge conference and to the pastor all marriages performed, baptisms administered, and other pastoral functions. If they reside outside the bounds of the annual conference where membership is held, they shall forward annually to the charge conference where membership is held a report of their Christian and ministerial conduct, signed by the district superintendent or the pastor of the affiliate charge conference where they reside.

6. *Appointment of Retired Ordained Ministers*—A retired ordained minister shall be eligible to receive an appointment when requested by the bishop and cabinet. A retired ordained minister appointed to a pastoral charge shall have neither a claim upon minimum compensation from the Commission on Equitable Compensation or similar conference agency, nor further pension credit. Compensation for a retired ordained minister shall be negotiated between the district superintendent and the pastoral charge or other appointment to which the retired ordained minister is appointed. Retired ordained ministers may serve on conference agencies.[67]

7. *Return to Effective Relationship*—A clergy member who has retired under the provisions of ¶ 357.2 may at his or her own request be made an effective member upon recommendation of the Board of Ordained Ministry, the bishop and cabinet, and by majority vote of the clergy members in full connection of the annual conference and thereby be eligible for appointment so long as he or she remains in the effective relation or until ¶ 357.1 applies. Each clergy member requesting return to effective relationship after voluntary retirement must meet the following conditions: (1) presentation of their certificate of retirement; (2) a satisfactory certificate of good health on the prescribed form from a physician approved by the Board of Ordained Ministry. However, any pension being received through the General Board

---

67. See Judicial Council Decisions 87, 531, 558.

of Pension and Health Benefits shall be discontinued upon their return to the effective relationship. The pension shall be reinstated upon subsequent retirement.

¶ 358. *Honorable Location*—1. An annual conference may grant clergy members in full connection certificates of honorable location at their own request, provided that the Board of Ordained Ministry shall have first examined their character and found them in good standing, and provided that the clergy session shall also pass on their character after the request is made, and provided further, that this relation shall be granted only to one who intends to discontinue service in the itinerant ministry. The Board of Ordained Ministry shall provide guidance and counsel to the locating member and family as they return to a new relationship in the local church. Upon recommendation of the Board of Ordained Ministry, an annual conference may offer transition assistance.

2. Associate members or clergy members in full connection located according to the provisions of this paragraph shall not continue to hold membership in the annual conference, and they shall surrender their certification of conference membership for deposit with the conference secretary. After consultation and with the written consent of the pastor in charge, and with the approval of the district superintendent and the staff-parish relations committee of a local church, located clergy members shall designate the local church in which they shall hold membership. Documentation of this consent and approvals shall be filed with the Board of Ordained Ministry of the annual conference that granted them honorable location. As clergy members of the charge conference, they shall be permitted to exercise ministerial functions only with the written permission of the pastor in charge. They shall have all the privileges of membership in the church where they elect to hold charge conference membership, except as set forth in the *Book of Discipline*. When approved by the executive committee of the Board of Ordained Ministry, a person on honorable location may be appointed *ad interim* by the bishop as a local pastor.[68] A copy of the annual report to the charge conference shall be forwarded to the registrar of the Board of Ordained Ministry of the annual conference that granted them honorable location in order for location to be continued. They shall report to the charge conference and the pastor all marriages performed, baptisms admin-

---

68. See Judicial Council Decision 366.

istered, and funerals conducted and shall be held amenable for their conduct and the continuation of their ordination rights to the annual conference that granted them honorable location.

Failure to submit the report for two consecutive years may result in termination of orders upon recommendation of the Board of Ordained Ministry and vote of the clergy session. The provisions of this paragraph shall not apply to persons granted involuntary location prior to the General Conference of 1976. The names of located members after the annual passage of their character shall be printed in the journal.

3. Ordained ministers on honorable location may request the annual conference to grant them the status of honorable location-retired.[69] Requests for retired status shall be stated in writing to the bishop, cabinet, and registrar of the Board of Ordained Ministry at least ninety days prior to the annual conference session. Those granted honorable location retired status shall be accountable for all ministerial services performed to the charge conference in which they hold membership. If such services have been performed, they shall report to that charge conference and exercise their ministry under the supervision of the pastor in charge therein as outlined in ¶ 358.2. They shall continue to be held amenable for their conduct, through accountability to their charge conference, to the annual conference in which charge conference membership is held.

¶ 359. *Administrative Location*—1. When an associate or full member clergyperson's effectiveness is in question, the bishop shall complete the following procedure:

a) Identify the concerns. These can include an associate or full member clergyperson's failed professional responsibilities or vocational ineffectiveness.

b) Hold supervisory conversations with the associate or full member clergyperson that identifies the concerns and designs collaboratively with the associate or full member clergyperson a corrective plan of action.

c) Upon evaluation, determine that the plan of action has not been carried out or produced fruit that gives a realistic expectation of future effectiveness (¶ 334.3).

2. If the process defined above (§1) has been completed and has failed to produce sufficient improvement, the bishop and the

---

69. See Judicial Council Decision 717.

district superintendents may request that an associate or full member be placed on administrative location without the consent of the clergy member. They shall provide to the clergy member and the Board of Ordained Ministry, in writing, specific reasons for the request. The conference relations committee of the Board of Ordained Ministry shall conduct a fair process hearing as set forth in ¶ 361.2 in any administrative location procedure. The committee shall report the result of the hearing to the full Board of Ordained Ministry for its action. Any recommendation to administrative location shall be presented from the Board of Ordained Ministry at the next following meeting of the clergy session for final action. Between sessions of the annual conference, an associate or full member may be placed on administrative location by the Board of Ordained Ministry. This interim action shall be subject to the approval of the clergy session of members in full connection with the annual conference at its next session.[70]

3. Administratively located clergy shall not continue to hold membership in the annual conference, and they shall surrender their certification of conference membership for deposit with the conference secretary. After consultation and with the written consent of the pastor in charge, and with the approval of the district superintendent and the staff-parish relations committee of a local church, clergy placed on administrative location shall designate a charge conference within the bounds of the annual conference that placed them on administrative location. Ministerial service shall be limited to that charge and shall be provided only with the written consent of the pastor in charge and the district superintendent and with the approval of the bishop and pastor/staff-parish relations committee. An annual report shall be made to the charge conference that includes all marriages performed, baptisms administered, and funerals conducted. A copy of the report shall be forwarded to the registrar of the Board of Ordained Ministry in order for location to be continued. They shall be held amenable by the annual conference within which the charge conference membership is held for their conduct and the continuation of their ordination rights. Failure to submit the report to the Board of Ordained Ministry for two consecutive years may result in termination of orders upon recommendation of the Board of Ordained Ministry and vote of the clergy session.

---

70. See Judicial Council Decision 695.

4. Ordained ministers on administrative location may request the annual conference to grant them the status of administrative location-retired. Requests for retired status shall be stated in writing to the bishop, cabinet, and registrar of the Board of Ordained Ministry at least ninety days prior to the annual conference session. Those granted administrative location-retired status shall be accountable to the charge conference in which they hold membership for all ministerial services performed. Ministerial service shall be limited to that charge and shall be provided only with the written consent of the pastor in charge and the district superintendent and with the approval of the bishop and pastor/staff-parish relations committee. If such services have been performed, they shall report to that charge conference and exercise their ministry under the supervision of the pastor in charge therein as outlined in ¶ 358.2. They shall continue to be held amenable for their conduct, through accountability to their charge conference, to the annual conference in which charge conference membership is held.

¶ **360.** *Withdrawal*—1. *Withdrawal to Unite With Another Denomination*[71]—When ordained members in good standing withdraw to unite with another denomination or to terminate their membership in the denomination, their certification of conference membership, and their written request to withdraw shall be deposited with the conference secretary.

2. *Withdrawal From the Ordained Ministerial Office*—Ordained members of an annual conference in good standing who desire to leave their ministerial office and withdraw from the conference may be allowed to do so by the annual conference at its session. The ordained minister's certifications of ordination and conference membership, and their written request to withdraw, shall be given to the district superintendent for deposit with the secretary of the conference, and his or her membership may be transferred to a church which he or she designates, after consultation with the pastor, as the local church in which he or she will hold membership.[72]

3. *Withdrawal Under Complaints or Charges*—When clergy members are named as respondents to a complaint under ¶ 362.1e and desire to withdraw from the membership of the annual conference, it may permit them to withdraw under the provisions of ¶ 2719.2. The clergy member's certifications of ordination and

---

71. See Judicial Council Decision 696.
72. See Judicial Council Decisions 552, 695, 1055.

conference membership shall be surrendered to the district superintendent for deposit with the secretary of the conference, and their membership may be transferred to a local church that they designate, after consultation with the pastor.[73]

Withdrawn under complaint or withdrawn under charges shall be written on the face of the credentials.

4. *Withdrawal Between Conferences*—In the event that withdrawal by surrender of the ministerial office, to unite with another denomination, or under complaints or charges, should occur in the interval between sessions of an annual conference, the clergy member's credentials, under the provisions of ¶ 360.1 and .3, shall be surrendered to the bishop or district superintendent along with a letter of withdrawal from the ordained ministry. Both the credentials and the letter of withdrawal shall be deposited with the secretary of the conference. This action shall be reported by the Board of Ordained Ministry to the annual conference at its next session.[74] The effective date of withdrawal shall be the date of the letter of withdrawal.[75]

Section XVI. Administrative Fair Process

¶ 361. 1. *Conference Relations Committee*—Each annual conference Board of Ordained Ministry shall establish a conference relations committee of at least three persons to hear requests for discontinuance of provisional members, involuntary leave of absence, administrative location, involuntary retirement, or other such matters as may be referred to them by the Board of Ordained Ministry (¶ 635). District superintendents shall not serve on the conference relations committee.

2. *Fair Process Hearings*—As a part of the holy covenant that exists within the membership and organization of The United Methodist Church, the following procedures are presented for the protection of the rights of individuals and for the protection of the Church in administrative hearings. The process set forth in this paragraph shall be followed whenever there is a request for discontinuance of provisional membership (upon appeal by the provisional member), involuntary leave of absence, administrative location, or involuntary retirement. Special attention shall

---

73. See Judicial Council Decision 691.
74. See Judicial Council Decision 552.
75. See Judicial Council Decision 691.

be given to the timely disposition of all matters and to ensuring racial, ethnic, and gender diversity in the committee dealing with the fair process hearing.

a) In any administrative proceeding the bishop or the bishop's designee and the respondent (the person against whom involuntary action [excluding complaints] is directed) shall have a right to be heard before any final action is taken.

b) Notice of any hearing shall advise the respondent of the reason for the proposed procedures with sufficient detail to allow the respondent to prepare a response. Notice shall be given not less than twenty days prior to the hearing.

c) The respondent shall have a right to be accompanied to any hearing by a clergyperson who is a member in full connection of the respondent's annual conference, in accordance with the appropriate disciplinary provisions. The clergyperson accompanying the respondent shall have the right to voice.[76]

d) In any administrative hearing, under no circumstances shall one party, in the absence of the other party, discuss substantive issues with members of the pending hearing body. Questions of procedure may be raised with the presiding officer of the hearing body.

e) The respondent shall have access, at least seven days prior to the hearing, to all records relied upon in the determination of the outcome of the administrative process.[77]

f) In the event that a clergyperson fails to appear for supervisory interviews, refuses mail, refuses to communicate personally with the bishop or district superintendent, or otherwise fails to respond to supervisory requests or requests from official administrative committees, such actions or inactions shall not be used as an excuse to avoid or delay any Church processes, and such processes may continue without the participation of such individual.

3. *Immunity From Prosecution*—In order to preserve the integrity of the Church's administrative process and ensure full participation in it at all times, the bishop, cabinet, Board of Ordained Ministry, witnesses, advocates, administrative review committee, clergy in full connection voting in executive session, and all others who participate in the Church's administrative process shall have immunity from prosecution of complaints brought against them

---

76. See Judicial Council Decisions 921, 972.
77. See Judicial Council Decision 974.

related to their role in a particular administrative process, unless they have committed a chargeable offense in conscious and knowing bad faith. The complainant/plaintiff in any proceeding against any such person related to their role in a particular judicial process shall have the burden of proving, by clear and convincing evidence, that such person's actions constituted a chargeable offense committed knowingly in bad faith. The immunity set forth in this provision shall extend to civil court proceedings, to the fullest extent permissible by the civil laws.

¶ **362.** *Complaint Procedures*—1. Ordination and membership in an annual conference in The United Methodist Church is a sacred trust. The qualifications and duties of local pastors, associate members, provisional members, and full members are set forth in *The Book of Discipline of The United Methodist Church,* and we believe they flow from the gospel as taught by Jesus the Christ and proclaimed by his apostles. Whenever a person in any of the above categories, including those on leaves of all types, honorable or administrative location, or retirement, is accused of violating this trust, the membership of his or her ministerial office shall be subject to review.

This review shall have as its primary purpose a just resolution of any violations of this sacred trust, in the hope that God's work of justice, reconciliation and healing may be realized in the body of Christ.

A just resolution is one that focuses on repairing any harm to people and communities, achieving real accountability by making things right in so far as possible and bringing healing to all the parties. In appropriate situations, processes seeking a just resolution as defined in ¶ 362.1c may be pursued. Special attention should be given to ensuring that cultural, racial, ethnic and gender contexts are valued throughout the process in terms of their understandings of fairness, justice, and restoration.

A complaint is a written and signed statement claiming misconduct as defined in ¶ 2702.1. When a complaint is received by the bishop, both the person making the complaint and the person against whom the complaint is made will be informed in writing of the process to be followed at that stage. When and if the stage changes, those persons will continue to be informed in writing of the new process in a timely fashion. All original time limitations may be extended for one 30-day period upon the consent of the complainant and the respondent.

a) Supervision—In the course of the ordinary fulfillment of the superintending role, the bishop or district superintendent may receive or initiate complaints about the performance or character of a clergyperson. A complaint is a written and signed statement claiming misconduct or unsatisfactory performance of ministerial duties.[78] The person filing the complaint and the clergyperson shall be informed by the district superintendent or bishop of the process for filing the complaint and its purpose.

b) Supervisory Response—The supervisory response of the bishop shall begin upon receipt of a formal complaint. The response is pastoral and administrative and shall be directed toward a just resolution among all parties. It is not part of any judicial process. The complaint shall be treated as an allegation or allegations during the supervisory process. At all supervisory meetings no verbatim record shall be made and no legal counsel shall be present. The person against whom the complaint was made may choose another person to accompany him or her with the right to voice; the person making the complaint shall have the right to choose a person to accompany him or her with the right to voice.

The supervisory response shall be carried out by the bishop or the bishop's designee in a timely manner, with attention to communication to all parties regarding the complaint and the process. At the determination of the bishop, persons with qualifications and experience in assessment, intervention, or healing may be selected to assist in the supervisory response. The bishop also may consult with the committee on pastor-parish relations for pastors, the district committee on superintendency for the district superintendents, appropriate personnel committee, or other persons who may be helpful.

When the supervisory response is initiated, the bishop shall notify the chairperson of the Board of Ordained Ministry that a complaint has been filed, of the clergyperson named, of the general nature of the complaint, and, when concluded, of the disposition of the complaint.

c) Just Resolution—The supervisory response may include a process that seeks a just resolution in which the parties are assisted by a trained, impartial third party facilitator(s) or mediator(s), in reaching an agreement satisfactory to all parties.[79]

---

78. See Judicial Council Decisions 763, 777.

79. See Judicial Council Decisions 691, 700, 751, 763, 768.

If the bishop chooses to initiate a mediated attempt to produce a just resolution, then the bishop, the person filing the complaint, the respondent, and other appropriate persons shall enter into a written agreement outlining the process, including any agreements on confidentiality. A process seeking a just resolution may begin at any time in the supervisory, complaint, or trial process. If resolution is achieved, a written statement of resolution, including any terms and conditions, shall be signed by the parties and the parties shall agree on any matters to be disclosed to third parties. A just resolution agreed to by all parties shall be a final disposition of the related complaint.

A process seeking a just resolution may begin at any time in the supervisory or complaint process. This is a not an administrative or judicial proceeding.

d) Suspension—When deemed appropriate, to protect the well-being of the person making the complaint, the congregation, annual conference, other context for ministry, and/or clergy, the bishop, with the recommendation of the executive committee of the Board of Ordained Ministry, may suspend the person from all clergy responsibilities, but not from an appointment, for a period not to exceed ninety days. With the agreement of the executive committee of the Board of Ordained Ministry, the bishop may extend the suspension for only one additional period not to exceed thirty days. During the suspension, salary, housing, and benefits provided by a pastoral charge will continue at a level no less than on the date of suspension.[80] The person so suspended shall retain all rights and privileges as stated in ¶ 334. The cost of supply of a pastor during the suspension will be borne by the annual conference.[81]

e) Referral or Dismissal of a Complaint—Upon receiving a written and signed complaint, the Bishop shall, within 90 days, carry out the supervisory response process outlined above. If within 90 days after the receipt of the complaint resolution is not achieved, the bishop shall either:

(1) Dismiss the complaint with the consent of the cabinet giving the reasons therefore in writing, a copy of which shall be placed in the clergyperson's file; or

(2) Refer the matter to the counsel for the church as a complaint.

---

80. See Judicial Council Decision 776.
81. See Judicial Council Decisions 534, 836.

f) Supervisory Follow-up and Healing—The bishop and cabinet shall provide a process for healing within the congregation, annual conference, or other context of ministry if there has been significant disruption by the complaint. This process may include sharing of information by the bishop or the bishop's designee about the nature of the complaint without disclosing alleged facts, which may compromise any possible forthcoming administrative or judicial process. When facts are disclosed, due regard should be given to the interests and needs of all concerned, including the respondent and complainant who may be involved in an administrative or judicial process. This process for healing may include a process of a just resolution, which addresses unresolved conflicts, support for victims, and reconciliation for parties involved.[82] This can take place at any time during the supervisory, complaint, or trial process.

g) A complaint may be held in abeyance with the approval of the Board of Ordained Ministry if civil authorities are involved or their involvement is imminent on matters covered by the complaint. The status of complaints held in abeyance shall be reviewed at a minimum of every 90 days by the bishop and the executive committee of the Board of Ordained Ministry to ensure that the involvement of civil authorities is still a valid impediment for proceeding with the resolution of a complaint. Abeyance of a complaint may be terminated by either the bishop or the Board of Ordained Ministry. The time in which a complaint is held in abeyance shall not count toward the statute of limitations. A clergyperson shall continue to hold his or her current status while a complaint is held in abeyance.

¶ **363.** *Disposition of Recommendations of Involuntary Status Change*—1. When there is a recommendation for an involuntary status change, the Board of Ordained Ministry shall take action in a timely manner. The recommendation shall be referred to the conference relations committee who shall conduct an administrative hearing following the fair process provisions of ¶ 361.2. The bishop or the Board of Ordained Ministry, as appropriate, shall designate the person to present the recommendation to the committee. The respondent shall be given an opportunity to address the recommendation in person, in writing, and with the assistance of a clergyperson who is a member in full connection of

---

82. See Judicial Council Decision 763.

the respondent's annual conference, and who shall have voice. Once the committee has heard the person designated to represent the recommendation, the respondent, and others as determined by the chairperson of the committee, it shall report its decision to the Board of Ordained Ministry. The board may affirm or reverse the decision of the committee.

Section XVII. Readmission to Conference Relationship

¶ **364.** *Readmission to Provisional Membership*—Persons who have been discontinued as provisional members under the provisions of ¶ 327.6 from an annual conference of The United Methodist Church or one of its legal predecessors may be readmitted by the annual conference in which they held previously such membership and from which they requested discontinuance or were discontinued, or its legal successor, or the annual conference of which the major portion of their former conference is a part, upon their request and recommendation by the district committee on ordained ministry, the Board of Ordained Ministry, and the cabinet after review of their qualifications, as required in ¶ 324, and the circumstances relating to their discontinuance. When reinstated by vote of the clergy members in full connection, their provisional membership in the conference shall be restored, they shall serve a minimum of two years of provisional membership according to ¶ 326 prior to ordination, and they shall be authorized by licensing and/or commissioning to perform those ministerial functions for which they are qualified.

¶ **365.** *Readmission After Honorable or Administrative Location*— Associate members or clergy members in full connection requesting readmission after honorable or administrative location must meet the following conditions:

1. Presentation of their certificate of location.

2. A satisfactory report and recommendation by the charge conference and pastor of the local church in which their membership is held.

3. A satisfactory certificate of good health on the prescribed form from a physician approved by the Board of Ordained Ministry. The Board of Ordained Ministry shall require psychological evaluation.

4. Recommendation by the district committee on ordained ministry, the Board of Ordained Ministry, and the cabinet after review of their qualifications, the circumstances relating to their

location and conduct during the period of time while on location. When reinstated by vote of the clergy members in full connection of the annual conference that granted the location, their membership in the conference shall be restored, and they shall be authorized to perform all ministerial functions. The conference Board of Ordained Ministry may require at least one year of service as a local pastor (elder and associate member) or approved ministry setting (deacon) prior to readmission to conference membership.

¶ **366.** *Readmission After Leaving the Ministerial Office*—Associate members or clergy members in full connection who have left the ministerial office under the provisions of ¶ 360 to an annual conference of The United Methodist Church or one of its legal predecessors may be readmitted by the annual conference in which they held previously such membership and to which they surrendered the ministerial office, or its legal successor, or the annual conference of which the major portion of the former conference is a part, upon their request and recommendation by the district committee on ordained ministry, the Board of Ordained Ministry, and the cabinet after review of their qualifications and the circumstances relating to the surrender of their ministerial office. A period of at least two years service as a local pastor (elder and associate member) or approved ministry setting (deacon) shall be required prior to readmission to conference membership. This service may be rendered in any annual conference of The United Methodist Church with the consent of the Board of Ordained Ministry of the annual conference in which members previously held membership. When reinstated by vote of the clergy members in full connection, their membership in the conference and their credentials shall be restored, and they shall be authorized to perform all ministerial functions.[83]

¶ **367.** *Readmission After Termination by Action of the Annual Conference*—Persons who have been terminated by an annual conference of The United Methodist Church or one of its legal predecessors may seek full membership in the annual conference in which they previously held membership and from which they were terminated, or its legal successor, or the annual conference of which the major portion of their former conference is a part, upon recommendation of the cabinet and completion of all requirements for full membership, including all requirements for election

---

83. See Judicial Council Decisions 515, 552.

to candidacy and provisional membership. The provisions of this paragraph shall apply to all persons terminated or involuntarily located prior to General Conference of 1976.

¶ 368. *Readmission After Involuntary Retirement*—Clergy members of an annual conference desiring to return to effective relationship after having been placed in involuntary retirement (¶ 357.3) must meet the following conditions:

1. Submit a written request for reinstatement to the Board of Ordained Ministry.

2. The Board of Ordained Ministry and the cabinet shall review the member's qualifications and the circumstances relating to his or her retirement.

3. Recommendation by the Board of Ordained Ministry, the bishop, cabinet, and a two-thirds vote of the clergy members in full connection of the annual conference that granted the involuntary retirement. A period of at least two years of service as a local pastor shall be required prior to readmission to conference membership.

4. Presentation of the certificate of retirement.

5. Presentation of satisfactory certificate of good health on the prescribed form from a physician approved by the Board of Ordained Ministry. The Board of Ordained Ministry may require a psychological evaluation. Any pension being received through the General Board of Pension and Health Benefits shall be discontinued upon their return to effective relationship. The pension shall be reinstated upon subsequent retirement.

Section XVIII. General Provisions

¶ 369. 1. The annual conference is the basic body of The United Methodist Church. The clergy membership of an annual conference shall consist of deacons and elders in full connection (¶¶ 329, 333), provisional members (¶ 327), associate members, affiliate members (¶¶ 344.4, 586.4), and local pastors (¶ 317). All clergy are amenable to the annual conference in the performance of their duties in the positions to which they are appointed.[84]

2. Both men and women are included in all provisions of the *Discipline* that refer to the ordained ministry.[85]

3. In all cases where district committees on ordained ministry, boards of ordained ministry, or clergy in executive session vote

---

84. See Judicial Council Decisions 327, 371.
85. See Judicial Council Decisions 317, 155.

on granting any status regarding license, ordination, or conference membership, it is understood that the requirements set forth herein are minimum requirements only. Each person voting is expected to vote prayerfully based on his or her personal judgment of the applicant's gifts, evidence of God's grace, and promise of future usefulness for the mission of the Church.[86]

4. All clergy members mentioned in ¶ 369.1 shall receive written communication about decisions made regarding their relationship with the annual conference.

5. There shall be an annual meeting of this covenant body, in executive session of clergy members in full connection with the annual conference, including both deacons and elders, at the site of the regular session of the annual conference, or at an alternative time and location determined by the bishop after consultation with the cabinet and the executive committee of the Board of Ordained Ministry, to consider questions relating to matters of ordination, character, and conference relations (¶¶ 605.7, 636).[87]

6. A special session of the annual conference may be held at such time and at such place as the bishop shall determine, after consultation with the cabinet and the executive committee of the Board of Ordained Ministry. A special clergy session shall have only such powers as stated in the call.

---

86. See Judicial Council Decision 536.
87. See Judicial Council Decisions 406, 555, 1009.

Chapter Three
THE SUPERINTENDENCY

Section I. The Nature of Superintendency

¶ 401. *Task*—The task of superintending in The United Methodist Church resides in the office of bishop and extends to the district superintendent, with each possessing distinct and collegial responsibilities. The mission of the Church is to make disciples of Jesus Christ for the transformation of the world (see Part IV, Section I). From apostolic times, certain ordained persons have been entrusted with the particular tasks of superintending. The purpose of superintending is to equip the Church in its disciple-making ministry. Those who superintend carry primary responsibility for ordering the life of the Church. It is their task to enable the gathered Church to worship and to evangelize faithfully.

It is also their task to facilitate the initiation of structures and strategies for the equipping of Christian people for service in the Church and in the world in the name of Jesus Christ and to help extend the service in mission. It is their task, as well, to see that all matters, temporal and spiritual, are administered in a manner that acknowledges the ways and the insights of the world critically and with understanding while remaining cognizant of and faithful to the mandate of the Church. The formal leadership in The United Methodist Church, located in these superintending offices, is an integral part of the system of an itinerant ministry.

Section II. Offices of Bishop and District Superintendent

¶ 402. *Special Ministry, Not Separate Order*—The offices of bishop and district superintendent exist in The United Methodist Church as particular ministries. Bishops are elected and district superintendents are appointed from the group of elders who are ordained to be ministers of Service, Word, Sacrament, and Order and thereby participate in the ministry of Christ, in sharing a royal priesthood that has apostolic roots (1 Peter 2:9; John 21:15-17; Acts 20:28; 1 Peter 5:2-3; 1 Timothy 3:1-7).

¶ 403. *The Role of Bishops and District Superintendents*—Bishops and superintendents are elders in full connection.

1. Bishops are elected from the elders and set apart for a ministry of servant leadership, general oversight and supervision

(¶ 401). As followers of Jesus Christ, bishops are authorized to guard the faith, order, liturgy, doctrine, and discipline of the Church. The role and calling forth of the bishop is to exercise oversight and support of the Church in its mission of making disciples of Jesus Christ for the transformation of the world. The basis of such discipleship of leadership (*episkopé*) lies in discipline and a disciplined life. The bishop leads therefore through the following disciplines:

a) A vital and renewing spirit. The role of the bishop is to faithfully practice, model and lead the spiritual disciplines of our faith and to call and inspire the clergy and laity within the Church to practice the Christian disciplines in their individual lives through the tradition of personal holiness. The bishop is to lead in public worship, in the celebration of the sacraments, and in the commendation of our faith.

b) An enquiring mind and a commitment to the teaching office. The role of the bishop is to continue to learn and to teach how to make disciples and lead faithful and fruitful congregations using scripture, spiritual disciplines, our Wesleyan heritage, and the history and doctrines of the Church.

c) A vision for the Church. The role of bishop is to lead the whole Church in claiming its mission of making disciples of Jesus Christ for the transformation of the world. The bishop leads by discerning, inspiring, strategizing, equipping, implementing, and evaluating the fulfillment of the mission of the church. Working in partnership with the Council of Bishops, the cabinet and lay and clergy leadership of the annual conference, and the professing members of the Church, the bishop urges the whole church to move toward the vision of sharing Christ with the world in fulfillment of our mission, faithful discipleship, and "an even better way" of being Christ's people in the world.

d) A prophetic commitment for the transformation of the Church and the world. The role of the bishop is to be a prophetic voice for justice in a suffering and conflicted world through the tradition of social holiness. The bishop encourages and models the mission of witness and service in the world through proclamation of the gospel and alleviation of human suffering.

e) A passion for the unity of the church. The role of the bishop is to be the shepherd of the whole flock and thereby provide leadership toward the goal of understanding, reconciliation, and unity within the Church—The United Methodist Church and the church universal.

f) The ministry of administration. The role of the bishop is to uphold the discipline and order of the Church by consecrating, ordaining, commissioning, supervising, and appointing persons in ministry to the Church and the world. As the presiding officer of the annual conference, the resident bishop provides order and leads in new opportunities for ministry within the annual conference. The bishop shares with other bishops the oversight of the whole church through the Council of Bishops and is held accountable through the Council of Bishops in collaboration with conference and jurisdictional committees on episcopacy.

2. District superintendents are elders in full connection appointed by the bishop to the cabinet as an extension of the superintending role of the bishop within the annual conference through the same disciplines and in accordance with their responsibilities designated in the *Book of Discipline* under the supervision of the resident bishop

Section III. Election, Assignment, and Termination of Bishops

¶ 404. *Provisions for Episcopal Areas*
1. In central conferences, the number of bishops shall be determined on the basis of missional potential, as approved by the General Conference on recommendation of the Standing Committee on Central Conference Matters. Before recommending changes in the number of episcopal areas, the Standing Committee on Central Conference Matters shall:

a) consider these criteria in the following order of priority:
(1) the number of charge conferences and the number of active clergy in episcopal areas;
(2) the geographic size of episcopal areas, measured by the square miles/square km, and the numbers of time zones and nations;
(3) the structure of episcopal areas, measured by the number of annual conferences, and the overall church membership in all annual, provisional annual, missionary conferences, and missions in episcopal areas.

b) conduct a further analysis of the context and missional potential of changes in episcopal areas.
2. In the jurisdictions, the number of bishops shall be determined on the following basis:
a) Each jurisdiction having 300,000 church members or fewer shall be entitled to five bishops and each jurisdiction having

more than 300,000 church members shall be entitled to one additional bishop for each additional 300,000 church members or major fraction thereof.

b) If the number of church members in a jurisdiction shall have decreased by at least 10 percent below the number of church members which had previously entitled the jurisdiction to its number of bishops, then the number of bishops to which it shall be entitled shall be determined on the basis of missional needs, as approved by the General Conference on the recommendation of the Interjurisdictional Committee on Episcopacy, provided however that said jurisdiction shall be entitled to no less than the number of bishops to which it would be entitled under subparagraph *a)* above. It shall be the responsibility of the affected jurisdiction, through its Committee on Episcopacy, to request consideration of its missional need for an exception, and in the absence of such a request, there shall be no obligation on the part of the Interjurisdictional Committee on Episcopacy to consider such an exception nor to make any report on such an exception to General Conference. In no case shall there be any constraint on General Conference's power to act in the absence of such a recommendation or to reject any recommendation that might be received.

c) If a jurisdiction, as a result of the provisions of this paragraph, shall have the number of bishops to which it had previously been entitled reduced, then the reduction in the number of bishops to which it is entitled shall be effective as of September 1 of the calendar year in which said reduction has been determined by the General Conference.

¶ **405.** *Election and Consecration of Bishops*—1. *Nomination*— An annual conference, in the session immediately prior to the next regular session of the jurisdictional or central conference, may name one or more nominees for episcopal election. Balloting at jurisdictional and central conferences shall not be limited to nominees of annual conferences nor shall any jurisdictional or central conference delegate be bound to vote for any specific nominee. Each jurisdictional or central conference shall develop appropriate procedures for furnishing information about nominees from annual conferences. This shall be done at least two weeks prior to the first day of the jurisdictional or central conference. Similar procedures shall be developed for persons nominated by ballot who receive ten votes, or 5 percent of the valid votes cast, and the information shall be made available to the delegates at the site of the conference.

2. *Process—a)* Jurisdictional and central conference delegates, in electing bishops, shall give due consideration to the inclusiveness of The United Methodist Church with respect to sex, race, and national origin. In addition, consideration shall be given to the nature of superintendency as described in ¶ 401.

b) The jurisdictional and central conferences are authorized to fix the percentage of votes necessary to elect a bishop. It is recommended that at least 60 percent of those present and voting be necessary to elect.

c) Consecration of bishops may take place at the session of the conference at which election occurs or at a place and time designated by the conference. The consecration service may include bishops from other jurisdictional and central conferences. It is strongly urged that the consecration service also include representatives from other Christian communions (see ¶¶ 124, 422.2).

¶ **406.** *Assignment Process—1. Jurisdictional Committee on Episcopacy*—The jurisdictional committee on episcopacy, after consultation with the College of Bishops, shall recommend the assignment of the bishops to their respective residences for final action by the jurisdictional conference; it shall not reach any conclusion concerning residential assignments until all elections of bishops for that session are completed and all bishops have been consulted. A bishop may be recommended for assignment to the same residence for a third quadrennium.

The date of assignment for all bishops is September 1 following the jurisdictional conference.[1]

A newly elected bishop shall be assigned to administer an area other than that within which his or her membership was most recently held, unless by a two-thirds vote the jurisdictional committee shall recommend that this restriction be ignored and by majority vote the jurisdictional conference shall concur.[2]

2. *Central Conference Committee on Episcopacy*—The central conference committee on episcopacy, after consultation with the College of Bishops, shall recommend the assignment of the bishops to their respective residences for final action by the central conference.[3]

---

1. See Judicial Council Decision 781.
2. See Judicial Council Decisions 48, 57, 416, 538.
3. See Judicial Council Decision 248.

3. *Special Assignments*—The Council of Bishops may, with consent of the bishop and the concurrence of the jurisdictional or central conference committee on episcopacy, assign one of its members for one year to some specific churchwide responsibility deemed of sufficient importance to the welfare of the total Church. In this event, a bishop shall be released from the presidential responsibilities within the episcopal area for that term. Another bishop or bishops, active or retired, and not necessarily from the same jurisdictional or central conference, shall be named by the Council of Bishops on recommendation of the College of Bishops of the jurisdiction involved to assume presidential responsibilities during the interim. In the event that more than one retired bishop is assigned to fulfill presidential responsibilities in one episcopal area, the Episcopal Fund shall be responsible only for the difference between the pensions paid the retired bishops and the remuneration of one active bishop. This assignment may be renewed for a second year by a two-thirds vote of the Council of Bishops and majority vote of the jurisdictional or central committee on episcopacy, and the consent of the bishop and the College of Bishops involved. The bishop so assigned shall continue to receive regular salary and support.

¶ **407.** *Vacancy in the Office of Bishop*—A vacancy in the office of bishop may occur due to death, retirement (¶ 408.1, .2, .3), resignation (¶ 408.4), judicial procedure (¶ 2712), leave of absence (¶ 410.1), or medical leave (¶ 410.4). In case assignment of a bishop to presidential supervision of an episcopal area is terminated by any of the above causes, the vacancy shall be filled by the Council of Bishops on nomination of the active bishops of the College of Bishops of the jurisdiction or central conference concerned, after consultation with the jurisdictional or central conference and annual conference committees on the episcopacy and the cabinet(s); or, if the vacancy should occur within twenty-four months of the episcopal assumption of presidential supervision of that area, the College of Bishops of the jurisdiction or central conference concerned may call a special session of the jurisdictional or central conference as provided in ¶ 521.2. When a bishop is elected under the provisions of this paragraph, the years remaining in the quadrennium within which the election occurs shall count as a full quadrennium for purposes of assignment. It is recommended that the previous bishop serving the vacant episcopal area not be appointed to serve in the interim.

¶ **408.** *Termination of Office*—An elder who is serving as a bishop up to the time of retirement shall have the status of a retired bishop.[4]

1. *Mandatory Retirement*—*a)* A bishop shall be retired on August 31 next following the regular session of the jurisdictional conference if the bishop's sixty-eighth birthday has been reached on or before July 1 of the year in which the jurisdictional conference is held.[5]

b) A bishop in a central conference shall be retired at a date no later than three months following the adjournment of General Conference, if the bishop's sixty-eighth birthday is reached on or before the opening day of his or her scheduled conference effective on January 1, 2016. This action becomes effective at the adjournment of General Conference 2016.[6]

c) Pension, as provided under the Clergy Retirement Security Program or the Global Episcopal Pension Program (or, in either case, any successor bishop pension or retirement plan or program), as either may apply, shall be payable as provided in such plan or program following the close of the jurisdictional or central conference.

d) If, however, the retired bishop accepts any one of the following assignments of churchwide responsibility, the General Council on Finance and Administration, after consultation with the Council of Bishops, shall set a level of compensation not to exceed a maximum determined by the General Conference on recommendation of the General Council on Finance and Administration, with the compensation costs borne by the Episcopal Fund: (1) assignment of a special nature with direct relationship and accountability to the Council of Bishops, or (2) assignment to a general agency or United Methodist Church-related institution of higher education. Assignment of retired bishops to United Methodist Church-related institutions of higher education must be at the initiative of the institutions, with service not to exceed the mandatory retirement ages of the institutions.

If a bishop is assigned to a general agency or United Methodist Church-related institution of higher education, that agency or United Methodist Church-related institution of higher education will pay 50 percent of the compensation established by the General

---

4. See Judicial Council Decisions 361, 407.
5. See Judicial Council Decisions 413, 578.
6. See Judicial Council Decision 1248.

Council on Finance and Administration for the position. The general agency or United Methodist Church-related institution of higher education shall further assume all responsibility for the bishop's operational and travel expenses related to the assignment.

Compensation for any special assignment shall cease after the bishop has reached the mandatory age of retirement for all ordained ministers (¶ 357.1) or completes the assignment, whichever comes first, except that retired bishops elected by the Council of Bishops as executive secretary and ecumenical officer may continue to be compensated for such special assignment(s) throughout the terms of office. No assignment to a jurisdiction, central conference, annual conference, or non-United Methodist agency shall qualify for additional compensation from the Episcopal Fund under the provisions of this paragraph. The status of a retired bishop on special assignment shall, for purposes of housing and other benefits, be that of a retired bishop.

2. *Voluntary Retirement—a)* Bishops who have completed twenty years or more of service under full-time appointment as ordained ministers or as local pastors with pension credit prior to the opening date of the session of the jurisdictional or central conference, including at least one quadrennium as bishop, may request the jurisdictional or central conference to retire them with the privilege of receiving their pension to the extent permitted under the Clergy Retirement Security Program or the Global Episcopal Pension Program (or, in either case, any successor bishop pension or retirement plan or program), as either may apply.

b) Vocational Retirement—A bishop who has served at least eight years in the episcopacy may seek retirement for vocational reasons and may be so retired by the jurisdictional or central conference committee on episcopacy on recommendation by the involved College of Bishops. Such bishops shall receive their pensions as provided in ¶ 408.2*a*. If the employing entity provides or makes health insurance available to employees, then the bishop who retires under this provision will be insured under that program, whether or not the bishop is required to pay the premium for that coverage, and the Episcopal Fund will assume no future obligation to provide health insurance for the bishop or the bishop's family. If the employing entity does not provide or make health insurance available to employees, either while employed or in retirement, then the bishop retiring under this provision will be provided with health and welfare benefits for retirees as specified from time to time by the General Council on Finance and Administration.

c) Bishops who have attained age sixty-two or have completed thirty years of service under full-time appointment as an elder or a bishop may request the jurisdictional or central conference to place them in the retired relation with the privilege of receiving their pension to the extent permitted under the Clergy Retirement Security Program or the Global Episcopal Pension Program (or, in either case, any successor bishop pension or retirement plan or program), as either may apply.

d) Any bishop who seeks a voluntary retired status shall notify the president of the Council of Bishops at least six months prior to the General Conference.

e) A bishop may seek voluntary retirement for health reasons and shall be so retired by the jurisdictional or central conference committee on episcopacy upon recommendation by the involved College of Bishops and upon presentation of satisfactory medical evidence. Such bishops shall receive their pensions to the extent permitted under the Clergy Retirement Security Program or the Global Episcopal Pension Program (or, in either case, any successor bishop pension or retirement plan or program), as either may apply.

3. *Involuntary Retirement—a)* A bishop may be placed in the retired relation regardless of age by a two-thirds vote of the jurisdictional or central conference committee on episcopacy if, after not less than a thirty-day notice in writing is given to the affected bishop and hearing held, such relationship is found by said committee to be in the best interests of the bishop and/or the Church. This action may or may not be taken because of the performance of the bishop, and the reason for the action must be clearly stated in the report of the committee. The provisions of ¶ 361.2 for fair process in administrative hearings shall apply to this administrative process. Written notice also should be given to the chairperson of the jurisdictional conference administrative review committee (¶ 539).

b) A bishop, for health reasons, may be retired between sessions of the jurisdictional or central conference by a two-thirds vote of the jurisdictional or central conference committee on episcopacy upon the recommendation of one third of the membership of the involved College of Bishops. The affected bishop, upon request, shall be entitled to a review of his or her health condition by a professional diagnostic team prior to action by the involved College of Bishops. Notification of action to retire shall be given by the chairperson and secretary of the jurisdictional or central conference committee on episcopacy to the secretary of the Council of Bishops and the treasurer of the Episcopal Fund. Appeal from this action may be made to the Judicial Council with the notice provisions being applicable as set forth in ¶ 2716. Upon such retirement, the bishop shall receive a pension to the extent permitted under the Clergy Retirement Security Program or the Global Episcopal Pension Program (or, in either case, any successor bishop pension or retirement plan or program), as either may apply.

4. *Resignation*—A bishop may voluntarily resign from the episcopacy at any time. A bishop may resign from the office by submitting his or her resignation to the Council of Bishops. The Council of Bishops shall have authority to take appropriate actions concerning matters relating to the resignation, including the appointment of an acting bishop to act until a successor is elected and assigned. The consecration papers of a bishop in good standing so resigning shall be properly inscribed by the secretary of the Council of Bishops and returned. He or she shall be furnished with a certificate of resignation, which shall entitle him or her to membership as a traveling elder in the annual conference (or its successor) in which membership was last held. Notification of this action shall be given by the secretary of the Council of Bishops to the chairperson and secretary of the jurisdictional or central conference committee on episcopacy. Pension benefits will be payable to the resigned bishop to the extent permitted under the Clergy Retirement Security Program or the Global Episcopal Pension Program (or, in either case, any successor bishop pension or retirement plan or program), as either may apply.

¶ **409.** *Status of Retired Bishops*—A retired bishop is a bishop of the Church in every respect and continues to function as a member of the Council of Bishops in accordance with the Constitution and other provisions of the *Discipline*.

1. Retired bishops may participate in the Council of Bishops and its committees, but without vote. They may preside over sessions of an annual conference, provisional annual conference, or mission if requested to do so by the bishop assigned to that conference, or in the event of that bishop's incapacity, by the presi-

dent of the College of Bishops to which the conference is related. Retired bishops elected by the Council of Bishops may serve as the executive secretary and the ecumenical officer of the Council. In emergency situations, where the resident bishop is unable to preside, the College of Bishops shall assign an effective or retired bishop to preside over the sessions of the annual conference (¶ 48). They may not make appointments or preside at the jurisdiction or central conference. However, when a retired bishop is appointed by the Council of Bishops to a vacant episcopal area or parts of an area under the provisions of ¶¶ 409.3, 410.1, or 410.3, that bishop may function as a bishop in the effective relationship.[7]

2. A retired bishop may be considered a member of an annual conference, without vote, for purposes of appointment to a local charge within the said conference.

3. A bishop retired under ¶ 408.1, .2 above may be appointed by the Council of Bishops upon recommendation of the involved College of Bishops to presidential responsibility for temporary service in an area in the case of death, resignation, disability, or procedure involving a resident bishop (¶ 2703.1). This appointment shall not continue beyond the next jurisdictional or central conference.

4. Colleges of Bishops are encouraged to work with prospective retirees and institutions across the connection on possible retirement assignments (e.g., bishop-in-residence), particularly assignments expressive of the office's residential, presidential, and missional nature.

¶ **410.** *Leaves*—1. *Leave of Absence*—A bishop may be granted a leave of absence for a justifiable reason for not more than six months in consultation with the area committee on episcopacy and with the approval of the College of Bishops, the jurisdictional or central conference committee on episcopacy, and the executive committee of the Council of Bishops. During the period for which the leave is granted, the bishop shall be released from all episcopal responsibilities, and another bishop chosen by the executive committee of the Council of Bishops shall preside in the episcopal area. Salary and other benefits shall be continued through the Episcopal Fund.

2. *Renewal Leave*—Every bishop in the active relationship shall take up to three months' leave from his or her normal episcopal

---

7. See Judicial Council Decision 248.

responsibilities for purposes of reflection, study, and self-renewal during each quadrennium. The College of Bishops, in consultation with the appropriate jurisdictional or central conference committee on episcopacy, shall coordinate details pertaining to such leaves.

3. *Sabbatical Leave*—A bishop who has served for at least two quadrennia may be granted a sabbatical leave of not more than one year for a program of study or renewal in consultation with the area committee on episcopacy and with the approval of the College of Bishops, the jurisdictional or central conference committee on episcopacy, and the executive committee of the Council of Bishops. During the period for which the sabbatical leave is granted, the bishops shall be released from the presidential responsibilities within the episcopal area, and another bishop or bishops shall be designated by the Council of Bishops to assume the presidential duties. The bishop shall receive one-half salary and, where applicable, housing allowance for the period of the leave.

4. *Medical Leave*—Bishops who by reason of impaired health are temporarily unable to perform full work may be granted a leave of absence for a justifiable reason for not more than six months in consultation with the area committee on episcopacy and with the approval of the College of Bishops, the jurisdictional or central conference committee on episcopacy, and the executive committee of the Council of Bishops. During the period for which the leave is granted, the bishop shall be released from all episcopal responsibilities, and another bishop chosen by the executive committee of the Council of Bishops shall preside in the episcopal area. Salary and other benefits shall be continued through the Episcopal Fund. If after the six-month time period is over the bishop is still unable to perform full work due to impaired health, disability benefits through the benefit program provided to the bishop should be applied for.

¶ **411.** *Expiration of Terms in Central Conferences*—In a central conference where term episcopacy prevails, bishops whose term of office expires prior to the time of compulsory retirement because of age and who are not reelected by the central conference shall be returned to membership as traveling elders in the annual conference (or its successor) of which they ceased to be a member when elected bishop. Their term of office shall expire at the close of the central conference at which their successor is elected, and they shall therefore be entitled to participate as a bishop in the consecration of the successor. The credentials of office as bishop shall be submitted to the secretary of the central conference, who shall make thereon the notation that the bishop has honorably completed the term of service for which elected and has ceased to be a bishop of The United Methodist Church.[8]

¶ **412.** *Review and Evaluation of Bishops*—In its review of the work, character, and official administration of the bishops under ¶ 524.3*a*, the jurisdictional or central conference committee on episcopacy shall establish and implement processes that provide, at least once each quadrennium, for each active bishop, a full and formal evaluation which will include self-evaluation, assessment by episcopal peers, and comment by persons affected by his or her superintendency (such as cabinets, lay leaders, directors of agencies served). Such processes shall include the participation of the conference or area committee on episcopacy. It shall be the duty of each jurisdiction's College of Bishops/central conference's College of Bishops, under the leadership of its president, to consult with and to cooperate with the committee in order to schedule and facilitate such reviews and evaluations as well as to address issues that may arise in the course of that work.

¶ **413.** *Complaints Against Bishops*—1. Episcopal leadership in The United Methodist Church shares with all other ordained persons in the sacred trust of their ordination. The ministry of bishops as set forth in *The Book of Discipline of The United Methodist Church* also flows from the gospel as taught by Jesus the Christ and proclaimed by his apostles (¶ 402). Whenever a bishop violates this trust or is unable to fulfill appropriate responsibilities, continuation in the episcopal office shall be subject to review. This review shall have as its primary purpose a just resolution of any violations of this sacred trust, in the hope that God's work of justice, reconciliation, and healing may be realized.

2. Any complaint concerning the effectiveness, competence, or one or more of the offenses listed in ¶ 2702 shall be submitted to the president of the College of Bishops in that jurisdictional or central conference. If the complaint concerns the president, it shall be submitted to the secretary of the College of Bishops. A complaint is a written statement claiming misconduct, unsatisfactory

---

8. See Judicial Council Decisions 61, 236, 370.

performance of ministerial duties, or one or more of the offenses listed in ¶ 2702.[9]

3. After receiving a complaint as provided in ¶ 413.2, the president and the secretary of the College of Bishops, or the secretary and another member of the college if the complaint concerns the president (or the president and another member of the college if the complaint concerns the secretary), shall, within ten days, consult the chair of the jurisdictional or central conference committee on episcopacy who shall appoint from the committee one professing member and one clergy member who are not from the same episcopal area; who are not from the episcopal area that the bishop under complaint was elected from or has been assigned to; and who are not of the same gender.

a) When deemed appropriate to protect the well-being of the complainant, the Church and/or bishop, the College of Bishops, in consultation with the jurisdictional or central conference committee on episcopacy, may suspend the bishop from all episcopal responsibilities for a period not to exceed sixty days. During the suspension, salary, housing, and benefits will continue.

b) The supervisory response is pastoral and administrative and shall be directed toward a just resolution. It is not a part of any judicial process. The supervisory response should be carried out in a confidential manner and should be completed within 120 days. There may be an extension of 120 days if the supervising bishop and the two jurisdictional or central conference episcopacy committee members appointed to the supervisory process shall determine that an extension will be productive. There may be a second extension of 120 days by the mutual written consent of the supervisory bishop, members of the jurisdictional or central conference episcopacy committee appointed to the supervisory process, the complainant, and the bishop under complaint.

The supervising bishop shall regularly advise all parties of the status of the process and shall notify all parties within seven days after a determination is made that the supervisory response will not lead to a resolution of the matter.

No verbatim record shall be made and legal counsel shall not be present, although the bishop against whom the complaint was made and the complainant both may choose another person to accompany him or her, with the right to voice. At the determina-

9. See Judicial Council Decision 1149.

tion of the president (secretary), persons with qualifications and experience in assessment, intervention, or healing may be selected to assist in the supervisory responses. Others may be consulted as well.

c) The supervisory response may include a process seeking a just resolution in which the parties are assisted by a trained, impartial third party facilitator(s) or mediator(s) in reaching an agreement satisfactory to all parties. (See ¶ 362.1*b*, *c*.) The appropriate persons, including the president of the College of Bishops, or the secretary if the complaint concerns the president, should enter into a written agreement outlining such process, including an agreement as to confidentiality. If resolution is achieved, a written statement of resolution, including terms and conditions, shall be signed by the parties and the parties shall agree on any matters to be disclosed to third parties. Such written statement of resolution shall be given to the person in charge of that stage of the process for further action consistent with the agreement.

d) (i) If the supervisory response results in the resolution of the matter, the bishop in charge of the supervisory response and the two episcopacy committee members appointed to the supervisory process (¶ 413.3) shall monitor the fulfillment of the terms of the resolution. If the supervisory response does not result in resolution of the matter, the president or secretary of the College of Bishops may either dismiss the complaint with the consent of the College of Bishops and the committee on episcopacy, giving the reasons therefore in writing, a copy of which shall be placed in the bishop's file, refer the matter to the committee on episcopacy as an administrative complaint pursuant to ¶ 413.3*e*, or refer the matter to counsel for the Church pursuant to ¶ 2704.1 to prepare a complaint to forward to the committee on investigation.

(ii) If within 180 days of the receipt of the complaint by the president or secretary of the College of Bishops (as specified in ¶ 413.2), the supervisory response does not result in the resolution of the matter, and the president or secretary of the College of Bishops has not referred the matter as either an administrative or judicial complaint, then the matter will move to:

(1) In the case of a bishop from one of the central conferences, a panel of three bishops, one from each continent, as selected by the Council of Bishops, or

(2) In the case of a bishop from one of the jurisdictional conferences, a panel of five bishops,

one from each jurisdictional conference, as selected by the Council of Bishops, who shall then continue the supervisory response process and, within 180 days, either dismiss or refer the complaint, as required above.

(iii) All costs associated with actions taken pursuant to paragraph (ii), above, will be paid by the Episcopal Fund.

(iv) The Council of Bishops may, at any time in the process, after a complaint is filed, including after a just resolution, remove the complaint from the College of Bishops to the Council of Bishops with a two-thirds vote by the Council.

e) Administrative Complaint—If the complaint is based on allegations of incompetence, ineffectiveness, or unwillingness or inability to perform episcopal duties, the president and secretary of the College of Bishops (or the two members of the college who are handling the complaint) shall refer the complaint to the jurisdictional or central conference committee on episcopacy.[10] The committee may recommend involuntary retirement (¶ 408.3), disability leave (¶ 410.4), remedial measures, other appropriate action, or it may dismiss the complaint. When the jurisdictional or central conference committee on episcopacy deems the matter serious enough and when one or more offenses listed in ¶ 2702 are involved, the committee may refer the complaint back to the president and secretary of the College of Bishops (or the two members of the college who are handling the complaint) for referral as a judicial complaint to the jurisdictional or central conference committee on investigation. The provisions of ¶ 361.2 for fair process in administrative hearings shall apply to this administrative process.

4. Any actions of the jurisdictional or central conference committee taken on a complaint shall be reported to the next session of the jurisdictional or central conference.

5. Each jurisdiction shall develop a protocol for the caring of lay, clergy, and staff determined to be affected by the processing of the complaint.

6. *Immunity From Prosecution*—In order to preserve the integrity of the Church's complaint process and ensure full participation in it at all times, the College of Bishops, the supervisory response team, the jurisdictional committee on episcopacy, witnesses, advocates, and all others who participate in the complaint

---

10. See Judicial Council Decision 784.

process regarding a bishop shall have immunity from prosecution of complaints brought against them related to their role in a particular complaint process, unless they have committed a chargeable offense in conscious and knowing bad faith. The complainant/plaintiff in any proceeding against any such person relating to their role in a particular complaint process shall have the burden of proving, by clear and convincing evidence, that such person's actions constituted a chargeable offense committed knowingly in bad faith. The immunity set forth in this provision shall extend to civil court proceedings, to the fullest extent permissible by the civil laws.

Section IV. Specific Responsibilities of Bishops

¶ 414. *Leadership—Spiritual and Temporal*—1. To lead and oversee the spiritual and temporal affairs of The United Methodist Church which confesses Jesus Christ as Lord and Savior, and particularly to lead the Church in its mission of witness and service in the world.

2. To strengthen the local church, giving spiritual leadership to both laity and clergy; and to build relationships with people of local congregations of the area.

3. To guard, transmit, teach, and proclaim, corporately and individually, the apostolic faith as it is expressed in Scripture and tradition, and, as they are led and endowed by the Spirit, to interpret that faith evangelically and prophetically.

4. To travel through the connection at large as the Council of Bishops (¶ 422) to implement strategy for the concerns of the Church.

5. To teach and uphold the theological traditions of The United Methodist Church.

6. To provide liaison and leadership in the quest for Christian unity in ministry, mission, and structure and in the search for strengthened relationships with other living faith communities.

7. To organize such missions as shall have been authorized by the General Conference.

8. To promote and support the evangelistic witness of the whole Church.

9. To discharge such other duties as the *Discipline* may direct.

10. To convene the Order of Deacons and the Order of Elders and work with the elected chairperson of each order.

11. To promote, support, and model generous Christian giving, with special attention to teaching the biblical principles of giving.

¶ **415.** *Presidential Duties*—1. To preside in the General, jurisdictional, central, and annual conferences.[11]

2. To provide general oversight for the fiscal and program operations of the annual conference(s). This may include special inquiry into the work of agencies to ensure that the annual conference and general church policies and procedures are followed.

3. To ensure fair process for clergy and laity as set forth in ¶ 2701 in all involuntary administrative and judicial proceedings through monitoring the performance of annual conference officials, boards, and committees charged with implementing such procedures.[12]

4. To form the districts after consultation with the district superintendents and after the number of the same has been determined by vote of the annual conference.[13] Any district may be designated to be a mission district, and the district superintendent of that district, or his or her designee, shall be the agent in charge of the mission status, nature, and goals of the district. If there is a district missionary organization, or if funds for the district are anticipated from a conference organization, those bodies shall also be asked to approve the method of organization for a mission district. A mission district may be designated when any of the following conditions exist: 1) Membership opportunities and resources are limited and not likely to result in regular status for an extended period of time. 2) A strategic demographic, cultural, or language opportunity for serving a limited population is present. 3) It is expected that long-term sustaining funding from sources outside the district will be necessary to enable the district to exist. 4) The district is geographically located in a remote location from other districts of the annual conference. When any of these conditions exist, the bishop, in consultation with the congregational development area of the annual conference, may designate any district a mission district. The mission district may be organized in the same manner and have the same rights and powers as any district.

5. To appoint the district superintendents annually (¶¶ 417-418).

---

11. See Judicial Council Decision 395.
12. See Judicial Council Decision 524.
13. See Judicial Council Decision 422.

6. To consecrate bishops; to ordain elders and deacons; to commission deaconesses, home missioners, and missionaries; and to see that the names of the persons commissioned and consecrated are entered on the journals of the conference and that proper credentials are furnished to these persons. As these services are acts of the whole Church, text and rubrics shall be used in the form approved by the General Conference.

7. To fix the appointments of deaconesses, home missioners, and missionaries and to see that the names and appointments are printed in the journals of the conference.

¶ **416.** *Working with Ordained, Licensed, Consecrated, and Commissioned Personnel*—1. To make and fix the appointments in the annual conferences, provisional annual conferences, and missions as the *Discipline* may direct (¶¶ 425-429).

2. To divide or to unite a circuit(s), station(s), or mission(s) as judged necessary for missional strategy and then to make appropriate appointments.

3. To announce the appointments of deaconesses, diaconal ministers, home missionaries, and laypersons in service under the General Board of Global Ministries.

4. To fix the charge conference membership of all ordained ministers appointed to ministries other than the local church in keeping with ¶ 344.

5. To transfer, upon the request of the receiving bishop, clergy member(s) of one annual conference to another, provided said member(s) agrees to said transfer; and to send immediately to the secretaries of both conferences involved, to the conference boards of ordained ministry, and to the clearing house of the General Board of Pension and Health Benefits, written notices of the transfer of members and of their standing in the Course of Study if they are undergraduates.[14]

6 To appoint associate members, provisional members, or full members to attend any school, college, or theological seminary listed by the University Senate, or to participate in a program of clinical pastoral education in a setting accredited by the Association for Clinical Pastoral Education or another accrediting agency approved by the General Board of Higher Education and Ministry. Such appointments are not to be considered as extension ministry appointments.

---

14. See Judicial Council Decisions 114, 254, 554.

7. To keep and maintain appropriate supervisory records on all district superintendents and other records on ministerial personnel as determined by the bishop or required by the *Discipline* or action of the annual conference. When a district superintendent is no longer appointed to the cabinet, the bishop shall give that person's supervisory file to the superintendent of record. Supervisory records shall be kept under guidelines approved by the General Council on Finance and Administration. The supervisory records maintained by the bishop are not the personnel records of the annual conference.

Section V. Selection, Assignment, and Term of District Superintendents

¶ **417.** *Selection and Assignment*—Inasmuch as the district superintendency is an extension of the general superintendency, the bishop shall appoint elders to serve as district superintendents. Prior to each appointment, the bishop shall consult with the cabinet and the committee on district superintendency of the district to which the new superintendent will be assigned (¶ 426) for the purpose of determining leadership needs of the annual conference and the district (¶ 401). In the selection of superintendents, bishops shall give due consideration to the inclusiveness of The United Methodist Church with respect to sex, race, national origin, physical challenge, and age, except for the provisions of mandatory retirement.

¶ **418.** *Limitations on Years of Service*—The normal term for a district superintendent shall be up to six years, but this may be extended to no more than up to eight years at the discretion of the bishop, in consultation with the cabinet and the district committee on superintendency.

No superintendent shall serve for more than eight years in any consecutive eleven years. No elder shall serve as district superintendent more than fourteen years. In addition, consideration shall be given to the nature of superintendency as described in ¶ 401.[15]

Section VI. Specific Responsibilities of District Superintendents

¶ **419.** As an extension of the office of bishop, the district superintendent shall oversee the total ministry of the clergy (including)

---

15. See Judicial Council Decisions 368, 512.

clergy in extension ministry and ministry beyond the local church) and of the churches in the communities of the district in their missions of witness and service in the world. This oversight requires the superintendent to use his or her gifts and skills related to spiritual and pastoral leadership, personnel leadership, administration, and program. The superintendent is the acting administrator of any pastoral charge in which a pastoral vacancy may develop, or where no pastor is appointed.

1. The Church expects, as part of the superintendent ministry, that the superintendent will be the chief missional strategist of the district and be committed to living out the values of the Church, including a mandate of inclusiveness, modeling, teaching, and promoting generous Christian giving, cooperating to develop Christian unity, and ecumenical, multicultural, multiracial, and cooperative ministries; and working with persons across the Church to develop programs of ministry and mission that extend the witness of Christ into the world.

2. The superintendent shall work with the bishop and cabinet in the process of appointment and assignment for ordained and licensed clergy, or assignment of qualified and trained laypersons, lay ministers or lay missioners (¶ 205.4)

3. The superintendent shall work with the district committee on ordained ministry to develop an effective and functioning system for recruitment and examination of candidates for ordained or licensed ministry, and the ongoing oversight of persons approved for licensing (¶ 348).

4. The superintendent shall establish working relationships with staff/pastor-parish relations committees, clergy, district lay leaders, and other lay leadership, to develop faithful and effective systems of ministry within the district. Through the use of charge conferences (¶ 246.4-5), congregational studies (¶ 213) and other gatherings, the superintendent shall seek to form creative and effective connections with the local congregations on his or her district.

5. The superintendent shall serve as an example of spiritual leadership by living a balanced and faithful life, and by encouraging both laity and clergy to continue to grow in spiritual formation through both personal and corporate worship and devotional practices, including participation in the sacraments.

6. In the framework of their supervisory responsibilities, superintendents shall offer support, care, and counsel to clergy

concerning matters affecting their effective ministry. Further, the superintendents shall encourage the building of covenant groups and communities among both the clergy and clergy families, and the laity on the district.

7. The superintendent shall seek to be in regular contact with the clergy on the district for counsel and supervision, and shall receive written or electronic reports of the clergy's continuing education, spiritual practices, current ministry work, and goals for future ministry.

8. The superintendent shall maintain the appropriate records of all clergy appointed to or related to the charges on the district (including clergy in extension ministry and ministry beyond the local church), as well as records dealing with property, endowments, and other tangible assets of The United Methodist Church within the district.

9. The superintendent, in consultation with the bishop and cabinet, shall work to develop the best strategic deployment of clergy possible in the district, including realignment of pastoral charges when needed and the exploration of larger parishes, cooperative parishes, multiple staff configurations, new faith communities, and ecumenical shared communities.

10. The district superintendent shall interpret and decide all questions of Church law and discipline raised by the churches in the district, subject to review by the resident bishop of the annual conference.

11. The superintendent shall cooperate with the conference Board of Ordained Ministry in its efforts to provide or arrange support and liaison for clergy in a time of a change in conference relationship or termination.

12. The superintendent shall serve at the pleasure of the bishop and assume other leadership responsibilities as the bishop determines for the health and effectiveness of the district and annual conference.

¶ **420.** *Renewal and Study Leave*—A district superintendent may take up to three months' leave from his or her normal superintendent responsibilities for purposes of reflection, study, and self-renewal once during his or her term as superintendent. The bishop and cabinet, in consultation with the committee on district superintendency, shall coordinate details pertaining to such leaves.

Section VII. Expressions of Superintendency

¶ 421. *Relationship Between Bishops and District Superintendents*—The offices of bishop and district superintendent are linked with each other in ways described elsewhere (¶ 402). The interdependence of the offices calls for a collegial style of leadership. However, both the office of bishop and that of district superintendent are embedded in their own contexts.

¶ 422. *Council of Bishops*—1. Bishops, although elected by jurisdictional or central conferences, are elected general superintendents of the whole Church. As all ordained ministers are first elected into membership of an annual conference and subsequently appointed to pastoral charges, so bishops become through their election members first of the Council of Bishops before they are subsequently assigned to areas of service. By virtue of their election and consecration, bishops are members of the Council of Bishops and are bound in special covenant with all other bishops. In keeping with this covenant, bishops fulfill their servant leadership and express their mutual accountability. The Council of Bishops is a faith community of mutual trust and concern responsible for the faith development and continuing well-being of its members.

2. The Council of Bishops is thus the collegial expression of episcopal leadership in the Church and through the Church into the world. The Church expects the Council of Bishops to speak to the Church and from the Church to the world and to give leadership in the quest for Christian unity and interreligious relationships.

3. In order to exercise meaningful leadership, the Council of Bishops is to meet at stated intervals. The Council of Bishops is charged with the oversight of the spiritual and temporal affairs of the whole Church, to be executed in regularized consultation and cooperation with other councils and service agencies of the Church.

4. The Council of Bishops may assign one of its members to visit another episcopal area or Methodist-related church. When so assigned, the bishop shall be recognized as the accredited representative of the Council of Bishops, and when requested by the resident bishop or president in that area or church, may exercise therein the functions of episcopacy.

¶ 423. *Conference of Methodist Bishops*—There may be a conference of Methodist bishops, composed of all the bishops elected by the jurisdictional and central conferences and one bishop or chief executive officer from each affiliated autonomous Methodist or united church, which shall meet on call of the Council of Bishops after consultation with other members of the conference of Methodist bishops. The travel and other necessary expense of bishops of affiliated autonomous Methodist or united churches related to the meeting of the Conference of Methodist Bishops shall be paid on the same basis as that of bishops of The United Methodist Church.

¶ **424.** *Cabinet*—1. District superintendents, although appointed to the cabinet and assigned to districts, are also to be given conference-wide responsibilities. As all ordained ministers are first elected into membership of an annual conference and subsequently appointed to pastoral charges, so district superintendents become through their selection members first of a cabinet before they are subsequently assigned by the bishop to service in districts.

2. The cabinet under the leadership of the bishop is the expression of superintending leadership in and through the annual conference. It is expected to speak to the conference and for the conference to the spiritual and temporal issues that exist within the region encompassed by the conference.

3. The cabinet is thus also the body in which the individual district superintendents are held accountable for their work, both for conference and district responsibilities.

4. In order to exercise meaningful leadership, the cabinet is to meet at stated intervals. The cabinet is charged with the oversight of the spiritual and temporal affairs of a conference, to be executed in regularized consultation and cooperation with other councils and service agencies of the conference.

5. The cabinet is to consult and plan with the district committee and conference Board of Ordained Ministry in order to make a thorough analysis of the needs of the district for clergy, implementing this planning with a positive and conscious effort to fill these needs (¶ 635.2*a*).

6. When the cabinet considers matters relating to coordination, implementation, or administration of the conference program, and other matters as the cabinet and director of connectional ministries, or equivalent, may determine, the director shall be present. The conference lay leader shall be invited to be present.

7. The cabinet shall assume leadership responsibility for ascertaining those places where ecumenical shared ministry would be an effective way of expressing the United Methodist presence in a community.

Section VIII. Appointment-Making

¶ 425. *Responsibility*—1. Clergy shall be appointed by the bishop, who is empowered to make and fix all appointments in the episcopal area of which the annual conference is a part. Appointments are to be made with consideration of the gifts and evidence of God's grace of those appointed, to the needs, characteristics, and opportunities of congregations and institutions, and with faithfulness to the commitment to an open itinerary. Open itinerary means appointments are made without regard to race, ethnic origin, gender, color, disability, marital status, or age, except for the provisions of mandatory retirement. Annual conferences shall, in their training of staff-parish relations committees, emphasize the open nature of itinerary and prepare congregations to receive the gifts and graces of appointed clergy without regard to race, ethnic origin, gender, color, disability, marital status, or age. The concept of itinerary is important, and sensitive attention should be given in appointing clergy with physical challenges to responsibilities and duties that meet their gifts and graces. Through appointment-making, the connectional nature of the United Methodist system is made visible.[16]

2. Appointment-making across conference lines shall be encouraged as a way of creating mobility and open itineracy. The jurisdictional committee on ordained ministry will cooperate with bishops and cabinets in providing information on supply and demand within the jurisdiction.

3. The United Methodist Church promotes and holds in high esteem the opportunity of an inclusive church (¶ 4. Article IV) with the formation of open itineracy (¶ 425.1).

4. Cross-racial and cross-cultural appointments are made as a creative response to increasing racial and ethnic diversity in the church and in its leadership. Cross-racial and cross-cultural appointments are appointments of clergypersons to congregations in which the majority of their constituencies are different from the clergyperson's own racial/ethnic and cultural background.

---

16. See Judicial Council Decision 492.

Annual conferences shall prepare clergy and congregations for cross-racial and cross-cultural appointments. When such appointments are made, bishops, cabinets, and boards of ordained ministry shall provide specific training for the clergypersons so appointed and for their congregations.

¶ **426.** *Consultation and Appointment-Making*—Consultation is the process whereby the bishop and/or district superintendent confer with the pastor and committee on pastor-parish relations, taking into consideration the criteria of ¶ 427, a performance evaluation, needs of the appointment under consideration, and mission of the Church. Consultation is not merely notification. Consultation is not committee selection or call of a pastor. The role of the committee on pastor-parish relations is advisory. Consultation is both a continuing process and a more intense involvement during the period of change in appointment.[17]

1. The process of consultation shall be mandatory in every annual conference.[18]

2. The Council of Bishops shall inquire annually of their colleagues about the implementation of the process of consultation in appointment-making in their respective areas.[19]

¶ **427.** *Criteria*—Appointments shall take into account the unique needs of a charge, the community context, and also the gifts and evidence of God's grace of a particular pastor. To assist bishops, cabinets, pastors, and congregations to achieve an effective match of charges and pastors, criteria must be developed and analyzed in each instance and then shared with pastors and congregations.

1. *Congregations*—The district superintendent shall develop with the pastor and the committees on pastor-parish relations of all churches profiles that reflect the needs, characteristics, and opportunities for mission of the charge consistent with the Church's statement of purpose. These profiles shall be reviewed annually and updated when appropriate to include:

a) The general situation in which a congregation finds itself in a particular setting: size, financial condition, quality of lay leadership, special needs for pastoral ministry, and history.

b) The convictional stance of the congregation: theology; prejudices, if any; spiritual life.

---

17. See Judicial Council Decisions 492, 1174.
18. See Judicial Council Decision 492.
19. See Judicial Council Decision 701.

c) The ministry of the congregation among its people for the sake of the community: service programs, basis for adding new members, reasons for losing members, mission to community and world, forms of witness.

d) The qualities and functions of pastoral ministry needed to fulfill the mission, goals, and special needs of the congregation.

2. *Pastors*—The district superintendent annually shall develop with the pastor profiles reflecting the pastor's gifts, evidence of God's grace, professional experience and expectations, and also the needs and concerns of the pastor's spouse and family. These profiles shall be reviewed annually and updated when appropriate to include:

a) Spiritual and personal sensibility: personal faith, call and commitment to ordained ministry, work through the institutional church, integration of vocation with personal and family well-being, lifestyle.

b) Academic and career background: nature of theological stance, experience in continuing education, professional experience, record of performance.

c) Skills and abilities: in church administration, leadership development, worship and liturgy, preaching and evangelism, teaching and nurturing, interpreting and promoting the connectional giving system, counseling and group work, ability to work in cooperation, ability in self-evaluation, and other relational skills.

d) Community context: the ability of the pastor to relate effectively to his or her community setting, such as rural, town, urban, suburban, and so forth.

e) Family situation.

3. *Community Context*—The district superintendent may develop community profiles with the pastor and the committee on pastor-parish relations. Sources of information for these profiles could include: neighborhood surveys; local, state, and national census data; information from annual conference committees on parish and community development; and research data from the Connectional Table and other Church agencies. Profiles may be reviewed annually and updated when appropriate to include:

a) General demographic data and trends including age, sex, and racial-ethnic composition of the community.

b) Economic trends, including the incidence of poverty.

c) Projected community changes.

d) Other sociological, economic, political, historical, and ecumenical aspects of the community surrounding the church.

¶ **428.** *Process of Appointment-Making*—The process used in appointment-making shall include:[20]

1. A change in appointment may be initiated by a pastor, a committee on pastor-parish relations, a district superintendent, or a bishop.

2. The bishop and the cabinet shall consider all requests for change of appointment in light of the profile developed for each charge and the gifts and evidence of God's grace, professional experience, and family needs of the pastor.

3. When a change in appointment has been determined, the district superintendent should meet together or separately with the pastor and the committee on pastor-parish relations where the pastor is serving, for the purpose of sharing the basis for the change and the process used in making the new appointment.

4. All appointments shall receive consideration by the bishop, the district superintendent(s), and the cabinet as a whole until a tentative decision is made.

5. The process used in making the new appointment shall include:

a) The district superintendent shall confer with the pastor about a specific possible appointment (charge) and its congruence with gifts, evidence of God's grace, professional experience and expectations, and the family needs of the pastor, identified in consultation with the pastor (¶ 427.2).

b) If the appointment is to a cooperative parish ministry or to a charge that is part of a cooperative parish ministry, the following shall be included in the consultation process:

(1) The prospective appointee shall be informed prior to the appointment that the charge under consideration is part of a cooperative parish ministry.[21]

(2) The coordinator or director of the cooperative ministry, or, if there is no coordinator or director, a representative of the staff of the cooperative ministry, shall be conferred with concerning the prospective appointment and shall have the opportunity to meet with the prospective appointee prior to the appointment being made.[22]

---

20. See Judicial Council Decision 701.
21. See Judicial Council Decision 556.
22. See Judicial Council Decision 556.

(3) The prospective appointee shall have demonstrated skills in cooperative Christian mission or show potential for the same to ensure that the cooperative venture is strengthened during the time of the appointee's leadership.

c) If the appointment is to a position other than pastor in charge, the following shall be included in the consultation process:

(1) The prospective appointee shall be informed prior to the appointment that the position under consideration is part of a multiple-staff ministry and shall be furnished an initial written job description approved by the committee on pastor-parish relations.

(2) The pastor in charge shall be conferred with concerning the prospective appointee.

(3) The prospective appointee and pastor in charge shall meet for discussion of the job description and mutual expectations.

6. The district superintendent shall confer with the receiving committee on pastor-parish relations about pastoral leadership (¶ 427.1).

7. When appointments are being made to less than full-time ministry, the district superintendent shall consult with the clergy person to be appointed and the committee on pastor-parish relations regarding proportional time, salary, and pension credit and benefit coverage.

8. If during this consultative process it is determined by the bishop and cabinet that this decision should not be carried out, the process is to be repeated until the bishop, basing his or her decision on the information and advice derived from consultation, makes and fixes the appointment.

9. A similar process of consultation shall be available to persons in appointments beyond the local church.

10. When the steps in the process have been followed and completed, the announcement of that decision shall be made to all parties directly involved in the consultative process, that is, the appointment cabinet, the pastor, and the committee on pastor-parish relations, before a public announcement is made.

¶ 429. *Frequency*—While the bishop shall report all pastoral appointments to each regular session of an annual conference, appointments to charges may be made at any time deemed advisable by the bishop and cabinet. Appointments are made with the expectation that the length of pastorates shall respond to the long-term pastoral needs of charges, communities, and pastors. The bishop and cabinet should work toward longer tenure in local church appointments to facilitate a more effective ministry.

¶ **430.** *Appointment of Deacons in Full Connection*—The deacons shall be appointed by the bishop in the annual conference where they are members in full connection. Appointments of the deacons are to be made in consideration of the gifts and evidence of God's grace of the deacon, needs of the community, and the gifts of the congregation and institutions. The appointment shall reflect the nature of the ministry of the deacon as a faithful response of the mission of the church meeting the emerging needs in the world (¶ 331). It may be initiated by the individual deacon in full connection, the agency seeking their service, the bishop, or the district superintendent.

Section IX. Ecumenical Relationships

¶ **431.1.** *Full Communion Relationships*

a) The Council of Bishops shall have the authority to enter into ecumenical agreements with other Christian bodies. However, all proposed denominational level agreements of formal "full communion" relationships and permanent membership in ecumenical organizations must be approved and ratified by General Conference, before coming into effect.

b) A formal "full communion" relationship is one that exists between two or more Christian churches that:

(1) recognize each other as constituent members of the one, holy, catholic and apostolic church, the body of Christ, as described in the Holy Scriptures and confessed in the church's historic creeds;

(2) recognize the authenticity of each other's sacraments and welcome one another to partake in the Eucharist,

(3) affirm the authenticity of each church's Christian ministry, and

(4) recognize the validity of each other's offices of ministry.

c) A formal "full communion" relationship commits the churches to working together as partners in mission toward fuller visible unity.

d) A formal "full communion" relationship is entered into in order to: (1) actively commit the participants to working together as partners in mission and co-laborers in the ministry of

Christ Jesus, and (2) as a visible witness to the unity of Christians in sharing the love of God among all peoples and throughout creation.

e) A formal "full communion" relationship does not mean there are no differences or distinctions between churches; but does mean that these differences are not church dividing.

f) It is understood and affirmed that informal relationships exist with other Christians at all levels throughout the church; these relationships are manifested in creative and dynamic ways and the body of Christ is enriched by the initiative and leadership that takes place at many levels. Formal "full communion" relationships entered into by General Conference build upon the faithful unity of Christians in local communities and throughout God's creation that bring the compassion, love, and witness into the lives of a multitude of persons. Formal and informal relationships among Christians are integral to authentic Christian ministry.

g) No membership in an ecumenical organization, statement or policy of an ecumenical organization of which The United Methodist Church is a part, or formal "full communion" agreement shall be construed as modifying, interpreting, or changing the doctrinal and disciplinary standards of The United Methodist Church.

h) When a "full communion" relationship has been approved by General Conference, it will remain in effect until an action by the General Conference is taken to change it.

2. *Liaison Role of the Council of Bishops*—1. In formal relations with other churches and/or ecclesial bodies, the Council of Bishops shall be the primary liaison for The United Methodist Church. The ecumenical officer of the Council of Bishops shall be responsible for these relationships.

3. The Office of Christian Unity and Interreligious Relationships shall consult with the Council of Bishops in establishing the guidelines for the administration of the Interdenominational Cooperation Fund (see ¶ 814).

4. The United Methodist representatives to ecumenical organizations in the following paragraphs shall be selected by the Council of Bishops. Such representatives shall be inclusive in terms of gender, race and ethnicity, age, persons with disabilities, and region. Representatives shall reflect consideration of balances required both by The United Methodist Church and the respective

ecumenical organization. Consideration shall be given to persons named to jurisdictional and central conference pools (see ¶ 705.1.*b, c*).

When proxies are needed to substitute for United Methodist representatives to a specific ecumenical organization, the ecumenical officer of the Council of Bishops is authorized to name such proxies. Consideration shall be given to United Methodists residing in the area of the ecumenical organization's meeting, and to the inclusivity of the delegation. The names of proxies shall be reported at the next meeting of the Council of Bishops.

Representatives and proxies from The United Methodist Church to various working groups of any of the ecumenical organizations in the following paragraphs shall be named by the ecumenical officer of the Council of Bishops.

5. Notwithstanding the other provisions of this section, should structural changes be voted between sessions of the General Conference by any of the ecumenical organizations in the following paragraphs, necessitating election of a new group of United Methodist delegates, the Council of Bishops is authorized to elect such delegates as may be required.

¶ **432.** *Financial Support*—United Methodist financial support of the ecumenical organizations in the following paragraphs shall be remitted from the Interdenominational Cooperation Fund through the General Council on Finance and Administration in accordance with ¶ 814. The general agencies of the Church may make such payments to these ecumenical organizations as they deem to be their responsibility and proportionate share in the cooperative programs. Such payments shall be reported to the General Council on Finance and Administration, and that Council shall include a summary report of United Methodist financial support in its annual financial report to the Church. United Methodist financial support of ecumenical dialogues and multilateral conversations, approved by the Council of Bishops, shall also be remitted from the Interdenominational Cooperation Fund in the same manner.

¶ **433.** *Methodist Unity*—1. *World Methodist Council*—*a)* The United Methodist Church is a member of the World Methodist Council, its predecessor Methodist and Evangelical United Brethren churches having been charter members of such body. The council is a significant channel for United Methodist relationships with other Methodist churches and with autonomous Methodist churches, affiliated autonomous Methodist churches, affiliated united churches formerly part of The United Methodist Church or its predecessor denominations, and other churches with a Wesleyan heritage.

b) Each affiliated autonomous Methodist church and each affiliated united church that is a member of the World Methodist Council may choose to send delegates either to the General Conference as proposed in ¶ 570.2, .3 or to the World Methodist Council (receiving from the General Administration Fund the expense of travel and per diem allowances thereto). But no such church shall be entitled to send delegations at the expense of the General Administration Fund to both the World Methodist Council and the General Conference.

2. *Pan-Methodist Commission*—Given the relationship and shared history of the denominations of the Wesleyan tradition in America, there shall be a Pan-Methodist Commission established jointly among The African Methodist Episcopal Church, The African Methodist Episcopal Zion Church, The African Union Methodist Protestant Church, The Christian Methodist Episcopal Church, The Union American Methodist Episcopal Church, and The United Methodist Church. The membership of the commission shall consist of nine persons from each member denomination, with each denomination naming three bishops, three clergypersons, and three laypersons to include at least one young adult. Each denomination will pay the expenses of its delegation to participate in the work of the commission.

The commission shall work to define, determine, plan, and, in cooperation with established agencies of the several denominations, execute activities to foster meaningful cooperation among the six Methodist denominations, and to explore possible union and related issues. The commission may develop one or more Pan-Methodist coalitions to further meaningful cooperation on a particular activity or issue.

Each quadrennium, the commission shall plan and convene a Consultation of Methodist Bishops. The commission shall report to each of its member denominations through their General Conferences. The commission may be expanded by the inclusion of other denominations of the Wesleyan tradition and the commission may establish guidelines to provide for such expansion. Before another Wesleyan or American Methodist denomination may become a part of the commission, it must have the approval of its general conference or equivalent.

3. *Striving Toward Union*—As a result of our heritage as a part of a people called Methodist, The United Methodist Church commits itself to strive toward closer relationship with other Methodist or Wesleyan churches wherever they may be found (¶ 6).

¶ **434.** *Covenantal or Conciliar Relationships*—The United Methodist Church strives toward greater Christian unity through its participation in councils of churches and/or covenantal relationships. The United Methodist Church may establish covenants with other Christian churches through bilateral or multilateral efforts.

1. *Churches Uniting in Christ*—The United Methodist Church is a member of Churches Uniting in Christ, its predecessor Methodist and Evangelical United Brethren churches having been involved in its very beginnings and in all its committees and plenary consultations. The United Methodist Church is in covenantal relationship with other churches in Churches Uniting in Christ.

2. *National or Regional Ecumenical Organizations*—*a) The National Council of the Churches of Christ in the U.S.A.*—The United Methodist Church is a member of the National Council of the Churches of Christ in the U.S.A., its predecessor Methodist and Evangelical United Brethren churches having been charter members of such body.

b) Other National or Regional Ecumenical Organizations—The Council of Bishops, shall be in dialogue with United Methodists in whatever countries they may reside, and shall coordinate, explore, and advocate United Methodist participation in regional ecumenical and interreligious organizations and shall address the Interdenominational Cooperation Fund funding of financial needs and the advisability of support of these organizations.

c) The United Methodist Church shall seek observer status in the National Association of Evangelicals. United Methodist observers to these bodies shall be appointed by the Council of Bishops.

3. *The World Council of Churches and Other International Ecumenical Organizations*—*a) World Council of Churches*—The United Methodist Church is a member of the World Council of Churches, its predecessor Methodist and Evangelical United Brethren churches having been charter members of such body.

b) Other International Ecumenical Organizations—The Council of Bishops shall be in dialogue with United Methodists in whatever countries they may reside, and shall coordinate, explore, and advocate United Methodist participation in international ecumenical and interreligious organizations and shall address the Interdenominational Cooperation Fund funding of financial needs and the advisability of support of these organizations.

c) The United Methodist Church shall seek observer status in the World Evangelical Fellowship. United Methodist observers to these bodies shall be appointed by the Council of Bishops.

¶ **435.** *The American Bible Society*—To encourage the wider circulation and use of the Holy Scriptures throughout the world and to provide for the translation, printing, and distribution essential thereto, the American Bible Society shall be recognized as a means of mission outreach for The United Methodist Church, for which appropriate entities of The United Methodist Church shall offer means for seeking the financial support needed for this program.

¶ **436.** As provided in ¶ 431.2, "In formal relations with other churches and/or ecclesial bodies, the Council of Bishops shall be the primary liaison for The United Methodist Church." Further, as provided in ¶ 403.1e), "The role of the bishop is to be the shepherd of the whole flock." Therefore, the bishops of The United Methodist Church are called to lead the Church in its ecumenical and interreligious ministries.

¶ **437.** In pursuit of its responsibilities and in order to deepen and expand the ecumenical and interreligious ministries of The United Methodist Church, the Council of Bishops shall receive the input and support of the Office of Christian Unity and Interreligious Relationships.

¶ **438.** *Membership*—Members of the OCUIR shall be elected by the Council of Bishops as follows:

1. The OCUIR shall be composed of two episcopal members as determined by the Council of Bishops, including the ecumenical officer of the Council of Bishops. One of the episcopal members shall be from a central conference.

2. One person from each jurisdiction, one person from the central conferences in Africa, one person from the central conferences in Europe, and one person from the central conference in The Philippines. The bishop who is not the ecumenical officer shall be counted as one of these eight persons. Each jurisdictional or central conference will nominate two candidates, and the Council of Bishops will elect members from this pool of nominees.

3. It is recommended that the Council of Bishops ensure that the United Methodist membership persons be inclusive of ethnic representation, youth, young adults, and women, with a minimum of five laity.

4. Two members with voice and vote from our Full Communion Ecumenical Partners

5. The chairperson and secretary of the Council of Bishops Leadership Team on Ecumenical and Interreligious Relations, or its successor group, shall be nonvoting members of the OCUIR Steering Committee.

¶ **439.** *Staff*—1. There shall be an ecumenical staff officer of The United Methodist Church to be selected by the Council of Bishops. The work of the OCUIR shall be facilitated by the ecumenical staff officer who shall be in charge of the day-to-day work of the OCUIR. The ecumenical staff officer shall be the OCUIR's principal administrative and executive officer.

2. Additional staff shall be selected in number and responsibility as determined by the Council of Bishops.

3. The ecumenical staff officer shall report to the ecumenical officer of the Council of Bishops. All other staff members shall report to and serve at the pleasure of the ecumenical staff officer.

4. The staff of the OCUIR shall be positioned in locations to be determined by the Council of Bishops.

¶ **440.** *Funding*—Funding for the ecumenical and interreligious ministries of the Church shall be provided by the Council of Bishops in one or more clearly identified line items in the Episcopal Fund budget request to General Conference.

¶ **441.** *Responsibilities and powers*—Responsibilities and powers of the OCUIR shall be as assigned by the Council of Bishops.

¶ **442.** *Full Communion With Other Churches*

1. To fulfill the vision of full communion between The United Methodist Church and the Evangelical Lutheran Church in America, there shall be a Joint Commission on ELCA/UMC Full Communion. The commission shall serve the following functions:

a) Coordinate the implementation of action taken by the two churches to achieve full communion.

b) Assist joint planning for mission.

c) Facilitate consultation and common decision making through appropriate channels in fundamental matters that the churches may face together in the future.

d) Report regularly and appropriately to each church.

The United Methodist membership of this commission shall be the ccumenical officer of the Council of Bishops and one lay and one clergy member of OCUIR elected by OCUIR.

2. The Council of Bishops shall receive reports of the ongoing partnership of The UMC in the central conferences that are in full communion with Lutheran Churches and other denominations in order to learn from each other how to "provide leadership toward the goal of understanding, reconciliation, and unity within the Church—The United Methodist Church and the church universal" (¶ 403.1e).

Section X. Committee on Faith and Order

¶ 443. There shall be a Committee on Faith and Order related and amenable to the Council of Bishops. This relationship shall be collaborative, with attention paid in particular to working with the persons designated by Council of Bishops.

¶ 444. *Purpose*—The Committee on Faith and Order shall give leadership to The United Methodist Church in reflecting upon, discerning and living out matters of faith, doctrinal teaching, order, and discipline in the midst of mission and ministry in the church and world. The committee shall be a visible expression of the commitment of The United Methodist Church to carry on informed theological reflection for the present time in dynamic continuity with the historic Christian faith, our common heritage as Christians grounded in the apostolic witness, and our distinctive Wesleyan heritage. The committee shall be charged with three broad responsibilities:

1. Upon request of the Council of Bishops, to support and provide resources to the council in its responsibility to "guard, transmit, teach, and proclaim, corporately and individually, the apostolic faith as it is expressed in Scripture and tradition, and, as they are led and endowed by the Spirit, to interpret that faith evangelically and prophetically" (¶ 414.3).

2. To lead and coordinate studies commissioned by the General Conference in matters related to the faith, doctrine, order, and discipline of the church.

3. To prepare and provide resources and study materials to The United Methodist Church as deemed appropriate.

¶ 445. *Responsibilities*—The responsibilities of the Committee on Faith and Order shall be:

1. To provide a venue and context for ongoing conversation on matters of faith, doctrine, order, and discipline.

2. To draw upon scholars and scholarship in biblical studies, biblical theology, systematic theology, historical theology, Christian ethics, Wesleyan studies, practical theology, missiology, and other areas thereby providing expertise and knowledge to lead and assist the church in addressing matters of faith and order critical to the life, ministry and mission of the church.

3. To provide research and resourcing for the Council of Bishops upon their request in matters related to faith, doctrine, order and discipline.

4. To receive and administer mandates from the General Conference for studies on matters that require significant inquiry into and application of the faith and order of the church.

5. To bring studies, materials, or publications as appropriate to the Council of Bishops or to the General Conference for approval and action.

6. To make provision for the preparation and dissemination of study documents and materials for the Church upon request of the Council of Bishops, or the General Conference.

7. To coordinate and provide for effective interaction and communication among various study committees, commissions, and teams when multiple studies have been mandated.

¶ **446.** *Authorities and Powers*—The Committee on Faith and Order shall have the authority and power to fulfill all the responsibilities noted in ¶¶ 444 and 445.

¶ **447.** *Membership*—The Committee on Faith and Order (CFO) shall be organized each quadrennium and shall be composed of sixteen persons.

1. Nominations to the CFO shall be made by the CFO Executive Committee, in consultation with the General Board of Higher Education and Ministry and the Office of Christian Unity and Interreligious Relationships, and sent to the Council of Bishops and to the entire Committee on Faith and Order for their review.

2. Four bishops shall serve as members, one of whom shall be the ecumenical officer of the Council of Bishops of The United Methodist Church and three other bishops as assigned by the Council of Bishops. At least one of the bishops shall be from central conferences.

3. New members of the committee shall be elected by the Council of Bishops at its spring meeting in the year of the Gen-

eral Conference each quadrennium. Election shall be for a term of eight (8) years, and no person shall serve as a member of the Committee on Faith and Order for more than sixteen (16) years in succession. The classes of membership shall be established so that the terms of service of 50 percent of the membership expire when their successors are seated at the organizational meeting of the committee following each General Conference.

4. The composition of the committee, and all sub-committees and teams, shall attend to lay and clergy status, racial/ethnic and gender diversity, and regional representation. It shall model effective representation of the theological diversity of The United Methodist Church. The Council of Bishops shall exercise oversight in the nomination and election of members with regard to inclusiveness, diversity, and representation. Vacancies occurring during any quadrennium shall be filled by the CFO Executive Committee in consultation with the Council of Bishops.

5. The committee may, in consultation and collaboration with the Council of Bishops, carry out any mandated study internally or may create such sub-committees and teams using members from within the committee and others beyond the committee as may be required by the volume and complexity of work.

6. Membership on the board of directors of any other general agency, or serving as a staff member of a general agency, does not make one ineligible to serve as a member of this committee, ¶¶ 710.5 and 715.6 to the contrary notwithstanding, and the limitations specified in ¶ 710.4 for membership on general agencies shall not apply to anyone as a result of membership on this committee.

¶ 448. *Organization*—The Committee on Faith and Order shall be organized as follows:

1. The committee shall elect from its episcopal membership a chairperson and from its total membership other officers as it may determine.

2. There shall be an executive committee of the CFO with powers as determined by the CFO.

3. The committee shall meet for organizational purposes each quadrennium prior to the end of the first quarter of the year following the year in which the General Conference is held.

4. The committee shall meet at least annually and at such other times as it shall deem necessary. A majority of members of the committee shall constitute a quorum.

¶ **449.** *Staffing*—Staff for the work of the Committee on Faith and Order shall be provided as determined by the Council of Bishops in consultation with the Executive Committee of the Committee on Faith and Order. The Council of Bishops may request staff assistance and consultation from agencies and other bodies of the Church.

¶ **450.** *Funding*—In collaboration with the Council of Bishops, the Committee on Faith and Order shall propose its budget as part of the Episcopal Fund, to be approved by General Conference.

This legislation or any portion of it approved by General Conference (¶¶ 443-450) shall take effect at the close of General Conference 2016.

Chapter Four

THE CONFERENCES

The United Methodist Church is a connectional structure maintained through its chain of conferences.

Section I. The General Conference

¶ **501.** *Definition of Powers*—The General Conference has full legislative power over all matters distinctively connectional (see ¶ 16, Division Two, Section II, Article IV, The Constitution). It has no executive or administrative power.

¶ **502.** *Composition*—1. The voting membership of the General Conference shall consist of:

a) An equal number of clergy and lay delegates elected by the annual conferences as provided in the *Discipline*. The missionary conferences and provisional annual conferences shall be considered as annual conferences for the purposes of this paragraph. Annual conferences are urged to seek inclusiveness (as defined in ¶ 140) in the election of delegates.[1]

b) Delegates from The Methodist Church in Great Britain and other autonomous Methodist churches with which concordat agreements have been established providing for mutual election and seating of delegates in each other's highest legislative conferences (¶¶ 13.2, 13.3; 574).

2. The number of delegates to which an annual conference is entitled shall be computed on a two-factor basis: the number of clergy members of the annual conference, and the number of members of local churches in the annual conference.[2]

The term *clergy members* as used in this paragraph shall refer to both active and retired members of the annual conference (¶ 602.1).

3. Delegates to the General Conference shall be elected at the session of the annual conference held not more than two annual conference sessions before the calendar year preceding the session of the General Conference. At least thirty days prior to the beginning of that calendar year, the secretary of the General Conference shall notify the bishop and the secretary of each annual

---

1. See Judicial Council Decisions 435, 592.
2. See Judicial Council Decisions 327, 333, 1051.

conference of the number of delegates to be elected by that annual conference.[3]

4. The secretary of each annual conference, using the certificate of election form supplied by the secretary of the General Conference, shall report to the secretary of the General Conference the names, addresses, and such other information as may be required for delegates and reserves elected by the annual conference.

5. The secretary of the General Conference shall prepare and send to each annual conference secretary credentials to be signed and distributed to the delegates and reserves elected by the annual conference.

¶ 503. *Presiding Officers*—The bishops shall be the presiding officers at the General Conference.

¶ 504. *Election of Secretary-Designate*—1. The Council of Bishops shall present a nomination from the ordained ministry or lay membership of The United Methodist Church for secretary-designate.

Other nominations shall be permitted from the floor. The election, if there be two or more nominees, shall be by ballot.

2. *Assumption of Office*—The secretary-designate shall assume the responsibilities of the office of secretary as soon after the adjournment of the General Conference as all work in connection with the session has been completed, including the corrections to the *Daily Christian Advocate*, which serves as the official journal of the General Conference. Upon publication, all translations of the *Daily Christian Advocate* shall be made available as a daily downloadable file, free of charge, on the denominational website. The exact date of the transfer of responsibility to the secretary-designate shall be determined by the Commission on the General Conference, but shall not be later than December 31, following the adjournment of the General Conference.

3. *Assigned Duties*—The secretary, in cooperation with the Commission on the General Conference, shall initiate procedures to prepare delegates from central conferences for full participation in the General Conference by providing information concerning both the operation of the General Conference and materials it will consider. As far as possible, the materials should be provided in the languages of the delegates. After consultation with the Council of Bishops, the secretary shall issue invitations to ecumenical representatives.

---

3. See Judicial Council Decisions 435, 592.

¶ **505.** *Rules of Order*—The Plan of Organization and Rules of Order of the General Conference shall be the Plan of Organization and Rules of Order as approved by the preceding General Conference until they have been altered or modified by the action of the General Conference.

¶ **506.** *Quorum*—When the General Conference is in session, it shall require the presence of a majority of the whole number of delegates to the General Conference to constitute a quorum for the transaction of business; but a smaller number may take a recess or adjourn from day to day in order to secure a quorum, and at the final session may approve the journal, order the record of the roll call, and adjourn *sine die*.

¶ **507.** *Petitions to General Conference*—Any organization, clergy member, or lay member of The United Methodist Church may petition the General Conference in the following manner:

1. The petition must be sent to the secretary of the General Conference or a designated petitions secretary. It shall be in typed or printed form, or other means approved by the secretary of the General Conference, and shall follow a format determined by that officer.

2. Each petition must address only one issue if the *Discipline* is not affected; if the *Discipline* is affected, each petition must address only one paragraph of the *Discipline*, except that, if two or more paragraphs in the *Discipline* are so closely related that a change in one affects the others, the petition may call for the amendment of those paragraphs also to make them consistent with one another. Petitions dealing with more than one paragraph in the *Discipline* that do not meet these criteria are invalid. Petitions that meet these criteria (composite petitions) shall not be separated into pieces.

3. Each petition must be signed by the person submitting it, accompanied by appropriate identification, such as address, local church, or United Methodist board or agency relationship. Each petition submitted by fax or electronic mail must identify the individual submitting it, accompanied by identification as above, and must contain a valid electronic mail return address or return fax number by which the submitter can be reached. Electronic signatures will be accepted in accordance with common business practice.

4. All petitions submitted to the General Conference, except those submitted by individual members of The United Methodist

Church and local church groups, which call for the establishment of new programs or the expansion of existing programs will be invalid unless accompanied by supporting data that address the issue of anticipated financial requirements of the program.

5. Petitions must be postmarked by a national postal service no later than 230 days prior to the opening session of the General Conference.

6. If petitions are transmitted by a means other than a national postal service, they must be in the hands of the petitions secretary no later than 230 days prior to the opening session of the General Conference.

Exceptions to the time limitations shall be granted for petitions originating from an annual conference session held between 230 and 45 days prior to the opening session of the General Conference, and for other petitions at the discretion of the Committee on Reference.

7. Petitions adopted and properly submitted by annual conferences, jurisdictional and central conferences, the Division on Ministries With Young People, or general agencies or councils of the Church, and petitions properly submitted by individual members (either clergy or lay) of The United Methodist Church and local church groups, provided that they have been received by the petitions secretary or secretary of the General Conference no later than 230 days before the opening of General Conference, shall be printed in the Advance Edition of the *Daily Christian Advocate*.

8. Petitions and/or resolutions not printed in the Advance Edition of the *Daily Christian Advocate* shall be printed or copied and provided to all delegates. Where the content of petitions is essentially the same, the petition will be printed once, with the first author named and the number of additional copies received printed. Upon publication, all translations of the Advance Edition of the *Daily Christian Advocate* shall be made available as a downloadable file, free of charge, on the denominational website

9. The secretary of the General Conference shall arrange for electronic access to all petitions, including General Conference action and the resulting impact on *The Book of Discipline of The United Methodist Church*, throughout the General Conference session. This access shall be available until the publication of the new edition of *The Book of Discipline of The United Methodist Church*. Implementation shall be according to guidelines established by the Committee on Plan of Organization and Rules of Order.

10. All petitions that have been approved by a legislative committee shall receive a vote by the plenary session at that year's General Conference.

11. All petitions that have been submitted to the General Conference shall receive a vote of a legislative committee.

¶ 508. *Legislation Effective Date*—All legislation of the General Conference of The United Methodist Church shall become effective January 1 following the session of the General Conference at which it is enacted, unless otherwise specified (¶ 543.19).

¶ 509. *Speaking for the Church*—1. No person, no paper, no organization, has the authority to speak officially for The United Methodist Church, this right having been reserved exclusively to the General Conference under the Constitution. Any written public policy statement issued by a general Church agency shall clearly identify either at the beginning or at the end that the statement represents the position of that general agency and not necessarily the position of The United Methodist Church (¶ 718).[4]

2. Any individual member called to testify before a legislative body to represent The United Methodist Church shall be allowed to do so only by reading, without elaboration, the resolutions and positions adopted by the General Conference of The United Methodist Church.

¶ 510. *Duties of the Secretary*—The secretary of the General Conference shall be responsible for the permanent record of the General Conference, which shall include:

1. Corrections to the *Daily Christian Advocate*. The editor will then file with the Commission on Archives and History two bound copies of the *Daily Christian Advocate* and corrections as the official record of General Conference. Bound copies shall also be made available at cost by The United Methodist Publishing House.

2. A *Book of Resolutions* to be edited by The United Methodist Publishing House. The book shall contain all valid resolutions of the General Conference. The preface of the *Book of Resolutions* shall include the guidelines for writing resolutions.

a) All valid resolutions of the General Conference of The United Methodist Church shall be published in each edition of the *Book of Resolutions*. There shall be a complete subject index and index of Scripture passages to all valid resolutions of the General Conference of The United Methodist Church in each edition of the

---

4. See Judicial Council Decision 458.

Book of Resolutions. Resolutions are official expressions of The United Methodist Church for eight years following their adoption, after which time they shall be deemed to have expired unless readopted. Those that have expired shall not be printed in subsequent editions of the *Book of Resolutions.* The *Book of Resolutions* shall be made available on the official website of The United Methodist Church.

b) The program boards and agencies shall review all valid resolutions and recommend to the General Conference the removal of time-dated material.

c) Resolutions to be an official part of the *Book of Resolutions* will require a 60 percent affirmative vote at General Conference.

3. The Advance Edition of the *Daily Christian Advocate* and the *Daily Christian Advocate.*

4. All original documents of a General Conference shall be filed with the General Commission on Archives and History.

¶ **511.** *Commission on the General Conference*—There shall be a Commission on the General Conference, hereinafter called the commission.

1. *Membership*—*a)* The voting members of the commission shall be elected quadrennially by the General Conference and shall consist of twenty-five members as follows: one person from each US jurisdiction, one person from each of the seven central conferences, one young adult, one youth, the chairperson of the host committee, and ten additional members. The additional members shall be allocated to reflect the proportionate membership based upon combined clergy and lay membership of the church.

b) Members shall be nominated from the elected delegates to the General Conference by the Council of Bishops prior to General Conference and elected by the General Conference for a term of eight years. Additional persons who meet the qualifications may be nominated from the floor of General Conference. The commission shall reflect a balance of clergymen and clergywomen, laywomen and laymen, and the diverse character of The United Methodist Church. Approximately half of the commission shall be elected by the General Conference each quadrennium.

c) If vacancies occur, the Council of Bishops shall elect geographically appropriate successors to serve through the next session of the General Conference and then nominate for election by the General Conference persons to serve any remainder term.

d) The secretary of the General Conference, the treasurer of the General Council on Finance and Administration, the business manager of the General Conference, and a bishop named by the Council of Bishops shall have the right to the floor without the privilege of voting. The business manager of the General Conference shall be the chief administrative officer of the commission.

2. *Officers*—The officers of the commission shall be a chairperson, a vice-chairperson, and a secretary, all of whom shall be elected by the commission at the quadrennial organizational meeting. They shall serve until the adjournment of the next succeeding quadrennial session of the General Conference after their election and until their successors are duly elected and qualified.

3. *Committees*—*a) Executive Committee*—There shall be an executive committee of the commission, consisting of the officers of the commission, the chairperson of the host committee, the bishop serving on the commission, the secretary of the General Conference, the business manager of the General Conference, and the chairperson and secretary of the Committee on the Plan of Organization and Rules of Order.

b) Committee on the Plan of Organization and Rules of Order—The commission shall organize a Committee on the Plan of Organization and Rules of Order from within its membership. The composition of the committee shall be determined by the commission. The committee shall be organized at the initial meeting of the commission following General Conference. It shall elect its own chairperson and secretary, who will serve on the commission's executive committee. The committee shall study and consider any proposed amendments to the Plan of Organization and Rules of Order and make needed changes and adaptations to be presented to the entire Commission on the General Conference for approval and submission to the General Conference. Any other matters relating to parliamentary order or procedure in the business of the General Conference may be referred to this committee.

4. *Responsibilities*—*a)* The commission shall select the site and set the dates of the General Conference up to four quadrennia in advance and shall send an official notice to all elected delegates announcing specifically the opening day and hour of the General Conference and anticipated time of adjournment.

b) The commission shall plan the schedule for the opening day of the Conference and shall further advise the delegates in advance of all such special events and orders of the day, the dates and times of which have been determined prior to the opening of the General Conference, in order that the delegates may have an overview of the General Conference program.

c) The commission, in cooperation with The United Methodist Publishing House, shall make all necessary arrangements for the publication of the Advance Edition of the *Daily Christian Advocate* and quadrennial reports of the Connectional Table and the general agencies of the church in English, French, Portuguese, and Kiswahili (standard), and for all delegates to have timely (90-day period) and convenient access to the most linguistically appropriate translation of these documents. The commission shall also make arrangements for daily schedules, petition lists, nominations information, and other high-importance information published in the English version of the *Daily Christian Advocate* to also be made available in each of these languages in a timely and convenient way.

d) The commission shall take necessary measures to assure full participation of all General Conference delegates including but not limited to providing accommodation for languages and physical challenges of the delegates, and access to approved licensed childcare during the session at or near the site of the General Conference for children of General Conference delegates.

e) The commission shall recommend to the General Conference the per diem allowance to be paid to the elected delegates for housing and meals.

f) The commission shall set the number of legislative committees and the assignment of legislative materials to those committees in consultation with the secretary of the General Conference and the business manager of the General Conference.

5. The secretary of the General Conference shall calculate the number of delegates to be elected by each annual conference, based on the factors specified in ¶ 502.1, 2, using the most recent clergy and professing lay membership figures reported by the local congregation to the annual conference and from the annual conference to the General Council on Finance and Administration through their conference journals, as follows:

a) One clergy delegate for the first 375 clergy members of the annual conference and one clergy delegate for each additional 375 clergy members or major fraction thereof,[5] and

---

5. See Judicial Council Decisions 327, 558.

b) One clergy delegate for the first 26,000 members of local churches of the annual conference and one clergy delegate for each additional 26,000 local church members or major fraction thereof, and

c) A number of lay delegates equal to the total number of clergy delegates authorized as above.

d) Every annual conference shall be entitled to at least one clergy and one lay delegate.

e) This formula is designated to comply with the Constitution, Division Two, Section II, Article I (¶ 13), which defines the minimum and maximum number of delegates to a General Conference. Should the computations provided in the paragraph result in a figure below the prescribed minimum or above the prescribed maximum for delegates, the Commission on the General Conference shall be authorized to remedy the situation by adjusting up or down the numbers of clergy members and members of local churches of the annual conference necessary to entitle an annual conference to elect delegates, any such adjustment to be proportionally the same for the two factors.[6]

Section II. The Jurisdictional Conference

¶ **512.** *Interjurisdictional Committee on Episcopacy*—1. There shall be an Interjurisdictional Committee on Episcopacy elected by the General Conference consisting of the persons nominated by their annual conference delegations to serve on the several jurisdictional committees on episcopacy.[7] The committee shall meet not later than the fifth day of the conference session and at the time and place set for their convening by the president of the Council of Bishops and shall elect from their number a chairperson, vice chairperson, and secretary. The function of this joint committee shall be to discuss the possibility of transfers of bishops across jurisdictional lines at the forthcoming jurisdictional conferences for residential and presidential responsibilities in the ensuing quadrennium; and to review on the basis of missional needs an application from a jurisdiction which, by number of its church members as provided in ¶ 404, would experience a reduction in the number of its bishops, and recommend the number of bishops to which that jurisdiction should be entitled to the

6. See Judicial Council Decisions 687, 1274.
7. See Judicial Council Decision 472.

General Conference for determination by the General Conference. This provision regarding missional needs is enabling, and it is not constraining on the power of General Conference to act in the absence of a recommendation from the committee.

It shall elect an executive committee consisting of the officers named above and two clergy and two laypersons from the nominees to each jurisdictional committee, elected by that committee to conduct consultations with bishops and others interested in possible episcopal transfers. One of the persons elected from each jurisdiction shall be the chairperson, or the chairperson's designee, of the jurisdictional committee. The executive committee shall meet at the call of the chairperson, and it shall have plenary power for the full committee between full committee sessions. It shall be responsible to the interjurisdictional committee, and in fulfillment of that responsibility and in the interest of continuity of the work of the committee, the outgoing chairperson, or the chairperson's designee, shall present a report to the newly seated committee on the previous quadrennium's work as well as recommendations on what the coming quadrennium's work might include.

A record of the proceedings of the committee shall be kept by the Office of Episcopal Services of the General Council on Finance and Administration.

2. A bishop may be transferred across jurisdictional lines only when that bishop has consented to such transfer and has served at least one quadrennium in or under assignment by the jurisdiction in which the bishop was elected. Such a transfer shall be concluded when the committee on episcopacy of each jurisdiction involved has approved the transfer(s) by a majority vote of those present and voting, insofar as the transfer(s) affects those jurisdictions. (See ¶ 49, Article V.)[8]

3. The Interjurisdictional Committee on Episcopacy shall be recognized as the official body through which cross-jurisdictional transfers shall be arranged. Should a bishop request transfer, the bishop has the option to identify the receiving jurisdiction. A jurisdiction may request that a specific bishop be transferred or may indicate a willingness to accept a bishop transferring from another jurisdiction. Request for transfer from either a bishop or jurisdictional committees on episcopacy shall be received by the Interjurisdictional Committee on Episcopacy by April 1 of the year

---

8. See Judicial Council Decision 745.

preceding the year of jurisdictional conferences. The Interjurisdictional Committee on Episcopacy will arrange consultation between bishop(s) requesting transfer and the appropriate jurisdictional committee(s) on episcopacy by January 1 of the year of jurisdictional conference(s). Once the jurisdictional committee(s) on episcopacy has taken action, jurisdictional conference secretaries shall inform the Interjurisdictional Committee on Episcopacy not later than August 1 following jurisdictional conferences.[9]

4. The Interjurisdictional Committee on Episcopacy will report to each General Conference the action taken during the previous quadrennium.

¶ **513.** *Equal Status*—All jurisdictional conferences shall have the same status and the same privileges of action within the limits fixed by the Constitution.

¶ **514.** *Membership*—The membership of each jurisdictional conference shall consist of an equal number of clergy and lay delegates elected by the annual conferences as provided in the *Discipline*. Consideration shall be given to electing an inclusive delegation (¶¶ 124, 140). The number of delegates to which an annual conference is entitled shall be twice the number of its General Conference delegates, except when the application of that formula results in a total number of delegates to a jurisdictional conference less than 100. In that event, the secretary of the General Conference shall adjust the number of delegates to the jurisdictional conference in the same proportion among the annual and missionary conferences of the jurisdiction to achieve a total of 100, ensuring that no annual or missionary conference shall be represented by fewer than four delegates.

¶ **515.** *Election of Delegates*—The clergy and lay delegates and reserves to the jurisdictional conferences shall be elected by ballot in accordance with the provisions of the Constitution.[10]

¶ **516.** *Deliberations*—The clergy and lay delegates shall deliberate in one body.

¶ **517.** *Convening Date*—Each jurisdictional conference shall meet within the period prescribed by the Constitution at such time and place as shall have been determined by the preceding jurisdictional conference or by its properly constituted committee.

¶ **518.** *Rules of Order*—The jurisdictional conference shall adopt its own procedure, rules, and plan of organization. It shall

---

9. See Judicial Council Decision 745.
10. See Judicial Council Decision 592.

take a majority of the whole number of delegates elected to make a quorum for the transaction of business; however, a smaller number may take a recess or adjourn from day to day and at the final session may approve the journal, order the record of the roll call, and adjourn *sine die.*

¶ **519.** *Expenses*—The jurisdictional conference shall provide for the expenses of its sessions.

¶ **520.** The jurisdictional conferences shall provide for the accounts of the jurisdictional treasurer for the preceding fiscal year to be audited by a certified public accountant within 150 days after the close of the conference fiscal year and to provide for the report to be distributed to each of the presiding bishops and conference treasurers and in the jurisdiction.

¶ **521.** *Special Sessions*—1. The jurisdictional conference may order a special session in such manner as it shall determine.

2. The College of Bishops of a jurisdiction by a two-thirds vote shall have authority to call a special session of the jurisdictional conference when necessary; provided, however, that if an episcopal area is left vacant by reason of death, retirement, or other cause within twenty-four months of the episcopal assumption of presidential supervision of that area, the College of Bishops may by majority vote convene within three months, after giving not less than thirty days' notice, a special session of the jurisdictional conference for the purpose of electing and consecrating a bishop and of considering any other matters specified in the call; and provided further, that in such case the current jurisdictional committee on episcopacy may recommend to the conference reassignment of one or more of the previously elected bishops.

3. The delegates to a special session of the jurisdictional conference shall be the delegates last elected by each annual conference.

4. A called session of the jurisdictional conference cannot transact any other business than that indicated in the call.

¶ **522.** *Presiding Bishops*—The jurisdictional conference shall be presided over by the bishops of the jurisdiction or a bishop of another jurisdiction or of a central conference. In case no bishop of the jurisdiction is present, the conference may elect a president from the clergy delegates.

¶ **523.** *Accountability*—Bishops elected by or administering in a jurisdictional conference shall be amenable for their conduct to their jurisdictional conference. Any bishop shall have the right of appeal to the Judicial Council.

¶ 524. *Jurisdictional Committee on Episcopacy*—1. There shall be a jurisdictional committee on episcopacy consisting of one clergy and one lay delegate to the jurisdictional conference from each annual conference elected by the jurisdictional conference upon nomination of their respective annual conference delegations.

The committee shall be convened by the president of the College of Bishops at the close of the jurisdictional conference to which the delegates have been elected. It shall serve through the succeeding jurisdictional conference.

The committee shall elect from its members a chairperson, a vice chairperson, and a secretary. It shall meet at least annually.

Should there be a vacancy in an annual conference's elected representation on the jurisdictional committee on episcopacy by death, resignation, election to the episcopacy, cessation of membership in the annual conference from which one is elected, or for other reasons that the annual conference delegation may determine, the annual conference delegation shall nominate another person to fill the vacancy. That person may begin to serve on the committee as a nominee until the jurisdictional conference can elect.

2. The jurisdictional conference shall provide funding for the expenses of the jurisdictional committee on episcopacy.

3. The jurisdictional committee on episcopacy shall:

a) Review and evaluate annually the work of the bishops, pass on their character and official administration, and report such evaluations and other findings to the jurisdictional conference for such action as the conference may deem appropriate within its constitutional warrant of power. The evaluation shall include those areas of responsibility outlined in ¶ 414, ¶ 415, and ¶ 416 as well as the bishop's leadership in the promotion and support of the full payment of apportionments. The committee may, in its sole discretion, also forward its report to the president of the College of Bishops, who shall then share the report with the Council of Bishops in executive session.

b) Recommend boundaries of the episcopal areas and the assignments of the bishops.[11]

c) Be available to the Council and College of Bishops for consultation on matters of mutual concern.

---

11. See Judicial Council Decision 517.

d) Determine the number of effective bishops eligible for assignment.

e) Receive and act upon requests for possible voluntary and involuntary retirement of bishops; however, as provided in ¶ 408.3*a*), the committee may initiate on its own motion the process of involuntary retirement when it is seen to be in the best interest of the Church.

f) Initiate or receive and act upon a request for transfer of one or more of the members of its jurisdiction's College of Bishops to another jurisdiction's College of Bishops or upon a request for transfer of a member of another jurisdiction's College of Bishops to its jurisdiction's College of Bishops. As provided in ¶ 512.2, no such transfer may be completed without the affirmative vote of a majority of the members of the committee present and voting.

g) Consult with the conference committees on episcopacy with respect to the needs for episcopal leadership and how best they can be fulfilled.

h) Establish a consultation process with each bishop regarding his or her episcopal assignment.

i) Prepare a report of its decisions, activities, and recommendations to be transmitted to its successor through the office of the secretary of the jurisdictional conference. The report shall be made available to delegates of the jurisdictional conference prior to the jurisdictional conference.

¶ 525. *Powers and Duties of Jurisdictional Conference*—The jurisdictional conference shall have powers and duties as described in the Constitution. It shall also have such other powers and duties as may be conferred by the General Conference. It shall act in all respects in harmony with the policy of The United Methodist Church with respect to elimination of discrimination based upon race.

¶ 526. *Definition of Church Members*—In all elections in a jurisdictional conference that are based on the number of church members within that jurisdiction, the number counted shall include lay members, clergy members, and bishops assigned to that jurisdiction.

¶ 527. *Annual Conference Journals*—The jurisdictional conference shall have authority to examine and acknowledge the journals of the annual conferences within its bounds and shall make such rules for the drawing up of the journals as may seem necessary.

¶ **528.** *Jurisdictional Conference Journals*—The jurisdictional conference shall keep an official journal of its proceedings, duly signed by the secretary and president or secretary of the College of Bishops, which shall be deposited in accordance with ¶ 1711.3 *j, k* and with the secretary of the General Conference. The printing shall be done at the expense of the jurisdiction.

JURISDICTIONAL AGENCIES

¶ **529.** *Agencies*—The jurisdictional conference shall have the authority to appoint or elect such agencies as the General Conference may direct or as it deems necessary for its work. Insofar as possible, the membership on councils, boards, and agencies of the jurisdictional conference shall include one-third clergy, one-third laywomen, and one-third laymen in keeping with the policies for general Church agencies, except for the Board of Ordained Ministry and the jurisdictional committee on episcopacy. Special attention shall be given to the inclusion of clergywomen, youth, young adults, older adults, single adults, persons with disabilities, persons from churches of small membership, and racial and ethnic persons. (See ¶ 710.9*a-c*.) Every board, standing committee, commission, council, and work area of the jurisdiction shall designate one of its members as its coordinator of witness ministries. These persons shall help the agencies of which they are members to engage in witness ministries and, in particular, to ask, "How are we intentionally reaching new people for Jesus Christ through our ministries?" and "How are we helping new people grow and mature as disciples of Jesus Christ through our ministries and areas of responsibility?"

¶ **530.** *Coordination of Programs*—In each jurisdiction of The United Methodist Church there may be a jurisdictional council on ministries or jurisdictional administrative council, or alternative structure, organized as the jurisdiction shall determine and with the authority to coordinate the programs of the general agencies within the jurisdiction.

¶ **531.** *Program Agencies*—In each jurisdiction there may be jurisdictional program agencies related to the general program agencies and the appropriate annual conference program agencies organized as the jurisdictional conference shall determine.

¶ **532.** *Archives and History*—1. There shall be a jurisdictional commission on archives and history, auxiliary to the general commission, to be composed of the chairperson of each annual conference commission on archives and history or the historian of each annual conference, the president of the jurisdictional historical society, and at least five members at large to be elected by the jurisdictional commission, or composed in a way the jurisdictional conference determines.

¶ **533.** *Jurisdictional Young People's Ministries*—1. Jurisdictions shall engage youth, young adults, and adults who work with them in creative partnership to:

a) Network youth, young adults and young people's ministries throughout the region,

b) Support young people's ministries in the annual conferences, and

c) Provide a process by which representatives are chosen and sent to the Global Young People's Convocation and the Division on Ministries With Young People.

2. Jurisdictions are encouraged to organize their Young People's Ministries in creative ways that work best for their context. The jurisdictional young people's ministries coordinator shall help design, maintain, and revise any processes to accomplish this work.

In any process or coordinating group for Jurisdictional Young People's Ministries, the following representation is encouraged:

a) Participants from each conference in the jurisdiction

b) Racial/ethnic representation that reflects the demographic make-up of the jurisdiction

c) Participants who bring a variety of theological and cultural perspectives

d) Youth and young adults who may or may not also be serving on Conference Councils of Youth/Young Adult Ministry

e) Adult workers who may or may not also be conference youth/young adult staff or similar designee

3. There shall be a jurisdictional young people's ministries coordinator who shall be accountable to the jurisdictional council on ministries or equivalent structure and the jurisdictional young people's ministries coordinating team. This coordinator may or may not be the same person as the adult representative to the Division on Ministries With Young People of the General Board of Discipleship.

4. *Responsibility to Choose Representatives to the Division on Ministries With Young People*—Using a process appropriate to each

jurisdiction's context, the Jurisdictional Young People's Ministries shall:

a) Choose one youth member to serve on the Division on Ministries With Young People of the General Board of Discipleship for a four-year term. Youth chosen to serve on the Division on Ministries With Young People shall be age sixteen or younger at the time of appointment.

b) Nominations shall come from annual conference councils on youth ministry or equivalent structure, local churches, districts, conference youth coordinators, or other interested clergy or laity.

c) The Jurisdictional Young People's Ministries should ensure that either the youth or young adult representative (who is elected in the jurisdictional election) will be a racial/ethnic young person.

d) As far as possible, members of the Division on Ministries With Young People from each jurisdiction shall be from two different annual conferences in that jurisdiction.

5. *Responsibility to Choose Representatives to Attend the Global Young People's Convocation*—In the year prior to the Global Young People's Convocation, Jursidictional Young People's Ministries shall choose five youth and one adult to serve as voting delegates to the Global Young People's Convocation.

6. Other suggested responsibilities for the Jurisdictional Young People's Ministries:

a) Initiate and support jurisdictional events (camps, conferences, workshops, and so forth).

b) Recommend priorities, concerns, and/or policies to the Division on Ministries With Young People.

c) Promote the establishment and awareness of the needs, concerns, issues, and so forth,of racial and ethnic persons through caucuses, camps, consultations, and so forth.

d) Promote the spiritual growth of participants in the jurisdictional young people's ministry events and activities.

e) Promote an evangelistic outreach with young people and through young people by providing educational opportunities and resources that increase their awareness, exposure, and engagement in the areas of mission, social justice, discipleship, leadership development, and spiritual formation as they relate back to their annual conference and local church.

f) Provide training and supportive experiences for conference young people's ministries personnel.

g) Enable communication between general and conference levels of young people's ministries.

¶ **534.** There may be a jurisdictional young-adult organization for the purpose of networking young adults throughout the region, supporting young-adult ministries in the annual conferences, and supporting young adult workers in their ministry.

¶ **535.** *Committee on Ordained Ministry*—There may be a jurisdictional committee on ordained ministry. This committee shall be comprised of the chair of the conference boards of ordained ministry or their representatives, the deans/presidents of the United Methodist seminaries in the jurisdiction, two representatives from the College of Bishops and three members at large, named by the committee to insure inclusivity. Deacons and laypersons shall be represented in the committee. When a jurisdictional board of higher education and ministry exists, this board may be a part of that structure. The duties of the committee may include: providing information on supply and demand and encouraging mobility across conference lines; to create a forum for the discussion of issues related to representative ministry; to deal with matters of enlistment and recruitment; to create dialogue with seminaries serving the jurisdiction; to enable ethnic ministries in the jurisdictions. Funding shall be provided through the jurisdictional conference and the annual conference boards of ordained ministry.

¶ **536.** *Constitution of United Methodist Women in the Jurisdiction—Article 1. Name*—In each jurisdiction there shall be a jurisdiction organization named United Methodist Women, directly related to the United Methodist Women's national organization.

Article 2. Authority—Each jurisdiction organization of United Methodist Women shall have authority to promote its work in accordance with the program and policies of the United Methodist Women's national organization.

Article 3. Membership—The voting membership of the jurisdiction organization of United Methodist Women shall be composed of the members of the Jurisdiction Leadership Team; three members elected by each conference organization, members of the board of directors of United Methodist Women and the members of the United Methodist Women Program Advisory Group in organizations within the jurisdiction; a representative of the jurisdiction Association of Deaconesses, Home Missioners/Home Missionaries; and all the active bishops of the jurisdiction.

Article 4. Meetings and Elections—a) There shall be a meeting of the jurisdiction organization of United Methodist Women during the last year of the quadrennium. At that time the jurisdiction president, members of the Jurisdiction Leadership Team and members of the board of directors of the United Methodist Women's national organization shall be elected according to the *Discipline* (¶¶ 647.6*d*, 1906).

b) There may be other gatherings as needed to fulfill the purpose.

*Article 5. Amendments—*Proposed amendments to the constitution shall be sent to the recording secretary of United Methodist Women for consideration by the board of directors. The last date for consideration of any amendments will be the last regular meeting of the board of directors before the date by which it must submit proposed legislation for action of the General Conference.

¶ **537.** *Committee on United Methodist Men—*In each jurisdiction there shall be a jurisdictional committee on United Methodist Men, auxiliary to the General Commission on United Methodist Men (¶ 2301).

The membership of the jurisdictional committee on United Methodist Men shall be composed of the elected officers, committee chairpersons, and ministry coordinators as defined by the organizations' bylaws as well as the conference president of United Methodist Men of each annual conference organization within the boundary of the jurisdiction.

Each jurisdictional committee on United Methodist Men shall have authority to promote its work in accordance with the policies and programs of the General Commission on United Methodist Men.

The jurisdictional committee on United Methodist Men shall elect the jurisdictional president during the last year of the quadrennium. The jurisdictional president shall serve on the General Commission on United Methodist Men (¶ 2303.1*b*). Jurisdictional presidents who serve less than a full quadrennial term may be re-elected for a full term. There may be meetings, retreats, and cooperative training events held by the jurisdictional committee on United Methodist Men.

The jurisdictional committee on United Methodist Men shall secure funds for the fulfillment of its purpose. All funds from whatever source secured by the jurisdictional committee on

United Methodist Men belong to the organization and shall be disbursed only in accordance with its constitution and/or by-laws and by its order.

a) The jurisdictional committee on United Methodist Men may have their own bank accounts.

b) It is recommended that there be an annual financial audit.

¶ **538.** *United Methodist Volunteers in Mission*—It is recommended that there be a jurisdictional volunteer-in-mission (UMVIM) coordinator for the purpose of coordination of volunteers, in collaboration with annual conference UMVIM and Disaster Response Coordinators within their jurisdiction and the Global Ministries Mission Volunteer Office. The jurisdictional coordinator may network to coordinate opportunities and resources for volunteers in collaboration with the General Board of Global Ministries and other UMC agencies as requested. The Jurisdictional UMVIM Coordinator may communicate the need for Early Response Teams within their region in collaboration with UMCOR.

¶ **539.** *Administrative Review Committee*—The jurisdictional conference shall establish from its membership an administrative review committee of at least three persons who are not members of the jurisdictional committee on episcopacy. Its only purpose shall be to ensure that the disciplinary procedures for any involuntary action recommended by the jurisdictional committee on episcopacy are properly followed. The entire administrative process leading to the action for change of status of the bishop shall be reviewed by the administrative review committee, and it shall report its findings to the jurisdictional committee on episcopacy and the jurisdictional conference prior to any action by those bodies. The administrative review committee shall notify the parties of the review process. The administrative fair process hearing procedures (¶ 361.2) should be followed by the administrative review committee. Prior to its report, if the committee determines that any error has occurred, it may recommend to the appropriate person or body that action be taken promptly to remedy the error, decide the error is harmless, or take other action.

Section III. Central Conferences

¶ **540.** *Authorization*—1. In territory outside the United States, annual conferences, provisional annual conferences, missionary conferences, mission conferences, and missions, in such numbers as the General Conference by a two-thirds vote shall determine, may be organized by the General Conference into central conferences or provisional central conferences, with such duties, privileges, and powers as are hereinafter set forth and as the General Conference by a two-thirds vote shall prescribe.

2. There shall be such central conferences as have been authorized or shall be hereafter authorized by the General Conference, provided that a central conference shall have a total of at least thirty clergy and thirty lay delegates on the basis of representation as set forth in this section, except as the General Conference may fix a different number.

3. The United Methodist Church shall have central conferences with ministries in the following countries:

a) Africa Central Conference: Angola, Botswana, Burundi, Ethiopia, Kenya, Malawi, Mozambique, Namibia, Rwanda, Swaziland, South Africa, South Sudan, Uganda, Zambia, Zimbabwe;

b) Central and Southern Europe Central Conference: Albania, Algeria, Austria, Belgium, Bulgaria, Croatia, Czech Republic, France, Hungary, Republic of Macedonia, Poland, Romania, Serbia, Slovak Republic, Switzerland, Tunisia;

c) Congo Central Conference: Central African Republic, Democratic Republic of Congo, Republic of Congo, Tanzania, Zambia;

d) Germany Central Conference: Germany;

e) Northern Europe and Eurasia Central Conference: Belarus, Denmark, Estonia, Finland, Kazakhstan, Kyrgyzstan, Latvia, Lithuania, Moldova, Norway, Russia, Sweden, Tajikistan, Ukraine, Uzbekistan;

f) Philippines Central Conference: Philippines;

g) West Africa Central Conference: Burkina Faso, Cameroon, Cote d'Ivoire, Guinea, Guinea-Bissau, Liberia, Mali, Niger, Nigeria, Senegal, Sierra Leone.

4. A provisional central conference may become a central conference upon the fulfillment of the necessary requirements and upon the authorization of the General Conference.

¶ **541.** *Composition*—1. The central conference shall be composed of clergy and lay members in equal numbers, the clergy members elected by the clergy members of the annual conference and the lay members by the lay members thereof. Their qualifications and the manner of election shall be determined by the central conference itself, subject only to constitutional requirements. Each annual conference and provisional annual conference shall be entitled to at least two clergy and two lay delegates, and no other selection of delegates shall be authorized that would provide for more than one clergy delegate for every six clergy members of an annual conference; except that a majority of the number fixed by a central conference as the ratio of representation shall entitle an annual conference to an additional clergy delegate and to an additional lay delegate. Each missionary conference and mission is authorized to elect and send one of its members to the central conference concerned as its representative, said representative to be accorded the privilege of sitting with the committees of the central conference, with the right to speak in the committees and in the regular sessions of the central conference, but without the right to vote. Representatives of missionary conferences or missions shall have the same claim for payment of expenses as is allowed to members of the central conference.[12]

2. In the case of a central conference, the rule of proportionate representation shall be applied by each annual conference.

¶ 542. *Organization*—1. The first meeting of a central conference shall be called by the bishop or bishops in charge at such time and place as they may elect, to which members of the annual conferences, provisional annual conferences, missionary conferences, and missions concerned shall be elected on the basis of representation as provided herein. The time and place of future meetings shall be determined by the central conference or its executive committee.

2. Each central conference shall meet within the year succeeding the session of the General Conference at such time and place as the central conference itself or its bishops may determine for the purpose of electing bishops when vacancies occur and for attending to other matters as required. The central conference has the right to hold such adjourned sessions as it may determine. The sessions of said conference shall be presided over by the bishops. In case no bishop is present, the conference shall elect a temporary president from among its own members. The bishops resident in a central conference or a majority of them, with the concurrence of the executive committee or other authorized committee, shall

12. See Judicial Council Decision 371.

have the authority to call an extra session of the central conference to be held at the time and place designated by them.[13]

3. The Council of Bishops may assign one or more of its number to visit any central conference or provisional central conference. When so assigned, the bishop shall be an accredited representative of the general Church, and when requested by a majority of the bishops resident in that conference may exercise therein the functions of the episcopacy.

4. The presiding officer of the central conference shall decide questions of order, subject to an appeal to the central conference, and shall decide questions of law, subject to an appeal to the Judicial Council, but questions relating to the interpretation of the rules and regulations made by the central conference for the governing of its own session shall be decided by the central conference.[14]

5. A central conference, where the laws of the land permit, shall have the power to organize and incorporate one or more executive committees, executive boards, or councils of cooperation, with such membership and such powers as may have been granted by the central conference for the purpose of representing it in its property and legal interests and for transacting any necessary business that may arise in the interval between the sessions of the central conference or that may be committed to said boards or committees by the central conference.

6. Each central conference within the bounds of which the General Board of Global Ministries has work shall maintain a cooperative and consultative relationship with the said board through a duly constituted executive committee, executive board, or council of cooperation; but the legal distinction between the General Board of Global Ministries and the organized church on the field shall always be kept clear.

¶ 543. *Powers and Duties*—1. To a central conference shall be committed for supervision and promotion, in harmony with the *Discipline* and interdenominational contractual agreements, the missionary, educational, evangelistic, industrial, publishing, medical, and other connectional interests of the annual conferences, provisional annual conferences, missionary conferences, and missions within its territory and such other matters as may be

---

13. See Judicial Council Decision 371.
14. See Judicial Council Decisions 375, 376, 381.

referred to it by said bodies or by order of the General Conference; and it shall provide suitable organizations for such work and elect the necessary officers for the same.

2. A central conference, when authorized by a specific enabling act of the General Conference, may elect one or more bishops from among the traveling elders of The United Methodist Church. The number of bishops to be elected by each central conference shall be determined from time to time by the General Conference.

3. When a central conference shall have been authorized to elect bishops, such elections shall be conducted under the same general procedure as prevails in the jurisdictional conferences for the election of bishops. A central conference shall have power to fix the tenure of bishops elected by the said central conference.[15]

4. The General Council on Finance and Administration shall determine the apportionment amounts for the annual conferences of the central conferences for the succeeding quadrennium based on calculation methodology approved by the General Conference upon recommendation by the Council. This determination shall be informed by consultation with the Council of Bishops.

5. A central conference, in consultation with the bishops of that central conference, shall fix the episcopal areas and residences and make assignments to them of the bishops who are to reside in that central conference. The bishops of a central conference shall arrange the plan of episcopal visitation within its bounds.

6. A central conference shall have authority to elect and support general officers in all departments of the work of the Church within the boundaries of the central conference but may not determine the number of bishops.

7. A central conference shall have power to make such changes and adaptations of the *Book of Discipline* as the special conditions and the mission of the church in the area require, especially concerning the organization and administration of the work on local church, district, and annual conference levels, provided that no action shall be taken that is contrary to the Constitution and the General Rules of The United Methodist Church, and provided that the spirit of connectional relationship is kept between the local and the general church. Subject to this restriction, a central conference may delegate to an annual conference within its

---

15. See Judicial Council Decisions 311, 430.

boundaries the power to make one or the other of the changes and adaptations referred to in this paragraph, upon the request of such annual conference.[16]

8. A central conference shall fix the boundaries of the annual conferences, provisional annual conferences, missionary conferences, and missions within its bounds, proposals for changes first having been submitted to the annual conferences concerned as prescribed in the *Discipline* of The United Methodist Church. No annual conference shall be organized with fewer than thirty-five clergy members except as provided by an enabling act for the quadrennium, which shall not reduce the number below twenty-five. Nor shall an annual conference be continued with fewer than twenty-five clergy members except as provided by an enabling act for the quadrennium.[17]

9. A central conference may advise its annual conferences and provisional annual conferences to set standards of character and other qualifications for admission of lay members.

10. A central conference shall have power to make changes and adaptations in procedure pertaining to the annual, district, and charge conferences within its territory and to add to the business of the annual conference supplementary questions considered desirable or necessary to meet its own needs.

11. A central conference shall have authority to examine and acknowledge the journals of the annual conferences, provisional annual conferences, missionary conferences, and missions located within its bounds and to make rules for the drawing up of the journals as may seem necessary.

12. A central conference shall have authority to adopt rules of procedure governing the investigation and trial of its clergy, including bishops, and lay members of the Church and to provide the necessary means and methods of implementing the said rules; provided, however, that the ordained ministers shall not be deprived of the right of trial by a clergy committee, and lay members of the Church of the right of trial by a duly constituted committee of lay members; and provided also, that the rights of appeal shall be adequately safeguarded.[18]

---

16. See Judicial Council Decision 313.
17. See Judicial Council Decisions 525, 541, 549.
18. See Judicial Council Decisions 310, 595.

13. A central conference is authorized to prepare and translate simplified or adapted forms of such parts of the ritual as it may deem necessary, such changes to require the approval of the resident bishop or bishops of the central conference.

14. A central conference shall have the power to conform the detailed rules, rites, and ceremonies for the solemnization of marriage to the statute laws of the country or countries within its jurisdiction.

15. Subject to the approval of the bishops resident therein, a central conference shall have the power to prescribe courses of study, including those in the vernaculars, for its ministry, both foreign and indigenous, including local preachers, lay servants, Bible women, deaconesses, teachers—both male and female—and all other workers whatsoever, ordained or lay. It shall also make rules and regulations for examination in these courses.

16. A central conference shall have authority to edit and publish a central conference *Discipline,* which shall contain in addition to the Constitution of the Church such sections from the general *Discipline* of The United Methodist Church as may be pertinent to the entire Church and also such revised, adapted, or new sections as shall have been enacted by the central conference concerned under the powers given by the General Conference.

17. In a central conference or provisional central conference using a language other than English, legislation passed by a General Conference shall not take effect until twelve months after the close of that General Conference in order to afford the necessary time to make adaptations and to publish a translation of the legislation that has been enacted, the translation to be approved by the resident bishop or bishops of the central conference. This provision, however, shall not exclude the election of delegates to the General Conference by annual conferences within the territory of central conferences or provisional central conferences.

18. A central conference is authorized to interpret Article XXIII of the Articles of Religion (*page 71*) so as to recognize the governments of the country or countries within its territory.

19. A central conference shall have power to authorize the congregations in a certain state or country to form special organizations in order to receive the acknowledgment of the state or country according to the laws of that state or country. These organizations shall be empowered to represent the interests of the Church to the authorities of the state or country according to the

rules and principles of The United Methodist Church, and they shall be required to give regular reports of their activities to their respective annual conferences.

20. A central conference may, with the consent of the bishops resident in that conference, enter into agreements with churches or missions of other denominations for the division of territory or of responsibility for Christian work within the territory of the central conference.

21. A central conference shall have the right to negotiate with other Protestant bodies looking toward the possibility of church union; provided that any proposals for church union shall be submitted to the General Conference for approval before consummation.[19]

¶ 544. [*Reserved*]

¶ 545. *Records and Archives*—1. The journal of the proceedings of a central conference, duly signed by the president and secretary, shall be sent for examination to the General Conference through its secretary. Two paper copies in every translation shall be sent without charge to the General Commission on Archives and History and the General Council on Finance and Administration, and one copy of a digital version shall be sent along with the paper copies, if available. It is recommended that the journal include memoirs of deceased clergy and deceased clergy spouses.

2. The secretary of a central conference in which one or more bishops have been chosen shall report to the secretary of the General Conference the names of the bishop or bishops and the residences to which they have been assigned by the central conference.

3. The secretary of each central conference shall submit a hardcopy of every translation and adaptation of the general *Discipline* or portion thereof in use in that central conference to the General Commission on Archives and History and the General Council on Finance and Administration.

¶ 546. *Property*—1. A central conference, through a duly incorporated property-holding body or bodies, shall have authority to purchase, own, hold, or transfer property for and on behalf of all the unincorporated organizations of The United Methodist Church within the territory of that central conference or on behalf

---

19. See Judicial Council Decision 350.

of other organizations of The United Methodist Church that have entrusted their property to that central conference.

2. A central conference shall have authority to make the necessary rules and regulations for the holding and management of such properties; provided, however, that *(a)* all procedure shall be subject to the laws of the country or countries concerned; *(b)* no transfer of property shall be made from one annual conference to another without the consent of the conference holding title to such property; and *(c)* the status of properties held by local trustees or other holding bodies shall be recognized.

3. A central conference shall not directly or indirectly, through its incorporated property-holding body or bodies, alienate property or proceeds of property without due consideration of its trusteeship for local churches, annual conferences, the General Board of Global Ministries, and other organizations, local or general, of the Church.

4. A central conference or any of its incorporated organizations shall not involve the General Board of Global Ministries or any organization of the Church in any financial obligation without the official approval of said board or organization. All invested funds, fiduciary trusts, or property belonging to an annual conference, a provisional annual conference, a missionary conference, or a mission, or any of its institutions, acquired by bequest, donation, or otherwise and designated for a specific use, shall be applied to the purpose for which they were designated. They shall not be diverted to any other purpose, except by the consent of the conference or mission involved and with the approval of the central conference concerned and civil court action when necessary. The same rule shall apply to similar funds or properties acquired by a central conference for specific objects. In cases involving the diversion of trust funds and properties within the territory of a central conference, the central conference concerned shall determine the disposition of the interests involved, subject to an appeal to the judicial court of the central conference.

¶ **547.** *Conference Agencies*—1. A central conference may have a standing committee on women's work. This committee should preferably be composed of the women delegates and such other persons as the central conference may elect. The duty of this committee shall be to study the relation of women to the Church and to devise ways and means of developing this portion of the

Church membership, to the end that it may assume its rightful responsibilities in the extension of the Kingdom. The committee shall make recommendations to the central conference regarding women's organizations within its areas. A central conference organization may become a member of the World Federation of Methodist Women and may elect a representative to the World Federation of Methodist Women within the provisions of the federation.

2. A central conference may organize a women's unit, after consultation with the committee on women's work, in connection with any annual conference or provisional annual conference within its bounds and provide a constitution and bylaws for it.

3. A central conference that adapts and edits the *Discipline* as provided in ¶ 543.16 shall establish a judicial court, which in addition to other duties that the central conference may assign to it shall hear and determine the legality of any action of the central conference taken under the adapted portions of the *Discipline* or of a decision of law by the presiding bishop of the central conference pertaining to the adapted portions of the *Discipline*, upon appeal by the presiding bishop or by one-fifth of the members of the central conference. Further, the judicial court shall hear and determine the legality of any action of an annual conference taken under the adapted portions of the *Discipline* or of a decision of law by the presiding bishop of the annual conference pertaining to the adapted portion of the *Discipline*, upon appeal of the presiding bishop or of such percentage of the members of the annual conference as may be determined by the central conference concerned.

4. A central conference may have a standing committee on young people's ministry. This committee shall be composed of youth, young adults, and adult leaders of youth or young-adult ministry from each annual conference in the central conference. The duty of this committee shall be to study the relation of young people to the Church and to devise ways and means of developing the Church's ministry for, with, and by young people. The committee shall make recommendations to the central conference regarding youth and young-adult organizations within its areas as well as elect delegates to the Global Young People's Convocation (¶ 1210).

5. Every board, standing committee, commission, council, and work area of the central conference shall designate one of its

members as its coordinator of witness ministries. These persons shall help the agencies of which they are members to engage in witness ministries and, in particular, to ask, "How are we intentionally reaching new people for Jesus Christ through our ministries?" and "How are we helping new people grow and mature as disciples of Jesus Christ through our ministries and areas of responsibility?"

¶ 548. *Bishops in Retired Relation*—1. An ordained minister who has served a term or part of a term as a bishop in a central conference where term episcopacy has prevailed shall, upon retirement from the effective relation in the ministry, be paid an allowance from the General Episcopal Fund in such sum as the General Council on Finance and Administration shall determine for the years during which the ordained minister served as a bishop.[20]

2. When former central conferences of The United Methodist Church become or have become autonomous churches or entered into church unions, retired bishops therein shall continue to have membership in the Council of Bishops if the retired bishops involved so desire.

Section IV. Provisional Central Conferences

¶ 560. *Authorization*—Annual conferences, provisional annual conferences, missionary conferences, and missions outside the United States that are not included in central conferences or in the territory of affiliated autonomous churches and that, because of geographical, language, political, or other considerations, have common interests that can best be served thereby, may be organized into provisional central conferences as provided in ¶ 540.1.[21]

The United Methodist Church shall have a provisional central conference with ministries in the following countries:

　　a) Southeast Asia and Mongolia Provisional Central Conference: Laos, Mongolia, Thailand, and Vietnam.

¶ 561. *Organization*—The organization of provisional central conferences shall conform to the regulations prescribed for central conferences insofar as they are considered applicable by the bishop in charge.

---

20. See Judicial Council Decision 394.
21. See Judicial Council Decision 525.

¶ **562.** *Powers*—The General Conference may grant to a provisional central conference any of the powers of a central conference except that of electing bishops.[22]

¶ **563.** Ad Interim *Provisions*—In the interval between General Conferences, the General Board of Global Ministries, upon the recommendation of the bishops in charge and after consultation with the annual conferences, provisional annual conferences, missionary conferences, and missions concerned, may make changes in the boundaries of a provisional central conference and may grant to a provisional central conference or to any of its component parts any of the powers of a central conference except that of electing bishops. All changes in boundaries and all grants of powers authorized by the General Board of Global Ministries shall be reported to the ensuing session of the General Conference and shall expire at the close of that session unless renewed by the General Conference.

¶ **564.** *Lay Membership*—An annual conference or a provisional annual conference in the field of a provisional central conference shall have the power to set standards of character and other qualifications for admission of its lay members.

¶ **565.** Ad Interim *Provisions for Conferences Outside the United States*—To annual conferences, provisional annual conferences, missionary conferences, and missions that are outside the United States and are not included in central conferences or provisional central conferences, the General Conference may grant any of the powers of central conferences except that of electing bishops; and in the interval between General Conferences, the General Board of Global Ministries may grant such powers when requested to do so by the bishop in charge and by the annual conference, provisional annual conference, missionary conference, or mission concerned.

¶ **566.** *Episcopal Supervision*—The General Conference shall make provision for the episcopal supervision of work in the territory outside the United States that is not now included in central conferences.

¶ **567.** The Council of Bishops may provide, if and when necessary, for episcopal visitation of mission fields not included in central or provisional central conferences.

---

22. See Judicial Council Decision 403.

Section V. Autonomous Methodist Churches, Affiliated Autonomous Methodist Churches, Affiliated United Churches, Covenanting Churches, Concordat Churches

¶ **570.** Churches located outside the boundaries of the jurisdictional conferences and which have entered into relationship with or have agreements with The United Methodist Church, including that of sending representatives to General Conference of The United Methodist Church are described as follows:

1. *Autonomous Methodist Churches*

a) A self-governing church of the Wesleyan tradition and which may or may not have entered into the Act of Covenanting with The United Methodist Church.

b) Autonomous Methodist churches are not entitled to send delegates to the General Conference of The United Methodist Church.

2. *Affiliated Autonomous Methodist Churches*

a) A self-governing Methodist church in whose establishment The United Methodist Church or one of its constituent members (The Evangelical United Brethren Church and The Methodist Church or their predecessors) has assisted and which by mutual agreement has entered into a Covenant of Relationship (in effect from 1968 to 1984) or an Act of Covenanting (see ¶ 573) with The United Methodist Church.

b) Each affiliated autonomous Methodist church shall be entitled to two delegates, one clergy and one layperson, to the General Conference of The United Methodist Church in accordance with ¶ 433.1*b*. They shall be entitled to all the rights and privileges of delegates, including membership on committees, except the right to vote. Such a church having more than 70,000 full members shall be entitled to one additional delegate. At least one of the three delegates shall be a woman. The bishop or president of the affiliated autonomous Methodist churches may be invited by the Council of Bishops to the General Conference.

3. *Affiliated United Churches*

a) A self-governing church which is formed by the uniting of two or more denominations, at least one of which shall have been related to The United Methodist Church or one of its constituent members (The Evangelical United Brethren Church and The Methodist Church or its predecessors).

b) Each affiliated united church shall be entitled to two

delegates, one clergy and one layperson, to the General Conference of The United Methodist Church in accordance with ¶ 433.1b. They shall be entitled to all the rights and privileges of delegates, including membership on committees, except the right to vote. Such a church having more than 70,000 full members shall be entitled to one additional delegate. At least one of the three delegates shall be a woman. The bishop or president of the affiliated united churches may be invited by the Council of Bishops to the General Conference.

4. *Covenanting Churches*

a) An autonomous Methodist church, an affiliated autonomous Methodist church, an affiliated united church, or another Christian church which has entered into a covenanting relationship with The United Methodist Church through an Act of Covenanting as described in ¶ 573.

b) The Act of Covenanting does not warrant that the covenanting churches shall be entitled to delegates at the General Conference of The United Methodist Church, or at the equivalent body of the covenant partner.

5. *Methodist Churches With Concordat Agreements*

a) Other Methodist churches which have Methodist heritage in common with The United Methodist Church or one of its constituent members (The Evangelical United Brethren Church and The Methodist Church or its predecessors) and which have entered into concordat agreements in accord with ¶ 574 with the purpose of manifesting the common Methodist heritage, affirming the equal status of the two churches and expressing mutual acceptance and respect, and creating opportunities for closer fellowship between the two churches, especially on the leadership level.

b) Such concordat agreement, with the exception of The Methodist Church of Great Britain (see ¶ 13.3), shall entitle the two churches to the following rights and privileges:

(1) The two churches, entering a concordant relationship, shall each elect two delegates, one clergy and one lay, to be seated in each other's General Conference or equivalent bodies with all rights and privileges. The agreements with the Methodist Church of Mexico and the Methodist Church of the Caribbean and the Americas shall be honored.

(2) The host church shall make provisions for hospitality, including room and board, for the delegates of the other

concordat church. Travel and other expenses shall be the responsibility of the visiting church.

¶ 571. *Autonomous Methodist Churches, Affiliated Autonomous Methodist Churches, and Affiliated United Churches*—1. Certificates of church membership given by clergy in one church shall be accepted by clergy in the other church.

2. When the requirements of such a Methodist church for its ordained ministry are comparable to those of The United Methodist Church, clergy may be transferred between its properly constituted ministerial bodies and the annual and provisional annual conferences of The United Methodist Church and their ordination(s) recognized as valid, with the approval and consent of the bishops or other appointive authorities involved in compliance with ¶ 347.

3. A program of visitation may be mutually arranged by the Council of Bishops in cooperation with the equivalent leadership of the autonomous Methodist church, affiliated autonomous Methodist church, and/or affiliated united church.

4. The Council of Bishops, in consultation with the General Board of Global Ministries and the Office of Christian Unity and Interreligious Relationships, shall work out plans of cooperation with these churches. The General Board of Global Ministries shall serve as the agent of The United Methodist Church for a continuing dialogue looking to the establishment of mission priorities with special reference to matters of personnel and finance.[23]

BECOMING AN AUTONOMOUS METHODIST,
AFFILIATED AUTONOMOUS METHODIST,
OR AFFILIATED UNITED CHURCH FROM CENTRAL CONFERENCES

¶ 572. When conferences outside the United States that are parts of The United Methodist Church desire to become an autonomous Methodist, affiliated autonomous Methodist, or affiliated united church, approval shall first be secured from the central conference involved and this decision be ratified by the annual conferences within the central conference by two-thirds majority of the aggregate votes cast by the annual conferences.[24]

1. The conference shall prepare a historical record with reasons why affiliation and/or autonomy is requested and shall con-

---

23. See Judicial Council Decision 692.
24. See Judicial Council Decisions 548, 1062.

sult with the Standing Committee on Central Conference Matters (¶ 2201) on proceedings for affiliation and/or autonomy.

2. The Standing Committee on Central Conference Matters and the conferences involved shall mutually agree on the confession of faith and the constitution of the new church. These shall be prepared with care and shall be approved by the conferences.

3. Preparation of its *Discipline* is the responsibility of the conference(s) desiring affiliation and/or autonomy.

4. Upon recommendation of the Standing Committee on Central Conference Matters, when all disciplinary requirements for affiliated and/or autonomous relationship have been met, the General Conference through an enabling act shall approve of and grant permission for the conference(s) involved to become an autonomous Methodist, affiliated autonomous Methodist, or affiliated united church.

5. Then the central conference involved shall meet, declare the present relationship between The United Methodist Church and the conference(s) involved dissolved, and reorganize as an autonomous Methodist, affiliated autonomous Methodist, or affiliated united church in accordance with the enabling act granted by the General Conference. The Standing Committee on Central Conference Matters shall assist in this process and, when the plans are consummated, report to the Council of Bishops. The proclamation of affiliated and/or autonomous status shall then be signed by the president of the Council of Bishops and the secretary of the General Conference.

6. A plan of cooperation shall be developed in accordance with ¶ 571.4.

Becoming a Covenanting Church

¶ **573.** 1. A covenanting relationship, whose elements were adopted by the 1992 General Conference in an action called an "Act of Covenanting Between Christian Churches and The United Methodist Church" may be established between autonomous Methodist churches, affiliated autonomous Methodist churches, affiliated united churches, or other Christian churches and The United Methodist Church.

a) The purpose of an Act of Covenanting with another Christian church is to encourage a new sense of global common cause, mutual support, mutual spiritual growth, common study of Scripture and culture, creative interaction as ministers in the mission of God's church, cross-fertilization of ideas about ways to be in that mission, sharing of resources, and exploration of new forms of service directed at old and emerging needs.

b) An Act of Covenanting will include recognition of our respective baptisms as different facets of the one baptism; recognition of one another as authentic expressions of the one holy, catholic, and apostolic church of Jesus Christ; recognition of the ordained ministries of the two churches; commitment to systematic participation in full eucharistic fellowship; and commitment to function in new ways of partnership, visitations, and programs.

c) For The United Methodist Church, oversight of the covenantal relationships is the responsibility of the Council of Bishops, while participation in specific projects is the responsibility of the appropriate general agency or agencies.

2. The Council of Bishops shall represent The United Methodist Church in developing an Act of Covenanting with a prospective partner church. The Council of Bishops shall make recommendations to General Conference as to the specific covenanting agreements. When approved by General Conference and by the chief legislative body of the partner church, the Act of Covenanting becomes effective when signed by the president of the Council of Bishops and the secretary of the General Conference of The United Methodist Church and by the authorized persons in the covenanting church. The text of each Act of Covenanting as adopted shall be printed in the appropriate General Conference journal or equivalent.[25]

CONCORDAT AGREEMENTS

¶ **574.** *Concordat Agreements*—1. With the exception of The Methodist Church of Great Britain, such concordats may be established by the following procedure:

a) The Methodist church shall, through its major decision-making body, request a concordat relationship with The United Methodist Church through the Council of Bishops. Concordats may also be initiated by The United Methodist Church acting through the Council of Bishops who shall, in cooperation with the Methodist church in question, ascertain that all disciplinary conditions are met and then prepare the necessary enabling legislation for adoption by the General Conference.

---

25. See Judicial Council Decision 692.

b) When such concordat agreement has been approved by the General Conference, the Council of Bishops shall prepare a statement of the concordat agreement to be signed by the president of the Council of Bishops, the secretary of the General Conference, and two representatives of the Methodist church with whom the concordat agreement is made. Such concordats shall be printed in the *Daily Christian Advocate* of that General Conference.

2. Such concordat agreement shall entitle the two churches to the following rights and privileges:

a) A program of mutual visitation may be arranged by the Council of Bishops in cooperation with the equivalent leadership of the other concordat church. The Council of Bishops may assign one or more of its members for episcopal visitation to concordat churches.

b) Clergy may be transferred between the two churches in accordance with ¶¶ 347.2*b* and 571.2.

Joining The United Methodist Church

¶ **575.** A church outside the United States may join The United Methodist Church when all of the following requirements are fulfilled:

1. Said church shall accept and approve the Constitution, Articles of Faith, *Discipline,* and polity of The United Methodist Church.

2. Said church, if it is within the boundaries of a central or provisional central conference, shall apply for membership in that conference. Such application shall be approved by the central or provisional central conference and by the General Conference. In the event that said church is not within the boundaries of an existing central or provisional conference, then its membership application shall be reviewed by the Council of Bishops and shall be approved by the General Conference.

3. Said church shall declare its own constitution and church order null and void.

4. The Standing Committee on Central Conference Matters shall advise and assist said church in this process and prepare the necessary enabling act for approval by the General Conference.

5. The General Conference shall approve legislation authorizing the necessary adjustments in the organization of the central or provisional central conference involved. In the event that said church is not within the boundaries of an existing central or

provisional central conference, then legislation shall be approved to either change boundaries of a contiguous conference or to establish a new central or provisional central conference.

6. The Standing Committee on Central Conference Matters shall assist said church in the process of becoming a part of The United Methodist Church, determine when all requirements are met, and report to the General Conference.

Section VI. Provisional Annual Conferences

¶ **580.** *Definition*—A provisional annual conference is a conference that, because of its limited membership, does not qualify for annual conference status.

¶ **581.** *Provisions*—Any missionary conference or mission established under the provisions of the *Discipline* may be constituted as a provisional annual conference by the General Conference, in consultation with the central conference, provisional central conference, or jurisdictional conference within which the missionary conference or mission is located, provided that:

1. No provisional annual conference shall be organized with fewer than ten clergy members or be continued with fewer than six clergy members.

2. The total financial support from the General Board of Global Ministries, including the Advance, shall not exceed an appropriate percentage as determined in consultation with the board.

3. The membership and contributions of the conference have shown a reasonable increase during the previous quadrennium and give evidence of an aggressive program for continued progress in both areas.

¶ **582.** *Organization*—A provisional annual conference shall be organized in the same manner and have the same powers and functions as an annual conference, subject to the approval of the presiding bishop; and its members shall share *pro rata* in the proceeds of The United Methodist Publishing House with members of the annual conferences, with the following exceptions:

1. The bishop having episcopal supervision of a provisional annual conference in a foreign or a home mission field may appoint a representative as superintendent, to whom may be committed specific responsibility for the representation of the General Board of Global Ministries in its relation to the indigenous church and also in cooperation with other recognized evangelical missions.

Such duties shall be exercised so as not to interfere with the work of the district superintendent. This superintendent may also be a district superintendent, provided the superintendent is a member of the said conference. The superintendent shall be responsible directly to the bishop appointed to administer the work in that episcopal area and shall make adequate reports of the work and needs of the field to the bishop and to the secretaries of the General Board of Global Ministries immediately concerned.

2. A provisional annual conference shall meet annually at the time appointed by the bishop. If there is no bishop present, the superintendent shall preside. In the absence of both, the presidency shall be determined as in an annual conference (¶ 603.6). The conference or a committee thereof shall select the place for holding the conference.

3. In a provisional annual conference receiving major funding from the General Board of Global Ministries, the assigned staff of the board shall provide consultation and guidance in setting up the annual budget and Advance projects within the conference and in the promotion of new mission projects. The conference, in making requests for appropriations for support, including grants and loans for building projects, shall submit to the General Board of Global Ministries a statement of the proposed annual budget and proposed financial plan for new mission and building plans. Items involving increased appropriations from the General Board of Global Ministries or increased askings from the Advance shall be subject to modifications by the General Board of Global Ministries.

4. A provisional annual conference shall elect one ordained minister and one layperson as delegates with full voting and other rights to the General Conference and to the jurisdictional conference. Delegates to central conferences shall be elected in accordance with ¶ 541.1.

¶ 583. *Board of Global Ministries*—In a provisional annual conference in the United States or the Virgin Islands, there shall be a conference board of global ministries constituted as in an annual conference and having the same duties and powers.

Section VII. The Missionary Conference

¶ 585. *Definition*—A conference is a missionary conference because of its particular mission opportunities, its limited membership and resources, its unique leadership requirements, its strategic regional or language considerations, and ministerial needs. The General Board of Global Ministries shall provide administrative guidance and major financial assistance, including attention to the distinctive property matters.

¶ **586.** *Organization*—A missionary conference shall be organized in the same manner and with the same rights and powers as an annual conference (¶¶ 601-604), but with the following exceptions:

1. The College of Bishops shall provide episcopal supervision for any missionary conference(s) within its jurisdictional boundaries as are organized. The bishop thus placed in charge and having episcopal supervision within the respective episcopal area in cooperation with the General Board of Global Ministries shall appoint a conference superintendent and/or district superintendents. Such conference and/or district superintendent(s) shall be an elder(s) and shall be subject to the same limitations on years of service as district superintendents (¶ 418). Years of service may be either consecutive or non-consecutive. Years of service as a conference and/or district superintendent in a missionary conference shall be counted toward the total of twelve years permitted in a regular annual conference.[26]

2. The General Board of Global Ministries shall give close supervision and guidance in setting up the administrative and promotional budgets and Advance projects within the conference and in the promotion of new mission projects. The conference, in making requests for appropriations for support and grants and loans for building projects, shall submit to the General Board of Global Ministries a statement of the proposed annual promotional and administrative budget and the proposed financial plan for new mission and building projects. New work and building projects involving increased appropriations from the General Board of Global Ministries shall first have the approval of the General Board of Global Ministries.

3. Missionary conferences shall elect clergy and lay delegates to General and jurisdictional conference on the same basis as annual conferences as provided in ¶¶ 502 and 514.

4. *a) Membership*—A missionary conference shall determine by majority vote whether it will establish the right of full ministerial membership. With approval and consent of the bishops or

26. See Judicial Council Decision 512.

other judicatory authorities involved, appointments are to be made by the resident bishop of the conference in which the clergyperson is to serve.

b) An ordained minister in full connection with an annual conference who is appointed to a missionary conference that has previously voted to include full membership under § 4*a* may choose either to request the bishop of the missionary conference to seek the transfer of his or her membership into full membership with the missionary conference or retain his or her membership in a home conference and be considered in an affiliated relationship to the missionary conference.

c) In a missionary conference which has not voted to include full membership, each United Methodist cleric appointed by the bishop shall retain his or her membership in a home conference and be considered in an affiliated relationship to the missionary conference.

d) Affiliated relationship shall entitle the ordained minister to the fellowship of the conference, to full participation in its activities, including holding office and representing the missionary conference in General and jurisdictional conferences. An affiliate member of a missionary conference shall not vote in his or her annual conference while retaining the affiliate relationship to a missionary conference. Such affiliate relationship to a missionary conference shall be only for the duration of the ordained minister's appointment to the conference.

An affiliate member elected to a General or jurisdictional conference from a missionary conference shall not be eligible to be elected to such position from the conference where his or her membership is held.

e) A missionary conference may elect into full ministerial membership those persons desiring full membership in accordance with ¶ 588.

f) A pastor under full-time appointment in a missionary conference, upon consultation with and the approval of the bishop and conference or district superintendent or cabinet, may waive his or her claim upon the conference minimum salary. This waiver is to be reviewed annually and is to be effective until the time of subsequent appointment.

g) In a missionary conference that has not established the right of full ministerial membership (§ 4*a*), if the missionary conference is part of an episcopal area consisting of two or more annual and missionary conferences, then for purposes of candidacy for ordination (¶¶ 310-314), provisional membership (¶¶ 324-327), and election to full conference membership (¶¶ 328-336), the missionary conference may function as a district of an annual conference in the same episcopal area, with and only with the approval of the presiding bishop, the Board of Ordained Ministry of the annual conference, and the committee on ordained ministry of the missionary conference. If the missionary conference does not have a committee on ordained ministry, then approval may be provided by the body of the missionary conference to which the functions of the committee on ordained ministry have been assigned.[27]

5. A missionary conference may include in its membership representation of such mission agencies within its boundaries as it deems advisable, provided, however, such representation shall not exceed a number equal to one-third of the total membership of the missionary conference and that such representatives shall be members of The United Methodist Church in accordance with constitutional requirements.[28]

6. In order to provide traditional and experimental ministries, the bishop of the missionary conference may appoint an effective elder to other than full-time pastoral appointment combined with secular employment. This will in no way affect the conference relationship. Pension and other benefits shall be provided in consultation with the parties involved and with the approval of the missionary conference.

7. A missionary conference that has not established the right of full ministerial membership may ordain indigenous racial and ethnic persons as deacons who, although they are not associate members, shall be accorded all the rights and privileges of associate membership in the missionary conference, provided that they have completed all of the necessary requirements for candidacy and such other requirements the missionary conference may establish. Further, these persons have the right to pursue transfer of their ministerial relationship to another annual conference as an associate member and to pursue a relationship of full connection under the guidance of that annual conference.

¶ 587. Only the General Conference can create a missionary conference or change a missionary conference to a provisional

27. See Judicial Council Decision 448.
25. See Judicial Council Decision 511.

annual conference or an annual conference. A petition to the General Conference for change in status from a missionary conference shall set forth details of the history and status of the conference and shall be accompanied by a report and recommendation of the General Board of Global Ministries.

¶ **588.** *Rights and Privileges*—Missionary conferences shall have the same rights as those given to the central conferences in ¶ 543.7, .8 to make such changes and adaptations regarding the ministry and ordination of ordained ministers as the effective use of indigenous leadership in the missionary conference may require, provided that no action shall be taken that is contrary to the Constitution and the General Rules of The United Methodist Church, and provided further that a missionary conference that does not have a board of ordained ministry must use the process prescribed in ¶ 586.4g) for approval of candidates for ordination.

Section VIII. Missions

¶ **590.** The purpose of a mission is to provide and develop ministry with a particular group or region whose potential and needs cannot be met within the existing structures and resources of annual or district conference(s). A mission may also be the initial stage in moving toward the formation of a provisional annual conference.

In accordance with the Wesleyan ecumenical spirit, in all phases of mission development, the initiating United Methodist entities will consult with, and where possible create cooperative relationships with, Wesleyan communions. They will promote relationships with other denominations serving in the area and with interdenominational and ecumenical organizations. Where appropriate, they will engage in dialogue with interfaith agencies and organizations.

¶ **591.** *Powers and Duties*—1. A mission is an organizational body for a field of work inside, outside, or across the structures of annual conferences, or provisional annual conferences.

2. A mission may be established by the General Board of Global Ministries, or by a central or annual conference in cooperation with the General Board of Global Ministries.

3. The boundaries for a mission established by a central or annual conference in cooperation with the General Board of Global Ministries are to be determined by the central or annual conference and the General Board of Global Ministries. If a mission

is established by the General Board of Global Ministries outside territories of central conferences, the General Board of Global Ministries will establish the boundaries.

4. *(a)* When the mission lies within the bounds of one episcopal area, the resident bishop shall preside over the mission. *(b)* When the mission crosses the boundaries of one or more episcopal areas, jurisdictions, or central conferences, the College(s) of Bishops, in consultation with the general secretary of the General Board of Global Ministries, shall assign a bishop to the mission. *(c)* When the mission lies outside the bounds of an established episcopal area in jurisdictions or central conferences, the Council of Bishops, in consultation with the general secretary of the General Board of Global Ministries, will assign a bishop to be its presiding officer.

5. The entity or entities establishing a mission, in collaboration with the assigned bishop, will seek a cooperative agreement with an annual conference which will serve as the correspondent annual conference to the mission for the purposes of ordination and conference membership as well as for local pastor licensing.

6. The annual meeting of the mission shall have the power to certify candidates for the ordained ministry, to receive and to examine mission pastors and local elders in mission, and to recommend to an annual conference proper persons for provisional or full membership and ordination.

7. The entity or entities initiating a mission shall be responsible for its administration and development and for making sure that the mission sets up, organizes and implements the necessary mechanisms and processes to fulfill the functions of the mission.

8. Neither the mission nor its officers shall assume financial obligations or make financial commitments on behalf of the General Board of Global Ministries without the board's written authorization.

9. Recommendations for a change of status of a mission shall be made by the entity or entities that established the mission.

¶ **592.** *Membership*—1. A mission shall be made up of all regularly appointed missionaries, both lay and clergy, local elders in mission, mission pastors, and other lay members. The mission shall determine the number of lay members and the method of their selection. In so doing, it shall ensure that all aspects of the mission's work are represented.[29]

---

29. See Judicial Council Decision 341.

2. In territories outside the boundaries of central or annual conferences, the bishop assigned to the mission and the General Board of Global Ministries recommend the educational requirements for local elders in mission, and mission pastors. Such recommendations and requirements shall be approved by the General Board of Higher Education and Ministry.

a) Local elders in mission are ordained members of the mission and are not members of an annual conference. Local elders in mission are limited in their itineration and sacramental authority to the bounds of the mission and as such are not eligible to transfer their credentials to another annual conference.

b) Mission pastors are members of the mission without being members of an annual conference. The mission shall determine the requirements for a mission pastor in order to most effectively utilize the indigenous leadership. Mission pastors are limited in their itineration to the bounds of the mission.

¶ **593.** *Missions—Annual Meeting—*1. A mission shall meet annually at the time and place designated by the bishop in charge, who shall preside. In the absence of the bishop, a superintendent of the mission shall preside. The presiding officer shall bring forward the regular business of the meeting and arrange the work.

2. The assigned bishop, in consultation with the entity or entities establishing a mission, may appoint one or more superintendents of the mission.

3. At the annual meeting, the bishop shall assign the missionaries, local elders in mission, and mission pastors to the several charges for the ensuing year; provided that transfer of missionaries related to the General Board of Global Ministries shall be completed only after consultation with the board.

4. A mission related to a central conference is authorized to elect and send one lay and one clergy to the central conference as its representative, with voice but not vote.

Section IX. The Annual Conference

¶ **601.** *Purpose—*The purpose of the annual conference is to make disciples of Jesus Christ for the transformation of the world by equipping its local churches for ministry and by providing a connection for ministry beyond the local church; all to the glory of God.

¶ **602.** *Composition and Character—*1. The clergy membership of an annual conference (¶ 369) shall consist of deacons and elders in full connection (¶ 333), provisional members (¶ 327), associate members, affiliate members (¶¶ 344.4, 586.4), and local pastors (¶ 317).[30] (See also ¶ 32.)

a) Clergy members in full connection shall have the right to vote on all matters in the annual conference except in the election of lay delegates to the General and jurisdictional or central conferences and shall have sole responsibility for all matters of ordination, character, and conference relations of clergy.[31]

b) Provisional clergy members shall have the right to vote in the annual conference on all matters except constitutional amendments, election of clergy delegates to the General and jurisdictional or central conferences and matters of ordination, character, and conference relations of clergy. Provisional clergy members who have completed all of their educational requirements may vote to elect clergy delegates to General and jurisdictional or central conferences.[32]

c) Associate clergy members shall have the right to vote in the annual conference on all matters except constitutional amendments, and matters of ordination, character, and conference relations of clergy. When associate members are members of the conference Board of Ordained Ministry, they have the right to vote at clergy session on matters of ordination, character, and conference relations of clergy (¶ 635.1). Affiliate clergy members shall have the right to vote in the annual conference on all matters except the constitutional amendments, election of clergy delegates to the General jurisdictional or central conferences, and matters of ordination, character, and conference relations of clergy.[32]

d) Full-time and part-time local pastors shall have the right to vote in the annual conference on all matters except constitutional amendments; election of delegates to the General and jurisdictional or central conferences and matters of ordination, character, and conference relations of clergy.[33] When local pastors are members of the Conference Board of Ordained Ministry, they have the right to vote at clergy session on matters of ordination, character, and conference relations of clergy (¶ 635.1). Local pastors who have completed course of study or an M. Div. degree and

30. See Judicial Council Decisions 477, 555, 1062.
31. See Judicial Council Decisions 406, 555, 686, 690.
32. See Judicial Council Decision 1181 and ¶ 35, Article IV.
33. See Judicial Council Decision 862.

have served a minimum of two consecutive years under appointment before the election may vote to elect clergy delegates to General and jurisdictional or central conferences.[34]

e) Each annual conference having campus ministers, chaplains and Wesley Foundation directors shall include the same in its lay and clergy annual conference composition. In districts where United Methodist laypersons serve as campus ministers/ directors of Wesley Foundations, they shall be added as district-at-large lay members to the annual conference. In districts where United Methodist clergy serve as chaplains, campus ministers, and directors of Wesley Foundations, the laypersons elected as their balancing counterpart shall be elected from either the campus ministry board of directors or a student from that ministry/ foundation. In making sure that such inclusion is adhered to, special consideration shall be given to the inclusion of United Methodist young adults who are active participants in campus ministry.

2. Consecrated diaconal ministers serve as lay members of the annual conference as long as they maintain this status in The United Methodist Church.

3. Persons who become associate members prior to January 1, 1997, shall be allowed to continue in this relationship and serve under the provision of the 1992 *Book of Discipline* as long as they hold this status.

4. The lay membership of the annual conference shall consist of a professing member elected by each charge, diaconal ministers, deaconesses, home missioners, the conference president of United Methodist Women, the conference president of United Methodist Men, the conference lay leader, district lay leaders,[35] the president or equivalent officer of the conference young adult organization, the president of the conference youth organization, one youth between the ages of twelve and eighteen and one young adult between the ages of eighteen and thirty from each district to be selected in such a manner as may be determined by the annual conference (in the case of central conferences, the youth member shall be not younger than twelve and not older than twenty-five and the young adult member shall be not younger than eighteen and not older than thirty-five), and the chair of the annual conference college student organization.

---

34. See Judicial Council Decision 1181 and ¶ 35. Article IV.
35. See Judicial Council Decisions 989, 1005.

If the lay membership should number less than the clergy members of the annual conference, the annual conference shall, by its own formula, provide for the election of additional lay members to equalize lay and clergy membership of the annual conference.[36]

Each charge served by more than one clergy member under appointment (including deacons in full connection for whom this is their primary appointment) shall be entitled to as many lay members as there are clergy members under appointment. The lay members shall have been members of The United Methodist Church for the two years preceding their election and shall have been active participants in The United Methodist Church for at least four years preceding their election (¶¶ 32, 251.2).

a) In the annual conference or the central conferences, the four-year participation and the two-year membership requirements may be waived for young persons under thirty years of age. Such persons must be members of The United Methodist Church and active participants at the time of election.

b) By authorization of a central conference, national diaconal ministers may be given the same privileges as a diaconal minister.[37]

5. The lay member or alternate, whoever was last seated in the annual conference, shall be seated in a special session of the annual conference when convened, provided that no local charge shall be deprived of its lay member due to death, serious illness, or cessation of membership. Under such circumstances, another lay member may be elected by the charge conference.[38] (See ¶ 32.)

6. The lay members of the annual conference shall participate in all deliberations and vote upon all measures except on the granting or validation of license, ordination, reception into full conference membership, or any question concerning the character and official conduct of ordained ministers, except those who are lay members of the Board of Ordained Ministry and committee on investigation. Lay members shall serve on all committees except those on ministerial relations.[39]

---

36. See Judicial Council Decision 1212.
37. See Judicial Council Decision 505.
38. See Judicial Council Decision 319.
39. See Judicial Council Decisions 109, 505.

7. When at any time a lay member is excused by the annual conference from further attendance during the session, the alternate lay member, if present, shall be seated. The lay member or the alternate shall be the lay member of the annual conference, and it shall be the duty of the lay member to report to the local church on actions of the annual conference.

8. It is the duty of every member and all provisional members and local pastors of the annual conference to attend its sessions and furnish such reports in such form as the *Discipline* may require. Any such person unable to attend shall report by letter to the conference secretary, setting forth the reason for the absence. Should any ordained minister in active service be absent from the session of the annual conference without a satisfactory reason for the absence, the matter shall be referred by the conference secretary to the Board of Ordained Ministry.

9. The following shall be seated in the annual conference and shall be given the privilege of the floor without vote: official representatives from other denominations invited by the annual conference; missionaries regularly assigned by the General Board of Global Ministries and serving within the bounds of the annual conference; lay missionaries regularly appointed by the General Board of Global Ministries in nations other than the United States; and certified lay missionaries from nations other than the United States; serving within the bounds of the annual conference.

10. If not otherwise a voting member of the annual conference, the conference chancellor shall be seated in the annual conference and shall be given the privilege of the floor without vote.

¶ 603. *Organization*—1. Annual conferences may become severally bodies corporate, whenever practicable, under the law of the countries, states, and territories within whose bounds they are located.[40]

2. The bishops shall appoint the times for holding the annual conferences.[41]

3. The annual conference or a committee thereof shall select the place for holding the conference, but should it become necessary for any reason to change the place of meeting, a majority of the district superintendents, with the consent of the bishop in charge, may change the place.

40. See Judicial Council Decision 108.
41. See Judicial Council Decision 1206.

4. The annual conference sessions shall be held in places that are accessible to people with disabilities.

5. A special session of the annual conference may be held at such time and in such place as shall have been determined by the annual conference after consultation with the bishop, or by the bishop with the concurrence of three-fourths of the district superintendents. A special session of the annual conference shall have only such powers as are stated in the call.[42]

6. The bishop assigned shall preside over the annual conference or, in case of inability, shall arrange for another bishop to preside. In the absence of a bishop, the conference shall by ballot, without nomination or debate, elect a president *pro tempore* from among the traveling elders. The president thus elected shall discharge all the duties of a bishop except ordination.

7. The annual conference at the first session following the General Conference or jurisdictional or central conferences (or, if it may desire, at the last session preceding the General, jurisdictional, or central conferences), utilizing such nominating procedure as the annual conference shall determine, shall elect a secretary and statistician to serve for the succeeding quadrennium. In the case of a vacancy in either office in the interim of the sessions, the bishop, after consultation with the district superintendents, shall appoint a person to act until the next session of the annual conference. (See ¶ 619 for election of the treasurer.)

8. The annual conference shall designate a chancellor, and may designate one or more associate chancellors. The chancellor and any associate chancellors must be members in good standing of a local church or an annual conference in the episcopal area, and be licensed to practice law in the episcopal area. The chancellor and any associate chancellors shall be nominated by the bishop and elected quadrennially by the annual conference. If a vacancy should occur during the quadrennium, the bishop shall fill the vacancy until the next session of the annual conference. The chancellor, assisted by the associate chancellors, if any, shall serve as legal adviser(s) to the bishop and the annual conference. Each annual conference shall report its election of the chancellor and any associate chancellors to the General Council on Finance and Administration.

---

42. See Judicial Council Decision 397.

9. The conference lay leader is the elected leader of conference laity and is an officer of the annual conference. The conference lay leader shall be a professing member of a local church in the annual conference. The conference lay leader shall participate in annual conference sessions as a partner in ministry with the bishop.

¶ 604. *Powers and Duties*—1. The annual conference, for its own government, may adopt rules and regulations not in conflict with the *Discipline* of The United Methodist Church, provided that in exercise of its powers, each annual conference shall act in all respects in harmony with the policy of The United Methodist Church with respect to elimination of discrimination.[43] (See ¶ 4, Article IV.)

2. An annual conference cannot financially obligate any organizational unit of The United Methodist Church except the annual conference itself.[44]

3. The annual conference may admit into clergy membership only those who have met all the disciplinary requirements for membership and only in the manner prescribed in the *Discipline*.[45]

4. The annual conference shall have power to make inquiry into the moral and official conduct of its clergy members. Subject only to the provisions of ¶¶ 2701-2719, the annual conference shall have power to hear complaints against its clergy members and may try, reprove, suspend, deprive of clergy office and credentials, expel, or acquit any against whom charges may have been preferred. The annual conference shall have power to locate a clergy member for failure to perform effectively and competently the duties of itinerant ministry.[46]

5. The status of a clergy member and of a provisional member and the manner and conditions of a transfer of a clergy member from one annual conference to another are governed by the section on the ordained ministry (Chapter Two).

6. Transfers of traveling preachers are conditioned on the passing of their character by the conference to which they are amenable. The official announcement that a preacher is transferred changes the preacher's membership so that all rights and

---

43. See Judicial Council Decisions 43, 74, 141, 318, 367, 373, 432, 435, 476, 536, 584, 590, 592, 699, 876, 1198.
44. See Judicial Council Decision 707.
45. See Judicial Council Decision 440.
46. See Judicial Council Decisions 534, 782.

responsibilities in the conference to which that preacher goes begin from the date of transfer. Such member of an annual conference shall not vote twice on the same constitutional question, nor be counted twice in the same year in the basis for election of delegates, nor vote twice in the same year for delegates to the General, jurisdictional, or central conferences.

7. Whenever clergy members, whether provisional members or in full connection, are transferred to another annual conference, either in connection with a transfer of the pastoral charge to which they are appointed or by reason of the dissolution or merger of the annual conference, they shall have the same rights and obligations as the other members of the conference to which they are transferred.

8. The annual conference shall have power to make inquiry into the financial status of the local churches, and where there is a deficit in finances, it may require the pastor and the lay member to appear before the appropriate committee and make explanation. Based upon its findings, it shall provide counsel to help the church overcome such a deficit position.

9. The annual conference shall have the power to make inquiry into the membership status of the local churches, and where no members have been received on confession of faith during the year, it may require the pastor and the lay member to appear before the appropriate agency and make explanation.

10. The annual conference shall give recognition to any new churches that have been organized during the year and shall, through the presiding bishop and the secretary, send to each new church a certificate of organization, which the district superintendent shall, on behalf of the conference, present to the new church in an appropriate ceremony.

11. The annual conference shall secure, during the course of its annual session, the answers to the questions for conducting annual conference sessions, and the secretary to the annual conference shall include the answers to these questions in the conference journal and in the report to the council on finance and administration.

12. If any annual conference initiates, joins, monitors, or terminates a boycott, the guidelines in *The Book of Resolutions*, 2008, should be followed. The General Conference is the only body that can initiate, empower, or join a boycott in the name of The United Methodist Church.

13. The annual conference may choose to adopt a conference-wide plan for compensation of pastors. Such a plan shall provide the method for setting and funding the salaries, and/or other compensation elements as specified in the plan, of the pastors appointed to the charges of the annual conference.

¶ 605. *Business of the Conference*—1. The session shall open with a period of devotion, followed by a call of the roll, including the roll of the local pastors.

2. The annual conference, to expedite the transaction of its business, may adopt an agenda as a basis of its procedure. Such agenda shall be prepared by the bishop, the district superintendents, the conference lay leader, and such others as the conference may name and shall be submitted to the conference for adoption.

3. Members for all standing committees, boards, and commissions of the annual conference shall be selected in such manner as the *Book of Discipline* may specifically require or as the annual conference may determine.[47] Attention shall be given to inclusiveness (¶¶ 124, 140).

For the purpose of adjusting tenure, a certain number of members may be elected or appointed for particular terms. Members shall hold office until their successors are elected. For the annual conference agencies provided for by the *Discipline*, see ¶ 610.1; and for the agencies established by the annual conference itself, see ¶ 610.2.

4. The business of the annual conference shall include receiving and acting upon reports from district superintendents, officers, standing and special committees, boards, commissions, and societies and also making such inquiries as the Council of Bishops shall recommend by the provision of a supplemental guide.[48]

5. The agenda of the annual conference shall provide time for an address or report that shall be the responsibility of the conference lay leader.

6. At the request of the general secretary of the General Board of Pension and Health Benefits, the agenda of the annual conference shall provide time for an address of or report from the General Board of Pension and Health Benefits in consultation with the annual conference board of pensions for the purpose of discussing benefit plans and related issues.

---

47. See Judicial Council Decision 559.
48. See Judicial Council Decision 367.

7. The annual conference shall make inquiry into the moral and official conduct of its ordained ministers and local pastors. In response to the inquiry whether all such persons are blameless in their life and official administration, the district superintendent may answer for all the preachers in the district in one answer, or the Board of Ordained Ministry may make inquiry of each district superintendent about each ordained minister in the district and make one report to the bishop and the conference in open session.[49] Questions relating to matters of ordination, character, and conference relations of clergy shall be the business of the clergy session. The actions of the clergy session shall be for and on behalf of the annual conference. The provisions of the *Book of Discipline* applicable to an annual conference shall also be applicable to the clergy session. All clergy members (¶ 602.1) of the annual conference and the lay members of the Board of Ordained Ministry may attend and shall have voice in the clergy session. Only the ordained clergy in full connection and the members of the Board of Ordained Ministry may vote (¶ 602.1*a*). Others may be admitted by express action of the clergy session, but shall not have vote, nor, unless specifically granted by the clergy session, shall have voice (¶ 333).[50]

8. At the conclusion of the examination of the standing of the ordained ministers and local pastors in the conference or at such later times as the bishop may designate, the presiding bishop may call to the bar of the conference the class to be admitted into full connection and receive them into conference membership after asking the questions to be found in ¶ 336. This examination of the ordained ministers and the passing of their characters may be the business of one session.

9. The annual conference shall adopt a comprehensive policy for handling sexual and gender harassment of clergy when laypersons are the perpetrators. This policy shall guide the local church in how to handle the report, how to care for the accuser and the accused, the victim and the perpetrator, the findings and settlement. It shall make provision for support of the pastor and for care of church members.

¶ **606.** *Records and Archives*—1. The annual conference shall keep an exact record of its proceedings according to the forms provided by the General, jurisdictional, and central conferences.

---

49. See Judicial Council Decisions 42, 406, 555.
50. See Judicial Council Decisions 686, 690, 769, 782, 1009.

If there are no archives of the annual conference, the secretary shall keep the bound copy or copies or a digital version to be handed on to the succeeding secretary. The conference shall send to its jurisdictional conference or central conference copies of the minutes of the quadrennium for examination.

2. Each annual conference shall send without charge to the General Council on Finance and Administration, the General Board of Pension and Health Benefits, the General Commission on Archives and History, the Central Conference or Jurisdictional Commission on Archives and History, and the Annual Conference Commission on Archives and History two printed copies or a digital version of its annual journal. In addition, the annual conference shall send one printed copy or a digital version of its annual journal to the Connectional Table and one printed copy or a digital version to United Methodist Communications. If available, one copy of a digital version of the journal shall be sent to the General Commission on Archives and History and one copy to United Methodist Communications.

3. The annual conference may form a committee on journal publication. The annual conference journal shall include the following divisions, in the following order:

    a) Officers of annual conference,

    b) Boards, commissions, committees; rolls of conference members,

    c) Daily proceedings,

    d) Business of the annual conference report (formerly known as the disciplinary questions),

    e) Appointments,

    f) Reports as ordered by the annual conference,

    g) Annual report of the district superintendents, if any.

    h) Memoirs as ordered by the annual conference following the guidelines of the General Commission on Archives and History,

    i) Roll of dead-deceased clergy members,

    j) Historical,

    k) Miscellaneous,

    l) Pastoral record (including the records of accepted local pastors in such manner as the conference may determine),

    m) Statistics,

    n) Index.

4. An annual conference in the United States and Puerto Rico shall include in its journal a list of the deaconesses and missionaries, clergy and lay, active and retired, who have gone from the conference into mission service or who are presently serving in such capacity within the bounds of the annual conference.

5. The annual conference journal shall include a listing of the consecrated diaconal ministers and their service records.

6. The secretary, treasurer, or other administrative officer named by the annual conference shall keep a complete service record of ordained and diaconal ministry personnel in the annual conference. Service records shall include but not be limited to biographical information supplied by the individual, a list of appointments, and a record of annual conference actions with regard to conference relationships. In addition to service records, the secretary, treasurer, or other administrative officer named by the annual conference shall keep descriptions of circumstances related to changes in conference relationships, credentials surrendered to the bishop or district superintendent, and confidential trial records.

7. The local church report to the annual conference shall be submitted on the prescribed forms no later than thirty days following the close of the calendar year. If the annual conference sets an earlier deadline for receiving the reports, the earlier deadline shall apply.

8. Official records of secretaries, statisticians, and treasurers shall be kept according to the forms prepared by the General Council on Finance and Administration so that official statistical and financial items shall be handled alike in all annual conferences and that uniformity of reporting shall be established as a worldwide church policy.

9. All records of candidates and ordained and diaconal ministry personnel maintained by the conference secretary, treasurer, or other administrative officer named by the annual conference, Board of Ordained Ministry, board of pensions, and the district committee on ordained ministry are to be kept on behalf of the annual conference in conformity with guidelines provided by the General Council on Finance and Administration, in consultation with the General Board of Higher Education and Ministry and the General Board of Pension and Health Benefits, and the following principles:

a) The annual conference is the owner of its personnel records and files;

b) Individuals in whose name a record is kept shall have access to the information contained in a record or file, with the exception of surrendered credentials and information for which a right-of-access waiver has been signed;

c) Access to unpublished records by persons other than the bishop, district superintendent, conference secretary, treasurer, or other administrative officer or the Board of Ordained Ministry, through its chair, board of pensions, through its chair, the district committee on ordained ministry, through its chair, counsel for the Church, and committee on investigation, through its chair, shall require written consent of the person in whose name a record is kept; access to trial records shall be governed by the provisions of ¶¶ 2712.5, 2713.5.[51]

¶ 607. *The Conference Lay Leader*

1. The conference lay leader is the elected leader of conference laity and will have responsibility for fostering awareness of the role of the laity both within the congregation and through their ministries in the home, workplace, community, and world in achieving the mission of the Church and enabling and supporting lay participation in the planning and decision-making processes of the annual conference, district, and local church in cooperation with the bishop, district superintendents, and pastors.

2. The conference lay leader shall relate to the organized lay groups in the conference such as United Methodist Men, United Methodist Women, United Methodist Youth, and Scouting Ministries, encourage and support their work, and help them coordinate their activities. The conference lay leader shall also have the general responsibility in: (1) developing the advocacy role for laity in the life of the Church; (2) increasing the participation of laity in the sessions and structure of the annual conference; and (3) encouraging laypersons in the general ministry of the Church.

3. The conference lay leader shall be the chairperson of the conference board of laity, or its equivalent structure, and shall be a member of the annual conference, the conference council on ministries or equivalent structure, the executive committee, if any, of the conference council on ministries, the conference committee on nominations, the conference committee on episcopacy, and the committee planning annual conference sessions; and may be

---

51. See Judicial Council Decisions 751, 765, 1024.

designated by virtue of office to membership on any conference agency by the annual conference.

4. The annual conference shall provide time for an address that shall be the responsibility of the conference lay leader.

5. The conference lay leader may serve on the conference Board of Ordained Ministry and will participate in the Service of Ordination at annual conference.

6. The conference lay leader shall meet with the cabinet when matters relating to the coordination, implementation, or administration of the conference program, or other matters as the cabinet may determine are on the agenda.

7. The conference lay leader will meet regularly with the bishop to discuss the state of the annual conference, the Church, and the needs for ministry both locally and globally.

8. The conference lay leader shall ensure that the annual conference has a conference director of Lay Speaking Ministries filled in the manner determined by the annual conference and the conference lay leader shall participate in Lay Servant Ministries.

9. The conference lay leader shall be elected for a term of not less than four years by the annual conference as the annual conference may determine. The method of nomination and term of office shall be determined by the annual conference. Associate lay leader(s), to work with the conference lay leader, may be elected by the annual conference as it may determine. The conference lay leader and associate lay leader(s) will receive reasonable reimbursement for approved dues and expenses necessary for the ministry.

10. The conference lay leader shall be a member of the Association of Annual Conference Lay Leaders.

¶ 608. *Connectional Ministries*—Each annual conference is responsible to focus and guide the mission and ministry of The United Methodist Church within its boundaries by:

1. envisioning the ministries necessary to live out the mission of the church in and through the annual conference;

2. creating and nurturing relationships and connections among the local, district, annual conference, and general Church ministries;

3. providing encouragement, coordination, and support for the ministries of nurture, outreach, and witness in districts and congregations for the transformation of the world;

4. ensuring the alignment of the total resources of the annual conference to its mission;

5. developing and strengthening ethnic ministries, including ethnic local churches and concerns;

6. providing for advocacy and monitoring functions to ensure that the church is consistent with its stated values.

It is recommended that each annual conference have a director of connectional ministries or designated person to focus and guide the mission and ministry of The United Methodist Church within the annual conference.

a) The director may be lay or clergy.

b) The director shall serve as an officer of the annual conference and shall sit with the cabinet when the cabinet considers matters relating to coordination, implementation, or administration of the conference program, and other matters as the cabinet and director may determine. Whether appointed or elected to this position, the director shall be amenable to the bishop, in consultation with the appropriate annual conference personnel body.

c) In partnership with the bishop and cabinet and the elected leadership of the conference, the director of connectional ministries shall have the following primary responsibilities:

(1) to serve as steward of the vision of the annual conference, including the development, clarification, interpretation, and embodiment of the vision;

(2) to serve as leader of the continuous process of transformation and renewal necessary for the annual conference to be faithful to our Christian identity in a changing world;

(3) to ensure alignment of the total resources of the conference to its vision;

(4) to ensure the connections among the local, district, annual conference, and general Church ministries for the purpose of networking, resourcing, and communicating their shared ministry.

¶ **609.** There shall be in each annual conference or episcopal area a director of communications or designated person to focus and guide the communications ministry of The United Methodist Church within the annual conference or episcopal area.

a) It is recommended that the director have the following primary responsibilities:

(1) to help identify, equip, and coordinate the work of a communications team (staff and/or volunteer);

(2) to develop and guide the implementation of strategies for effective communication among annual conference agencies, districts, and local churches;

(3) to promote and coordinate activities to enhance the awareness and reputation of the Church;

(4) to help guide the strategy to interpret the conference budget and other benevolences;

(5) to provide guidance and training in effective communications for annual conference, district, and/or local church leaders;

(6) to lead the conference in developing effective relationships with the news media within the annual conference;

(7) to guide conference leaders in developing and implementing an effective communication strategy under the connectional ministry;

(8) to lead the conference in using new and emerging technologies as tools for ministry;

(9) to provide the connectional relationship between the conference and United Methodist Communications.

b) It is recommended that the director or designated person be a part of the extended cabinet (or equivalent leadership structure) to provide advice and counsel concerning communications strategies relating to the conference program, apportionment and benevolence interpretation, crisis management, and other matters as the cabinet and director may determine.

CONFERENCE AGENCIES

¶ **610.** The annual conference is responsible for structuring its ministries and administrative procedures in order to accomplish its purpose (¶ 601), with the exception of the mandated provisions of ¶¶ 611, 635, 636, 637, 639, 640, 647, 648. In so doing it shall provide for the connectional relationship of the local church, district, and conference with the general agencies. It will monitor to ensure inclusiveness—racial, gender, age, and people with disabilities—in the annual conference. Every board, standing committee, commission, council, and work area of the annual conference shall designate one of its members as its coordinator of witness ministries. These persons shall help the groups of which they are members to engage in witness ministries and, in particular, to ask, "How are we intentionally reaching new people for Jesus Christ through our ministries?" and "How are we helping new people grow and mature as disciples of Jesus Christ through our ministries and areas of responsibility?"

1. Annual conferences are permitted the flexibility to design conference and district structures in ways that best support the mission of making disciples of Jesus Christ in an increasingly diverse global community and that place secondary any prescribed structure, except for the mandated entities in ¶ 610 above. In doing so, an annual conference shall provide for the functions and General Conference connections with all general agencies provided by the *Discipline* as follows: *a)* There shall be clear connections between the General Conference agencies, annual conference program and administrative entities, and the local congregations. These connections shall be identified in the business questions of the annual conference each year. *b)* There shall be clear checks and balances regarding program functions and financial/administration functions within the annual conference. These structural matters will be defined and approved by the annual conference session. Further, conferences are permitted to create contextually appropriate structures that encourage collaboration and partnerships among all program, administrative, and financial entities. Annual conferences may fund their ministries in ways that reflect conference priorities and structures, as approved by the annual conference in the budgeting process. All disciplinary references to "equivalent structures" shall be defined by this paragraph.

2. The annual conference may appoint additional committees for the purpose of promoting the work of The United Methodist Church within the bounds of the said annual conference and may prescribe their membership and their powers and duties.

3. Each annual conference may make its agencies of such size as its work may require, provided that consideration shall be given to the inclusion of lay and clergypersons from small membership churches. All local pastors serving charges are eligible for election or appointment to such agencies, except those dealing with qualifications, orders, and status of clergy and local pastors.

4. Whenever possible, meetings scheduled by the annual conference and its districts, boards, or committees should be held in places that are accessible to persons with disabilities even if this means scheduling meetings outside church-related facilities.

5. In the nomination and election of the membership on councils, boards, and agencies of the annual conference, special attention shall be given to the inclusion of clergywomen, youth (¶ 256.3), young adults, older adults, persons from churches with small memberships, people with disabilities, and racial and ethnic

persons, in keeping with policies for general Church agencies. It is further recommended that the membership of such agencies, except for the Board of Ordained Ministry, include one-third clergy, one-third laywomen, and one-third laymen, who are professing members of local churches.[52]

6. Members of general agencies (¶ 701) shall serve as ex officio members of the corresponding annual conference agency or its equivalent structure (see ¶ 710.4, .6). If this results in a person being a member of more than one annual conference agency in violation of either annual conference policy or another provision of the *Book of Discipline*, the person shall choose the annual conference agency on which to serve.

7. It is strongly recommended that the annual conference provide for child and dependent care both during the sessions of the annual conference and during meetings of the annual conference boards and agencies. Child and dependent care should follow the annual conference policy of child protection. If no policy is in place, care should be given to keep all people safe, and procedures should be followed as suggested by the General Board of Discipleship and the General Council on Finance and Administration.

8. Whenever possible, meetings scheduled by the annual conference and its districts, boards, or committees shall be held at a time and place that accommodates young people's schooling schedules.

The Conference Council on Finance and Administration

¶ **611.** In each annual conference there shall be a conference council on finance and administration, hereinafter called the council, or other structure to provide for the functions of this ministry and maintain the connectional relationships (¶ 610.1).

¶ **612.** The council's purpose, membership, organization, and relationships shall be as follows:

1. *Purpose*—The purpose of the council shall be to develop, maintain, and administer a comprehensive and coordinated plan of fiscal and administrative policies, procedures, and management services for the annual conference.[53]

2. *Membership*—*a)* Each annual conference shall elect, at its session next succeeding the General Conference or jurisdictional

---

52. See Judicial Council Decisions 446, 558.
53. See Judicial Council Decision 1054.

conference, a conference council on finance and administration, or other structure to provide for the functions of this ministry. It is recommended that it be composed of not less than five nor more than twenty-one members; it is recommended that there be at least one layperson more than clergy included on the voting membership of the council.[54] Persons shall be nominated for membership in a manner determined by the conference in accordance with ¶ 610.5. It is recommended that churches of less than two hundred members be represented on the conference council on finance and administration. The term of office shall begin with the adjournment of the annual conference session at which they are elected and shall be for a period of four years and until their successors are elected.

b) No member or employee of any conference agency and no employee, trustee, or director of any agency or institution participating in the funds of any conference budget shall be eligible for voting membership on the council.[55] Any vacancy shall be filled by action of the council until the next conference session, at which time the annual conference shall fill the vacancy.

c) The following shall be ex officio members of the council in addition to the number set by the annual conference under ¶ 612.2*a*: (1) the conference treasurer/director of administrative services, without vote; (2) any members of the General Council on Finance and Administration who reside within the bounds of the conference, with vote unless voting membership is in conflict with another provision of the *Book of Discipline*, in which case their membership shall be without vote; in either case, they shall not be eligible to serve on an agency receiving funding; (3) the presiding bishop, without vote; (4) a district superintendent chosen by the cabinet, without vote; and (5) the director of connectional ministries or equivalent, or another representative of the conference council on ministries, without vote.

d) The executive director of the conference or area United Methodist foundation may be included in the membership, without vote.

3. *Officers*—The council shall elect from its voting membership a president, a vice president, a secretary, and such other officers as it may deem necessary. Consideration shall be given to inclusiveness (¶¶ 124, 140). The conference treasurer/director of

---

54. See Judicial Council Decision 441.
55. See Judicial Council Decisions 10, 493.

administrative services (¶ 619) shall be the treasurer of the council. The treasurer/director of administrative services shall not be eligible for voting membership on the council and shall not be eligible for election to any of those offices that are to be filled by voting members of the council.

4. No member of the council shall vote on or take part in deliberations on significant matters directly or indirectly affecting her or his business, income, or employment, or the business, income, or employment of his or her immediate family.

5. *Organization—a)* Whether the conference chooses to organize the council as provided in ¶ 612 or to assign its functions to another structure as authorized in ¶ 611, the restrictions set forth in ¶ 612.2*b*, .4 shall apply to the members of any conference structure that has responsibility for the following functions:

(1) Preparing annual conference budgets or other funding recommendations.

(2) Nominating the annual conference treasurer/ director of administrative services or other officer having the functions described in ¶ 619.

(3) Having authority and supervision over the work of the conference treasurer/director of administrative services.

(4) Having fiscal oversight responsibilities, such as are described in ¶¶ 613.5 through 613.11, and 616-618, for annual conference funds.

b) The council may establish committees and task forces and define their duties and authority as it deems necessary for fulfilling its purpose and responsibilities.

c) The annual conference may enact bylaws governing meetings, quorum, and other matters of procedure for the council, or it may authorize the council to enact such bylaws; in any event, such bylaws shall not be in conflict with the *Book of Discipline*.

d) If deemed necessary for the fulfillment of its functions and if so authorized by the annual conference, the council may be incorporated.

6. *Amenability*—The council shall be amenable and report directly to the annual conference.[56]

7. *Relationships—a)* The council and the annual conference council on ministries shall cooperate in the development of the conference benevolences budget (¶ 614.3).

---

56. See Judicial Council Decisions 551, 560.

b) In the interest of developing and implementing coordinated annual conference policies in the areas of fiscal management and administrative services, the council shall serve in a liaison role among conference agencies with responsibilities in these areas. It shall be authorized to convene representatives of annual conference administrative and clergy support agencies for the purpose of consulting on matters of mutual concern, such as the coordination of fiscal management, fundraising activities, and administrative services in the annual conference.

¶ **613.** *Responsibilities*—The council shall have authority and responsibility to perform the following functions:

1. To recommend to the annual conference for its action and determination budgets of anticipated income and proposed expenditures for all funds that provide for annual conference clergy support, annual conference administrative expenses, and annual conference benevolence and program causes (¶ 614).[57]

2. To receive, consider, report, and make recommendations to the annual conference regarding the following prior to final decision by the annual conference: *(a)* any proposal to raise capital funds for any purpose; *(b)* funding considerations related to any proposal that may come before the conference; *(c)* any requests to conduct a special conference-wide financial appeal, whether by special collections, campaigns, or otherwise in the local churches of the conference.

3. To recommend to the annual conference for its action and decision the methods or formulas by which apportionments to churches, charges, or districts for duly authorized General, jurisdictional, conference, and district funds shall be determined (¶ 615.4).[58]

4. To consult and cooperate with the commission on communication in providing district superintendents, pastors, and appropriate officers of the local churches and charge conferences with interpretive aids or other materials to assist in gaining understanding and support of the conference budget and other approved conference causes. This shall include the theology and discipline of financial giving.

5. To develop policies governing the investment of conference funds (except for pension funds as provided in ¶ 1508), whether in debt or equity, short-term or long-term instruments, with the aim

57. See Judicial Council Decisions 521, 551, 560, 590, 744.
58. See Judicial Council Decision 983.

of maximizing funds available for mission in a manner consistent with the preservation of capital, the Policies Relative to Socially Responsible Investments (¶ 717), and the Social Principles of the Church. A statement of such policies shall be printed in the conference journal at least once in each quadrennium.

6. To recommend to the annual conference procedures for funding local churches, including the theology of financial giving.

7. To advise local churches about making their church buildings, facilities, and programs accessible.

8. To recommend to the annual conference for its action procedures for dealing responsibly with situations in which budgeted funds, as approved by the annual conference, are inadequate to meet emerging missional needs or unforeseen circumstances.

9. To review at least quarterly and to account to the annual conference for the disbursement of funds in accordance with budgets approved by the conference.

10. To recommend to the annual conference for its action and determination the conditions under which it may borrow funds for current expense purposes and the maximum amount of such borrowing.

11. To have authority and supervision over the conference treasurer/director of administrative services subject to ¶ 619; to establish policies governing the treasurer/director's work.

12. To work in cooperation with other annual conference agencies for the design and implementation of a plan by which the annual conference may designate the conference treasury as a central treasury for funds designated for any or all conference agencies participating in conference funds.

13. To establish uniform and equitable policies and practices in the employment and compensation of personnel, in consultation and cooperation with other conference agencies that employ staff, unless the annual conference has designated another agency to carry this responsibility. These policies and practices shall be in accordance with the Social Principles (¶ 162*A, E, F,* and *I*). In addition, the council shall recommend that the annual conference provide, effective on and after January 1, 2006, 100 percent vested pension benefits of at least three percent of compensation for lay personnel of the annual conference who work at least 1,040 hours per year, are at least 21 years of age, and have at least one year of permanent service. The annual conference shall have authority to provide such pension benefits through either a denominational

pension program administered by the General Board of Pension and Health Benefits or another pension program administered by another pension provider.

14. To cooperate with the General Council on Finance and Administration and with the General Board of Discipleship in promoting and standardizing the financial recording and reporting system in the local churches of the conference.

15. To cooperate with the General Council on Finance and Administration in order to provide leadership, training, and encouragement in the areas of church business administration for individuals and organizations of The United Methodist Church by: (1) distributing information regarding certification as a church business administrator; and (2) listing in the council's report to the annual conference the names of persons certified as church business administrators by the General Council on Finance and Administration who are employed within the bounds of the annual conference.

16. To make recommendations to the annual conference for its action and determination regarding plans to initiate or cause to be organized a foundation or similar organization for the purpose of securing, conserving, or expending funds for the direct or indirect benefit or support of the annual conference, or of any conference agency, or any of its programs or work. The council shall have opportunity to make its recommendations regarding such plans if the foundation or similar organization is: (1) proposed to be organized by the annual conference itself, whether acting alone or in concert with other annual conferences; (2) proposed to be organized by any conference council, board, commission, committee, or other agency; (3) to make use of the name *United Methodist* in its title or solicitation; or (4) proposed for the purpose of soliciting gifts primarily from the United Methodist constituency.

17. To perform such other administrative and fiscal functions and services as the annual conference may assign.

18. To ensure that no apportioned conference funds are expended for the use of alcoholic beverages.

19. To ensure that no annual conference board, agency, committee, commission, or council shall give United Methodist funds to any gay caucus or group, or otherwise use such funds to promote the acceptance of homosexuality or violate the expressed commitment of The UMC "not to reject or condemn lesbian and gay members and friends" (¶ 161G). The council shall have the

right to stop such expenditures. This restriction shall not limit the Church's ministry in response to the HIV epidemic, nor shall it preclude funding for dialogs or educational events where the Church's official position is fairly and equally represented.[59]

¶ **614.** *Budgets*—The council shall recommend to the annual conference for its action and determination budgets of anticipated income and proposed expenditures for all funds to be apportioned to the churches, charges, or districts.[60]

Prior to each regular session of the annual conference, the council shall make a diligent and detailed study of the needs of all the conference agencies and causes asking to be included in the budget of any conference fund. The chairperson of each conference agency, or other duly authorized representative, shall have opportunity to represent the claims of that agency before the council.

1. *Clergy Support Budgets*—*a)* It shall be the duty of the council, unless otherwise provided, to estimate the total amount necessary to furnish a sufficient and equitable support for the district superintendents of the conference, including base compensation, travel, staff, office, and housing. The council shall report specific recommendations to the annual conference for conference action (¶ 669.4*a*).[61]

b) The council shall report to the annual conference at each session the Episcopal Fund apportionment to the annual conference under the methodology approved by the General Conference and shall include in its recommended clergy support budget the amount determined by the treasurer of the General Council on Finance and Administration as necessary to meet this apportionment.

c) Based on recommendations from the episcopal residence committee (¶ 638.4), the council shall recommend the amount to be raised as the annual conference share of the cost of the bishop's housing.

d) After consultation with the conference board of pensions, the council shall report to the annual conference the amounts computed by that agency as necessary to meet the needs for pensions and benefit programs of the conference. Such amounts need not be derived solely from apportionments.[62]

---

59. See Judicial Council Decision 1054.
60. See Judicial Council Decisions 551, 560, 744, 1054, 1172.
61. See Judicial Council Decisions 590, 591, 1013.
62. See Judicial Council Decision 1132.

e) It shall recommend to the annual conference an amount determined in consultation with the commission on equitable compensation to be used for compliance with the approved schedule of equitable base compensation for pastors (¶ 625.3).

f) It shall recommend to the annual conference estimates of the amounts needed for any other programs of clergy support the conference may adopt, such as a Sustentation Fund (¶ 626) or provision for the moving expenses of pastors.

2. *Administration Budget—a)* The council shall recommend to the annual conference estimates of the amounts needed for administrative expenses of the conference, including its own expenses and those of the conference treasurer's office. It shall consult with the conference agencies and officers to be included in the administrative budget regarding the estimated budgets of their expenses and base its conference administration budget recommendations on information thus received.

b) It shall include in its estimates recommendations regarding the conference's share of an area expense fund, if any, and apportionments for administration properly made by the jurisdictional conference and the General Conference (¶ 811.4).

3. *Conference Benevolences Budget—a)* In preparing the conference benevolences budget, the council, working together with the conference council on ministries or alternative structure as provided in ¶ 614.3*b*, shall make diligent effort to secure full information regarding all conference benevolence and service causes that none may be neglected, jeopardized, or excluded. Basing its judgment of needs upon the information secured, the council shall recommend to the annual conference for its action and determination the total amount to be apportioned for the conference benevolences budget. After receiving the recommendations of the conference council on ministries or alternative structure, the council shall also recommend the amount or the percentage of the total of the conference benevolences budget that shall be allocated to each cause included in the said budget. Such recommendations should reflect agreement with the conference council on ministries or alternative structure on program agency allocations as specified below.[63]

b) The council on finance and administration and the annual conference council on ministries shall work together to

---

63. See Judicial Council Decisions 521, 551, 582.

establish and follow a procedure that shall preserve the following principles:

(1) It is the responsibility of the conference council on finance and administration to establish the total amount to be recommended to the annual conference as the conference benevolences budget and, within that amount, the total sum to be recommended for distribution among the conference program agencies. It is likewise the responsibility of the council to study the budget requests for any agencies or causes to be included in the conference benevolences budget other than the conference program agencies, including the requests of the conference council on ministries, and to give the chairpersons or other authorized representatives of such agencies and causes opportunity to represent their claims before the council.[64]

(2) It is the responsibility of the conference council on ministries to study the budget requests of the conference program agencies and to recommend to the conference council on finance and administration amounts to be allocated from the conference benevolences budget to each such agency, within the total established by the conference council on finance and administration.[65]

(3) It is the responsibility of the conference council on finance and administration to present the conference benevolences budget recommendations to the annual conference. The recommended allocations to conference program agencies should reflect agreement between the council and the conference council on ministries or alternative structure.[66]

c) The term *conference benevolences* shall include those conference allocations and expenditures directly associated with the program, mission, and benevolent causes of annual conference program agencies and institutions. Annual conference program agencies and institutions shall be defined as those agencies with responsibilities parallel to those of the program-related general agencies (¶ 703) and institutions whose work is within the field of responsibility of one or more of those agencies. Administrative expenses that are directly related to the program, mission, and benevolent causes of conference program agencies, including the expenses of the conference council on ministries or alternative structure, may also be included in the conference benevolences

64. See Judicial Council Decisions 521, 551.
65. See Judicial Council Decisions 521, 551.
66. See Judicial Council Decision 551.

budget. The term *conference benevolences* shall not include allocations and expenditures for other conference agencies and officers whose work is primarily administrative. It shall likewise not include annual conference clergy support funds as set forth in ¶¶ 620-628, allocations and expenditures of conference agencies responsible for administering clergy support funds, or apportionments made to the annual conference by the General or jurisdictional conferences.

d) The council, on receiving from the treasurer of the General Council on Finance and Administration a statement of the amount apportioned that annual conference for World Service, may recommend that the conference combine the total World Service apportionment, without reduction for the quadrennium, and the approved conference benevolences budget (¶ 614.3*a*). If combined the sum of these two amounts shall be known as World Service and Conference Benevolences, and the combined budget thus established shall include a statement of the percentage for World Service and the percentage for conference benevolences.[67] (See also ¶ 619.1*a*(2).)

4. *Other Apportioned Causes*—The council shall include in its budget recommendations specific amounts recommended for all other funds properly apportioned to the annual conference for the support of duly authorized general or other connectional funds. The budget recommendations shall likewise include any other amounts to be apportioned to the districts, charges, or churches by the annual conference for conference or district causes of any kind.

5. *Special Appeals*—*a)* No annual conference agency or interest, including any related agency or institution such as a school, college, university, hospital, home, housing project, or other service institution, shall make a special conference-wide appeal to the local churches for funds without the approval of the annual conference upon recommendation of the council, except in case of an extreme emergency, when such approval may be given by a two-thirds vote of the district superintendents and of the council, acting jointly. Neither shall special conference-wide appeals to local churches for funds be made by such boards, interests, agencies, or institutions that are not related to the annual conference in which the appeal is to be made, unless approval for such an appeal is granted by the annual conference upon recommendation of the

---

67. See Judicial Council Decisions 348, 1135, 1146, 1172.

council. The annual conference approvals specified in this paragraph shall not be required for special church-wide financial appeals that have been approved under the provisions of ¶ 819, for solicitations that have been approved under the provisions of ¶ 812.3, or for any other general fund promotion or appeal authorized by the General Conference or approved and conducted under other provisions of the *Book of Discipline*.

b) When application is made to the council for the privilege of a special conference-wide financial appeal, whether by special collections, campaigns, or otherwise, the council shall investigate the application and its possible relation to other obligations of the conference and in the light of the facts make recommendations to the conference for its action and determination. If application for privilege of a special appeal is made directly to the conference, the application shall be referred to the council before final action is taken.

c) The council may include in its budget recommendations to the annual conference amounts to be considered as goals for special appeals or other nonapportioned causes.

6. The council shall make its budget recommendations to the annual conference in a format based on guidelines suggested by the General Council on Finance and Administration.

¶ **615.** *Apportionments*—When a change to the apportionment formula or method is proposed, the council should provide for a study of the proposed change's effects. After its study, which may include resources supplied by the General Council on Finance and Administration, the council shall recommend such formula or method to the annual conference for its action and determination which shall include the approved budgeted amounts for clergy support, administration, World Service, Conference Benevolences, and other apportioned causes (¶ 614.1-.4), the sum of which shall be apportioned to the districts, churches, or charges of the conference.[68]

1. The council, on receiving from the General Council on Finance and Administration a statement of the amount or methodology for apportioning to the annual conference for the several general funds as authorized by the General Conference, shall apportion the same to the several districts, charges, or churches by whatever method the conference may direct. The council shall

---

68. See Judicial Council Decisions 983, 1172.

make every effort for the full payment of these apportionments as a part of the Church's shared financial covenant.[69]

2. The council shall recommend to the annual conference for its action and determination whether the apportionments referred to in this paragraph shall be made by the council to the districts only or to the churches or charges of the conference. If the apportionments are made to the districts only, then the distribution to the churches or charges of each district shall be made as provided in ¶ 614.3. The conference may order that the district superintendents make the entire distribution to all the churches or charges of the conference.

3. Should the annual conference make the apportionments to the districts only, the distribution to the churches or charges of each district shall be made by its district board of stewards, composed of the district superintendent as chairperson and the district stewards elected by the several charge conferences (¶ 247.14). In that case, the board, meeting on call of the district superintendent as soon as practicable after the adjournment of the annual conference, shall make the distribution to the churches or charges of the district using such methods as it may determine, unless the annual conference shall have determined the method of distribution to the churches or charges.

4. If the council recommends an apportioned fund that combines two or more general apportioned funds with one another, or that combines one or more general apportioned funds with funds other than a general apportioned fund, the recommendation and consequent annual conference actions shall include: (1) a statement of the amount of each general fund apportionment included in the combined fund, and (2) a statement of the percentage of the combined fund total that corresponds to each general fund apportionment.

5. If an annual conference establishes an apportioned fund that combines funds subject to proportional payment under ¶ 622 with funds not subject to proportional payment, it shall establish procedures to ensure that the proportional payment provisions of ¶ 622 are observed.

6. If an annual conference establishes an apportioned fund that combines support for several distinct causes, it shall make available to local churches information identifying the causes supported by the fund.

---

69. See Judicial Council Decisions 1135, 1146, 1172.

¶ **616.** *Depository*—The council shall be responsible for designating a depository or depositories for conference funds.

¶ **617.** *Auditing*—The council shall have the following authority and responsibility with respect to the auditing of the financial records of the conference and its agencies:

1. To have the accounts of the conference treasurer for the preceding fiscal year audited by a certified public accountant within 150 days after the close of the conference fiscal year and to receive, review, and report such audit to the annual conference.

As a part of the audit, the accountant shall confer with the presiding bishop of the annual conference and the president of the council.

2. To require and review at least annually audited reports, in such detail as it may direct, from all conference agencies and from all agencies, institutions, and organizations receiving any financial support from conference funds or from any authorized conference-wide appeal.

3. To require and review at least annually, in such detail as it may direct, compiled or audited reports of all funds received or administered by districts or district agencies, including funds held or administered by treasurers or officers other than the conference treasurer. Based on its review of such audits, the council may make such recommendations to the annual conference as it deems appropriate.

4. The council may establish an audit review committee to review all of the reports and audits required by ¶ 617.1, .2. If the council chooses to establish such a committee, at least half of its members should be persons who are not members of the council and who are chosen for their expertise in areas related to the work of the committee. Consideration shall be given to inclusiveness (¶¶ 124, 140) in the selection of persons to serve on the committee.

¶ **618.** *Bonding*—The council shall have the following authority and responsibility with respect to the bonding of conference and conference agency officers and staff whose responsibilities include the custody or handling of conference funds or other negotiable assets:

1. The council shall provide for the fidelity bonding of the conference treasurer and other staff under its authority and supervision in amounts it judges to be adequate.

2. In the case of those agencies, institutions, and organizations for which the conference treasurer does not serve as trea-

surer, the council shall have authority to require fidelity bonding of their treasurers in such amounts as it deems adequate and to withhold payment of the allocation of any such agency, institution, or organization until evidence of the required bonding has been submitted.

3. The council may provide, or require any conference agency to provide directors' and officers' liability insurance in amounts it judges to be adequate.

4. The council shall require compliance with the policies established as provided by this paragraph and shall report annually to the annual conference on such compliance.

¶ 619. *Conference Treasurer/Director of Administrative Services*—Each annual conference, on nomination of its council on finance and administration, shall at the first session of the conference after the quadrennial session of the General Conference or jurisdictional conference, or at such other times as a vacancy exists, elect a conference treasurer or conference treasurer/director of administrative services.[70] The treasurer or treasurer/director shall serve for the quadrennium or until a successor shall be elected and qualify. If a vacancy should occur during the quadrennium, the council shall fill the vacancy until the next session of the annual conference. After consultation with the bishop in charge, the council may remove the treasurer or treasurer/director from office for cause and fill the vacancy until the next session of the conference. The treasurer/director shall be directly amenable to the council. The treasurer/director may sit with the council and its committees at all sessions and have the privilege of voice but not vote.

1. As conference treasurer, this officer shall have the following functions:

a) The conference treasurer shall receive and disburse, in accordance with the actions of the annual conference and the provisions of the *Book of Discipline*, remittances from local church treasurers for all duly authorized General, jurisdictional, annual conference, and district causes.[71]

(1) Local church treasurers shall remit monthly to the conference treasurer all amounts contributed in each local church for: *(a)* the World Service Fund and the Conference Benevolences fund, whether apportioned separately or as one combined fund;

---

70. See Judicial Council Decision 185.
71. See Judicial Council Decisions 456, 591.

(b) all other funds authorized by the General Conference and apportioned to the annual conferences by the General Council on Finance and Administration; *(c)* all other jurisdictional, annual conference, and district funds or causes apportioned in accordance with ¶ 615, unless otherwise directed by the annual conference; *(d)* special Sunday offerings (¶ 262); *(e)* special appeals (¶¶ 614.5, 819); *(f)* Advance Special Gifts (¶ 822); *(g)* World Service Special Gifts (¶ 820); *(h)* Youth Service Fund (¶ 1208); and *(i)* all other General, jurisdictional, annual conference, and district funds not otherwise directed.[72]

(2) *The World Service Fund and the Conference Benevolences Fund*—(*a*) If apportioned as one combined fund, the treasurer shall each month divide the total amount received from local churches for World Service and Conference Benevolences, setting aside the proper amount for World Service and the proper amount for conference benevolences, according to the ratio of each established by the annual conference in the total World Service and Conference Benevolences budget (¶ 614.3*c*).[73]

(*b*) Whether apportioned separately or as one combined fund, the treasurer shall, from the share received for conference benevolences, credit monthly the accounts of the several agencies or causes included in the conference benevolences budget or make monthly remittances to the treasurers of such agencies or causes according to the rightful share and proportion of each (¶ 614.3*a*) or according to a payment schedule approved by the conference council on finance and administration, which shall provide that the total allocated to each agency or cause during the year shall be equal to the rightful share and proportion of each.

(*c*) Whether apportioned separately or as one combined fund, the treasurer shall remit each month to the treasurer of the General Council on Finance and Administration the total share received during the month for World Service. When the share so designated for World Service during a year exceeds the amount apportioned to the annual conference, the entire share contributed for World Service shall be remitted in regular order to the treasurer of the General Council on Finance and Administration before the end of the fiscal year.[74]

---

72. See Judicial Council Decision 591.
73. See Judicial Council Decision 332.
74. See Judicial Council Decision 400.

(*d*) If an annual conference establishes an apportioned fund which combines two or more general funds with one another, or which combines one or more general church funds with funds other than general church funds, the conference treasurer shall allocate to the general church funds amounts at least equal to the percentage of receipts set under ¶ 614.3-.5. Amounts so allocated shall be remitted at least monthly to the treasurer of the General Council on Finance and Administration.

(3) The treasurer shall, as far as practicable, remit monthly to the several district superintendents the amount due each of them (¶ 614.1*a*).

(4) The treasurer shall likewise credit or remit each month all funds received and payable for other jurisdictional, annual conference, and district causes in accordance with budgets adopted by the annual conference.

(5) The conference treasurer shall remit each month to the treasurer of the General Council on Finance and Administration the amounts received during the month for the General Administration Fund, the Episcopal Fund, the Interdenominational Cooperation Fund, the Black College Fund, the Ministerial Education Fund, World Service Special Gifts, Advance Special Gifts, general Church special Sunday offerings (¶ 262), special churchwide appeals (¶ 819), and all other general causes not otherwise directed.

b) The conference treasurer may serve as treasurer for any or all agencies served by a conference central treasury (¶ 613.11). The treasurer shall enter the proper credits to each at the end of each month's business. Disbursements from funds allocated to any conference agency shall be made only on proper order from the agency.[75]

c) The treasurer shall prepare at regular intervals such financial statements and reports as may be required for the bishop in charge, the district superintendents, the annual conference, the council, the agencies served by the conference central treasury and its officers, and the treasurer of the General Council on Finance and Administration.

(1) The treasurer shall make each month a full report of all general funds handled to the treasurer of the General Council on Finance and Administration and to the presiding bishop of the conference.

---

75. See Judicial Council Decision 400.

(2) The treasurer shall prepare annually a report of all receipts, disbursements, and balances of all funds under his or her direction, which report shall be printed in the conference journal.

d) The treasurer may be authorized by the council to invest funds in accordance with policies and procedures established by the council (¶ 613.5). A listing of securities held shall be printed annually in the conference journal.

e) The treasurer shall provide counsel and guidance to local church business administrators, treasurers, financial secretaries, and committees on finance in the development of standardized financial recording and reporting systems (¶ 613.13).

f) The treasurer shall perform such other staff services as the council may require in the fulfillment of its functions and responsibilities.

2. As director of administrative services, this officer may have responsibility in one or more of the following areas: office management; payroll and personnel services; the provision of administrative services for annual conference officers and agencies; property management with respect to property owned by the annual conference or any of its agencies; and such other responsibilities of an administrative nature as the council, by mutual agreement with other annual conference officers and agencies, may assign. The director shall be present when the cabinet considers matters relating to conference administration related to the conference treasurer's or conference treasurer/director of administrative services' responsibilities, and other matters as the cabinet and director may determine. The director shall not be present during the cabinet discussions on matters related to the making of appointments.

3. The council shall have authority and supervision over the director and shall, after consultation with those annual conference officers and agencies for whom the director might be expected to perform services, define his or her specific responsibilities and do regular evaluation.

PASTORAL SUPPORT

¶ **620.** Assumption of the obligations of the itineracy, required to be made at the time of admission into the traveling connection, puts upon the Church the counter obligation of providing support for the itinerant ministry of the Church. In view of this, the claim for pastoral support in each pastoral charge shall include provisions for the support of pastors, district superintendents, bishops, and conference claimants.[76]

¶ **621.** *Apportionment Distribution*—Each annual conference shall determine what plan and method shall be used in distributing the apportionments to its several districts and charges for the Episcopal Fund (¶ 818.1), for the support of district superintendents and conference claimants, and for the Equitable Compensation Fund (¶ 625).[77]

¶ **622.** When the apportionments for bishops, district superintendents, conference claimants, and the Equitable Compensation Fund for the several districts and charges have been determined, payments made to the same in each pastoral charge shall be exactly proportional to the amount paid on the clergy base compensation (¶ 818.3). The treasurer or treasurers of each pastoral charge shall accordingly make proportional distribution of the funds raised in that charge for the support of the ordained ministry and shall remit monthly if practicable and quarterly at the latest the items for bishops, district superintendents, conference claimants, and the Equitable Compensation Fund to the proper treasurer or treasurers.[78]

¶ **623.** *Base Compensation*—The several charge conferences shall determine the pastor's base compensation according to the provisions of ¶ 247.13. "Base Compensation" shall be defined in "Guidelines: A Resource for the Conference Commission on Equitable Compensation" prepared by The National Association of Commissions on Equitable Compensation (NACEC) and made available by the General Council on Finance and Administration (GCFA) either in print or on the GCFA website.

¶ **624.** *Payment Obligation*—1. Each church or charge has an obligation to pay the base compensation, the benefits adopted by the annual conference, and other ministerial support (including housing) adopted by the charge conference, to its pastor(s). If it becomes apparent that a church or charge will be unable to so provide the base compensation, support, and benefits adopted by the charge conference, the church or charge SPRC chair, finance chair, or treasurer, shall immediately notify, both in writing and verbally, the pastor, district superintendent, and congregation.

---

76. See Judicial Council Decisions 306, 455, 579.
77. See Judicial Council Decisions 208, 455.
78. See Judicial Council Decisions 320, 401.

This communication shall indicate all avenues explored to meet the base compensation, support, and benefits, including requesting consideration for a short-term emergency subsidy grant from the Equitable Compensation Fund (¶ 625.7). If it becomes necessary to reduce a pastor's compensation, it shall occur at the end of the conference appointment year.

2. In the event the annual conference has no arrearage policy in place, all such claims shall be subject to, and controlled by, the civil laws applicable to such claims in the state in which the claim arises. Any pastor who does not receive a full scheduled payment of the approved compensation shall immediately report such, in writing, to the church or charge SPRC chair, church council chair, and district superintendent. Failure to report in a timely fashion may result in surrender of any/all arrearage claims, subject to the annual conference arrearage policy (¶ 625.2d).

¶ **625.** *Equitable Compensation*—1. There shall be in each annual conference a commission on equitable compensation or other structure to provide for these functions and maintain the connectional relationships. It shall be composed of an equal number of lay and clergypersons, including at least one layperson and one clergyperson from churches of fewer than two hundred members, who are nominated by the conference nominating committee and elected by and amenable to the annual conference. It is recommended that in selection of commission members, consideration shall be given to inclusiveness. In addition, one district superintendent named by the cabinet shall be a member.

2. It is the purpose of the commission on equitable compensation to support full-time clergy serving as pastors in the charges of the annual conference by: *(a)* recommending conference standards for pastoral support; *(b)* administering funds to be used in base compensation supplementation; and *(c)* providing counsel and advisory material on pastoral support to district superintendents and committees on pastor-parish relations; and *(d)* submitting an arrearage policy to be adopted by the annual conference. For pastors receiving equitable compensation, once the base compensation supplementation has been paid by the annual conference, and the minimum base compensation and base compensation supplementation has been received by the pastor, the annual conference shall have no further financial obligation or responsibility to the pastor, the charge or anyone else regarding the pastor's compensation.

3. The commission shall carefully study the needs for additional support within the conference and the sources of income and shall recommend annually to the conference for its action a schedule of minimum base compensation for all full-time pastors or those clergy members of the annual conference appointed less than full-time to a local church, subject to such rules and regulations as the conference may adopt (¶ 338.1, .2).[79]

4. In some instances, for missional reasons, consideration may be given by the conference commission on equitable compensation to make funds available for the deacon in full connection when the primary appointment is to a local church.

5. Consistent with the provisions of this paragraph, the primary responsibility for the payment of pastoral base compensation remains with individual pastoral charges.

6. On recommendation of the commission on equitable compensation, the annual conference may authorize the utilization of the Equitable Compensation Fund to provide for supplementing base compensation beyond the minimum base compensation schedule. Special attention shall be given to ethnic pastors serving ethnic ministries, with particular attention given to Native American pastors serving Native American ministries. In all cases (ethnic or nonethnic), emphasis shall be given to funding entry-level appointments in a teaching parish in a station church, circuit, or cooperative parish and/or equivalent, or to a cooperative parish.

7. In consultation with the Commission on Equitable Compensation, the council on finance and administration shall recommend to the conference its estimate of the amount required to support the schedule of minimum base compensation and base compensation supplements for the pastors, as adopted by the conference. The conference council on finance and administration shall apportion the amount approved by the conference as an item of clergy support to the districts or the charges as the conference may direct (¶ 614.1e).[80]

8. The Equitable Compensation Fund, secured as described above in ¶¶ 614.1e and 625.7, shall be disbursed under the direction of the Commission on Equitable Compensation.

9. The Equitable Compensation Fund, secured as described in ¶¶ 614.1e and 625.7, shall be used to provide each pastor who

---

79. See Judicial Council Decision 579.
80. See Judicial Council Decisions 90, 179, 1013.

receives less than the minimum base compensation with an additional amount sufficient to make the base compensation approved by the pastoral charge plus the supplemental aid or income from other sources equal to the minimum base compensation approved by the conference. An annual conference may set a maximum amount to be used in attaining such minimum base compensation in any given case, and it may set its own policy regarding the number of years for which a pastoral charge is eligible to receive equitable base compensation funds, provided that no member in good standing who is appointed to a pastoral charge is denied the minimum base compensation (¶ 342).[81]

10. In light of our constitutional commitment to Ecumenical Relations (Division One—General, ¶ 6, Article VI), the commission should give consideration in setting standards for clergy support for those ministers who have had their orders recognized for service in The United Methodist Church (¶ 346.2) and whose years of service include ministry exercised in other denominations, especially those coming from the churches of the Pan-Methodist Commission and other member churches of the Churches Uniting In Christ.

11. The commission shall assemble and distribute to the charges and the district superintendents advisory material for use in the process of negotiating the total of each pastoral support package, the schedule of minimum base compensation, and other information relevant to the establishment of more equitable base compensation by all the charges of the conference.

12. The guidelines of the annual conference program of equitable clergy support shall, insofar as possible, be observed by the bishops and district superintendents in arranging charges and making appointments. Each full-time pastor or those clergy members of the annual conference appointed less than full-time under episcopal appointment to a local church are eligible for participation in the annual conference program of equitable base compensation (¶ 342.1, .2).

13. The commission may suggest to the annual conference for its consideration equitable base compensation ranges for the pastors and/or charges, and the annual conference may suggest such equitable base compensation ranges to the charges for their consideration.

---

81. See Judicial Council Decisions 456, 579, 587, 1013.

¶ **626.** *Sustentation Fund*—An annual conference may establish a sustentation fund for the purpose of providing emergency aid to the clergy of the conference who may be in special need. On recommendation of the conference council on finance and administration, the amount needed for this purpose may be apportioned to the pastoral charges as the conference may determine. The fund, if established, shall be administered jointly by the bishop, the appropriate district superintendent, and the chairperson of the commission on equitable compensation or the chairperson of such other agency as the annual conference may determine.

¶ **627.** *Pastors' Expenses and Allowances*—Local churches shall report to the annual conference, in the manner indicated on the annual conference report form, expenditures for the following purposes: (1) amounts reimbursed to pastors for expenses incurred by them in the fulfillment of their professional responsibilities; (2) amounts paid to or for pastors as allowances (including housing allowance) in addition to base compensation. Local churches are encouraged to consider guidelines provided by the annual conference and/or the General Council on Finance and Administration in setting and reporting the amounts of such allowances and reimbursements.

¶ **628.** *Compensation for Extension Ministries*—Every clergy member of an annual conference appointed to extension ministry shall furnish annually to the conference secretary at such time as the secretary shall direct a statement of his or her total compensation (including base compensation, travel, automobile, housing, and other expenses allowed and paid) for the year then ending, and said compensation of all clergy appointed to extension ministry shall be published in the journal of the annual conference.[82] When this information is not furnished, the appointment of the clergyperson shall be subject to review by the resident bishop and the cabinet.

OTHER CONFERENCE AGENCIES

¶ **629.** *Conference Board of Church and Society*—1. The annual conference shall organize a board of church and society or other structure to provide for the functions of this ministry and maintain the connectional relationship between the General Board of Church and Society and the conference, district, and local church,

---

82. See Judicial Council Decisions 345, 465.

as well as for church and society responsibilities related to the objectives and scope of work of the General Board of Church and Society as set forth in ¶¶ 1002-1004.

2. The conference board of church and society or equivalent structure shall be composed of those persons as determined by the annual conference, including, by virtue of their offices, the mission coordinator for social action of the conference United Methodist Women and members of the General Board of Church and Society from the annual conference who shall serve within limits set by ¶¶ 610.6 and 710.6. The conference board of church and society or equivalent structure shall also name a conference Peace with Justice Coordinator who will be responsible for administering the conference Peace with Justice Special Sunday Offering receipts and for coordinating peace and justice ministries. Guidelines for inclusiveness in the membership shall be followed (¶ 610.5).

3. The conference board, in cooperation with the General Board of Church and Society and the annual conference council on ministries, shall develop and promote programs on church and society within the bounds of the conference that include prison ministry and reform concerns. To this end, it may divide its membership into committees of approximately equal size patterned after the organization of the General Board of Church and Society. Committees of the board shall have responsibility to cooperate with one another to advance the respective and mutual concerns of their respective areas in social education, service, witness, and action.

4. The conference board of church and society shall serve to connect the General Board of Church and Society and the district and local churches in relating the gospel of Jesus Christ to the members of the Church and to the persons and structures of the communities, nation, and world in which they live. Program shall be developed that provides education and action on issues confronting the Church consistent with the Social Principles and the policies adopted by the General Conference.

5. The board shall estimate annually the amount necessary for support of its work and shall report this amount according to the procedure of the annual conference. The work of the board may be considered a benevolence interest of the Church within the conference.

6. The annual conference may employ a person or persons to further its purposes. Two or more annual conferences may coop-

erate in developing their programs and in employing one or more persons.

¶ **630.** *Conference Board of Discipleship*—The annual conference shall organize a board of discipleship or other *equivalent* structure to provide for these functions and maintain the connectional relationship between the General Board of Discipleship and the conference, district, and local church, and to provide for discipleship functions related to the objectives and scope of work of the General Board of Discipleship as set forth in ¶¶ 1101, 1102. The person or persons serving as member(s) of the General Board of Discipleship shall be member(s) of the conference board of discipleship and may be granted voting privileges.

1. *General Responsibilities—a)* To lead and assist the congregations and districts in the conference in their efforts to communicate and celebrate the redeeming and reconciling love of God as revealed in Jesus Christ to persons of every age, ethnic background, and social condition; to invite persons to commit their lives to Christ and to his church; and to enable persons to live as Christian disciples in the world.

b) To foster and promote a holistic approach to the development of Christian disciples. This shall include such ministries as Christian education and other small-group ministries; camping, retreat, and outdoor activities; evangelism; stewardship; worship; lay development; Christian spiritual formation and devotional life; age-level, life-span, and family-life ministries; leadership education; and such other areas of work as the annual conference may determine.

c) To foster and promote camping experiences for persons with disabilities, including camps specifically designed for persons with disabilities, and the participation of persons with disabilities, when feasible, in camps sponsored by the district and conference.

d) To provide training for clergy and laity in ministries with persons with disabilities, including the areas of the Sunday school, camps and retreats, and faith development.

e) To provide guidance and training for related district leaders and agencies and for local church councils, officers, and committees.

f) To develop a unified and comprehensive program for leadership training to serve all age groups in the home, church, and community.

    g) To provide continued training for pastors in effective ministry with children, child and faith development of children, and interpretation of curriculum resources.

    h) To enable and strengthen the ministry with and to youth at all levels of the Church.

    i) To determine the necessary directors, coordinators, or designated leaders for discipleship responsibilities at the annual conference level, including the maintenance of linkage with the General Board of Discipleship and related district committees within the annual conference.

    2. *Responsibilities in the Area of Christian Education—a)* To develop and promote a conference program of Christian education for the whole life span, to lead, assist, and support congregations and districts in developing systems for educational and small-group ministries that give children, youth, young adults, adults, older adults, and families knowledge of and experience in the Christian faith and the spiritual disciplines as motivation for Christian service in the Church, the community, and the world. This may include guidance and training for district leaders responsible for Christian education and for local church ministry areas and commissions on education, superintendents of the church school, church school division superintendents, church school teachers, and other leaders in the educational ministry of local churches.

    b) To develop and maintain an organized system for communicating and working with persons responsible for Christian education programs in local churches, districts, jurisdictions, and the General Board of Discipleship.

    c) To provide training for confirmation leaders and to equip local congregations in confirmation experiences and in the use of approved resources.

    d) To encourage the observance of the first Sunday of Christian Education Week, or some other day designated by the annual conference, in each local church as Christian Education Sunday for the purpose of emphasizing the importance of Christian education and for receiving an offering for the work of Christian education. (See ¶ 265.1.)

    e) To develop and recommend to the annual conference plans for the acquisition or disposition of conference camps and/or retreat properties in accordance with standards of camping developed by the General Board of Discipleship (¶ 1109.10).

f) To promote church school extension by: (1) encouraging the development of new United Methodist church schools; (2) starting new classes; (3) expanding teaching and learning opportunities in the congregation and community.

g) To assist local congregations in initiating programs of teacher recruitment, development, training, and retraining in biblical, theological, and ethical thinking as well as in the procedures and methods of Christian education.

h) To cooperate in the promotion of knowledge about the support for all schools, colleges, universities, and seminaries related to the conference, the United Methodist Student Movement, and the campus ministry of the conference, region, or area through the establishment and support of such programs as may be approved by the annual conference in harmony with the policies and procedures of the General Board of Higher Education and Ministry.

3. *Responsibilities in the Area of Evangelism—a)* To plan and promote an effective, comprehensive ministry of evangelism for people of all ages.

b) To create an understanding of, interest in, and commitment to evangelism throughout the conference.

c) To provide for the training of clergy and laypersons in leadership in ministries of evangelism, the distribution of promotional literature, the encouragement and enlistment of local church participation in an ongoing ministry of evangelism, and the support of church revitalization and new church development.

d) To give guidance to the groups responsible for the work of evangelism in the districts and to the ministry area of evangelism in the local church.

e) To give particular emphasis to the promotion of ministries of evangelism, which may include ministries in jails and prisons with offenders, victims, and their families, in order that all persons living in a community where there is a local United Methodist church, and who are without a church affiliation or who make no profession of faith, will be included within the nurturing and caring responsibility of that local church.

f) To recommend annually, in consultation with the Board of Ordained Ministry, to the conference and to the bishop in charge the appointment of certain effective members of the conference as general evangelists, provided that such persons shall meet the standards set for general evangelists by the General Board of

Discipleship. This person shall serve as an ex officio member of the conference board of discipleship area of evangelism. In the event that there is more than one general evangelist in said annual conference, at least one shall be selected by the conference committee on nominations.

g) To recommend and endorse the ministry of said general evangelist to the pastors and leadership of the annual conference.

4. *Responsibilities in the Area of Worship—a)* To be responsible for the concerns of worship for people of all ages within the annual conference.

b) To foster the use of the best resources for worship at conference meetings and in all the churches of the conference, promote the use of *The United Methodist Hymnal* (1989) and *The United Methodist Book of Worship* (1992) in all the churches of the conference. To plan and promote seminars and demonstrations on cooperative planning for worship involving pastors and musicians, forms of worship, and the use of music and other arts, with particular emphasis on congregational singing. This includes cooperating with the resident bishop, who has primary responsibility for planning all worship services at each annual conference.

c) To provide exhibits at the conference sessions, cooperate with the General Board of Discipleship, the conference council on ministries, the conference chapter of The Fellowship of United Methodists in Music and Worship Arts, and the Order of St. Luke in promoting seminars and training events in the area of worship, including music and other arts.

d) To assist local congregations in discovering and recruiting persons to serve as musicians (instrumentalists, singers, and song leaders) and in developing the skills of those serving in local congregations in cooperation with the General Board of Discipleship. This focus shall include persons who work full-time, part-time, and especially as volunteers in church music.

5. *Responsibilities in the Area of Stewardship—a)* To plan and promote a comprehensive program of stewardship for people of all ages throughout the conference in such areas as stewardship education, proportionate giving and tithing, funding the Church's ministries, planned giving, time and abilities, economics and money management, and lifestyle.

b) To interpret the biblical and theological basis for stewardship.

c) To promote giving consistent with a Christian lifestyle.

d) To develop funding concepts within annual conference, district, and local church consistent with sound stewardship principles and the doctrine of The United Methodist Church.

e) To educate the local church that tithing is the minimum goal of giving in The United Methodist Church.

f) To design and schedule training events, distribute promotional material, and enlist local church participation in a year-round program of stewardship.

g) To give guidance to the ministry area of stewardship in the districts and to the ministry area of stewardship and the committee on finance in the local church.

h) To develop a program that will create concern on the part of every local church for the ecological and environmental problems that confront the world and to motivate them to accept responsibility for aiding in the solution of such problems.

i) To participate in the work of national and jurisdictional organizations related to stewardship, such as the National Association of Stewardship Leaders and the National Association of United Methodist Foundations.

6. *Responsibilities in the Area of Spiritual Formation*—It is recommended that a separate committee be established to carry out the following responsibilities:

a) To promote spiritual formation and the development of the devotional life for families and people of all ages, *clergy and laity,* throughout the conference.

b) To conduct seminars and training events in the areas of private and corporate prayer.

c) To encourage and assist with the distribution and use of resources for spiritual formation as provided by The Upper Room and the General Board of Discipleship.

d) To encourage every local church to have a prayer coordinator to promote prayer and mobilize the local church to pray.

e) To encourage every local church to have a prayer room or designated place for prayer and prayer resources.

f) To encourage intentional prayer for pastoral leadership of the local church.

¶ 631. *Conference Board of Laity*—1. There shall be in every annual conference a conference board of laity or other equivalent structure to provide for these functions and maintain connectional relationship.[83] It shall provide for the ministry of the laity

---

83. See Judicial Council Decision 835.

related to the objectives of the General Board of Discipleship as set forth in ¶¶ 1101-1126.

2. The purpose of the conference board of laity shall be:

a) To foster an awareness of the role of the laity both within the local congregation and through their ministries in the home, workplace, community, and world in achieving the mission of the Church; to develop and promote programs to cultivate an adequate understanding of the theological and biblical basis for lay life and work among the members of the churches of the annual conference.

b) To develop and promote stewardship of time, talent, and possessions within the annual conference in cooperation with the conference council on ministries or other appropriate conference bodies.

c) To provide for the training of lay members of annual conference.

d) To provide support and direction for the ministry of the laity on the local, district, and annual conference levels and to promote the observance of Laity Sunday.

e) To provide organization, direction, and support for the development of local church leaders.

3. The following membership of the board is recommended: the conference lay leader, associate conference lay leaders, the conference director of Lay Speaking Ministries, the conference scouting coordinator, and the presidents and two representatives elected by each of the conference organizations of United Methodist Men, United Methodist Women, United Methodist Young Adults, and the conference council on youth ministries; and in addition, the district lay leaders, two laymen, two laywomen, and two youth elected by the annual conference upon nomination of the conference nominating committee, a district superintendent designated by the cabinet, the director of the conference council on ministries, and the presiding bishop. Special attention shall be given to the inclusion of people with disabilities and racial and ethnic persons. All members shall be professing members of local churches.

4. The conference lay leader shall chair the board. Other officers shall be elected as the board shall deem necessary.

5. The board shall relate to Lay Servant Ministries and other organized lay groups in the conference, such as United Methodist Men, United Methodist Women, United Methodist Young Adults,

and United Methodist Youth and shall support their work and help them coordinate the activities of the organized laity of the conference.

6. *Conference Committee on Lay Servant Ministries—a)* Every annual conference is encouraged to create a conference committee on Lay Servant Ministries or other equivalent structure to fulfill the requirements of ¶¶ 266-268 and to relate to the conference board of laity and the General Board of Discipleship as per ¶ 1116 and others that might apply.

b) The purpose of a conference committee on Lay Servant Ministries is to set criteria and guidelines for district committees on Lay Servant Ministries, to develop lay servant courses and approve courses developed by district committees, and to organize conference-wide lay servant events.

c) A conference committee on Lay Servant Ministries will consist, at a minimum, of the district directors of Lay Servant Ministries or their equivalent.

d) There will be a conference director of Lay Speaking Ministries. This position will be filled in a manner to be determined by the annual conference. This position shall be filled by a certified lay servant. The conference director will chair the committee. Other officers will be elected by the committee as the committee deems necessary.

7. *Responsibilities in the Area of Ministry of the Laity—a)* To develop and promote programs to cultivate an adequate understanding of the theological and biblical basis for ministry of the laity among the members of the churches of the annual conference; to give special emphasis to programs and services that will enable laity of all ages to serve more effectively as leaders in both church and community.

b) To provide support and direction for such lay programs as Lay Servant Ministries, the observance of Laity Day, and the work of lay leaders on the local and district levels.

c) To give support and direction to the conference and district program for local church leadership development, coordinating and developing training experiences that will enable persons of all ages to serve more effectively as members of local church councils on ministries, church councils, and the committees, commissions, and task forces related to these groups.

d) To organize a conference committee on Lay Servant Ministries that will fulfill the requirements of ¶¶ 266-268 on behalf of the conference. This committee shall set guidelines and criteria to be used by district committees (see ¶ 669).

¶ **632.** *Conference Committee on Ethnic Local Church Concerns*—1. There shall be in every annual conference a conference committee on ethnic local church concerns or other structure to provide for these basic functions and to maintain connectional relationship.

2. It shall provide for these functions:

a) Keeping the vision of ethnic local church concerns before the annual conference;

b) Providing guidance and resources to churches in the annual conference as they minister with and to ethnic constituencies;

c) Coordinating annual conference strategies related to ethnic local church concerns including general church emphases and initiatives;

d) Providing a forum for dialogue among the ethnic constituencies, as well as with annual conference agencies;

e) Providing training for annual conference and congregational leaders;

f) Promoting and interpreting ethnic local church concerns to the annual conference; and

g) Working with annual conferences to identify and nurture leaders, lay and clergy, of ethnic communities.

3. The membership of this committee shall be nominated and elected by established procedures of the annual conference. The annual conference shall determine the number and composition of the membership of the committee. It is recommended that the committee be constituted so that the majority of the membership be representative of racial and ethnic people, reflecting the racial and ethnic constituencies and local churches of the annual conference (¶ 705.3). Care should be taken, where feasible, to ensure balance of membership with clergy and laity, men and women, youth and young adults.

¶ **633.** *Conference Board of Global Ministries*—1. The annual conference shall organize a board of global ministries or other structure to maintain the connectional relationship and provide for global ministries responsibilities related to the objectives and scope of work of the General Board of Global Ministries as set forth in ¶¶ 1302-1303.

2. The conference board of global ministries or equivalent structure shall be composed of those persons as determined by the annual conference and shall fulfill those responsibilities as assigned. The mission coordinator of education and interpretation of the conference United Methodist Women, by virtue of office, shall be a member of the conference board of global ministries.

The chairperson of the conference board of global ministries shall work with the conference secretary of global ministries to relate the annual conference board of global ministries to the objectives and scope of work of the General Board of Global Ministries. A person or persons serving as member(s) of the General Board of Global Ministries from the annual conference shall, by virtue of their office, be member(s) of the conference board of global ministries (see ¶¶ 610.6 and 710.6).

3. There shall be a conference secretary of global ministries who shall be a member of the annual conference board and may be a member of the annual conference council on ministries or equivalent structure.

The conference secretary of global ministries shall work with the chairperson of the conference board of global ministries to relate the annual conference board of global ministries to the objectives and scope of work of the General Board of Global Ministries.

4. *a)* The annual conference and the General Board of Global Ministries shall cooperate in carrying out the policies and promoting all phases of the work as related to the scope of the board as set forth in ¶ 1302.

b) Responsibilities—(1) To designate the necessary committees, sections, or commissions and individual secretaries, coordinators, or other leaders for global ministries responsibilities at the annual conference level.

(2) To interpret to the annual conference the programs, plans, and policies of the General Board of Global Ministries and to plan and promote emphases on global ministries. To undergird with education, constructive evaluation, communication, and cultivation the total program of the General Board of Global Ministries.

(3) To receive reports of the liaison to the annual conference from the General Board of Global Ministries.

(4) To interpret to the General Board of Global Ministries the mission program, priorities, and concerns of the annual

conference and the local churches to enable the board to fulfill its responsibilities as an extension of the local church.

(5) To plan and promote various kinds of meetings and experiences throughout the conference for the purpose of developing a spirit of mission and participation in global ministries for training, education, and leadership development of mission leaders and persons in the field of human services and health and welfare ministries.

(6) To cooperate with the General Board of Global Ministries in its program outside the United States.

(7) To identify with all who are alienated and dispossessed and to assist them in achieving their full human development—body, mind, and spirit—including encouraging and implementing affirmative action programs.

(8) To engage in direct ministries to human need, both emergency and continuing institutional and noninstitutional, however caused.

(9) To cooperate with the conference organization of United Methodist Women in helping to equip all women for full participation in the mission of the Church.

(10) To cultivate, through the channels of the Church other than United Methodist Women, the Advance Special Gifts for ministries administered by designated units of the General Board of Global Ministries, including United Methodist Committee on Relief (UMCOR).

(11) To promote the development of covenant relationships between local churches and General Board of Global Ministries personnel.

(12) To encourage, maintain, and strengthen the relationships between the annual conference and agencies related to the appropriate divisions and departments of the General Board of Global Ministries and provide a channel through which these agencies shall report to the annual conference.

(13) To develop and implement Church financial support of conference mission projects and programs, and health and welfare ministries, with particular emphasis on benevolent care and Golden Cross, education and social service ministries, and World Communion Scholarships.

(14) To enable, encourage, and support the development of congregations, cooperative parishes, community centers, education and human services, and health and welfare ministries

so that they may be units of mission in urban and rural areas and partners with others in the worldwide mission of the Christian church.

(15) To encourage and support specialized urban and town and country ministries enabling comprehensive mission related to broad metropolitan and rural issues, services ministering to the needs of persons, and supportive programs strengthening the local church.

(16) To assist districts and local churches in exploring and developing new methods and direct service ministries as changing conditions and societal forms demand.

(17) To cooperate with Church and secular leaders at all levels in strategic planning, developing programs, and advocating legislation that impacts community and national issues.

(18) To envision and engage in imaginative new forms of mission appropriate to changing needs and to share the results of experimentation.

(19) To develop strategies in response to critical community issues, with special attention to the needs of ethnic and language groups, people with disabilities, people in transitional relationships, the working poor, and those living under repressive systems

(20) To support United Methodist Committee on Relief's refugee ministry by promoting an annual conference refugee committee that relates to the annual conference board of global ministries and encourages, advises, and assists churches with their refugee programs.

(21) To support the United Methodist Committee on Relief's World Hunger/Poverty Ministry by encouraging annual conferences to appoint an annual conference hunger coordinator and form an annual conference hunger committee that relates to the annual conference board of global ministries.

(22) To appoint annual conference disaster response coordinators to assist the United Methodist Committee on Relief by encouraging the formation of an annual conference disaster response committee that relates to the annual conference board of global ministries and includes, when possible, members of the General Board of Global Ministries from the annual conference. The membership of the Disaster Response Committee may include district disaster response coordinators and the conference director of communications or member of the commission on communica-

tions. Annual conference and district disaster response coordinators shall receive training at least once a quadrennium.

(23) To assist the program of Church and Community Ministry in setting goals, developing programs, providing funding, and evaluating the ministries.

(24) To cooperate with the General Board of Global Ministries in the recruitment and support of missionaries and to cooperate with the appropriate conference units such as a Conference Committee on Mission Personnel or an equivalent body in the promotion and recruitment of persons for health and welfare service careers and other Church-related occupations.

(25) To review and certify applications to the General Board of Global Ministries for loans, donations, and grants; to administer such funds for their designated purposes in accordance with the established guidelines; and to participate with the General Board of Global Ministries in planning and evaluation processes related to these funds.

(26) To cultivate gifts for those special Sunday offerings that are administered through the General Board of Global Ministries.

(27) To strive to ensure mutual representation between the annual conference unit responsible for health and welfare ministries and each health and welfare institution related to the annual conference where such representation is called for by mutual agreement of the institution and the annual conference.

(28) To encourage the health and welfare institutions and programs within the annual conference related to a connectional unit of The United Methodist Church to utilize the programmatic standards, self-study, and peer review appropriate to Church-related institutions and programs and available to them through organizations that will promote excellence in Christian ministry and mission and enhance the quality of services offered.

(29) To assist the annual conference in assessing needs in health and welfare ministries. To assist the annual conference in development of health and welfare services in local communities and within the annual conference.

(30) To work with the General Board of Global Ministries in leadership development programs and the promotion of health and welfare ministries, and to work with the United Methodist Association of Health and Welfare Ministries in leadership

development programs and the promotion of health and welfare ministries.

(31) To promote Christian, financial, and professional standards in health and welfare ministries within the annual conference.

(32) To aid in planning and developing a religious ministry in annual conference-related institutions and programs and, wherever practical, in state and other institutions and programs not related to the conference where there is a need.

(33) To serve in an advisory capacity to the conference nominating processes where the annual conference participates in the selection of trustees for health and welfare institutions and programs related to the annual conference.

(34) To provide a channel through which health and welfare programs and institutions report to the annual conference.

(35) To promote an annual Golden Cross offering or other means of giving to be received in every local church on a day or days designated by the annual conference in support of the health and welfare ministries within the annual conference. This offering shall provide financial support to care for sick persons, older persons, children and youth, and people with disabilities. Special emphasis shall be given to aiding those ministries that provide direct financial assistance to persons in need. Promotion also should include all units of the General Board of Global Ministries related to health and welfare ministries.

(36) To make available program and other resources to local churches to help ensure physical accessibility of church buildings.

5. The annual conference shall establish a committee on parish and community development or assign this responsibility to an existing agency in the annual conference that will fulfill the responsibilities related to the objectives and scope of the General Board of Global Ministries (¶ 1313). The committee shall initiate and develop programs with institutional and voluntary ministries related to the work of the board. The committee may form subcommittees for these areas. The committee shall be accountable to the conference board of global ministries, or to such other agency as the conference may determine. The chairperson of the committee and the chairpersons of the subcommittees shall be members of the conference board of global ministries or such body to which the committee shall be amenable.

a) The committee shall include persons involved in significant types of parish and community ministries, lay and clergy representatives of rural, town, and urban small-membership churches, the area or conference superintendent or director of parish development, representatives of related church agencies and groups, and at-large community representatives.

b) The general responsibilities of the committee shall include research, evaluation, planning and strategy development, policy formulation, program implementation, local and national liaison (denominational and ecumenical) related to parish and community development, and such other functions as the conference or agency to which the committee is accountable may determine.

c) Responsibilities of the subcommittee on institutional and voluntary ministries related to the General Board of Global Ministries may include developing a relationship to all such institutional and voluntary ministries within the annual conference; consulting with them in cooperative planning and strategy for the implementation of national mission concerns relative to needs in the area of social welfare as implemented through the ministries of community centers, residences, health-care agencies, schools, and other educational agencies; and working with funding sources to provide the support needed for effective service in such agencies.

d) In annual conferences where church and community workers are assigned through the General Board of Global Ministries, responsibilities of the subcommittee on church and community ministry shall include reviewing and evaluating projects; serving as liaison between projects and the General Board of Global Ministries; and securing consultative and financial support for workers.

e) Responsibilities of the subcommittee on congregational development shall include encouraging and supporting the development of new and established congregations; conducting research studies and community surveys that plan for and assist with developing innovative strategies for mission; and reviewing, evaluating, and making recommendations for loans, donations, and grants from the General Board of Global Ministries. The subcommittee also shall encourage greater use of such pastoral ministry models as tentmaking/bi-vocational ministries, part-time local pastors, and cooperative ministries by advocating for the removal of impediments to their use and emphasizing the pastors' proven ability to produce effective nurture, outreach, and witness ministries as the primary criterion for appointment.

f) Responsibilities of the subcommittee on town and country ministries shall include mission development and ministry in town and country areas with a population of less than 50,000. These shall include incorporated areas of 10,000 to 50,000; towns, villages, and incorporated areas with 10,000 or fewer; and rural areas with population density of 200 or fewer persons per square mile, fulfilling the functions outlined in ¶ 633.5*h.*

g) Responsibilities of the subcommittee on urban ministries shall include long-range mission strategy development and ministry for metropolitan communities with a population of more than 50,000, fulfilling the functions outlined in ¶ 633.5*h.*

h) Responsibilities of the subcommittees on town and country ministries and urban ministries shall include the following:

(1) consulting with the bishop, cabinet, area or conference superintendent/director of parish development, district representatives of town and country ministries and urban ministries, and the conference agencies in the development of policies for cooperative parish ministries, securing of funding for staff, and in initiating and strengthening these ministries;

(2) developing a comprehensive related missional strategy for the mission of the annual conference, the districts, and the local churches and reporting this plan to the annual conference for consideration, with the understanding that the plan may relate to a regional mission organization for purposes of larger geographical coordination; and

(3) initiating and/or assisting with programs to deal with needs such as:

(*a*) local church and community outreach organization and development;

(*b*) ministries with specialized constituencies and sectors of community life, agricultural and industrial production, and other issue-oriented ministries;

(*c*) the development and strengthening of regional and/or national networks and/or associations;

(*d*) ethnic and language groups;

(*e*) churches in transitional communities;

(*f*) small membership churches;

(*g*) the impact of oppressive systems on town and country and urban people and their communities; and

(h) to fulfill other functions as related to the objectives and scope of work of the General Board of Global Ministries as set forth in ¶ 1314.

i) Responsibilities of the subcommittee on the small membership church shall include the following: (1) being informed about needs and opportunities of the small membership church in rural, town, and urban settings in the total life of the conference; (2) calling for representation by small membership churches in the decision-making structures of the annual conference; (3) informing and sensitizing leadership at all levels of the conference on issues that affect small membership churches; (4) enlisting the support of the bishop, cabinet, council on ministries, and conference staff on policies, plans, and practices that affect small membership churches; (5) working with the subcommittees on town and country ministries and urban ministries within the parish and with the community development committee to develop and implement strategies for the nurturing, outreach, and witness ministries of small membership churches.

j) In metropolitan areas with a population of more than 50,000, consideration shall be given to the establishment of a metropolitan commission whose purpose shall be to promote long-range planning and to provide a coordinating framework for United Methodism's mission strategy for that metropolitan area. The membership may include the bishop or bishop's representative, the district superintendents involved, a selected group of clergy and laypersons representing the annual conference board of global ministries and the annual conference committee on urban ministry, the conference commission on religion and race, the annual conference United Methodist Women and United Methodist Men, representatives from community-based ministries, representatives from district council(s) on ministries, representatives from other boards and agencies deemed appropriate, and groups and individuals who have skills and experience enabling them to fulfill creative planning and strategy functions for United Methodism in the metropolitan area.

When the metropolitan area includes more than one annual conference, representatives shall be elected from each conference's constituent boards and agencies to the metropolitan commission.

6. There may be a volunteer-in-mission coordinator who will coordinate the volunteer-in-mission ministries of the annual

conference in cooperation with the General Board of Global Ministries' mission volunteers office and the jurisdictional volunteer-in-mission office.

    a) The coordinator shall be elected annually and shall be a member of the annual conference board of global ministries.

    b) The coordinator will be responsible to:

        (1) match volunteers with mission opportunities;

        (2) be responsive to volunteers' desire to serve;

        (3) train and mobilize volunteers for mission volunteer service;

        (4) disseminate information on what is happening in the area of short-term volunteer-in-mission programs.

    ¶ **634.** *Conference Board of Higher Education and Campus Ministry*—1. There shall be in each annual conference a board of higher education and campus ministry or other structure to provide for these functions and maintain the connectional relationships. The number of members shall be determined by the annual conference, including representation from appropriate constituencies.[84]

    2. The annual conference board of higher education and campus ministry or equivalent structure shall provide for the connectional relationship between the Division of Higher Education of the General Board of Higher Education and Ministry and the conference, district, and local church and shall provide for a ministry in higher education related to the objectives and scope of work of the General Board of Higher Education and Ministry and the Division of Higher Education. A person serving as a member of the General Board of Higher Education and Ministry from that annual conference shall, by virtue of his or her office, be a member of the conference board of higher education and campus ministry or equivalent structure (see ¶¶ 610.6 and 710.6).

    3. The annual conference chairperson of higher education and campus ministry or equivalent structure shall be a member of the annual conference council on ministries.

    4. The responsibilities of an annual conference board of higher education and campus ministry or equivalent structure include:

    a) General Responsibilities—(1) To interpret and promote the United Methodist ministries in higher education that are supported by the general Church and those specifically related to the annual conference.

---

84. See Judicial Council Decision 1171.

(2) To recommend the policies guiding the annual conference in its program of ministry in higher education.

(3) To train and provide resources for district committees and local church ministry areas of higher education and campus ministry.

(4) To apprise United Methodists of their historic commitment to and present mission in higher education.

(5) To work with the annual conference council on ministries and with districts and local churches to interpret and promote higher education ministries supported by special Sundays and funds: Africa University Fund, Black College Fund; Hispanic, Asian, and Native Americans (HANA) Educational Ministries; Ministerial Education Fund, Native American Ministries Sunday, United Methodist Student Day; World Communion Sunday; and other funds and special days related to higher education ordered by the General Conference or annual conference.

(6) To promote use of the United Methodist Loan Fund and to designate appropriate persons to represent the United Methodist Loan Fund on campuses, such persons normally being Wesley Foundation directors or ecumenical campus ministers supported by the annual conference; to provide the Office of Loans and Scholarships with the names and addresses of those persons; and to apprise students of alternative ways to apply for loans in the event there is no campus minister.

(7) To evaluate schools, colleges, universities, and campus ministries related to the annual conference, with concern for the quality of their performance, the integrity of their mission, and their response to the missional goals of the general Church and the annual conference.

(8) To promote the education award programs provided by The United Methodist Church, including the United Methodist Higher Education Foundation's award programs.

(9) To confer at once with representatives of the General Board of Higher Education and Ministry to determine what resources and aid the board may be able to provide and to enable the Division of Higher Education to carry out its responsibilities in the event that any educational institution, Wesley Foundation, or other campus ministry moves to sever or modify its connection with the Church or violates the rules adopted by the division in accordance with ¶ 1413.3.

(10) To provide that two or more annual conferences may, on recommendation of their boards of higher education and campus ministry or equivalent structures, join in constituting an area or regional committee or commission on higher education and campus ministry, the membership, scope, and functions of which shall be determined by the cooperating conferences in consultation with their bishop or bishops. The area committee or commission shall include a majority of its members from the participating annual conference boards of higher education and campus ministry or equivalent structure with appropriate representation of college presidents, campus ministers, students, and ethnic persons.

b) Fiscal Responsibilities—In addition to its general responsibilities, the annual conference board of higher education and campus ministry shall carry out the following fiscal duties:

(1) To present to the council on ministries and then to the council on finance and administration of the annual conference the financial needs for adequate support of the schools, colleges, universities, theological schools, campus Christian movements, Wesley Foundations,[85] and other campus ministries related to the annual conference for apportionment to the churches within the conference.

(2) To determine the distribution of the funds received from undesignated gifts, returns from special days, annual conference and district Advance Specials for higher education and scholarships of the United Methodist Higher Education Foundation.

(3) To establish, where appropriate, foundations or other means to ensure the ongoing support of the annual conference program of ministry in higher education.

(4) To counsel United Methodist schools, colleges, universities, and campus ministries related to the annual conference with regard to their charters and constitutions, reversionary clauses, and liability.

(5) To counsel United Methodist institutions about property and endowments entrusted to the institutions and to maintain and enforce trust and reversionary clauses in accordance with the provisions of the Division of Higher Education under ¶ 1413.3c.

---

85. See Judicial Council Decision 191.

(6) To monitor fiduciary and legal relationships with United Methodist schools, colleges, universities, and campus ministries and to assist annual conferences in their responsibilities in these matters.

(7) To administer the scholarship funds rebated to the annual conference by the Office of Loans and Scholarships in accordance with the guidelines of that office.

(8) To encourage the establishment of loan and scholarship funds in the annual conference and local churches and to administer the loan and scholarship funds of the annual conference.

c) Responsibilities with Schools, Colleges, and Universities— In addition to its general responsibilities, the annual conference board of higher education and campus ministry or equivalent structure shall carry out the following duties with regard to United Methodist schools, colleges, and universities:

(1) To make known to the district, subdistricts, and all local churches the names and location of all United Methodist educational institutions and, wherever possible, provide resources interpreting their work and special missions.

(2) To assist institutions related specifically to the annual conference in their efforts to raise funds, scholarships, recruit students, and extend services to the annual conference.

(3) To assume responsibility, after consultation with the annual conference committee on nominations and the nominating committee of the institution's board of trustees, for the nomination of those trustees who are to be nominated and elected by the annual conference to the boards of trustees of United Methodist schools, colleges, and universities. In the event that the annual conference confirms or elects trustees nominated by trustee-nominating committees, to consult with those committees, having special concern for the selection of persons who will appropriately address the financial, missional, and educational progress of the institution.

(4) To provide for interpretation of the programs of United Methodist schools, colleges, and universities throughout the educational program of the annual conference, especially in cooperation with those committees and persons responsible for youth and young-adult ministries.

(5) To interpret systematically to the districts, subdistricts, and local churches the conference program with United

Methodist schools, colleges, and universities, encouraging their support and participation.

(6) To represent the annual conference in its relationship to United Methodist schools, colleges, and universities, especially those related to the annual conference.

d) Responsibilities with Campus Ministries—In addition to the general responsibilities listed above, the annual conference board of higher education and campus ministry or equivalent structure shall have the following responsibilities with regard to campus ministry:

(1) To have available the names and addresses of all campus ministries supported by The United Methodist Church and to supply the names and addresses of campus ministries supported by the annual conference to all districts and local churches.

(2) To ensure that each Wesley Foundation or campus ministry shall have a board of directors or a local church committee which provides for planning and implementing a program of mission and ministry to the campus. It will also be the responsibility of the board of directors or local church committee:

(*a*) to establish a budget to present to the board of higher education and campus ministry, and to be responsible for the fund-raising needs of the Wesley Foundation or campus ministry;

(*b*) to have a personnel committee to confer with and counsel the campus minister and staff, to evaluate for effective ministry, to develop and approve written job descriptions for all staff, to interview campus minister candidates and to recommend candidates for appointment or hiring to the board of higher education and campus ministry, the district superintendent and the bishop, to establish all personnel policies, to examine and recommend candidates for ordained or licensed ministry to the district committee on ordained ministry, faithfully adhering to the provisions of ¶ 310.2*b*);

(*c*) when determined that a Wesley Foundation board may hold property, to review the adequacy of the property, liability, and crime insurance coverage, to establish policies on the use of property by outside organizations, to receive and administer all bequests made to the Wesley Foundation or campus ministry according to standards established by the board of higher education and campus ministry or equivalent structure and the annual conference, and the relevant civil governmental authorities and to provide for the upkeep of all properties;

(d) to be encouraged to establish a Wesley Foundation, or campus ministry, permanent endowment fund in accord with the policies established by the board of higher education and campus ministry and the annual conference;

(e) to have fiscal oversight of all income and expenditures of the campus ministry, to develop sound accounting practices, and to ensure proper record keeping and reporting according to the policies set by the board of higher education and campus ministry;

(f) to review and recommend covenants and agreements with ecumenical campus ministries and university organizational policies.

(3) To ensure representation of the annual conference board or equivalent structure on the boards of all campus ministries supported by the annual conference.

(4) To interpret systematically to the districts, subdistricts, and local churches the conference program of campus ministry as a ministry to the whole campus (students, faculty, staff, and administration), encouraging their support and urging United Methodist students of all ages to participate.

(5) To support the development of the United Methodist Student Movement (UMSM) within the annual conference, including the organization of a UMSM student council and the appointment of a UMSM adviser, and to encourage student participation in the UMSM and other related student Christian organizations, both nationally and globally.

(6) To hold the Wesley Foundation board of directors responsible for the direction and administration of the foundation in accordance with the policies and objectives of the annual conference board of higher education and campus ministry or equivalent structure and the standards of the Division of Higher Education of the General Board of Higher Education and Ministry.

(7) To ensure that the Wesley Foundation board of directors is related functionally and cooperatively to the United Methodist local church or churches in the immediate vicinity of the college or university and to the council on ministries or other organization of the district in which it is located.

(8) To determine whether or not Wesley Foundation boards of directors, when incorporated, may hold property and to ensure such property is held and administered according to *The*

Book of Discipline of The United Methodist Church and the laws of the state in which the foundation is located.

(9) To determine the policies for nomination and election by the annual conference of Wesley Foundation boards of directors.

(10) To determine, in consultation with local boards, the personnel needs of Wesley Foundations; to institute standards for professional staff in accordance with the policies, standards and goals of the Division of Higher Education of the General Board of Higher Education and Ministry.

(11) To encourage the development of a permanent endowment fund for Wesley Foundations and campus ministries; and to set polices and investment standards, in consultation with the conference foundation, for permanent endowment funds for Wesley Foundations and campus ministries.

(12) To establish procedures for selection and termination of professional staff in Wesley Foundations; to determine a procedure for a national search; and to consult with the bishop and cabinet when securing the appointment of ministerial staff members.

(13) To cooperate with the district superintendents in the gathering of names and addresses of college students from charge conferences in the districts to send to Wesley Foundations, United Methodist-related campus ministries, and United Methodist chaplaincies at the schools where the students are attending.

(14) To develop policies and procedures for the planning, financing, and construction of any Wesley Foundation or campus ministry building, in consultation with the appropriate boards and agencies of the annual conference and in accordance with the policies, and standards of the Division of Higher Education of the General Board of Higher Education and Ministry.

(15) To oversee the management and financial support of the annual conference program of campus ministry in Wesley Foundations, local churches, and ecumenical campus ministries, in accordance with the policies, standards, and goals of the Division of Higher Education of the General Board of Higher Education and Ministry.

(16) To determine where new campus ministries are needed after the completion of extensive study by an appointed task force to assess the potential of campus ministry on a university or college campus in accordance with the policies, standards,

and goals of the Division of Higher Education of the General Board of Higher Education and Ministry. Such study shall include but not be limited to: the unique missional opportunities and needs of the campus, student demographics of the university or college, number and size of other denominational campus ministries, student life plan of the university or college, long-range development plan of the campus, fiscal and facilities needs, support and cooperation of nearby United Methodist churches and district, and other items that may impact the campus ministry's ability to fulfill the mission of the church on campus.

(17) Prior to the discontinuation of a Wesley Foundation or campus ministry the board of higher education and campus ministry shall conduct an assessment of its potential as outlined in ¶ 634.4*d*) and ¶ 1413.3*c*). A recommendation to the annual conference for discontinuation shall include proposals for the future use of any property of the Wesley Foundation or campus ministry and for the disposition of any real, personal, tangible and intangible property. Any proceeds from the sale of Wesley Foundation or campus ministry property shall be reserved for other campus ministry needs in the annual conference.

(18) To establish and review covenants and agreements for ecumenical campus ministry and to ensure that they are in harmony with the policies, standards, and goals of the Division of Higher Education and the annual conference board of higher education and campus ministry or equivalent structure.

(19) To oversee the management of the annual conference program of campus ministry in Wesley Foundations, local churches, and ecumenical campus ministries; to determine where new campus ministries are needed, and to plan for their establishment and financial support.

(20) To provide resources for local churches and districts with programs of ministry with students or to campuses and, where those programs receive financial support from or are designated as ministries on behalf of the annual conference, to ensure that the policies, standards, and goals of the conference board of higher education and campus ministry or equivalent structure are observed.

(21) To establish the procedures for the nomination and election of United Methodist college students as lay members to annual conference, and to encourage the election of United Methodist college students to General conference.

(22) To work closely in cooperation with local church and annual conference young adult councils and programs to offer a cohesive approach to ministry with young adults.

e) Public Policy—In addition to its general responsibilities, the annual conference board of higher education and campus ministry shall have the following duties with regard to public policy and relationships to the state:

(1) To provide counsel, guidance, and assistance to United Methodist schools, colleges, universities, and campus ministries within the annual conference regarding their relationships to the state.

(2) To interact with public higher education as it reflects on the wholeness of persons and the meaning of life.

(3) To identify and work with the annual conference, church-related colleges, and campus ministries on issues of public policy that bear on higher education, such as issues bearing on access, equity, academic freedom, peace, and justice.

¶ **635.** *Conference Board of Ordained Ministry*—1. Each annual conference at the first session following the General Conference, shall elect for a term of four years a Board of Ordained Ministry. At least six ordained elders and deacons in full connection and, when possible, at least two associate members or local pastors who have completed the Course of Study shall be included as members of the board with voice and vote. Each annual conference shall elect at least one-fifth laypersons, which may include diaconal ministers, and may at its discretion elect further lay members, up to one-third of the membership of the board. All laypersons shall be professing members of local churches in the annual conference. The board membership shall include women and ethnic persons, at least one ordained clergyperson in the retired relationship, at least one ordained clergyperson in extension ministry, and when possible at least one young adult clergyperson in full connection age 35 or younger, and a district superintendent named by the bishop to represent the cabinet. No district superintendent or extended cabinet member shall be the chairperson of the Board of Ordained Ministry. Two-thirds of the members who are elders shall be graduates of seminaries listed by the University Senate.

a) Members shall be nominated by the presiding bishop after consultation with the chairperson of the board, the executive committee, or a committee elected by the board of the previous quadrennium, and with the cabinet. To ensure adequate board membership, consultation shall include an evaluation of the workload of the board in meeting disciplinary and annual conference responsibilities. Vacancies shall be filled by the bishop after consultation with the chairperson of the board. An elected board member may serve a maximum of three consecutive four-year terms. The chair of the Order of Deacons, the chair of the Order of Elders, and the chair of the Fellowship of Local Pastors and Associate Members shall be members of the Board of Ordained Ministry (§ 1c) and its executive committee.

b) This board shall be directly amenable to the annual conference, notwithstanding its organizational relationship within any other program or administrative unit of the annual conference. The annual conference council on finance and administration shall recommend adequate administrative funds for the board and its staff in light of its workload.

c) The board shall organize by electing from its membership a chairperson, registrars, and such other officers as it may deem necessary. A vocational discernment coordinator may be named to coordinate the candidacy mentoring process. The board shall designate its executive committee, which shall include elders, deacons, and laity. The board shall organize in such manner as to care for its responsibilities, including the needs of certified persons, diaconal ministers, local pastors, deacons, and elders. The organization of the board shall include a committee to fulfill the governance responsibilities for diaconal ministers (see *The Book of Discipline,* 1992, ¶¶ 301-317 and 734) and shall provide for certification in specialized ministry careers under the guidelines of the General Board of Higher Education and Ministry (see ¶ 1421). The board may include in its organization a division of deacons and a division of elders.

d) Each annual conference Board of Ordained Ministry shall establish a Conference Relations Committee of at least three persons to hear requests for discontinuance of provisional members, involuntary leave of absence, administrative location, involuntary retirement, or other such matters as may be referred to them by the Board of Ordained Ministry. District superintendents shall not serve on the Conference Relations Committee.

e) To ensure maximum contact with and support of persons in appointments beyond the local church, the board shall maintain relationships with all general agencies that have responsibility for persons in such appointments.

f) The board shall meet at least once prior to its meeting at the time of the annual conference session and may set a deadline prior to annual conference for transacting its business.

g) The board shall select from its own membership an official representative to serve as a member of each district committee on ordained ministry, which shall function as subcommittees of the board.

h) The board shall provide orientation for new members, including distribution of any available written guidelines.

2. The duties of the annual conference Board of Ordained Ministry shall be:

a) To assume the primary responsibility for the enlistment and recruitment of ministerial leadership for our churches and other ministry settings by working in consultation with the cabinet and the General Board of Higher Education and Ministry to study and interpret the ordained, licensed, certified, and assigned ministerial leadership needs and resources of the annual conference, with due regard to the inclusive nature of the Church. It shall, with the assistance of the local church committee on pastor-parish relations, conference agencies, and every ordained, licensed, certified, and assigned leader of the conference, enlist women and men of all races and ethnic origins for ministry as a vocation and guide those persons in the process of education, training, and discernment of the most appropriate path for their ministry, recommending colleges and schools of theology listed by the University Senate, licensing school, and other approved educational opportunities. Persons recruited should have an understanding of and appreciation for persons of different racial and ethnic heritages.

b) To renew a culture of call in the church by giving strategic leadership to annual conferences, districts, congregations, campus ministries, camps, and other appropriate ministries, especially among youth and young adults

c) To seek from a school of theology information about the personal and professional qualities of an applicant for provisional membership or of a provisional member; provided, however, that the applicant or member consent to the provision of such information.

d) To receive annual reports on the progress made by each ministerial student enrolled in a theological school and to record credit for work satisfactorily completed.

e) It shall require a transcript of credits from each applicant before recognizing any of the applicant's educational claims. In case of doubt, the board may submit a transcript to the General Board of Higher Education and Ministry for evaluation.

f) The board shall annually appoint and train a sufficient number of mentors in each district in consultation with the district superintendent.

g) To guide the candidate for ordained ministry who is not enrolled in a theological school and who is pursuing the Course of Study as adopted by the General Board of Higher Education and Ministry.

h) To examine all applicants as to their fitness for the ordained ministry and make full inquiry as to the fitness of the candidate for: (1) annual election as local pastor; (2) election to associate membership; (3) election to provisional membership; and (4) election to full conference membership.

i) To provide all candidates for ordained ministry a written statement on the disciplinary and annual conference requirements for the local pastor, provisional, and full membership.

j) To interview and report recommendation concerning: (1) student local pastors; (2) certified candidates for ordination as deacons; and (3) certified candidates for ordination as elders.[86]

k) To assign a board member to serve as liaison to retired clergy in the conference.

l) To interview applicants and make recommendation concerning: (1) changes from the effective relation to a leave of absence or retirement; (2) return to the effective relation from other relations; (3) honorable location; (4) readmission of located persons and persons discontinued from provisional membership; (5) sabbatical leave; (6) medical leave; (7) appointment as a student; (8) termination; and (9) changes to or from less than full-time ministry.

The board shall keep a record of these changes and the reason behind them and place a copy in the permanent records of the annual conference maintained by the secretary of the conference.

---

86. See Judicial Council Decisions 405, 1263.

m) To ensure confidentiality in relation to the interview and reporting process. The personal data and private information provided through the examinations of and by the Board of Ordained Ministry will not be available for distribution and publication. There are occasions when the Board of Ordained Ministry would not report privileged information, which in the judgment of the board, if revealed in the executive session of clergy members in full connection with the annual conference, would be an undue invasion of privacy without adding measurably to the conference's information about the person's qualifications for ordained ministry. However, it is the right of the executive session of the clergy members in full connection with an annual conference to receive all pertinent information, confidential or otherwise, related to the qualifications and/or character of any candidate or clergy member of the conference.[87]

n) To be in consultation with the bishop through the chairperson or the executive committee regarding transfers. This consultation is to be at the bishop's initiative and, where possible, to take place prior to transfers into the annual conference.

o) To provide support services for all those in ministerial leadership, including ordained, licensed, certified, and assigned; to provide career development, including personal and career counseling, continuing education, formation in servant leadership and continuing spiritual growth in Christ, assistance in preparation for retirement, and all matters pertaining to clergy morale. In providing such support, the board, in cooperation with the cabinet, shall give training and guidance to each local committee on pastor-parish relations regarding its work and role.

p) To work with and support the Order of Deacons, the Order of Elders, and the Fellowship of Local Pastors and Associate Members (see ¶ 323), including receiving reports, offering financial support, and coordinating these groups' activities with the continuing formation offerings of the board. The board may delegate continuing formation responsibility to the groups by mutual agreement, with final approval, evaluation, and budgeting remaining with the board.

q) To provide a means of evaluating the effectiveness of ministerial leaders in the annual conference (¶¶ 604.4, 349). Suggested guidelines will be provided by the General Board of Higher

---

87. See Judicial Council Decision 406.

Education and Ministry, Division of Ordained Ministry. In cooperation with the cabinet, the board shall develop standards of effectiveness for ministerial leaders, whether ordained, licensed, certified, or assigned, serving as pastors of congregations in that annual conference.

r) To interpret the high ethical standards of ordained ministry set forth in the *Discipline* and to study matters pertaining to character (¶ 605.7).

s) To recommend to the full members of the annual conference for validation special ministries for which members seek appointment.

The appointment to such ministries is the prerogative of the bishop and the cabinet.

t) To provide continuing support and management of consecrated diaconal ministers using the policies described in ¶¶ 301-317 of the 1992 *Book of Discipline*.

u) To care for the administration of professional certification established by the General Board of Higher Education and Ministry through (1) enlisting and recruiting clergy and laity to become certified in Christian education, music, youth, evangelism, and other areas established by the General Board of Higher Education and Ministry; (2) determining whether applicants meet the standards established by the General Board of Higher Education and Ministry; (3) to recommend to the annual conference board and the General Board of Higher Education and Ministry; (4) to renew or discontinue professional certification biannually based on a review of their ministry; and (5) to report annually to the annual conference for publication in the conference journal a roster of all persons certified in professional careers for which they have received certification, including places of service address.

v) To report annually to the annual conference for publication in the conference journal a roster of all persons certified as Lay Ministers.

w) To administer the portion of the Ministerial Education Fund for use by the annual conference in its programs of enlistment, basic professional educational aid, continuing formation, ethnic ministry and language training, and professional growth of ordained ministers. Priority shall be given to scholarships for seminary students preparing for ordination.

x) To cooperate with the General Board of Higher Education and Ministry and assist in: (1) the interpretation of current legislation concerning ordained ministry; (2) the interpretation and promotion of the Ministerial Education Fund; (3) the promotion and observance of Ministry Sunday; and (4) the supplying of a record of all information, recommendations, and action on each candidate for ordained ministry after each session of the annual conference; (5) the promotion and addition of standards required for certification in specialized ministry careers.

y) To promote in the annual conference and/or jurisdictional conference a system of financial aid to ministerial students. A conference transferring a person with less than three years of active service into another conference may require reimbursement either from the person or from the receiving conference for outstanding obligations for theological education financed through conference funds.

z) To report in a timely manner any change in the conference relationship of a clergy member of the conference to the conference board of pensions.

3. The board shall elect a registrar and such associate registrars as it may determine; one such associate registrar to be given responsibility for candidacy, including giving leadership to the training and guidance of mentors in each district. A staff executive may be named by the board to fulfill the functions of registrar.

a) The registrar shall keep full personnel records for all candidates for ordained ministry under the care of the board, including essential biographical data, transcripts of academic credit, instruments of evaluation, and, where it applies, psychological and medical test records, sermons, theological statements, and other pertinent data.

b) Pertinent information and recommendations concerning each candidate shall be certified to the annual conference in duplicate; one copy of this record shall be kept by the registrar and one copy shall be mailed after each conference session to the General Board of Higher Education and Ministry. The registrar shall forward an acknowledgment of transfer to the pastor of the local church where each newly elected provisional and associate member held membership.

c) The registrar shall keep a record of the standing of the students in the Course of Study and report to the conference when required. This record shall include the credits allowed students for work done in accredited schools of theology, in approved Course of Study schools, or Course of Study correspondence.

d) The registrar shall file in the bishop's office for permanent record a copy of circumstances involving the discontinuance of provisional membership or termination of the local pastor status.

e) The records and files of the Board of Ordained Ministry are kept on behalf of the annual conference and shall be maintained under guidelines provided by the General Council on Finance and Administration in consultation with the General Board of Higher Education and Ministry and the General Board of Pensions.

4. Administrative costs of the Board of Ordained Ministry shall be a claim on the conference operating budget. The Board of Ordained Ministry shall have direct access to the conference council on finance and administration in support of its program.

¶ **636.** *Conference Administrative Review Committee*—There will be an administrative review committee composed of three clergy in full connection and two alternates who are not members of the cabinet, the Board of Ordained Ministry, or immediate family members of the above. The committee shall be nominated by the bishop and elected quadrennially by the clergy session of members in full connection with the annual conference. Its only purpose shall be to ensure that the disciplinary procedures for discontinuance of provisional membership (¶ 327.6), involuntary leave of absence (¶ 354), involuntary retirement (¶ 357.3), or administrative location (¶ 359) are properly followed. Additionally, if in the event of unresolved issues related to medical leave (¶ 356.4) a fair process hearing (¶ 361.2) occurs, the administrative review committee shall ensure that fair process was followed. The entire administrative process leading to the action for change in conference relationship shall be reviewed by the administrative review committee, and it shall report its findings to the clergy session of members in full connection with the annual conference prior to any action of the annual conference. The administrative review committee shall notify the parties of the review of the process. The administrative fair process hearing procedures (¶ 361.2) should be followed by the administrative review committee. Prior to its report, if the committee determines that any error has occurred, it may recommend to the appropriate person or body that action be taken promptly to remedy the error, decide the error is harmless, or take other action.[88]

---

88. See Judicial Council Decision 921.

¶ **637.** *Conference Committee on Episcopacy*—1. There shall be a conference committee on episcopacy elected quadrennially by the annual conference at the session following the General Conference. The committee's membership shall number at least seven, but no more than seventeen. One-fifth of the committee's membership shall be appointed by the bishop. In addition to the lay and clergy members of the jurisdictional committee on episcopacy, who shall be ex officio members with vote, it is recommended that the committee consist of the following: one-third laywomen, one-third laymen, and one-third clergypersons, provided that one layperson shall be the conference lay leader. All lay members shall be professing members of local churches. Special attention shall be given to the inclusion of racial and ethnic persons, youth (¶ 256.3), young adults, older adults, and people with disabilities. No member of the staff of the annual conference or any of its agencies, nor an immediate family member of such staff, shall serve as a member of the committee, except that a member of the jurisdictional committee on episcopacy or the conference lay leader shall not be disqualified from membership as a result of this provision.[89]

Two or more conferences under the presidency of a single bishop may decide to have one committee on episcopacy, in which case each annual conference shall be represented as stated in the preceding paragraph and shall each elect its own representatives.

2. The committee shall meet at least annually. It shall be convened by the bishop and shall elect a chairperson, a vice chairperson, and a secretary. The bishop and/or chairperson are authorized to call additional meetings when desired.

3. The functions of the conference committee on episcopacy shall be:

a) To support the bishop of the area in the oversight of the spiritual and temporal affairs of the Church, with special reference to the area where the bishop has presidential responsibility.

b) To be available to the bishop for counsel.

c) To assist in the determination of the episcopal needs of the area and to make recommendations to appropriate bodies.

d) To keep the bishop advised concerning conditions within the area as they affect relationships between the bishop and the people of the conference agencies.

---

89. See Judicial Council Decisions 711, 778.

e) To interpret to the people of the area and to conference agencies the nature and function of the episcopal office.

f) To engage in annual consultation and appraisal of the balance of the bishop's relationship and responsibilities to the area and annual conferences, the jurisdiction, general Church boards and agencies, and other areas of specialized ministry, including, at all levels, concern for the inclusiveness of the Church and its ministry with respect to sex, race, and national origin, and understanding and implementation of the consultation process in appointment-making.

g) To report needs for episcopal leadership to the jurisdictional committee on episcopacy through the duly elected conference members of that committee.

4. The conference council on finance and administration shall make provision in its budget for the expenses of this committee.

¶ **638.** *Episcopal Residence Committee*—1. The provision of housing for effective bishops in the jurisdictional conferences shall be the responsibility of the annual conference or conferences comprising the episcopal area to which the bishop is assigned.

2. In each episcopal area in the jurisdictional conferences there shall be an episcopal residence committee or other structure to provide for this function and maintain the connectional relationship. The committee shall be composed of the following persons:

a) The chairperson or designate of the conference committee on episcopacy from each conference.

b) The president or designate of the conference council on finance and administration from each annual conference.

c) The president or designate of the conference board of trustees from each annual conference.

d) Consultants without vote, with specific expertise related to the tasks of the committee, may be utilized.

3. The chairperson of the episcopal residence committee shall be the representative of the committee on episcopacy of the annual conference in which the episcopal residence is currently located.

4. It shall be the responsibility of the episcopal residence committee:

a) To make recommendations to the annual conference(s) regarding the purchase or sale of an episcopal residence.

b) To prepare an annual budget covering the cost of providing the episcopal residence, which may also include utilities, insurance, and normal costs of upkeep in maintaining the residence.

c) To forward the proposed budget to each conference council on finance and administration, including a recommendation for the proportionate share of the proposed budget to be borne by that annual conference, such proportionate share to be approved by each annual conference as it acts on budget recommendations (¶ 614).

d) To supervise the expenditure of funds allocated from all sources for expenses related to the provision of the episcopal residence and to account for such expenditures annually to each annual conference in the episcopal area.

e) To give oversight in all matters related to upkeep, maintenance, improvements, and appropriate insurance coverages for the episcopal residence.

5. Titles to properties held as episcopal residences shall be held in accordance with ¶ 2514.

¶ **639.** *Conference Board of Pensions*—1. *Authorization*—There shall be organized in each annual conference a conference board, auxiliary to the General Board of Pension and Health Benefits, to be known as the conference board of pensions, hereinafter called the board, that shall have charge of the interests and work of providing for and contributing to the support, relief, assistance, and pensioning of clergy and their families, other church workers, and lay employees of the institutions, organizations, and agencies within that annual conference of The United Methodist Church, except as otherwise provided for by the general board.

2. *Membership*—*a)* It is recommended that the board be composed of not less than twelve members not indebted to pension and benefit funds, plans, and programs; one-third laywomen, one-third laymen, and one-third clergy; and in accordance with ¶ 605.3 elected for a term of eight years and arranged in classes as determined by the annual conference; and in addition thereto, any clergy member of the conference or lay member of a church within the conference who is a member of the General Board of Pension and Health Benefits. Active and retired participants in pension and benefit funds, plans, and programs, whether or not currently receiving benefits, and not indebted as provided above, are eligible to serve on the board. All lay members shall be professing members of local churches. A vacancy in the membership of the board may be filled by the board for the remainder of the

conference year in which the vacancy occurs, subject to the same qualifications before provided; and at its next session the conference shall fill the vacancy for the remainder of the unexpired term.

b) The members shall assume their duties at the adjournment of the conference session at which they were elected.

3. *Organization*—The board shall organize by electing a chairperson, vice chairperson, secretary, and treasurer, who shall serve during the ensuing quadrennium or until their successors shall have been elected and qualified. These officers shall constitute an executive committee; *provided,* however, that three members may be added thereto by the board. The duty of the executive committee shall be to administer the work of the board during the conference year in the interim between regular or special meetings of the board. The office of secretary may be combined with that of treasurer. The treasurer may be a person who is not a member of the board, in which case the person shall be an ex officio member of the executive committee, without vote. Calls for special meetings of the board shall be issued by the secretary on request of the chairperson, or the vice chairperson when the chairperson is unable to act.

4. *Proportional Payment*—The board shall compare the records of the amounts paid by each pastoral charge for the support of pastors and for pension and benefit programs, computing the proportional distribution thereof and keeping a permanent record of defaults of the churches of the conference that have failed to observe the following provisions pertaining to proportional payment, and shall render annually to each church that is in default a statement of the amounts in default for that and preceding years.[90]

a) When the apportionment to the pastoral charges for the pension and benefit program of the annual conference has been determined, payments made thereon by each pastoral charge shall be exactly proportionate to payments made on the salary or salaries of the ordained minister or clergy serving it.

b) The treasurer of the pastoral charge shall be primarily responsible for the application of proportional payment; but in the event of the treasurer's failure to apply it, the pastor shall adjust cash salary and payment according to the proper ratio, as provided above, before the pastor enters the respective amounts in the statistical report to the annual conference.

---

90. See Judicial Council Decisions 50, 250, 390, 401, 471.

c) The conference statistical tables shall provide separate columns for reporting the amount apportioned to each pastoral charge for pension and benefit purposes and the amount paid thereon.

d) It shall not be permissible for a pastor to receive a bonus or other supplementary compensation tending to defeat proportional payment.

5. *Reports to and Responsibilities Regarding the General Board*— The board shall have the powers and responsibilties with respect to the General Board of Pension and Health Benefits described in ¶ 1506 and shall report to the general board immediately following the session of the conference, in such form as required by the general board, the names and years of service approved for pre-1982 pension credit for each eligible person and the names and addresses of clergy who are members of funds, plans, or programs administered by the general board.

Moreover, annually, the board or other authorized agency shall submit, annually, its group health care plan data, to the extent the board maintains a group health care plan, de-identified as necessary, including, but not limited to, financial soundness, claims experience and other cost drivers, plan designs and coverage, and eligibility criteria to the General Board of Pension and Health Benefits.

6. *Annual Conference Retiree Health Care Access*—The board or other agency authorized by the annual conference shall respect the health and wholeness of the annual conference's clergypersons, who have retired in accordance with ¶ 357.1, ¶ 357.2*b*, ¶ 357.2*c*, or ¶ 357.2*d* other than as applied to ¶ 357.2*a* of the *Book of Discipline* and lay employees of the annual conference who have retired in accordance with the annual conference's retirement policy, and are eligible for Medicare, and their spouses. The board or agency shall provide access to Medicare supplement plans and prescription drug coverage plans. Access for retirees and their spouses may include, but shall not be limited to (i) sponsoring an employer retiree health care plan that supplements Medicare; (ii) participating in a multiple employer retiree health care plan that supplements Medicare; (iii) securing individuals' eligibility under group contracts with Medicare supplement plan providers or exchanges; (iv) subsidizing the costs of coverage for retired clergypersons and retired lay employees and their spouses enrolled in Medicare Part D plans or Medicare Advantage plans;

(v) providing subsidies toward or group relationships with providers of individual Medicare supplement and other retiree coverage policies; and (vi) providing fixed dollar retiree health benefits through health reimbursement arrangements, stipends, or otherwise. Providing access does not compel an annual conference to fund such coverage (i.e., coverage can be retiree-pay-all); however, an annual conference may fund or subsidize the cost of coverage (e.g., through premium payment, premium reimbursement, contributions to a health reimbursement arrangement, stipend, or grant) for its retired clergy and lay employees in its discretion. Additional eligibility may be determined by the annual conference; for example, for early retirees and surviving dependents.

7. *Annual Conference Group Health Care Plans*—The board or other agency authorized by the annual conference shall sponsor or participate in a group health care plan, which local churches may adopt for their full-time appointed clergy, or which the annual conference may require its local churches to adopt, that covers the annual conference's own full-time clergy employees and its full-time lay employees in the United States. Clergy appointed to an appointment extending the ministry of the local United Methodist church under ¶ 344.1, except those serving in positions for which the annual conference is responsible under ¶ 344.1*a*(1), and lay employees who are not employees of the annual conference, such as lay employees of local churches and lay employees of district and jurisdictional offices, need not be covered under the preceding sentence, but may be covered by the local church or other common-law employer adopting the plan, at the discretion of the annual conference. For the purpose of this paragraph, group health care plan shall mean a health insurance plan, group health care plan, or multiple-employer health care plan that covers benefits for major medical and hospitalization expenses. The board or authorized agency may recommend additional eligibility for its group health care plan in its discretion.

Alternatively, in the event that federal law or state law governing health care plans and health insurance establishes coverage options for those persons without employer-provided coverage that ensure access, regardless of health status or condition, to affordable coverage through health insurance exchanges, connectors, single-payer systems, or other mechanisms, the board may cease maintaining its group health care plan to the extent such coverage is available to its clergy and lay employees. In such event, the board nevertheless shall provide continued administrative support (e.g., through cafeteria plans, employer-adopted exchange plans, or health reimbursement arrangements) for participation in the exchanges or alternative systems, and recommend an appropriate and adequate level of Church financial support (e.g., in the form of local church, employer, or annual conference contributions toward premiums, additional compensation, or apportionments) of full-time clergy and full-time lay employees of the conference toward the purchase of such coverage through these alternative mechanisms to the extent individuals' coverage may not be subsidized by government agencies, particularly considering (a) the tax advantages of employer-provided financial support toward health care coverage, and (b) the reduced availability of government subsidies for clergy whose compensation is near or above denominational average compensation.

In addition, the board or authorized agency shall provide and maintain health and wellness programs for the annual conference's full-time clergy and full-time lay employees.

¶ **640.** Each annual conference shall have a board of trustees, whose membership and duties are detailed in ¶ 2512.1-.8.

¶ **641.** 1. In each annual conference there shall be a conference commission on archives and history. The number of members of the commission and their terms of office shall be as the conference may determine and may include an ex officio representative of each United Methodist heritage landmark in its bounds. It shall be the duty of the commission to collect, preserve, and make accessible the historically significant records of the annual conference and its agencies, including data relating to the origin and history of the conference and its antecedents; to encourage and assist the local churches in preserving their records, compiling their histories, and celebrating their heritage; to provide for the permanent safekeeping of the historical records of all abandoned or discontinued churches in the bounds of the annual conference and its antecedents (see ¶ 2549.3); to maintain a fire-safe historical and archival depository and to see that all items that obviously will have value for future history are properly preserved therein; to provide for the ownership of real property and to receive gifts and bequests; to nominate to the General Commission on Archives and History buildings, locations, or structures within the annual conference for designation as historic sites or heritage landmarks; to maintain contact with officially designated historic sites and heritage landmarks in their bounds; to assist the bishop or the appropriate conference committee in planning for the historical hour and other appropriate historical observances at annual conference sessions; to establish retention and disposition schedules for annual conference and local church records under standards or guidelines developed by the General Commission on Archives and History; to cooperate with and report, when requested, to the general and jurisdictional commissions on archives and history; and to engage with other Wesleyan, Methodist, or Evangelical United Brethren-related denominations in lifting up our joint heritage.

2. The commission may organize a conference historical society and encourage membership therein for the purpose of promoting interest in the study and preservation of the history of the conference and its antecedents. The officers of the conference commission on archives and history may be the officers of the conference historical society. Membership in the historical society shall be established as the society may determine. Membership may include the payment of dues as the society may direct, and in return, members shall receive official publications and publicity materials issued by the commission and the society and other such benefits as may be deemed suitable.

3. Each annual conference may have a historian to undertake specific duties as may be designated by the commission. The annual conference historian may be a member of the annual conference commission on archives and history.

4. The annual conference commission on archives and history shall work with the ethnic congregations of the conference to develop and preserve the historical records of those congregations and antecedent conferences.

¶ 642. 1. Each annual conference shall create appropriate structures related to Christian unity and interreligious relationships to provide for these functions and maintain the connectional relationships with the Council of Bishops. The annual conference structure will report each year to the conference in such manner as the conference may direct. The responsibilities of this annual conference structure for Christian unity and interreligious relationships may be assigned to an existing or newly created multifunctional agency.

2. It is recommended that this annual conference structure be composed of two United Methodists from each district (comply-

ing with ¶ 610.5), one of whom shall be district coordinator for Christian unity and interreligious relationships and shall serve as liaison with local church ministry areas on Christian unity and interreligious relationships. Additional members may include persons from The United Methodist Church or other member churches of Churches Uniting in Christ as directed by the conference to ensure ecumenical expertise and interchange with other agencies. Laypersons from The United Methodist Church shall be professing members of local churches. Ex officio members of the annual conference structure for Christian unity and interreligious relationships shall include the conference ecumenical officer(s), if elected, and any United Methodists residing within the conference bounds who are members of the following: Office of Christian Unity and Interreligious Relationships of the Council of Bishops, the governing board of the National Council of the Churches of Christ in the U.S.A., the World Methodist Council, the United Methodist delegation to the most recent World Council of Churches Assembly, and the United Methodist delegation to the most recent plenary meeting of Churches Uniting in Christ.

3. There shall be a representative of this structure who serves as one of the conference representatives to state councils or conferences of churches.

4. The duties of the annual conference structure shall be to act in cooperation with the annual conference council on ministries, and, as it may recommend, and to take initiative in ecumenical and interreligious relationships as follows:

a) To interpret, advocate, and work for the unity of the Christian church in every aspect of the life of the conference and its churches and to encourage dialogue and cooperation with persons of other living faiths.

b) To recommend to the conference the goals, objectives, and strategies and to assist the conference, in cooperation with the bishop and the cabinet, in the development of ecumenical relationships and planning for mission with other judicatories, particularly in the establishment of new churches, yoked congregations, and in the process of local church union efforts.

c) To stimulate participation in and evaluation of mission programs ecumenically planned and implemented, such as experimental parishes, ecumenical parish clusters, ecumenical task forces, and united ministries in higher education, and in other issue-oriented tasks.

d) To stimulate conference, district, and congregational participation in councils, conferences, or associations of churches, in coalition task forces, and in interreligious groups through ecumenical educational or shared-time programs, jointly approved curriculum resources, interreligious study programs, or ecumenical community action projects such as institutional ministries and media communications, and various other modes of interchurch cooperation.

e) To participate in the selection of conference delegates to state councils or conferences of churches, which participation may include nomination, in cooperation with the conference nominating committee, for conference election of the delegates to these bodies; to select representatives to district, area, and regional ecumenical and interreligious task groups and workshops; and to act as the body to which such delegates are accountable by receiving and acting on their reports and recommendations.

f) To promote and interpret the work of national and world ecumenical bodies such as the National Council of the Churches of Christ in the U.S.A., the World Council of Churches, Churches Uniting in Christ, and the World Methodist Council; and to cooperate in and provide leadership for specific ecumenical experiences of worship and celebration such as the Week of Prayer for Christian Unity, Pentecost Sunday, World Communion Sunday, Reformation Sunday, and other appropriate occasions.

g) To stimulate understanding and conversations with all Christian bodies, to encourage continuing dialogue with Jewish and other living-faith communities, and to encourage an openness of mind toward an understanding of other major world religions.

h) To fulfill other functions assigned by the annual conference and to respond to such requests as may be made by its leadership.

¶ 643. 1. There shall be in each annual conference including those in central conferences a conference commission on religion and race or other structure to provide for these functions and maintain the connectional relationships. It shall follow the general guidelines and structure of the General Commission on Religion and Race as outlined in ¶¶ 2002 and 2008, where applicable.

2. The basic membership of the annual conference commission shall be nominated and elected by established procedure of the respective annual conferences. Each annual and central conference shall determine the number and composition of the total

membership. Care shall be taken to ensure that membership is selected based primarily on the passion and expertise possessed in the areas of training, resource development, evaluation, consultation, and strategic planning in the areas of diversity, intercultural competency, racial and ethnic justice, reconciliation and equity, and communicating/advocacy for change. The total membership shall have an equitable balance in the number of laymen, laywomen, and clergypersons. It is strongly urged that the conference commissions be constituted to reflect the widest sense of racial, ethnic, tribal, and cultural diversity relevant to that area. Selection of commission members shall ensure adequate representation of women, youth, young adults, older adults, and persons with disabilities. Members of the General Commission on Religion and Race residing in the annual conference shall be ex officio members of the annual conference commission on religion and race with vote.

3. The annual conference commissions including those in central conferences shall assume responsibility for such matters as:

a) Interpreting the intent of all responsibilities given to annual conference and central conference commission on religion and race so that the responsibilities reflect the context for ministry and realities of the areas in which they serve.

b) Supporting and providing programs of education in areas of intercultural competency, institutional equity and vital conversations at every level of the conference.

c) Partnering with annual and central conference boards and agencies as they seek to develop vital conversations, programs, and policies of racial/institutional equity and intercultural competency.

d) Reviewing and making appropriate recommendations for total inclusiveness and equity within the conference staff and on all of the conference boards, agencies, commissions, and committees. Reports will be made yearly to the annual conference.

e) Providing resources and training to enable the work of the local church ministry area of religion and race as specified in ¶ 252.2*b*, with particular emphasis placed on pastors and congregations involved in cross-racial/cross-cultural ministry. In the case of annual conferences within central conferences, cross-racial/cross-cultural ministry may include tribes, ethnic communities, and cultural/language groups.

f) Consulting with the Board of Ordained Ministry and the cabinet to ensure racial/ethnic inclusion and equity in the recruitment, credentialing, and itineracy processes of the conference. The executive committee of the Board of Ordained Ministry and cabinet shall meet at least once per year in joint sessions with the Conference Commission on Religion and Race to create and assess long-term plans for identifying and developing clergy leadership who will serve the growing racial and ethnic populations in the Church.

g) Consulting with local churches that are experiencing changing demographics in the neighborhoods where they are located, which demographics may be different from the church's racial/ethnic constituency, and that have a desire to be in ministry with their community.

h) Coordinating conference leadership in and in support of racial and social justice movements impacting local communities in consultation and partnership with other entities within and outside the conference boundaries.

i) Partnering with the appropriate denominational bodies to assist in resolution of complaints of racial/ethnic discrimination made by clergy or laity.

4. The annual conference commission on religion and race shall develop an adequate budget for its operation as a commission, which shall be included within the annual conference budget.

5. The annual conference commission on religion and race, or other structure to provide for its function and connectional relationship, shall have vote and voice in the decision-making unit of the conference such as the conference connectional ministries or equivalent structure.

¶ **644.** There shall be in each annual conference, including the central conferences, a conference commission on the status and role of women or other structure to provide for these functions and maintain the connectional relationships.[91]

1. The responsibility of this commission shall be in harmony with the responsibility of the general commission (see ¶ 2103), with the following objectives established as guidelines for adaptation to the needs of the respective annual conferences:

a) To be informed about the status and role of all women in the total life of the conference. Data shall be gathered that relate to all structural levels of the conference, including the local church. Such information will be regularly updated and disseminated.

---

91. See Judicial Council Decision 712.

b) To initiate cooperation with United Methodist Women at the annual conference level and other levels as appropriate in order to achieve full participation of women in the decision-making structures.

c) To develop ways to inform and sensitize the leadership within the conference at all levels on issues that affect women, which shall be projected into and through all districts within the conference by the commission.

d) To focus on major priorities of issues related to women, which may include sexual harassment policies and procedures, and to enlist the support of the bishop, cabinet, and conference staff in policies, plans, and practices related to those priorities.

e) To advise the general commission about the progress and effectiveness of efforts to achieve full participation of women in the life of the Church.

f) To participate in connectional programs and plans initiated or recommended by the general commission, and to utilize the resources available from the general commission as needed.

2. The basic membership of the conference commission shall be nominated and elected by established procedures of the respective annual conferences. Each annual conference shall determine the number and composition of the total membership. All must be members of The United Methodist Church. Special consultants without vote may be used as resource persons. It is recommended that the addition of the at-large membership ensure that the total membership maintain a balance of one-third laywomen, one-third laymen, and one-third clergy. The majority of the commission shall be women, including both clergy and lay. In an annual conference where there is not a sufficient number of clergywomen to meet the recommended balance, additional laywomen shall be elected beyond the one-third proportion to bring the total membership to a majority of women. A person or persons serving as member(s) of the General Commission on the Status and Role of Women from that annual conference shall, by virtue of their office, be member(s) of the conference commission on the status and role of women (see ¶¶ 610.6 and 710.6). Selection of commission members shall ensure adequate representation of racial and ethnic groups, youth, young adults, older adults, and persons of varying lifestyles.

At least one member shall be named by the conference United Methodist Women.

3. The chairperson of the commission shall be a woman.

4. The commission shall propose a budget and submit it for inclusion in the budget of the annual conference according to procedures for funding of all boards, commissions, and agencies of the annual conference.

¶ 645. There shall be in each annual conference a conference commission on the small membership church, or the responsibilities of the small membership church commission may be assigned to an existing or newly created multifunctional agency of the council or other structure that cares for the functions of support, nurture, and growth of small membership churches and their relationships to the conference, districts, and other local churches. Where these responsibilities are assigned to new or existing agencies within the conference, the individual(s) responsible for the functioning of the commission shall be designated by the annual conference and included in the listing of conference officers.

1. The responsibility of this commission shall be in harmony with the responsibility of the general commission, with the following objectives established as guidelines for adaptation to the needs of the respective annual conference:

a) To be informed about the needs and opportunities of the small membership church in rural, suburban, and urban settings in the total life of the conference. Specific data shall be gathered that relate to all structural levels of the conference, including the local church. This data shall include, but not be limited to, demographics, membership, information on the formation and effectiveness of cooperative ministries, information about pastoral tenure, compensation, and other factors that affect the vitality of the small membership churches. Such information will be regularly updated and disseminated to bishops, district superintendents, and to relating conference boards and agencies, the General Board of Global Ministries, and the General Board of Discipleship.

b) To ensure representation from small membership churches in the decision-making structures of the annual conference.

c) To develop ways to inform and sensitize the leadership within the annual conference at all levels on issues that affect small membership churches, which shall be projected into and through all districts within the annual conference by the commission.

d) To focus on major issues related to small membership churches and to enlist the support of the bishop, cabinet, and conference staff in policies, plans, and practices impacting those issues.

e) To advise the general commission on the progress and effectiveness of efforts to achieve full participation of laity and clergy from small membership churches in the life of the Church.

f) To participate in connectional programs and plans initiated or recommended by the general commission as needed.

2. The basic membership of the conference commission shall be nominated and elected by established procedures of the annual conferences. All must be members of The United Methodist Church. Special consultants without vote may be used as resource persons.

3. The commission shall propose a budget and submit it for inclusion in the budget of the annual conference according to procedures for funding of all boards, commissions, and agencies of the annual conference.

¶ 646. In each annual conference there shall be a commission on communication or other structure to provide for these functions and maintain the connectional relationship. It shall include persons with skills in communications nominated for membership in a manner determined by the conference in accordance with ¶ 610.5.

The commission shall be a service agency to meet the communication, publication, multimedia, public and media relations, interpretation, and promotional needs of the annual conference. It may be responsible for providing resources and services to conference agencies, districts, and local churches in the field of communication. The commission shall have a consultative relationship with agencies and bodies within the conference structure.

¶ 647. *United Methodist Women—Constitution of United Methodist Women in the Conference*

Article 1. Name—In each annual conference there shall be a conference organization named United Methodist Women, directly related to the jurisdictional and national organizations of United Methodist Women.

Article 2. Function—The function of the conference organization of United Methodist Women shall be to work with the district and local organizations of United Methodist Women to develop programs to meet the needs and interests of women and the concerns and responsibilities of the global Church; to encourage and support spiritual growth, missionary outreach, and

Christian social action; and to promote the plans and responsibilities of the United Methodist Women's national organization.

Article 3. Authority—Each conference organization of United Methodist Women shall have authority to promote its work in accordance with the plans, responsibilities, and policies of the United Methodist Women's national organization.

Article 4. Membership—The conference organization of United Methodist Women shall be composed of members of United Methodist Women existing within the conference. The resident bishop shall be an ex officio member of the conference organization of United Methodist Women and of the Leadership Team or equivalent structure.

Article 5. Leadership Team—The conference organization shall elect such leaders as may be needed to fulfill the Purpose, including at least a president, a treasurer, a secretary, and a Committee on Nominations. Additional committees and teams may be formed to fulfill the Purpose in accordance with this constitution and guidance from the United Methodist Women's national organization as set forth in the bylaws of the conference organizations of United Methodist Women.

Article 6. Meetings and Elections—*a)* There shall be an annual meeting of the conference organization of United Methodist Women. At the annual meeting, the Leadership Team shall review the conference events and priorities of the prior year, propose a plan of activities and priorities for the following year, including a supporting budget, elect members of the Leadership Team as needed to implement the plan, and set the pledge amount for the following year.

b) The voting body of the annual meeting of the conference organization shall be composed of members of United Methodist Women organizations existing within the bounds of the conference as determined by the conference organization; members of the conference and district leadership teams; and members of the board of directors of United Methodist Women and the United Methodist Women Program Advisory Group and the jurisdictional leadership team residing within the bounds of the conference.

c) At the annual meeting of the conference organization prior to the quadrennial meeting of the jurisdictional organization, three members of the Leadership Team or their designees shall be elected according to provisions in ¶ 536.3 for membership in the jurisdiction organization.

d) At the annual meeting of the conference organization prior to the quadrennial meeting of the jurisdictional organization, the conference organization shall nominate two women for membership on the board of directors of the United Methodist Women's national organization, the names to be sent to the jurisdiction organization according to ¶ 536.4.

Article 7. Relationships—a) The president of the conference organization of United Methodist Women is a member of the annual conference, as set forth in ¶ 32.

b) The conference organization shall name representatives from among its membership to serve on the various boards, councils, commissions, and committees of the annual conference as the constitutions and bylaws of such agencies provide.

c) The conference organization shall encourage women to participate in the total life and work of the Church and shall support them in assuming positions of responsibility and leadership.

Article 8. Amendments—Proposed amendments to this constitution may be sent to the recording secretary of the United Methodist Women's national organization for consideration by the board of directors. The last date for consideration of any amendments will be the last regular meeting of the board of directors before the date by which it must submit proposed legislation for action of the General Conference.

¶ **648.** *United Methodist Men—Constitution of United Methodist Men in the Conference*

Article 1. Name—In each annual conference there shall be a conference organization named United Methodist Men, auxiliary to the jurisdictional committee on United Methodist Men and to the General Commission on United Methodist Men (¶ 2301).

Article 2. Function—The function of the conference organization of United Methodist Men shall be to build and support the district organizations of United Methodist Men in developing resources to meet the needs and interests of men and the responsibilities of discipleship; to empower personal witness and evangelism; to enable outreach in individual and group mission and ministry; to encourage and support spiritual growth and faith development; and to promote the objectives and responsibilities of the General Commission on United Methodist Men. In the absence of a district organization, the conference organization, in consultation with the district superintendent, shall fulfill the district responsibilities (¶ 671).

Article 3. Authority—Each conference organization of United Methodist Men shall have the authority to promote its work in accordance with the plans, responsibilities, and policies of the General Commission on United Methodist Men.

Article 4. Membership—The conference organization of United Methodist Men shall be composed of all men of local churches or charges (chartered or unchartered) within the bounds of the conference and all clergy.

Article 5. Officers and Committees—a) The conference organization shall elect a president, at least one vice president, a secretary, and a treasurer.

b) The resident bishop shall serve as the honorary president and be a member of the conference organization and its executive committee.

c) The conference lay leader (or designated representative) shall be a member of the conference organization and its executive committee.

d) Additional officers (including civic youth-serving agencies/scouting coordinator) and committees shall be elected or appointed in accordance with the guidelines of the General Commission on United Methodist Men and/or the bylaws of the conference organization of United Methodist Men.

Article 6. Meetings and Elections—a) There shall be an annual meeting of the conference organization of United Methodist Men, at which time there shall be presented an annual report and a program plan designed to meet the needs of the men of the conference. Officers and committees shall be elected in accordance with the requirements of the organization's bylaws.

b) The voting body of the annual meeting of the conference shall be determined by the organization's bylaws but shall include conference and district officers and committee chairpersons as determined, members of the General Commission on United Methodist Men, and members of the jurisdictional committee on United Methodist Men residing within the bounds of the conference.

Article 7. Relationships—a) The president of the conference organization of United Methodist Men is a member of the annual conference, as set forth in ¶ 32.

b) The president of the conference organization of United Methodist Men shall represent the conference organization on the jurisdictional committee on United Methodist Men. In the absence of the president a designated vice president may represent the conference organization.

c) Designated officers or members shall represent the conference organization on the various agencies, councils, commissions, and committees of the annual conference as the constitutions, bylaws, and rules of such agencies provide.

d) The conference organization shall encourage men to participate in the total life and work of the Church and shall encourage them to assume positions of responsibility and leadership as part of their discipleship.

Article 8. Finances—The Conference United Methodist Men shall secure funds for the fulfillment of its purpose. All funds from whatever source secured by the Conference United Methodist Men belong to the organization and shall be disbursed only in accordance with its constitution and/or bylaws and by its order.

a) Conference United Methodist Men may have their own bank accounts.

b) It is recommended that there be an annual financial audit.

Article 9. Amendments—Proposed amendments to this constitution may be sent to the recording secretary of the General Commission on United Methodist Men prior to the last annual meeting of the commission in the third year of the quadrennium.

Article 10. Connectional Reporting and Accountability—*a)* Each annual conference United Methodist Men shall have on file a current copy of their constitution and bylaws with the General Commission on United Methodist Men.

b) Each annual conference shall submit an annual report to the General Commission on United Methodist Men. This report will be presented by the conference president at the spring meeting of the National Association of Conference Presidents and shall include but not be restricted to:

1. Annual goals and progress toward those goals in the last 12 months.
2. A review of the work in evangelism, mission, and spiritual growth within the annual conference or beyond.
3. A listing of training events conducted at a conference, district, and local church level to expand men's ministry in all levels of the church.

4. An assessment of the General Commission on United Methodist Men to include the annual conference UMM's appraisal of the commission's goals and the commission's progress toward those goals in the last 12 months.

5. A report of the significant challenges to men's ministry and the significant successes of men's ministry to be shared with other conference organizations of UMM.

These reports will become part of the internal review process of the General Commission on United Methodist Men and each conference report shall be shared with the annual conference leadership by the conference president.

¶ 649. 1. In each annual conference there shall be a conference council on youth ministry or other equivalent structure to provide for these functions and maintain the connectional relationships, or the responsibilities outlined below may be assigned to such organization that follows the same membership requirements as the annual conference provides pursuant to ¶ 610.1. Its purpose shall be to strengthen the youth ministry in the local churches and districts of the annual conference. For administrative purposes, the council shall be related to the annual conference council on ministries or equivalent structure. (See ¶¶ 1201-1212 for the Division on Ministries With Young People.)

2. *Membership*—No more than one-third of the membership of the council shall be adults, one of whom may be the conference lay leader or his or her representative. It is strongly recommended that the membership of the council include an equal number of persons with respect to race, ethnicity, gender and social status as defined by the annual conference or episcopal area. Where ethnic or language conferences overlap nonethnic conferences, provision shall be made for the inclusion of members of the ethnic or language conferences and vice-versa. Those serving on the conference council on youth ministry or equivalent structure shall be baptized or professing members of The United Methodist Church.

3. *Responsibilities—a)* To initiate and support plans, activities, and projects that are of particular interest to youth.

b) To be an advocate for the free expression of the convictions of youth on issues vital to them.

c) To support and facilitate, where deemed needed, the formation of youth caucuses.

d) To cooperate with the boards and agencies of the annual conference, receiving recommendations from and making recommendations to the same.

e) To recommend to the annual conference committee on nominations qualified youth for membership on boards and agencies.

f) To elect and certify annual conference representatives to the jurisdictional youth ministry organization convocation.

g) To promote, introduce and encourage youth in the annual conference to become active in Wesley Foundations or United Methodist campus ministries when they attend a college or university and to become aware of opportunities to attend United Methodist-related colleges and universities.

h) To cooperate with Wesley Foundations, United Methodist campus ministries and United Methodist-related colleges and universities to assist annual conference youth in the transition to college life.

i) To receive and set the policy and criteria for its portion of the Youth Service Fund (¶ 1212). No more than one-third shall be used for administrative purposes; at least one-third shall be used for projects within the geographic bounds of the annual conference; and at least one-third shall be used for projects outside the geographic bounds of the annual conference.

j) To establish the policy for Youth Service Fund education and be responsible for its promotion throughout the annual conference, in cooperation with the Division on Ministries With Young People of the General Board of Discipleship.

k) To establish a project review committee as an advisory committee with regard to the use of the Youth Service Fund receipts for projects. It is recommended that the committee be composed of at least 50 percent racial and ethnic group persons.

l) To participate with the appropriate conference agencies in the nomination of the conference coordinator of youth ministry, who shall serve as its adviser.

m) To promote an evangelistic outreach with youth and through youth by providing educational opportunities and resources that increase their awareness, exposure, and engagement in the areas of mission, social justice, discipleship, leadership development and spiritual formation as they relate back to their local church.

¶ 650. 1. In each annual conference there shall be a conference council on young-adult ministry or equivalent structure. Its purpose shall be to strengthen the young-adult ministry in the local churches and districts of the annual conference. For administrative purposes, the council shall be related to the annual conference council on ministries or alternative structure.

2. *Membership*—The membership of the council shall be young adults (as defined by annual conference or episcopal area). It is recommended there be one young adult elected by each district of the conference. There may also be members at large nominated by the conference nominating committee. It is strongly recommended that the membership of the council include an equal number of persons with respect to race, ethnicity, gender, and social status as defined by annual conference or episcopal area, as well as persons of both genders to ensure inclusiveness. Those serving on the conference council on young-adult ministry shall be members of The United Methodist Church. At least one-half of the members shall be laypersons who are professing members of The United Methodist Church. Members should represent the diversity of young adults in the general population, including college students, working persons, single, and married.

3. *Responsibilities—a)* To initiate and support plans and activities and projects that are of particular interest to young adults who are college students, working persons, single, and married.

b) To be an advocate for the free expression of the convictions of young adults on issues vital to them.

c) To support and facilitate, where deemed needed, the formation of young-adult caucuses.

d) To cooperate with the boards and agencies of the annual conference, including Wesley Foundations, United Methodist-related campus ministries and chaplaincies, in assisting graduating college students in the transition to congregational life, and receiving recommendations from and making recommendations to the same to provide for the needs of young adults in The United Methodist Church.

e) To recommend to the annual conference committee on nominations qualified young adults for membership on boards and agencies.

f) To participate with the conference council on ministries in the nomination of the conference coordinator of young-adult ministry, who shall serve as its adviser.

¶ **651.** 1. In each annual conference there may be a conference council on older adult ministries. Its purpose shall be to strengthen the older-adult ministries in the local churches and districts of the annual conference. For administrative purposes, the council shall be related to the annual conference board of discipleship, or the annual conference board of laity, or equivalent structure.

2. *Membership*—The majority of the membership of the council should be older adults. It may also include persons (regardless of age) who, because of their specialized interests, education, training, and experience, have developed a passion for ministry with older adults. Those serving on the conference council on older-adult ministries shall be professing members of The United Methodist Church and shall include both laypersons and clergy. There may also be members-at-large, nominated by the conference nominating committee and elected by the annual conference, to achieve racial, ethnic, gender, and geographic inclusiveness and to assure participation by people with specialized interests, education, training, and experiences. The conference lay leader (or designee), the conference coordinator of older-adult ministries (if any), and a cabinet representative shall serve ex officio with vote. Members should represent the diversity of older adults in the general population, including retired persons, working persons, persons with disabilities, persons with chronic illnesses, single persons, widowed persons, married persons, persons living in a variety of residential settings, and persons with a wide variety of family situations.

3. *Responsibilities*—*a)* To initiate and support ministries, plans, activities, and projects that are of particular interest to older adults, including retired persons, working persons, persons with disabling conditions, persons with chronic illnesses, single persons, widowed persons, married persons, persons living in a variety of residential settings, and persons with a wide variety of family situations.

b) To advocate on behalf of older adults.

c) To support and facilitate, where appropriate, the formation of older-adult caucuses.

d) To identify the needs, concerns, and potential contributions of older adults in the annual conference and its districts.

e) To cooperate with the boards and agencies of the annual conference in receiving and making recommendations to provide for the needs of older adults in The United Methodist Church.

f) To recommend to the annual conference committee on nominations qualified and motivated older adults for membership on boards and agencies.

g) To participate with the annual conference board of discipleship, or the annual conference board of laity, or equivalent structure in the nomination of the coordinator of older-adult ministries for election by the annual conference.

h) To educate and keep before the annual conference and its districts the lifelong process of aging with emphases on the quality of life, intergenerational understandings, and faith development.

i) To serve as a focal point for supplying information and guidance on older-adult ministries within the annual conference and its districts.

j) To support the development of resources that will undergird older-adult ministries within the annual conference and its districts.

¶ 652. Each annual conference shall establish a procedure by which it will manage clergy medical leave. The annual conference may establish a joint committee on clergy medical leave. If the annual conference establishes such a committee, it should be composed of at least two representatives each from the Board of Ordained Ministry and the conference board of pensions, who may be elected by those boards at the beginning of each quadrennium and at other times when vacancies occur, and a district superintendent appointed from time to time by the bishop to represent the cabinet. The joint committee shall be encouraged to include in its composition a person with a disability, preferably someone under appointment. Unless and until other members are elected, the chairperson and registrar of the Board of Ordained Ministry and the chairperson and secretary of the conference board of pensions, or others designated by them, shall be authorized to represent their respective boards. The committee shall organize at the beginning of each quadrennium by the election of a chairperson and a secretary. If the annual conference does not establish a joint committee, the annual conference's established policy and process for managing clergy medical leave nonetheless should involve the Board of Ordained Ministry, the conference board of pensions and representation from the cabinet.

The duties of the annual conference, with respect to clergy medical leave, or the joint committee on clergy medical leave, or its equivalent, shall be:

a) To study issues related to clergy medical leave in the annual conference.

b) To provide for a continuing personal ministry to any clergy on medical leave of the conference and to aid them in maintaining fellowship with the members of the conference.

c) To provide advice and support to and, where appropriate advocacy for, clergy on medical leave in (i) applying for and securing disability benefits from the Comprehensive Protection Plan and government programs, (ii) exploring possible sources of interim financial assistance before disability benefits can be obtained, (iii) establishing rehabilitation and return-to-service programs, and (iv) assessing the need for and providing reasonable accommodations.

d) To make recommendations to the Board of Ordained Ministry, the conference board of pensions, and the cabinet on matters related to clergy medical leave, including steps for the prevention of the need for medical leave, the process of granting medical leave, benefits, grants, or other assistance, and programs of rehabilitation.

e) To cooperate with and give assistance to the General Board of Pension and Health Benefits in its administration of the Clergy Retirement Security Program, the Comprehensive Protection Plan and other benefit plans for clergy on medical leave, and to the extent applicable assist with the disability benefits and other benefits provided under those plans.

¶ **653.** There shall be in each annual conference a committee on disability concerns or other structure to provide for the functions of this ministry and maintain the connectional relationships.

1. The basic membership of the committee shall be nominated and elected by established procedures of the respective annual conference. Each annual conference shall determine the number and composition of the total membership. Membership shall include persons with physical disabilities and persons with mental disabilities.

2. It shall be the responsibility of this committee:

a) To be aware of, and advocate for, the role of persons with disabilities in ministry, including ordained and diaconal ministries and local church and annual conference leadership positions.

b) To advocate for and help develop programs within the annual conference that meet the needs of persons with disabilities.

c) To be informed about current ministries within the annual conference that are related to persons with disabilities.

d) To develop ways to sensitize persons in leadership positions on issues that affect persons with disabilities and therefore the entire Church.

e) To foster cooperation among ministries within the annual conference that focus on specific disabilities (deaf, deafened, hard of hearing, development disabilities, mental retardation, mental illness, visual impairment, physical disabilities, etc.).

f) To be a resource for local churches who are attempting to develop ministries that are attitudinally and architecturally accessible.

g) To promote the full inclusion of persons with disabilities in the life of the local church and the annual conference.

h) To participate in jurisdictional accessibility associations in the sharing of knowledge and resources.

¶ 654. There shall be an annual conference committee on Native American ministry or other structure to provide for these ministries and maintain the connectional relationships. The basic membership of the committee shall be nominated and elected by established procedure of the respective annual conferences. Each annual conference shall determine the number and composition of the total membership. Where possible, the membership shall consist of a majority of Native Americans. It shall be the responsibility of this committee to determine the distribution of the Native American Ministries Sunday offering, coordinate the promotion of Native American Ministries Sunday, and monitor Native American ministries within the annual conference. Each committee shall report on how the offering funds have benefited Native Americans in their annual conference. Annual reports, including the amount of the total receipts from the Native American Ministries Sunday offerings, should be forwarded to the conference council on ministries and to the Connectional Table.

Every local church at charge conference shall designate by nomination and election a minimum of one person per charge (without regard to race or ethnic origin) or a designated member of an established church committee to represent the need for better awareness of Native American contributions in the local church. These names are to be submitted to the district superintendent at charge conference to be given to the annual conference committee on Native American ministry.

¶ **655.** The annual conference is encouraged to establish a committee on Hispanic/Latino Ministries or other structure to support the development, implementation, and evaluation of a Hispanic/Latino Ministries comprehensive plan of action and the strategies for working with the Hispanic/Latino persons of all generations in the community. The membership of the committee shall be nominated and elected by the established procedures of the respective annual conference. The committee shall include at least one-third Hispanic/Latino persons.

In those conferences where a committee on Hispanic/Latino ministries or other structures is adopted, there shall be strategies to: (1) strengthen existing ministries and congregations, (2) start new congregations and ministries, including intentional ministries with children and youth, (3) identify, equip, and deploy elders, local pastors, lay missioners, lay certified ministers, and other lay leaders who can serve in this mission and ministry, (4) identify financial and material resources to support and maintain its implementation. The plan shall be based on a clear analysis of the socioeconomic, cultural, and religious realities of the community where the conference is located. The Conference Comprehensive Plans for Hispanic/Latino Ministries in the Jurisdictional Annual Conferences are encouraged to be ready by the 2016 General Conference.

¶ **656.** 1. There may be a conference Advance program, established and carried out in the same spirit of partnership as the general Advance program.

2. A conference Advance Special Gift is one made to a conference Advance Special project within bounds of the annual conference or episcopal area authorized by an annual conference upon recommendation by the conference board of global ministries or its equivalent structure and consistent with the goals of the Advance. The funds as received shall be administered by the conference board of global ministries or such structure as designated by the conference.

3. An annual conference may undertake a conference-wide campaign for a lump sum to be applied to its missionary and

church extension. The funds so received shall be designated as conference Advance Specials and shall be administered by the conference board of global ministries or equivalent structure. Local churches shall report their contributions as conference Advance Specials.

4. With the approval of the annual conference, a district within the conference may authorize and promote Advance Specials for church extension and missionary needs within the district, such funds to be administered by a district committee on mission organized for that purpose or by a similar body set up by the district. Such special funds secured and administered on a district level shall be reported by each local church to the annual conference as conference Advance Specials.

5. Local churches shall report their contributions to general Advance Specials and conference Advance Specials to the charge conference and in the manner indicated on the annual conference report form.

¶ 657. The annual conference is encouraged to establish a committee on criminal justice and mercy ministries (CJAMM) to accomplish the following: (1) raise awareness and generate local church involvement; (2) identify existing programs; (3) promote criminal justice ministries; and (4) serve as a resource and connectional link with local churches, general program agencies, and ecumenical groups, and use prison ministry and prison reform resources made available through the general agencies. The purpose is to promote a ministry to persons of all genders and ages who are in prison, to the families of those in prison, and to the victims of crime and their families and to be an advocate for prison concerns. The CJAMM committee may relate to the board of global ministries and/or the board of church and society, which shares social justice concerns. The results of the work in this area will be reported to the annual conference.

Section X. The District Conference

Upon approval of the annual conference, the term *subdistrict* may be used in the references to district in ¶¶ 658-672.

¶ 658. A district conference shall be held if directed by the annual conference of which it is a part and may be held upon the call of the district superintendent, which call shall specify the time and place.

¶ **659.** 1. A district conference shall be composed of members as determined and specified by the annual conference, giving attention to inclusiveness (see ¶¶ 124, 140).

2. The district conference may choose its own order of business. The secretary duly elected shall keep an accurate record of the proceedings and submit it to the annual conference for examination.

3. The district conference shall issue certificates of candidacy for the ordained ministry on recommendation of the district committee on ordained ministry and shall consider for approval the reports of this committee.

4. The district conference may incorporate a district union, under the laws of the state in which it is located, to hold and administer district real and personal property, receive and administer church extension and mission funds for use within the district, and exercise such other powers and duties as may be set forth in its charter or articles of incorporation as authorized by the annual conference having jurisdiction over said district. If a district union is so incorporated, it shall also assume the power and duties of the district board of trustees (¶ 2518.2). All such district unions chartered or incorporated by districts of the churches that joined and united in adopting the Constitution of The United Methodist Church are declared to be disciplinary agencies of The United Methodist Church as though originally created and authorized by that Constitution and may act for or as a district conference when convened for that purpose by the district superintendent, who shall be its executive secretary, or by its president or other executive officer.

5. If any district or conference initiates, joins, monitors, or terminates a boycott, the guidelines in *The Book of Resolutions*, 2008, should be followed. The General Conference is the only body that can initiate, empower, or join a boycott in the name of The United Methodist Church.

¶ **660.** 1. The district lay leader is the elected leader of the district laity and shall be a professing member of a local church. The district lay leader shall provide for the training of local church lay leaders for their ministries in the local churches in relation to ¶ 249. The district lay leader shall have responsibility for fostering awareness of the role of the laity both within congregations and through their ministries in the home, workplace, community, and world in achieving the mission of the Church, and supporting and enabling lay participation in the planning and decision-making processes of the district and the local churches in cooperation with the district superintendent and pastors.

2. The district lay leader shall be elected as determined by the annual conference for a term of not less than four years. The method of nomination and the maximum term of office shall be determined by the annual conference.

There may be one or more associate district lay leader(s) within a district. The associate district lay leader(s) shall be elected as determined by the annual conference. The method of nomination and the maximum term of office shall be determined by the annual conference. The district lay leader and the associate district lay leader(s) may be reimbursed for their approved expenses.

3. The district lay leader will meet regularly with the district superintendent to discuss the state of the district, the Church, and the needs for ministry both locally and globally.

4. The district lay leader is a member of annual conference (see ¶ 32).

5. The district lay leader shall be a member of the conference board of laity or equivalent structure.

6. The district lay leader shall work with the district superintendent to ensure that there is a district director of Lay Servant Ministries and shall serve on the district committee on Lay Servant Ministries.

7. The district lay leader is a member of the district conference and shall be a member of the district council on ministries or alternative structure and its executive committee. The district lay leader shall also be a member of the committee on district superintendency of the district.

8. The district lay leader may serve as a lay member of the district committee on ordained ministry (or equivalent agency) and the district board of church location and building (or equivalent agency).

9. The district lay leader shall relate to the organized lay groups in the district such as United Methodist Women, United Methodist Men, and United Methodist Youth and support their work and their activities.

10. The district lay leader may designate persons to serve as proxy in any of the above groups except the annual conference, the district conference, district council on ministries, and the district

council on ministries executive committee, district committee on ordained ministry, and the district board of church location and building.

¶ 661. Each district of an annual conference may organize to develop, administer, and evaluate the missional life, advocacy needs, and ministries of the Church in and through the district. It shall maintain connectional relationships, organize to develop and strengthen ethnic ministries, including ethnic local churches and concerns, and provide encouragement, coordination, and support for local churches in their ministries of nurture, outreach, and witness in accordance with the mission of The United Methodist Church. Every board, standing committee, commission, council, and work area of the district shall designate one of its members as its coordinator of witness ministries. These persons shall help the groups of which they are members to engage in witness ministries and, in particular, to ask, "How are we intentionally reaching new people for Jesus Christ through our ministries?" and "How are we helping new people grow and mature as disciples of Jesus Christ through our ministries and areas of responsibility?"

¶ 662. The district superintendent, after consultation with the conference board, may appoint a district director of church and society. Also, if desirable, a district may create a committee on church and society of laypersons and clergy, to work with the district superintendent to further the purposes of the conference board. The mission coordinator for social action of the district United Methodist Women shall be an ex officio member.

¶ 663. The district superintendent, after consultation with the annual conference ethnic local church concerns committee, may appoint a district director of ethnic local church concerns. This director would become a member of the district council on ministries or its structural counterpart. A district may establish a committee on ethnic local church concerns comprised of laypersons and clergy to work with the district superintendent to implement the annual conference's comprehensive plan as it relates to that district and to further the purposes of the annual conference committee.

¶ 664. The district superintendent, after consultation with the annual conference commission on religion and race, may appoint a district director of religion and race. A district may establish a committee on religion and race to work with the district superintendent to further the purposes of the annual conference commission in the district. The district director, if appointed, shall be a member of the annual conference commission on religion and race. (See ¶ 643.2.)

¶ 665. The district superintendent, after consultation with the conference council on young-adult ministries or equivalent structure, if available, may appoint a district coordinator of young-adult ministries. This coordinator would become a member of the district committee on ministries or its structural counterpart. Also, if desirable, a district may create a committee on young-adult ministries to work with the district superintendent to further the purposes of increasing young adult participation in local churches. The district coordinator, if appointed, shall be a member of the annual conference council on young-adult ministries or equivalent structure.

¶ 666. There shall be a district committee on ordained ministry.

1. The district committee on ordained ministry shall be amenable to the annual conference through the Board of Ordained Ministry. All members shall be nominated annually by the district superintendent in consultation with the chairperson or executive committee of the Board of Ordained Ministry and approved by the annual conference. Interim vacancies shall be filled by the district superintendent. The committee shall be composed of at least three professing members of local churches, a representative from the Board of Ordained Ministry who may be named chairperson; the district superintendent, who shall not be the chairperson, and at least six other clergy in the district. The clergy shall include elders and deacons, and where possible, women and ethnic clergy, a deacon or elder who is age 35 or younger, an associate member, and may include one local pastor who has completed the Course of Study. All persons named to the district committee on ordained ministry shall be members with vote. The conference Board of Ordained Ministry shall provide orientation for new members, including education regarding the ministry and roles of all clergy and distribution of any available written guidelines.

2. The district committee on ordained ministry shall elect its officers at the first meeting following the annual conference session when the members are elected.

3. The committee shall maintain a list of all persons who have declared their candidacy for the ordained ministry and are pursuing candidacy studies with a candidacy mentor. A duplicate

list shall be forwarded to the annual conference registrar for candidacy; such list being made current at least prior to each session of the annual conference.

4. The committee, through the Board of Ordained Ministry, shall seek ways to make reasonable accommodations for cultural and ethnic/racial realities and language translations as candidates meet the requirements for candidacy, including interviews, psychological assessments, criminal background, and credit checks.

5. The committee shall offer counsel to candidates regarding pre-theological studies.

6. The committee shall supervise all matters dealing with candidacy for the ordained ministry and with the license for local pastor.

7. The vote of the committee on matters of candidacy shall be by individual written ballot of the committee present. A three-fourths majority vote is required for certification. All other matters of candidacy shall be by a simple majority vote.[92]

8. The committee shall maintain a service record and file on every local pastor and candidate for the ordained ministry until the individual becomes an associate or provisional member of the annual conference, at which time a copy of the files shall be forwarded to the registrar of the Board of Ordained Ministry. The records and files of the committee are kept on behalf of the annual conference and shall be maintained under guidelines provided by the General Council on Finance and Administration in consultation with the General Board of Higher Education and Ministry and the General Board of Pension and Health Benefits.

9. The committee shall recommend to the Board of Ordained Ministry those persons who qualify for associate and provisional membership, for license or continuance as local pastors, and for restoration of credentials. All persons shall have been professing members of The United Methodist Church or a baptized participant of a recognized United Methodist campus ministry or other United Methodist ministry setting for a minimum of one (1) year.

10. The committee shall examine all persons who apply in writing for certification or renewal of certificate. Where there is evidence that their gifts, evidence of God's grace, and usefulness warrant and that they are qualified under ¶¶ 315-319, and on

92. See Judicial Council Decision 586.

recommendation of their charge conference or the conference Board of Ordained Ministry, the committee shall issue or renew their certificate.

11. The committee shall examine all persons who apply in writing to be certified as lay ministers. When there is evidence that their gifts, evidence of God's grace and usefulness, warrant and that they are qualified under ¶ 268, and on recommendation of their charge conference, the committee shall recommend their certification or recertification. The district committee shall report annually to the annual conference through the annual conference Board of Ordained Ministry a roster of all persons certified as lay ministers.

12. All persons interviewed by the district committee shall be informed of decisions and recommendations as soon as possible, both orally and in writing.

13. The committee shall assist the conference Board of Ordained Ministry in providing support services for all clergy under appointment within the district.

¶ **667.** Each district of an annual conference may organize a district board of laity or alternative structure.

1. The purpose of the district board of laity shall be:

a) To foster an awareness of the role of laity both within the local congregation and through their ministries in the home, workplace, community, and world in achieving the mission of the Church.

b) To work with the district lay leader in: (1) developing and promoting an increased role for laity in the life of the local church, (2) increasing the participation of laity in the sessions and programs of the district and local churches in cooperation with the district superintendent and pastors, and (3) encouraging lay-persons to participate in the general ministry of the Church in the world. (See ¶ 661.)

c) To develop and promote stewardship of time, talent, and possessions within the district in cooperation with the district council on ministries.

2. The membership of the board shall include the district lay leader, associate district lay leader(s), district director of Lay Servant Ministries, and may include the district superintendent, district president of United Methodist Women, district president of United Methodist Men, district president of United Methodist Youth, district president of United Methodist Young Adults,

and, where organized, the district president of the Older Adult Council, and others as deemed necessary. Special attention shall be given to the inclusion of women, men, youth, young adults, and older adults; people with disabilities; and racial and ethnic group persons.

3. The district lay leader shall chair the board. Other officers shall be elected as the board shall deem necessary.

4. The board shall relate to the lay servant program and to the organized groups in the district such as the United Methodist Women, United Methodist Men, United Methodist Youth, and United Methodist Young Adults and shall support their work and help them coordinate their activities.

¶ **668.** *District Committee on Lay Servant Ministries*—Districts are encouraged to create a district committee on Lay Servant Ministries related to the annual conference through the conference committee on Lay Servant Ministries. There shall be a district director of Lay Servant Ministries filled in a manner determined by the district. This position shall be filled by a certified lay servant.

1. The purpose of the district committee on Lay Servant Ministries is to plan and supervise the program within the district.

2. The committee is chaired by the district director of Lay Servant Ministries. In addition to the director, membership of the committee will include the district lay leader, the district superintendent, and an instructor of lay servant courses. Other resource people may be added as needed.

3. The responsibilities of a district committee on Lay Servant Ministries are to provide basic training for local church lay servants and advanced courses for certified lay servants as recommended by the General Board of Discipleship, or as approved by the conference committee on Lay Servant Ministries; to decide who will be recognized as certified lay servants; to help match lay servants and certified lay ministers with service opportunities; and to support and affirm lay servants and certified lay ministers as they serve.

4. The district committee shall plan advanced courses for lay servants that will enable certified lay servants to maintain that recognition.

5. The district committee will report to the pastor and charge conference of each certified lay servant the courses that have been satisfactorily completed by the certified lay servant.

¶ 669. *Committee on District Superintendency*—There shall be a committee on district superintendency.

1. *Membership*—This committee shall be composed of eleven members, including the district lay leader, and two persons appointed by the district superintendent. It is recommended that the remaining members of the committee consist of two laywomen, two laymen, two clergy, and two at-large members, all of whom should be selected with special attention to the representation of racial and ethnic persons, youth (¶ 256.3), young adults, older adults, and people with disabilities. At least three of the eleven persons shall be clergy, and seven shall be laypersons. All laypersons shall be professing members of a local church.

2. *Selection*—The members shall be selected in such manner as may be determined by the district conference or, where there is no district conference, by the annual conference. The district committee shall be authorized to co-opt members as advisory members who have expertise in areas of special need. The bishop of the area, or his or her authorized representative, shall be an ex officio member of said committee.

3. *Meeting*—The district committee shall meet at least annually and upon call of the district superintendent and/or the chairperson of the committee. The committee shall elect a chairperson, vice chairperson, and secretary.

4. *Purpose*—The purpose of the committee on district superintendency shall be to support the district superintendent of the district in the oversight of the spiritual and temporal affairs of the Church, with special reference to the district where the superintendent has responsibilities. In fulfilling this purpose, the committee shall give attention to the following responsibilities:

    a) To advocate for adequate budget-support services for the district superintendent, such as adequate secretarial support, travel, continuing education, and parsonage needs (¶ 614.1*a*).

    b) To be available for counsel.

    c) To keep the district superintendent advised concerning conditions within the district as they affect relations among the district superintendent, the laity, the clergy, and the district agencies.

    d) To establish a clearly understood process for observing the district superintendent's ministry with direct evaluation and feedback, with special concern for the inclusiveness of the Church and its ministry with respect to sex, race, and national origin, and implementation of the consultative process in appointment-making.

e) To consult with the district superintendent concerning continuing education and to arrange with the cabinet and bishop for the necessary time and financial assistance for the attendance of the district superintendent at such continuing education events as may serve his or her professional and spiritual growth.

f) To interpret to the people of the district and to the district boards and agencies the nature and function of the district superintendency.

5. *Consultation*—The district committee and the district superintendent shall engage in an annual consultation and appraisal of the work of the district superintendent in the district and shall serve in an advisory relationship with the bishop of the area.

¶ **670.** *United Methodist Women—Constitution of United Methodist Women in the District*

Article 1. Name—In each district there shall be a district organization named United Methodist Women, auxiliary to the conference and national organizations of United Methodist Women.

Article 2. Responsibilities—The responsibilities of the district organization of United Methodist Women shall be to work with United Methodist Women members and local organizations of United Methodist Women existing within the district to develop programs to meet the needs and interests of women and the concerns and responsibilities of the global Church; to encourage and support spiritual growth, missionary outreach, and Christian social action; and to promote the plans and responsibilities of the conference and national organizations of United Methodist Women.

Article 3. Authority—Each district organization of United Methodist Women shall have authority to promote its work in accordance with the plans, responsibilities, and policies of the conference and national organizations of United Methodist Women.

Article 4. Membership—The district organization of United Methodist Women shall be composed of members of United Methodist Women existing within the district. The district superintendent shall be an ex officio member of the district organization of United Methodist Women and of its leadership team or equivalent structure.

Article 5. Leadership Team—The district organization shall elect as its leaders those persons who are needed to help the organization to fulfill the Purpose, including at least a president, a treasurer, a secretary, and a Committee on Nominations. Additional committees or teams may be formed to fulfill the Purpose in accordance with this constitution and guidance from the conference and national organizations of United Methodist Women.

Article 6. Meetings and Elections—There shall be an annual meeting of the district organization of United Methodist Women to adopt a program designed to meet the needs of the women of the district in harmony with the Purpose, the plans and responsibilities of the conference and national organizations of United Methodist Women, to elect members of the Leadership team and the Committee on Nominations, to transact the necessary business, and to receive pledges made for the ensuing year.

Article 7. Relationships—a) The district organization of United Methodist Women shall designate members to serve on the various boards, councils, commissions, and committees of the district and/or the annual conference as the constitution and bylaws of such agencies provide.

b) The district president shall be a member with vote of the conference Leadership Team.

c) The district organization shall encourage women to participate in the total life and work of the Church and shall support them in assuming positions of responsibility and leadership.

Article 8. Amendments—Proposed amendments to this constitution may be sent to the recording secretary of the United Methodist Women's national organization for consideration by the board of directors. The last date for consideration of any amendments will be the last regular meeting of the board of directors before the date by which it must submit proposed legislation for action of the General Conference.

¶ 671. *United Methodist Men—Constitution of United Methodist Men in the District*

Article 1. Name—In each district there shall be a district organization named United Methodist Men, auxiliary to the conference organization of United Methodist Men and the General Commission on United Methodist Men (¶ 2301).

Article 2. Responsibilities—The responsibilities of the district organization of United Methodist Men shall be to work with local units of United Methodist Men in developing resources to meet the needs and interests of men and the responsibilities of discipleship; to empower personal witness and evangelism; to enable outreach in individual and group mission and ministry; to encourage and support spiritual growth and faith development; and to promote the objectives and responsibilities of the conference organization and the General Commission on United Methodist Men. The district organization shall also encourage and promote the chartering and annual recertification of local units through the General Commission on United Methodist Men (¶¶ 2302 and 256.6).

Article 3. Authority—Each district organization of United Methodist Men shall have the authority to promote its work in accordance with the plans, responsibilities, and policies of the conference organization and the General Commission on United Methodist Men.

Article 4. Membership—All men and clergy of local churches or charges (chartered and unchartered) of the district shall be considered members of the district organization.

Article 5. Officers and Committees—*a)* The district organization shall elect a president, at least one vice president, a secretary, and a treasurer.

b) Additional officers (including civic youth-serving agencies/scouting coordinator) and committees shall be elected or appointed in accordance with the guidelines of the General Commission on United Methodist Men and/or the bylaws of the district organization of United Methodist Men.

c) The district superintendent shall be a member of the district organization and of its executive committee.

d) The district lay leader (or designated representative) shall be a member of the district organization and of its executive committee.

Article 6. Meetings and Elections—There shall be an annual meeting of the district organization of United Methodist Men, at which time there shall be presented an annual report as well as a program plan designed to meet the needs of the men of the district. Officers and committees shall be elected in accordance with the requirements of the organization's bylaws.

Article 7. Relationships—*a)* Designated officers or members shall represent the district organization of United Methodist Men on the various boards, councils, commissions, and committees of the district as the constitutions, bylaws and rules of such agencies provide.

b) The district president shall be a member of the conference executive committee.

c) The district organization shall encourage men to participate in the total life and work of the Church and shall encourage them to assume positions of leadership as part of their discipleship.

Article 8. Finances—The District United Methodist Men shall secure funds for the fulfillment of its purpose. All funds from whatever source secured by the District United Methodist Men belong to the organization and shall be disbursed only in accordance with its constitution and/or bylaws and by its order.

a) District United Methodist Men may have their own bank accounts.

b) It is recommended that there be an annual financial audit.

Article 9. Amendments—Proposed amendments to this constitution may be sent to the recording secretary of the General Commission on United Methodist Men prior to the last annual meeting of the commission in the third year of the quadrennium.

Article 10. Connectional Reporting—*a)* Each district shall file a current copy of their constitution with the conference organization of United Methodist Men.

b) Each district shall submit an annual report to the conference organization of United Methodist Men prior to its annual meeting.

¶ **672.** Each district of an annual conference may organize a district council on youth ministry.

1. *Purpose*—The purpose of the district council on youth ministry is defined as follows: to assist local churches in ministry for, with, and by junior high and senior high youth more effectively; to serve as a channel of communication and involvement among the youth ministry in the local churches, the conference council on youth ministry, and the general agencies of the Church; to initiate youth programs for the district to influence the total programming of the district and conference as it relates to the concerns and needs of youth; and to take primary responsibility for promoting and raising money for the Youth Service Fund.

2. *Membership*—Each district may determine the membership and the method of election of its district council on youth ministry in consultation with the conference council on youth ministry. It is recommended that the membership include the following: *a)* no more than one-third of the membership shall be adults; *b)* an equal number of persons with respect to race, ethnicity, gender, and social status as defined by the annual conference or episcopal area;

c) the district youth coordinator, to be a member by virtue of his or her office; and *d)* representatives on the conference council on youth ministry.

3. *Functions*—The functions of the district council on youth ministry may be determined by the annual conference council on youth ministry and/or the district council on youth ministry. The following functions may be incorporated in its work:

a) To study the needs of the junior high and senior high youth ministry of the local churches in the district and help them establish and provide more effective ministry in and through the district.

b) To keep local churches informed of the work of the whole Church in youth ministry and to challenge each church to full participation.

c) To serve as a two-way channel of communications between the local church youth and the annual conference and to assist local church youth in communication with one another.

d) To cooperate with the programming and ministry of the district council on ministries as it serves to provide leadership training to persons in the district.

e) To assist in the implementation of the program of the annual conference and particularly of the annual conference council on youth ministry.

f) To serve as an advocate for the free expression of youth in the district and local churches of the district.

g) To provide leadership training.

h) To promote, introduce and encourage youth in the district to become active in Wesley Foundations or United Methodist campus ministries when they attend a college or university and to become aware of opportunities to attend United Methodist-related colleges and universities.

i) To cooperate with Wesley Foundations, United Methodist campus ministries, and United Methodist-related colleges and universities to assist district youth in the transition to college life.

j) To promote, educate, and be a resource to local churches on Youth Service Fund.

k) To participate with the district superintendent and the conference coordinator of youth ministry, who shall serve as its adviser. The district council on youth ministry's responsibilities shall include organizing, programming, consulting with local churches, and nurturing adult workers with youth in the district.

Chapter Five

ADMINISTRATIVE ORDER

Section I. General Provisions

¶ **701.** *Agencies and General Agencies*—1. Connectionalism is an important part of our identity as United Methodists. It is a vital web of interactive relationships (¶ 132) that includes the agencies of the Church, as defined in ¶¶ 701.2 and 701.3, with the purpose of equipping local churches for ministry and by providing a connection for ministry throughout the world, all to the glory of God. It provides us with wonderful opportunities to carry out our mission in unity and strength.

2. We experience this connection in many ways, including our systems of episcopacy, itineracy, property, and mutual cooperation and support. Our connectional system performs at least three essential tasks: embracing God's mission for the church as making disciples for Jesus Christ; organizing our whole Church to enable local congregations, the primary arena for mission, faithfully and fruitfully to make disciples for Jesus Christ; and ensuring that all components in the connection carry out their appropriate responsibilities in ways that enable the whole United Methodist Church to be faithful in its mission. The term *agency*, wherever it appears in the *Book of Discipline*, is a term used to describe the various councils, boards, commissions, committees, divisions, or other units constituted within the various levels of Church organization (General, jurisdictional, central, annual, district, and charge conferences) under authority granted by the *Book of Discipline*; the term does not and is not meant to imply a master-servant or principal-agent relationship between these bodies and the conference or other body that creates them, except where the authority is specifically granted.

3. General agencies, in particular, are important to our common vision, mission, and ministry. They provide essential services and ministries beyond the scope of individual local congregations and annual conferences through services and ministries that are highly focused, flexible, and capable of rapid response. The general agencies of The United Methodist Church are the regularly established councils, boards, commissions, committees, or other units with ongoing responsibilities that have been constituted by the General Conference. Not included are such commissions and

committees as are created by the General Conference to fulfill a special function within the ensuing quadrennium, ecumenical groups on which The United Methodist Church is represented, or committees related to the quadrennial sessions of the General Conference.[1] The term general agency or agency, wherever it appears in the *Book of Discipline* in reference to a general agency, does not and is not meant to imply a master-servant or principal-agent relationship between such a body and the General Conference or any other unit of the denomination, or the denomination as a whole.

¶ **702.** *Amenability and Program Accountability*—1. All the general agencies of The United Methodist Church that have been constituted by the General Conference are amenable to the General Conference, except as otherwise provided.

2. Each organization, group, committee, council, board, and agency of the general Church shall adopt a code of ethics and policies that embody and live out our Christian values regarding conflict of interest, confidentiality, whistleblower protection, record retention and document destruction, and nepotism applicable to both members and employees.

3. Between sessions of the General Conference, the following general agencies are accountable to the Connectional Table for those functions that are outlined in the 900 ¶¶s: the General Board of Church and Society, the General Board of Discipleship, the General Board of Global Ministries, the General Board of Higher Education and Ministry, the General Commission on Religion and Race, the General Commission on the Status and Role of Women, the General Commission on Archives and History, the General Commission on United Methodist Men, and the General Commission on Communication in matters pertaining to their program responsibilities.

4. The Connectional Table shall review and evaluate the effectiveness of the general program-related agencies and connectional structures of the church as they collectively seek to aid annual conferences and local churches as they fulfill the mission of The United Methodist Church to make disciples of Jesus Christ for the transformation of the world.

5. Questions and concerns about programs, projects, or decisions of a particular agency may be addressed to that agency, with

---

1. See Judicial Council Decision 139.

copies to the Connectional Table. Agencies shall acknowledge receipt of requests for information within ten days and provide information requested within thirty days or as soon thereafter as it is available.

6. If any district, annual conference, or general agency initiates, joins, monitors, or terminates a boycott, the guidelines in the 2008 *Book of Resolutions* should be followed. The General Conference is the only body that can initiate, empower, or join a boycott in the name of The United Methodist Church.

7. In all matters of accountability episcopal oversight as provided in ¶ 422 is assumed.

¶ **703.** *Definitions, Structures, and Titles*—1. *General Council*— An organization created by the General Conference to perform defined responsibilities of review and oversight on behalf of the General Conference in relation to the other general agencies and to perform other assigned functions shall be designated as a general council. General councils are amenable and accountable to the General Conference and report to it. The General Council on Finance and Administration is a council.

(Note: The Council of Bishops and Judicial Council are authorized by the Constitution and are not created by the General Conference.)

2. *General Board*—A continuing body of the Church created by the General Conference to carry out assigned functions of program, administration, and/or service shall be designated as a general board.

3. *General Commission*—An organization created by the General Conference for the fulfillment of a specific function for an indefinite period of time.

4. *Study Committee*—An organization created by the General Conference for a limited period of time for the purpose of making a study ordered by the General Conference. The Connectional Table shall provide for coordination with and among the study committees except where General Conference otherwise designates.

5. *Program-Related General Agencies*—The general boards and commissions that have program and/or advocacy functions shall be designated as program-related general agencies. These agencies are amenable to the General Conference, and between sessions of the General Conference are accountable to the Connectional Table for those functions outlined in the 900 ¶¶s: the

General Board of Church and Society, the General Board of Discipleship, the General Board of Global Ministries, the General Board of Higher Education and Ministry, the General Commission on Religion and Race, the General Commission on United Methodist Men, and the General Commission on the Status and Role of Women. In all matters of accountability, episcopal oversight as provided in ¶ 422 is assumed.

6. *Administrative General Agencies*—The general boards and commissions that have primarily administrative and service functions shall be designated as administrative general agencies. These agencies are the General Board of Pension and Health Benefits, The United Methodist Publishing House, and the General Commission on Archives and History, and General Commission on Communication, the last two of which also carry program-related responsibilities for which they are accountable to the Connectional Table.

7. Each general agency, unless otherwise provided, shall adopt the following executive staff titles:

a) General Secretary—the chief staff officer of a general agency. Each general agency is entitled to only one general secretary, who is its chief administrative officer.

b) Deputy General Secretary—the chief staff officer assigned to oversight of a major programmatic or administrative unit(s), or with major programmatic or administrative responsibilities with a general agency.

c) Associate General Secretary—the associate staff officer of a general agency or the chief staff officer of a division or a department of a general agency.

d) Assistant General Secretary—the assistant staff officer of a general agency or the chief staff officer of a section or office of a general agency.

e) Treasurer—the staff financial officer of a general agency, entrusted with the receipt, care, and disbursement of agency funds. In some general agencies there may be associate and/or assistant treasurers. There are general agencies in which "treasurer" is not a staff title but is an officer elected from the voting membership of the agency.

8. *Theme*—A theme is a theological focus, missional emphasis, prophetic statement, or program catalyst for ministry. A theme enhances programs or ministries basic to the life of the Church

and serves as a rallying point for constituents involved in those programs.

9. *Missional Priority*—A missional priority is a response to a critical need in God's world that calls The United Methodist Church to a massive and sustained effort through primary attention and ordering or reordering of program and budget at every level of the Church, as adopted by the General Conference or in accord with ¶ 806.1*b*(2). This need is evidenced by research or other supporting data, and the required response is beyond the capacity of any single general agency or annual conference. However, the ongoing priority of The United Methodist Church both in program and budget is to proclaim the good news that salvation comes through Jesus Christ.

10. *Special Program*—A special program is a quadrennial emphasis initiated by a general program-related agency in accordance with ¶ 905, approved by General Conference, and assigned to a general program-related agency. The program shall be designed in response to a distinct opportunity or need in God's world that is evidenced by research or other supporting data and shall propose achievable goals within the quadrennium.

11. *Program*—A program is an ongoing or special activity designed and implemented to fulfill a basic disciplinary responsibility of a general agency accountable to the Connectional Table.

12. *Association or Fellowship*—Organizations not created by nor officially related to the General Conference and intended to provide professional relationships conducive to sharing professional techniques and information for groups within the denomination shall be designated as associations or fellowships.

¶ **704.** *Financial Accountability of General Agencies*—All general agencies receiving general church funds (see ¶ 810.2) shall account for receipts and expenditures of funds in a format designed by the General Council on Finance and Administration. A quadrennial report of such accounting shall be included in the report of the General Council on Finance and Administration to the General Conference. The report will include, in fully descriptive form, the amount of remuneration, in cash, and in cash value of any in-kind benefits provided to all executive employees, clergy and lay, of all general agencies, where executives shall include at least those persons in positions described in ¶ 703.7. No information in the report will be considered to be confidential, and in keeping with the spirit of ¶ 702.4, all information therein will be made available upon request.

Annual reports shall be made available by the respective agencies upon the request of annual conferences and local church councils or boards. The annual reports prepared by the agencies shall include a listing of organizations, individuals, associations, fellowships, coalitions, consultants, programs, and entities not formally part of the Church, and the amount (expended annually) of monetary and in-kind contributions. The listing shall include, but not be limited to, office space, printing, staff assistance, purchases, travel expense, and other forms of financial assistance that have been granted to such entities.

¶ 705. *General Agency and Connectional Table Membership*—The people of God are called to faithful discipleship in the name of Jesus Christ. "He gave some apostles, some prophets, some evangelists, and some pastors and teachers. His purpose was to equip God's people for the work of serving and building up the body of Christ" (Ephesians 4:11-12). In response to God's call, some are called forth from local congregations to fulfill the common mission of The United Methodist Church as an expression of the Church made visible in the world. This call includes the invitation to some to be in ministry with others who together seek to fulfill the vision for the Church as members of general Church bodies. Such persons come to this ministry as servants of the whole Church.

The following provisions shall govern the nomination and election of the voting membership of those general Church bodies to which the jurisdictional conferences elect and central conferences nominate members.[2] All lay voting members of general agencies and the Connectional Table shall be professing members of The United Methodist Church and active in local churches unless otherwise specified by the *Book of Discipline*. All provisions pertaining to the nomination and election of general agency and Connectional Table members shall take effect immediately upon the adjournment of the General Conference that enacts them. The secretary of the General Conference shall coordinate the processes pertaining to nominations and elections of general agency and Connectional Table members.

---

2. See Judicial Council Decisions 467, 1090, 1095.

1. *Nominations by Conferences—a)* Each annual and missionary conference in the United States, upon recommendation from a committee composed of the bishop and the General and jurisdictional conference delegation, and having allowed opportunity for nominations from the floor, shall elect persons to be submitted to a jurisdictional pool. The jurisdictional nominating committee shall select persons for election to the following general Church bodies: Connectional Table; General Board of Church and Society; General Board of Discipleship; General Board of Global Ministries; General Board of Higher Education and Ministry; General Board of Pension and Health Benefits; The United Methodist Publishing House; Office of Christian Unity and Interreligious Relationships; General Commission on Communication; General Commission on Religion and Race; and the General Commission on the Status and Role of Women. Jurisdictional conferences may decide that persons elected by the annual and missionary conferences in the United States for inclusion in the jurisdictional pool shall not serve as members of the jurisdictional nominating committee.

b) Each annual and missionary conference in the United States shall nominate the persons most recently elected as delegates to the General Conference to the jurisdictional pool. In addition, it may nominate at least fifteen and not more than forty-five persons to the jurisdictional pool, including, where available, at least two racial and ethnic persons from each of the ethnic groups Asian American, African American, Hispanic American, Native American, Pacific Islanders; and where available at least one and not more than five persons in each of the following seven categories: (1) clergy (including at least one woman), (2) laywomen, (3) laymen, (4) youth (¶ 710.3), (5) young adults (¶ 710.3), (6) older adults, and (7) persons with disabilities. Elected members of General and jurisdictional delegations, and others nominated by their annual conference shall list all of the categories for which they qualify, i.e., nationality, age, gender, ethnic origin, etc., and shall be eligible to be nominated by the jurisdictional nominating committee to a general Church body in any one of the categories for which a delegate is qualified.

c) Each central conference or a body authorized by it shall nominate to each general program board membership at least one person from each of the following three categories: (1) clergy, (2) laymen, and (3) laywomen to form a pool from which each board is to elect the additional members that are to come from the central conferences pursuant to ¶ 705.4c. These lists shall be sent to the Connectional Table for use by the general agencies in electing additional members.

d) All nominees shall list one to three preferences for membership. In addition all nominees shall prepare an up to one-hundred-word biographical statement listing experience, gifts, training, and other qualifications for general agency membership. Biographical statements for all persons in the central and jurisdictional conference pools shall be available to the nominating committee members in the meeting at which they make their nominations. Names and biographical data of all persons nominated by the annual and missionary conferences in the United States or the central conferences, but not elected, shall be forwarded by the jurisdictional or central conference secretary to the Connectional Table to be used by the general agencies as a pool from which additional members may be elected (§§ 4e, 5b).[3]

2. *Additional Nominations*—In addition to the foregoing provisions (¶ 705.1), the Division on Ministries With Young People of the General Board of Discipleship shall nominate ten youth and ten young adults (¶ 710.3) to each jurisdictional pool, inclusive of race, ethnicity, gender, size of church, and persons with disabilities.

3. Members of the general agencies and the Connectional Table shall be elected using the following provisions:

a) Each jurisdiction shall elect members of the general agencies and the Connectional Table as provided in ¶¶ 705.4, 705.5, and 906.1. Persons within any jurisdiction elected by the United Methodist Women's national organization to serve as members of the General Board of Global Ministries (¶ 1906) shall be counted in, and not be additional to, the total number of members allocated to each jurisdiction for purposes of determining proportional distribution, but United Methodist Women members are additional to the membership prescribed in ¶ 1311.1. The secretary of the General Conference shall offer to each jurisdiction a suggested fair and equitable allocation of members to the annual and missionary conferences within each jurisdiction; however, each jurisdiction shall determine for itself how members will be allocated among the annual and missionary conferences of the jurisdiction.

---

3. See Judicial Council Decisions 520, 538.

b) Each general agency may elect at least one member with vote and voice from among the member churches of the Pan-Methodist Commission. In addition, each general agency is permitted to elect at least one member with voice but not vote from among our Full Communion Ecumenical Partners. These members would be in addition to those otherwise specified in ¶ 705.3*a* above. The Council of Bishops shall assist general agencies if they choose to elect such representatives.

c) It is recommended that, to the extent possible, at least 10 percent of the voting membership of each general agency be youth and young adults (¶ 256.3), and that the number of youth be equal to the number of young adults. Youth and young adult members of general agencies shall serve with vote except when local laws prohibit them from voting on corporate matters under consideration (see ¶ 2506.1) in which case and for which purpose youth and young adult members shall serve as non-director representatives with voice, but not vote, until they reach the legal age to serve as voting members for this purpose, at which time they shall become voting members for all purposes. The youth and young adult membership of each general board, agency, and the Connectional Table shall be inclusive (consistent with ¶¶ 705.3*d* and 2506.1).

d) It is recommended that the membership of each of the general agencies seeks to be inclusive based on gender, racial and ethnic persons, age, persons with disabilities, and size of church. In order to ensure adequate representation of racial and ethnic persons (Asian American, African Americans, Hispanic Americans, Native Americans, Pacific Islanders), it is recommended that a jurisdiction's membership on each general agency be at least 30 percent racial and ethnic persons and incorporate one-third clergy, one-third laymen, and one-third laywomen (except as provided in ¶¶ 1105, 1311). The episcopal members shall not be counted in the computation of the clergy membership.

e) The membership of the General Commission on United Methodist Men shall be elected in accordance with ¶ 537 and ¶ 2303.3. Other paragraphs of the *Discipline* notwithstanding, members of the commission holding membership by virtue of office may serve a maximum of three consecutive terms.

4. *General Program Board Membership—a)* Each general program board shall have the number of members specified in ¶¶ 1006, 1105, 1311, and 1407.

    b) Jurisdictional Membership—Each jurisdiction shall elect the number of persons listed in the specific legislation for membership on each of the four general program boards. In the jurisdictional nominating process for membership on those boards, special attention shall be given to the inclusion of clergywomen, youth (¶ 256.3), young adults, older adults, people with disabilities, and persons from small membership churches. In order to ensure adequate representation of racial and ethnic persons (Asian Americans, African Americans, Hispanic Americans, Native Americans, Pacific Islanders), it is recommended that at least 30 percent of a jurisdiction's membership on each general program board be racial and ethnic persons. It is further recommended that the jurisdiction membership on each program board incorporate one-third clergy, one-third laymen, and one-third laywomen (except as provided in ¶¶ 1105.1, 1311.2; see also ¶¶ 1311.6, 1407). The episcopal members shall not be counted in the computation of the clergy membership.[4]

    c) Central Conference Membership—The total central conference membership, including central conference bishops, in general Church bodies shall be allocated as follows: four members on the General Commission on Religion and Race; three each (one from each region: Philippines, Europe, Africa) on the General Commission on Archives and History, the General Commission on Communication, the General Commission on United Methodist Men, and The United Methodist Publishing House; three each on the General Council on Finance and Administration; seven each (one from each Central Conference) on the Connectional Table, and the General Board of Church and Society; three on the General Board of Higher Education and Ministry; four (at least one from each region from the Philippines, Europe, and Africa) on the General Board of Discipleship and the General Commission on the Status and Role of Women; and eleven on the General Board of Global Ministries, only two of whom shall be bishops. It is recommended that the aggregate central conference membership on the program boards be composed of one-third clergy (half of whom shall be women), one-third laymen, and one-third laywomen. The central conference membership, excluding episcopal members, shall be elected by the Council of Bishops, except that central conference membership (except bishops) to the Global

---

4. See Judicial Council Decisions 446, 451, 467.

Ministries board of directors shall be nominated and elected by the central conferences as provided in ¶¶ 1311.1 and 1311.5*b*)

d) Episcopal Membership—The episcopal membership of the general program boards shall be nominated by the Council of Bishops and elected by the General Conference. At least one of the episcopal members of each general agency, with the exception of the General Board of Pension and Health Benefits, shall be a central conference bishop and, in the case of the General Board of Global Ministries, two central conference bishops (from two of three regions: Africa, Europe, Philippines). (See ¶ 1311.6.)

e) Additional Membership—Additional members shall be elected by each general program board in order to bring into the board persons with special knowledge or background that will aid in the work of the agency, to consider differing theological perspectives, and to perfect the representation of racial and ethnic persons, youth (¶ 710.3), young adults (¶ 710.3), older adults, women and men, people with disabilities, and persons from small-membership churches. After the election of central conference members as provided in ¶ 705.4*c*, and with the exception of the General Commission on the Status and Role of Women (¶ 2104.1*b*), the remaining number of additional members shall be allocated by the secretary of the General Conference so as to insure to the extent possible that membership of each board reflects the proportionate membership of the jurisdictions based upon the combined clergy and lay membership, excluding episcopal members. In the determination of proportionate allocation, minor fractions shall be rounded down and major fractions rounded up to the nearest integer, and there shall be no minimum number of additional members assigned to any jurisdiction. Insofar as possible, the nominating committee shall select from the jurisdictional nominating pool for the election of persons to fill the additional membership positions from their jurisdictions insuring diversity as otherwise provided in *The Book of Discipline* (¶ 705.4*b*). Each general program board shall elect additional members as specified in general program board membership paragraphs. Insofar as possible, no more than one person shall be elected from each episcopal area. It is recommended that such additional membership shall maintain the one-third laymen, one-third laywomen, and one-third clergy balance.[5]

5. See Judicial Council Decisions 446, 520, 601.

f) Liaison Representatives—The Methodist Church of Puerto Rico (*Iglesia Metodista Autonóma Affiliada de Puerto Rico*) will have one liaison representative, at its own expense, to each of the general program agencies of The United Methodist Church.

g) Status of Liaison Representatives—Because of the special nature of the relationship between the Methodist Church of Puerto Rico and the general agencies of The United Methodist Church as established in the Concordat between the two churches, the liaison representatives of the Methodist Church of Puerto Rico to the general agencies of The United Methodist Church will serve with voice and vote and be afforded the same status on those agencies as though they were members, except as provided in ¶ 705.4*f*).

5. *Other General Agencies*—*a*) Each jurisdictional conference shall elect members from the jurisdictional pool nominated by the annual and missionary conferences in the United States (¶ 705.1) in accordance with the specific membership provisions of those agencies as set forth in the *Book of Discipline:* General Board of Pension and Health Benefits (¶ 1502.1*a*), The United Methodist Publishing House (¶ 1602), Office of Christian Unity and Interreligious Relationships (¶ 437), General Commission on Communication (¶ 1807), General Commission on the Status and Role of Women (¶ 2104), and General Commission on Religion and Race (¶2003). With the exception of the General Board of Pension and Health Benefits (¶ 1502.1) and The United Methodist Publishing House (¶ 1602.1) the number of additional members to be elected shall be allocated by the secretary of the General Conference so as to insure to the extent possible that membership of each agency reflects the proportionate membership of the jurisdictions based upon the combined clergy and lay membership, excluding episcopal members. In the determination of proportionate allocation, minor fractions shall be rounded down and major fractions rounded up to the nearest integer, and there shall be no minimum number of additional members assigned to any jurisdiction. Insofar as possible the nominating committee shall select from the jurisdictional nominating pool for the election of persons to fill the additional membership positions from their jurisdictions insuring diversity as otherwise provided in *The Book of Discipline* (¶ 705.4*b*).

b) Episcopal and additional members, if any, of the general agencies listed in ¶ 705.5*a* shall be nominated and elected by the procedures specified in the paragraphs listed in ¶¶ 705.1*b*,

705.1*d*, and 705.4*e*. The agencies shall consider names forwarded to them by the Connectional Table as having been nominated by the annual and missionary conferences in the United States or in the central conferences, but not elected by these conferences to general agency membership. Additional names may be considered in order to perfect the representation as provided in ¶ 705.4*e*.

¶ **706.** *Nomination of Additional Board Members*—1. Giving due consideration to inclusiveness (see ¶¶ 124, 140), each jurisdiction shall designate one clergy, one laywoman, and one layman whom it has elected to a general program agency to nominate the additional members of that program agency (¶ 705.4). The members thus designated by the five jurisdictions in each general program agency shall constitute a committee to nominate additional members for that agency and shall be convened as provided in ¶ 706.2. The number of additional members shall be allocated by the secretary of the General Conference so as to insure to the extent possible that membership of the program agency reflects the proportionate membership of the jurisdictions based upon the combined clergy and lay membership, excluding episcopal members. In the determination of proportionate allocation, minor fractions shall be rounded down and major fractions rounded up to the nearest integer, and there shall be no minimum number of additional members assigned to any jurisdiction. In so far as possible, the nominating committee shall select from the jurisdictional nominating pool for the election of persons to fill the additional membership positions from their jurisdictions insuring diversity as otherwise provided in *The Book of Discipline* (¶ 705.4*b*). In place of the process outlined in this paragraph, the General Commission on the Status and Role of Women will use the procedures in ¶ 2104.1*b*) to select additional members.

2. A bishop designated by the president of the Council of Bishops shall convene the committee as soon as practical after jurisdictional elections have been completed. The committee shall, in so far as possible, use the names forwarded to it by the jurisdictions as having been nominated by the annual and missionary conferences in the United States to their jurisdictional pool as well as names from caucuses and other appropriate groups. To aid the committee, biographical data submitted by the annual conferences (¶ 705.1*d*) shall be made available from the jurisdictional conference secretaries. In addition, general agencies shall submit

to the committee names and biographical data of persons eligible for reelection who are willing to serve.

3. The committee shall complete its work prior to the organizational meeting (¶ 707) of any of the agencies listed in ¶ 703.5 and report by mail to the previously elected members of each of those agencies the names of persons nominated as additional members of that agency. All members shall be elected and seated before an agency proceeds to the election of officers or any other business.

¶ 707. *Meetings*—1. In those years in which the General Conference holds its regular session, all general program agencies shall meet, organize, and conduct such business as may properly come before the agency not later than ninety days after the close of the jurisdictional conferences. Each organizational meeting shall be convened by a bishop designated by the president of the Council of Bishops.

2. All councils, boards, commissions, and committees established by a General, jurisdictional, central, annual, or other conference shall meet and organize as promptly as feasible following the selection of their members.

3. Unless otherwise specified in the *Discipline* or by the establishing conference, every council, board, commission, and committee shall continue in responsibility until its successor council, board, commission, or committee is organized.

¶ 708. *Organization*—1. Each program board shall elect a president and one or more vice presidents from the voting membership of the board, and a secretary, treasurer, and such other officers as it deems appropriate, giving consideration to inclusiveness (¶¶ 124, 140), provided that all officers shall be members of The United Methodist Church.

2. Each program board shall elect chairpersons for its divisions, departments, or other subunits from the voting membership of the board. The divisions, departments, or other subunits shall elect a vice chairperson, a secretary, and such other officers as it deems appropriate.

3. Officers of boards, divisions, and departments, or other subunits who do not serve on the board of directors as voting members shall be elected for the quadrennium or until their successors are elected.

4. No person shall serve as president or chairperson of more than one general agency or division, department, or the structural counterpart thereof.

5. Staff of program boards shall not be eligible to serve as officers of corresponding General Conference legislative committees.

¶ **709.** *Divisions and Subunits*—The membership of each program board shall be divided among the divisions or other subunits of the board in such number as the board determines.

¶ **710.** *Membership Qualifications*—1. Members of all general agencies shall be professing members of The United Methodist Church except as provided in ¶ 705.3*b*.

2. Members of all general agencies shall be persons of genuine Christian character who love the Church, are morally disciplined and loyal to the ethical standards of The United Methodist Church as set forth in the Social Principles, and are otherwise competent to serve as members of general agencies.

3. All youth representatives (¶ 256.3) elected to general agencies shall be at the time of organizational board meetings twelve to sixteen years of age. All young adults (¶ 256.3) elected to general agencies shall be at the time of organizational board meetings seventeen to twenty-eight years of age. Youth and young adult members serve with the voting limitations of ¶ 705.3*c*), as conditioned by ¶ 2506.1. All older-adult representatives (¶ 705.1*b*(6)) shall be at the time of organizational board meetings at least sixty-five years of age.

4. A voting member of a general agency shall be eligible for membership on that agency for no more than two consecutive four-year terms. The four-year term shall begin at the first organizational meeting of that agency following General Conference. Service of more than one year in fulfilling an unexpired or vacated position shall be considered as a full four-year term. To provide a continuing membership on these agencies, it is recommended that each nominating and electing body give special attention to continuing and effective membership on these agencies. If a general agency is merged with another agency, the years served by members prior to the merger shall be counted as part of the maximum specified above.[6]

A person who has been a voting member of general agencies for four consecutive quadrennia shall be ineligible for election to a general agency in the succeeding quadrennium. The foregoing shall not apply to episcopal members.

5. No person shall serve at the same time on more than one general agency or any part thereof, except where the *Discipline*

---

6. See Judicial Council Decision 495.

specifically provides for such interagency representation; provided, however, that if this limitation would deprive a jurisdiction of its full episcopal representation on an agency, it may be suspended to the extent necessary to permit such representation. (See ¶ 906.1*a*.)

6. A voting member of a general agency, by virtue of such membership, shall become an ex officio (voting) member of the corresponding agency or its equivalent structure, if any, in the annual conference in accordance with the provisions of ¶ 610.6; unless such membership would conflict with ¶ 612.2*c*(2). Elected members of the General Board of Higher Education and Ministry may serve as ex officio members on both corresponding boards of their annual conference: the Board of Ordained Ministry and the board of higher education. They shall be voting members, however, only on the conference board of higher education unless nominated by their resident bishop to be a voting member of the conference Board of Ordained Ministry pursuant to ¶ 635.1*a*.

7. No person who receives compensation for services rendered or commissions of any kind from an agency shall be eligible for voting membership on that agency.[7]

8. No elected member, officer, or other employee shall vote on or take part in deliberations on significant matters directly or indirectly affecting his or her business, income, or employment, or the business, income, or employment of a member of his or her immediate family.

9. *a*) If any clergy member of a General or jurisdictional agency who was elected to represent a certain annual conference ceases to be a member of that annual conference, or if any lay member so elected changes permanent residence to a place outside the bounds of that annual conference, that member's place shall automatically become vacant.

b) If any clergy member of a general agency who was chosen to represent a certain jurisdiction ceases to be a member of an annual conference in that jurisdiction, or if any lay member so elected changes permanent residence to a place outside the bounds of that jurisdiction, that member's place shall automatically become vacant.

c) If any clergy member of a jurisdictional agency ceases to be a member of an annual conference in that jurisdiction, or if

---

7. See Judicial Council Decision 139.

any lay member so elected changes permanent residence to a place outside the bounds of the jurisdiction, that member's place shall automatically become vacant.

10. If a member of a general agency is absent from two consecutive meetings of the agency without a reason acceptable to the agency, that person shall cease to be a member thereof. In that case the person shall be so notified, and that place shall be filled in accordance with the appropriate provisions of the *Discipline*.

¶ 711. *Dismissal of Members and Employees*—The councils, boards, committees, or commissions elected, authorized, or provided for by the General Conference shall have full power and authority to remove and dismiss at their discretion any member, officer, or employee thereof:

1. Who has become incapacitated so as to be unable to perform official duties.

2. Who is guilty of immoral conduct or breach of trust.

3. Who for any reason is unable to or who fails to perform the duties of the office or for other misconduct that any council, board, committee, or commission may deem sufficient to warrant such dismissal and removal.

In the event that any member, officer, or employee of such council, board, committee, or commission, elected, authorized, or provided for by the General Conference, is found guilty of any crime involving moral turpitude by any federal, state, or county court or pleads guilty thereto, then the council, board, committee, or commission of which that person is a member, officer, or employee shall be and is hereby authorized to remove such member, officer, or employee so convicted; and the place so vacated shall be filled as provided in the *Discipline*.

¶ 712. *Vacancies*—Unless otherwise specified, vacancies on general agencies occurring during the quadrennium shall be filled as follows: an episcopal vacancy shall be filled by the Council of Bishops; a vacancy in the jurisdictional or central conference membership shall be filled by the corresponding College of Bishops (the replacement must be a member of the same annual conference of the person being replaced), with notice of the vacancy sent by the agency to the secretary of the Council of Bishops; a vacancy in the additional membership shall be filled by the agency itself. When the vacancy has been filled, the secretary of the agency will immediately notify the new member's annual conference secretary.

¶ **713.** *Election of General Secretaries of Program Agencies and Termination of General Agency Staff*—The general secretary of each general program agency that is accountable to the Connectional Table shall be elected quadrennially by ballot of the board of the agency involved. The balloting shall be secret, but the presiding officer shall announce to the membership the results of the election, including the number of votes for election, against election, and in abstention. The termination of employment of an agency's general secretary must be approved by the agency's board. Absent a contrary action by, or policy of, the agency's board, the agency's general secretary may terminate the employment of all other agency staff, including elected staff.

¶ **714.** Each general agency shall appoint such other staff as may be necessary by a process to be determined by the agency.

¶ **715.** *Provisions Pertaining to Staff*—1. No elected general program agency staff shall hold the same position more than twelve years. Years of service prior to January 1, 1989, are not counted. The agency responsible for the election of such staff may annually suspend this provision by a two-thirds ballot vote.[8]

2. Official travel of the staffs of agencies shall be interpreted to include all travel that is necessary in the performance of official duties directly related to the agency functions. No staff person shall accept honoraria for such official duties. A staff member may accept an engagement not related to the functions of the employing agency when such an engagement does not interfere with official duties; the staff member may accept an honorarium for services rendered in connection with such engagements.

3. Normal retirement for all general agency staff personnel shall be at age sixty-five or the completion of forty years of service to The United Methodist Church in an elective, appointive, or employed capacity. Mandatory retirement for elective and appointive staff shall be at age seventy-two. There shall be no mandatory retirement age for other employed staff. All general agency staff personnel may elect to retire from the employing general agency at any time in accordance with the policy in place at the general agency or, if the general agency has a voting representative on the Committee on Personnel Policies and Practices of the General Council on Finance and Administration, with the policy established by the General Council on Finance and Admin-

---

8. See Judicial Council Decision 858.

istration upon recommendation of the Committee on Personnel Policies and Practices.

4. Provisions of the Retirement Plan for General Agencies, shall be reviewed, with recommendations, by the Committee on Personnel Policies and Practices (¶ 807.12b).

a) Each general agency shall sponsor or participate in a group health care plan that covers the agency's full-time clergy and full-time lay employees in the United States. For the purpose of this paragraph, group health care plan shall mean a health insurance plan, group health care plan, or multiple-employer health care plan that provides benefits for major medical and hospitalization expenses. The sponsoring general agency may determine additional eligibility for the group health care plan in its discretion.

Alternatively, in the event that federal law or state law governing health care plans and health insurance establishes coverage options for those persons without employer-provided coverage that ensure access, regardless of health status or condition, to affordable coverage through health insurance exchanges, connectors, single-payer systems, or other mechanisms, the general agency may cease maintaining its group health care plan to the extent such coverage is available to its clergy and lay employees. In such event, the general agency nevertheless shall provide continued administrative and financial support of full-time clergy and full-time lay employees toward the purchase of such coverage through these alternative mechanisms to the extent such individuals' coverage may not be subsidized by government agencies, i.e., because their compensation exceeds certain thresholds, particularly considering the tax advantages of employer-provided financial support toward health care coverage.

In addition, general agencies shall develop and maintain health and wellness programs for their full-time clergy and full-time lay employees. Moreover, each general agency shall annually submit its health plan data to the extent the general agency maintains a group health care plan, de-identified as necessary, including, but not limited to, financial soundness, claims experience and other cost drivers, plan designs and coverage, and eligibility criteria to the General Board of Pension and Health Benefits.

b) Each general agency shall respect the health and wholeness of its clergypersons and lay employees, who have retired in accordance with the general agency's retirement policy, and their spouses, by providing access to Medicare supplement plans and prescription drug coverage plans. Access for retirees and their spouses may include, but shall not be limited to (i) sponsoring an employer retiree health care plan that supplements Medicare; (ii) participating in a multiple employer retiree health care plan that supplements Medicare; (iii) securing individuals' eligibility under group contracts with Medicare supplement plan providers or exchanges; (iv) subsidizing the costs of coverage for retired clergypersons and lay employees and their spouses enrolled in Medicare Part D plans or Medicare Advantage plans; (v) providing subsidies toward and group relationships with providers of individual Medicare supplement and other retiree coverage policies; and (vi) providing fixed dollar retiree health benefits through health reimbursement arrangements, stipends, or otherwise.

c) Each general agency must submit a generally accepted financial valuation, such as in accordance with Statement of Financial Accounting Standard No. 106, as amended, of its projected medical liabilities for its population covered by its employer retiree health care plan to the General Board of Pension and Health Benefits biennially.

d) On or before December 31, 2013, and then annually thereafter, each general agency must develop and implement a formal comprehensive funding plan for funding its annual benefit obligations relating to its annual retirement, welfare and health plan obligations (including those obligations of the General Council on Finance and Administration (GCFA) for bishops) as well as its projected pension and retiree medical liabilities (including those obligations of GCFA for bishops). The funding plan or plans shall be submitted to the General Board of Pension and Health Benefits for review and be published along with a favorable written opinion of the General Board of Pension and Health Benefits in an addendum to the agency's annual financial report. In addition, the General Board of Pension and Health Benefits shall include general agency benefits and benefits for bishops in its quadrennial report to General Conference concerning the long-term benefit liabilities of the denomination. Therefore, each general agency shall provide to the General Board of Pension and Health Benefits information periodically requested. Each general agency shall document in writing its policy regarding the portability of retiree health care eligibility, coverage, cost-sharing, and benefits and communicate the policy to its clergy and lay employees and incoming clergy and lay employees from annual conferences or other general agencies. For the purpose of this paragraph, portability encompasses credit given for service outside the general agency within the denomination to clergy and lay employees toward (i) eligibility for health care coverage in retirement and (ii) accrual of employer subsidies toward or employer cost-sharing of the cost of health care coverage

5. All general secretaries, deputy general secretaries, associate general secretaries, assistant general secretaries, and treasurers of all general agencies and the publisher of The United Methodist Church shall be professing members of The United Methodist Church. This provision shall not apply to persons employed prior to the 2004 General Conference.[9]

6. No member of the staff of a general agency shall be eligible for voting membership on any general or jurisdictional agency of The United Methodist Church, except where the *Discipline* specifically provides for such interagency representation.

7. Elected staff shall be allowed voice, but not vote in the agency and its subunits.

8. All elected staff persons of general agencies shall be persons who model themselves after the servanthood of Jesus Christ. They shall be persons of genuine Christian character who love the Church and are committed to the oneness of the body of Christ, are morally disciplined and shall uphold the doctrinal and ethical standards of The United Methodist Church as set forth in the Doctrinal Standards (¶ 104) and Social Principles, and are competent to administer the affairs of a general agency.

9. Prior to any interviews of clergypersons for general board or agency staff positions, the bishop of the clergyperson under consideration shall be consulted at the initiative of the general agency. When a clergyperson's employment with a general agency is terminated, the general agency shall have no further obligation to provide compensation or benefits to the terminated clergyperson, except as provided or permitted by the General Council on Finance and Administration's uniform personnel policies described in ¶ 807.12*a*.

¶ **716.** *Nondiscrimination Policies*—1. It shall be the policy of The United Methodist Church that all agencies and institutions, including hospitals, homes, and educational institutions, shall:

---

9. See Judicial Council Decision 426.

(*a*) recruit, employ, utilize, recompense, and promote their professional staff and other personnel in a manner consistent with the commitment of The United Methodist Church to women and men of all races and ethnic origins, including persons with disabilities; (*b*) fulfill their duties and responsibilities in a manner that does not involve segregation or discrimination on the basis of race, color, age, sex, or disability, including HIV status; and (*c*) provide for adequate representation by laity.

2. All agencies and institutions shall, insofar as reasonably possible, schedule and hold all events, including designated places of lodging and meals for the events, in accessible settings that adequately accommodate persons with disabilities. They are encouraged to include persons with disabilities in the planning and presentation of events.

If for any reason whatsoever any event is scheduled or held in a facility that does not so conform, all notices of the meeting will include plainly stated advice to that effect, or alternatively may bear a logo consisting of the international symbol for access placed inside a slashed circle. The term *event* shall be given a broad interpretation and shall include, by way of example, scheduled conferences, seminars, and other meetings to which persons are invited or called to attend as representatives of the Church or its various institutions and agencies.

¶ **717.** *Sustainable and Socially Responsible Investments*—In the investment of money, it shall be the policy of The United Methodist Church that all general boards and agencies, including the General Board of Pension and Health Benefits, and all administrative agencies and institutions, including hospitals, homes, educational institutions, annual conferences, foundations, and local churches, make a conscious effort to invest in institutions, companies, corporations, or funds with policies and practices that are socially responsible, consistent with the goals outlined in the Social Principles. All United Methodist institutions shall endeavor to seek investments in institutions, companies, corporations, or funds that promote racial and gender justice, protect human rights, prevent the use of sweatshop or forced labor, avoid human suffering, and preserve the natural world, including mitigating the effects of climate change. In addition, United Methodist institutions shall endeavor to avoid investments in companies engaged in core business activities that are not aligned with the Social Principles through their direct or indirect involvement with the production of anti-personnel weapons and armaments (both nuclear and conventional weapons), alcoholic beverages or tobacco; or that are involved in privately operated correctional facilities, gambling, pornography or other forms of exploitative adult entertainment. The boards and agencies are to give careful consideration to environmental, social, and governance factors when making investment decisions and actively exercise their responsibility as owners of the companies in which they invest. This includes engaging with companies to create positive change and hold them accountable for their actions, while also considering exclusion if companies fail to act responsibly.

¶ **718.** *Record Maintenance*—Each general agency shall keep a continuous record of its advocacy roles, coalitions, and other organizations supported by membership or funds, and endorsement or opposition of federal or state legislation. Information concerning these activities shall be available to United Methodist churches upon written request. Organizations not officially related to the General Conference may take positions only in their own names and may not speak for a general agency or the denomination as a whole (¶ 509.1).

¶ **719.** *Decisions for Program Expenditures*—All programs or general funds administered by any general agency of The United Methodist Church (¶ 701) that are proposed to be used within an annual conference shall be implemented or disbursed only after consultation with the presiding bishop, the director of connectional ministries or equivalent, the Council on Ministries, and the appropriate district superintendent(s) of that annual conference. Consultation in matters of program implementation, funding, and relationships among various agencies, conferences, and other bodies of the Church requires communication, including written documentation, in which each party reveals plans and intents in such a way as to assure dialogue and mutual awareness, even if not agreement.[10]

¶ **720.** *International and Ecumenical Settings*—The General Board of Global Ministries shall facilitate and coordinate the program relationships of other program agencies of The United Methodist Church with colleague churches and agencies in nations other than the United States. The resources of the General Board of Global Ministries shall also be available to the Council of

---

10. See Judicial Council Decision 518.

Bishops in the implementation of its responsibilities as defined in ¶ 416.2, .3. Central conferences of The United Methodist Church may request program and other assistance through direct relationships with the program agencies of The United Methodist Church.

¶ **721.** *Program and Fiscal Year*—1. The program and fiscal year for The United Methodist Church shall be the calendar year.

2. Unless otherwise specified in the *Discipline* for a specific purpose, the term *quadrennium* shall be deemed to be the four-year period beginning January 1 following the adjournment of the regular session of the General Conference.[11]

¶ **722.** *Restrictions on Closed Meetings*—In the spirit of openness and accountability, all meetings of councils, boards, agencies, commissions, and committees of the Church at all levels of the church, including subunit meetings and teleconferences, shall be open. Regardless of local laws or customs, all participants shall be notified at the beginning of any meeting, including telephone or video conference calls, if the meeting is being recorded electronically and of the intended use of such recording. Portions of a meeting may be closed for consideration of specific subjects if such a closed session is authorized by an affirmative public vote of at least three-fourths of the voting members present. The vote shall be taken in public session and recorded in the minutes. Documents distributed in open meetings shall be considered public.

Great restraint should be used in closing meetings; closed sessions should be used as seldom as possible. Subjects that may be considered in closed session are limited to real estate matters; negotiations, when general knowledge could be harmful to the negotiation process; personnel matters;[12] issues related to the accreditation or approval of institutions; discussions relating to pending or potential litigation or collective bargaining; communications with attorneys or accountants; deployment of security personnel or devices; and negotiations involving confidential third-party information. Meetings of the committee on pastor-parish or staff-parish relations are to be closed meetings pursuant to ¶ 258.2e. While it is expected that the General Conference, the Judicial Council, and the Council of Bishops will live by the spirit of this paragraph, each of these constitutional bodies is governed by its own rules of procedure.

---

11. See Judicial Council Decision 559.
12. See Judicial Council Decision 869.

A report on the results of a closed session shall be made immediately upon its conclusion or as soon thereafter as is practicable.

¶ **723.** *Translation of Church Name*—The name of The United Methodist Church may be translated by any central conference into languages other than English. The United Methodist Church in the Central and Southern Europe Central Conference and the Germany Central Conference may use the name *Evangelisch-methodistische Kirche.*

¶ **724.** *Church Founding Date*—The United Methodist Church (¶ 141) has become the successor to all rights, powers, and privileges of The Evangelical United Brethren Church and The Methodist Church. The two churches, from their beginnings, have had a close relationship.

The Methodist Church, the first of the two churches to organize, dates from the Christmas Conference of 1784. Therefore, The United Methodist Church recognizes as its founding date the year 1784.

All General Conferences shall be designated not in numerical sequence from any particular date, but merely by the calendar years in which they are respectively held. An annual conference, local church, or other body within The United Methodist Church that is composed of uniting units with differing dates of origin shall use as the date of its founding the date of founding of the older or oldest of the uniting units while remaining sensitive to the recording of the entirety of the Church's history, including all information regarding the younger unit.

Section II. General Council on Finance and Administration

¶ **801.** The work of the Church requires the support of our people. Participation through service and gifts is a Christian duty, a means of grace, and an expression of our love to God. In order that all members of The United Methodist Church may share in its manifold ministries at home and abroad and that the work committed to us may prosper, the following financial plan has been duly approved and adopted.

¶ **802.** *Name*—There shall be a General Council on Finance and Administration of The United Methodist Church, hereinafter called the council.

¶ **803.** *Incorporation*—The council shall be incorporated in such state or states as the council shall determine. This corporation shall be the successor corporation and organization to the

Council on World Service and Finance (including the Council on World Service and Finance of The United Methodist Church, an Illinois corporation; the World Service Commission of the Methodist Episcopal Church, an Illinois corporation; the General Council of Administration of The Evangelical United Brethren Church, an Ohio corporation; the Board of Administration, Church of the United Brethren in Christ, an Ohio corporation) and the Board of Trustees.

This corporation shall receive and administer new trusts and funds, and so far as may be legal be the successor in trust of: The Board of Trustees of The United Methodist Church; The Board of Trustees of The Evangelical United Brethren Church, incorporated under the laws of Ohio; The Board of Trustees of the Church of the United Brethren in Christ, incorporated under the laws of Ohio; The Board of Trustees of The Evangelical Church, an unincorporated body; The Board of Trustees of The Methodist Church, incorporated under the laws of Ohio; The Trustees of The Methodist Episcopal Church, incorporated under the laws of Ohio; The Board of Trustees of The Methodist Episcopal Church, South, incorporated under the laws of Tennessee; and The Board of Trustees of The Methodist Protestant Church, incorporated under the laws of Maryland; and so far as may be legal, as such successor in trust, it is authorized to receive from any of its said predecessor corporations all trust funds and assets of every kind and character—real, personal, or mixed—held by them or any one of them, or to merge into itself any one or more of its said predecessor corporations. Any such trusts and funds coming to it as successor corporation, either by transfer or by merger, shall be administered in accordance with the conditions under which they have been previously received and administered by said predecessor corporations or unincorporated body.

¶ **804.** *Amenability*—The council shall report to and be amenable to the General Conference, and it shall cooperate with the Connectional Table in the compilation of budgets for program agencies participating in World Service Funds, as defined in ¶ 806.1.

¶ **805.** *Organization*—1. *Membership*—The twenty-one voting members of the council shall be elected quadrennially.

    a) Sixteen voting members of the council shall be elected by the General Conference and be nominated as follows:

(1) two bishops nominated by the Council of Bishops;

(2) eleven persons from the jurisdictions, nominated by the college of bishops in each jurisdiction based upon an allocation by the secretary of the General Conference so that the membership of the council reflects the proportionate membership of the jurisdictions based upon their combined clergy and lay membership; and

(3) three persons from the central conferences—one from Africa, one from Europe, and one from the Philippines—nominated by the Council of Bishops.

b) It is recommended that in selecting the voting members from the jurisdictions and central conferences attention be given to ensuring representation of racial and ethnic groups and young people, and that approximately one-third be clergy in full connection, one-third be laymen, and one-third be laywomen.

c) Five voting members of the council shall be nominated and elected by the council in such a manner as set forth in the council's bylaws, provided, not more than one of these five voting members shall be from the same jurisdictional or central conference. These five voting members shall be selected for the purpose of bringing to the council special knowledge, experience, or diversity.

d) The general secretaries who serve as the chief executive officers of the general agencies and the president/chief executive officer of The United Methodist Publishing House may sit with the council and shall have the right to the floor without the privilege of voting.

e) The voting members, including bishops, shall not be eligible for membership on, or employment by, any other general agency of The United Methodist Church (¶ 701.2), except where the *Book of Discipline* specifically provides for such interagency representation. Members shall also be guided by such conflict-of-interest policies and provisions as may from time to time be adopted by the General Conference or by the council itself.

f) Members shall serve until their successors are elected and qualified.

g) Vacancies occurring between sessions of the General Conference shall be filled by the council on nomination of the College of Bishops of the jurisdiction concerned (see ¶ 712) if the vacancy is among members chosen to represent a jurisdiction, or, in the event of a vacancy among the episcopal or central conference representative members, on nomination of the Council of Bishops. Vacancies among the five voting members nominated and elected by the council shall be filled in such a manner as set forth in the council's bylaws.

2. *Meetings*—The council shall meet at least annually and at such other times as are necessary on call of the president or on written request of one-fifth of the members. Eleven voting members shall constitute a quorum.

3. *Officers*

a) The council shall elect from its membership a president, a vice president, and a recording secretary, whose duties shall be prescribed in its bylaws.

b) The council shall elect quadrennially, in such manner as it shall provide in its bylaws, a general secretary, who shall also be the treasurer and chief executive officer of the council. The general secretary shall have the right to the floor at all meetings of the council and its committees without the privilege of voting.

4. *Committees*—*a) Committee on Audit and Review*—The council shall appoint a Committee on Audit and Review, no members of which shall be officers of the council, and at least half of whom shall not be members of the council, whose duty it shall be to review audits of all treasuries receiving general Church funds (see ¶ 810.2) in accordance with all established auditing standards, including the funds of the council, related policies with financial implications, and the utilization of financial assets in achieving the stated mission of the entity as defined by the General Conference, the governing board, and donor designations. Not included are the audits of the General Board of Pension and Health Benefits and The United Methodist Publishing House. In any matter of possible or potential financial impropriety reported to the committee by the auditors, the committee chair shall immediately inform the president and general secretary of the General Council on Finance and Administration and the president and general secretary of the applicable agency. If any matter involves the president or general secretary of the General Council on Finance and Administration (GCFA) or the applicable agency, the committee shall determine other reporting avenues within GCFA or the applicable agency, as appropriate. The committee shall report its findings to the next meeting of the council.

b) Committee on Personnel Policies and Practices—The council shall organize a committee consisting of three representatives from the General Council on Finance and Administration, one of whom shall serve as chairperson, and one representative of each of the following agencies: the General Board of Church and Society, the General Board of Discipleship, the General Board of Global Ministries, the General Board of Higher Education and Ministry, the General Commission on Archives and History, the General Commission on Communication, the General Commission on Religion and Race, the General Commission on the Status and Role of Women, and the General Commission on United Methodist Men. Each of the aforementioned representatives shall be selected by the council, board, or commission represented from its membership. The general secretary of the council, or his or her designee, shall sit with this committee with voice but not vote.

The committee shall have duties and responsibilities as defined in ¶ 807.12*b*.

c) Committee on Legal Responsibilities and Corporate Governance—The council shall organize a committee composed of six persons: three members of the council, two active annual conference chancellors, and one at-large attorney. The committee shall be amenable to the council and shall make recommendations to the council regarding the fulfillment of its responsibilities defined in ¶ 807.9 and its exercise of appropriate principles of corporate governance. The Legal Services Department of the council shall be responsible to the Committee on Legal Responsibilities and Corporate Governance.

d) Other Committees—The council shall establish such other committees and task forces as needed for the performance of its duties.

5. *Staff*—On nomination of the general secretary, the council may elect deputy and/or associate general secretaries, who shall work under the direction of the general secretary.

6. *Financial Support*—a) Financial support from general church funds for the work of the council shall be from the following sources: (1) an on-ratio allocation from the General Administration Fund, in an amount determined by the General Conference; (2) fixed charges against the World Service Fund, the Episcopal Fund, the Interdenominational Cooperation Fund, and such other general funds as the General Conference may

authorize, on recommendation of the council. Fixed charges shall be in proportion to the funds' receipts.

b) The council shall submit to each quadrennial session of the General Conference budgets of estimated income and expense for the four years of the ensuing quadrennium. Prior to the beginning of each fiscal year, the council shall approve a budget for its operation for the following year. In the event of unanticipated circumstances, the council may amend a budget it had previously approved for its own operation.

c) The council shall report to each quadrennial session of the General Conference the amounts of its actual income and expenditures for the four preceding years.

¶ **806.** *Fiscal Responsibilities*—All monies contributed by a local church to any of the general funds of the Church, as listed or defined in ¶ 810.1, and such other funds as may have been authorized by the General Conference shall be held in trust by the council and distributed only in support of the ministries of the respective funds. The council shall be accountable to The United Methodist Church through the General Conference in all matters relating to the receiving, disbursing, and reporting of such funds, and agencies receiving such funds shall be fiscally accountable to the council. In the exercise of its fiscal accountability role, the council shall have the authority and responsibility to perform the following functions:

1. It shall submit to each quadrennial session of the General Conference, for its action and determination, budgets of expense for each of the general funds of the Church, as listed or defined in ¶ 810.1, and such other general funds as the General Conference may establish. It shall also make recommendations regarding all other funding considerations to come before General Conference. Actual receipts for each fund for the quadrennium then ending shall be the basis for all budgeting procedures and comparisons for the coming quadrennium.

a) The council shall make recommendations to the General Conference as to the amount and distribution of the Episcopal Fund and General Administration Fund, and, in consultation with the Connectional Table, other apportioned general funds.

b) In the case of the World Service Fund, Ministerial Education Fund, Black College Fund, Africa University Fund, and Interdenominational Cooperation Fund, the General Council on Finance and Administration and the Connectional Table shall proceed in the following manner to develop budget recommendations as they relate to allocations to the general program agencies of the Church and funding level recommendations:

(1) The General Council on Finance and Administration shall establish the estimated amount available for distribution from the World Service Fund among the general program agencies and through the other funds.

(2) The Connectional Table will review the program priorities, missional priorities, and special programs and the estimated amount available to the general program agencies, and then establish the amounts to be distributed to those agencies from the annual World Service allocation. The Connectional Table will review both the funding priorities and the estimated amount available to the other funds and then establish the amounts to be distributed to each.

(3) The General Council on Finance and Administration will review the recommended allocations to the several general program agencies within the total sum of the World Service Fund budget, and the funding levels for each of the other listed apportioned funds. When the General Council on Finance and Administration and the Connectional Table agree, these allocations and total sum will be included in the World Service budget and the funding levels of all these listed general apportioned funds will be recommended to the General Conference by the General Council on Finance and Administration.

c) It shall recommend the formulas by which all apportionments to the annual conferences shall be determined, subject to the approval of the General Conference.

d) Before the beginning of each year, the General Council on Finance and Administration shall estimate and communicate to the Connectional Table the sum available at that time from World Service contingency funds to meet requests for additional funding from the general program agencies. The Connectional Table shall be authorized to approve allocations to the general program agencies for additional program funding up to the limit so established. No money shall be allocated by the Connectional Table from this source for general administrative costs, fixed charges, or capital outlay without approval by the General Council on Finance and Administration.

e) The Connectional Table shall receive from the General Council on Finance and Administration copies of the proposed annual budgets of the general program agencies, in order that it may review such budgets in relation to the program proposals made by those agencies in their quadrennial budget requests.

2. It shall receive and disburse in accordance with budgets and/or directives approved by the General Conference all funds raised throughout the Church for any of the general funds of the Church, as listed or defined in ¶ 810.1, and for any other fund or funds, as directed by the proper authority.

3. *Accounting and Reporting*—It shall require all agencies receiving general Church funds (see ¶ 810.2) to follow uniform accounting classifications and procedures for reporting. It shall include in its quadrennial report to the General Conference a fiscal report for each such agency receiving general Church funds.

4. *General Agency Budget Review*—It shall require annually one month in advance of its annual meeting, or as is deemed necessary, and in such form as the council may require, statements of proposed budgets of all treasuries receiving general Church funds (see ¶ 810.2). It shall review the budget of each treasury receiving general Church funds in accordance with guidelines that it shall establish and communicate to the agencies, including the relationship between administration, service, and promotion, and consideration of evaluations from the Connectional Table on the missional effectiveness of the general program-related agencies and connectional structures of the Church. In the interest of sound fiscal management, the council will ensure that expenditures of agencies receiving general Church funds do not exceed receipts and available reserves, and this within a budget approved by the council.

5. *General Agency Audits*—It shall require an annual audit of all treasuries receiving general Church funds (see ¶ 810.2), following such auditing procedures as it may specify. It shall select the auditing firm for these annual audits based on a recommendation by the Committee on Audit and Review.

6. *Internal Audit Functions*—It shall establish and conduct the internal auditing functions for all treasuries receiving general Church funds (see ¶ 810.2).

7. It shall establish policy governing the functions of banking, payroll, accounting, budget control, and internal auditing for all agencies receiving general Church funds (see ¶ 810.2). The council may, upon mutual consent of the agencies involved, perform the functions of banking, check preparation, and payroll on behalf of an agency in order to maximize efficiency of operation.

8. It shall review for approval plans for financing all international or national conferences and convocations to be held under the auspices of any general agency receiving general Church funds (see ¶ 810.2).

9. It shall be responsible for ensuring that no board, agency, committee, commission, or council shall give United Methodist funds to any gay caucus or group, or otherwise use such funds to promote the acceptance of homosexuality or violate the expressed commitment of The United Methodist Church "not to reject or condemn lesbian and gay members and friends" (¶ 161G). The council shall have the right to stop such expenditures.[13] It shall not limit the Church's ministry in response to the HIV epidemic.

10. It shall be responsible for ensuring that no board, agency, committee, commission, or council shall expend United Methodist funds in a manner that violates the expressed commitment of The United Methodist Church to "oppose the use of late-term abortion known as dilation and extraction (partial-birth abortion) and call for the end of this practice [with rare exceptions]" (¶ 161K). The council shall have the right to stop such expenditures.

11. In keeping with the Church's historic stand on total abstinence, the council shall seek to ensure that no apportioned general funds are expended for the use of alcoholic beverages.

12. It shall develop general investment policies and guidelines for all agencies receiving general Church funds (see ¶ 810.2), following consultation with those agencies. The council, in its oversight capacity, shall review those agencies' compliance with the general investment policies and guidelines. Upon their review, the council may recommend that an agency take certain actions to conform with these policies and guidelines. These guidelines are recommended for all Church organizations. If requested by an agency, the council shall provide consultation and assistance on the development of specific investment policies and the selection of investment counselors and managers. The council shall review, on at least an annual basis, the performance of all invested funds of all agencies receiving general Church funds. The council shall have complete authority to manage any portfolio of less than $5,000,000 and may, upon request by the agency, manage larger portfolios. The council and general agencies are encouraged to invest in institutions, companies, corporations, or funds that make

---

13. See Judicial Council Decisions 597, 1264.

a positive contribution toward the realization of the goals outlined in the Social Principles of The United Methodist Church (¶¶ 160-166).

13. The Committee on Audit and Review (¶ 805.4*a*), on behalf of the council, shall monitor the compliance of treasuries receiving general Church funds (see ¶ 810.2) with the fiscal accountability policies and practices set forth in ¶ 806, the personnel policies and procedures set forth in ¶ 807.12, the general policies set forth in ¶¶ 811.1-3, .6, 819, and all applicable accounting standards and practices. The committee will also review recommendations made by the independent and/or internal auditors under ¶ 805.4*a*, with respect to matters of possible or potential financial impropriety or violation of policies and procedures. The council shall have authority to implement actions which it may approve based on recommendations from the committee.

a) If the committee finds that there are violations of such policies, practices, or recommendations, it shall request, within a specified timeline, a written response to the committee's findings, with the written response to include additional information and/or proposed corrective action.

b) After receiving the response, the committee may take one or more of the following actions:

(1) It may determine that the response and any additional information supplied is sufficient to explain the issue or situation that occasioned the initial finding, and that no further action is needed.

(2) It may determine that the proposed corrective action is sufficiently responsive to the issue or situation, and that, when implemented, no further action will be needed. It shall also notify the president and general secretary of the council of its findings, in writing.

(3) It may determine that the response is insufficient to address the issue or situation. In that case, it may recommend the type of corrective actions that it believes necessary to address the issue or situation adequately, along with a timeline for reporting corrective action taken. It shall also notify the president and general secretary of the council of its findings, in writing.

(4) It may prepare an informational report on the matter for those members of the council who have been assigned responsibility for reviewing the annual budget. It shall also notify

the president and general secretary of the council of its findings, in writing.

  c) It may recommend to the General Council on Finance and Administration for its action, with notice of the recommendation given to the appropriate leadership of the treasury involved, one or more of the following steps:

    (1) Continuing monitoring by the council's internal audit department, at the expense of the treasury involved, until the committee finds that the issue has been satisfactorily resolved.

    (2) Withholding of an appropriate amount of funding from general fund receipts that would otherwise be payable to the treasury, until the council, on recommendation of the committee, finds that the issue has been satisfactorily resolved.

    (3) Reporting of any unresolved issues to the next session of the General Conference, along with recommendations for General Conference action.

  ¶ 807. *Other Fiscal Responsibilities*—The council shall have the following additional fiscal responsibilities:

  1. To receive, collect, and hold in trust for the benefit of The United Methodist Church, its general funds, or its general agencies any and all donations, bequests, and devises of any kind, real or personal, that may be given, devised, bequeathed, or conveyed to The United Methodist Church as such or to any general fund or agency of The United Methodist Church for any benevolent, charitable, or religious purposes, and to administer the same and the income therefrom in accordance with the directions of the donor, trustor, or testator.

  2. To take such action, in cooperation with the Board of Discipleship, as is necessary to encourage United Methodists to provide for their continued participation in World Service, in one or more of the World Service agencies, or in other general Church benevolence funds or interests, through current and planned giving, including wills and trusts.

  3. *a)* When the use to be made of any such donation, bequest, or devise of under $50,000 is not otherwise designated, the same shall be added to and become a part of the World Service Contingency Fund, which shall be held and administered by the council.

  b) Any such donation, bequest, or devise of $50,000 or more not otherwise designated shall be added to the "Permanent Fund" of The United Methodist Church. This fund shall be held and administered by the council, as the General Conference shall direct.

4. Where annual conferences, individually or in groups, have established United Methodist foundations, the council may provide staff leadership on request to advise in matters of financial management, to the end that foundation assets shall be wisely managed on behalf of the Church.

5. To make recommendations to the General Conference, in consultation with the Connectional Table and the Council of Bishops, regarding any offerings to be received in connection with special days observed on a church-wide basis. These recommendations shall include the number and timing of such special days with offerings, the amount, if any, to be established as a goal for each such offering, the causes to be benefited by each, the method by which the receipts on each such offering shall be distributed among the causes benefiting from it, and the method by which such receipts shall be remitted and reported by local churches. All such recommendations are subject to the approval of the General Conference.

6. To establish general policy governing the ownership, sale, rental, renovation, or purchase of property by a general agency in the United States. The council shall consider the plans of any general agency proposing to acquire or sell real estate or erect a building or enter into a lease in the continental United States and determine whether the proposed action is in the best interest of The United Methodist Church. On the basis of that determination it shall approve or disapprove all such proposed actions. In the case of such proposed action by a general program agency, it shall solicit and consider the recommendation of the Connectional Table. If either the General Council on Finance and Administration or the Connectional Table disapproves, the agency shall delay the project until it can be considered by the next General Conference. Nothing in the foregoing shall include the operational requirements of The United Methodist Publishing House, the General Board of Pension and Health Benefits, or United Methodist Women.

7. To establish a procedure for making a quadrennial review, initiating proposals and/or responding to proposals by the general agencies regarding the location of headquarters and staff and reporting the same to the General Conference.

8. To exercise on behalf of the General Conference a property reporting function by receiving reports annually from general agencies of the Church concerning property titles, values, debts, general maintenance, lease or rental costs, space usage, and such

other information as the council may deem relevant. The council may consult and advise with the general agencies concerning any property problems that may arise. A summary of the property data shall be reported to each quadrennial General Conference. This provision shall apply to headquarters buildings but not to properties that are part of the program responsibilities of the General Board of Global Ministries or to any of the properties of The United Methodist Publishing House or United Methodist Women.

9. To take all necessary legal steps to safeguard and protect the interests and rights of the denomination; to maintain resources related to the denominational interests of The United Methodist Church, and to make provisions for legal counsel where necessary to protect the interests and rights of the denomination. The council shall have the authority to pursue policies and procedures necessary to preserve the tax-exempt status of the denomination and its affiliated organizations.[14]

10. To supervise the use of the official United Methodist insignia and preserve the integrity of its design, in cooperation with the General Commission on Communication. It shall maintain appropriate registration to protect the insignia on behalf of the denomination. The insignia may be used by any official United Methodist agency, including local churches, to identify United Methodist work, programs, and materials. The use indicates the identity of The United Methodist Church, with the cross proclaiming Jesus Christ as its foundation, and the two flames descending to one point celebrating its origin when two denominations became one, and affirming its readiness to go forth to the ends of the earth to all people to make disciples of Jesus Christ for the transformation of the world, as the anointing of the Holy Spirit with "individual flames of fire" sent forth the apostles speaking the language of people wherever they went. In order to preserve the integrity of its design, the insignia should not be altered or modified. Users of the insignia must ensure that it stands independent from and is not covered by or layered over other designs or words. Any commercial use of the design requires express prior authorization in writing by an appropriate officer of the General Council on Finance and Administration and shall be used only in accordance with guidelines and fees set forth by the General Council on Finance and Administration.[15]

---

14. See Judicial Council Decision 458.
15. See Judicial Council Decision 828.

11. To supervise the use of the name "United Methodist" and maintain the appropriate registrations of this name on behalf of the denomination.

12. *a)* The council shall: (1) require each general agency as listed in ¶ 805.4*b*, including itself, to follow uniform policies and practices in the employment and remuneration of personnel, recognizing differences in local employment conditions (these policies and practices shall be consistent with the Social Principles and resolutions of The United Methodist Church); and (2) be authorized to gather from all general agencies, at such intervals and in such format as it may determine, information regarding salary remuneration and pay equity and the number of agency employees and staff. Information related to the remuneration of specific employees may be released only by the employing agency or employee.

b) The Committee on Personnel Policies and Practices (¶ 805.4*b*) shall: (1) review annually the uniform policies and practices referred to in ¶ 807.12*a*, (2) annually recommend to the council an appropriate salary schedule, based upon responsibilities, for personnel of the councils, boards, and commissions represented on the committee; and (3) recommend annually to the council a schedule of benefits for an employee benefit program for personnel of each general agency as listed in ¶ 805.4b.

c) The Committee on Audit and Review shall (1) receive from agencies and institutions receiving general Church funds (see ¶ 810.2) statements regarding their compliance with the policies stated or referenced in ¶¶ 807.12*a* and 811.1; and (2) receive from all general agencies information necessary to evaluate pay equity. Based on these statements, and in consultation with and upon the advice of the General Commission on Religion and Race and the General Commission on the Status and Role of Women, the committee shall prepare for the General Council on Finance and Administration reports and recommendations deemed appropriate by the committee, in accordance with the procedures set forth in ¶ 806.12.

d) In the event it is determined by the council that an agency or institution receiving general Church funds is not in compliance with the policies stated or referenced in ¶¶ 807.12*a* and 811.1, the council shall notify in writing the agency so named and suspend, after a three-month period of grace, an appropriate amount of future funding until the agency or institution complies.

13. To maintain a consultative service to assist general agencies in planning and making arrangements for national meetings, conferences, and convocations.

14. To establish and supervise definitions and policies for general agencies receiving general church funds regarding the collection, processing, and distribution of certain authoritative data of the denomination, such as contact information for local churches, clergy, and leadership of The United Methodist Church, in collaboration with the Council of Bishops and in consultation with the general agencies.

15. To maintain the authoritative database for the general agencies receiving general Church funds (see ¶ 810.2) of the official data of all bishops; ordained and consecrated ministers in effective relation; local pastors, including retired ordained ministers serving charges; charges, local churches, parishes, fellowships, and new church starts; and such lists of General, jurisdictional, and conference boards, commissions, and committees, and officers of same, and of such other officers as the council may determine necessary. No one other than authorized bodies or officers of the Church shall be permitted to use these records.

16. To establish an electronic means that local churches shall use to collect, prepare, and report, in an accurate and timely manner, their statistical information to the council. It shall provide for the distribution of such information to annual conferences, the general planning and research agencies of the Church, and other interested parties. The council may establish an appropriate schedule of fees and charges to defray the cost of such information distribution services.

17. To assist and advise the jurisdictions, annual conferences, districts, and local churches in all matters relating to the work of the council. These matters shall include, but shall not be limited to, business administration, investment and property management, information technology, and auditing. The council may perform certain functions for the jurisdictions, annual conferences, districts, or local churches if the particular organization so elects and a suitable plan of operation can be determined. In accordance with ¶ 810.1, any assistance or resources provided by the council hereunder shall be in-kind and not a direct grant of funds.

18. To provide guidance and consultation to individuals providing services to the Church in the following areas: local church business administration; administrative assistance; equitable

compensation; information technology; and legal guidance to annual conferences. Such guidance and consultation may, as the council deems appropriate, include: establishing relevant professional standards, training programs, continuing education, and certifications; encouraging participation in associations related to these services (for example, the Professional Association of United Methodist Church Secretaries, the United Methodist Network of Practice, the National Association of Commissions on Equitable Compensation of The United Methodist Church, the United Methodist Information Technology Association, and the United Methodist Church Conference Chancellors Association, or similar organizations); and providing staff and/or in-kind services to such associations.

19. To institute, manage, and maintain an insurance program available, where approved by regulatory agencies, to all United Methodist local churches in the United States and, where acceptable on an underwriting basis, to all United Methodist annual conferences, agencies, and institutions in the United States.

20. To designate a staff member who, in cooperation with the general secretary, will fulfill such responsibilities as may be needed to assist the Commission on the General Conference with preparation for sessions of the General Conference. In fulfilling this role, the staff member will function as the commission's business manager and shall be related operationally to the Commission.

21. To provide guidance and consultation to churches, conferences and other United Methodist organizations on fund-raising campaigns conducted via the Internet and social media where capital can be solicited from a large pool of potential donors, also known as crowd funding. The General Council on Finance and Administration shall prepare a list of approved crowd funding websites. This consultation shall be limited to churches and conferences residing in the United States.

¶ 808. *Conference Payments of Apportioned Funds*—1. The treasurer of the General Council on Finance and Administration shall, not less than ninety days prior to the session of each annual conference or as soon thereafter as practical, transmit to the presiding bishop thereof, to the president of the conference council on finance and administration, and to the conference treasurer a statement of the apportionments to the conference for the World Service Fund, the General Administration Fund, the Episcopal Fund, the Interdenominational Cooperation Fund, the Ministerial Education Fund, the Black College Fund, the Africa University Fund, and such other funds as may have been apportioned by the General Conference.

2. The treasurer shall keep an account of all amounts remitted by the conference treasurers and from other sources intended for the funds listed in ¶ 810.1 and any other fund so directed by the proper authority, and shall disburse the same as authorized by the General Conference and directed by the council. A separate account shall be kept of each such fund, and none of them shall be drawn on for the benefit of another fund.

3. If more than the amount approved by the General Conference for a fund total, or for a line item within a fund total, is received in any given year, the excess funds shall be held in trust by the council in an apportionment stabilization fund. All monies placed in such a fund shall be considered as fund balances restricted by the General Conference to the fund(s) or line item(s) in which the surplus occurred. They shall be held by the council until such time as shortfalls in such receipts occur during the same quadrennium, at which time they shall be released to compensate for the shortfalls. If undistributed funds remain in an apportionment stabilization fund at the end of the quadrennium, the council shall recommend, for action by the next General Conference, the disposition of any remaining fund balances, provided that those recommendations shall be consistent with the purposes for which the funds were raised.

¶ 809. *Annual Reports by the General Treasurer to the Annual Conferences of All General Church Expenditures*—The treasurer shall report annually to the council and to the respective conference councils as to all amounts received and disbursed during the year. The treasurer shall also make to each quadrennial session of the General Conference a full report of the financial transactions of the council for the previous four fiscal years. The treasurer shall be bonded for such an amount as may be determined by the council. The books of the treasurer shall be audited annually by a certified public accountant selected by the General Council on Finance and Administration upon recommendation by the Committee on Audit and Review (¶ 805.4*a*).

General Funds

¶ 810. *Definition of General Funds*—1. The terms *general fund(s)* and *general Church fund(s),* wherever they appear in the *Book of Discipline,* refer to: the World Service Fund; the General

Administration Fund; the Episcopal Fund; the Interdenominational Cooperation Fund; the Ministerial Education Fund; the Black College Fund; the Africa University Fund; World Service Special Gifts; general Advance Special Gifts; the World Communion Fund; the Human Relations Day Fund; the United Methodist Student Day Fund; the UMCOR Sunday Fund[16]; Peace with Justice Sunday Fund; Native American Ministries Sunday Fund; the Youth Service Fund; and such other funds as may have been established by the General Conference and have been specifically authorized by the General Conference to be raised on a church-wide basis. They are restricted assets and are not funds of local churches, annual or jurisdictional conferences, or other units of the denomination. Such general funds are to be disbursed for the purpose or purposes set forth in ¶¶ 812-824 and budgets or similar directives adopted for the respective funds by the General Conference. The General Council on Finance and Administration, in the fulfillment of its fiscal responsibilities pursuant to ¶ 806, shall only have authority to disburse monies contributed to any of these funds in a manner specifically authorized by the *Book of Discipline* or for a purpose set forth in the budget or directives adopted by the preceding General Conference for that particular fund. The General Council on Finance and Administration's Committee on Audit and Review shall review the internal and external audits of these funds and report the results of its findings to the treasuries receiving these funds, the General Council on Finance and Administration, and/or any other entity it deems appropriate. The provisions of ¶ 806.13 shall apply to this function of the Committee on Audit and Review.

2. The terms *agency(ies) receiving general Church funds* and *treasury(ies) receiving general Church funds,* as used in ¶¶ 701-824 of the *Book of Discipline,* refer to agencies whose operational or administrative budgets are directly supported, in whole or in part, by allocations from one or more general Church funds. For the purposes of ¶¶ 701-824, the General Board of Pension and Health Benefits, The United Methodist Publishing House, and United Methodist Women shall be deemed not to be agencies or treasuries whose operational or administrative budgets are directly supported, in whole or in part, by allocations from one or more general Church funds.

---

16. Changed from One Great Hour of Sharing Fund to be consistent with General Conference 2016 Calendar Items 53 and 54 (*DCA* page 2101).

¶ **811.** *General Policies*—1. The General Council on Finance and Administration is authorized to withhold approval of a portion or all of the budget of any agency or any Church-related institution receiving general Church funds (see ¶ 810.2) until such agency or Church-related institution shall submit to the council in writing its established policies of: *(a)* recruiting, employing, utilizing, recompensing, and promoting professional staff and other personnel without regard to race, ethnicity, age, or gender; *(b)* fulfilling its duties and responsibilities in a manner that does not involve segregation or discrimination on the basis of race, ethnicity, age, or gender; and *(c)* insofar as possible, purchasing goods and services from vendors who are in compliance with such policies as are described in sections *(a)* and *(b)* of this paragraph. In the fulfillment of this directive, the council shall take the following steps: (1) collaborate with the General Commission on Religion and Race and the General Commission on the Status and Role of Women in the development of a certification form to be submitted to the council by agencies and institutions receiving general Church funds; (2) review copies of such certifications with the two commissions; (3) in consultation with the two commissions determine adequate recommendations regarding possible noncompliance with these policies by agencies and institutions receiving general Church funds; and (4) in collaboration with the General Commission on Religion and Race and the General Commission on the Status and Role of Women, the General Council on Finance and Administration shall determine fair and just recommendations for withholding funds from agencies and church-related institutions that are non-compliant.

2. It may withhold approval of any item or items in the budget or budgets receiving general Church funds (see ¶ 810.2) that in its judgment represent unnecessary duplication of administrative functions and services. Such functions and services shall include, but not be limited to, accounting, databases, equipment, human resources, information technology, maintenance, and meeting planning. In cooperation with and on recommendation of the Connectional Table, it may withhold approval of any such item that represents unnecessary duplication of program within an agency or between two or more agencies. If the council finds that there is such duplication in existing activities, it shall promptly direct the attention of the agencies involved to the situation and shall cooperate with them in correcting the same, and it may

decline to supply from general fund receipts money to continue activities that have been held to duplicate each other unnecessarily or plainly violate the principle of correlation as applied to the total benevolence program of the Church.

3. An agency of The United Methodist Church receiving general Church funds (see ¶ 810.2) proposing to borrow funds for a period in excess of twelve months or in an amount in excess of 25 percent of its annual budget or five hundred thousand dollars, whichever amount is smaller, whether for building or current expense purposes, shall submit such proposal, accompanied by a plan for amortization, to the council for approval. If the council disapproves, the agency shall delay such borrowing until it can be considered by the next General Conference.

4. The apportionments for all apportioned general Church funds, as approved by the General Conference, shall not be subject to reduction either by the annual conference or by the charge or local church (¶ 615.1).[17]

5. Individual donors or local churches may make contributions to the support of any cause or project that is a part of the work of any general Church agency. Such miscellaneous gifts shall be sent to the General Council on Finance and Administration, which shall then forward the gift to the agency for which it is intended. Agencies receiving miscellaneous gifts shall acknowledge receipt of the gift to the donor. No agency shall solicit or cultivate gifts for any cause or project in a Churchwide appeal that has not been approved for support through World Service Special Gifts (¶ 820), general Advance Special Gifts (¶ 822), or a special appeal (¶ 819).

6. No general council, board, commission, or committee receiving general Church funds (see ¶ 810.2) shall initiate or cause to be organized without approval of the General Council on Finance and Administration a foundation, endowment fund, or similar organization for the purpose of securing, conserving, or expending funds for the direct or indirect benefit or support of any general agency or any of its programs or work. Foundations, endowment funds, and similar organizations related directly or indirectly to any general Church agency receiving general Church funds shall report annually to the council in a manner determined by the council.

---

17. See Judicial Council Decisions 818, 1146.

¶ 812. *The World Service Fund*—The World Service Fund is basic in the financial program of The United Methodist Church. World Service on apportionment represents the minimum needs of the general agencies of the Church. Payment in full of these apportionments by local churches and annual conferences is the first benevolent responsibility of the Church.[18]

1. The council shall recommend to each quadrennial session of the General Conference the amount of the annual World Service budget for the ensuing quadrennium and the method by which it shall be apportioned to the annual conferences. In cooperation with the Connectional Table, it shall prepare and recommend a plan of distribution of World Service receipts among the World Service agencies, in accordance with the procedures described in ¶ 806.1b. In the planning of the World Service budget, it shall be the role of the General Council on Finance and Administration to facilitate sound fiscal and administrative policies and practices within and among the general agencies of the Church. It shall be the role of the Connectional Table to relate the budget requests of the program agencies to one another in such a way as to implement the program and mission of the Church.

2. The general secretary or other duly authorized representative of each agency of The United Methodist Church seeking support from the World Service Fund and the authorized representative of any other agency for which requests are authorized by the General Conference shall have the right to appear before the council at a designated time and place to represent the cause for which each is responsible, provided such representation has been previously made to the Connectional Table.

3. The World Service agencies shall not solicit additional or special gifts from individual donors or special groups, other than foundations, unless approval for such solicitation is first secured from the council.

4. The General Commission on Communication shall promote the World Service Fund.

¶ 813. *General Administration Fund*—1. The General Administration Fund shall provide for the expenses of the sessions of the General Conference, the Judicial Council, special commissions and committees constituted by the General Conference, and other administrative agencies and activities recommended for inclusion

18. See Judicial Council Decision 818.

in the general administration budget by the General Council on Finance and Administration and approved by the General Conference. Any agency or institution requiring or desiring support from the General Administration Fund shall present its case to the council at a time and place indicated by council officers. The council, having heard such requests, shall report the same to the General Conference with recommendations for its action and determination.

2. The treasurer of the council shall disburse the General Administration Fund as authorized by the General Conference and as directed by the council. Where the General Conference has not allocated definite sums to agencies receiving money from the General Administration Fund, the council or a committee designated by the General Council on Finance and Administration shall have authority to determine the amount to be allocated to each.

3. The expenses of the Judicial Council shall be paid from the General Administration Fund, within a budget submitted annually by the Judicial Council to the General Council on Finance and Administration for its approval and subject to the requirement of ¶ 813.4.

4. The General Administration Fund, and all payments made from this fund, shall be subject to the financial, accounting, and auditing requirements of ¶ 806.

5. The General Commission on Communication shall promote the General Administration Fund.

¶ 814. *Interdenominational Cooperation Fund*—1. This fund shall provide United Methodist support of the basic budgets of those organizations that relate to the ecumenical responsibilities of the Council of Bishops. Those organizations are described in Chapter Three, Section IX—Ecumenical Relationships in ¶¶ 431-442.

2. The Council of Bishops, shall recommend to the General Council on Finance and Administration the amounts of the several annual allocations from the Interdenominational Cooperation Fund budget. The council shall recommend to the General Conference the amounts to be included in the annual Interdenominational Cooperation Fund budget.

3. The Council of Bishops shall determine annually the designations of all funds for ecumenical agencies to be paid from the following year's Interdenominational Cooperation Fund budget that have not been specifically designated by the prior General Conference. The Council of Bishops shall communicate such designations

to the General Council on Finance and Administration prior to the beginning of the fiscal year made the subject of such designations. The General Council on Finance and Administration shall then disburse funds to each recipient in accordance with such designations during that fiscal year to the extent funds are available.

4. The fund shall also provide for the expenses of representatives chosen by the Council of Bishops to attend meetings and committees of such ecumenical agencies. The General Council on Finance and Administration shall reimburse such expenses from vouchers approved by persons designated by the ecumenical officer of the Council of Bishops.

5. *Disbursement of Funds to Ecumenical Organizations*—*a)* The General Council on Finance and Administration shall remit monthly to each organization included in the approved Interdenominational Cooperation Fund budget an on-ratio share of the fund's net receipts, after the payment of any fixed charges.

b) In the interim between sessions of the General Conference, exceptions to this directive may occur under one of the following circumstances:

(1) If the organization is unable to fulfill, or ceases to fulfill, the purpose or purposes which were the basis for the Council of Bishops' original recommendation for funding.

(2) If the organization ceases to exist.

c) If the Council of Bishops determines that such circumstances warrant, it may recommend to the General Council on Finance and Administration that funding for the organization be suspended or reduced, either indefinitely or for a specified period of time. The Council shall then reduce or suspend remittance of fund receipts to the organization until such time as the Council of Bishops determines that the circumstances which led to reduction or suspension of payments no longer exist. The Council of Bishops shall then recommend to the General Council on Finance and Administration whether remittances to the organization are to be resumed in amounts based on current Interdenominational Cooperation Fund receipts only, or whether amounts previously withheld should be disbursed along with the amounts payable from current receipts.

d) If funding to an organization is reduced or suspended, the funds which otherwise would have been disbursed shall be held by the General Council on Finance and Administration until the Council of Bishops recommends that they be restored to the organization or used to support a similar ecumenical organization. If the funds are not expended prior to the next session of the General Conference, the General Council on Finance and Administration, after consultation with the Council of Bishops, shall report to the General Conference the amount of funds being held and may recommend, for General Conference action, the disposition of the funds.

6. Before the beginning of each calendar year, the General Council on Finance and Administration shall determine and communicate to the Council of Bishops the sum available from the Interdenominational Cooperation Fund Contingency Reserve to be allocated to meet emerging needs of ecumenical agencies.

7. The General Commission on Communication shall promote the Interdenominational Cooperation Fund.

¶ **815.** *Black College Fund*—The General Council on Finance and Administration shall recommend to the General Conference the sum that the Church shall undertake for the Black colleges and the method by which it shall be apportioned to the annual conferences. The purpose of the fund is to provide financial support for current operating budgets and capital improvements of the Black colleges related administratively to the Church.

1. The treasurer of the General Council on Finance and Administration shall remit monthly receipts for this fund to the General Board of Higher Education and Ministry for distribution to those Black colleges whose eligibility under adopted guidelines of management, educational quality, and measurement by announced objectives shall be the precondition of participation. These guidelines and a formula for distribution shall be revised and administered by the Division of Higher Education of the General Board of Higher Education and Ministry, in consultation with the Council of Presidents of the Black Colleges. The formula for distribution is as follows;

a) Five-sixths of the receipts of the fund shall be distributed to the colleges to assist in supporting their current operating budgets:

(1) 75 percent of the five-sixths operating portion shall be shared equally by each college.

(2) 20 percent of the five-sixths operating portion shall be distributed on the basis of enrollment.

(3) The remaining 5 percent of the five-sixths operating portion shall be distributed equally to each college annually

for long-range planning, special academic programs, and meeting challenge grants in complying with the guidelines for support established by the General Conference.

b) One-sixth of the fund receipts shall be set aside for capital improvements, to be distributed by the General Board of Higher Education and Ministry on the basis of need and matching funds.

2. In the interim between sessions of the General Conference, the guidelines for support and formula for distribution may be changed as necessary upon recommendation of the Council of Presidents of the Black Colleges and the General Board of Higher Education and Ministry and with the consent of the General Council on Finance and Administration.

3. Promotion of the Black College Fund shall be by the Division of Higher Education and in consultation with the Council of Presidents of the Black Colleges, in cooperation with and with the assistance of the General Commission on Communication, the cost being a charge against the Black College Fund receipts and within a budget approved by the Division of Higher Education and the General Council on Finance and Administration.

4. An annual conference may make direct and/or designated gifts for current expense or capital funds purposes to one or more of these colleges, but only after it has met its full Black College Fund apportionment. There may be reasonable exceptions to this restriction, but such exceptions shall be negotiated with the General Board of Higher Education and Ministry prior to implementation.

¶ 816. *The Ministerial Education Fund*—The council shall recommend to the General Conference the sum that the Church shall undertake for the Ministerial Education Fund and the method by which it shall be apportioned to the annual conferences, in accordance with the provisions adopted by the 1968 General Conference in establishing the Ministerial Education Fund. The purpose of the fund is to enable the Church to unify and expand its program of financial support for the recruitment and education of ordained and diaconal ministers and to equip the annual conferences to meet increased demands in this area. The maximum amount possible from this fund shall go directly for programs and services in theological education, the enlistment and continuing education of ordained and diaconal ministers, and courses of study. When these funds are used to finance continuing education events sponsored by the Board of Ordained Ministry of an annual conference, such events may be open to laity for their attendance and participation at the option of the Board of Ordained Ministry of each annual conference.

1. Of the total money raised in each annual conference for the Ministerial Education Fund, 25 percent shall be retained by the annual conference that raised it, to be used in its program of ministerial education as approved by the annual conference and administered through its Board of Ordained Ministry. The Board of Ordained Ministry will confer concerning use of the Ministerial Education Fund. Administrative costs of the Board of Ordained Ministry shall be a claim on the conference's operating budget. No annual conference that participated in a 1 percent plan or other conference program of ministerial student scholarships and loan grants prior to the establishment of this fund shall receive less for this purpose than it received in the last year of the quadrennium preceding the establishment of the fund, provided the giving from that conference for ministerial education does not fall below the level achieved in the quadrennium preceding the establishment of the fund.

a) "Service Loans" from the conference portion of the Ministerial Education Fund may be considered repaid if the recipients served five years in the connection in appointments approved by their bishop.[19]

b) In case the recipients of these loans do not satisfy the terms of the "Service Loans" by service in the "connection," they would make arrangements to repay the loans with the conferences from which they received their loans.

2. Of the total money raised in each annual conference for the Ministerial Education Fund, 75 percent shall be remitted by the conference treasurer to the treasurer of the council for distribution to the General Board of Higher Education and Ministry for support of ministerial education and shall be administered by that board. It shall be distributed as follows:

a) At least 75 percent of the amount received by the divisions shall be distributed to the theological schools of The United Methodist Church on a formula established by the General Board of Higher Education and Ministry after consultation with the theological schools. United Methodist theological schools where less than 40 percent of the regular rank faculty are United Meth-

---

19. See Judicial Council Decision 1175.

odist or another historic Wesleyan denomination will forfeit 1/3 of their Ministerial Education funding, which will go back to the General Board of Higher Education and Ministry to be distributed as scholarship aid for certified candidates for United Methodist ordained ministry enrolled in United Methodist institutions of theological education that have been approved by the Commission on Theological Education. All money allocated to the theological schools shall be used for current operations, not for physical expansion. Ministerial Education funds allocated to United Methodist theological schools for current operations shall only be used for:

—United Methodist student scholarships

—Faculty and staff salaries and benefits for those who prepare United Methodist students (implementing the curriculum required in ¶ 324.4) for ordained ministry or service as local pastors through the Course of Study program.

All United Methodist theological schools receiving Ministerial Education Fund allocations shall submit annual reports to the General Board of Higher Education and Ministry detailing how the Ministerial Education Fund allocations were spent.

b) The remaining portion of the amount received shall be used for supplemental distributions to the theological schools and for board use in its program of ministerial enlistment and development. The General Board of Higher Education and Ministry will recommend to the general secretary of the General Board of Higher Education and Ministry appropriate funding for divisional programs of ministerial enlistment and development.

c) Beginning in the 2009-2012 quadrennium, the General Board of Higher Education and Ministry shall facilitate the creation of United Methodist Ministerial Education Funds in the central conferences, including the development and provision of funds for this new initiative. The purpose of this initiative is to improve and strengthen the existing indigenous structures for theological education in order to create a sustainable system of education for central conference clergy.

3. Annual conferences shall regard this fund as a priority to be met before any additional benevolences, grants, or funds are allocated to a theological school or school of religion.[20]

4. The General Commission on Communication shall promote the Ministerial Education Fund.

---

20. See Judicial Council Decision 545.

¶ **817.** *Central Conference Theological Education Fund*—There shall be a Central Conference Theological Education Fund. Funds for this purpose shall be provided from the World Service Fund.

a) There shall be a Commission on Central Conference Theological Education Fund elected by the Council of Bishops to determine policies and procedures for this fund. It shall approve disbursements from this fund. The commission will include one person from each central conference, and shall include members of the Council of Bishops, members of Boards of Ordained Ministry, representatives of theological schools, representatives from the General Board of Higher Education and Ministry, the General Board of Global Ministries, and the Standing Committee on Central Conference Matters. The Council of Bishops shall take into consideration both geographical and proportional representation when selecting the members of the commission.

b) It shall be used in central conferences outside the United States to in any or all of the following ways at the discretion of the commission: (1) development of theological schools; (2) development of courses of study; (3) development of libraries and contextually developed resources; (4) scholarships and faculty development; (5) support for associations and networks of faculty and schools; (6) support for new and innovative approaches to theological education.

c) The General Board of Higher Education and Ministry will administer this fund.

d) All money collected from the central conference apportionments for the General Administration Fund in excess of $750,000 (the costs of the Standing Committee on Central Conference Matters, including its work on the *General Book of Discipline*) is to be directed to the Central Conference Theological Education Fund.

THE EPISCOPAL FUND

¶ **818.** *Purpose*—1. The Episcopal Fund, raised in accordance with ¶ 818.3, shall provide for the salary and expenses of effective bishops from the date of their consecration and for the support of retired bishops and surviving spouses and minor children of deceased bishops. Subject to the approval of the General Council on Finance and Administration, the treasurer shall have authority to borrow for the benefit of the Episcopal Fund such amounts as may be necessary for the proper execution of the orders of the

General Conference. The General Commission on Communication shall promote the Episcopal Fund.

2. *Requirements*—The council shall recommend to each quadrennial session of the General Conference for its action and determination: (1) the amounts to be fixed as salaries of the effective bishops or a formula by which the council shall fix the salaries; (2) a schedule of such amounts as may be judged adequate to provide for their office expense; (3) provision for an annual operating budget for the Council of Bishops, including the salaries and office and travel expenses of the executive secretary and the ecumenical officer of the Council of Bishops; (4) guidelines governing the payment of bishops' travel expenses, including all travel authorized by the Council of Bishops; (5) the amounts needed to fund the Clergy Retirement Security Program or the Global Episcopal Pension Program (or, in either case, any successor bishop pension or retirement plan or program); and (6) provisions for allowance for the surviving spouses and for the support of minor children of deceased bishops. From the facts in hand, the council shall estimate the approximate total amount required annually during the ensuing quadrennium to provide for the items of episcopal support mentioned above and shall report the same to the General Conference. This amount as finally determined shall be the estimated episcopal budget. The administration of the Episcopal Fund budget as determined by the General Conference shall be under the direction and authority of the General Council on Finance and Administration, including annual fiscal statements and audits. Nothing in this paragraph shall preclude the annual conference or conferences of an episcopal area from including in their budgets amounts for an area expense fund.

3. *Proportionality*—The amount apportioned to a charge for the Episcopal Fund shall be paid in the same proportion as the charge pays its pastor (see also ¶ 622).[21]

4. *Bishops' Salaries*—The treasurer of the General Council on Finance and Administration shall remit monthly to each effective bishop one-twelfth of the annual salary as determined by the General Conference, less such deductions or reductions from the salary as each bishop may authorize. Allowances for retired bishops and for the surviving spouses and minor children of deceased bishops shall be paid in equal monthly installments.

---

21. See Judicial Council Decisions 320, 1298.

5. *Housing Expenses*—The General Council on Finance and Administration shall provide an annual grant from the Episcopal Fund to share in the costs of providing the episcopal residence owned by the annual or central conference(s) in the episcopal area. The amount of such grant is to be approved by the General Conference on recommendation of the council. The Episcopal Fund shall not make a payment directly to a bishop for housing. It shall go to the annual conference(s) for episcopal residence housing purposes. The treasurer of the General Council on Finance and Administration shall remit the annual housing grant to the respective annual or central conference(s) in the episcopal area. The treasurer shall also remit periodic installments of the amount approved by the council as office expenses to each bishop, or to the office designated by the bishop to receive such payments.

6. *Episcopal Expense Reimbursement and Honoraria Policies*— The treasurer of the council shall pay monthly the claim for the official travel of each bishop upon presentation of an itemized voucher with such supporting data as may be required by the General Council on Finance and Administration. *Official travel* of an effective bishop shall be interpreted to include: (1) all visitations to local churches and to institutions or enterprises of The United Methodist Church within the area; (2) such travel outside the area, but within the jurisdiction, as is approved by the College of Bishops; and (3) such other travel as may be consistent with guidelines approved by the General Conference as being within the meaning of *official travel*. No part of the expense and no honoraria for any such visitations shall be accepted from local churches or enterprises or institutions of The United Methodist Church, such expense being a proper claim against the Episcopal Fund. Nothing in this interpretation is intended to preclude special or nonofficial engagements of a bishop other than the oversight of the temporal and spiritual affairs of the Church, such as series of lectures in educational institutions, baccalaureate addresses, and preaching missions for several days' duration when such engagements do not interfere with official duties, nor does it preclude the acceptance of honoraria for such services.

7. *Audit of Episcopal Area Offices*—Fiscal reporting and audit procedures of each area office shall be determined according to a schedule as set forth by the council upon recommendation of a committee designated by the General Council on Finance and Administration.

8. *Episcopal Pensions*—The pensions for the support of retired bishops elected by General, jurisdictional, or central conferences and the surviving spouses and minor dependent children of such deceased bishops shall be administered by the General Council on Finance and Administration in consultation with the General Board of Pension and Health Benefits and in accordance with such program and procedures as may from time to time be determined by the General Council on Finance and Administration with the approval of the General Conference. For service years beginning January 1, 1982, and thereafter, the pensions for the support of bishops elected by jurisdictional conferences and those of their surviving spouses and dependent children shall include the benefits provided by the Clergy Retirement Security Program (or any successor bishop pension or retirement plan or program) and the Comprehensive Protection Plan of the General Board of Pension and Health Benefits. The pensions for the support of bishops elected by central conferences and those of their surviving spouses and, for service years beginning before January 1, 1982, the pensions for the support of bishops elected by jurisdictional conferences and those of their surviving spouses shall both include the benefits provided by the Global Episcopal Pension Program.

9. *Episcopal Group Health Care Plan*—The General Council on Finance and Administration shall sponsor or participate in a group health care plan that covers bishops elected by jurisdictional conferences, in the United States. For the purpose of this paragraph, group health care plan shall mean a health insurance plan, group health care plan, or multiple-employer health care plan that provides benefits for major medical and hospitalization expenses. The General Council on Finance and Administration may recommend additional eligibility for the group health care plan in its discretion.

Alternatively, in the event that federal law or state law governing health care plans and health insurance establishes coverage options for those persons without employer-provided coverage that ensure access, regardless of health status or condition, to affordable coverage through health insurance exchanges, connectors, single-payer systems, or other mechanisms, the General Council on Finance and Administration may cease maintaining its group health care plan for bishops to the extent such coverage is available to the bishops. In such event, the General Council on Finance and Administration nevertheless shall provide continued administrative and financial support of bishops toward the purchase of such coverage through these alternative mechanisms to the extent individuals' coverage may not be subsidized by government agencies, i.e., because their compensation exceeds certain thresholds, particularly considering the tax advantages of employer-provided financial support toward health care coverage.

In addition, the Council of Bishops shall provide and maintain health and wellness programs for bishops. Moreover, annually, the General Council on Finance and Administration shall submit Episcopal health plan data, to the extent the General Council on Finance and Administration maintains a group health care plan for bishops, de-identified as necessary, including, but not limited to, financial soundness, claims experience and other cost drivers, plan designs and coverage, and eligibility criteria to the General Board of Pension and Health Benefits.

10. *Episcopal Retiree Health Care Access*—The General Council on Finance and Administration shall respect the health and wholeness of retired bishops in the United States and their spouses by facilitating access to Medicare supplement plans and prescription drug coverage plans. Access for retirees and their spouses may include, but shall not be limited to (i) sponsoring an employer retiree health care plan that supplements Medicare; (ii) participating in a multiple employer retiree health care plan that supplements Medicare; (iii) securing individuals' eligibility under group contracts with Medicare supplement plan providers or exchanges; (iv) subsidizing the costs of coverage for retirees and their spouses enrolled in Medicare Part D plans or Medicare Advantage plans; (v) providing subsidies toward and group relationships with providers of individual Medicare Supplement and other retiree coverage policies; and (vi) providing fixed dollar retiree health benefits through health reimbursement arrangements, stipends, or otherwise. The General Council on Finance and Administration must submit a generally accepted financial valuation, such as in accordance with Statement of Financial Accounting Standard No. 106, as amended, of its projected medical liabilities for the retired population covered by the Episcopal Group Health Care Plan to the General Board of Pension and Health Benefits, biennially.

11. *Bishops Whose Service Is Interrupted*—Should any effective bishop in the interim of the quadrennial sessions of the jurisdictional conference be relieved by the College of Bishops of the

jurisdiction from the performance of regular episcopal duties on account of ill health or for any other reason, the president of the said College of Bishops shall so notify the treasurer of the Episcopal Fund. Beginning ninety days after such notification, the said bishop shall receive at least the minimum regular pension allowance of a retired bishop; the amount of such benefit for which the Episcopal Fund is responsible shall be reduced by the amount of any disability benefit payable from the Comprehensive Protection Plan of the General Board of Pension and Health Benefits. Such pension allowance shall continue until the regular duties of an effective bishop are resumed or until the bishop's status shall have been determined by the jurisdictional conference. Assignment of another bishop or bishops to perform the regular episcopal duties of a bishop so disabled or otherwise incapacitated, for a period of sixty days or more, shall be interpreted as a release of the said bishop from the performance of regular episcopal duties.

12. *Retired Bishops Appointed to* Ad Interim *Service*—Should any retired bishop, in the interim of the quadrennial sessions of the jurisdictional conference, be called into active service and assigned to active episcopal duty (¶ 406.3), that bishop shall be entitled to remuneration for such service. The Episcopal Fund shall be responsible for the difference between the pension of the retired bishop and the remuneration of an active bishop. In the event of such assignment of a retired bishop to active episcopal duty, the president or secretary of the Council of Bishops shall notify the treasurer of the Episcopal Fund. The treasurer of the Episcopal Fund shall make remittance accordingly.

FINANCIAL APPEALS BEYOND THE GENERAL FUNDS

¶ **819.** *Special Churchwide Financial Appeals*—1. Any general appeal to the Church at large for financial support for any cause, agency, institution, or purpose shall be subject to the provisions of this paragraph. Appeals in conjunction or partnership with other corporations for projects that are believed to be consistent with the established mission and ministry of The United Methodist Church shall also be subject to the provisions of this paragraph. Appeals to special or limited groups such as alumni of an educational institution are not included.

2. Any general board, cause, agency, or institution or any organization, group, officer, or individual of The United Methodist Church or to which The United Methodist Church contributes

financial support desiring or proposing to make a special church-wide financial appeal during the quadrennium shall present a request for authorization to make such appeal to the General Council on Finance and Administration at the time budgets for the ensuing quadrennium are being considered. All such appeals shall be reviewed by the Connectional Table, and its actions shall be reported to the General Council on Finance and Administration. The council shall then report such request to the General Conference with a recommendation for its action thereon.

3. In the interim between the quadrennial sessions of the General Conference, such proposed churchwide financial appeal shall require the approval of the General Council on Finance and Administration, the Connectional Table and the Council of Bishops. In case of emergency, the executive committee, if any, of these bodies may act in such matter for the body itself, but only by a three-fourths vote.

4. All requests for approval of a special churchwide financial appeal, whether as a request for General Conference action or in the interim between sessions of General Conference, shall include a proposed budget for a promotion of the appeal, including proposed promotional expenditures and the sources of funding (see ¶ 1806.13).

5. Any individual or agency authorized to make a churchwide appeal for funds shall channel all gifts through the General Council on Finance and Administration.

6. The General Council on Finance and Administration may withhold payment of the allocation from any general fund to any agency or institution that it finds to be in violation of the provisions of this paragraph.

¶ **820.** *World Service Specials*—1. World Service Specials are official programs within The United Methodist Church through which support may be designated for projects approved by the General Conference and in the interim by the General Council on Finance and Administration and the Connectional Table.

2. A World Service Special donation is a designated financial contribution made by an individual, local church, organization, district, or annual conference to a project authorized as a World Service Special project. All general boards and commissions (see ¶ 810.2) except those units of the General Board of Global Ministries authorized to receive general Advance Specials are authorized to recommend World Service Special projects for approval,

provided the project is specifically related to one or more of the disciplinary functions of the recommending agency.

3. General guidelines governing the types of projects that may be recommended as World Service Special projects shall be approved by the General Conference on recommendation of the Connectional Table and the General Council on Finance and Administration.

4. The World Service Specials program shall be under the administrative supervision of the General Council on Finance and Administration, and programmatic supervision of the Connectional Table, which jointly shall: *(a)* establish project approval criteria consistent with the guidelines adopted by the General Conference; *(b)* establish the process by which projects may be recommended and approved; *(c)* approve projects to receive World Service Special support; and *(d)* provide adequate staff administration and program accountability.

5. Churches and individuals shall give priority to the support of World Service and conference benevolences and other apportioned funds. World Service Special giving shall be voluntary and in addition to the support of apportioned funds. World Service Specials shall not be raised as a part of a fund apportioned by an annual conference.

6. Local church treasurers shall remit World Service Special donations in full to annual conference treasurers, who shall remit each month to the General Council on Finance and Administration the total amounts received during the month as World Service Specials. The council shall remit such funds in full to the administering agencies, which shall acknowledge the receipt of every donation to the donor or the local church.

7. General promotion of this program, for purposes of name identification and visibility, shall be the responsibility of the General Commission on Communication.

8. Specific cultivation of approved projects shall be done by the administering agencies to specific audiences that have demonstrated their interest and concern for the ministry contained in the approved project. Expenses for specific cultivation shall be borne by the administering agencies. No promotional or cultivation expenses shall be paid from World Service Special receipts. Such expenses shall not exceed amounts approved by the General Council on Finance and Administration under guidelines approved by the General Conference.

¶ **821.** *General Directives, World Service Specials, and UMCOR Sunday*—The following general directives shall be observed in the promotion and administration of World Service Specials and UMCOR Sunday:

1. In the appeal and promotion of World Service Specials and UMCOR Sunday offerings, there shall be no goals or quotas except as they may be set by the annual conferences for themselves.

2. The treasurer of the General Council on Finance and Administration shall be treasurer of World Service Specials and UMCOR Sunday.

3. Promotional expenses for World Service Specials shall be borne by the respective participating agencies in proportion to the amount received by each in World Service Specials. The causes of World Service Specials shall be coordinated with other financial appeals and shall be promoted by the General Commission on Communication.

4. The appeals for World Service Specials shall be channeled through bishops, district superintendents, and pastors. Details of the procedure shall be determined by the General Commission on Communication in consultation with representatives of the recipient agencies or entities.

5. In each annual conference, World Service Specials and UMCOR Sunday shall be promoted by the appropriate conference agency with the appropriate general agency and the General Commission on Communication.

6. Should a clear emergency arise or an appropriate outreach opportunity emerge requiring urgent response between sessions of the General Conference, any feature of the structure and administration of World Service Specials may be altered on the approval of a majority of the Council of Bishops and of the General Council on Finance and Administration in consultation with the Connectional Table. The executive committee, if any, of each of these bodies may act in such matter for the body itself, but only by a three-fourths vote.

¶ **822.** *The Advance*—1. The Advance for Christ and His Church (hereafter referred to as the Advance) is an official program within The United Methodist Church through which support may be designated for projects approved by the Advance Committee of the General Board of Global Ministries (hereafter referred to as the Advance Committee). Cultivation for the Advance shall be through channels of the church other than United Methodist Women who have other means of mission giving.

2. A general Advance Special Gift is a designated financial contribution made by an individual, local church, organization, district, or conference to a project authorized for this purpose by the Advance Committee.

a) Gifts as Advance Specials may be made for specific projects or purposes authorized by the Advance Committee.

b) Gifts as Advance Specials may be made for broadly designated causes (such as a type of work, a country, or a region) or for use as block grants to a certain country or administrative unit, provided such causes are authorized by the Advance Committee. In such case the administering agency shall provide the donor with information about the area to which the funds have been given and, where practicable, establish communication with a person or group representative of that type of work.

c) Rather than being given to a specific project, an Advance Special Gift may be given to the mission program units of the General Board of Global Ministries or the United Methodist Committee on Relief. In such cases the program unit shall determine the Advance Special project(s) to which such a gift shall be allocated.

3. Funds given and received as a part of the general Advance shall be subject to the following conditions:

a) Churches and individuals shall give priority to the support of the World Service Fund and conference benevolences and other apportioned funds. Advance giving shall be voluntary and in addition to the support of apportioned funds.

b) Funds shall be solicited or received only for authorized projects. Programs and institutions having general Advance Special projects shall promote only the projects approved and shall ask that gifts be remitted in the manner described in ¶ 822.4 below.

c) Donor-designated gifts received through the Advance shall be used solely for project support and are not to be used for general Church administration or promotional costs. Donors will be offered the option to add an additional contribution to cover administrative costs.

d) Advance Special Gifts shall not be raised as a part of a fund apportioned by an annual conference. (For conference Advance Special Gifts, see ¶ 656.)

e) Upon receipt of funds for a general Advance Special, the General Board of Global Ministries shall communicate promptly with the donor, acknowledging receipt of the gift and suggesting avenues for communication if communication has not already been established.

4. Receipts for general Advance Specials shall be remitted by the local church treasurer to the conference treasurer, who shall make remittance each month to the participating agencies in a manner determined by the treasurer of the General Council on Finance and Administration. Individuals may remit directly to respective program units in a manner determined by the treasurer of the General Council on Finance and Administration, including online giving, with these remittances reported to the General Council on Finance and Administration.

¶ **823.** *General Directives, Advance Specials*—The following general directives shall be observed in the promotion and administration of the Advance:

1. In the appeal and promotion of Advance Specials, there shall be no goals or quotas except as they may be set by the annual conferences for themselves.

2. The treasurer of the General Council on Finance and Administration shall be treasurer of the Advance. The treasury function for the Advance is performed by the treasurer of the General Board of Global Ministries on behalf of the General Council on Finance and Administration.

3. Promotional expenses for Advance Specials shall be borne by the respective participating units in proportion to the amount received by each in Advance Specials. The causes of the Advance shall be coordinated with other financial appeals and shall be promoted by the General Commission on Communication.

4. The appeal for Advance Specials shall be channeled through bishops, district superintendents, pastors, and other individuals. Details of the procedure shall be determined by the General Commission on Communication in consultation with the designated unit of the General Board of Global Ministries and the Advance Committee.

5. In each annual conference the conference board of global ministries (if any; see ¶ 633), in cooperation with the General Board of Global Ministries, shall promote Advance Specials through conference and district secretaries of global ministries, conference and district mission events, and other effective means as it may determine.

¶ **824.** *General Church Special Sunday Offerings*—The following are the churchwide special Sundays with offerings to be used in support of general Church causes:

1. *Human Relations Day*—Historically, Human Relations Day has been celebrated with an offering on the Sunday before the observance of Martin Luther King Jr.'s birthday. Congregations are encouraged to observe Human Relations Day on this date or on another date appropriate to the local church. The purpose shall be to further the development of better human relations. The observance shall be under the general supervision of the General Board of Global Ministries and the General Board of Church and Society. In connection with Human Relations Day, the General Commission on Communication shall conduct a churchwide appeal. The treasurer of the General Council on Finance and Administration shall allocate net receipts, after payment of promotional expenses (see ¶ 263.1). Funds shall be administered by the agencies under which approved programs are lodged.

2. *UMCOR Sunday*—Historically, UMCOR Sunday[22] has been celebrated with an offering on the Fourth Sunday in Lent. Congregations are encouraged to observe UMCOR Sunday on this date or on another date appropriate to the local church. The purpose shall be to share the goodness of life with those who hurt (¶ 263.2). The observance shall be under the general supervision of the United Methodist Committee on Relief, General Board of Global Ministries (¶ 1315.1c(5), in accordance with the following directives:

a) All local churches shall be fully informed and encouraged to receive a freewill offering in behalf of the relief program.

b) Insofar as possible, planning and promotion of One Great Hour of Sharing[22] shall be done cooperatively with other denominations through the National Council of the Churches of Christ in the U.S.A. Offering receipts shall be administered by The United Methodist Church. In connection with UMCOR Sunday,[23] the General Commission on Communication shall conduct a churchwide appeal. The treasurer of the General Council on Finance and Administration shall allocate net receipts after payment of promotional expenses. Funds shall be administered by the agency under which approved programs are lodged.

---

22. One Great Hour of Sharing is now called UMCOR Sunday in The United Methodist Church. See General Conference 2016 Calendar Item 53 (*DCA* page 2101).

23. Changed from One Great Hour of Sharing to be consistent with General Conference 2016 Calendar Item 53 (*DCA* page 2101).

3. *United Methodist Student Day*—Historically, United Methodist Student Day has been celebrated with an offering on the last Sunday in November. Congregations are encouraged to observe United Methodist Student Day on this date or on another date appropriate to the local church. The offering shall support United Methodist scholarships and the United Methodist Student Loan Fund (¶ 263.4). The observance shall be under the general supervision of the General Board of Higher Education and Ministry. In connection with United Methodist Student Day, the General Commission on Communication shall conduct a churchwide appeal. The treasurer of the General Council on Finance and Administration shall allocate net receipts, after payment of promotional expenses. Funds shall be administered by the agency under which approved programs are lodged.

4. *World Communion Sunday*—Historically, World Communion Sunday has been celebrated with an offering on the first Sunday of October. Congregations are encouraged to observe World Communion Sunday on this date or another date appropriate to the local church. The purpose shall be to assist racial and ethnic persons pursuing various avenues of ministry. In connection with World Communion Sunday, the General Commission on Communication shall conduct a churchwide appeal according to the following directives:

a) Each local church shall be requested to remit as provided in ¶ 824.8 all of the communion offering received on World Communion Sunday and such portion of the communion offering received at other observances of the sacrament of the Lord's Supper as the local church may designate.

b) The treasurer of the General Council on Finance and Administration shall allocate net receipts, after payment of promotional expenses, to be divided as follows: 50 percent World Communion Scholarships; 35 percent Ethnic Scholarship Program, and 15 percent Ethnic In-Service Training Program. Funds shall be administered by the General Board of Global Ministries and the General Board of Higher Education and Ministry, in consultation with various ethnic groups (¶ 263.3).

5. *Peace with Justice Sunday*—Historically, Peace with Justice Sunday has been celebrated with an offering on the first Sunday after Pentecost. Congregations are encouraged to observe Peace with Justice Sunday on this date or on another date appropriate to the local church. The purpose shall be to witness "to God's

demand for a faithful, just, disarmed, and secure world" (¶ 263.5). The observance shall be under the general supervision of the General Board of Church and Society. In connection with Peace with Justice Sunday, the General Commission on Communication shall conduct a churchwide appeal.

a) The annual conference treasurer shall retain 50 percent of the monies for Peace with Justice Ministries in the annual conference, to be administered by the conference board of church and society or an equivalent structure.

b) The annual conference treasurer shall remit the remaining 50 percent of the monies to the General Council on Finance and Administration.

c) The treasurer of the General Council on Finance and Administration shall allocate net receipts, after payment of the promotional expenses, to the General Board of Church and Society under which approved programs are lodged.

6. *Native American Ministries Sunday*—Historically, Native American Ministries Sunday has been celebrated with an offering on the Third Sunday of Easter. Congregations are encouraged to observe Native American Ministries Sunday on this date or on another date appropriate to the local church. The purpose shall be to develop and strengthen Native American ministries in the annual conferences and in Native American rural, urban, and reservation ministries and communities relating to the General Board of Global Ministries, and to provide scholarships for Native Americans attending United Methodist schools of theology (¶ 263.6). The observance shall be under the general supervision of the General Board of Global Ministries and the General Board of Higher Education and Ministry. In connection with Native American Ministries Sunday, the General Commission on Communication shall conduct a churchwide appeal. The treasurer of the General Council on Finance and Administration shall allocate net receipts, after payment of promotional expenses. Funds shall be administered by the agencies under which approved projects are lodged.

7. The General Commission on Communication shall promote all authorized churchwide special Sundays with offerings in consultation with participating agencies. Promotional expenses for each offering shall be a prior claim against the receipts of the offering promoted. In each case, such expenses shall be within a budget approved by the General Council on Finance and Administration upon recommendation of the General Commission on

Communication after consultation with participating agencies. In the promotion of these offerings, the spiritual implications of Christian stewardship shall be emphasized.

8. Receipts from all authorized churchwide special Sunday offerings shall be remitted promptly by the local church treasurer to the annual conference treasurer, who shall remit monthly to the treasurer of the General Council on Finance and Administration. Local churches shall report the amount of the offerings in the manner indicated on the annual conference report form.

Section III. Connectional Table

¶ **901.** *Name*—There shall be a Connectional Table in The United Methodist Church where ministry and money are brought to the same table to coordinate the mission, ministries, and resources of The United Methodist Church. Effective January 1, 2005, the Connectional Table shall be assigned the primary responsibilities, general policies and practices found in the relevant 700 paragraphs.

¶ **902.** *Incorporation*—The Connectional Table shall be incorporated in such state or states, as the Connectional Table shall determine. This corporation shall be the successor corporation and organization to the General Council on Ministries of The United Methodist Church, an Ohio corporation, and the Program Council of The United Methodist Church.

¶ **903.** *Amenability*—The Connectional Table shall report and be amenable to the General Conference.

¶ **904.** *Purpose*—The purpose of the Connectional Table (CT) is for the discernment and articulation of the vision for the church and the stewardship of the mission, ministries, and resources of The United Methodist Church as determined by the actions of the General Conference and in consultation with the Council of Bishops. As part of the total mission of the church, the CT is to serve as a steward of the vision and resources for mission and ministry, provide fiscal responsibility, and establish policies and procedures to carry out the mission of the church.

¶ **905.** *Objectives*—The essential functions of the Connectional Table are:

1. To provide a forum for the understanding and implementation of the vision, mission, and ministries of the global church as determined in consultation with the Council of Bishops and/or the actions of the General Conference.

2. To enable the flow of information and communication

among annual conferences, jurisdictions, central conferences, general agencies, and the Council of Bishops.

3. Consistent with actions of the General Conference, to coordinate the program life of the church with the mandates of the gospel, the mission of the church, and the needs of the global community by listening to the expression of needs, addressing emerging issues, and determining the most effective, cooperative, and efficient way to provide optimum stewardship of ministries, personnel, and resources.

4. To review and evaluate the missional effectiveness of general program-related agencies and connectional structures of the church as they collectively seek to aid annual conferences and local churches as they fulfill the mission of The United Methodist Church to make disciples of Jesus Christ for the transformation of the world.

5. To recommend to the General Conference such changes and implementing legislation as may be appropriate to ensure effectiveness of the general agencies.

6. To provide leadership in planning and research, assisting all levels of the church to evaluate needs and plan strategies to carry out the mission of the church.

7. In order to be accountable, along with the General Council on Finance and Administration, to The United Methodist Church through the General Conference, the Connectional Table shall have the authority and responsibility in the following matters:

a) To collaborate with the General Council on Finance and Administration in the preparation of budgets for the apportioned funds as provided for in ¶¶ 806.1 and 810.1.

b) To receive from the General Council on Finance and Administration and approve all general agency budget reviews.

c) To review and approve special offerings and church-wide appeals.

¶ **906.** *Organization of the Connectional Table*—1. *Membership*—The voting members of the Connectional Table shall consist of 49 persons as follows:

a) Twenty-eight persons elected through jurisdictional and central conferences, one from each of the central conferences by their own nomination processes and 21 from the jurisdictional conferences elected by the jurisdictional nomination process. Jurisdictional membership shall include one person from each jurisdiction and the balance of the jurisdictional members shall be allocated by the Secretary of the General Conference so as to insure to the extent possible that the members represent the proportionate membership of the jurisdictions based upon the combined clergy and lay membership.

b) An effective bishop, selected by the Council of Bishops, serves as the chair of the Connectional Table.

c) The ecumenical officer of the Council of Bishops and the presidents of the following agencies: General Board of Church and Society, General Board of Discipleship, General Board of Global Ministries, General Board of Higher Education and Ministry, General Commission on Religion and Race, General Commission on Status and Role of Women, General Commission on United Methodist Men, General Commission on Communication, and General Commission on Archives and History, program-related agencies that are accountable to the Connectional Table (as expressed in ¶ 702.3). The chairperson of the Commission on the General Conference, the chairperson of the Standing Committee on Central Conference Matters, and the president of the General Council on Finance and Administration shall also sit with voice and vote on the Connectional Table.

d) One youth and one young adult elected by the Connectional Table upon nomination by the membership of the Division on Ministries With Young People from among its members shall serve on the Connectional Table.

e) One member from each of the racial/ethnic caucuses as elected by the Connectional Table upon nomination from: Black Methodists for Church Renewal, Methodists Associated to Represent Hispanic Americans, Native American International Caucus, National Federation of Asian American United Methodists and Pacific Islanders National Caucus United Methodist.

f) The general secretaries of the above-named agencies and the General Board of Pension and Health Benefits, the United Methodist Women, the publisher of The United Methodist Publishing House, and the secretary of General Conference shall sit at the Table and have the right of voice but no vote.

g) Jurisdictional, central conferences, and other groups involved in the nominating and election of persons to the Connectional Table shall ensure the diversity objectives of, insofar as possible, fifty percent clergy, fifty percent laity, fifty percent female, fifty percent male, not less than thirty percent members of racial/ethnic groups (excluding central conference members), and not less than ten percent youth and young adults, ensuring diversity as otherwise provided in ¶ 705.4*b*.

h) Vacancies of members elected from central and jurisdictional conferences occurring between sessions of the general conference shall be filled by the College of Bishops where the vacancy occurred, in so far as possible from the same annual conference.

i) Members shall meet all the membership qualifications as expressed in ¶ 710.

2. *Meetings*—The Connectional Table shall meet at least semiannually and at such other times as are necessary on call of the president or on written request of one-fifth of the members. One more than half of the voting membership shall constitute a quorum.

3. *Officers*—The officers of the Connectional Table, other than the chair, shall be elected from the Connectional Table and shall serve for a quadrennium or until their successors are duly elected.

4. *Internal Structure*—The Connectional Table shall determine its own internal structure as it deems appropriate for the performance of its duties.

5. *Staff*—The Connectional Table shall determine the support staff that it deems appropriate to facilitate its work.

¶ **907.** *Effective Date*—The organizational plan for the Connectional Table shall be effective January 1, 2005.

Section IV. General Board of Church and Society

¶ **1001.** *Name*—There shall be a General Board of Church and Society in The United Methodist Church, as an expression of the mission of the Church.

¶ **1002.** *Purpose*—The purpose of the board shall be to relate the gospel of Jesus Christ to the members of the Church and to the persons and structures of the communities and world in which they live. It shall seek to bring the whole of human life, activities, possessions, use of resources, and community and world relationships into conformity with the will of God. It shall show the members of the Church and the society that the reconciliation that God effected through Christ involves personal, social, and civic righteousness.

¶ **1003.** *Objectives*—To achieve its purpose, the board shall:

1. Project plans and programs that challenge the members of The United Methodist Church to work through their own local

churches, ecumenical channels, and society toward personal, social, and civic righteousness;

2. Assist the district and annual conferences with needed resources in areas of such concerns;

3. Analyze the issues that confront persons, communities, nations, and the world; and

4. Encourage Christian lines of action that assist humankind to move toward a world where peace and justice are achieved.

¶ **1004.** *Responsibilities*—The prime responsibility of the board is to seek the implementation of the Social Principles and other policy statements of the General Conference on Christian social concerns.

Furthermore, the board and its executives shall provide forthright witness and action on issues of human well-being, justice, peace, and the integrity of creation that call Christians to respond as forgiven people for whom Christ died. In particular, the board shall conduct a program of research, education, and action on the wide range of issues that confront the Church.

The board shall analyze long-range social trends and their underlying ethical values. It shall explore systemic strategies for social change and alternative futures. It shall speak its convictions, interpretations, and concerns to the Church and to the world.

The board shall develop, promote, and distribute resources and conduct programs to inform, motivate, train, organize, and build networks for action toward social justice throughout society, particularly on the specific issues prioritized by the board. Special attention shall be given to the nurture of the active constituency of the board. The board will encourage an exchange of ideas on strategy and methodology for social change. Through conferences, districts, coalitions, and networks, it will assist Church members as they identify and respond to critical social issues at community, regional, national, and international levels. The board shall promote education, prayer, and advocacy on behalf of our brothers and sisters in Christ around the world who suffer persecution for their faith.

All the above shall be consistent with the Social Principles and policies adopted by the General Conference.

The board shall maintain close relationships with the General Commission on Religion and Race, the General Commission on the Status and Role of Women, and the Appalachian Development Committee as they seek to coordinate denominational support and cooperation with various movements for racial, sexual, and social justice, according to guidelines stated in the *Book of Discipline*. In cooperation with ecumenical agencies and other appropriate boards and agencies, the board shall encourage and promote ministries and models of mediation and conflict resolution, both ecumenically and within the agencies and institutions of The United Methodist Church.[24]

The board shall facilitate and coordinate the legislative advocacy activities in the United States Congress of other general agencies of The United Methodist Church that receive General Church funds.

¶ **1005.** *Incorporation*—The General Board of Church and Society shall be a corporation existing under the laws of the District of Columbia and shall be the legal successor and successor in trust of the corporations, boards, departments, or entities known as the General Board of Christian Social Concerns of The United Methodist Church; the Department of Christian Social Action of The Evangelical United Brethren Church; the Board of Christian Social Concerns of The Methodist Church; the Division of General Welfare of the General Board of Church and Society of The United Methodist Church; the Division of General Welfare of the General Board of Christian Social Concerns of The United Methodist Church; the Division of Alcohol Problems and General Welfare of the Board of Christian Social Concerns of The Methodist Church; the Division of Temperance and General Welfare of the Board of Christian Social Concerns of The Methodist Church; the Board of Temperance of The Methodist Church; the Board of Temperance, Prohibition, and Public Morals of The Methodist Episcopal Church; the Board of World Peace of The Methodist Church; the Commission on World Peace of The Methodist Church; the Commission on World Peace of The Methodist Episcopal Church; the Division of World Peace of the General Board of Church and Society of The United Methodist Church; the Board of Social and Economic Relations of The Methodist Church; the Division of Human Relations of the General Board of Church and Society of The United Methodist Church.

¶ **1006.** *Organization*—1. The General Board of Church and Society shall have sixty-two members, constituted in accordance

---

24. See Judicial Council Decision 387.

with ¶ 705.3*d*, and shall be organized as specified in its bylaws and in harmony with ¶¶ 702-710 of the General Provisions. The membership shall be constituted as follows:

a) Jurisdictional Members—Clergy, laywomen, and laymen shall be elected to the board by the jurisdictional conference upon nomination from the annual conference in accordance with ¶ 705.5*b*, based on the following formula: North Central—7, Northeastern—8, South Central—11, Southeastern—12, and Western—3.

b) Central Conference Members—Six central conference members shall be elected to the board on nomination by the Council of Bishops, according to the provisions in ¶ 705.4*c*.

c) Episcopal Members—Six episcopal members, including at least one from the central conferences, shall be named by the Council of Bishops.

d) Additional Members—(1) *United Methodist*—Additional members are nominated by a committee composed of three persons from each jurisdiction (one clergy, one laywoman, and one layman) elected by the jurisdictional conference. They shall elect up to nine additional members to ensure inclusivity and expertise.

(2) The board may elect one of the additional members with vote from among our Full Communion Ecumenical Partners.

¶ **1007.** *Vacancies*—Vacancies in the board membership shall be filled by the procedure defined in ¶ 712.

¶ **1008.** *Financial Support*—1. The General Conference shall determine and provide the funding for the board in accord with policies and procedures of ¶ 806.

2. Either on behalf of its total work or on behalf of one of its programs, the board may solicit and create special funds, receive gifts and bequests, hold properties and securities in trust, and administer all its financial affairs in accordance with its own rules and provisions of the *Book of Discipline*. Funds vested in any of the predecessor boards shall be conserved for the specific purposes for which such funds have been given.

¶ **1009.** *Staff*—1. The general secretary shall be the chief administrative officer of the board, responsible for the coordination of the total program of the board, the supervision of staff, and the administration of the headquarters office. The general secretary shall be an ex officio member of the executive committee without vote and shall sit with the board when it is in session, with voice but without vote.

2. All other staff are to be elected or appointed in a manner prescribed by the board consistent with the affirmative action policies of the Church and the board.

¶ **1010.** *Headquarters*—The headquarters location shall be determined in accordance with ¶ 807.7. A United Nations Office shall be maintained in cooperation with the General Board of Global Ministries and the United Methodist Women's national organization.

¶ **1011.** *Bylaws*—The General Board of Church and Society shall provide its own bylaws, which shall not violate any provisions of the Constitution or the *Book of Discipline*. The bylaws may be amended by a two-thirds vote of the members present and voting thereon at a regular or special meeting, provided that notice of such amendment has previously been given to the members.

Section V. General Board of Discipleship

¶ **1101.** *Purpose*—1. There shall be a General Board of Discipleship, the purpose of which is found within the expression of the total mission of the Church. Its primary purpose shall be to assist annual conferences, districts, and local churches of all membership sizes in their efforts to win persons to Jesus Christ as his disciples and to help these persons to grow in their understanding of God that they may respond in faith and love, to the end that they may know who they are and what their human situation means, increasingly identifying themselves as children of God and members of the Christian community, to live in the Spirit of God in every relationship, to fulfill their common discipleship in the world, and to abide in the Christian hope.

2. The board shall use its resources to enhance the meaning of membership as defined in ¶¶ 216-220, which emphasizes the importance of the identification of church membership with discipleship to Jesus Christ. The board shall seek to enable congregations to carry out their primary task and shall provide resources that support growth in Christian discipleship. In doing its work, the board shall listen to the needs and requests of the Church, conduct research, design and produce resources, offer training, and deliver resources. All of this is to support congregations in their

primary task of reaching out and receiving all who will respond, encouraging people in their relationship with God and inviting them to commitment to God's love made known in Jesus Christ, providing opportunities for them to be nurtured and formed in the Christian faith, and supporting them to live lovingly and justly in the power of the Holy Spirit as faithful disciples. The board, through all activities, shall lead and assist congregations in becoming inclusive communities of growing Christians, celebrating and communicating to persons of every age, racial and ethnic background, and social condition the redeeming and reconciling love of God as revealed in Jesus Christ.

3. Members of the General Board of Discipleship shall assume fiduciary, strategic, and generative governing functions. Fiduciary responsibilities include ensuring financial, legal, and ethical stewardship of tangible assets; accountability for stated performance standards; ensuring the annual evaluation of the general secretary; and providing counsel to the general secretary regarding evaluation and deployment of staff. Strategic responsibilities include ensuring that priorities, goals, achievement markers, and agency resources are aligned with the mission, vision, and values of the agency. Generative responsibilities include long-range analysis and planning in accordance with agency mission, vision, and values; setting direction and priorities for the agency; and exploring options in order to amend priorities when needed.

4. Members of the General Board of Discipleship (GBOD) are to be dedicated Christian leaders who have a heart for the local church and a passion for making disciples. They must be willing to invest time and skills to support the work of the board, including interpreting and articulating the GBOD strategy in a variety of contexts. They must engage in regular and intentional conversation with networks and individuals throughout the church to ensure that the wide diversity of people and perspectives present in The United Methodist Church are considered as the board carries out its responsibilities. They must be committed to supporting and implementing the mandates and foci of the general church as well as the General Board of Discipleship.

¶ 1102. *Responsibilities*—All the responsibilities assigned to the units within the board shall be considered to be the responsibilities of the board. In addition to these, the board shall have authority to:

1. Provide for special publications directed toward the local church nurture, outreach, witness ministries, age-level and family ministries, ministry group representatives, the ministry group chairpersons, the pastor, and the other local church officers for whom the board has primary responsibility.

2. Manage and produce *The Upper Room* daily devotional guide and a wide range of other resources to help people grow in their relationship with God.

3. Provide systems of resources and support to users of resources that will assist people in the historic disciplines of the Church, i.e., Christian education, evangelism, lay ministries, spiritual growth, stewardship, and worship. These resources will address ministry concerns across children, youth, and adult ages and family groupings and across programmatic and administrative functions of the congregation in order to improve ministry and the quality of Christian leadership for the future ministry of the Church.

4. Develop and provide resources, training, and consultation for pastors of congregations. These resources will focus on equipping pastors for their spiritual and visioning leadership role with their congregations and their role as partners with the laity.

5. Develop and provide resources, training, and consultation for pastors and congregational leaders as they enhance and evaluate the ministries of the laity and initiate new forms of ministry that nurture faith, build Christian community, and equip people for ministry in daily life.

6. Provide resources and training that will assist annual conference leaders in building, improving, and sustaining systems that develop spiritual leaders for congregations.

7. Provide resources and training that will assist leaders in planning and administering comprehensive children, youth, young-adult, adult, and older-adult ministries that encourage lifelong learning and growth in faith, that strengthen understanding of God and relationship with God and other people, and that lead to spiritual maturity in faith and in practice.

8. Provide representation in ecumenical and interdenominational agencies as they relate to the work of the board.

9. Respond to requests and needs for ministries throughout the world, in consultation with conferences and appropriate agencies.

10. Engage in research, experimentation, innovation, and the testing and evaluation of programs, resources, and methods to discover more effective ways to help persons achieve the purpose set forth in ¶ 1101. This responsibility will include authority for experimentation and research in all areas of ministry assigned to the General Board of Discipleship and will encourage cooperation with other agencies in the conduct of such research and experimentation. This research and experimentation may be assigned to appropriate units within the board.

11. Ensure that ethnic local church concerns shall be an integral part of the total life of the board, providing guidance, resourcing, and training so that these concerns are incorporated in all areas of discipleship in the local church.

¶ **1103.** The board shall provide such bylaws as necessary to facilitate the work of the board, which shall not violate any provisions of the *Discipline* and which may be amended by a two-thirds vote of the members present and voting thereon at a regular or special meeting; provided that written notice to such amendment has been given to the members and the vote thereon shall be delayed at least one day. The board shall have the power and right to do any and all things that shall be authorized by its charter(s) and by the *Book of Discipline*. It shall have authority to develop and carry out its responsibilities as described in ¶ 1102; to buy, acquire, or receive by gift, devise, or bequest property—real, personal, and mixed; to hold, mortgage, sell, and dispose of property; to sue and be sued; to borrow money in case of necessity in a manner harmonious with ¶¶ 806-807; to develop and maintain ecumenical relations to carry out its responsibilities; and to administer its affairs through the board and its various units and committees.

¶ **1104.** *Incorporation*—1. The General Board of Discipleship shall be a corporation existing under the laws of Tennessee and shall be the legal successor and successor in trust of the corporations known as the General Board of Evangelism of The United Methodist Church and the General Board of Laity of The United Methodist Church, and it shall further be responsible for the performance of the functions previously conducted by the Commission on Worship of The United Methodist Church, the Division of the Local Church, and the Division of Curriculum Resources of the General Board of Education of The United Methodist Church.

2. The General Board of Discipleship is authorized to take such action as is appropriate under the corporation laws of Ten-

nessee so as to accomplish the end result stated above, and under which the General Board of Discipleship shall be one legal entity.

3. The divisions of the General Board of Education were not incorporated separately; it is the intent, however, that responsibility for the functions delegated to the divisions by prior legislative action be transferred consistent with the separation of the divisions between the General Board of Discipleship and the General Board of Higher Education and Ministry. In the division of the assets of the General Board of Education, it is the intent that all assets be used in keeping with the original intent and purpose for which they were established or acquired, and so be assigned as appropriate to the General Boards of Discipleship and Higher Education and Ministry, respectively. It is further intended that the annuities, bequests, trusts, and estates formerly held by the General Board of Education be used for the benefit and use of the General Boards of Discipleship and Higher Education and Ministry (in accord with their purposes as defined in the *Discipline*), respectively, as their interests may appear, and that real estate titles be authorized to be conveyed as appropriate and apportioned where indicated.

4. In the event that the intent of the original donor of existing annuities, bequests, trusts, and estates cannot clearly be determined in relation to the interests of the two boards, such assets shall be divided equally between the two boards.

5. It is further intended that should additional assets accrue to the former General Board of Education by reason of annuities, bequests, trusts, and estates not now known and where the intent of the donor can be clearly ascertained, the assets shall be used in keeping with the original intent and purpose for which they were established or acquired and so be assigned as appropriate to the General Boards of Discipleship and Higher Education and Ministry, respectively.

6. It is further intended that should additional assets accrue to the former General Board of Education by reason of annuities, bequests, trusts, and estates not now known and where the intent of the original donor cannot be clearly determined in relation to the interests of the two boards, such assets shall be divided equally between the two boards.

7. The spiritual formation responsibilities of the general board as described in ¶ 1115 may be carried out primarily by its subsidiary The Upper Room, incorporated in the State of Tennessee as a nonprofit, charitable organization that relates to the Gen-

eral Board of Discipleship (GBOD) and whose board members are elected by the GBOD. The Upper Room is authorized, subject to ¶ 1107, to establish long-range investments and engage in fund-raising that shall guarantee, insofar as possible, a continuous flow of financial resources for the development of devotional literature, programs, and experiences.

8. The president of the board, the general secretary, and the treasurer shall have the power to execute on behalf of the board legal paper such as conveyances of real estate, releases on mortgages, transfer of securities, contracts, and all other legal documents.

¶ **1105.** *Organization*—1. The board shall consist of twenty-two members constituted in accordance with ¶ 705.3 of the General Provisions. It shall be organized to accomplish its work through elected officers as prescribed in ¶ 708. The membership shall be constituted as follows:

a) Jurisdictional Members—Each jurisdiction shall elect one member to the board in accordance with ¶ 705.3*a*. Before election, nominated members will be informed of the fiduciary, strategic, and generative responsibilities they will be assuming upon election so that they may clearly understand the time and resource commitment they are making. Other paragraphs of the *Discipline* notwithstanding, the secretary of the General Conference shall offer to each jurisdiction a suggested member allocation to ensure that, when combined with the board members from the central conferences, the resulting membership will reflect a balance of clergy, laywomen, and laymen. The secretary will also establish an equitable rotation to ensure that over the course of several quadrennia each jurisdiction will have the opportunity to elect a laywoman, a layman, and a clergy member.

b) Central Conference Members—The Council of Bishops shall elect three members from the central conferences in accordance with ¶ 705.4*c*, one each from Africa, Europe, and the Philippines.

c) Episcopal Members—The Council of Bishops will nominate two bishops to be members in accordance with ¶ 705.4*d*.

d) Division on Ministries With Young People—The Division on Ministries With Young People will elect two members, one youth and one young adult as defined by the age qualifications for the Division on Ministries With Young People in accordance with ¶ 1207.

e) Additional Members—Other paragraphs of the *Discipline* notwithstanding, the members of the board shall elect ten additional members based on expertise needed to accomplish the fiduciary, generative, and strategic work of the board. Particular attention will be given to ensuring an inclusive board membership that is sensitive to the wide diversity of people and perspectives throughout The United Methodist Church. The board may select these members from any jurisdiction or central conference in The United Methodist Church. Before election, nominated members will be informed of the fiduciary, strategic, and generative responsibilities they will be assuming upon election so that they may clearly understand the time and resource commitment they are making.

2. *Liaison Representative*—The board will name a liaison representative according to ¶ 705.4*f* and may name other individuals as liaison representatives to provide networking and advice related to areas of mutual concern. When invited to board meetings, they shall have voice but not vote.

3. The board shall determine and establish the appropriate organization of the board and its staff in order to best carry out the work of the board.

¶ **1106.** *Financial Support*—1. The financial support of the board shall be determined as follows: the General Conference shall determine and provide the budget for the board in accord with procedures defined in ¶ 806.

2. The board shall have authority to receive and administer funds, gifts, or bequests that may be committed to it for any portion of its work and to solicit, establish, and administer any special funds that may be found necessary for the carrying out of its plans and policies in accordance with ¶ 811.3. In the investment of any funds, the board shall adhere to the specific investment guidelines adopted by the General Conference.

3. When special missions are conducted or special projects are undertaken by the board, offerings and contributions may be received toward defraying expenses.

4. In the discharge of its responsibility for Christian education in The United Methodist Church, the board may establish and provide for participation by church school groups in a fund (or funds) for missions and Christian education in the United States and overseas. Plans for the allocation of, administration of, and education for this fund(s) shall be developed cooperatively

by such means as the board shall determine in consultation with the General Board of Global Ministries.

¶ **1107.** *Financial Relationship of The Upper Room to the General Board of Discipleship*—1. The funds for the fulfillment of the responsibilities of *The Upper Room* shall be derived from sales of resources, gifts, devises, bequests, annuities, events, and funds raised from subscribers, customers, foundations, and other limited groups of faithful subscribers, supporters, and interested parties (as defined in ¶ 819.1).

2. No funds, property, or other investments either now in hand or hereafter accumulated by *The Upper Room* or other devotional and related literature hereafter produced by *The Upper Room* shall be used for the support of other features of the board's work, but all funds from the sale of such publications shall be conserved by the board for the purpose of preparing and circulating such literature and cultivating the devotional life; provided, however, that this shall not prevent the setting up of a reserve fund out of such income as a protection against unforeseen emergencies.

3. Administrative support services are provided to *The Upper Room* by the General Board of Discipleship (GBOD) on a reimbursable basis. As a subsidiary of the GBOD, *The Upper Room* participates in the general church pension and benefits programs and receives administrative, financial, and personnel-related services from the General Council on Finance and Administration to the same extent as GBOD.

¶ **1108.** *Christian Education*—1. The board shall have general oversight of the educational interests of the Church as directed by the General Conference. The board shall be responsible for the development of a clear statement of the biblical and theological foundations of Christian education, consistent with the doctrines of The United Methodist Church and the mission of the board. The board shall devote itself to strengthening and extending the teaching ministry of the Church through research; testing new approaches, methods, and resources; evaluation; and consultation.

2. Through the ministry of Christian education, United Methodist congregations shall reach out to people of all ages as they are, encourage them to commit themselves to Christ and membership in his church, provide opportunities for them to grow in faith and to connect that faith with their daily lives, and equip them to live as God's people in the world. Opportunities for Christian education shall include educational aspects of all the general areas and

interests of the denomination, such as evangelism, stewardship, missions, Christian social action, and Bible instruction. The ministry of Christian education shall be developed as a comprehensive, unified, and coordinated program for children, youth, adults, and families in local churches. It shall be promoted and administered by the board in cooperation with those agencies responsible for Christian education in jurisdictions, annual conferences, districts, and local churches. It shall give careful consideration to the needs of all churches, such as small and large membership churches, rural and urban settings, and ethnic populations.

¶ **1109.** *Education Responsibilities and Standards*—The board shall organize as may be necessary for carrying on the educational ministry throughout the whole life span of persons. The board shall:

1. Formulate and interpret the philosophy of Christian education based on biblical, theological, and educational foundations (consistent with the Doctrinal Standards and General Rules of The United Methodist Church, ¶ 104) as they relate to the church school and related activities; individual or group study; fellowship, education, and action groups for children, youth, and adults; related educational programs provided by civic youth-serving agencies; weekday preschools and kindergartens; daycare centers; choirs, drama groups, mission studies; education for leisure; outdoor education; camping; education of persons with developmental disabilities and others of special need; special Bible study groups; confirmation and church membership training.

2. Develop educational approaches in a variety of settings that appeal to persons of different ages, lifestyles, learning needs, and theological perspectives.

3. Develop educational approaches that will enable persons of different racial, ethnic, and cultural groups to appropriate the gospel for their own life situations.

4. Promote church school extension in a variety of ways, such as providing resources and training that help persons in sponsoring new church schools, starting new church school classes, and expanding teaching and learning opportunities in the congregation and the community.

5. Provide resources and support services for pastors, parents, educational leaders, teachers, and others responsible for teaching and learning with persons across the life span at the local church, district, and conference levels.

6. Provide resources and support services for teacher recruitment, development, and training in biblical, theological, and ethical thinking, as well as in procedures and methods; work with the colleges and seminaries of the Church wherever possible to forward the common interest in the training of professional Christian educators and the training of ministerial students in local church Christian education; provide national camp training events and assist jurisdictions and annual conferences in designing, guiding, and resourcing camp training programs and outdoor Christian education.

7. Set standards and provide guidance concerning programming, leadership, and grouping for the various educational settings of the Church, including the church school.

8. Establish guidelines for the organization and administration of the church school, for recording and reporting membership and attendance of the church school, and for the equipment, arrangement, and design for church school buildings and rooms, with particular attention given to the needs of persons with disabilities.

9. Provide resources and services related to the training and work of local church directors, ordained and diaconal ministers, and associates of Christian education and educational assistants.

10. Provide assistance and information for groups and organizations with direct oversight for United Methodist-related camp/retreat centers and ministries, to help them with their responsibility to establish standards, policies, and procedures related to physical facilities, program, and leadership. To the extent possible, all camps/retreat centers shall be accessible to persons with disabilities.

11. Cooperate with the General Board of Higher Education and Ministry as they develop standards for certifying professional ministry careers as provided in ¶ 1421.2c and promote the continuing growth of local church staff related to educational ministries.

12. Provide resources, models, and training to support annual conferences and local churches as they help people make decisions related to their general Christian vocation as well as their specific occupations or careers.

13. Review and recommend for approval the curriculum plans developed in cooperation with the other boards and agencies in the Curriculum Resources Committee and interpret and support the curriculum developed by the committee.

14. Promote the observance of Christian Education Sunday (¶¶ 265.1, 1806.12).

¶ **1110.** *Cooperation*—1. The board shall cooperate with other general boards and agencies in the promotion of stewardship, evangelism, worship, mission education, and social action, and in the evaluation of these ministries from the perspective of sound educational procedure.

2. The board, in cooperation with the General Board of Global Ministries, shall be responsible for developing a unified program of mission education for all age groups in the local church. The mission education program shall include provisions for the following:

a) Linking emerging philosophies of mission and of education through information flow and cooperative work of the respective staffs and boards;

b) Developing and interpreting varied styles of mission education appropriate to different groups, including age groupings and the various racial and ethnic cultures;

c) Curriculum planning for education in mission, providing mission information about projects supported by The United Methodist Church (including ecumenical projects) through the church school resources, and preparing curricular and other materials for mission education;

d) Participating with various agencies in the design, development, and promotion of ecumenical mission education resources;

e) Developing and interpreting educational approaches and channels for mission giving of children, youth, and adults, such as the Children's Fund for Christian Mission;

f) Developing and interpreting models for new approaches to mission study and educational participation in mission;

g) Providing information regarding educational criteria to the staff of the General Board of Global Ministries for use in certifying leaders for schools of mission;

h) Disseminating a comprehensive listing of mission resources for leaders;

i) Cooperating with the General Board of Higher Education and Ministry and the General Board of Global Ministries in providing an emphasis on mission education in the schools of theology through United Methodist courses on history, polity, and doctrine now required for candidates considering ordination or consecration.

3. The board shall have authority to cooperate with other agencies of the Church, with defined organizations, and with ecumenical agencies to promote the ministry of Christian education.

4. The board is authorized to cooperate with the General Board of Global Ministries in the planning and execution of programs for the strengthening and development of the town and country, urban, and ethnic local church ministries of The United Methodist Church and of interdenominational cooperation in these fields.

¶ **1111.** *Evangelism*—The board shall have general oversight of the evangelism ministries of the Church as directed by the General Conference. Evangelism is central to the mission of the Church. *Evangelism* is defined in the *Book of Discipline,* ¶ 630.1.

The board shall share the blessing of the gospel of the Lord Jesus Christ with people of all age groupings and the various racial and ethnic cultures by the development, promotion, and support of all phases of evangelism throughout The United Methodist Church.

¶ **1112.** *Evangelism Responsibilities*—In response to God's love in Jesus Christ, the board shall have general oversight of the evangelism ministries of The United Methodist Church by the envisioning and developing of resources and by training and consultation in various settings. The board shall:

1. Set forth an adequate biblical and theological basis and understanding for the personal, corporate, and social aspects of evangelism, consistent with the doctrine and tradition of The United Methodist Church, and it shall communicate and interpret the same to the membership of the Church.

2. Give emphasis to the development, interpretation, and promotion of ministries of evangelism at the conference, district, and local church levels so that persons who are not active Christian disciples through any local church will be invited and cared for by a United Methodist church.

3. Provide resources and training for strategies, ministries, and programs in evangelism, including resources for the local church ministry of evangelism (¶ 254).

4. Cooperate with other program agencies of the Church in supporting and equipping both clergy and laity at all levels in involvement in evangelism, church growth, and new congregational development.

5. Provide and encourage research in what creative congregations of various membership sizes and settings are doing in effective evangelism that can serve as models for other churches, and foster experimentation and demonstration of additional evangelistic approaches, consistent with the nature of the Christian gospel and the Church, at all levels of the Church's life, including new congregations and all racial and cultural groups.

6. Provide resources and services for those serving as pastors, diaconal ministers, directors of evangelism, general evangelists, and other professionals in evangelism in local churches.

7. Set standards for elders desiring to serve as general evangelists. The board shall send copies of these standards quadrennially to the bishops, district superintendents, conference boards of discipleship, and general evangelists. An elder who feels called by God to be a general evangelist should prepare definitely for such service under the guidance of the annual conference to which that person belongs.

8. Relate and provide liaison services to denominational and ecumenical associations and fellowships of evangelism.

9. Seek mutual cooperation among and with the seminaries of the Church and the General Board of Higher Education and Ministry in the training and nurturing of persons for ministry and in continuing education where the responsibilities intersect.

10. Communicate with other agencies in whose programs the subject matter of evangelism would be included, and provide counsel, guidance, and resources for the implementation of such programs.

11. Participate in and cooperate with the work of the Curriculum Resources Committee of the board for the inclusion of evangelism concepts and resources in local church study curriculum.

12. Provide consultation with conferences, districts, local congregations, and other agencies to develop strategies in evangelism for outreach, church revitalization, and new congregational development.

13. Work with the General Board of Global Ministries for the extension of the Church. To this end there shall be a Joint Committee on Congregational Development with equal representation of members from the General Board of Discipleship and the General Board of Global Ministries, which shall meet regularly for mutual learning, developing strategies for Church extension, and providing resources and assistance to conferences and districts in

the field of new congregational development and congregational revitalization.

¶ **1113.** *Worship Responsibilities*—The board shall: 1. Set forth and interpret the biblical and theological basis for corporate worship with people of all age groupings and the various racial and ethnic cultures through resources, programs, and training materials consistent with the doctrines of The United Methodist Church, and cultivate the fullest possible meaning in the corporate worship celebrations of the Church to the glory of God, including liturgy, preaching, the sacraments, music, related arts, and the observance of the liturgical seasons of the Christian Year.

2. Develop standards and resources for the conduct of public worship in the churches, including liturgy, preaching, the sacraments, music, and related arts.

3. Make recommendations to the General Conference regarding future editions of a book of worship and a hymnal and, as ordered, provide editorial supervision of the contents of these publications, which shall be published by The United Methodist Publishing House. The hymnals of The United Methodist Church are *The United Methodist Hymnal* (1989), *Mil Voces Para Celebrar: Himnario Metodista* (1996), and *Come, Let Us Worship: The Korean-English United Methodist Hymnal* (2000). The ritual of the Church is that contained in *The United Methodist Hymnal* (1989), *The United Methodist Book of Worship* (1992), *Mil Voces Para Celebrar: Himnario Metodista* (1996), and *Come, Let Us Worship: The Korean-English United Methodist Hymnal* (2000).

4. Prepare revisions of the ritual of the Church and approved orders of worship for recommendation to the General Conference for adoption.

5. Work with other North American Christian denominations through the Consultation on Common Texts in the continuing development of a common calendar and lectionary, and encourage the voluntary use of the *Revised Common Lectionary* and resources based upon it.

6. Prepare and sponsor the publication of supplemental orders and texts of worship.[25]

7. Maintain a cooperative but not exclusive relationship with The United Methodist Publishing House in the preparation and publication of worship resources.

---

25. See Judicial Council Decision 445.

8. Advise the general agencies of the Church in the preparation, publication, and circulation of orders of service and other liturgical materials bearing the imprint of The United Methodist Church, encouraging use of racial and ethnic worship resources and incorporation of language that recognizes the several constituencies of the Church. (See ¶ 4.)

9. Counsel with the editors of the periodicals and publications of The United Methodist Church concerning material offered in the fields of worship, including preaching, music, and the other liturgical arts.

10. Participate in and cooperate with the Curriculum Resources Committee of the board for the inclusion of worship concepts and resources in local church study curriculum.

11. Encourage in the schools of theology and pastors' schools, and other settings, the offering of instruction in the meaning and design of worship. This should include the worship practices and expressions of various styles (i.e., traditional, contemporary), cultures, and races.

12. Counsel with those responsible for planning and conducting the worship services of the General Conference and other general assemblies of the Church.

13. Give guidance to, provide resources for, and encourage the continuing growth of those persons responsible for music leadership in the local church, i.e., directors, ordained ministers, associates, music assistants, and those volunteering in music and the other worship arts. (See ¶ 1405.7.)

14. Cooperate with the Fellowship of United Methodists in Music and Worship Arts and The Order of St. Luke in affirming the sacramental life embracing liturgy, preaching, music, and other arts appropriate for the inclusive worship life of the Church.

15. Develop performance standards for associates, directors, and ministers of music in cooperation with the General Board of Higher Education and Ministry, and cooperate with the General Board of Higher Education and Ministry in the development of standards and requirements for certification of directors, associates, and ministers of music as provided in ¶ 1405.7.

¶ 1114. *Stewardship Responsibilities*—1. To interpret the biblical and theological basis for stewardship through programs, resources, and training materials for people of all ages consistent with the doctrines of The United Methodist Church.

2. To provide education, counsel, resourcing, and training for the local church stewardship ministry group chairperson, commission on stewardship, board of trustees, endowment and permanent fund committees, wills and estate planning committees, memorial committees, committee on finance, committee on finance chairperson, financial secretaries, and treasurers, and to develop program resources and training materials for use with and by the above-named persons and/or groups (see ¶ 807.17). Matters relating to procedures involving official records, forms, and reporting of statistical and financial information shall be the responsibility of the General Council on Finance and Administration.

3. To create within The United Methodist Church a deepening commitment to personal and corporate Christian stewardship, which includes the use and sharing of talents and resources and the practice of a Christian lifestyle.

4. To develop strategies, provide resources, and implement actions that lead to a continuing improvement in the level of giving of United Methodists in providing adequate support for the mission of the Church.

5. To counsel in the area of stewardship and finance with jurisdictional and annual conference program agencies relative to their organizational structure and program responsibilities and assist them in their interpretation of program and resources.

6. To provide counsel, resources, and guidance to conference and area foundations as they fulfill their stewardship functions and to associations such as the National Association of United Methodist Foundations and the National Association of Stewardship Leaders.

7. To call together regularly United Methodist general agency leaders whose programs include the subject matter of stewardship to work toward common language, consistent stewardship theology, and cooperative efforts, in cooperation with the General Council on Finance and Administration.

¶ **1115.** *Spiritual Formation Responsibilities of The Upper Room—* 1. To develop resources that foster an international community of people and congregations who are seeking God, building a vision of new life in Christ, nurturing one another by sharing experiences of God's love and guidance, and encouraging one another in Christian action to transform the world.

2. To explore and communicate a biblically and theologically informed vision of the spiritual life that encourages and supports

spiritual leaders in the church who can guide people of all ages into a more vital, intimate, and transforming relationship with God through Christ.

3. To maintain and extend the worldwide ministry of *The Upper Room* and other resources, which are available in an increasing number of languages and which address the spiritual needs of people throughout their life and continue to embody the interdenominational character of the ministry of *The Upper Room*.

4. To cooperate with all other units within the board, as well as other groups within United Methodism, and other denominations whose concerns are related to the spiritual life.

¶ **1116.** *Ministry of the Laity*—The board shall interpret and spread through the Church all the rich meanings of the universal priesthood of believers, of Christian vocation, and of the ministry of the laity in daily life.

The United Methodist Church has the responsibility of training and enabling the *laos*—the whole body of its membership—to enter into mission and to minister and witness in the name of Jesus Christ, the Head of the Church. Although all units of the Church have some responsibility for this imperative, the General Board of Discipleship has a preeminent responsibility in that it is charged with developing discipleship. To this end, the board shall:

1. Help develop an adequate understanding of the theological and biblical basis for ministry of the laity.

2. Develop and interpret ministry of the laity both inside and outside the institutional Church.

3. Provide resources and support services for the development and improvement of leadership in the local church, except as specifically delegated to other agencies, and especially for those persons who serve as members of charge conferences, church councils, councils on ministries, committees on pastor-parish relations, personnel committees, committees on lay leadership, those who serve as lay leaders, lay members of annual conferences, and leaders of related organizations in local churches, districts, annual conferences, and jurisdictions.

4. Assist congregations, districts, and annual conferences in equipping persons for leadership in community ministries.

5. Provide resources and suggested plans for the observance of Laity Sunday in the local church.

6. Provide support to conference director and district director of Lay Servant Ministries, to conference and district committees

on Lay Servant Ministries, and to the Association of Conference Directors of Lay Servant Ministries. In consultation with the conference directors, set standards for certified lay servants, certified lay speakers, and certified lay ministers and provide teaching resources for use by annual conference and district committees.

7. Provide support services to conference and district lay leaders and conference and district boards of laity or equivalent structures, to the Association of Annual Conference Lay Leaders, and to other appropriate associations and conference and district officers and agencies.

8. Initiate a process of coordination and collaboration in developing a comprehensive approach to leadership development and training within all program areas for which the General Board of Discipleship has responsibility.

9. Encourage ordained elders to select and train laity to distribute the consecrated Communion elements to sick or homebound persons following a service of Word and Table. This distribution also may apply to laypersons who have been assigned pastoral roles in a church or in more than one church by the district superintendent.

¶ **1117.** *Christian Discipleship Formation Responsibilities*—The board shall interpret and promote group ministries in local congregations in order to support the formation of Christian disciples focused on the transformation of the world.

1. *Small-Group Ministries*—Recognizing the diverse means of grace necessary in forming Christian disciples, the General Board of Discipleship shall assist local congregations in developing a comprehensive system of small-group ministries by:

a) providing resources, training, and support services for leaders of small-group ministries that support people in their search for God, in their yearning for community, and in their desire to be formed as Christian disciples;

b) providing resources and support services for groups such as cell groups, life groups, care groups, or small groups that equip people throughout the life span for faithful Christian living in the world, and especially those areas for which the General Board of Discipleship has responsibility. When developing resources, attention should be given to the impact of the oral and visual cultures in which we live and to the importance of stories of transformation.

2. *Accountable Discipleship*—Affirming that our Wesleyan heritage embraces a distinct emphasis of mutual accountability, the General Board of Discipleship shall encourage accountability in congregations by:

a) promoting the General Rule of Discipleship: "To witness to Jesus Christ in the world, and to follow his teachings through acts of compassion, justice, worship, and devotion, under the guidance of the Holy Spirit"[26];

b) advocating the formation of Covenant Discipleship Groups or equivalent models applicable to the cultural context of the Central Conferences for all ages throughout the church by providing resources, training, and support services that ground leadership in the richness of our Wesleyan tradition;

c) providing resources, training, and support services for revitalizing the role of class leaders so that they may interpret the General Rule of Discipleship to all church members and assist the pastor in fostering mutual accountability throughout the congregation and other ministries;

d) providing consultative services to jurisdictions, conferences, and districts in the introduction and development of Covenant Discipleship Groups and class leaders in congregations.

¶ **1118.** *Ethnic Local Church Concerns*—The board shall function as an advocate for programs and concerns of ethnic local churches. It shall coordinate efforts to keep the needs of the membership of ethnic churches uppermost in the minds of its membership. The board will ensure that adequate resources—fiscal, human, and programmatic—are used to support and encourage the ministries of the ethnic local churches.

¶ **1119.** *Age-Level, Life-Span, and Family Ministries*—The board will provide for an integrated and coordinated approach in development of resources and service support for ministries with children, youth, adults of all ages, and families. Through its services to administrative and coordinating leaders, the board will assist congregations and conferences to:

a) Build knowledge for development of ministries that support the primary task of the local congregation;

b) Provide for the development and nurture of persons at all age levels and stages of growth and for families in diverse configurations;

---

26. Adapted version of Wesley's General Rules; see Gayle Turner Watson's *A Guide to Covenant Discipleship Groups* (Discipleship Resources, 2000), p. 12.

c) Assist individuals and families in spiritual development and growth; and

d) Promote the making and keeping of covenants as foundations for family living.

The board will also engage in research and testing, consultation and training, and collaborative planning so as to enhance the delivery of resources and services to leaders with age-level and family ministries responsibilities.

1. *Comprehensive Children's Ministries*—The board will assist congregations and conferences in developing comprehensive ministries for and with children. Such ministries may include, but shall not be limited to, the following: Sunday school and vacation Bible school, weekday ministries for preschool and elementary ages, fellowship and neighborhood groups, scouting ministries, and short-term studies and activities within and outside the church facilities. Ministries should focus on biblical foundations, prayer and spiritual formation, community service, personal worth through Jesus Christ, human sexuality, values, United Methodist studies, creative and fine arts, multicultural awareness, outreach to others, and celebration of significant moments in children's lives.

Responsibilities may include such supportive tasks as: assisting congregations to be advocates on behalf of children; identifying the needs and concerns of children, their families and congregations; assessing the status of ministries with children in The United Methodist Church; collecting and disseminating pertinent data on issues, models, and programs that inform the leaders in congregations and church structures to strengthen the quality of life of children.

2. *Comprehensive Young People's Ministries*—There shall be a comprehensive approach to development and implementation of youth and young-adult ministry programming at all levels of the Church. The comprehensive approach is based on the understanding of the primary task of young people's ministry: to love young people where they are, to encourage them in developing their relationship to God, to provide them with opportunities for nurture and growth, and to challenge them to respond to God's call to serve in their communities. Four component parts undergird this comprehensive ministry:

a) Curriculum—Through the Curriculum Resources Committee (¶ 1121), the General Board of Discipleship shall ensure the availability of curriculum and leaders' guides for use in a variety of settings suitable for the needs of all young people, age specific depending on the U. S. or central conference definitions;

b) *Program Resources*—Additional and supplemental guidebooks and other program aids shall be developed and promoted for effective young people's ministries programs in the local church and at the district, conference, jurisdictional, and general Church levels;

c) *Leadership Training and Networking*—Leadership training shall be provided to encourage and support adult workers with young people in their roles as teachers, counselors, advisers, and enablers at all levels of the Church. Networking shall be developed through ongoing communication to include workshops, social media, online platforms and publications between leaders in young people's ministries across the denomination for the enhancement of skills and the sharing of effective models and resources;

d) *Structures*—Active and effective structures for young people's ministries programming shall be promoted and maintained at all levels of the United Methodist connection, as identified in the U. S. and central conferences. These structures will encourage the full involvement of young people in leadership and membership and for the advocacy of young people's concerns in all areas of Church life, planning, and administration.

3. *Comprehensive Adult Ministries*—The board will assist congregations and conferences in developing comprehensive ministries by, with, and for adults. In keeping with the primary task of the board, adult ministries may include but need not be limited to: education and ministries with young adults, middle adults, older adults, and single adults (i.e., widowed, always single, separated, and divorced), and intergenerational programs involving adults. Such a plan would include biblical foundation and study, developmental stages and tasks of adults, faith development and spiritual formation, and leadership training in various models of adult educational ministries.

Responsibilities may include such supportive tasks as: identifying the needs and concerns of adults (i.e., young adults, middle adults, older adults, and single adults); assessing the status of ministries by, with, and for adults in The United Methodist Church; collecting and disseminating pertinent data on issues, models, and programs that inform the leaders in local congregations, districts, conferences, boards, and agencies to strengthen the quality of faith and life of adults.

4. *Comprehensive Family Ministries*—The board will assist congregations and conferences in developing comprehensive ministries with families. In alignment with the primary task, the ministries may assist families in the following areas: spiritual formation and development, marital growth ministries, parenting, human sexuality, care giving, and issues affecting the quality of family life. Such a plan would include: biblical exploration and study, as well as theological and experiential understandings of family life and the evolving patterns of family living. Ministries with families will focus on persons rather than structures.

The board may organize and administer a Committee on Family Life. The committee will provide an arena for information sharing, collaborative planning, and/or cooperative programming in alignment with the purpose and responsibilities of representative participants. The committee will serve as advocates for ministries with families in all boards and agencies.

Responsibilities may include such supportive tasks as: identifying the needs and concerns of families and of congregations, assessing the status of ministries with families in The United Methodist Church, collecting and disseminating pertinent data on issues, models, and programs that inform the work of the boards and agencies to strengthen the quality of family life. The committee will relate to and provide liaison services to ecumenical and interdenominational agencies in the area of family life.

¶ **1120.** *General Provisions for the Committee on Older Adult Ministries*—1. There shall be a Committee on Older Adult Ministries, which shall be administratively related to the General Board of Discipleship.

2. *Purpose*—The committee will provide a forum for information sharing, cooperative planning, and joint program endeavors as determined in accordance with the responsibilities and objectives of the participating agencies. The committee shall serve as an advocate for older-adult concerns and issues and shall serve to support ministries by, with, and for older adults throughout The United Methodist Church and its affiliated agencies and in the larger society.

3. *Responsibilities*—The responsibilities of the committee shall include the following:

a) Identify the needs, concerns, and potential contributions of older adults.

b) Promote a plan of comprehensive ministry by, with, and for older adults in local churches that includes spiritual growth, education, training, mission, service, and fellowship.

c) Encourage and support the development of resources and programs that will undergird local church ministries by, with, and for older adults.

d) Advocate development and implementation of policies and service designed to impact systems and concepts that adversely affect older adults.

e) Educate and keep before the Church the lifelong process of aging, with emphasis on the quality of life, intergenerational understanding and interaction, and faith development.

f) Encourage and support the development of resources and programs that can be used by annual conferences, jurisdictions, central conferences, and the denomination at large in training and equipping older adults for new roles in the ministry and mission of the Church.

g) Serve as focal point for supplying information and guidelines on older-adult ministries to local churches.

h) Encourage coordination and networking opportunities among agencies responsible for the development of resources, programs, and policies relating to older-adult ministries.

i) Support and advocate the provisions contained in *The Book of Resolutions* of The United Methodist Church related to aging.

j) Support and encourage resource development for the celebration of an annual Older Adult Recognition Day.

k) Develop and administer a program of financial grants for older-adult ministries throughout The United Methodist Church.

4. *Membership*—The committee shall be composed of one board member and one staff member from each of the following agencies: the General Board of Discipleship, the General Board of Global Ministries, the General Board of Church and Society, the General Board of Higher Education and Ministry, and the General Board of Pension and Health Benefits; one member (board or staff) from each of the following: the Commission on the Status and Role of Women, the Commission on Religion and Race, the General Commission on United Methodist Men, The United

Methodist Publishing House, the General Commission on Communication, United Methodist Women; one active or retired bishop representing the Council of Bishops, and one central conference representative; five older adults, one to be selected by each jurisdictional College of Bishops; and no more than three members to be selected by the committee for expertise and/or professional qualifications, and no more than three additional members to be selected by the committee for inclusiveness (racial/ethnic, disability, age, gender, laity, clergy, or geographic distribution). Staff and/or board members will provide appropriate liaison and reports to their respective agencies. Board members and central conference and jurisdiction representatives shall serve no more than two consecutive terms (one term equals four years). Each board and agency will be responsible for travel, lodging, and other expenses incurred by representatives attending meetings of the Committee on Older Adult Ministries.

5. *Meetings*—The committee will meet at least once a year in conjunction with a meeting of the General Board of Discipleship.

¶ **1121.** *Duties and Responsibilities of the Curriculum Resources Committee*—There shall be a Curriculum Resources Committee, organized and administered by the General Board of Discipleship, which shall be responsible for the construction of plans for curriculum and curriculum resources to be used in the Christian educational ministry of the Church and other study settings. (See ¶ 258.1.)

1. The Curriculum Resources Committee shall carefully review and act on the plans constructed and proposed by the staff of Church School Publications based upon research, including ideas from the Curriculum Resources Committee and other persons in United Methodist educational ministries.

2. The plans for curriculum and curriculum resources shall be designed to help local churches carry out the Church's educational ministry.

3. The plans for curriculum and curriculum resources shall be consistent with the educational philosophy and approach formulated for the educational ministry of the Church by the General Board of Discipleship and shall reflect a unity of purpose and a planned comprehensiveness of scope. They shall be designed to support the total life and work of the Church, shall teach Christian truth consistent with the Doctrinal Standards and General Rules of The United Methodist Church (¶ 104), and shall reflect

the official positions of The United Methodist Church as authorized by the General Conference.

¶ **1122.** *Curriculum Requirements*—When the plans for curriculum and curriculum resources have been approved by the General Board of Discipleship, the editorial staff of Church School Publications shall be responsible for the development of curriculum resources based on the approved plans. The curriculum resources shall be based on the Bible, shall reflect the universal gospel of the living Christ, shall be in agreement with United Methodist doctrine as delineated in ¶¶ 104 and 105 of the *Book of Discipline*, and shall be designed for use in the various settings that are defined by the board.

¶ **1123.** *Authority of the Curriculum Resources Committee to Review Teaching Resources of General Agencies*—The Curriculum Resources Committee may review, approve, and recommend existing or projected resources from other agencies. The committee shall make certain that all approved materials conform to United Methodist doctrine as delineated in ¶¶ 104 and 105 of the *Book of Discipline*. All curriculum resources that are approved by the General Board of Discipleship shall be authorized for use in the teaching and learning ministries of the Church.

¶ **1124.** *Relationship of the Curriculum Resources Committee to the General Board of Discipleship and to The United Methodist Publishing House*—1. The Curriculum Resources Committee shall be related to the General Board of Discipleship as follows:

The committee shall be responsible to the board with respect to educational philosophy and approaches and shall seek to maintain the standards set by the board.

2. The Curriculum Resources Committee shall be related to The United Methodist Publishing House as follows:

a) The publisher of The United Methodist Publishing House or the chairperson of the board of The United Methodist Publishing House may sit with the General Board of Discipleship for consideration of matters pertaining to joint interests of the Curriculum Resources Committee and The United Methodist Publishing House and shall have the privilege of the floor without vote.

b) The United Methodist Publishing House shall publish, manufacture, and distribute the curriculum resources prepared by the editorial staff of Church School Publications. The United Methodist Publishing House and the General Board of Discipleship shall be responsible jointly for interpretation and support of these resources.

c) The work of the Curriculum Resources Committee shall be financed by The United Methodist Publishing House.

3. The committee shall exercise this additional relationship:

The committee may cooperate with The United Methodist Publishing House and the General Board of Discipleship in educational research, in the development of experimental resources, and in the evaluation of resources that are provided for the teaching and learning ministries of the church.

¶ **1125.** *Editor of Church School Publications*—1. The editor of Church School Publications shall be responsible for the administration of the work of the Curriculum Resources Committee and the editorial staff of Church School Publications, the general editorial policy, and the final determination of editorial content of the church school publications.

2. The editor shall be elected by the General Board of Discipleship upon nomination by a joint committee composed of the president of the General Board of Discipleship, the chairperson of the Curriculum Resources Committee, one other member of the General Board of Discipleship representing educational concerns, the chairperson and two other members of The United Methodist Publishing House. The election of the editor shall be subject to confirmation by the board of The United Methodist Publishing House.

3. The editor shall be responsible to the General Board of Discipleship for seeing that the content of church school publications is consistent with the educational philosophy formulated by the board.

¶ **1126.** *Membership of the Curriculum Resources Committee*—1. The Curriculum Resources Committee shall consist of eight voting members elected quadrennially by the General Board of Discipleship as follows:

a) A bishop not serving on the General Board of Discipleship and with experience in teaching and learning ministries, to be nominated by the Council of Bishops.

b) Seven members, nominated by the board, at least three of whom are members of the General Board of Discipleship. Up to four additional members shall be selected for expertise in educational ministries and knowledge of the various concerns of congregations in teaching and learning ministries.

c) The publisher of The United Methodist Publishing House and the general secretary of the General Board of Discipleship shall be ex officio members of the Curriculum Resources Committee with the privilege of voice but without vote.

d) The chairperson of the committee shall be a member of the General Board of Discipleship.

2. The Curriculum Resources Committee shall include staff of Church School Publications and of the General Board of Discipleship, with the privilege of voice but without vote. The Curriculum Resources Committee may select other people to assist in its work, including people nominated by other boards, agencies, and general commissions of the Church. Members of other boards, agencies, and general commissions will serve at their own expense.

3. The committee may prepare such bylaws and operating guidelines as are necessary to facilitate the work of the committee.

Section VI. Division on Ministries With Young People

¶ **1201.** There shall be a Division on Ministries With Young People of the General Board of Discipleship.

¶ **1202.** *Purpose*—The purpose of the Division on Ministries With Young People is to empower young people as world-changing disciples of Jesus Christ, to nurture faith development, and to equip young leaders by

1. Developing youth/young adult spiritual leaders of local congregations to transform lives by making disciples of Jesus Christ;

2. Challenging The United Methodist Church to embrace, confirm, and celebrate God's call on the lives of young people;

3. Cultivating and nurturing life-giving ministries where influence and worth are not limited by age or experience;

4. Advocating for the issues and concerns of young people in the church and the global community;

5. Empowering young people to work as agents of peace, justice, and mercy;

6. Building a network of support and providing resources that connect the diverse experiences of youth and young adults in local ministries and communities across the globe.

¶ **1203.** *Responsibilities*—The responsibilities of the Division on Ministries With Young People shall be:

1. to promote and maintain active and effective systems for youth and young-adult ministry programming at the local church, district, conference, jurisdictional/central conference, and general church levels for the full involvement of young people in leadership and membership;

2. to advocate for the needs and concerns of young people throughout all arenas of church life, planning, and administration. Attention shall be given to the vast array of the life realities of young people;

3. to develop and support three constituency networks: a Network for United Methodist Youth, a Network for United Methodist Young Adults, and a Network for United Methodist Workers With Young People (may include youth workers, youth pastors, campus ministers, conference staff, chaplains, young adult workers, and so forth). These networks will provide ongoing communication and connectional links between local churches and other arenas of church life, relational ties to the denomination and one another, and resources for the spiritual formation of young people;

4. to provide leadership training models and resources that will support youth, young adults, and adult workers with young people to be full and active participants in the life and mission of the Church;

5. to plan and carry out a quadrennial global young people's convocation and to provide program resources and support services for regional and national convocations;

6. to provide administrative oversight to the grants for ministries with young people distributed in consultation with the General Board of Church and Society, General Board of Discipleship, General Board of Global Ministries, and General Board of Higher Education and Ministry;

7. to provide administrative oversight to the Youth Service Fund;

8. to recommend youth and young adults to nomination committees of general boards and agencies, considering suggestions from annual conference councils on youth and young-adult ministry (¶¶ 649.3e and 650.3e) and other appropriate organizations;

9. to collaborate with appropriate boards and agencies to provide young people with effective strategies and opportunities to live out their faith through ministries of peace, justice, and mercy in vocational choices and other avenues of service;

10. to collaborate with appropriate boards and agencies to strengthen the church's challenge for young people to respond to God's call to licensed and ordained ministry and to support young clergy through the development of networks and other appropriate resources;

11. to collaborate with appropriate boards and agencies to encourage the participation of young people in appropriate denominational, ecumenical, and interreligious relationships and deliberations.

¶ **1204.** *Authority and Accountability*—The Division on Ministries With Young People shall be accountable to the General Board of Discipleship in programming, personnel, and administration. The division shall have the authority to determine and interpret program directions that support its mandate. These program directions shall be in harmony with the charter of the General Board of Discipleship (GBOD) and have the GBOD's approval.

¶ **1205.** *Relationship of the Division on Ministries With Young People to the General Board of Discipleship*—The Division on Ministries With Young People shall be related to the General Board of Discipleship as follows: Two members of the Division on Ministries With Young People shall be elected to the board, one youth and one young adult as defined by the age qualifications for the Division on Ministries With Young People in accordance with ¶ 1207.

¶ **1206.** *Structure*—The Division on Ministries With Young People shall be organized around three basic units: United Methodist Youth, United Methodist Young Adults, and United Methodist Workers With Young People.

¶ **1207.** *Membership*—The membership of the Division on Ministries With Young People shall be inclusive with respect to gender, race/ethnicity, lay/clergy, and vocation.

1. Membership shall be as follows:

a) Twelve youth—1 youth, elected by the youth organization of each central conference (according to the age definition of each central conference, but not to exceed the age of 24); 1 youth, sixteen or younger at the time of election, elected by the jurisdictional youth convocation;

b) Twelve young adults—1 young adult elected by the young adult organization of each central conference (according to the age definition of each central conference, but not to exceed the age of 35); 1 young adult elected by the jurisdictional conference;

c) Twelve adult workers with young people—1 adult from each central conference, appointed by the central conference nominating committee; 1 adult from each jurisdiction, elected by the jurisdictional conference;

d) Additional Members:

(1) One member of the General Board of Discipleship;

(2) Two members of the United Methodist Student Movement steering committee (¶ 1412.2*g*);

(3) up to 5 additional members who, as determined by the General Board of Discipleship, may be nominated by the division to ensure inclusiveness and expertise.

(4) One bishop selected by the Council of Bishops.

2. *Resource People*—The division shall be responsible for connecting and highlighting the work of general agencies and other United Methodist entities in youth and young-adult ministry. In order to effectively carry out that charge, one staff person (or board member when staff are not available) from the following entities shall be present (with voice but not vote) at meetings of the division. These representatives shall attend at the expense of the sending agency and shall relate the priorities of the division to their agency and serve as resource people to the division:

a) General Board of Church and Society

b) General Board of Discipleship

c) General Board of Global Ministries

d) General Board of Higher Education and Ministry

e) General Commission on Religion and Race

f) General Commission on the Status and Role of Women

g) General Commission on United Methodist Men

h) General Council on Finance and Administration

i) Connectional Table

j) United Methodist Communications

k) United Methodist Publishing House

l) United Methodist Women

¶ **1208.** *Youth Service Fund*—There shall be a Youth Service Fund.

1. *Organization*—The Youth Service Fund shall be a means of stewardship education and mission support of youth within The United Methodist Church. As a part of the Fund's cultivation, youth shall be challenged to assume their financial responsibilities in connection with the total program and budget of the church of which they are members. Local church treasurers shall

send the full amount of Youth Service Fund offerings to the treasurer of the annual conference, who shall retain 70 percent of the amount for distribution by the annual conference council on youth ministry. The annual conference treasurer shall send the remaining 30 percent monthly to the treasurer of the General Council on Finance and Administration to be forwarded to the General Board of Discipleship, Division on Ministries With Young People. All other Youth Service Fund money raised in the annual conference shall be divided in the same manner and distributed in the same way.

2. *Project Review*—The youth network of the Division on Ministries With Young People shall constitute a project review committee to advise the network in the selection of projects. The project review committee shall be comprised of youth and adult worker members of the Division on Ministries With Young People in a ratio of at least five youth to one adult as determined by the Division on Ministries With Young People. The projects shall be chosen according to the policies and criteria established by the youth network of the Division on Ministries With Young People.

3. A minimum of 70 percent of the general portion of the Youth Service Fund shall be used to fund Youth Service Fund projects; the remaining amount shall be used for office resourcing and Youth Service Fund promotion and interpretation. United Methodist Communications shall assist the Division on Ministries With Young People in the promotion and interpretation of the Youth Service Fund.

¶ **1209.** *Grants for Ministries With Young People*—There shall be grants made available to local churches, affiliated organizations, campus ministries, districts, annual conferences, provisional conferences, jurisdictional conferences, and central conferences of The United Methodist Church.

1. *Purpose*—The purpose of these grants is to fund dynamic, creative ministries with young people that can serve as model programs for other organizations throughout the connection.

2. *Project Review*—The Division on Ministries With Young People shall constitute a project review committee made up of three youth, three young adults, and three adult workers with young people who are members of the division. The committee may also include one staff representative and one board member each from the General Board of Church and Society, the General Board of Discipleship, the General Board of Global Ministries,

and the General Board of Higher Education and Ministry. The Division on Ministries With Young People shall establish criteria in consultation with the four participating program boards and in relation to the purposes of the division and the program boards.

¶ 1210. *Global Young People's Convocation*—There shall be a Global Young People's Convocation.

1. *Purpose*—The Global Young People's Convocation shall be a global event held once every four years for the purpose of celebrating the mission and vitality of young people in The United Methodist Church, raising the joys and concerns of young people from the global community, developing young people as leaders for effective ministry in local churches and communities of faith, highlighting emerging trends in youth and young-adult ministry, and providing a common forum that embraces the global reality of the church.

2. *Legislation*—During the convocation there shall be opportunities for jurisdiction and central conference delegations and individuals to propose legislation in an appropriate forum. This forum shall be made up of delegations as defined under "Voting members." Legislation brought to the forum shall relate to issues of concern to young people. Legislation adopted by the forum may be referred to the Division on Ministries With Young People or sent to the General Conference of The United Methodist Church carrying the name "United Methodist Young People's Convocation." All legislation, petitions, and programming must be in accordance with ¶ 806.9 and ¶ 806.11.

3. *Membership*—The membership at the forum of the United Methodist Young People's Convocation shall be inclusive in nature and selected as follows:

a) Voting members

(1) Five youth (ages 12-18) from each jurisdiction and five youth from each central conference according to the age definition of each central conference. These youth shall be chosen by the process outlined by each Jurisdictional Young People's Ministry and by central conference youth organizations in the year preceding the Global Young People's Convocation.

(2) Five young adults (ages 19-30) from each jurisdiction and five young adults from each central conference according to the age definition of each central conference. These young adults shall be chosen by the process outlined by each Jurisdic-

tional Young People's Ministry and central conference young-adult organizations.

(3) Two adult workers with young people from each jurisdiction and two youth and young-adult workers from each central conference. These adults shall be chosen by the process outlined by each Jurisdictional Young People's Ministry and by central conference youth organizations in the year preceding the Global Young People's Convocation.

b) Nonvoting members (In all cases, nonvoting members will have the status of voice without vote.)

(1) Youth and young-adult members of the general agencies

(2) Members and staff of the Division on Ministries With Young People

(3) Additional members from jurisdictions, central conferences, and ecumenical partners

4. *Expenses*—The expenses for the Global Young People's Convocation are to be borne by participants wherever possible. An adequate funding plan shall be devised by the Division on Ministries With Young People to ensure the full participation of elected delegates to Global Young People's Convocation. It is strongly recommended that jurisdictions, central conferences, and annual conference councils on youth and young-adult ministries, or equivalent structures, secure funding for Convocation participants who are elected from said conference. A limited amount of need-based scholarships shall be made available through the Division on Ministries With Young People to promote the full participation of the body.

¶ **1211.** *Staff*—1. The Division on Ministries With Young People shall have as its chief staff officer an Associate General Secretary. This staff officer shall be nominated by the personnel committee of the General Board of Discipleship for election by the board. The search committee shall be chaired by the General Secretary of the General Board of Discipleship and composed of equal representation from the General Board of Discipleship and the Division on Ministries With Young People.

2. All other staff members of the division will be elected or appointed in a manner prescribed by the board (¶ 714).

¶ **1212.** *Division Funding*—The operating funds for the division shall be derived from three main sources: World Service

Fund, self-funding programs, and the general portion of the Youth Service Fund.

Section VII. General Board of Global Ministries

¶ **1301.** There shall be a General Board of Global Ministries, hereinafter referred to as the board, the purpose of which is found within the expression of the total mission of the Church. It is a missional instrument of The United Methodist Church, its annual conferences, missionary conferences, and local congregations in the context of a global setting.

The Church in mission is a sign of God's presence in the world. By the authority of God and the power of the Holy Spirit, the Church:

1. Joins God's mission to reclaim, restore, and redeem the life of all creation to its divine intention;

2. Confesses by word and deed the redeeming activity of God in Christ among the whole human family;

3. Seeks to embody and realize the potential of new life in Christ among all human beings; and

4. Looks forward in faith and hope for the fulfillment of God's reign and the completion of God's mission.

¶ **1302.** *Responsibilities*—1. To discern those places where the gospel has not been heard or heeded and to witness to its meaning throughout the world, inviting all persons to newness of life in Jesus Christ through a program of global ministries.

2. To encourage and support the development of leadership in mission for both the Church and society.

3. To challenge all United Methodists with the New Testament imperative to proclaim the gospel to the ends of the earth, expressing the mission of the Church; and to recruit, send, and receive missionaries, enabling them to dedicate all or a portion of their lives in service across racial, cultural, national, and political boundaries.

4. To plan with others and to establish and strengthen Christian congregations where opportunities and needs are found, so that these congregations may be units of mission in their places and partners with others in the worldwide mission of the Christian church.

5. To advocate the work for the unity of Christ's church through witness and service with other Christian churches and through ecumenical councils.

6. To engage in dialogue with all persons, including those of other faiths, and to join with them where possible in action on common concerns.

7. To assist local congregations and annual conferences in mission both in their own communities and across the globe by raising awareness of the claims of global mission and by providing channels for participation.

8. To address the concerns of women organized for mission and to help equip women for full participation both locally and globally in the Church and the world.

9. To engage in direct ministries to human need, both emergency and continuing, institutional and noninstitutional, however caused.

10. To work within societies and systems so that full human potential is liberated and to work toward the transformation of demonic forces that distort life.

11. To identify with all who are alienated and dispossessed and to assist them in achieving their full human development-body, mind, and spirit.

12. To envision and engage in imaginative new forms of mission appropriate to changing human needs and to share the results of experimentation with the entire Church.

13. To facilitate the development of cooperative patterns of ministry so that the unified strength of local congregations and other units of the Church in designated areas can respond with more effective ministries of justice, advocacy, compassion, and nurture.

14. To affirm Volunteers in Mission as an authentic form of personal missionary involvement and devise appropriate structure to interpret and implement opportunities for mission volunteers in the global community.

15. To facilitate the receiving and assignment of missionaries from churches in nations other than the United States in cooperation with the other general agencies and with annual conferences.

¶ 1303. *Objectives*—1. The objectives of the board shall be:

a) To plan for the implementation of the responsibilities of the board in the missional outreach of The United Methodist Church.

b) To establish the appropriate organization of the board and staff to accomplish its program and fulfill the responsibilities of the board.

c) To determine, in cooperation with mission constituencies, the areas to be served and the nature of the work to be undertaken.

d) To determine policy and program, to establish goals and priorities, to project long-range plans, to evaluate the program and services of the board as to the progress made in fulfilling its purpose in accordance with ¶¶ 1301 and 1302, and to seek to achieve its objectives through the programs of the board.

e) To coordinate and harmonize the work of the board.

f) To elect or appoint, according to the bylaws, the staff of the board.

g) To assign responsibility and delegate authority to staff and to provide oversight of the staff.

h) To receive and properly administer all properties, trust funds, permanent funds, annuity funds, and other special funds.

i) To receive, secure, appropriate, and expend funds to underwrite its program and fulfill its responsibilities.

j) To receive and act upon the reports of its units, committees, and their staff.

k) To make a report of its activities during the quadrennium to the General Conference.

l) To develop and maintain cooperative relations with other general agencies and with jurisdictional, central, annual, and missionary conferences.

m) To be responsible for implementing a policy stating that The United Methodist Church is not a party to any comity agreement that limits the ability of any annual conference in any jurisdiction to develop and resource programs of ministry of any kind among Native Americans, including the organization of local churches where necessary.

2. The board shall develop and maintain cooperative working relationships with churches and ecumenical agencies on matters of mutual concern in the implementation of disciplinary responsibilities.

3. The board shall facilitate and coordinate the program relationships of other program agencies of The United Methodist Church with churches and agencies in nations other than the United States.

¶ **1304.** *Authority*—The board shall have authority to make bylaws and regulate its proceedings in accordance with the *Book of Discipline.* Bylaws may be amended by a two-thirds vote of the members at a regular or special meeting, provided that required notice of such amendment has previously been given to the members. The board shall have the power and right to do any and all things that shall be authorized by its charter, except when there is duplication of activities from one agency to another. It shall have authority to develop and carry out its responsibilities as described in ¶ 1302; to buy, acquire, or receive by gift, devise, or bequest property—real, personal, and mixed; to hold, mortgage, sell, and dispose of property; to sue and be sued; to borrow money in case of necessity in accordance with ¶¶ 806-807; to develop and maintain ecumenical relations to carry out its responsibilities; and to administer its affairs through the board and its various units and committees.

¶ **1305.** *Incorporation*—1. The board shall be incorporated and shall implement its responsibilities through its corporate structure and the corporate structures of the entities that it controls or that are administratively organized as divisions or departments of the board.

2. The board or another entity described in ¶ 1305.1 shall be the successor to the following corporations: the Board of Missions of The Evangelical United Brethren Church, the Home Missions and Church Erection Society of the Church of the United Brethren in Christ, the Foreign Missionary Society of the United Brethren in Christ, the Missionary Society of The Evangelical Church, and the Board of Church Extension of The Evangelical Church, and as such successor it shall be and is authorized and empowered to receive from its said predecessor corporations all trust funds and assets of every kind and character—real, personal, or mixed—held by them, and it shall and hereby is authorized to administer such trusts and funds in accordance with the conditions under which they have been previously received and administered by the said predecessor corporations.

In the case of administering "conditional donations secured by trust agreements and mortgages" issued prior to 1980, the General Board of Global Ministries of The United Methodist Church may negotiate payment of less than original value of any outstanding notes that are associated with former conditional grants or donations secured by trust agreements or mortgages.

3. The board or another entity described in ¶ 1305.1 shall have control of all the work formerly controlled and administered by the following: the Board of Health and Welfare Ministries; the

Board of Missions of The United Methodist Church; the Board of Missions and Church Extension of The Methodist Church; the Missionary Society, the Board of Foreign Missions, the Board of Home Missions and Church Extension, the Board of Missions, and the Board of Church Extension of The Methodist Episcopal Church, South; the Board of Missions of The Methodist Protestant Church; the Board of Missions of The Methodist Church; such other incorporated or unincorporated divisions and departments and their predecessors as may have been merged into the board; and such other corporations or agencies of the General Conference as do similar work; but this list shall not be construed as exhaustive.

4. Subject to the limitations hereinafter specified, any corporations within the board shall be subject to the supervision and control of the General Conference of The United Methodist Church in all things not inconsistent with the Constitution and laws of the United States and of the states of incorporation.

5. The board shall have the authority to create those subsidiary units or sections needed in the fulfillment of designated functions.

¶ **1306.** *Executive Committee*—There shall be an executive committee, which shall exercise the powers of the board *ad interim*, and whose membership and responsibilities shall be determined by the board's bylaws.

¶ **1307.** *Corporate Officers*—The board shall elect as its corporate officers a president, one vice president, a general treasurer, a corporate secretary, and such other officers as it shall deem necessary. The board shall determine the powers and duties of the officers.

¶ **1308.** *Elected Staff*—1. The board shall elect the general secretary for a quadrennial term by ballot. As chief staff officer of the board, the general secretary shall have direct involvement in staff selections.

2. The board shall elect, for quadrennial terms, a general treasurer/chief operating officer and as many executive directors as the board thinks are appropriate to carry out its work.

3. The board's personnel committee, in consultation with the general secretary, shall recommend candidates for the positions described in the preceding sub-paragraph 2.

4. The general secretary may add positions to the cabinet in consultation with the board's personnel committee.

¶ **1309.** *Personnel Policies*—1. *Selection*—The staff of the board shall be selected on the basis of competency and with representation of ethnic and racial groups, young adults, and women, in accordance with policies in ¶ 714.

2. *Staff Participation of Women—a)* Of the cabinet-level staff positions within the board, a minimum of 40 percent shall be occupied by women.

b) A minimum of 40 percent of all elected staff, as well as a minimum of 40 percent of the appointed staff, shall be women.

¶ **1310.** *Properties, Trusts, and Annuities*—1. All properties, trust funds, annuity funds, permanent funds, and endowments now or formerly held and administered by the Board of Missions, the Board of Health and Welfare Ministries, and the United Methodist Committee on Relief of The United Methodist Church; the Board of Missions of The Methodist Church; the Board of Missions of The Evangelical United Brethren Church or their successors; and their respective divisions and departments or their successors shall be carefully safeguarded. The board shall endeavor to invest in institutions, companies, corporations, or funds that make a positive contribution toward the realization of the goals outlined in the Social Principles of The United Methodist Church and to administer such investments in the best interest of those persons and causes for which said funds were established. Such properties, trust funds, annuity funds, permanent funds, and endowments shall be transferred to the board from merged boards and societies only when such transfers can be made in accordance with the laws of the states where the several boards and societies are chartered and on the recommendation of the board and the approval of such boards and societies. Funds of the board and its preceding corporations and societies that are subject to appropriation shall be appropriated only on recommendation of the board. (See ¶ 806.12.)

2. Former Evangelical United Brethren mission agencies located within the United States not directly owned by the board, which receive more than 50 percent of their charitable donations through United Methodist channels of giving shall be governed by a board of trustees or directors of whom two-thirds of its elected voting membership shall be members of The United Methodist Church.

3. The financial affairs of the board shall be as follows:

a) The income of the board shall be derived from apportionments, assessments, or askings distributed to jurisdictions, annual conferences, and pastoral charges by the budget-making process of the General Conference in such manner as the General

Conference may prescribe, and from church schools, gifts, donations, freewill offerings, annuities, bequests, specials, and other sources from which missionary and benevolence funds are usually derived, in accordance with *The Book of Discipline* and actions of the General Conference.

b) All contributions to and income on all funds of the board should be used for current expenses and annual appropriations unless otherwise designated by the donor.

4. Askings shall be received from the fields, and budgets shall be prepared by the board, consistent with its constitution and charter, and the budget shall be presented to the Connectional Table in accordance with ¶ 806.

¶ **1311.** *Membership*—The policies, plans of work, management, business, and all affairs of the board shall be governed and administered by it according to the following conditions:

1. The basic members (clergy, laity) are elected by the jurisdiction upon the nomination of the annual conferences.

The jurisdictions shall use the following formula when electing members: Northeastern Jurisdiction—3; Southeastern Jurisdiction—4; Western Jurisdiction—2; North Central Jurisdiction—3; and South Central Jurisdiction—3. Each central conference shall nominate one member to the basic membership of the board for a total of seven (7). The additional members of the board shall be nominated and elected in accordance with the board's bylaws. There may be up to five (5) additional members from the five jurisdictions, one of whom shall be from either the Oklahoma Indian Missionary Conference or the Rio Grande Annual Conference, unless they are already represented in the basic membership of the board. There shall be two (2) additional members from the central conferences

2. The United Methodist Women shall elect three members of its board of directors to serve as directors of the General Board of Global Ministries with voice and without vote.

3. The composition of the board and its units should reflect the major recognized categories of Church members. (See ¶ 705.) A minimum of one-half of the membership should be women.

4. Members of the board shall be distributed across the component units and standing committees in accordance with the board's bylaws. The members elected by the United Methodist Women shall serve on the program committees of the board with voice and without vote.

5. *a)* Except as provided below in subparagraph 1311.5*b*, the term of office of all members whose election is provided for in this paragraph shall begin and the board shall organize at a meeting to be held within ninety days after the adjournment of the last meeting of the several jurisdictional conferences held after the adjournment of the General Conference.

b) The term of office of each basic member elected by the central conferences shall begin immediately following the central conference meeting at which he or she was elected to the board. The term of office of any additional members nominated by the central conferences shall begin at the board meeting at which he or she is elected in accordance with the bylaws. Unless otherwise specified in the *Discipline* or the board's bylaws, the term of office of each member whose election is provided for in this paragraph shall end when his or her successor takes office as provided for in this paragraph.

6. On nomination of the Council of Bishops, the General Conference shall elect three bishops from the five jurisdictions and two bishops from two of the three central conference regions (Africa, Europe, Philippines) to the board. Each jurisdiction and each central conference region shall have representation from this category on the board at least once within a three-quadrennia period. Except as provided in the preceding sentence, bishops shall not be permitted to serve as members of the board.

7. The general secretary, the general treasurer, and the deputy general secretaries of the board shall be members without vote.

8. Salaried members of staff of any agency receiving appropriation funds from the board shall not be eligible to serve as voting members of the board, except in order to fulfill the provisions of ¶ 705.

¶ **1312.** *Relationship to the United Methodist Women*—The board shall elect three of its directors to serve as members of the United Methodist Women Program Advisory Group.

¶ **1313.** *Advance Committee*—The Advance for Christ and His Church is the designated giving channel of The United Methodist Church. The Advance Committee shall have general oversight of the Advance for Christ and His Church (¶ 822).

1. The Advance Committee shall be organized under the authority and direction of the board as determined by the bylaws of the board

2. *General Advance Special Projects*—It shall be the responsibility of the Advance Committee to determine which projects are approved to receive general Advance Special Gifts (¶ 822.2). The Advance fosters partnership between those who give and those who receive, and it affirms the right of persons to determine the priority of their own needs.

MISSION PROGRAM AREAS

¶ 1314. *Program Areas*—The program responsibilities within the General Board of Global Ministries shall be assigned to its units as it seeks to enhance the involvement of all United Methodists in Christian mission and develop ways to facilitate this mission involvement. The membership of the program areas shall be constituted in accordance with the bylaws of the General Board of Global Ministries.

The General Board of Global Ministries shall engage in mission programming around the following areas:

1. Congregational and Community Development

a) Evangelization among people who have not heard or heeded the gospel.

b) Strategic new mission initiatives and establishing new congregations where United Methodism and/or cooperative church relationships do not exist.

c) Leadership development, including identifying, preparing, training, and empowering persons for leadership in the church and community so that vital mission-oriented congregations may be developed.

d) Resourcing leadership training programs and administering scholarships, including the World Communion Scholarship Program.

e) Church growth, including revitalization of existing congregations and faith communities, and congregational development, particularly among racial and ethnic congregations and congregations in transitional communities/neighborhoods. Congregational development shall be carried out in cooperation with the General Board of Discipleship through a Joint Committee on Congregational Development composed of equal representation from the General Board of Global Ministries and the General Board of Discipleship, which shall meet at least annually to expedite cooperation between these two boards in the field of congregational development of both new congregations as well as the revitalization of existing congregations, with a priority given to racial and ethnic congregations.

f) Church and community development, including grants, loans and technical assistance for programs of self-development and self-determination pertaining to social needs arising from concerns for ethnic and cultural pluralism, economic and sexual exploitation, and political and racial oppression.

g) Community-based programs in areas such as agricultural mission, communications, student and youth ministries.

h) Development of strong local and regional organizations for community development with the capacity to network and become part of an internationally related program.

i) To foster and facilitate cooperative patterns of ministry, including cooperative parishes, metropolitan ministries, rural and town and country ministries.

j) Administering funding and other forms of resource sharing for projects and programs—especially those serving women, children, and youth of partner churches and ecumenical bodies.

2. Connectional and Ecumenical Relationships

a) Working with denominational, ecumenical, and secular coalitions, as appropriate, to develop new patterns of joint mission.

b) Identification and analysis of the missional concerns that shape the conditions under which the church is called to engage in God's mission.

c) Development of and sustaining cooperative relationships and mission partnerships that include sharing of opportunities and resources, networking and collaboration. This includes the maintaining and fulfilling of connectional relationships with annual conferences, missionary conferences, and central conferences; autonomous, affiliated autonomous, and united churches; and ecumenical church bodies.

d) Developing missional relationships in countries where The United Methodist Church has no commitments by pursuing a working agreement with the church or churches, a united mission organization, or ecumenical bodies related to the area, if such exists. If these approaches are not available, the board may participate in the formation of a new United Methodist denominational structure, in which case it may request the Council of Bishops to provide any necessary episcopal oversight.

e) Liaising with each central conference and its conferences, both annual and provisional, and each affiliated autonomous Methodist church or united church, and where applicable, requesting that these bodies make provision for liaison functions with the board.

f) Providing information and assisting in developing action and advocacy for global justice, peace, and freedom through working cooperatively with other agencies of the Church; other denominations; and ecumenical, interfaith, and secular coalitions. The General Board of Global Ministries will maintain its special consultative status with the United Nations and its collaborations with United Methodist Women and the General Board of Church and Society through the United Methodist Office at the Church Center for the UN.

g) Fostering interaction of churches and ecumenical groups for the purpose of mutuality in the definition and implementation of Christian mission and international concerns.

3. Mission Education and Interpretation

a) Providing opportunities for United Methodists to understand the global mission of The United Methodist Church and for personal and corporate witness through involvement in and support of this mission.

b) Initiating and developing programs and resources that will encourage persons of particular cultures to become receivers and bearers of the gospel across boundaries and to live faithfully within a multicultural world.

c) Engaging in programs of mission interpretation, including training mission interpreters.

d) Training of connectional mission leaders to fulfill their responsibilities.

e) Working with schools of theology and professors of mission, in cooperation with the General Board of Higher Education and Ministry, in providing an emphasis on education for mission.

f) Cooperating with the General Board of Discipleship, especially the Curriculum Resources Committee, in providing opportunities for mission involvement and understanding of all age levels.

g) Initiating and developing special programs and resources through which children and youth may understand the mission of the Church.

h) Working with ecumenical agencies in fulfilling mission education responsibilities.

i) Providing opportunities for United Methodists to gather and witness as a global church.

4. Mission Service

a) Planning for and developing a broad range of mission volunteer opportunities for short-term assignments, including promoting and interpreting the need for volunteers with a variety of skills and abilities; working in close relationship with conference and jurisdictional officers (i.e., volunteers in mission, disaster response) to assist in identifying, developing, and supporting opportunities for mission volunteer service.

b) Promoting opportunities for mission service related to the General Board of Global Ministries throughout the constituencies of the Church, through the recruitment, selection, preparation, commissioning, and assignment of all categories of mission personnel, with necessary supervision and support of these persons in assignments in the widest variety of church and ecumenical partners in the United States and around the globe.

c) Relating to persons in mission of partner churches.

5. Global Health

a) Engaging in, supporting, facilitating, advocating, and partnering with others (including UM organizations and ecumenical, interfaith, and secular organizations, as appropriate) to provide global and local health ministries that, in the spirit of Jesus Christ, foster abundant health for all, including holistic physical, mental and spiritual well-being, regardless of religion, nationality, culture, race, ethnicity, gender, sexual orientation, or physical or mental disability.

b) Combating preventable diseases of poverty and supporting comprehensive community-based health care.

c) Convening, mobilizing, resourcing, and equipping United Methodists to engage in, support, and advocate holistic health ministries, locally and globally.

d) Encouraging awareness of the gifts, graces, assets, and needs of persons with special physical, mental, and other developmental needs, fostering a culture of inclusivity within The United Methodist Church as a place where people with special needs will be embraced in all aspects of worship, leadership, and ministry.

e) Encouraging and supporting congregations to respond effectively and compassionately to those affected by substance abuse and related violence.

UNITED METHODIST COMMITTEE ON RELIEF

¶ **1315.** 1. *General Provisions—a) Purpose*—The United Methodist Committee on Relief ("UMCOR") exists to assist United Methodists and churches to become involved globally in direct ministry to persons in need through programs of relief, rehabilitation, and service, including issues of displaced persons, hunger and poverty, disaster response, and disaster risk reduction; and to assist organizations, institutions, and programs related to annual conferences and other units of The United Methodist Church in their involvement in direct service to such persons in need.

b) Authority—UMCOR is a not-for-profit corporation whose directors are elected by the General Board of Global Ministries. UMCOR shall operate in a manner consistent with the policies set by the General Board of Global Ministries and in accordance with the bylaws of the General Board of Global Ministries and UMCOR.

c) Responsibilities—The responsibilities of UMCOR shall be as follows:

(1) seek to address human need in the spirit of Jesus Christ;

(2) provide immediate relief of acute human need and respond to the suffering of persons in the world caused by disaster;

(3) work cooperatively with the appropriate conference units, ecumenical bodies, interdenominational agencies and other partners in the identification of, advocacy for, and assistance with ministries with displaced persons, hunger and poverty, disaster response, and disaster risk reduction;

(4) administer these ministries described in subparagraph three (3) above in the spirit of Jesus Christ, preserving the dignity of persons without regard to religion, race, nationality, or gender, and seek to enhance the quality of life in the human community;

(5) work cooperatively with The General Commission on Communication in promotion of the UMCOR Sunday;

(6) initiate printed, audiovisual, electronic, and other resources to interpret, support, and communicate with confer-

ences and churches concerning appeals for help and information related to ministries with displaced persons, hunger and poverty, disaster response, and disaster risk reduction; and

(7) assist and train conference coordinators and other partners to address emerging and ongoing issues related to displaced persons' ministries, root causes of hunger and poverty, disaster relief, disaster risk reduction, and rehabilitation;

d) *Response to Requests for Disaster Funding*—UMCOR shall respond to a disaster response proposal only if the request for such funds comes from either (i) an appropriate body related to The United Methodist Church, preferably an annual conference, or (ii) an appropriate body of an entity that is not related to The United Methodist Church. UMCOR will review disaster response proposals for compliance with international or national standards for humanitarian assistance. UMCOR will review proposals for funding to repair places of worship or church property damaged by disasters in consultation with conference disaster response coordinators, bishops, and district superintendents in The United Methodist Church, or with persons in similar positions from other religious institutions, and will arrange an onsite visit to evaluate and initiate an ongoing consultative process when appropriate.

e) *Limitation of Responsibility*—UMCOR shall not be responsible, legally or morally, for the debts, contracts, or obligations or for any other financial commitments of any character or description created, undertaken, or assumed by any institution or interest related to a unit of The United Methodist Church, whether or not such institution or interest shall be approved, accepted, or recognized by UMCOR or shall be affiliated with UMCOR, or whether or not the promotion or establishment of the same shall be approved by the constitution of UMCOR. No such institution or interest related to a unit of The United Methodist Church and no officer or member of UMCOR shall have any authority whatsoever to take any action directly or by implication at variance with, or deviating from, the limitation contained in the preceding sentence hereof, except as UMCOR may directly own and manage an institution in its own name.

Section VIII. General Board of Higher Education and Ministry

¶ **1401.** There shall be a General Board of Higher Education and Ministry, hereinafter referred to as the board.

¶ 1402. *Incorporation*—The General Board of Higher Education and Ministry shall be a corporation under the laws of Tennessee and shall be responsible for the functions previously conducted by the Division of Higher Education of the General Board of Education and the Commission on Chaplains and Related Ministries of The United Methodist Church.

The General Board of Higher Education and Ministry is authorized to take such action as is appropriate under the corporation laws of Tennessee so as to accomplish the end result stated above, and under which the General Board of Higher Education and Ministry shall be one legal entity.

The divisions of the General Board of Education were not incorporated separately; it is the intent, however, that responsibility for the functions delegated to the divisions by prior legislative action be transferred consistent with the separation of the divisions between the General Board of Discipleship and the General Board of Higher Education and Ministry. In the division of the assets of the General Board of Education, it is the intent that all assets be used in keeping with the original intent and purpose for which they were established or acquired, and so be assigned as appropriate to the General Boards of Discipleship and Higher Education and Ministry, respectively. It is further intended that the annuities, bequests, trusts, and estates formerly held by the General Board of Education be used for the benefit and use of the General Boards of Discipleship and Higher Education and Ministry (in accord with their purposes as defined in the *Discipline*), respectively, as their interests may appear, and that real estate titles be authorized to be conveyed as appropriate and apportioned where indicated.

In the event that the intent of the original donor of existing annuities, bequests, trusts, and estates cannot be clearly determined in relation to the interests of the two boards, such assets shall be divided equally between the two boards.

It is further intended that should additional assets accrue to the former General Board of Education by reason of annuities, bequests, trusts, and estates not now known and where the intent of the donor can be clearly ascertained, the assets shall be used in keeping with the original intent and purpose for which they were established or acquired and so be assigned as appropriate to the General Boards of Discipleship and Higher Education and Ministry, respectively.

It is further intended that should additional assets accrue to the former General Board of Education by reason of annuities, bequests, trusts, and estates not now known and where the intent of the original donor cannot be clearly determined in relation to the interests of the two boards, such assets shall be divided equally between the two boards.

¶ 1403. *Amenability and Accountability*—The board shall be amenable to the General Conference, and between sessions of the General Conference it shall be accountable to the Connectional Table.

¶ 1404. *Purpose*—The board exists, within the expression of the total mission of the Church, for the specific purpose of preparing and assisting persons to fulfill their ministry in Christ in the several special ministries, ordained and diaconal; and to provide general oversight and care for campus ministries and institutions of higher education, including schools, colleges, universities, and theological schools.

¶ 1405. *Objectives*—All the objectives assigned to the divisions shall be considered to be the objectives of the board. In summary, the board shall have authority:

1. To maintain the historic mission of The United Methodist Church in higher education and to serve as advocate for the intellectual life of the Church.

2. To seek to understand and communicate the significance of the Christian mission in higher education and ministry throughout the world as the context in which values and Christian lifestyle are shaped.

3. To encourage a Christian presence in institutions related to The United Methodist Church.

4. To ensure that the board's programs and policies address the needs and concerns for ministry with racial and ethnic persons and people with disabilities.

5. To provide counsel, guidance, and assistance to annual conferences through their boards of ordained ministry and higher education and campus ministry, and other such program units as may be organized in the annual conferences.

6. To study needs and resources for ordained and diaconal ministries, including identification of new types of ministry.

7. To develop and maintain standards and procedures for certification in professional ministerial careers and for ordination into the ordained ministry.

8. To promote and give direction to work among racial and ethnic groups, and people with disabilities for enlistment, training, and placement of persons in the professional Church-related ministries.

9. To coordinate and make visible information about career assessment opportunities and continuing education that will assist persons in professional Church-related ministries with their professional growth and development.

10. To recruit, endorse, and provide general oversight of United Methodist ordained ministers, including persons who speak languages in addition to English, who desire to serve as chaplains in specialized institutional ministry settings in both private and governmental sectors.

11. To represent The United Methodist Church in, and provide liaison with, United Methodist ordained ministers certified by professional certifying and accrediting organizations related to ministry in specialized settings.

12. To plan and implement a continuing ministry to United Methodist laity in institutions and armed forces who are separated from their local churches.

13. To develop and provide services directed to enlistment for specialized Church-related ministries, professional growth and development, and counseling.

14. To offer personnel and placement assistance for persons involved in professional Church-related ministries.

15. To conduct research on human needs to be met by the Church through its resources in higher education.

16. To provide for the allocation of funds to institutions and to programs related to the board.

17. To maintain adequate fiduciary and legal relationships with institutions and ministries and to assist annual conferences and other judicatories in their responsibilities in these matters.

18. To provide counsel, guidance, and assistance to institutions of higher education in their relationships with governmental agencies.

19. To guard property and endowments entrusted to the institutions and to maintain and enforce adequate trust and reversionary clauses.

20. To monitor and interact with public higher education in terms of its reflection on the wholeness of persons and the meaning of life, and to study and inform constituencies of public

policy issues related to higher education, both independent and public.

21. To promote, in cooperation with the General Commission on Communication, churchwide special Sundays and funds: Africa University Fund, Black College Fund, Ministerial Education Fund, Native American Ministries Sunday, United Methodist Student Day, World Communion Sunday, and other funds and special days ordered by the General Conference.

22. To evaluate United Methodist higher education and professional Church-related ministries with concern for the quality of their performance and the integrity of their mission.

23. To provide standards and support for and interpretation of the work of United Methodist theological schools.

24. To analyze needs of those in Church-related ministries for continuing education, including assessment of effectiveness, professional growth and development, and funding.

25. To provide professional ministerial courses of study for orderly entrance into ordained ministry. In providing these courses of study, consideration shall be given to languages other than English and to persons with disabilities.

26. To provide for a continuing discussion of the theological bases for professional Church-related ministries and higher education.

27. To provide such services as will create a climate of acceptance and empowerment for women, racial and ethnic persons, and people with disabilities in higher education and professional Church-related ministries, and to be alert to the necessity of advocacy in behalf of these professional ministries in questions of equity and justice.

28. To provide counsel, guidance, and assistance to professional associations and fellowships related to diaconal and other Church-related special ministries.

29. To interpret, promote, and administer the loan and scholarship programs of the board, and to cooperate with the General Board of Global Ministries in matters related to the World Communion Scholarship Program.

30. To engage in research related to personnel needs and interpretation of occupational opportunities in the Church.

31. To provide such support agencies as are deemed necessary to carry out the functions of the board.

32. To give priority to the planning and policy development functions of the board on behalf of the Church.

¶ **1406.** *Responsibilities*—The responsibilities of the General Board of Higher Education and Ministry shall be:

1. To establish and review the objectives of the General Board of Higher Education and Ministry within the wider mission of The United Methodist Church.

2. To establish appropriate organizational structures within the board and staff to achieve established objectives, including writing bylaws, electing officers, establishing committees, electing staff, and filling vacancies in accord with ¶ 712.

3. To determine policy and program, establish goals and priorities, project long-range plans, and evaluate program and services of the board.

4. To give direction to the staff and to delegate authority to board executives through general oversight of the administration.

5. To report the activities of the board to The United Methodist Church through appropriate agencies of the General and jurisdictional conferences.

6. To develop and maintain cooperative relationships with ecumenical agencies and other denominations for the full discharge of the objectives of the board.

7. To cooperate with other agencies in The United Methodist Church in the fulfillment of the programs of the General Conference.

8. To develop and maintain cooperative relationships with higher educational institutions, campus ministries, chaplains and related ministries, and diaconal ministries throughout the world in collaboration with the General Board of Global Ministries.

9. Upon request, to provide resources and technical assistance in higher education throughout the world in collaboration with churches of the Wesleyan tradition.

10. In cooperation with the General Council on Finance and Administration, to develop long-range investments and fund-raising projects within the Church that shall guarantee, insofar as possible, the continuous flow of resources for United Methodist higher education for the decades and the centuries to come. In developing such long-range investments, the board shall adhere to the specific investment guidelines adopted by the General Conference.

11. To promote awareness of and concurrence with "Policies Relative to Socially Responsible Investments" (¶ 717), the Social

Principles (¶¶ 160-166), and *The Book of Resolutions of The United Methodist Church.*

¶ **1407.** *Organization*—1. The membership shall be twenty-two persons, constituted in accordance with ¶ 705.3*a* and .4 of the General Provisions.

2. The membership shall be constituted as follows:

a) Jurisdictional Members—Each jurisdiction shall elect one member to the board. Other paragraphs of the *Book of Discipline* notwithstanding, the secretary of the General Conference shall offer to each jurisdiction a suggested member allocation to ensure that, when combined with the board members from central conferences, the resulting membership will reflect a balance of clergymen and clergywomen, laywomen and laymen. The secretary will also establish an equitable rotation to ensure that over the course of several quadrennia, each jurisdiction will have the opportunity to elect a laywoman, a layman, a clergywoman, and a clergyman.

b) Central Conference Members—Three central conference members shall be elected to the board on nomination by the Council of Bishops according to the provisions in ¶ 705.4c. There shall be alternate members of the central conferences selected to ensure consistent representation at board meetings.

c) Episcopal Members—Three episcopal members shall be named by the Council of Bishops, including at least one from the central conferences (see ¶ 705.4*d*).

d) Additional Members—United Methodist—Additional members are nominated by a committee composed of one person from each jurisdiction elected by the jurisdictional conference. They shall elect up to eleven additional members from the jurisdictions to ensure inclusivity and expertise. It is recommended that at least four (4) of the additional members be racial and ethnic persons from historically underrepresented groups.

e) If a vacancy occurs in the board, it shall be filled in accordance with ¶ 712.

f) Liaison Representatives—The board may name other individuals as liaison representatives to provide networking and advice related to the areas of mutual concern. When invited to board meetings, they shall have voice but not vote.

¶ **1408.** 1. *Divisions*—The board shall provide for a Division of Higher Education and a Division of Ordained Ministry providing support for ordained clergy, local pastors, and diaconal ministers. Further, the board is authorized to alter its organization to adjust to changing circumstances, within the parameters of responsibility established by the *Book of Discipline.*

2. *Offices*—The board, in implementing the objectives (¶¶ 1403, 1405), shall have authority to establish and maintain the following offices: *(a)* Interpretation, and *(b)* Loans and Scholarships.

¶ **1409.** *Provision for Funding*—1. The work and program of the board shall be supported from the general benevolences of the Church and the Ministerial Education Fund. Funds received by the board for the divisions from the Ministerial Education Fund shall be restricted to the support of theological schools and the Division of Ordained Ministry in the development of their programs of enlistment, basic professional degree programs, and continuing education (in accordance with ¶ 816.2*a* and *b*).

2. Administration and other programs of the divisions shall be supported solely from World Service moneys. The associate general secretaries shall recommend through the general secretary of the board to the General Council on Finance and Administration the amount of financial support that should be allocated for the divisions.

DIVISION OF HIGHER EDUCATION

¶ **1410.** *Duties and Responsibilities*—1. Higher education is a significant part of our Wesleyan heritage, our present task, and our future responsibility. The Church continues its historic mission of uniting knowledge and vital piety by maintaining educational institutions and a campus ministry, and through them an intellectual, spiritual, and material ministry to all persons within the academic community without respect to sex, race, creed, or national origin.

2. There shall be a Division on Higher Education representing The United Methodist Church in its relationships with educational institutions and the campus ministry. The division shall have an advisory relationship to all United Methodist-affiliated institutions, including universities, colleges, secondary and special schools, Wesley Foundations, and similar organizations as well as ecumenical campus ministry groups. The division will, on request, serve in an advisory and consultative capacity to all agencies of the Church owning or administering educational institutions and campus ministry units.

3. The nominating committee of the board shall, insofar as possible, provide representation for nomination as members of the Division of Higher Education an equitable number of persons directly related to the areas of concern of the division.

4. Principal objectives of the division are:

a) To determine the nature of the United Methodist mission in and through its elementary, secondary, and higher educational institutions and campus ministries.

b) To develop policy that enables The United Methodist Church to engage effectively in higher education throughout the world.

c) To encourage the Church in programs designed to nurture and sustain educational institutions and campus ministry units as invaluable assets in the ongoing life of the Church.

d) To promote the United Methodist Student Movement, along with other Methodist and ecumenical student Christian movements around the world, and a concerned Christian ministry of the educational community; to witness in the campus community to the mission, message, and life of Jesus Christ; to deepen, enrich, and mature the Christian faith of college and university students, faculty, and staff through commitment to Jesus Christ and the Church and to assist them in their service and leadership to the world, in and through the Church.

e) To interpret both the Church and its educational institutions and campus ministry to each other; to help the agencies of the Church and higher education participate in the greater realization of a fully humane society committed to freedom and truth, love, justice, peace, and personal integrity.

f) To foster within educational institutions the highest educational standards, effective programs of Church relationships, the soundest business practices, the finest ethical and moral principles, and especially Christian ideals; to help people experience release from enslavement, fear, and violence; to help people live in love; and to raise the awareness of and sensitivity to persons with special needs.

g) To preserve and protect resources, property, and investments of The United Methodist Church or any conference, agency, or institution thereof, in any educational institution, Wesley Foundation, or other campus ministry unit founded, organized, developed, or assisted under the direction or with the cooperation of The United Methodist Church.

h) To relate to professional organizations of higher education and campus ministry on behalf of The United Methodist Church.

i) To enable the division's constituencies to develop an interest in and response to public policies bearing on higher education, both independent and public.

j) To provide resources and suggest guidelines for annual conference boards of higher education and campus ministry.

5. The division shall appoint personnel, including an assistant general secretary for campus ministry, an assistant general secretary for schools, colleges, and universities, and an assistant general secretary for the Black College Fund, and it shall establish such committees and commissions as may be necessary for effective fulfillment of its objectives. It may adopt such rules and regulations as may be required for the conduct of its business.

¶ **1411.** *Responsibilities to General and Annual Conferences—* The Division of Higher Education will cooperate with and assist the General and annual conferences and their respective boards and area commissions organized in behalf of educational institutions and the campus ministry. (For annual conference boards, see ¶ 634.2.)

1. The division shall:

a) Provide for the cooperative study of plans for maximum coordination of the work of United Methodist higher education with the Church's mission in Christian education.

b) Direct attention of Church members to the contribution of United Methodist educational institutions and campus ministry units to the life and character of students, faculty, and staff and to the place the institutions and campus ministry have in the preservation and propagation of the Christian faith for our time.

2. The division shall assess institutional and campus ministry relationships with and responsibilities to the Church, and it shall aid in the determination of the degree of active accord between institutional and campus ministry policies and practices and the policies of the Church as expressed in the *Discipline* and in General Conference enactments.

3. The division shall assist educational societies and foundations related to the annual conferences for the promotion of Christian higher education and the campus ministry, and it shall recognize such societies and foundations as auxiliaries of the division when their objectives and purposes, articles of incorpo-

ration, and administrative policies shall have been approved by the annual conference within whose boundaries they have been incorporated.

4. The division should provide the connectional relationship whenever agencies of the General Church wish to enter into discussion with or make inquiry into United Methodist-related schools, colleges, and universities.

5. The division shall direct attention to the work and needs of those educational institutions that stand in special relationship to The United Methodist Church and shall request support for them. Due recognition shall be given to the needs of the Black colleges historically related to The United Methodist Church. (See ¶¶ 815, 1420.)

6. The division shall approve changes in institutional sponsorship and relationships to the general or annual conferences, including separation from United Methodist program boards, from the general or one or more annual conferences, or from the University Senate as the certifying agency of The United Methodist Church.

¶ 1412. *Responsibilities to Educational Institutions*—The Division of Higher Education shall establish policy and practice providing for consultation with and support of United Methodist educational institutions, campus ministry units, and annual conference boards of higher education and campus ministry in matters of institutional study and evaluation, promotion, interpretation, management, program, and finance.

1. The division shall, in cooperation with the University Senate:

a) Study trends in higher education, the needs of the Church, and public and private educational opportunities and requirements and make recommendations to the educational institutions and state commissions or other bodies or publics concerned with higher education.

b) Recommend and approve plans for institutional cooperation, consolidation, or merger between or among United Methodist-related colleges and/or between them and institutions of other denominations that ensure that the interests of The United Methodist Church are adequately protected.

c) Investigate the objectives, academic programs, educational standards, personnel policies, plant and equipment, business and management practices, financial program, public relations, student personnel services, student development programs, religious life, and Church relations of any educational institution claiming or adjudged to be related to The United Methodist Church.

d) Evaluate and classify institutions in order to authenticate relatedness to the Church and determine eligibility for Church financial support.

2. The division shall, in regard to campus ministry, Wesley Foundations, and ecumenical campus ministry groups, provide a structure within the division in order to:

a) Assist in development of plans for the systematic evaluation of these units in cooperation with their regularly constituted boards of directors or trustees and with conference boards of higher education and campus ministry, and with area or regional committees or commissions on Christian higher education and campus ministry or appropriate ecumenical agencies.

b) Study the trends in programming and funding in campus ministry, review reports from the United Methodist Campus Ministers Association (UMCMA), conference agencies and local units, and interpret these findings to the constituency as appropriate and to The United Methodist Church.

c) Affirm its commitment to an ecumenical approach to campus ministry; encourage local, campus, state, regional, and global units of that ministry to work toward ecumenical programming and structures where appropriate to provide counsel and support to conference boards and agencies in reviewing, evaluating, and strengthening existing and proposed local and regional ecumenical covenants for campus ministry; and ensure that ecumenical covenants and procedures for these units are on file with the annual conference boards of higher education and campus ministry.

d) Develop standards and policies for the professional staff of Wesley Foundations, campus ministries and chaplaincies and provide educational and training opportunities for campus ministers and chaplains.

e) Establish policies and guidelines for the work and responsibilities of oversight of the annual conference board of higher education and ministry programs of campus ministry in Wesley Foundations, local churches, and ecumenical campus ministries, and the work and responsibilities of local Wesley Foundations and campus ministry boards of directors.

f) Establish procedures and guidelines for the establishment of a new Wesley Foundation or campus ministry unit and the planning and construction of Wesley Foundation or campus ministry buildings.

g) Recognize and cooperate with agencies with whom relationships may serve to further the objectives of the division.

h Provide for representation and participation, as deemed necessary, with other national and international ecumenical campus ministry agencies and associations.

i) Provide services to meet specific denominational needs.

j) Relate college and university students of The United Methodist Church to the United Methodist Student Movement and such Methodist and ecumenical student organizations around the world as may be appropriate.

3. The division shall, as it seeks to interpret higher education:

a) Promote the Church's mission in higher education, including the special missions and educational ministries to ethnic groups, people with disabilities, and other peoples disadvantaged by world conditions.

b) Promote Christian instruction and provide opportunity for Christian service.

c) Encourage educational institutions and campus ministry units to inculcate human and humane values consistent with the gospel and the public good.

d) Foster the development of Christian community within the life of educational institutions and campus ministry units.

e) Make use of the existing Church organization and publications for interpreting the mission of higher education.

f) Participate in the World Communion Scholarship program.

g) Design and organize the promotion of United Methodist Student Day to recognize United Methodist students in higher education.

¶ **1413.** *Financial Support of Higher Education*—1. In recognition of its heritage and the mandate to maintain its mission in higher education and in light of emergent fiscal concerns, The United Methodist Church affirms its commitment to higher education and to the means by which it can be continuously supported and renewed.

2. The Division of Higher Education shall be empowered to take such action as may be necessary to:

   a) Promote the financial support of Christian higher education within the Church.

   b) Create arrangements that shall provide for the flow of supporting funds from the whole Church to the institutions affiliated with the Church as affirmed by the University Senate (¶ 1416).

   c) Develop corporations, or other fiscal or fiduciary agencies, for the purpose of financing, creating, recycling, managing, or otherwise caring for institutions and campus ministry units or their assets and liabilities.

   3. The division, in regard to fiscal matters, shall:

   a) Study the financial status of United Methodist educational institutions and campus ministry units, encourage the Church to give them continuous support, and provide consultative services in fiscal affairs and other aspects of institutional management. The division shall study all appropriate related data and may recommend to each conference or agency the support levels appropriate for each related institution or institutions.

   b) Appropriate such funds as are available for the support of educational institutions, Wesley Foundations, or other campus ministry units related to The United Methodist Church under such rules as the board may adopt.

   c) Take such action as is necessary to protect or recover resources, property, and investments of The United Methodist Church or any conference, agency, or institution thereof, in capital or endowment funds of any educational institution, Wesley Foundation, or other campus ministry unit founded, organized, developed, or assisted under the direction or with the cooperation of The United Methodist Church should any such institution discontinue operation or move to sever or modify its connection with the Church or violate the terms of any rules adopted by the board or the terms of any such grant of new capital or endowment funds made by The United Methodist Church or any conference, agency, or institution thereof. In order to carry out its duties under this paragraph, the division shall, at its discretion, investigate, audit, and review all necessary records and documents of any educational institution claiming or adjudged by the division to be related to The United Methodist Church. In the event any such educational institution, Wesley Foundation, or other campus ministry unit shall endeavor to discontinue operation or move to sever or modify its connection with the Church or violate the rules adopted by the division in accordance with ¶ 1413.3*b*, it shall be the duty of the trustees and the administrators of such institutions, along with the conference agency on higher education and the resident bishop of the conference in which such institution is located, to confer at the earliest possible opportunity with appropriate representatives of the division to determine what resources and aid the division may be able to provide and to permit the division to carry out its responsibilities under this paragraph.

d) (1) Foster and aid through a special apportionment the United Methodist institutions historically related to education for African Americans. It shall have authority to institute plans by which colleges sponsored by the division may cooperate with or may unite with colleges of other denominations or under independent control, provided that the interests of The United Methodist Church are adequately protected. (2) Encourage such Black colleges to secure adequate endowments for their support and maintenance. Whenever the division is assured that their support will be adequate and the property will be conserved and perpetuated for Christian education under the auspices and control of The United Methodist Church, it may transfer the colleges to boards of trustees under such conditions as the General Board of Higher Education and Ministry may prescribe, which shall include the right of reversion to the board under conditions prescribed by the board.

University Senate

¶ **1414.** *Organization and Membership*—1. The University Senate is an elected body of professionals in higher education created by the General Conference to determine which schools, colleges, universities, and theological schools meet the criteria for listing as institutions affiliated with The United Methodist Church.[27]

2. The senate shall be composed of twenty-seven (27) voting members who, at the time of election, are actively engaged in the work of education through employment in an educational institution and are fitted by training and experience for the technical work of evaluating educational institutions. Election is for the quadrennium, except in cases where conflict of interest arises as a result of change in employment. Nine (9) of these members shall be elected quadrennially by the National Association of Schools

---

27. See Judicial Council Decision 589.

and Colleges of The United Methodist Church—seven of whom shall be chief executive officers of United Methodist-related educational institutions, the other two holding other positions relevant to academic or financial affairs or Church relationships; six (6) by the General Board of Higher Education and Ministry—two of whom shall be chief executive officers of United Methodist-related higher educational institutions, two holding other positions relevant to academic or financial affairs, and two holding positions relevant to Church relationships; four (4) by the General Conference—two of whom shall be chief executive officers of United Methodist-related educational institutions at the time of their election, the other two holding other positions relevant to academic or financial affairs or Church relationships; four (4) by the senate itself, without limitation other than the general provisions of this paragraph; and four (4) shall be appointed by the Council of Bishops—two of whom shall be chief executive officers of United Methodist-related educational institutions, the other two holding other positions relevant to academic or financial affairs or Church relationships. Each of the five electing bodies shall elect at least one woman.

Members elected by the General Conference shall be nominated and elected by the following procedure: Twelve persons shall be nominated by the Council of Bishops, six of whom shall be chief executive officers of United Methodist-related educational institutions, the other six holding other positions relevant to academic or financial affairs or Church relationships. At the same daily session at which the above nominations are announced, additional nominations may be made from the floor but at no other time. From these nominations, the General Conference shall elect without discussion, by ballot and by plurality vote, the four persons to serve on the senate, two from each of the two categories of nominees. Should a vacancy occur in the members elected by General Conference in the interim prior to the next General Conference, the Council of Bishops shall appoint a replacement taken from the remaining nominees. The election process shall be repeated at each succeeding General Conference. Care should be taken that women, racial and ethnic persons, and representatives from the United Methodist-related Black colleges and graduate theological seminaries shall be members of the senate. If a member (other than the four elected by the General Conference) retires from educational work, or for any other cause a vacancy occurs during the quadrennium, it shall be filled by the agency by which the retiring member was elected at its next meeting. The general secretary of the General Board of Higher Education and Ministry and the associate general secretaries of the Divisions of Higher Education and Ordained Ministry of that board shall serve as ex officio members of the senate, with voice but without vote. There shall be one staff representative on the senate from the General Board of Global Ministries, with voice but without vote, named by the general secretary of the General Board of Global Ministries.

3. The associate general secretary of the Division of Higher Education shall be the executive secretary of the senate. The general secretary of the board shall convene it for organization at the beginning of each quadrennium. The senate shall elect its own officers, including a president, a vice president, and a recording secretary, and it may appoint such committees and commissions and delegate to them such powers as are incident to its work. Thereafter, it shall meet semiannually at such time and place as it may determine. Special meetings may be called on the written request of five members or at the discretion of the president and the executive secretary.

4. After consultation with the officers of the senate, the Division of Higher Education shall provide in its annual budget for the expense of the senate as it may deem sufficient, except that expenses incurred by the senate on behalf of any other board of the Church shall be borne by that board.

¶ 1415. *Purposes and Objectives*—1. To establish the criteria that must be met by schools, colleges, universities, and theological schools to achieve and retain listing as institutions affiliated with The United Methodist Church.

2. To support the development of institutions whose aims are to address and whose programs reflect significant educational, cultural, social, and human issues in a manner reflecting the values held in common by the institutions and the Church.

3. To provide an effective review process to ensure that schools, colleges, universities, and theological schools listed by the University Senate and qualifying for Church support have institutional integrity, well-structured programs, sound management, and clearly defined Church relationships.[28]

---

28. See Judicial Council Decision 589.

4. To establish effective annual reporting procedures that will provide the senate with the data necessary to complete its review of the institutional viability and program integrity of member institutions.

5. At the conclusion of each General Conference a complete set of the *Daily Christian Advocate* for that General Conference shall be sent to each theological school approved by the University Senate.

¶ 1416. *Institutional Affiliation*[29]—1. Approval by the senate is prerequisite to institutional claim of affiliation with The United Methodist Church.

2. Every effort shall be made by both the annual conferences and institutions to sustain and support each other, but identification of an institution with The United Methodist Church shall depend upon its approval by the senate. The senate shall provide adequate guidelines and counsel to assist institutions seeking initial or renewed affiliation.

3. Only institutions affiliated with The United Methodist Church through approval by the senate shall be eligible for funding by annual conferences, General Conference, general boards, or other agencies of The United Methodist Church.

4. To qualify for affiliation with The United Methodist Church, institutions must maintain appropriate academic accreditation.

5. Assessment of Church relationships shall be a part of the process for those institutions seeking approval of the senate for affiliation with The United Methodist Church. Inasmuch as declarations of Church relationships are expected to differ one from the other, and because of the diversity in heritage and other aspects of institutional life, declarations of Church relationship will necessarily be of institutional design.

¶ 1417. *Annual Reports of Approved Institutions*—1. Each year the senate shall publish a list classifying United Methodist-affiliated institutions. These institutions shall include secondary schools, colleges, universities, graduate theological seminaries, and special schools.

2. The senate shall also prepare annually a list of approved schools, colleges, universities, and graduate theological seminaries for use by annual conference boards of ordained ministry in determining candidate educational eligibility for admission into full connection.

---

29. See Judicial Council Decision 589.

3. An institution that chooses to disaffiliate with The United Methodist Church for any reason shall: *a)* inform the University Senate as soon as possible after discussions begin concerning disaffiliation; *b)* inform all appropriate United Methodist judicatories; and *c)* seek technical and legal assistance from the Division of Higher Education regarding fiduciary issues.

4. The senate shall publish annually, with its list of United Methodist-affiliated institutions, the names of institutions of other historic Methodist Churches that wish to participate in research projects, the insurance program, and technical services of the General Board of Higher Education and Ministry. Such institutions shall be designated as "associate" institutions.

¶ **1418.** *Consultative Services*—1. Support for approved institutions shall include, through the appropriate divisions of the General Board of Higher Education and Ministry, consulting teams with skills in comprehensive institutional design, management, governance, and program.

2. Support for approved institutions shall include an interpretation of and consultation on data in the annual institutional reports.

3. The Division of Higher Education shall report annually to the senate on the level and types of institutional support rendered by related conferences and agencies and shall evaluate such support, including specific responses of conferences and agencies to recommended levels.

UNITED METHODIST HIGHER EDUCATION FOUNDATION

¶ **1419.** The United Methodist Higher Education Foundation is incorporated in the State of Tennessee as a nonprofit, charitable organization with permanent ties to the Division of Higher Education, which elects its board of trustees. The general purpose of the foundation is to foster the growth and development of institutions of higher education by encouraging persons and corporations to provide financial support and by acting as a foundation for such support. The foundation is also authorized to serve as a trustee and administrator of gifts and bequests designated by donors to specific institutions.

COUNCIL OF PRESIDENTS OF THE BLACK COLLEGES

¶ **1420.** *Council of Presidents of the Black Colleges*—1. There shall be an organization known as the Council of Presidents of the

Black Colleges. It shall be composed of all the presidents of the United Methodist institutions historically related to the education of African Americans and with a current relationship to The United Methodist Church.

2. *Purposes and Objectives*—The purpose of the council shall be to:

    a) Help identify and clarify the roles of these colleges in higher education and in The United Methodist Church.

    b) Promote fund-raising efforts through the Church.

    c) Study, review, and discuss programs of member institutions.

The council shall have a minimum of two regular meetings in each calendar year and shall be amenable to the Division of Higher Education in the implementation of its responsibilities.

Division of Ordained Ministry

¶ **1421.** *Duties and Responsibilities of the Division of Ordained Ministry*—The Division of Ordained Ministry shall be responsible for leading and serving the church in inviting, equipping, and supporting faithful and effective spiritual leaders from all cultural, ethnic, and racial backgrounds, who serve as ordained deacons and elders, licensed local pastors, diaconal ministers, certified persons in specialized ministries, and clergy endorsed for extension ministries in order to fulfill the mission of The United Methodist Church and the proclamation of the gospel of Jesus Christ. The division's work includes all men and women who are serving in categories of appointment by a bishop. This responsibility shall be discharged in active relationship with bishops, schools of theology, annual conference boards of ordained ministry, cabinets, jurisdictional boards or committees on ordained ministry, central conferences, ethnic caucuses, and other appropriate bodies. This division shall be responsible for the promotion of theological education and its support for the whole church.

In fulfillment of this responsibility and in accordance with the disciplinary requirements established for each region of the church in the world, the division will organize its work around the following core responsibilities:

1. *Administration—a)* Provide leadership in the interpretation of the need for ministry in The United Methodist Church in ways that are appropriate to each region of the church in the world. The interpretation of ministry includes the ministry of deacons,

elders, local pastors, those approved for extension ministries, and certified for specialized ministries.

b) Maintain contact with the constituencies of the division through gatherings of the chairs of the Order of Deacons and the Order of Elders and the Fellowship of Local Pastors, personal communication, newsletters, and other consultative services.

c) In consultation with ethnic constituencies, work with boards of ordained ministry, district committees on ordained ministry, and other appropriate agencies by developing guidelines, training, and resources for their work; providing guidance and counseling in the examination of ministerial students; and interpreting current disciplinary legislation concerning ordained and licensed ministry.

d) Provide resources and training to conference boards of ordained ministry and similar recognized bodies in their responsibility for administering the standards, requirements, examination, and interviews for ordination and certification in ministry careers.

e) Provide the connectional relationship whenever agencies of the general Church wish to enter into discussion with or make inquiry into the work of United Methodist seminaries.

f) Study and coordinate mutual ministry between United Methodist schools of theology and annual conferences in the fulfillment of their responsibilities for the education and formation of candidates for ordained, licensed, and certified ministries.

g) Lead in the Church-wide interpretation and promotion of the Ministerial Education Fund, and support other funds and programs that assist in training persons for ordained ministry.

h) Relate to the University Senate and its Commission on Theological Education in the review and approval of non-United Methodist seminaries for candidates for ordination as elder and deacon.

i) Cooperate with other agencies and ethnic groups within The United Methodist Church in matters related to the calling, training, and support of ministerial leadership throughout the church.

j) Participate in professional, ecumenical, national, and international associations that support professional ministry.

k) Cooperate with the General Council on Finance and Administration and boards of ordained ministry concerning legal issues, policies of professional ethics, and other matters related to the practice of ministry.

l) Foster cooperative relationships among persons in the diaconate of The United Methodist Church and their colleagues in other Christian churches.

2. *Enlistment, Candidacy, and Conference Relations*—The division shall: *a)* Lead the church in lifting up God's call to set-apart ministry in The United Methodist Church through discernment and enlistment programs.

b) Study ministerial needs and resources in The United Methodist Church and cooperate with the general boards and agencies, and other appropriate ethnic and cultural groups, in the interpretation of ministry as a vocation, in an effort to enlist suitable persons for ordained, licensed, and certified ministry.

c) Study the ministerial needs of the annual and central conferences in terms of pastoral leadership, the ministry of the deacon, and certified ministries, including candidacy statistics, retirement trends, retention of clergy, and the changing demand for ministerial supply.

d) Study the ministerial needs of the world and provide resources for the enlistment of persons for service in ministries beyond the local church.

e) Provide program materials and training resources for the enlistment and support of candidates for ordained, licensed, and certified ministry.

f) Work with ethnic centers related to the United Methodist seminaries, general church initiatives, and the ethnic caucuses to enlist racial and ethnic persons as candidates for ordained, licensed, and certified ministry.

3. *Theological Education*—The division shall: *a)* Develop and maintain the educational programs and standards for those who are ordained as deacons and elders, licensed as local pastors, and certified for specialized ministries in The United Methodist Church and shall disseminate the approved courses and standards to appropriate oversight bodies and boards.

b) Certify the course offerings in United Methodist history, doctrine, and polity as specified in ¶ 335.(3), and provide the University Senate and boards of ordained ministry with a list of the courses approved.

c) Prescribe a theological studies program which will include basic graduate theological studies for those preparing for ordination as a deacon, an advanced course of studies program for local pastors preparing for ordination as an elder, and a curriculum of studies for those seeking certification in areas of specialized ministry.

d) Prescribe a Course of Study for local pastors that include the studies for license for pastoral ministry and the Course of Study curriculum. All work in the Course of Study shall be taken in programs approved by the Division of Ordained Ministry. Upon approval of the conference Board of Ordained Ministry, a candidate may complete up to one-half of the work through online courses developed by the Division of Ordained Ministry.

e) Identify the areas of need for specialized ministries; provide standards and educational programs that may lead to certification in those areas; and review the qualifications of persons recommended for certification by conference boards of ordained ministry.

f) Consult with the schools of theology and programs of pastoral training in the central conferences concerning pastoral needs, the relationship between United Methodist seminaries in the central conferences and the United States, and other resources for training pastors to serve in the central conferences.

g) Promote attending United Methodist seminaries for theological training in the Wesleyan tradition.

h) Cooperate with the Office of Loans and Scholarships, the Higher Education Foundation, the World Communion Scholarship Program, and other funding agencies in regard to scholarship assistance for racial and ethnic students preparing for ordained ministry.

4. *Support, Supervision, and Accountability*—The division shall:
a) Provide guidance and resources for the continuing education, spiritual formation, and career development for elders, deacons, diaconal ministers, chaplains and pastoral counselors, and persons certified for specialized ministries serving in local churches, extension ministries, and other appointment settings in the church and world.

b) Support and cooperate with bishops and district superintendents in the fulfillment of their ministry of superintending by (1) providing jointly with the Connectional Table and the Council of Bishops for the training of new district superintendents; (2) providing ongoing training and support for bishops and superintendents in their work; and (3) developing resources to assist clergy, superintendents, and local churches in assessment and evaluation of ministry, including providing tools for staff-parish relations committees, pastors, boards of ordained ministry, and cabinets on ensuring effective cross-racial and cross-cultural appointments.

c) Encourage and resource conference boards of ordained ministry, the Order of Deacons and the Order of Elders, and the Fellowship of Local Pastors for the ongoing support of persons in ordained, consecrated, licensed, and certified ministry in The United Methodist Church.

d) Provide guidance to cabinets and other annual conference agencies to ensure conditions of employment, support, and benefits commensurate with their training, ability, and experience for those ordained, consecrated, licensed, or certified for ministerial service.

e) Support members of the endorsed community through relationships to certifying bodies and professional organizations; linking congregations, conferences, and church structures with persons in specialized settings; assisting persons in receiving specialized training for ministry in pastoral care and pastoral counseling settings; and providing retreats, convocations, and other special programs.

f) Lead the church in the acceptance and support of women of all ethnic and racial groups in ordained and licensed ministry.

g) Give attention to the specific needs of clergy with disabilities.

h) Work with bishops, cabinets, boards of ordained ministry, the Order of Deacons and the Order of Elders, the Fellowship of Local Pastors, and other church agencies in maintaining the professional and ethical standards of ministry in The United Methodist Church.

i) Encourage and support the continuing education, spiritual formation, and career development of effective spiritual leaders of all races and ethnic origins.

5. *Endorsement*—The division shall: *a)* Identify, assess, and support chaplains and clergy who show demonstrated ability to provide pastoral care in health-care settings, children's homes, retirement homes, prisons, workplaces, counseling centers, and the military.

b) Establish standards required for endorsed persons in the areas of specialized education, training and skills, and when required, professional certification, to ensure that The United

Methodist Church provides quality pastoral care to patients, residents, prisoners, workers, counselees, and military personnel and their families.

c) Maintain policies and procedures to provide Ecclesiastical Endorsement for associate members, deacons and elders under appointment to ministries of chaplaincy and pastoral care where endorsement is required.

(1) The Division of Ordained Ministry, through its endorsing committee, the United Methodist Endorsing Agency, has the authority to grant and remove endorsement and to adopt appropriate rules of procedure, to include procedure for appeals.

(2) An endorsing committee consisting of elected members of the Division of Ordained Ministry and chaired by a bishop shall represent The United Methodist Church in all endorsing procedures.

(3) Endorsement is the credential which certifies that a clergyperson performs a valid ministry of The United Methodist Church and has presented evidence of required specialized education, training, skills, and, when required, professional certification necessary to perform that ministry. Once the clergyperson no longer serves in that particular setting, the endorsement is withdrawn.

d) Establish and follow procedures for ecclesiastical approval for persons in the military student chaplain candidate programs, intermittent chaplaincy with the Department of Veterans Affairs, and other identified entities.

e) Maintain programs for the oversight and advocacy of endorsed/approved persons.

f) Provide general oversight for all those under endorsement, particularly those serving outside the bounds of their annual conferences.

g) Assure conference boards of ordained ministry concerning the validity of ministry of clergy serving under endorsement.

h) Verify annually, to bishops and conference boards of ordained ministry, those clergy under endorsement and where necessary request their reappointment.

i) Establish and maintain standards for ecclesiastical endorsement.

(1) Establish standards for endorsements for all ministry settings in ¶ 344.1*b*.

(2) Provide standards for use by annual conference boards of ordained ministry to determine the appropriateness of other extension ministry settings not identified in ¶ 344.1, and will assist, as requested, to evaluate specific settings.

(3) Provide advocacy for persons appointed under ¶ 344.1*d* and encourage new efforts to widen the understanding of ministry through the development of new extension ministry settings.

(4) Coordinate with certifying bodies in the development of standards for pastoral care certification in a variety of ministry settings.

j) Link congregations, conferences, and church agencies with those persons in extension ministry settings.

k) Advise congregations, conferences, and church agencies in the development of programs of pastoral care in extension ministries.

l) Interpret extension ministries to the church and serve as an advocate for persons in extension ministries under its endorsement.

m) Assist in providing a ministry to United Methodist laity in or associated with the military, particularly outside the continental United States. The Division of Ordained Ministry, with the General Board of Discipleship, the General Board of Global Ministries, and other agencies of the Church, shall work together to prepare materials, programs, and continuing ministries that include retreats, confirmation classes, and other pastoral functions.

n) Receive and distribute funds and special gifts as have been or shall be given specifically for the support of endorsing agency responsibilities.

o) Sponsor the Chaplains Supplemental Pension Grant Fund for certain endorsed clergy, with administration and oversight provided by the General Board of Pension and Health Benefits.

6. *Constituency Relationships*—Establish three teams (elders and local pastors, deacons and diaconal ministers, chaplains and endorsed clergy) to relate directly with the constituents of the Division of Ordained Ministry to resource, support and interpret the work of the Division of Ordained Ministry. Each team shall be led by a member of that particular constituency.

SCHOOLS OF THEOLOGY OF THE UNITED METHODIST CHURCH

¶ **1422.** *Goals*—1. United Methodist schools of theology share a common mission of preparing persons for leadership in the ministry of The United Methodist Church; of leading in the ongoing reflection on Wesleyan theology; and of assisting the church in fulfilling its mission to make disciples of Jesus Christ for the transformation of the world. They contribute to the life of the global United Methodist connection through theological education for the sake of the worldwide mission of the church. These schools of theology are maintained for the education of ordained and lay leadership, for the interpretation of the Christian faith and United Methodist tradition through biblical and theological research, and for prophetic leadership. The General Board of Higher Education and Ministry provides leadership and support in this common mission and in the development of relationships among the schools of theology in the U.S.A. and the central conferences and the various agencies of the general Church.

2. All candidates for ordination as deacon or elder in The United Methodist Church are strongly encouraged to attend United Methodist schools of theology since these schools share with the General Board of Higher Education and Ministry and the conference boards of ordained ministry in the work of preparing persons for ordination and leadership in The United Methodist Church.

3. *Schools of theology of The United Methodist Church located in the U.S.A.*—*a*) Schools of theology of The United Methodist Church located in the U.S.A. exist to serve The United Methodist Church, primarily in the United States, but with concern for the witness of the church around the world. In addition to their commitment to United Methodism, they also serve students of other denominations in witness to United Methodism's ecumenical relationships. As denominational schools, they have a historic relationship to the denomination and are officially related to The United Methodist Church through the Board of Higher Education and Ministry and the approval of the University Senate. The following schools comprise this network of United Methodist schools of theology in the U.S.A.: Boston University School of Theology, Claremont School of Theology, Duke Divinity School, Candler School of Theology, the Theological School-Drew University, Gammon Theological Seminary (ITC), Garrett-Evangelical Theological Seminary, Iliff School of Theology, Methodist Theological

School in Ohio, Perkins School of Theology, Saint Paul School of Theology, United Theological Seminary (Dayton, Ohio), and Wesley Theological Seminary. They are accountable to the Church through the General Board of Higher Education and Ministry and the University Senate. Therefore, agencies of the church seeking to monitor the use of the schools will do so in cooperation with the General Board of Higher Education and Ministry, Division of Ordained Ministry.

b) These schools of theology shall receive financial support for the current operating expenses from the annual conferences in the U.S.A. through the Ministerial Education Fund, administered by the Division of Ordained Ministry, General Board of Higher Education and Ministry. (See ¶ 816.2.) The Ministerial Education Fund shall be regarded by the annual conferences in the U.S.A. as a priority to be met before any additional benevolence, grants, or funds are allocated to other theological schools or schools of religion.[30]

c) In fulfilling their task of preparing persons for effective service for Christ and the church, The United Methodist schools of theology located in the U.S.A. shall acquaint students with the current polity, theology and programs of The United Methodist Church and shall offer practical experience in administration, evangelism, stewardship, and other areas which will prepare them for effective Christian ministry in a multicultural society. Each school of theology, in consultation with the General Board of Higher Education and Ministry, Division of Ordained Ministry, shall provide the courses in United Methodist history, doctrine, and polity specified in ¶ 335.(3) and seek to form persons for ministry in the Wesleyan tradition.

d) Any institution seeking affiliation with The United Methodist Church for the preparation of candidates for ordination must first present its plan to the General Board of Higher Education and Ministry, Division of Ordained Ministry for approval and recommendation to the University Senate, which alone can grant affiliation and listing as a United Methodist school of theology. A select number of non-United Methodist schools of theology may be granted approval for the preparation of candidates for ordination under the criteria of the University Senate.

4. *Schools of Theology of The United Methodist Church located in the Central Conferences—a)* In order to meet the needs for theo-

---

30. See Judicial Council Decision 545.

logical education and clergy training in their regions, the central conferences establish schools of theology to serve the United Methodists in their distinct cultural, social, and linguistic context. Schools of theology and programs of clergy training are also established by General Board of Global Ministries and the General Board of Higher Education and Ministry to serve the needs of the central conferences. These schools may be supported through the central conference and/or the General Board of Global Ministries and/or the General Board of Higher Education and Ministry and are accountable to the appropriate bodies for their program and their relationship to the denomination.

b) Additional schools of theology and pastoral training may be established by the central conference, General Conference, General Board of Higher Education and Ministry, or the General Board of Global Ministries and accountability depends on the founding documents of the institutions.

5. The United Methodist Church also shares in global theological education through ecumenical schools of theology where The United Methodist Church is a partner. Though not United Methodist-related, these institutions serve on behalf of United Methodists in those regions and may relate to the General Board of Global Ministries and/or General Board of Higher Education and Ministry, in accordance with their charter and mission.

¶ **1423.** *Education of Ordination Candidates*—The United Methodist schools of theology share with the conference boards of ordained ministry the responsibility for the education and formation of candidates for admission to the annual conferences.

Section IX. General Board of Pension and Health Benefits

GENERAL ADMINISTRATION

¶ **1501.** *Establishment*—1. *a)* There shall be a General Board of Pension and Health Benefits of The United Methodist Church, hereinafter called the general board, having the general supervision and administration of the support, relief, and assistance and pensioning of clergy of this denomination, lay workers of the various units of the Church, and their families.

b) The general board shall be the successor to the General Board of Pensions of The United Methodist Church, the Board of Pensions of The Evangelical United Brethren Church, and the General Board of Pensions of The Methodist Church.

2. The general board shall have authority to establish, maintain, and discontinue the location of its headquarters office and such auxiliary offices as it shall deem proper and advisable.

3. The general board shall report to and be amenable to the General Conference.

¶ 1502. 1. *Membership—a)* The membership of the general board shall be composed of two bishops, elected by the Council of Bishops; sixteen members elected by the jurisdictional conferences from the annual conference nominations on a ratio providing for an equitable distribution among the various jurisdictions, based on the combined clergy and laity membership thereof, as determined by the secretary of the General Conference; six members, with not more than two from the same jurisdiction, elected by the General Conference on nomination of the Council of Bishops; and eight additional members for the purpose of bringing to the general board special knowledge or background, not more than two from the same jurisdiction, nominated and elected by the general board in such manner as it shall provide in its bylaws.

b) The aforementioned electing bodies shall give consideration during the nominating process to equitable representation on the basis of race, color, age, gender, and people with disabilities.

c) The general secretary of the general board shall be an ex officio member thereof, without vote.

d) The terms of all members so elected shall be four years, to take effect at the first meeting of the general board following the General Conference, hereinafter referred to as the organizational meeting.

(1) Members shall serve during the terms for which they are elected and until their successors shall have been elected and qualified.

(2) Other paragraphs of the *Discipline* notwithstanding, members of the general board may serve a maximum of three consecutive terms.

(3) In case a vacancy occurs between regular sessions of the jurisdictional conferences for any cause, the general board shall fill the vacancy for the unexpired term from that jurisdiction in the representation of which the vacancy occurs, except in the case of members elected by the General Conference or the general board where such vacancies would be filled by the general board in the manner prescribed by its bylaws without regard to geographic or jurisdictional representation.

2. *Officers*—*a)* The general board shall elect from its membership at its organizational meeting a chairperson, a vice chairperson, and a recording secretary whose duties shall be prescribed in its bylaws.

b) The general board shall elect quadrennially, in such manner as it shall provide in its bylaws and policies, a general secretary, who shall be the chief executive officer of the general board.

c) Other offices that are deemed desirable and in the best interest of the general board for carrying out its purposes may be created by the general board, and persons may be elected or appointed to fill such offices.

d) A vacancy in any of these offices shall be filled by the general board for the remainder of the unexpired term in a manner prescribed in its bylaws.

3. *Meetings*—The general board shall hold at least one meeting in each calendar year.

a) The place and time of all meetings shall be designated by the general board, but if it fails to do so, then the time and place shall be designated by the chairperson.

b) It shall convene at such other times on call of the chairperson, on written request by one-fifth of its members, or on written request by a majority of its executive committee.

c) A majority of the members of the general board shall constitute a quorum.

4. *Committees*—The general board shall establish the following committees:

a) Executive Committee—An executive committee shall be elected by the general board from its membership. During the periods between the meetings of the general board, its business and affairs shall be managed by the executive committee.

b) Committee on Audit and Review—A committee on audit and review shall be elected by the general board. The committee on audit and review shall be responsible for reviewing the financial audits and related policies of the general board and its constituent legal entities.

c) Committee on Appeals—A committee on appeals shall be elected by the general board. The committee on appeals shall hear appeals from participants in the funds, plans, and programs administered by the general board. Decisions of the committee on appeals shall be final and not reviewed by the full general board.

d) Other Committees—The general board shall have the authority to establish, from time to time, such other standing committees or special committees as provided in its bylaws.

e) Committee Membership—The general board shall elect the membership of its standing committees in accordance with its bylaws. The membership of any special committees shall be selected in accordance with the resolution establishing such special committee.

f) Committee Members at Large—The general board shall have the authority to elect additional members to its committees, not to exceed one-half of the committee membership, for the purpose of bringing to those committees special knowledge or background. These committee members at large shall have full voice and vote on the committee, but they shall have voice, but not voting privileges, on the general board.

¶ **1503.** *Legal Entities*—1. Subject to the continuing control and direction of the General Conference of The United Methodist Church as set forth from time to time in the *Discipline,* the general board is authorized and empowered to cause the operations of the General Board of Pension and Health Benefits to be carried on and the general authorizations defined in ¶ 1504 to be achieved in such manner, through or by means of such agencies or instrumentalities, and by use of such procedures as the general board may from time to time determine to be necessary, advisable, or appropriate, with full power and authority in the premises to take all such action and to do all such other acts and things as may be required or found to be advisable. In particular, and without limiting the generality of the foregoing, the general board is authorized and empowered, for the purposes of this paragraph:

a) To use, manage, operate, and otherwise utilize all property and assets of every kind, character, and description of any corporation(s) created by the general board pursuant to ¶ 1503.2 below, as well as all income from such property and assets and the avails thereof, all with liability or obligation to account for such property and assets, the use thereof, the income therefrom, and avails thereof only to the General Conference of The United Methodist Church.

b) To cause a corporation(s) created by the general board pursuant to ¶ 1503.2 to take all such action and to do all such things as the general board may deem necessary or advisable to carry out the intent and purposes of this paragraph. The governing body of said corporation(s) from time to time shall take all action that the general board deems necessary or advisable to carry out the intent and purpose of this paragraph, unless local law would require such governing bodies to make independent decisions with respect to particular actions.

2. The general board is authorized and empowered in its discretion at any time it may deem such action to be desirable or convenient to create corporations or other legal entities through which it shall fulfill its responsibilities described hereunder.

a) The general board is authorized and empowered in its discretion to cause its general operations to be conducted through a corporation, the name of which shall be the General Board of Pension and Health Benefits of The United Methodist Church, Incorporated in Illinois.

b) The general board is authorized and empowered in its discretion to cause its general trust operations to be conducted through a corporation, the name of which shall be the UMC Benefit Board, Inc.

c) If the general board creates and directs more than one legal entity, it is authorized and empowered at its discretion at any time it may deem such action desirable or convenient to take action in the name of said legal entities to surrender the charter or charters of one or several or all of said legal entities or to merge, consolidate, or affiliate such corporations, or any of them, in compliance with appropriate state or federal laws.

d) The governing bodies of such legal entities shall be determined by the general board in conformance with applicable local law. A majority of the members of the governing bodies shall be elected from the membership of the general board.

e) The legal entities created under this paragraph are agencies or instrumentalities through which the denomination known as The United Methodist Church provides benefits, investment services, and other services outlined in ¶ 1504 below in the name of the General Board of Pension and Health Benefits.

¶ **1504.** *Authorizations*—The General Board of Pension and Health Benefits is authorized and empowered to provide administrative, trust, and investment support to The United Methodist Church and its constituent boards, agencies, conferences, organizations, and other institutions in their efforts to provide support, relief, and assistance, and pension, welfare, and other benefits for clergy of this denomination, lay workers of the various units of the Church, and their families. Subject to the provisions of ¶ 2506 herein the general board shall perform its duties and responsibilities in the spirit of the Church's mandate for inclusiveness and racial and social justice. In particular, and without limiting the generality of the foregoing, the general board, directly or through any entity created by it, is authorized and empowered:

1. To operate, manage, and administer the mandatory benefit funds, plans, and programs established by the General Conference: *(a)* the Ministerial Pension Plan, amended and restated effective January 1, 2007, as the Clergy Retirement Security Program; *(b)* the Retirement Security Program for General Agencies of The United Methodist Church, amended and restated effective January 1, 2010, as the Retirement Plan for General Agencies; and *(c)* the Comprehensive Protection Plan. The provisions of these mandatory benefit programs shall be incorporated by reference into the *Discipline* and shall have the full force of law as if printed in the *Discipline*. No proposal shall be made to the General Conference that changes a benefit presently in effect without first securing through the General Board of Pension and Health Benefits an actuarial opinion concerning the cost and other related aspects of the proposed change.

2. To create, amend, operate, manage, administer, and terminate nonmandatory relief, assistance, and benefit funds, plans, products, and programs for interested members, conferences, local churches, boards, agencies, institutions, and other affiliated units of The United Methodist Church.

3. To continue the operation, management, and administration of relief, assistance, and benefit funds, plans, and programs created prior to 1981.

4. To make reports to the General Conference with respect to the support, relief, assistance, and pension, welfare, and other benefits for clergy of this denomination, lay workers of the various units of the Church, and their families.

5. To adopt rules, regulations, and policies for the administration of the relief, assistance, and benefit funds, plans, and programs that the general board administers, in all matters not specifically covered by General Conference legislation or by reasonable implication, and to prescribe such forms and records as are needed for the administration of such funds, plans, and programs.

6. To prepare and publish benefit summaries, manuals, and other publications or media related to the funds, plans, and programs administered by the general board.

7. To compile and maintain complete service records of clergy members in full connection, associate members, and provisional members, and of local pastors whose service may be related to potential annuity claims of the annual conferences of The United Methodist Church situated within the boundaries of the United States and Puerto Rico. Such service records shall be based on answers to the Business of the Annual Conference questions as published in the journals of the annual conferences situated within the boundaries of the United States and Puerto Rico and in the General Minutes of The United Methodist Church, or in comparable publications of either or both of the uniting churches, and from information provided by annual conference boards of pensions. The conference boards of pensions shall be responsible for providing census data when requested by the general board on participants and their families, including but not limited to such data as birth dates, marriage dates, divorce dates, and dates of death.

8. The general board shall have the authority to allocate the costs of the mandatory benefits plans among the annual conferences situated within the boundaries of the United States and Puerto Rico, in accordance with the terms of the appropriate benefits plan.

a) The general board shall have authority to determine the liabilities allocated to and contributions due from each annual conference, in accordance with the terms of the appropriate plan.

b) The general board shall have the authority to collect from each annual conference the amount required by the clearinghouse to provide benefits pursuant to the terms of the appropriate benefits plan. Each annual conference shall provide funds to meet its benefit responsibilities to clergy serving the annual conference and their spouses, as applicable, who are members of other annual conferences on the same basis as it provides pension payments for beneficiaries related directly to itself.

c) The general board is authorized and empowered to make all the rules concerning details that may be necessary to implement the foregoing.

9. On request of an annual conference or conference organization or agency of The United Methodist Church, to receive

therefrom distributable and reserve pension funds and to make the periodic pension payments to the beneficiaries of such annual conference, conference organization, board, or agency, in accordance with a schedule of distribution, which shall be provided for the guidance of the general board in making such payments. The general board shall report annually the details of transactions under this provision. The general board shall be entitled to recover the cost of performing such services.

10. To administer the Chartered Fund for the benefit of all the annual and provisional annual conferences in The United Methodist Church, the boundaries of which are within the United States, its territorial and insular possessions, and Cuba, unless the General Conference shall order otherwise. Once a year the net earnings of the fund, after provision for depreciation, shall be divided equally among such annual and provisional annual conferences in accordance with the restrictive rule contained in ¶ 22.

11. To order and direct that the income from the General Endowment Fund for Conference Claimants (formerly known as the General Endowment Fund for Superannuates of The Methodist Episcopal Church, South) held by the UMC Benefit Board, Inc., shall be distributed on account of service of conference claimants rendered in an annual conference of The United Methodist Church; provided, however, that such distribution shall be restricted to annual conferences that, directly or through their predecessor annual conferences, participated in raising this fund, in proportion to the number of approved years of annuity responsibility of each annual conference as shall be determined by the General Board of Pension and Health Benefits.

12. To distribute on the basis it determines the appropriations from the net earnings of the publishing interests that are contributed to the pension programs of The United Methodist Church and of the several annual conferences.

13. To create such legal entities in order to obtain, accept, receive, manage, and administer any and all assets or property, absolute or in trust, for the purpose of providing for, aiding in, and contributing to the support, relief, assistance, and pension, welfare, and other benefits for clergy of this denomination, lay workers of the various units of the Church, and their families and for other purposes stated in the trust instrument.

14. To discharge its fiduciary duties with respect to a benefit fund, plan, or program solely in the interest of the participants and beneficiaries and for the exclusive purpose of providing benefits to participants and their beneficiaries and defraying reasonable expenses of administering the plan, with the care, skill, prudence, and diligence under the circumstances then prevailing that a prudent person acting in a like capacity and familiar with such matters would use in the conduct of an enterprise of a like character and with like aims.

15. To receive, hold, manage, merge, consolidate, administer, invest, and reinvest all connectional relief, support, and benefit funds. The general board is encouraged to invest in institutions, companies, corporations, or funds that make a positive contribution toward the realization of the goals outlined in the Social Principles of the Church, subject to other provisions of the *Discipline*, and with due regard to any and all special contracts, agreements, and laws applicable thereto. Among the tools the general board may use are shareholder advocacy, selective divestment, and advocacy of corporate disinvestment from certain countries or fields of business.

16. To receive, hold, manage, administer, and invest and reinvest, by and through its constituent corporations, endowment funds or other funds of an annual conference, local church, board, agency, or other unit affiliated with The United Methodist Church that have been designated for the funding of relief, support, or benefit funds, plans, or programs, and endowment funds or other funds of such units not so designated. The general board is encouraged to invest in institutions, companies, corporations, or funds that make a positive contribution toward the realization of the goals outlined in the Social Principles of the Church; provided, however, that at no time shall any part of the principal of the endowment funds be appropriated by the general board for any other purpose. The general board shall annually provide to such units an accounting of such funds.

17. To receive, hold, manage, administer, invest and reinvest, funds of and offer administrative services to other nonprofit organizations.

18. To collect, receive, and administer such gifts, devises, and bequests, and other funds as may be specifically designated for the general board or any constituent corporation of the general board by donors, subject to the rules, regulations, and policies

of the general board with respect thereto. All undesignated gifts, devises, bequests, and donations shall be collected, received, and administered under the direction of the general board.

19. To charge the various trusts, funds, plans, and programs for which it is responsible an administrative fee for its general services and to charge reasonable and appropriate transactional fees for specific services provided to a unit of the Church or to a participant or beneficiary. The general board shall not use for operational or administrative purposes moneys allocated from any of the general Church funds of The United Methodist Church.

20. To create, administer, and encourage funding for the programs of the Central Conference Pension Initiative, in consultation with the General Council on Finance and Administration, and supported by a multi-agency task force.

21. To support the health as wholeness of the clergy and lay workers of the denomination, and thereby mitigate the frequency and duration of disability and incapacity, by collecting, analyzing, and disseminating the group health care plan data and health and wellness program information submitted by annual conferences, the General Council on Finance and Administration for bishops, and general agencies. The General Board of Pension and Health Benefits shall use the collected group health care plan data and health and wellness program information to *(a)* establish denomination-wide benchmarks and standards; *(b)* identify and disseminate best practices for healthy lifestyles and health and disability costs management; *(c)* provide reports of data; *(d)* share data and analyses with the denomination; *(e)* advise about health care plan designs, coverage, financial soundness, and wellness programs and initiatives; and *(f)* recommend health and wellness strategies and guidelines for annual conferences, the General Council on Finance and Administration for bishops in the United States, and general agencies.

22. To cause its operations to be carried on and the objectives defined above to be achieved in such manner by use of such procedures as the general board may from time to time determine to be necessary, advisable, or appropriate, with full power and authority in the premises to take all such action and to do all such other acts and things as may be required or found to be advisable.

¶ 1505. *General Agency Pension Credit*—Pension for service approved for pension credit by an agency of The United Methodist Church receiving financial support from the general Church funds shall be provided by the employing agency in uniformity with that provided by other agencies under one of the pension funds, plans, or programs administered by the General Board of Pension and Health Benefits of The United Methodist Church; provided, however, that where service has been rendered in two or more agencies, the total pension benefit shall be calculated as if all such service had been with one agency, and the final agency shall provide any additional pension benefits necessary to accomplish this; furthermore, such agency may not make any arrangement with a life insurance company or any other entity for the purchase of annuities for the benefit of individual effective or retired employees or take any steps to nullify, in whole or in part, the pension plans or program of The United Methodist Church by making contracts with outside parties.

Annual Conference Administration

¶ **1506.** *Powers, Duties, and Responsibilities of Annual Conferences*
1. The annual conferences have the following powers, duties, and responsibilities with respect to clergy benefit plans administered by the General Board of Pension and Health Benefits: *(a)* executing an adoption agreement, including making any optional elections; *(b)* enrolling clergy; *(c)* making contributions; *(d)* determining the appointment status of a clergyperson for a given period, including the classification of the clergyperson and his or her full-time or part-time status; *(e)* reporting on a clergyperson's compensation; *(f)* determining a clergyperson's conference relationship status, including the termination thereof; *(g)* determining a clergyperson's leave of absence status; *(h)* reporting on any waivers of plan participation made by a clergyperson; and *(i)* determining the retirement status of a clergyperson, including determining how many years of service a clergyperson has earned toward the number prescribed in the *Book of Discipline* to qualify for retirement.
2. The annual conference, on recommendation of the conference Board of Pensions, shall determine the admissibility and validity of pre-January 1, 1982 service approved, or compensation considered, for pension credit, subject to the provisions of the *Discipline* and the rules and regulations of the pension and benefit funds, plans, and programs of The United Methodist Church.[31]

---

31. See Judicial Council Decisions 81, 360, 379.

3. Concerning the normal conditions for pension credit and pro rata pension credit, the following provisions shall apply for service rendered prior to January 1, 1982, in determining approval for pension credit, eligibility for pension, and allocation of responsibility:

a) *Full Pension Credit*—Full pension credit may be granted for persons not meeting some or all of the above conditions by a three-fourths vote of those present and voting in the annual conference on recommendation of the conference board of pensions.[32]

b) Service of a local pastor prior to 1982 may be approved for pension credit only by vote of the annual conference, on recommendation of the conference board of pensions, after consultation with the district superintendents. If such credit is granted, it should be included under the *Discipline* question, "What other personal notation should be made?"

c) Upon recommendation of the conference board of pensions and by a three-fourths vote of those present and voting in the annual conference, pension credit may be granted to a clergy member in full connection, provisional member, or associate member of the conference on account of full-time service previously rendered as an approved local pastor or approved supply pastor to an institution, organization, or agency, which in the judgment of the annual conference rendered to it some form of service sufficient to warrant pension credit; provided, however, that such institution, organization, or agency shall accept and pay such apportionment as the conference may require.

4. If the conference board of pensions so recommends, a pension shall be payable on account of pension credit for service prior to 1982 for an ordained minister from another Christian denomination who shall have rendered not less than four consecutive years of full-time service with pension credit for service prior to 1982 or with full participation in the Comprehensive Protection Plan since 1981, or a combination thereof, in one annual conference while qualified under ¶ 346.2, who has attained the age of voluntary retirement for a conference clergy member.

5. The annual conference, on recommendation of the conference board of pensions, shall have the power to revise, correct, or adjust a clergyperson's record of pension credit as set forth in his or her service record to align such record with the *Discipline* and

---

32. See Judicial Council Decision 386.

Supplement One of the Clergy Retirement Security Program (or any successor clergy pension or retirement plan or program). Prior to the revision of such record, the General Board of Pension and Health Benefits may be requested to review relevant data and report its findings thereon. Such revisions, corrections, and adjustments shall be published in the journal of the annual conference in answer to Business of the Annual Conference questions and shall be reported to the General Board of Pension and Health Benefits by the conference board of pensions.[33]

6. Each annual conference shall develop, adopt, and implement a formal comprehensive funding plan or plans for funding all of its benefit obligations. The funding plan or plans shall be submitted annually to the General Board of Pension and Health Benefits for review and be approved annually by the annual conference, following the receipt and inclusion of a favorable written opinion from the General Board of Pension and Health Benefits. In addition, the General Board of Pension and Health Benefits shall present a quadrennial report to General Conference concerning the long-term benefit liabilities of the denomination. Therefore, each annual conference shall provide to the General Board of Pension and Health Benefits information periodically requested.

7. The responsibility for pension for service approved for pension credit under Supplement One of the Clergy Retirement Security Program (or any successor clergy pension or retirement plan or program) shall rest with the annual conference in which the service was rendered; provided, however, that in the event of mergers, unions, boundary changes, or transfers of churches, such responsibility shall rest with the successor annual conference within whose geographical boundaries the charge is located.[34]

8. Pension for service approved for pension credit by an annual conference shall be provided by the annual conference under one of the pension funds, plans, or programs administered by the General Board of Pension and Health Benefits of The United Methodist Church.

9. An annual conference may not make any arrangement with a life insurance company for the purchase of annuities for the benefit of individual effective or retired clergy or take any steps to nullify, in whole or in part, the pension plans and programs of

---

33. See Judicial Council Decision 386.
34. See Judicial Council Decisions 203, 389, 523.

The United Methodist Church by making contracts with outside parties.[35]

10. *Other Annual Conference Organizations—a)* Annual conferences, hereinafter called conferences, are authorized to establish, incorporate, and maintain investment funds, preachers' aid societies, and organizations and funds of similar character, under such names, plans, rules, and regulations as they may determine, the directors of which shall be elected or otherwise designated by the conference, where permissible under the laws of the state of incorporation, and the income from which shall be applied to the support of the pension, health, and welfare benefit programs for clergy through the conference board of pensions.[36]

b) Distributable pension, health, and welfare benefit funds from all sources shall be disbursed by or under the direction of the conference board of pensions, excepting only such funds as are otherwise restricted by specific provisions or limitations in gifts, devises, bequests, trusts, pledges, deeds, or other similar instruments, which restrictions and limitations shall be observed.

c) It shall not be permissible for any conference or permanent fund organization thereof to deprive its beneficiaries who are beneficiaries in other conferences of the privilege of sharing in the distribution of the earned income of such funds through the clearinghouse administered by the General Board of Pension and Health Benefits.

d) Each conference, on recommendation of its conference board of pensions or one of the organizations mentioned in § *a* above, may select a Sunday in each year to be observed in the churches as Retired Ministers Day, in honor of the retired clergy, their spouses, and the surviving spouses of clergy in recognition of the Church's responsibility for their support. The bishop may request each conference in the area to insert a Retired Ministers Day in its calendar.

11. A conference board of pensions may make special grants to clergy or former clergy of an annual conference who have served under appointment in that conference; or to their spouses, former spouses, surviving former spouses, or surviving dependent children (including adult dependent children). A report of such special grants shall be made annually to the annual conference.

---

35. See Judicial Council Decision 716.
36. See Judicial Council Decision 218.

12. Clergy members in full connection, provisional members, and associate members in an annual conference who voluntarily withdraw from the ministry of The United Methodist Church to enter the ministry of another church or denomination, on the attainment of age sixty-two and on recommendation of the conference board of pensions and a three-fourths vote of those present and voting in any annual conference in which approved service was rendered prior to January 1, 1982, or the legal successor, may be recognized and granted approved pension service rendered in that conference.

13. The responsibility for providing pension on account of service rendered prior to January 1, 1982, in a missionary conference, provisional annual conference, or former mission within the United States or Puerto Rico that has been approved for pension credit shall rest jointly with: *(a)* the missionary conference, provisional annual conference, or former mission concerned, *(b)* the General Board of Pension and Health Benefits with funds provided by the General Council on Finance and Administration, and *(c)* the General Board of Global Ministries. The revenue for pension purposes covering such service shall be provided by the aforesaid parties in accordance with such plan or plans as may be mutually agreed to by them.

14. Pension and benefit contributions are the responsibility of the Plan Sponsor for participants in the Clergy Retirement Security Program (or any successor clergy pension or retirement plan or program) and the Comprehensive Protection Plan. Unless otherwise determined by vote of the annual, missionary, or provisional conference, the treasurer of a local church or pastoral charge shall remit such contributions related to the participant's compensation that is provided from local church funds to the Plan Sponsor. If compensation from the local church or pastoral charge is supplemented from other church sources, pension and benefit contributions related to such supplements shall be paid from that same source. If the entire compensation for a participant is from a salary-paying unit other than a local church or a pastoral charge, the unit responsible for compensation shall remit the pension and benefit contributions to the Plan Sponsor. Nothing in this paragraph shall be understood as preventing an annual, missionary, or provisional conference from raising part or all of the annual contributions for the Clergy Retirement Security Program (or any successor clergy pension or retirement plan or program) or

the Comprehensive Protection Plan by an apportionment to the churches of the conference and remitting payments to the General Board of Pension and Health Benefits on behalf of all the pastors covered; there is no time limit on this provision.

15. Effective January 1, 2007, pension contributions will be determined in accordance with the provisions of the Clergy Retirement Security Program (or any successor clergy pension or retirement plan or program). Actual compensation, limited by 200 percent of the denominational average compensation, is the basic contribution base of the Comprehensive Protection Plan.

16. An annual conference may establish a pension support fund to be administered by the conference board of pensions. Local churches may request pension assistance from this fund when special circumstances arise that result in nonpayment of pension contributions and/or apportionments for pension and benefit purposes. The board shall present its estimate of the amount required to the conference council on finance and administration, which shall include it in its recommendation to the conference. If the amount is approved by the conference, it shall be apportioned as an item of clergy support.

17. The annual conference board of pensions, in consultation with the General Board of Pension and Health Benefits, shall have the responsibility to enroll clergy of the annual conference in the Clergy Retirement Security Program (or any successor clergy pension or retirement plan or program) and the Comprehensive Protection Plan in accordance with the provisions of such plans.

18. Optional provisions contained in the Clergy Retirement Security Program (or any successor clergy pension or retirement plan or program) and Comprehensive Protection Plan may be adopted by vote of the annual conference subsequent to the receipt of a recommendation from the conference board of pensions. Effective January 1, 2007, contributions and credited service are determined in accordance with the provisions of the Clergy Retirement Security Program (or any successor clergy pension or retirement plan or program).

19. On or before December 31, 2008, each annual conference's board of pensions or other agency authorized by the annual conference must submit a generally accepted financial valuation, such as in accordance with Statement of Financial Accounting Standard No. 106, as amended, of its projected medical liabilities for its population covered by its employer retiree health care plan

to the General Board of Pension and Health Benefits, and must submit a similar report biennially thereafter.

20. On or before December 31, 2008, each annual conference shall document in writing its policy regarding the portability of retiree health care eligibility, coverage, cost-sharing, and benefits and communicate the policy to its clergy and lay employees and incoming clergy and lay employees from other annual conferences or general agencies. For the purpose of this paragraph, portability encompasses credit given for service outside the annual conference within the denomination to clergy and lay employees toward (a) eligibility for health care coverage in retirement and (b) accrual of annual conference subsidies toward or annual conference cost-sharing of the cost of health care coverage.

¶ 1507. *Financing Pension and Benefit Programs*—The annual conference shall be responsible for annually providing moneys in the amount necessary to meet the requirements of the pension and benefit funds, plans, and programs of the conference.

1. The board shall compute the amount to be apportioned annually to meet the requirements of the pension and benefit programs of the conference.

2. After consultation with the board, the conference council on finance and administration shall report to the annual conference the amounts computed by the board that are required to meet the needs of the pension, benefit, and relief programs of the conference.

3. Distributable pension funds from all sources, unless restricted by specific provisions or limitations, shall be disbursed by, or under the direction of, the conference board of pensions.

4. The board may accumulate a fund from the income for pension purposes in order to stabilize the pension program of the conference.[37]

¶ 1508. *Policies Related to Conflict of Interest and Investment Management*—The following rules shall apply to the financial administration of annual conference pension and pension-related funds:

1. A member of the board connected or interested in any way with the securities, real estate, or other forms of investment sold to or purchased from such funds, or with an insurance program or a contract under consideration by the board, shall be ineligible

---

37. See Judicial Council Decision 50.

to participate in the deliberation of the investment committee or of the board or to vote in connection therewith.

2. No officer or member of a conference agency handling such funds shall receive a personal commission, bonus, or remuneration, direct or indirect, in connection with the purchase or sale of any property the loan of any money, the letting of any annuity or insurance contract, the making or acceptance of any assignment, pledge, or mortgage to secure the payment of any loan, or for the purchase or sale of any securities or other properties from or to that agency, or be eligible to obtain a loan in any amount from funds committed to the care of that agency. No investment shall be purchased from or sold to any member of the board or any member of the family of a member of the board.

3. To prevent development of any conflict of interest or preferential treatment and to preserve goodwill and confidence throughout the Church, no local church, Church-related institution, or organization thereof shall be eligible to obtain a loan in any amount from such funds.[38]

4. The principle of diversification of investments shall be observed, with the agency encouraged to invest in institutions, companies, corporations, or funds that make a positive contribution toward the realization of the goals outlined in the Social Principles of our Church, however with primary consideration given to the soundness and safety of such investments.

5. Real property may hereafter be accepted as consideration for gift annuity agreements only with the stipulation that the annuity shall not exceed the net income from the property until such property shall have been liquidated. Upon liquidation, the annuity shall be paid upon the net proceeds at the established annuity rate.

6. An annual conference agency handling such funds shall not offer higher rates of annuity than those listed in the annuity schedule approved by the General Board of Pension and Health Benefits.

7. *a)* There shall be printed in the annual conference journal a list of the investments held by each agency handling such funds directly or indirectly under the control of the annual conference, or such list may be distributed directly to the members of the annual conference at their request.

---

38. See Judicial Council Decision 145.

b) The conference board of pensions shall require an annual audit of pension and pension-related funds setting forth the total asset value of such funds and the distribution of income from such funds from persons and organizations appointed or employed for the management of these funds.

8. The borrowing of money in any conference year by a conference corporation or organization to enable the conference board of pensions to meet the requirements of the pension and benefit programs shall be done only on authority of the conference granted by three-fourths vote of the members present and voting.

9. *Depositories and Bonding—a)* The conference board of pensions shall designate a bank or banks or other depository or depositories for deposit of the funds held by the board and may require a depository bond from such depository or depositories.

b) The board, through the conference council on finance and administration, shall provide a fidelity bond in suitable amount for all persons handling its funds.

¶ **1509.** *Joint Distributing Committees*—1. *Authorizations*—Whenever two or more annual or provisional annual conferences are to be merged, in whole or in part, there shall be elected by each conference affected a distributing committee of three members and three alternates, which shall act jointly with similar committees from the other conference or conferences. The joint distributing committee thus formed shall have power and authority: *(a)* to allocate the pension responsibility involved; *(b)* to distribute equitably the permanent funds and all other pension assets of the conference or conferences affected, taking into consideration the pension responsibility involved, such distribution to be made within twelve months of the date of the dissolution of the committee as provided in ¶ 1509.3*d; (c)* to the extent not otherwise previously provided for by the conference or conferences involved, to apportion or distribute equitably any other assets or property and any other liabilities or obligations. It shall be governed by the legal restrictions or limitations of any contract, trust agreement, pledge, deed, will, or other legal instrument.

2. *Organization*—The committee shall be convened by the general secretary of the General Board of Pension and Health Benefits, or by some other officer of that board designated by the general secretary in writing, and shall elect from its membership a chairperson, a vice chairperson, and a secretary.

3. *Powers, Duties, and Responsibilities*—*a)* The committee shall determine the number of years of service approved for pension credit rendered in the conferences that will lose their identity in the merging of conference territories, and the findings of the committee shall be final unless substantial evidence to the contrary is presented, and the annuity payments by the continuing conference or conferences shall be made accordingly. The determination of pension benefits in The United Methodist Church shall recognize all pension rights to which clergy are entitled under the pension plans in existence at the time of Church union and shall recognize all approved service that has been rendered in The Evangelical United Brethren Church and The Methodist Church prior to the date of Church union.

b) The committee shall keep complete minutes of its transactions, and a copy thereof shall be filed with the secretary of each annual conference involved and with the General Board of Pension and Health Benefits.

c) Until the committee's work shall have been completed, the corporate organization of each conference in the process of merger shall be maintained. After the committee shall have completed its work, the officers of such corporation, subject to the completion of its business, shall dissolve or merge it, in accordance with applicable corporate laws, after being authorized to do so by the conference involved.

d) The committee, having completed its work in connection with the merger or mergers for which it was organized and having filed copies of its findings and actions with the secretaries of the conferences involved for publication in the respective conference journals, and with the General Board of Pension and Health Benefits, shall be dissolved; subject, however, to recall by the general secretary of the General Board of Pension and Health Benefits in the event of the discovery and presentation to the general board of data substantially at variance with those previously submitted, for the purpose of reviewing such data and possible revision of its previous actions.

4. Whenever a single annual conference or provisional annual conference is to be divided into two or more conferences, the provisions of ¶ 1509 shall be applied, provided the distributing committee members of each resulting conference shall be named subsequent to the effective date of the division and no later than the first regular annual session of such conferences.

Section X. The United Methodist Publishing House

¶ **1601.** *Authorization and Establishment*—The United Methodist Publishing House comprises the publishing interests of The United Methodist Church. It shall have responsibility for and supervision of the publishing and distribution for The United Methodist Church. The United Methodist Publishing House shall, through agencies or instrumentalities it deems necessary, achieve the objectives set forth in ¶ 1613. The United Methodist Publishing House shall provide publishing and distribution services for other agencies of The United Methodist Church and shall share with other agencies of The United Methodist Church in the total program of The United Methodist Church, as well as share in the total ecumenical program in the area of publishing for the advancement of the cause of Christ and his Kingdom as The United Methodist Publishing House shall determine to be appropriate. All matters related to the work of The United Methodist Publishing House shall be under the direction of the Board of The United Methodist Publishing House.

¶ **1602.** *Membership*—1. The Board of The United Methodist Publishing House, hereinafter called the board, shall consist of up to twenty-five members as follows:

a) *Episcopal members*—Two bishops, one from the central conferences and one from the jurisdictional conferences named by the Council of Bishops.

b) *Jurisdictional members*—Fifteen members elected by the jurisdictional conferences based on the following formula: North Central—3, Northeastern—2, South Central—3, Southeastern—6, and Western—1.

c) *Central Conference Members*—Two members elected by the Council of Bishops.

d) *Additional members*—Up to six additional members may be elected by the board, with consideration given to representation of women and racial and ethnic groups not elected by the jurisdictions, and to special knowledge specific to the work of the publishing house. It is recommended that where possible persons elected by each jurisdiction be inclusive of women and racial/ethnic groups—Asian Americans, African Americans, Hispanic Americans, Native Americans, and Pacific Islanders.

e) At least two persons who are young adults at the time of election shall be elected each quadrennium.

f) Membership on the board shall be equally divided, as far as practicable, between clergy and laity.

g) Other paragraphs of the *Discipline* notwithstanding, jurisdictional and central conference membership shall also be by classes based on term of office for one, two, or three quadrennia, attention being given to the principle of rotation so that, as far as practicable, one third of the membership shall be elected each quadrennium.[39] The principle of rotation is also applicable to the executive committee.

h) In case a vacancy occurs between sessions of the jurisdictional conferences for any cause, the board shall fill the vacancy for the unexpired term from that jurisdiction in the representation of which the vacancy occurs, except in the case of members elected by the board where such vacancies would be filled by the board in the prescribed manner without regard to geographic or jurisdictional relationship.

i) The president/CEO of The United Methodist Publishing House shall be an ex officio member of the board without vote.

¶ 1603. *Annual Meeting*—The board shall hold at least one meeting in each calendar year. The place and time of all meetings shall be designated by the board, but if it fails to do so, then the time and place shall be designated by the chairperson. It shall convene at such other times on call of the chairperson or by the board or by the executive committee. At all meetings of the board, a majority of the members shall constitute a quorum.

¶ 1604. *Record of Proceedings*—The board shall keep a correct record of its proceedings and make written report thereof to the Church through the General Conference.

¶ 1605. *Tenure of Board Members and Officers*—The members of the board and all officers of the board elected by it shall hold office until their successors are chosen and the new board is duly organized.

¶ 1606. *Executive Committee*—The board is authorized to perfect its organization from its membership, including the offices of chairperson, vice chairperson, and secretary. The board shall elect from its membership at the quadrennial organizational meeting an executive committee of eight members, including the chairperson, vice chairperson, and secretary of the board, who shall serve, respectively, as chairperson, vice chairperson, and secretary of the

---

39. See Judicial Council Decision 593.

committee. Special attention shall be given to representation of racial and ethnic groups and women. Not more than three members of the executive committee shall be from any one jurisdiction, and there shall be at least one member from each of the five jurisdictional conferences. The U.S. bishop serving on the board shall be an ex officio member, and the president/CEO of The United Methodist Publishing House shall be an ex officio member without vote. Any vacancy occurring in the membership of the executive committee shall be filled by it, subject to confirmation by the board at its next meeting.

¶ 1607. *Powers and Duties of the Executive Committee*—The executive committee shall have and may exercise all the powers of the board except those expressly reserved by the board and/or by the *Discipline* for board action.

¶ 1608. *Successor in Interest*—The board shall be the successor in interest to and carry on the work of the Board of Publication of The Evangelical United Brethren Church and the General Board of Publication of The Methodist Church.

¶ 1609. *Powers and Duties of the Board*—1. The board is empowered and authorized in its discretion to carry out its general operations under the corporate name of The United Methodist Publishing House.

2. The board is authorized and empowered in its discretion at any time it may deem such action to be desirable or convenient to create an additional corporation(s), in compliance with appropriate state corporation laws.

3. If the board creates and directs more than one corporate entity, it is authorized and empowered in its discretion at any time it may deem such action desirable or convenient to take corporate action in the name of said corporations to surrender the charter or charters of one or several or all of said corporations or to merge, consolidate, or affiliate such corporations, or any of them, in compliance with appropriate state laws.

¶ 1610. *Board Members as Trustees*—The members of the board shall serve and act as directors or trustees of the corporation(s) named or authorized in ¶ 1609.

¶ 1611. *Agency Status*—The corporation(s) named or authorized in ¶ 1609 is an agency or instrumentality through which The United Methodist Church conducts its publishing and distribution in the name of The United Methodist Publishing House in accordance with the objectives set forth in ¶ 1613. The corporation(s) shall comply with the policies set forth in ¶ 715.

¶ 1612. *Report to General Conference*—The board shall examine carefully the affairs of The United Methodist Publishing House and make written report thereof to the Church through the General Conference.

¶ 1613. *Objectives*—The objectives of The United Methodist Publishing House shall be: the advancement of the cause of Christianity throughout the world by disseminating religious knowledge and useful literary, scientific, and educational information in the form of books, tracts, multimedia, electronic media, and periodicals; the promotion of Christian education; the implementation of any and all activities properly connected with the publishing, production in a variety of media, and distribution of an array of print, video, digital resources, and many types of supplies for ministry used by individuals, leaders, congregations, and other entities of the church to advance the ecumenical outreach of Christianity, and such activities as the General Conference may direct and the board may authorize.

¶ 1614. *Direction and Control*—The United Methodist Publishing House shall be under the direction and control of the board, acting through a president/CEO elected quadrennially by the board, and a publisher who shall be elected annually as the publisher of The United Methodist Church, and such other officers as the board may determine.

¶ 1615. *Appropriation of Net Income*—The net income from the operations of The United Methodist Publishing House, after providing adequate reserves for its efficient operation and allowing for reasonable growth and expansion, shall be appropriated by the board and distributed annually on the basis of a just plan provided by the General Board of Pension and Health Benefits to the several annual conferences for the persons who are and shall be conference claimants. The just plan may encompass disproportionate allocations to annual conferences where there is a disparate need relative to other annual conferences, as, for example, in developing nations relative to developed nations.

¶ 1616. *Designation of Net Income*—The net income from the operations of The United Methodist Publishing House shall be appropriated to no other purpose than its own operating requirements and for persons who are or shall be conference claimants as provided in ¶ 22 and ¶ 1615.[40]

---

40. See Judicial Council Decisions 322, 330.

¶ **1617.** *Board Members as Successors*—The members of the board and their successors in office are declared to be the successors of the incorporators named in the charters of The Methodist Book Concern issued by the States of New York and Ohio and in the charter of the Board of Publication of the Methodist Protestant Church issued by the State of Pennsylvania. The president/CEO of the board, elected from time to time under this or any subsequent *Discipline*, is declared to be the successor in office of the Book Agents of The Methodist Episcopal Church, South, named in the charter issued to the corporation of that name by the State of Tennessee.

¶ **1618.** *Powers and Duties of the Board*—Subject to the provisions of ¶ 1614 and to the continuing control and direction of the General Conference of The United Methodist Church as set forth from time to time in the *Discipline*, the board is authorized and empowered to cause the operations of The United Methodist Publishing House to be carried on and the objectives defined in ¶ 1613 to be achieved in such manner, through or by means of such agencies or instrumentalities and by use of such procedures as the board may from time to time determine to be necessary, advisable, or appropriate, with full power and authority in the premises to take all such action and to do all such other acts and things as may be required or found to be advisable. In particular, and without limiting the generality of the foregoing, the board is authorized and empowered, for the purposes of this section:

1. To use, manage, operate, and otherwise utilize all property and assets of every kind, character, and description of any corporation(s) created by the board pursuant to ¶ 1609.2, as well as all income from such property and assets and the avails thereof, all with liability or obligation to account for such property and assets, the use thereof, the income therefrom, and avails thereof, only to the General Conference of The United Methodist Church or as it shall direct.

2. To cause a corporation(s) created by the board pursuant to ¶ 1609.2 to take all such action and to do all such things as the board may deem necessary or advisable to carry out the intent and purposes of this paragraph. The governing body of said corporation(s) from time to time shall take all action that the board deems necessary or advisable to carry out the intent and purposes of this paragraph. The board shall cause all legal obligations of said corporation(s) to be met, fulfilled, and performed.

3. To continue to exercise the powers and administer the duties and responsibilities conferred on it as an agency of The United Methodist Church through the corporation named The United Methodist Publishing House, incorporated under the laws of the State of Illinois in accord with authority delegated to it by the General Conference of 1952, or through such other means and agencies as it may from time to time determine to be expedient and necessary in order to give full effect to the purposes expressed in this section.[41]

¶ **1619.** *Ownership and Control of Assets*—1. The property, assets, and income of the Illinois corporation shall be held by it, under the direction of the board, as an agency of The United Methodist Church and shall at all times be subject to the control and direction of the General Conference of The United Methodist Church as set forth from time to time in the *Discipline*.

2. In carrying out and executing its operations and functions, the board of The United Methodist Publishing House shall be entitled to hold, use, manage, operate, and otherwise utilize all property and assets of every kind, character, and description of the corporation(s) identified in ¶ 1618.1 (other than its corporate powers and franchises) and all income therefrom and avails thereof for the purposes and objectives defined in this section.

3. The Illinois corporation and any corporation(s) created by the board pursuant to ¶ 1609.2 shall from time to time take all such action as the board deems necessary or advisable to carry out the intent and purposes of this paragraph and section.

4. The board of The United Methodist Publishing House shall be liable for and shall execute and satisfy all legal obligations of the corporation(s) created by the board pursuant to ¶ 1609.2, but neither it nor the board shall have or be under any obligation to account for principal and income to any such other corporation or to otherwise report to any of them.

¶ **1620.** *Dissolution of The Evangelical Press and Otterbein Press*—Pursuant to the Declaration of Union of The Evangelical United Brethren Church and The Methodist Church and under the authority of ¶¶ 939, 950-954 of *The Book of Discipline of The United Methodist Church, 1968,* The Otterbein Press, an Ohio corporation, and The Evangelical Press, a Pennsylvania corporation, have been legally dissolved and their charters have been surren-

---

41. See Judicial Council Decision 330.

dered. The proceeds of their corporate assets have been and are being administered pursuant to said disciplinary provisions.

¶ **1621.** *Corporate Officers*—The officers of the corporation(s) under the direction of the board shall be elected in accordance with the bylaws.

¶ **1622.** *Corporate President*—The chief executive officer (CEO) elected pursuant to ¶ 1614 shall also be elected the president of the corporation(s) under the direction of the board.

¶ **1623.** *Salaries for Corporate Officers*—The board shall fix the salaries of the officers of the corporation(s) and shall report the same quadrennially to the General Conference.

¶ **1624.** *Quarterly Financial Reports*—The board shall require the president/CEO to submit quarterly to the executive committee and annually to the board written reports of the financial condition and operating results of The United Methodist Publishing House.

¶ **1625.** *Authority to Extend Activities*—The president/CEO and the board shall have authority to extend the activities of The United Methodist Publishing House in such manner as they may judge to be for the best interests of the Church.

¶ **1626.** *Fidelity Bonding of President/Chief Executive Officer and Corporate Officers*—The board shall require the president/CEO and other corporate officers to give bond conditioned on the faithful discharge of their respective duties. It also shall authorize the execution of a blanket bond covering all staff personnel whose responsibilities justify such coverage. The amount of the bonds shall be fixed by the board, and the bonds shall be subject to the approval of the board. The premiums shall be paid by The United Methodist Publishing House, and the chairperson of the board shall be the custodian of the bonds.

¶ **1627.** *Power to Suspend Officers*—The board shall have power to suspend, after hearing, and to remove, after hearing, the president/CEO, publisher, or any of the officers for misconduct or failure to perform the duties of their offices.

¶ **1628.** *Book Editor*—The board shall elect annually a book editor, who shall be designated chief content officer. The book editor shall have joint responsibility with the publisher for approving manuscripts considered for publication. The book editor shall edit or supervise the editing of all books and materials of our publication. In the case of church school publications and official forms and records, the book editor shall collaborate with the appropriate agencies or groups whenever such collaboration is mutually desirable and beneficial. The book editor shall perform such other editorial duties as may be required by the board.

¶ **1629.** *Salary of Book Editor*—The board shall fix the salary of the book editor.

¶ **1630.** *Suspension of Book Editor*—The board shall have power to suspend or remove, after hearing, the book editor for misconduct or failure to perform the duties of the office.

¶ **1631.** *Editor of Church School Publications*—There shall be an editor of Church School Publications, elected as set forth in ¶ 1125.

¶ **1632.** *Duties of Editor of Church School Publications*—The editor of Church School Publications shall be responsible for the preparation of all curriculum materials as set forth in ¶ 1125.

¶ **1633.** *Church School Curriculum*—The curriculum of the church school shall be determined by the Curriculum Resources Committee, which shall include in its membership the publisher and an associate publisher named by The United Methodist Publishing House.

¶ **1634.** *Salary of Editor of Church School Publications*—The board shall fix the salary of the editor of Church School Publications and shall have full financial responsibility for all expenses connected with this work.

¶ **1635.** *Publications of the Curriculum Resources Committee*—The publications of the Curriculum Resources Committee shall be manufactured, published, and distributed through The United Methodist Publishing House. In matters involving financial responsibility, the final determination in every case shall lie with the board. After consultation with the publisher, the editor of Church School Publications shall prepare a complete budget for this work, including salaries of assistants and office secretaries and travel, etc., to be effective when approved by the board, and shall direct its operation from year to year.

¶ **1636.** *Service of the Entire United Methodist Church*—There shall be one complete, coordinated system of literature published by the board for the entire United Methodist Church. This literature is to be of such type and variety as to meet the needs of all groups of our people. The publisher and such other staff as the board and president/CEO shall determine shall consult with the general program agencies, the General Commission on Communication, and the Connectional Table with regard to their publishing needs in order to avoid unnecessary overlapping and duplication.

¶ **1637.** *Financial Feasibility*—The board and the publisher shall have authority to decline to publish any item of literature when in their judgment the cost would be greater than should be borne by The United Methodist Publishing House.

¶ **1638.** *Board Participation*—The editor of Church School Publications (¶ 1125) and a member of the General Board of Discipleship designated by its president shall have the right to sit with the board and shall have the privilege of the floor without vote for the consideration of matters pertaining to their joint interests.

¶ **1639.** *Cooperative Publications*—The United Methodist Publishing House shall explore and engage in cooperative publication of United Methodist church school curriculum resources wherever both The United Methodist Publishing House and the Curriculum Resources Committee of the General Board of Discipleship find this to be practicable and in harmony with related editorial and publishing policies.

¶ **1640.** *Use of Distribution System by General Agencies*—It is recommended that all general agencies of The United Methodist Church use the distribution system of The United Methodist Publishing House for distribution of resources, materials, and supplies needed for use in the local church.

¶ **1641.** *Real Estate Purchases*—The United Methodist Publishing House shall not buy any real estate costing in excess of $500,000 and shall not sell or exchange any real estate having a fair market value in excess of $500,000 except by the order of the General Conference or, between sessions of the General Conference, by a two-thirds vote of all the members of the board. In either case, such vote shall be taken at a regular or called meeting of the board, and if at a called meeting, the purpose of this meeting shall have been stated in the call. The erection of a new building or improvement, alteration, or repair of an existing building or the purchase of real estate for retail purposes involving an expenditure of not more than $500,000, or the sale or exchange of real estate used by the publishing house for retail purposes that has a fair market value of not more than $500,000, may be authorized by the vote of a majority of the executive committee. These provisions shall not prevent the making of investments on mortgage security or the protection of the same or the collection of claims and adjustments.

Section XI. General Commission on Archives and History

¶ 1701. *Authorization and Establishment*—The name of the official historical agency of The United Methodist Church shall be the General Commission on Archives and History.

¶ 1702. *Incorporation*—The General Commission on Archives and History shall be incorporated under the laws of whatever state the commission may determine.

¶ 1703. *Purpose*—1. The purpose of the commission shall be to promote and care for the historical interests of The United Methodist Church at every level. It shall gather, preserve, and hold title to library and archival materials, and it shall disseminate interpretive materials on the history of The United Methodist Church and its antecedents. It shall cooperate with other bodies, especially the Historical Society of The United Methodist Church, the African American Methodist Heritage Center, the World Methodist Historical Society, and the World Methodist Council in areas of mutual concern. It shall maintain archives and libraries in which shall be preserved historical records and materials of every kind relating to The United Methodist Church and shall see that such holdings are available for responsible public and scholarly use. It shall provide guidance for the proper creation, maintenance, and disposition of documentary record material at all levels of The United Methodist Church (see ¶ 1711.1*b*). It shall provide support, direction, and encouragement for the work of annual conference and jurisdictional historical agencies and organizations by developing and making available historical, interpretive, and training media. It shall develop policies and resources for the designated United Methodist Historic Sites and United Methodist Heritage Landmarks. It shall provide general supervision for the observance of Heritage Sunday (see ¶ 264.1). It shall engage with other Wesleyan, Methodist, or Evangelical United Brethren-related denominations in lifting up our joint heritage.

2. The commission shall be accountable to the Connectional Table for all programmatic assignments.

3. The commission shall have responsibility for and supervision of its archives and historical libraries and other depositories of similar character, if any, established by The United Methodist Church.

4. The commission shall promote collection and dissemination of information and materials concerning the historic witness

made individually and collectively by women, racial and ethnic peoples, and other constituencies not covered extensively in traditional historical documentation in the worldwide life of The United Methodist Church and its antecedents.

5. The commission shall develop and make available interpretive materials such as handbooks, services of worship and celebrations of historical events, training films, and other media helpful to annual conferences and local churches.

6. Once each quadrennium, the commission may hold a historical convocation, to which may be invited members of jurisdictional and annual conference historical agencies and organizations; appropriate faculty and students in institutions of higher education related to The United Methodist Church; members of the Historical Society of The United Methodist Church; members of other Wesleyan, Methodist, and Evangelical United Brethren-related historical organizations; and such other persons, groups, or organizations as may be interested.

¶ 1704. *Membership*—1. The commission shall be constituted quadrennially, and its members and all officers elected by it shall hold office until their successors have been chosen. The commission may fill interim vacancies during a quadrennium where not otherwise provided by the *Discipline.*

2. The commission shall be composed of twenty-four members in the following manner: ten members elected by the General Conference on nomination of the Council of Bishops, in which two shall be from the central conferences; two bishops (one of whom shall come from the central conferences); five presidents of the jurisdictional commissions on archives and history, or where no commission exists or any disciplinary conflict arises, a person designated by the jurisdictional College of Bishops; and, other paragraphs of the *Discipline* notwithstanding, seven additional members elected by the general commission, at least one of whom may be from a central conference, ensuring that all three regions of the central conferences are represented. It is recommended that careful consideration be given to people with special interests and skills in the history of United Methodism and that careful consideration be given to inclusiveness, including representation from men, women, age levels, and all racial and ethnic groups.

¶ 1705. *Meetings*—The commission shall meet annually at such time and place as it may determine, subject to the provisions of the act of incorporation. The commission may hold special meetings on the call of the president. A majority of the members of the commission shall constitute a quorum.

¶ **1706.** *Officers*—The commission shall elect from its membership a president, vice president, secretary, and such other officers as may be needed. The president shall be a bishop. The officers shall perform the duties usually incident to their positions.

¶ **1707.** *Staff*—The commission shall elect a general secretary and such other staff officers as may be needed. The general secretary shall be the executive and administrative officer and shall carry on the work of the commission, keep the records and minutes, serve as editor of official publications of the commission, supervise the depositories, make an annual report to the commission, and furnish such reports as are required to the General Conference and General Conference agencies. The general secretary shall attend meetings of the commission and the executive committee and shall have the privilege of the floor without vote. Archivists, curators, and librarians employed by the commission shall be responsible to the general secretary. They shall attend meetings of the commission and the executive committee when it is deemed necessary by the general secretary. When in attendance, they shall have the privilege of the floor without vote.

¶ **1708.** *Executive Committee*—There shall be an executive committee, composed of the president, vice president, secretary, and two members from each of the three standing committees-Heritage Landmarks, Archives and Library, and History and Interpretation. The executive committee shall perform the duties and exercise the authority of the commission between meetings. Its minutes shall be submitted to the commission for approval. The executive committee and the commission may vote on any matter by mail. Mail polls shall be directed by the general secretary, who shall state clearly the propositions to be voted on and announce the results to all the members.

¶ **1709.** *Finances*—The commission shall be financed by appropriations of the General Conference; the sale of literature and historical materials; subscriptions to the commission's official publications; dues from associate members; and gifts, grants, and bequests of interested individuals and organizations.

¶ **1710.** *Historical Society of The United Methodist Church*—1. The general commission shall endorse and encourage the Historical Society of The United Methodist Church and encourage membership therein for the purpose of promoting interest in the study, preservation, and dissemination of the history and heritage of The United Methodist Church and its antecedents. The Historical Society shall be encouraged to enlist the support and cooperation of commission on archives and history (or equivalent) at the annual conference, jurisdictional conference, and general Church levels as well as other interested agencies and organizations in the promotion of the historical interests of the Church. The society shall be financially self-supporting through dues and other sources, except for such services as may be provided by the General Conference Commission on Archives and History.

2. Membership in the Historical Society shall be established as the society may determine. Membership shall entail the payment of such dues as the society may direct, in return for which members shall receive publications and other benefits as are deemed suitable.

¶ **1711.** 1. *Archival Definitions—a) Archives,* as distinguished from libraries, house not primarily books, but documentary record material.

b) Documentary record material shall mean all documents, minutes, journals, diaries, reports, pamphlets, letters, papers, manuscripts, maps, photographs, books, audiovisuals, sound recordings, magnetic or other tapes, electronic data processing records, artifacts, or any other documentary material, regardless of physical form or characteristics, made or received pursuant to any provisions of the *Discipline* in connection with the transaction of Church business by any general agency of The United Methodist Church or of any of its constituent predecessors.

c) General agency of The United Methodist Church or of its constituent predecessors shall, in turn, mean and include every Church office, Church officer, or official (elected or appointed)—including bishop, institution, board, commission, bureau, council, or conference—at the national level.

2. *Custodianship of Records*—The church official in charge of an office having documentary record material shall be the custodian thereof, unless otherwise provided.

3. *Procedures—a)* The general commission shall establish a central archives of The United Methodist Church and such regional archives and record centers as in its judgment may be needed.

b) The bishops, General Conference officers, the Judicial Council, general boards, commissions, committees, and agencies of The United Methodist Church shall deposit official minutes or journals, or copies of the same, in the archives quadrennially and shall transfer correspondence, records, papers, and other archival materials described above from their offices when they no longer have operational usefulness. No records shall be destroyed until a disposal schedule has been agreed upon by the General Commission on Archives and History and the agency. When the custodian of any official documentary record material of a general agency certifies to the General Commission on Archives and History that such records have no further use or value for official and administrative purposes and when the commission certifies that such records appear to have no further use or value for research or reference, then such records may be destroyed or otherwise disposed of by the agency or official having custody of them. A record of such certification and authorization shall be entered in the minutes or records of both the commission and the agency. The General Commission on Archives and History is hereby authorized and empowered to make such provisions as may be necessary and proper to carry this paragraph into effect.

c) The commission shall have the right to examine the condition of documentary record material and shall, subject to the availability of staff and funds, give advice and assistance to Church officials and agencies in regard to preserving and disposing of documentary record material in their custody. Officials of general agencies shall assist the commission in the preparation of an inventory of records in their custody. To this inventory shall be attached a schedule, approved by the head of the agency having custody of the records and the commission, establishing a time period for the retention and disposal of each series of records. So long as such approved schedule remains in effect, destruction or disposal of documentary record material in accordance with its provisions shall be deemed to have met the requirements of ¶ 1711.3*b.*

d) The commission is authorized and directed to conduct a program of inventorying, repairing, and microfilming among all general agencies of The United Methodist Church for security purposes that documentary record material which the commission determines has permanent value and to provide safe storage for microfilm copies of such material. Subject to the availability of funds, such program may be extended to material of permanent value of all agencies of The United Methodist Church.

e) The general boards, commissions, committees, and agencies of The United Methodist Church shall place two copies, as they are issued, of all their publications, of whatever kind, in the archives or in lieu thereof shall file a statement with the archivist affirming that they are preserving copies of all such items in their own libraries or depositories.

f) Official documents, or copies thereof, such as articles of incorporation, constitutions, bylaws, and other official papers of the boards and agencies of The United Methodist Church shall be deposited in the archives.

g) Whoever has the custody of any general agency records shall, at the expiration of the term of office, deliver to the successor, custodian, or, if there be none, to the commission all records, books, writings, letters, and documents kept or received in the transaction of official general agency business. This will also apply to the papers of temporary and special general Church committees.

h) The bishops, General Conference officers, and the general boards, commissions, committees, and agencies of The United Methodist Church are urged to counsel with the central archivist concerning the preservation of all materials.

i) Jurisdictional, central, and annual conference secretaries shall deposit, without charge, two paper copies of their respective conference journals quadrennially or annually, as the case may be, with the General Commission on Archives and History and in the archives of the central, jurisdictional, and annual conference as appropriate. One copy of a digital version of the journal will be sent to the General Commission on Archives and History, if available.

j) Secretaries of jurisdictional and annual conference boards, commissions, committees, and agencies shall deposit annually, or as often as they meet, copies of their minutes (as distinguished from reports that are printed separately or in the jurisdictional and annual conference journals) in the central archives or in the appropriate regional archives.

k) Bishops, General Conference officers, general agency staff personnel, missionaries, and those ordained ministers and laypersons in positions of leadership and influence at any level of the Church are urged to deposit or bequeath their personal papers to the archives of the general commission.

l) Organizations and individuals may negotiate appropriate restrictions on the use of materials that they deposit in the archives.

m) Upon recommendation of its executive committee, the commission may authorize the transfer of materials to an organization, agency, or family.

n) All materials in the archives shall be available for research and exhibition, subject to such restrictions as may be placed on them.

¶ 1712. *Historic Sites and Heritage Landmarks*—1. *a) Historic Sites*—*Historic sites* are buildings, locations, or structures that are specifically related to a significant event, development, or personality in the history of an annual, central, or jurisdictional conference (or its antecedents). Historic sites are designated by formal action of the annual, central, or jurisdictional conference within whose regions the site is located. Such designation shall first be considered and reviewed by the respective commission on archives and history (or equivalent). After action by the annual, central, or jurisdictional conference to designate a building, structure, or location as a historic site, the president or chairperson of the commission on archives and history (or equivalent) shall advise the General Commission on Archives and History of the action taken and provide such documentation as may be required. The general commission in turn shall provide an official historic site marker, keep a register of all historic sites, and maintain an ongoing file of pertinent information concerning them.

b) Heritage Landmarks—*Heritage landmarks* of The United Methodist Church are buildings, locations, or structures that are specifically related to significant events, developments, or personalities in the overall history of The United Methodist Church or its antecedents. They must have distinctive historic interest and value for the denomination as a whole, as contrasted with local or regional historic significance. Ordinarily, buildings, locations, or structures that have achieved historic significance within the preceding fifty years shall not be considered for designation as a heritage landmark.

c) Designation of Heritage Landmarks—All nominations for the designation of buildings, locations, and structures as United Methodist heritage landmarks shall be made by the annual, central, or jurisdictional conference commission on archives and history (or equivalent) within whose regions they are located. Such nominations shall be referred for consideration to the General Commission on Archives and History, in accord with guidelines established by the commission. Through its Committee on Heritage Landmarks, the commission shall consider the merits of each nomination and shall make such recommendation as it deems appropriate to the ensuing General Conference for its action and determination.

The commission shall recommend only a building, location, or structure for designation as a heritage landmark that has been registered as a historic site by an annual, central, or jurisdictional conference and has met the requirements established by the commission. The commission shall keep a register of all duly designated heritage landmarks and maintain an ongoing file of pertinent information concerning them.

d) Quadrennial Review—The commission shall be responsible for making a quadrennial review of the existing duly designated heritage landmarks, according to the criteria that it shall prepare and which shall be compatible with the *Book of Discipline*. The commission shall further be responsible for recommending to the General Conference the redesignation or reclassification of the designated heritage landmarks as such action may be appropriate in keeping with such criteria.

2. *Present Heritage Landmarks*—The present heritage landmarks of The United Methodist Church (and the year of their designation by General Conference) are: Acuff's Chapel, between Blountville and Kingsport, TN (1968); Albright Memorial Chapel, Kleinfeltersville, PA (1968); Asbury Manual Labor School and Mission, Ft. Mitchell, AL (1984); Barratt's Chapel, near Frederica, DE (1968); Bethune-Cookman College, Daytona Beach, FL (1984); Bishop John Seybert/Flat Rock Cluster, Flat Rock and Bellevue, OH (1992); Boehm's Chapel, Willow Street, PA (1984); College of West Africa, Monrovia, Liberia (2012); Cokesbury College, Abingdon, MD (1984); Cox Memorial United Methodist Church, Hallowell, ME (1992); Deadwood Cluster, Deadwood, SD (1984); Edward Cox House, near Bluff City, TN (1968); First Evangelical Association Church Building and Publishing House, New Berlin, PA (1988); First United Methodist Church, Johnstown, PA (1996); Green Hill House, Louisburg, NC (1968); Gulfside Assembly, Waveland, MS (2016); Hanby House, Westerville, OH (1988); John Street Church, New York City (1968); John Wesley's American Parish, Savannah, GA (1976); Keywood Marker, Glade Spring, VA (1988); Isaac Long's Barn, Landis Valley, Lititz, PA (2008); Lovely Lane Chapel, Baltimore, MD (1972); Mary Johnston Hospital, Manila, The Philippines (2012); McMahan's Chapel, Bronson,

TX (1972); Methodist Hospital, Brooklyn, NY (1972); Newtown Indian United Methodist Church, Okmulgee, OK (2012); Old McKendree Chapel, Jackson, MO (1968); Old Mutare Mission, Zimbabwe (2012); Old Otterbein Church, Baltimore, MD (1968); Old Stone Church Cemetery and Site, Leesburg, VA (1968); Organization of The Methodist Episcopal Church, South, Louisville, KY (1984); Pearl River United Methodist Church, Madison County, MS (2016); Peter Cartwright United Methodist Church, Pleasant Plains, IL (1976); Rehoboth Church, near Union, WV (1968); Robert Strawbridge's Log House, near New Windsor, MD (1968); Rutersville Cluster, Rutersville, TX (1988); St. George's Church, Philadelphia, PA (1968); St. Simon's Island, GA (1968); Simpson House, Philadelphia, PA (2012); Wesley Foundation, University of Illinois, Champaign, IL (1996); Town of Oxford, GA (1972); United Brethren Founding Sites Cluster, Frederick, Keedysville, and Beaver Creek, MD (2000); United Methodist Building on Capitol Hill, Washington, DC (2016); Wesleyan College Cluster, Macon, GA (1992); Whitaker's Chapel, near Enfield, Halifax County, NC (1972); Willamette Mission, near Salem, OR (1992); Woman's Foreign Missionary Society founding site, Boston, MA (2004); Wyandot Indian Mission, Upper Sandusky, OH (1968); and Zoar United Methodist Church, Philadelphia, PA (1984).

Section XII. General Commission on Communication

¶ 1801. As United Methodists, our theological understanding obligates us, as members of the body of Christ, to communicate our faith by speaking and listening to persons both within and outside the Church throughout the world, and to utilize all appropriate means of communication.

The responsibility to communicate is laid upon every church member, every pastor, every congregation, every annual conference, every institution, and every agency of the Church. Within this total responsibility, there are certain functions that the General Conference has assigned to the General Commission on Communication, to be performed in behalf of all through the talents and resources at its command.

¶ 1802. *Name*—There shall be a General Commission on Communication of The United Methodist Church, which for communication and public relations purposes may be designated as United Methodist Communications (UMCom).

¶ **1803.** *Incorporation*—The General Commission on Communication is successor to the Joint Committee on Communications, incorporated in the State of Ohio, and shall be authorized to do business as United Methodist Communications (UMCom). It is authorized to create such other corporate substructures as the commission deems appropriate to carry out its functions.

¶ **1804.** *Amenability and Accountability*—The General Commission on Communication shall be amenable to the General Conference. As an administrative general agency that carries significant program functions in addition to its many service and support responsibilities, the commission shall be accountable to, report to, and be evaluated by the Connectional Table in program matters and shall be accountable to and report to the General Council on Finance and Administration in financial matters.

¶ **1805.** *Purpose*—The General Commission on Communication shall lead the Church in communication. It shall meet the communication, public relations, and marketing needs of the entire Church, reflecting the cultural and racial diversity within The United Methodist Church. It shall provide communication resources and services to local churches and annual conferences. It shall have a consultative relationship with all general agencies of the Church and with any structures for communication and public relations at the jurisdictional, episcopal area, annual conference, district, or local church level.

¶ **1806.** *Responsibilities*—Communication is a strategic function necessary for the success of the mission of The United Methodist Church. Specific responsibilities and functions of the General Commission on Communication and its staff are as follows:

1. It shall be the official newsgathering and distributing agency for The United Methodist Church and its general agencies. In discharging its responsibilities, in keeping with the historic freedom of the press, it shall operate with editorial freedom as an independent news bureau serving all segments of church life and society, making available to both religious and public news media information concerning the Church at large.

2. It shall have primary responsibility on behalf of the denomination to relate to the public media in presenting the Christian faith and work of the Church to the general public through the most effective communication channels. It will provide such structures and strategies as are deemed helpful to the Church in its witness through the media. It shall unify and coordinate

public media messages and programs of United Methodist general agencies.

3. It shall give special attention to television, including broadcast television, cable, videotape, videodisc, and satellite. It shall provide counsel and resources to annual conferences—and through conferences, to districts and local churches—to develop and strengthen their television ministries. Responsibilities of the commission shall include program production and placement, and relationships to commercial broadcasters at the national level in the United States.

4. It shall create and participate in partnerships with national, international, interdenominational, interfaith, and other organizations working in communications as deemed relevant to the mission and ministry of The United Methodist Church.

5. It shall have responsibility to work toward promotion and protection of the historic freedoms of religion and the press, and it shall seek to increase the ethical, moral, and human values of media structures and programs.

6. It shall have general supervision over the public relations strategy and activity for The United Methodist Church.

7. It shall plan, create, produce or cause to be produced, and distribute or cause to be distributed resources that are informative and vital to the religious life of all United Methodists. It shall work with all United Methodist agencies in coordinating resources produced for strategic Church initiatives.

8. It shall oversee a comprehensive communication system for the Church, providing a total view of communication structure and practices, including telecommunications. It shall create networks of communicators at all levels, including local church, district, conference, jurisdiction, and general church. These networks may include periodic consultations for such purposes as idea exchange, information sharing, joint planning, and monitoring and evaluating the total Church's communication enterprises. With respect to the use of computers for communication purposes, the agency shall cooperate with the General Council on Finance and Administration.

9. It shall provide guidance, resources, and training for the local church coordinator of communications (¶ 255[3]), provided that training at the local level shall be through and in cooperation with annual conferences.

10. It shall educate and train in communication principles and skills, including the following: *(a)* national workshops and training experiences in communication skills related to various media; *(b)* consultation with and assistance to annual conferences, districts, and racial and ethnic groups in training local church persons, especially the local church coordinator of communications; *(c)* training experiences for bishops, personnel of general Church agencies, and other groups on request; *(d)* providing and facilitating apprenticeship, internship, and scholarship programs for church communicators; and *(e)* counseling schools of theology and other institutions of higher education about the training of faculty, candidates for the ordained ministry, and laypersons in the principles and skills of communication, media resource development, and media evaluation.

11. It shall determine and implement, after consultation with the General Council on Finance and Administration, policy for the marketing of all financial causes demanding churchwide promotion or publicity.

12. It shall be the central agency marketing throughout the Church the following general Church funds: World Service Fund (¶ 812.1), Africa University Fund (¶ 806.2), Black College Fund (¶ 815), Episcopal Fund (¶ 818.1), General Administration Fund (¶ 813), Interdenominational Cooperation Fund (¶ 814), Ministerial Education Fund (¶ 816), Human Relations Day (¶¶ 824.1 and 263.1), UMCOR Sunday (¶¶ 821, 824.2 and 263.2), Native American Ministries Sunday (¶¶ 824.6 and 263.6), Peace with Justice Sunday (¶¶ 824.5 and 263.5), World Communion Sunday (¶¶ 824.4 and 263.3), United Methodist Student Day (¶¶ 824.3 and 263.4), the Advance for Christ and His Church (¶¶ 822 and 823), World Service Special Gifts (¶ 820), Christian Education Sunday (¶ 265.1), Golden Cross Sunday (¶ 265.2), Rural Life Sunday (¶ 265.3), Disability Awareness Sunday (¶ 265.4), Youth Service Fund (¶ 1208), and all other general Church funds approved by the General Conference, as well as any emergency appeals authorized by the Council of Bishops and the General Council on Finance and Administration (¶ 819). In the marketing of these causes, this agency shall consult with and is encouraged to use content material provided by the program agency responsible for the area and with the agency responsible for the administration of the funds. Budgets for the above funds shall be developed in cooperation with the General Council on Finance and Administration. In cases

where the General Conference assigns a portion of the marketing responsibility to some other agency, such marketing work shall be subject to coordination by the General Commission on Communication. The cost of marketing the funds, as set in the approved marketing budget, shall be a charge against receipts, except that the cost of marketing general Advance Specials shall be billed to the recipient agencies in proportion to the amount of general Advance Special funds received by each (¶ 823.3), and the cost of marketing World Service Special Gifts shall be borne by administering agencies (¶ 820.8). The administration of the money thus set aside for marketing shall be the responsibility of the General Commission on Communication.

13. It shall undertake the marketing of any cause or undertaking, financial or otherwise, not herein mentioned demanding Church-wide promotion or publicity, provided such action is approved by the Council of Bishops and the General Council on Finance and Administration, or their respective executive committees, if any. The General Council on Finance and Administration shall determine the source of the funding for any such authorized promotions.

14. Appeals for giving that are made to United Methodists shall be consistent with the aims of Christian stewardship. The General Commission on Communication and the General Board of Discipleship will cooperate in order that programs and resource materials of the two agencies may be in harmony in their presentation of Christian stewardship.

15. It shall provide content for clergy and laity in local congregations in a variety of accessible formats to promote understanding and appreciation of the global, connectional Church, to develop support for and encourage participation in initiatives, ministries, and missions of the general Church and its agencies, and to provide resources and information to assist local congregations and their leaders in carrying out their ministries. This agency shall obtain from the churches or district superintendents the names of church leaders entitled to receive this content so as to compile a subscription list.

16. It shall lead in communication study and research, applying findings from the professional and academic communities to the work of the Church, and in evaluative communication research. It shall cooperate with other agencies and other levels of the Church in communication research and development work and share the findings of study and research.

17. It shall represent United Methodist interests in new technological developments in the field of communication, including research, the evaluation of new devices and methods, and the application of technological developments to the communication services of the Church.

18. It may develop information, resources, databases, and services that provide channels of communication to and from all levels of the Church.

19. It shall provide resources, counsel, and staff training for area, conference, and district communication programs and develop guidelines in consultation with persons working in areas, conferences, and districts.

20. It shall produce materials for program interpretation in cooperation with the Connectional Table and the general program boards, including the official program calendar of the denomination.

21. The General Commission on Communication shall be charged with planning and implementation of the official United Methodist presence on and use of the Internet, the World Wide Web, or other computer services that can connect United Methodist conferences, agencies, and local churches with one another and with the larger world.

22. The General Commission on Communication shall be responsible for setting the official brand guidelines of The United Methodist Church. Such branding guidelines shall be consistent with the standards established by the General Council on Finance and Administration to preserve the integrity of the denomination's intellectual property (see ¶¶ 807.10-.11, 2502). The commission shall work with the General Council on Finance and Administration to ensure the use of the cross and flame logo at every level of the church (see ¶ 807.10).

¶ 1807. *Organization*—1. *Membership*—The membership of the General Commission on Communication shall be composed of twenty-seven members as follows:

a) Two bishops, including one from the United States and one from the central conferences named by the Council of Bishops.

b) Eleven members elected by the jurisdictional conferences based on the following formula: North Central—2, Northeastern—2, South Central—3, Southeastern—3, and Western—1. It is recommended that at least one of the persons elected by the jurisdictional conferences be a racial or ethnic person.

c) A total of seven members of the central conferences, plus one bishop referenced above, named by the Council of Bishops.

d) Seven additional members elected by the commission to ensure membership of persons with expertise in communication.

e) The additional members shall be nominated by a committee composed of one commission member designated from each jurisdiction and one of the member bishops.

f) In order to ensure inclusiveness, the composition of the commission shall reflect the major recognized categories of Church members (see ¶ 705.3c).

2. *Meetings*—The commission shall hold at least one meeting in each calendar year. Fifteen members shall constitute a quorum.

3. *Officers*—The commission shall elect a president, at least one vice president, a recording secretary, and such other officers as it determines.

There may be an executive committee comprised of not more than one-third of the total membership of the commission and elected by the commission. The membership of the executive committee shall be representative of the composition of the commission.

4. *Internal Organization*—The General Commission on Communication is empowered to create internal structures as it deems appropriate for effective operation.

5. *Staff*—The commission shall elect annually a general secretary upon nomination by the executive committee or a nominating committee and shall elect such deputy general secretaries as needed, and it shall provide for election or appointment of other staff. The general secretary shall cooperate with the Connectional Table for program services and with the general secretary of the General Council on Finance and Administration for financial services.

¶ **1808.** *Finance*—The General Conference shall provide for the financial needs of the General Commission on Communication upon recommendation by the General Council on Finance and Administration. The commission shall consult with the Connectional Table in the area of program matters in development of an annual budget, which shall be reported to the General Council on Finance and Administration for approval.

Section XIII. United Methodist Women

¶ **1901.** There shall be an organization called United Methodist Women in The United Methodist Church in the United States, organized at the local church, district, conference, jurisdiction, and national levels.

¶ **1902.** *Purpose*—United Methodist Women shall be actively engaged in fulfilling the mission of Christ and the Church and United Methodist Women's national organization shall interpret the Purpose of United Methodist Women for the whole organization. With continuing awareness of the concerns and responsibilities of the Church in today's world, United Methodist Women shall support ministry with and advocate for the oppressed and dispossessed with special attention to the needs of women, children, and youth; shall work to build a supportive community among women; and shall engage in activities that foster growth in the Christian faith, mission education, and Christian social involvement throughout the organization.

¶ **1903.** *Responsibilities*—United Methodist Women's national organization shall:

1. Recommend program and policies to local, district, conference, and jurisdiction organizations of United Methodist Women.

2. Interpret the role and responsibility of United Methodist Women in fulfilling the mission of Christ and the Church.

3. Express the concerns of women organized for mission.

4. Provide resources and opportunities for women that enrich their spiritual life and increase their knowledge and understanding of the needs of the world and their responsibility in meeting those needs.

5. Secure funds through the channels of United Methodist Women for God's mission in the world, with special concern for the needs and responsibilities of women, children, and youth.

6. Project plans specially directed toward leadership development of women through appropriate planning with the other organizations of the church and ecumenical community.

7. Strengthen the Church's challenge to men and women to respond to God's call by serving as missionaries, deaconesses or home missioners, and in all other avenues of service and leadership in the church.

8. Enlist women in activities that have a moral and religious significance for the public welfare and that contribute to the establishment of a just global society.

9. Administer the Office of the Deaconess and Home Missioner Order.

10. Strengthen and support direct ministries to human need, both emerging and continuing, through national mission institutions working on behalf of women, children, and youth, and compassion response around the world.

11. Provide leadership and support for persons serving as regional missionaries.

12. Work with the other agencies of the Church and community in areas of common concern and responsibility. A United Nations Office shall be conducted in cooperation with the General Board of Church and Society.

13. Give visible evidence of oneness in Christ by uniting in fellowship and service with other Christians, including the World Federation of Methodist and Uniting Church Women, Church Women United, and other similar groups, thereby strengthening the ecumenical witness and program of the Church.

14. Participate in developing mission theology.

¶ **1904.** *Authority*—The Board of Directors of United Methodist Women shall meet at least annually and at such other times as it may deem necessary and shall have the authority to:

1. Make its bylaws and regulate its proceedings in harmony with its charter; buy and sell property; solicit and accept contributions, and appropriate its funds; decide on policy matters pertaining to the homes for retired workers that are owned by United Methodist Women. Organize jurisdiction, conference, district, and local church organizations of United Methodist Women, which shall be directly related to the national organization.

2. Make constitutions and recommend bylaws for United Methodist Women at local, district, conference, jurisdiction levels.

3. Appropriate funds received through United Methodist Women.

4. Serve as the national official policy-making body of United Methodist Women, with the officers of the national organization designated as the national officers.

¶ **1905.** *Successor entity*—United Methodist Women shall be the name of the organization of The United Methodist Church formerly known as Women's Division of the General Board of Global Ministries of The United Methodist Church, which shall succeed to, control, and be responsible for the work formerly carried out by the Woman's Society of Christian Service of The Methodist Church, the Women's Society of World Service of The Evangelical United Brethren Church, the Women's Society of Christian Service of The United Methodist Church, and those other organizations of women of similar purposes that have operated in the churches forming the United Methodist tradition, including the Women's Missionary Association of the Church of the United Brethren in Christ; the Woman's Missionary Society of The Evangelical Church; the Woman's Foreign Missionary Society, the Woman's Home Missionary Society, the Wesleyan Service Guild, and the Ladies' Aid Societies of The Methodist Episcopal Church; the Woman's Missionary Society, the Woman's Board of Foreign Missions, the Woman's Board of Home Missions, and the Woman's Missionary Council of The Methodist Episcopal Church, South; and the Woman's Convention of the Board of Missions of The Methodist Protestant Church. This list shall not be construed as exhaustive.

¶ **1906.** *Membership of the Board of Directors*—United Methodist Women shall have a board of directors composed of 25 members as follows: 20 shall be laywomen elected by the jurisdiction organizations of United Methodist Women at quadrennial meetings (¶ 536.4); and five shall be laywomen elected by the board of directors. The staff cabinet of United Methodist Women shall be members ex officio, without vote.

¶ **1907.** *Organization*—The board of directors of United Methodist Women may elect an executive committee of such membership as it may determine, which shall exercise the powers of the board *ad interim*. The members of the staff cabinet of United Methodist Women shall be members of the executive committee, ex officio without vote. The board of directors of United Methodist Women shall be organized into sections or committees as the directors shall determine.

¶ **1908.** *Assembly*—There may be an assembly of United Methodist Women. The board of directors of United Methodist Women shall determine the time and place of meeting and the purpose of the Assembly.

¶ **1909.** *Finances*—The funds for the fulfillment of the responsibilities of United Methodist Women shall be derived from annual voluntary pledges, offerings, gifts, devises, bequests, annuities, or money received through special emphases and meetings held in the interest of United Methodist Women. All funds, except those designated for local purposes, shall be forwarded through the channels of giving of the organization to the treasurer of United Methodist Women's national organization. The board of directors of United Methodist Women shall allocate undesignated funds it receives for the work of its various sections and committees as well as for grants and allocations to other organizations within the church and the world as may be necessary or useful for the fulfillment of its Purpose.

¶ **1910.** *Relationship to the General Board of Global Ministries*— The board of directors of United Methodist Women shall elect three members to serve as directors of the General Board of Global Ministries with voice and without vote. The elected United Methodist Women directors shall serve on the program committees as defined in the General Board of Global Ministries' bylaws.

¶ **1911.** *United Methodist Women Program Advisory Group*— United Methodist Women shall organize a Program Advisory Group to provide input at regular intervals to the board of directors about the program and planning of the organization. The Program Advisory Group shall have between 80-90 members including all members of the board of directors of United Methodist Women, the jurisdiction presidents, a representative from each conference organization of United Methodist Women not already represented on the board (elected on nomination of the conference nominating committee), two members of the Order of Deaconess and Home Missioner elected by the order, seven to ten directors from other agencies of The United Methodist Church including three members elected by the General Board of Global Ministries and up to five members selected by the board of directors of United Methodist Women for diversity of age, experience, cultural background, race, physical ability, and employment status. United Methodist Women's regional missionaries, a representative from the World Federation of Methodist and Uniting Church Women and a representative of its North America Region shall be ex officio members, with voice and without vote. The national president of United Methodist Women shall convene the sessions of this group, which may be organized in committees, groups, or teams as needed to accomplish its work.

¶ **1912.** *Constitution of United Methodist Women*—For the Constitution of United Methodist Women in the jurisdiction, see ¶ 536; for the Constitution of United Methodist Women in the conference, see ¶ 647; for the Constitution of United Methodist Women in the district, see ¶ 670; for the Constitution of United Methodist Women in the local church, see ¶ 256.5.

Office of Deaconess and Home Missioner

¶ 1913. *General Provisions*—1. There shall be in The United Methodist Church the Office of Deaconess and Home Missioner. The purpose of the Office of Deaconess and Home Missioner shall be to express representatively the love and concern of the believing community for the needs in the world and to enable, through education and involvement, the full ministry and mission of the people of God. Deaconesses and home missioners function through diverse forms of service directed toward the world to make Jesus Christ known in the fullness of his ministry and mission, which mandate that his followers:

a) Alleviate suffering;

b) Eradicate causes of injustice and all that robs life of dignity and worth;

c) Facilitate the development of full human potential; and

d) Share in building global community through the church universal.

2. Deaconesses, who are laywomen, and home missioners, who are laymen, are professionally trained persons who have been led by the Holy Spirit to devote their lives to Christlike service under the authority of the Church. They are approved through a process established by United Methodist Women, consecrated and commissioned by a bishop at settings approved by the board of directors of United Methodist Women. They shall have a continuing relationship to The United Methodist Church through United Methodist Women.

Deaconesses and home missioners are available for service with any agency or program of The United Methodist Church. Deaconesses and home missioners may also serve in other than United Methodist Church agencies or programs, provided that approval is given by United Methodist Women in consultation with the bishop of the receiving area.

3. Full-time service is the norm for the ministry of a deaconess or home missioner, meaning that the person's entire vocational time is devoted to work of ministry in the field of labor to which one is appointed by the bishop.

a) Appointments for deaconesses and home missioners shall be recommended in consultation with the bishop of the area, in accordance with the policies and procedures of United Methodist Women.

b) The appointment shall be fixed by the bishop (¶ 415.7) at the session of annual conference and printed in the list of appointments in the annual conference journal.

c) The annual conference secretary shall:

(1) Keep a record of all persons in the annual conference who have been commissioned and/or consecrated to the Office of Deaconess or Home Missioner.

(2) Publish annually in the annual conference journal the list of appointments of deaconesses and home missioners.

4. A deaconess or home missioner shall hold church membership in a local church within the conference where her or his appointment is located and shall be a voting member of the charge conference of that church. Those serving in appointments with a general board or connectional agency of The United Methodist Church or where annual conference borders meet may hold church membership in an annual conference within reasonable distance of the office location at which they serve. A deaconess or home missioner whose appointment is located outside the boundaries of an annual conference may hold her or his church membership in a local church in her or his home conference or in the local church in the annual conference in which she or he last held her or his church membership.

5. Deaconesses and home missioners shall be seated at the sessions of the annual conference with voice and vote as lay members of the annual conference in accordance with ¶¶ 32 and 602.4.

6. Deaconesses and home missioners shall be subject to the administrative authority of the program or agency to which they are appointed. In matters of their assignment they are subject to the authority of United Methodist Women and may not contract for service that would nullify this authority.

7. Each deaconess or home missioner shall enroll in a pension plan. The rights of any deaconess or home missioner in any prior or existing agreement or pension plan shall be fully protected.

8. A deaconess or home missioner may request a leave of absence according to the administrative guidelines and procedures of United Methodist Women.

9. Involuntary termination for a deaconess or home missioner shall follow the procedural guidelines as set forth in ¶ 2702.

¶ **1914.** *Deaconess and Home Missioner Order*—Individuals consecrated and commissioned to the Office of Deaconess and Home Missioner in The United Methodist Church form a covenant community as laity in service as an order. Like other orders in the church, they respond to a calling from God. In their distinct tradition, they commit to a lifetime vocation in full-time ministries of love, justice, and service. In covenant with one another, they nurture and care for each other in their individual ministry calls and in community. They share a common study and are prepared based upon their unique gifts.

¶ **1915.** *Home Missionaries*—All persons commissioned to the office of home missionary shall retain that office with all of the rights and privileges pertaining thereto.

¶ **1916.** *Committee on Deaconess and Home Missioner Service*— United Methodist Women's national organization will organize the Committee on Deaconess and Home Missioner Service.

1. The Committee on Deaconess and Home Missioner Service shall be composed of one bishop (active or retired) named by the Council of Bishops; two representatives of the Order of Deaconess and Home Missioner, named by the Order; two representatives of United Methodist Women, named by the board of directors of United Methodist Women; and one representative of the National Association of Deaconesses, Home Missioners, and Home Missionaries, named by the Association. The committee may name additional members as it deems necessary, but will consist of no more than twelve persons in total.

2. There may be an executive committee and other committees as necessary for carrying out the duties of the Committee on Deaconess and Home Missioner Service.

3. The work of the committee shall be carried out in accordance with the bylaws as approved by the board of directors of United Methodist Women.

¶ **1917.** *Supporting the Work of Deaconesses and Home Missioners*—United Methodist Women's national organization shall retain staff whose primary assignment is to represent deaconesses and home missioners on a national level and to maintain a community of professionally competent persons who are committed to service under authority of the Church. At least one of the executive staff assigned to the work of deaconess and home missioner shall be a deaconess or home missioner.

1. All administrative policies and procedures that pertain to deaconesses and home missioners shall also apply to home missionaries and be administered by the executive staff with primary

assignment to the work with deaconesses and home missioners (¶¶ 1913-1917).

2. There may be a national association of deaconesses, home missioners, and home missionaries in relationship with United Methodist Women.

3. There may be jurisdictional organizations of deaconesses, home missioners, and home missionaries and their support constituencies.

¶ **1918.** *Ecclesiastical Support*—Ecclesiastical support is an affirmation provided by The United Methodist Church to employers and professional certification organizations that a deaconess/ home missioner is in good standing and has the appropriate professional training and equipping for ministry in specialized settings. Ecclesiastical support acknowledges a covenant of mutual commitment, accountability and support between The United Methodist Church, through United Methodist Women, and the deaconess/home missioner. Deaconesses and home missioners who are called to and professionally trained for chaplain or counseling ministry are eligible for ecclesiastical support for service in ministries not requiring them to administer the sacraments. The ecclesiastical support approval policies, guidelines, and process for those commissioned/consecrated deaconesses and home missioners are administered by the administrative office for the Office of Deaconess and Home Missioner with United Methodist Women.

Section XIV. General Commission on Religion and Race

¶ **2001.** *Authorization and Establishment*—There shall be a General Commission on Religion and Race.

1. *Amenability and Accountability*—The general commission shall be amenable to the General Conference of the United Methodist Church. Between sessions of the General Conference, the commission shall be accountable to the Connectional Table by reporting and interpreting activities designed to fulfill the purpose of the commission and by cooperating with the council in the fulfillment of its legislated responsibilities.

¶ **2002.** *Purpose*—The purpose of the General Commission on Religion and Race shall be to challenge, lead, and equip the people of The United Methodist Church to become interculturally competent, to ensure institutional equity and to facilitate vital conversations about religion, race, and culture.

¶ **2003.** *Membership*—The total membership of the commission shall be twenty-one board members constituted in accordance with ¶ 705.3 of the General Provisions of the *Book of Discipline.* The board shall be organized to accomplish its work through elected officers as prescribed in ¶ 708. The membership shall be composed of:

1. Two bishops, including one from the central conferences, named by the Council of Bishops in accordance with ¶ 705.4*d*.

2. Each jurisdiction shall elect two members to the board in accordance with ¶ 705.3*a*. It is recommended that persons elected by each jurisdiction include persons who have demonstrated expertise in the areas of finance, program planning and evaluation, education, advocacy, and racial justice; and have indicated a desire to actively support the work assigned to the General Commission on Religion and Race. Other paragraphs of the *Discipline* notwithstanding, the secretary of the General Conference shall offer to each jurisdiction a suggested member allocation to ensure that when combined with the board members from the central conferences, the resulting membership will reflect a balance of clergy and laity, men and women. The secretary will also establish an equitable rotation to ensure that over the course of several quadrennia each jurisdiction will have the opportunity to elect a laywoman, a layman, and a clergy member.

3. Three central conference members named to the board by the Council of Bishops according to the provisions in ¶ 705.4*c*.

4. Other paragraphs of the *Discipline* notwithstanding, the members of the board shall elect six additional members based on the expertise needed to accomplish the fiduciary, generative, and strategic work of the board. Consideration should be given to achieving jurisdictional, lay/clergy, gender, racial/ethnic, and age balance.

¶ **2004.** *Vacancies*—Vacancies in the commission membership shall be filled by the procedure defined in ¶ 712 of the General Provisions.

¶ **2005.** *Officers*—The General Commission on Religion and Race shall elect as its officers a president, a vice president, a secretary, and such other officers as it shall deem necessary.

¶ **2006.** *Staff*—The General Commission on Religion and Race shall elect its general secretary quadrennially by written, electronic, or other means of secret balloting (¶ 713). The commission shall select by whatever process it chooses the additional staff needed to assist the general secretary in carrying out the commission's responsibilities.

¶ **2007.** *Finances*—The General Council on Finance and Administration shall make provision for the support of the work of the commission, including provision for a general secretary and associated staff and an office for the commission.

¶ **2008.** *Responsibilities*—The General Commission shall equip, hold accountable, and partner with the Council of Bishops, jurisdictions, central conferences, annual conferences, local churches, general agencies, and other connectional structures of The United Methodist Church and shall assume responsibilities for such matters as:

1. Empowering visible and prophetic leadership at every level of the Global Church with regards to race, ethnicity, and culture.

2. Providing training, resources, and consultation at all levels of the Global Church in order to:

a. Increase interculturally competent leaders who can engage in ministries that promote intentional diversity at every level of the Church.

b. Expand contextually relevant local church ministry in order to reach more people, younger people, and more diverse people.

c. Promote anti-racism efforts and challenge issues of privilege.

d. Work with cabinets, local churches, and Boards of Ordained Ministry to develop and support cross-racial/cross-cultural and multicultural ministries.

e. Engage in vital conversations about the realities of race and culture in local and global contexts through consultations, research, reports, and annual conference training.

3. Identifying and responding to global racism, ethnocentrism, and tribalism in order for the Church to more effectively move its mission forward in a diverse and global society.

4. Administering the CORR (Commission on Religion and Race) Action Fund. The CORR Action Fund is established by the General Conference of The United Methodist Church for the empowerment of diversity, inclusion, and racial justice work within and outside the Church. The fund:

a) is available through grants to congregations, connectional structures, and other groups.

b) shall be administered by the General Commission on Religion and Race on behalf of The United Methodist Church. The General Commission shall be responsible for developing guidelines and policies regarding grants and for evaluation of projects receiving support.

5. Providing resources and consultations for just and equitable policies and processes at every level of the Global Church.

Section XV. General Commission on the Status and Role of Women

¶ **2101.** There shall be a General Commission on the Status and Role of Women in The United Methodist Church.

¶ **2102.** *Purpose*—The primary purpose of the General Commission on the Status and Role of Women shall be to challenge The United Methodist Church, including its general agencies, institutions, and connectional structures, to a continuing commitment to the full and equal responsibility and participation of women in the total life and mission of the Church, sharing fully in the power and in the policy-making at all levels of the Church's life.

Such commitment will confirm anew recognition of the fact that The United Methodist Church is part of the universal church, rooted in the liberating message of Jesus Christ, that recognizes every person, woman or man, as a full and equal part of God's human family.

The general commission shall function as an advocate with and on behalf of women individually and collectively within The United Methodist Church; as a catalyst for the initiation of creative methods to redress inequities of the past and to prevent further inequities against women within The United Methodist Church; and as a monitor to ensure inclusiveness in the programmatic and administrative functioning of The United Methodist Church.

¶ **2103.** *Responsibility*—The general commission shall be charged with the responsibility of fostering an awareness of issues, problems, and concerns related to the status and role of women, with special reference to their full participation in the total life of the Church at least commensurate with the total membership of women in The United Methodist Church.

1. In the fulfillment of its mandate, this commission shall have the authority to initiate and utilize such channels, develop such plans and strategies, and assign staff as may be required in the implementation of the following primary needs across The

United Methodist Church: leadership enablement, resources and communication, affirmative action and advocacy roles, and interagency coordination.

Such plans and strategies related to these needs shall be directed toward the elimination of sexism in all its manifestations from the total life of The United Methodist Church, including general agencies as well as the various connectional channels and structures that reach the local church. The commission shall work with the respective agencies as needs may determine in achieving and safeguarding representation and participation of women, including racial and ethnic groups.

2. The commission, through its various research and monitoring processes, shall continue to gather data, make recommendations, and suggest guidelines for action as appropriate to eradicate discriminatory policies and practices in any form or discriminatory language and images wherever found in documents, pronouncements, publications, and general resources.

3. The commission shall stimulate ongoing evaluation procedures and receive progress reports toward the end of effecting the guidelines in § 2 above in all responsible bodies of the Church.

4. The commission shall establish and maintain a working relationship with annual conference commissions, taking into account the objectives and guidelines for conferences in ¶ 644.1 and seeking to develop and strengthen the leadership of the conference for the realization of these objectives within the general context of the responsibilities of the general commission (¶ 2103.1).

5. The commission shall recommend plans and curricula for new understanding of theology and biblical history affecting the status of women. The commission shall also be encouraged to explore the relationships between spiritual gifts and women in the Bible.

6. The commission shall create needed policies and recommendations and program for immediate and long-range implementation related to the enhancement of the role of women in professional and voluntary leadership in the Church.

7. The commission shall serve in an advocacy role to ensure openness and receptivity in matters related to women's role in the Church's life, with particular attention to the contributions of clergy and lay professional women, racial and ethnic women, and those experiencing changing lifestyles. The commission in its role as advocate shall assist the local church, annual conferences,

the councils, boards, commissions, schools of theology, and other related institutions on eradicating the problems of sexual harassment by developing policies and procedures for addressing these problems.

8. The commission shall generate active concern and give full support toward immediate efforts in the fulfillment of the following directive: Councils, boards, commissions, committees, personnel recruitment agencies, schools of theology, and other related institutions are directed to establish guidelines and policies for specific recruitment, training, and full utilization of women in total employment, which includes but is not limited to pastoral and related ministries, health and welfare ministries, and faculties and staffs of seminaries and other educational institutions.

9. Advise the General Council on Finance and Administration (¶ 811.1) with regard to the policies and practices of agencies and Church-related institutions receiving general Church funds concerning their implementation of the denomination's policy of inclusiveness and nondiscrimination on the basis of gender. This shall be done by: (1) consulting with the council in development, review, and maintenance of the certification form to be submitted to the council by agencies and institutions receiving general Church funds; (2) reviewing annually the submissions of certifications of compliance with ¶ 811.1*a, b,* and *c;* and (3) recommending to the council acceptance of the certifications, or other appropriate action, including withholding approval of the entire budget of an agency or institution because of noncompliance with ¶ 811.1*a, b,* or *c.*

10. The commission shall provide resources for the local church ministry group on the status and role of women.

11. The commission shall assist in addressing the problem of sexual misconduct in the church. The commission shall provide leadership in providing resources for the prevention of and education about misconduct of a sexual nature, training opportunities for clergy and laity, policy and procedural recommendations for transformative and administrative fair processes, victim/survivor support, and congregational healing. The commission shall promote interagency coordination through its leadership of the Interagency Sexual Ethics Task Force and by assisting annual conferences, local churches, councils, boards, commissions, schools of theology, and other related institutions in witnessing to healthy boundaries within ministerial relationships.

¶ **2104.** *Membership*—1. The policies, plans, and administration of the work of the general commission shall be determined by its membership, which shall be composed of nineteen persons in accord with the following guidelines:

a) Jurisdictional membership shall be nominated and elected by the jurisdictional conferences, ensuring that the pluralism and diversity of the Church's membership is reflected in the representation of racial and ethnic minorities and various age categories. Each jurisdiction shall elect one person for membership. Before election, nominated members will be informed of the fiduciary, strategic, and generative responsibilities they will be assuming upon election so that they may clearly understand the time and resource commitment they are making. Other paragraphs of the *Discipline* notwithstanding, the secretary of the General Conference shall offer to each jurisdiction a suggested member allocation to ensure that, when combined with the board members from central conferences, the resulting membership will reflect a balance of clergywomen and clergymen, laywomen and laymen. The secretary will also establish an equitable rotation to ensure that over the course of several quadrennial each jurisdiction will have the opportunity to elect a laywoman, a layman, a clergywoman, and a clergyman.

b) There shall be nine additional members elected by the general commission, in accord with the provisions of ¶ 705.3*a*. The election of the additional members shall take into account the need to provide adequate representation of racial, ethnic, and national origin groups; persons with disabilities; persons from the various age categories, and to include persons of special competence, and striving for proportional representation among the jurisdictions. It is recommended that the addition of the at-large membership ensure that the total membership maintains a balance, 50 percent clergy (including the range of clergy as defined in ¶ 142) and 50 percent lay, as well as majority membership of women. It is further recommended that such additional members shall maintain a membership total of at least 10 percent youth and 10 percent young adults. Before election, nominated members will be informed of the fiduciary, strategic, and generative responsibilities they will be assuming upon election so that they may clearly understand the time and resource commitment they are making.

c) There shall be two bishops, including at least one from the central conferences, named by the Council of Bishops.

d) There shall be three central conference members, not including the central conference bishop, named to the board by the Council of Bishops according to the provisions in ¶ 705.4*c.*

e) The general commission shall be authorized to fill vacancies in its membership during the quadrennium.

f) Members who do not meet the requirements of ¶ 2506.1 shall serve with voice and vote, except in matters related to the fiduciary responsibilities of the board, in which they shall have voice only and not vote in accordance with the laws of the state of incorporation (Illinois).

g) The board may name other individuals as liaison representatives to provide networking and advice related to the areas of mutual concern. Likewise, United Methodist Women may name one or two such liaison representatives who may serve for a full quadrennium. When present at board meetings, liaison representatives shall have voice but not vote.

2. Members of the General Commission on the Status and Role of Women shall assume fiduciary, strategic, and generative governing functions. Fiduciary responsibilities include ensuring financial, legal, and ethical stewardship of tangible assets; accountability for stated performance standards; ensuring the annual evaluation of the general secretary; and providing counsel to the general secretary regarding evaluation and deployment of staff. Strategic responsibilities include ensuring that priorities, goals, achievement markers, and agency resources are aligned with the mission, vision, and value of the agency. Generative responsibilities include long-range analysis and planning in accordance with agency mission, vision, and values; setting direction and priorities for the agency; and exploring options in order to amend priorities when needed.

3. Members of the General Commission on the Status and Role of Women (GCSRW) are to be dedicated Christian leaders who have a passion for ensuring the full and equal participation of women at all levels of the Church. They must be willing to invest time and skills to support the work of the board, including interpreting and articulating GCSRW strategy in a variety of contexts. They must engage in regular and intentional conversation with networks and individuals throughout the Church to ensure that the wide diversity of people and perspectives present in The United Methodist Church are considered as the board carries out its responsibilities. They must be committed to supporting and

implementing the mandates and foci of the general Church as well as the General Commission on the Status and Role of Women.

¶ 2105. *Officers*—The president of the general commission shall be a woman elected by the total commission from its membership. Other officers shall be elected as the commission determines.

¶ 2106. *Meetings*—The general commission shall meet annually, with such additional meetings as needs demand.

¶ 2107. *Funding*—The funds for carrying out the general commission's purpose shall be authorized by the General Conference.

¶ 2108. *Staff*—The general commission shall elect quadrennially by ballot its general secretariat or general secretary who shall provide executive, administrative, and program staff leadership (¶ 713). The commission shall elect such other staff members as needs require within the General Conference mandates and the authority vested in the commission to develop policies and programs directed toward the realization of its purpose.

¶ 2109. *Relationships*—In order to fulfill its responsibilities and the directives of the General Conference, the general commission shall work with the Council of Bishops, the general agencies, institutions, and other appropriate structures and channels at all levels of the Church.

Section XVI. Standing Committee on Central Conference Matters

¶ 2201. *General Provisions*—1. The General Conference recognizes the differences in conditions that exist in various areas of the world and the changes taking place in those areas. There shall be a Standing Committee on Central Conference Matters serving as an independent coordinating body. The General Board of Global Ministries shall be the facilitating agency to the standing committee. The standing committee shall serve as the coordinating body to study the structure and supervision of The United Methodist Church in its work outside the United States and its territories and its relationships to other Church bodies.

2. The standing committee shall meet at least twice within the quadrennium in order to review, consider, and develop resolutions and petitions related to central conferences and may be called into session during General Conference as needed. It shall review and prepare such recommendations as it considers necessary for presentation directly to the General Conference. The com-

mittee shall submit its report and recommendations in accordance with the timelines governing general agencies for submission of petitions and resolutions. All resolutions and petitions related to central conferences presented to the General Conference shall be referred to the committee for consideration, and the committee shall report its recommendations directly to the General Conference. On matters dealing with the determination of episcopal areas (¶ 404.1), affiliation and autonomy (¶ 572), and joining The United Methodist Church (¶ 575), the committee shall report directly to the General Conference.

3. Other paragraphs of the *Discipline* notwithstanding, members may serve for three (3) four-year terms and may serve on one other general agency. The standing committee shall be composed of one bishop from each jurisdiction and from each central conference named by the Council of Bishops; one ordained minister and one layperson from each jurisdiction and from each central conference who are delegates to the General Conference and named by the Council of Bishops; central conferences with more than three episcopal areas shall elect additional members, lay or clergy, up to the total number of episcopal areas in the central conference; one bishop, one ordained minister, and one layperson who are members of the General Board of Global Ministries and named by the General Board of Global Ministries. The central conference bishop assigned to the Office of Christian Unity and Interreligious Relationships shall also be a member of this committee. Special attention shall be given to the inclusion of women, lay, clergy, youth, and young adults. The chairperson of the committee shall be a central conference bishop and shall also serve as a member of the Connectional Table. (This legislation will take effect immediately upon action by General Conference for the membership of the Standing Committee on Central Conference Matters for 2016-2020.)

4. The Standing Committee on Central Conference Matters will convene at the conclusion of the General Conference at which it was elected and continue its work through the following General Conference. To facilitate transition, incoming members shall participate in the deliberations of the committee during such General Conference, having voice but no vote until the organizing meeting.

5. The General Council on Finance and Administration shall recommend to the General Conference for its action and

determination a provision in the budget of an appropriate general Church fund for the expenses incurred by the standing committee.

Section XVII. General Commission on United Methodist Men

¶ **2301.** There shall be a General Commission on United Methodist Men in The United Methodist Church.

The general commission shall be amenable to the General Conference of The United Methodist Church. Between sessions of the General Conference, the general commission shall be accountable to the Connectional Table by reporting and interpreting activities in its purpose (¶ 702.3).

¶ **2302.** *Purpose*—The General Commission on United Methodist Men shall have primary oversight for the coordination and resourcing of men's ministry within The United Methodist Church.

1. United Methodist Men exists to declare the centrality of Christ in every man's life. Men's ministry leads to the spiritual growth of men and effective discipleship. This purpose is served as men are called to model the servant leadership of Jesus Christ.

2. Individual and group strategies form the foundation of UMMen ministry:

a) enhance Evangelism, Mission, and Spiritual Life (EMS), as men become servant leaders.

b) advocate programs that train men within local churches to promote specific ministries including prayer, missions, stewardship, and civic/youth-serving ministries.

c) forge pastoral partnerships by men committed to the effective support and service of clergy and local congregations.

d) enhance organizational strength by effective leadership, resources, membership growth, and financial accountability.

e) assist men in their ever-changing relationships, roles and responsibilities in their family setting, workplace, and society.

f) cultivate leadership among men for a policy of no tolerance of sexual harassment in family, church, workplace and society

g) understand the organization, doctrines, and beliefs of The United Methodist Church.

h) fulfill the membership vows through commitment to prayer, presence, gifts, service, and witness in congregational life.

i) fulfill the Great Commission with and through The United Methodist Church as one part of the body of Christ.

3. To provide support services to promote the ministry and growth of United Methodist Men:

a) provide specific and optional models for men in the local church, district, annual conference, and jurisdiction;

b) maintain effective communications and cooperation with the National Association of Conference Presidents of United Methodist Men and other national organizations representing the central conferences and other worldwide Methodist liaisons;

c) promote the annual certification of local church men's ministry and the chartering/annual renewal of local church men's units (¶ 256.6) with the General Commission on United Methodist Men.

4. To provide resources that assist men in their growing relationship with the Lord Jesus Christ and his church:

a) programs of evangelism that are geared to men's needs in cooperation with all areas of the Church dealing with the area of evangelism that model to men that witness is an integral part of daily life;

b) programs of mission in cooperation with all areas of the Church dealing with missional opportunities enabling men for outreach and service as an integral part of their Christian discipleship;

c) programs of spiritual life in cooperation with areas of faith development will assist men to realize that witness and outreach, with mission and ministry, become extensions of their faith development and their personal relationship to God through Jesus Christ;

d) programs of stewardship in cooperation with the area of stewardship that will lead men to an understanding of their responsibility as stewards of God's creation and personal stewardship of time, talent, money, and prayer;

e) programs that affirm the role of men in their family situations;

f) to advocate, research, and develop programs for The United Methodist Church to minister to and through men;

g) program partnership with The Upper Room in the Living Prayer Center ministry, including support for toll free telephone service and promotion. At all levels of the United Methodist Men's network there shall be prayer advocates;

h) United Methodist Men shall be in partnership with other general agencies and be a resource for men engaged in restorative justice and prison ministries.

5. The General Commission will provide resources and support for the office of Civic Youth-Serving Agencies/Scouting Ministries:

    a) to provide training of local church, district, annual conference, and jurisdictional scouting coordinators;

    b) to promote and counsel with youth-serving organizations selected at the discretion of the commission;

    c) to coordinate, promote, and resource as needed annual conference Bishop's Dinners for Scouting.

¶ **2303.** *Membership*—1. The commission shall consist of twenty (20) voting members as defined in ¶ 705.3 in the General Provisions and ¶ 537. Other paragraphs of the *Discipline* notwithstanding, members of the commission holding membership by office or organization, may serve a maximum of three consecutive terms. The membership shall be composed of:

    a) three bishops, including at least one from the central conferences, named by the Council of Bishops;

    b) the five (5) jurisdictional presidents of United Methodist Men;

    c) the president of the National Association of Conference Presidents of United Methodist Men;

    d) two central conference members named by the Council of Bishops;

    e) the president of the United Methodist Men Foundation;

    f) eight (8) members at large elected by the commission for inclusiveness, expertise, and balance, which should include at least one young person under the age of 30 and at least two members of the commission from the previous quadrennium.;

    g) The commission may include one representative from a men's ministry from a Pan-Methodist Church.

2. *Vacancies*—Vacancies in the general commission membership shall be filled by procedures defined in ¶ 712 of the General Provisions.

3. *Officers*—The General Commission on United Methodist Men shall elect as its officers a president, vice president, secretary, treasurer, and other such officers as it shall deem necessary. In addition, the president of the National Association of Conference Presidents of United Methodist Men shall also be considered an officer.

4. *Staff*—The General Commission on United Methodist Men shall elect quadrennially by ballot its general secretary, who shall

provide executive, administrative, and programmatic leadership
(¶ 713). The commission shall elect such other staff members as
needs require within the General Conference mandates and the
authority vested in the commission to develop policies and programs directed toward the realization of its purpose.

5. *Meetings*—The general commission shall meet annually,
with such additional meetings as needs demand.

6. *Funding*—The General Council on Finance and Administration shall make provision for the necessary support of the work
of the commission by providing World Service Funds to complement the direct revenue and contributions from United Methodist
Men.

7. *Advisory panel*—The commission may create an advisory
panel consisting of representatives of affiliated organizations.

Section XVIII: JUSTPEACE Center for Mediation and Conflict Transformation

¶ **2401.** 1. *Mission*—JUSTPEACE Center for Mediation and
Conflict Transformation is a mission of The United Methodist
Church to engage conflict constructively in ways that strive for
justice, reconciliation, resource preservation and restoration of
community in and through The United Methodist Church and
with the Church universal to the world in which we live.

2. *Relationship With the Church*—JUSTPEACE shall be an
incorporated resource of The United Methodist Church. It shall
be accountable to the General Conference and in order to fulfill
its mission be authorized to seek and create relationships with
the agencies and organizations of The United Methodist Church
and other organizations, while preserving its role as an impartial
entity. JUSTPEACE shall be proactive in its efforts to transform
conflict by accepting invitations to intervene in conflicts, train
church leaders and members of annual conference conflict transformation teams in conflict transformation, connect and nurture a
community of practitioners, and develop resources.

3. *Financial Support*—Either on behalf of its total work or
on behalf of a specific program, JUSTPEACE may charge fees,
solicit and create special funds or endowments, receive gifts and
bequests, hold properties and securities in trust, and administer
all its financial affairs in accordance with its own rules and relevant provisions of the *Book of Discipline.*

Chapter Six
CHURCH PROPERTY

Section I. All Titles—In Trust

¶ **2501.** *Requirement of the Trust Clause for All Property*—1. All properties of United Methodist local churches and other United Methodist agencies and institutions are held, *in trust*, for the benefit of the entire denomination, and ownership and usage of church property is subject to the *Discipline*. This trust requirement is an essential element of the historic polity of The United Methodist Church or its predecessor denominations or communions and has been a part of the *Discipline* since 1797. It reflects the connectional structure of the Church by ensuring that the property will be used solely for purposes consonant with the mission of the entire denomination as set forth in the *Discipline*. The trust requirement is thus a fundamental expression of United Methodism whereby local churches and other agencies and institutions within the denomination are both held accountable to and benefit from their connection with the entire worldwide Church.

In consonance with the legal definition and self-understanding of The United Methodist Church (see ¶ 141), and with particular reference to its lack of capacity to hold title to property, The United Methodist Church is organized as a connectional structure, and titles to all real and personal, tangible and intangible property held at jurisdictional, annual, or district conference levels, or by a local church or charge, or by an agency or institution of the Church, shall be held in trust for The United Methodist Church and subject to the provisions of its *Discipline*. Titles are not held by The United Methodist Church (see ¶ 807.1) or by the General Conference of The United Methodist Church, but instead by the incorporated conferences, agencies, or organizations of the denomination, or in the case of unincorporated bodies of the denomination, by boards of trustees established for the purpose of holding and administering real and personal, tangible and intangible property.

2. The trust is and always has been irrevocable, except as provided in the *Discipline*. Property can be released from the trust, transferred free of trust or subordinated to the interests of creditors and other third parties only to the extent authority is given by the *Discipline*.

3. Local churches and other United Methodist agencies and institutions may acquire, hold, maintain, improve, and sell property for purposes consistent with the mission of the Church, unless restricted or prevented by the *Discipline*.

¶ **2502.** *Registration of the Name* United Methodist—The words *United Methodist* are not to be used as, or as a part of, a trade name or trademark or as a part of the name of any business firm or organization, except by corporations or other business units created for the administration of work undertaken directly by The United Methodist Church. The General Council on Finance and Administration is charged with supervision and registration of "United Methodist" and the denomination's insignia (¶ 807.10 and ¶ 807.11).

¶ **2503.** *Trust Clauses in Deeds*—1. Except in conveyances that require that the real property so conveyed shall revert to the grantor if and when its use as a place of divine worship has been terminated, all written instruments of conveyance by which premises are held or hereafter acquired for use as a place of divine worship or other activities for members of The United Methodist Church shall contain the following trust clause:[1]

In trust, that said premises shall be used, kept, and maintained as a place of divine worship of the United Methodist ministry and members of The United Methodist Church; subject to the Discipline, *usage, and ministerial appointments of said Church as from time to time authorized and declared by the General Conference and by the annual conference within whose bounds the said premises are situated. This provision is solely for the benefit of the grantee, and the grantor reserves no right or interest in said premises.*

2. All written instruments by which premises are held or hereafter acquired as a parsonage for the use and occupancy of the ministers of The United Methodist Church shall contain the following trust clause:

In trust, that such premises shall be held, kept, and maintained as a place of residence for the use and occupancy of the ordained ministers of The United Methodist Church who may from time to time be entitled to occupy the same by appointment; subject to the Discipline *and usage of said Church as from time to time authorized and declared by the General Conference and by the annual conference within whose bounds the said premises are situated. This provision is solely for the benefit of the grantee, and the grantor reserves no right or interest in said premises.*

---

1. See Judicial Council Decision 688.

3. In case the property so acquired is to be used for both a house of worship and a parsonage, the provisions of both trust clauses specified in §§ 1 and 2 above shall be inserted in the conveyance.

4. In case the property so acquired is not to be used exclusively for a place of worship, or a parsonage, or both, all written instruments by which such premises are held or hereafter acquired shall contain the following trust clause:

In trust, that said premises shall be kept, maintained, and disposed of for the benefit of The United Methodist Church and subject to the usages and the Discipline *of The United Methodist Church. This provision is solely for the benefit of the grantee, and the grantor reserves no right or interest in said premises.*

5. When property is acquired from another United Methodist entity or organization, whether it is to be used as a place of divine worship, parsonage, or other use, all written instruments by which such premises are held or hereafter acquired shall contain the following trust clause:

In trust, that said premises shall be held, kept, maintained, and disposed of for the benefit of The United Methodist Church and subject to the usages and the Discipline *of The United Methodist Church.*

6. However, the absence of a trust clause stipulated in §§ 1, 2, 3, 4, or 5 above in deeds and conveyances executed previously or in the future shall in no way exclude a local church or church agency, or the board of trustees of either, from or relieve it of its connectional responsibilities to The United Methodist Church. Nor shall it absolve a local church or church agency or the board of trustees of either, of its responsibility and accountability to The United Methodist Church, including the responsibility to hold all of its property in trust for The United Methodist Church; provided that the intent of the founders and/or a later local church or church agency, or the board of trustees of either, is shown by any or all of the following:

a) the conveyance of the property to a local church or church agency (or the board of trustees of either) of The United Methodist Church or any predecessor to The United Methodist Church;

b) the use of the name, customs, and polity of The United Methodist Church or any predecessor to The United Methodist Church in such a way as to be thus known to the community as a part of such denomination; or *c)* the acceptance of the pastorate of ordained ministers appointed by a bishop or employed by the superintendent of the district or annual conference of The United Methodist Church or any predecessor to The United Methodist Church.

¶ **2504.** *Effect of Union*—Nothing in the Plan of Union at any time after the union is to be construed so as to require any existing local church of any predecessor denomination to The United Methodist Church to alienate or in any way to change the title to property contained in its deed or deeds at the time of union, and lapse of time or usage shall not affect said title or control. Title to all property of a local church, or charge, or agency of the Church shall be held subject to the provisions of the *Discipline,* whether title to the same is taken in the name of the local church trustees, or charge trustees, or in the name of a corporation organized for the purpose, or otherwise.

¶ **2505.** *Oil, Gas, and Mineral Leases*—Subject to and in accordance with the laws of the state, province, or country, the governing body of any church unit or agency owning land in trust for The United Methodist Church as provided in this *Discipline* may lease said land for the production of oil, gas, coal, and other minerals, upon such terms as it may deem best; provided, however, that such production shall not interfere with the purpose for which said land is held. The moneys received from such leases as rentals, royalties, or otherwise shall be used so far as practicable for the benefit of the church unit and for the promotion of the interests of The United Methodist Church. The lessee shall have no control over or responsibility for the payments made under such lease.

Section II. Compliance With Law

¶ **2506.** *Conformity With Local Law—Church Corporations—* 1. All provisions of the *Discipline* relating to property, both real and personal, and relating to the formation and operation of any corporation, and relating to mergers are conditioned upon their being in conformity with the local laws, and in the event of conflict therewith the local laws shall prevail; provided, however, that this requirement shall not be construed to give the consent of The United Methodist Church to deprivation of its property without due process of law or to the regulation of its affairs by state statute where such regulation violates the constitutional guarantee of freedom of religion and separation of church and state or violates the right of the Church to maintain its connectional structure. *Local laws* shall be construed to mean the laws of the country, state, or other like political unit within the geographical bounds of which the church property is located.[2]

2. Any corporation which is or has been formed or is controlled by a church agency (¶ 701), acting alone or with another church agency, shall include in its articles of incorporation (or charter) and its bylaws ("corporate documents") the following:

a) identification of the sponsoring church agency or agencies ("sponsor(s)") to which it relates and the relationship of the corporation to its sponsor(s),

b) recognition that its corporate powers are subject to the *Discipline* to the same extent as its sponsor(s), and

c) recognition that the corporation's powers cannot exceed those given by the *Discipline* to its sponsor(s).

3. The corporate documents shall contain language consistent with the Internal Revenue Code to protect its tax-exempt status. Also, the corporate documents shall name the corporation's sponsor(s) as the recipient(s) of corporate property in the event the corporation is abandoned, discontinued, or ceases to exist as a legal entity. The corporate documents shall also include a reference to the provisions of ¶ 2501.

4. The corporate documents shall contain provisions prohibiting the corporation's trustees, directors, or officers from changing the corporation's connectional relationship to its sponsor(s) without the sponsor(s)' consent, or otherwise acting in a manner contrary to the purpose of its sponsor(s) or the *Discipline*.

¶ **2507.** *The Terms* Trustee, Trustees, *and* Board of Trustees— *Trustee, trustees,* and *board of trustees,* as used herein or elsewhere in the *Discipline,* may be construed to be synonymous with *director, directors,* and *board of directors* applied to corporations.

¶ **2508.** *Conformity of Deeds and Conveyances with Local Law*— In order to secure the right of property, with the appurtenances thereof, of the churches and parsonages of The United Methodist Church, care shall be taken that all conveyances and deeds be drawn and executed in due conformity to the laws of the respective states, provinces, and countries in which the property is situated and also in due conformity to the laws of The United Methodist Church. Deeds shall be registered or recorded directly upon their execution.

---

2. See Judicial Council Decision 315.

¶ **2509.** *Instituting and Defending Civil Action*—Because of the nature of The United Methodist Church (¶ 141), no individual or affiliated church body or unit, nor any official thereof, may commence or participate in any suit or proceeding in the name of or on behalf of The United Methodist Church, excepting, however, the following:

1. The General Council on Finance and Administration or any person or church unit served with legal process in the name of The United Methodist Church may appear for the purpose of presenting to the court the nonjural nature of The United Methodist Church and to raise issues of lack of jurisdiction of the court, lack of capacity of such individual or unit to be served with process, and related constitutional issues in defense of denominational interests.

2. Any denominational unit authorized to hold title to property and to enforce trusts for the benefit of the denomination may bring suit in its own name to protect denominational interests.

¶ **2510.** *Limitation of Financial Obligations*—No conference, council, board, agency, local church, or other unit can financially obligate the denomination or, without prior specific consent, any other organizational unit thereof.

Section III. Audits and Bonding of Church Officers

¶ **2511.** All persons holding trust funds, securities, or moneys of any kind belonging to the General, jurisdictional, annual, or provisional annual conferences or to organizations under the control of the General, jurisdictional, annual, or provisional annual conferences shall be bonded by a reliable company in such good and sufficient sum as the conference may direct. The accounts of such persons shall be audited at least annually by a recognized public or certified public accountant. A report to an annual conference containing a financial statement that the *Discipline* requires to be audited shall not be approved until the audit is made and the financial statement is shown to be correct. Other parts of the report may be approved pending such audit.

Section IV. Annual Conference Property[3]

¶ **2512.** 1. *Conference Trustees*—Each annual conference may be incorporated in its own name if permitted by local law. It shall

---

3. For authority regarding property held by general agencies of the Church, see ¶ 807.6, .8.

have a board of trustees, which shall be incorporated if the conference itself is not incorporated. In either case, the board shall consist of twelve persons, and it is recommended that one-third be clergy, one third laywomen, and one-third laymen, in accordance with the provisions of ¶ 610.5.[4] Said persons must be of legal age as determined by law, and lay members shall be members in good standing of local churches within the bounds of the conference. Such persons shall be the directors of the corporation. They shall be elected by the conference for staggered terms of four years, except for the first board, one-fourth of whom shall be elected for a term of one year, one-fourth for a term of two years, one-fourth for a term of three years, and one-fourth for a term of four years, and shall serve until their successors have been elected; provided, however, that existing incorporated trustees of any annual conference may continue unaffected while the charter or articles of incorporation are amended to bring them into conformity with this paragraph.

2. The board of trustees shall meet at least annually and organize by electing a president, vice president, secretary, and treasurer, whose duties shall be those usually pertaining to such offices. They shall be amenable to the annual conference. Vacancies occurring between sessions of an annual conference shall be filled as follows: Upon nomination by the conference committee on nominations, the district superintendents shall, by majority vote, elect a trustee to serve until the next annual conference. Vacancies shall be filled by the annual conference for the unexpired term.[5]

3. The board of trustees shall have the following authority with respect to the properties of the annual conference and its agencies:

a) The said corporation shall receive, collect, and hold in trust for the benefit of the annual conference any and all donations, bequests, and devises of any kind or character, real or personal, that may be given, devised, bequeathed, or conveyed to the said board or to the annual conference as such for any benevolent, charitable, or religious purpose, and shall administer the same and the income therefrom in accordance with the directions of the donor, trustor, or testator and in the interest of the church, society, institution, or agency contemplated by such donor, trustor, or testator,

---

4. See Judicial Council Decision 446.
5. See Judicial Council Decision 1170.

under the direction of the annual conference. When the use to be made of any such donation, bequest, or devise is not otherwise designated, the same shall be used as directed by the annual conference.

b) When so directed by the annual conference, the said corporation may receive and hold in trust for and on behalf of the annual conference, its districts, or any of its agencies any real or personal property previously acquired by the conference, its districts, or its agencies to be used in carrying out their mission, ministry, and program. When such property is in the form of investable funds, the board of trustees may consider placing the funds for investment and administration with the United Methodist conference or area foundation serving that conference or, in the absence of such a foundation, with the United Methodist Church Foundation. A conscious effort shall be made to invest in a manner consistent with the Social Principles and the creation of an investment policy. With respect to such properties, the board shall take no action that would alter or interfere with their missional or programmatic use or function unless such action is specifically directed by the annual conference. The provisions of this subsection shall not apply to educational or health and welfare institutions whose properties are held in their own name or in the name of their own duly elected boards of trustees or directors; nor shall they apply to the property of local churches except as such local church property may have been declared discontinued or abandoned under the provisions of ¶ 2549.

c) Except as restricted in § 3*b*, the board shall have the power to invest, reinvest, buy, sell, transfer, and convey any and all funds and properties that it may hold in trust, subject always to the terms of the legacy, devise, or donation.

d) Unless the annual conference provides otherwise, any contract, deed, bill of sale, mortgage, or other necessary written instrument needed to implement any resolution authorizing proposed action regarding annual conference property may be executed by and on behalf of the annual conference board of trustees by any two of its officers, who thereupon shall be duly authorized to carry out the direction of the annual conference; and any written instrument so executed shall be binding and effective as the action of the annual conference.

e) The conference board of trustees is encouraged to invest in institutions, companies, corporations, or funds that make a positive contribution toward the realization of the goals of the Social Principles of our Church. The board of trustees shall act as a socially responsible investor and report annually to the annual conference regarding its carrying out of this responsibility. Among the tools the board may use are shareholder advocacy, selective divestment, advocacy of corporate disinvestment from certain countries or fields of business, and affirmative investments (as in affordable housing, care of the environment, minority business and banks, and so forth), as well as other appropriate strategies.

f) Funds committed to this board may be invested by it only in collateral that is amply secured and after such investments have been approved by the said board or its agency or committee charged with such investment, unless otherwise directed by the annual conference.[6]

4. The board may intervene and take all necessary legal steps to safeguard and protect the interests and rights of the annual conference anywhere and in all matters relating to property and rights to property whether arising by gift, devise, or otherwise, or where held in trust or established for the benefit of the annual conference or its membership.

5. It shall be the duty of the pastor within the bounds of whose charge any such gift, bequest, or devise is made to give prompt notice thereof to said board, which shall proceed to take such steps as are necessary and proper to conserve, protect, and administer the same; provided, however, that the board may decline to receive or administer any such gift, devise, or bequest for any reason satisfactory to the board. It shall also be the duty of the pastor to report annually to the board of trustees of the annual conference a list of all property, including real, personal, or mixed, within the charge belonging to or which should be under the control or jurisdiction of the said board.

6. The board shall make to each session of the annual conference a full, true, and faithful report of its doings, of all funds, monies, securities, and property held in trust by it, and of its receipts and disbursements during the conference year. The beneficiary of a fund held in trust by the board shall also be entitled to a report at least annually on the condition of such fund and on the transactions affecting it.

---

6. See Judicial Council Decisions 160, 190.

7. *Establishment of Annual Conference Policy With Regard to Gov-ernment Efforts to Designate Church-Owned Property as Landmarks*—The board, after consultation with the conference commission on archives and history, or alternate structure, shall develop a policy for an annual conference response, on behalf of any local church, Church-related agency, or district or annual conference board of trustees located within the bounds of the annual conference, to any governmental effort to designate a property held in trust for the benefit of The United Methodist Church (¶ 2501) by any such board of trustees as a cultural, historical, or architectural landmark.

8. In cooperation with the General Council on Finance and Administration, related annual conference agencies and institutions, and local churches, to make recommendations to the annual conference regarding the development, promotion, and review of a broad general program of insurance protection, except for employee benefit programs.

¶ 2513. *United Methodist Foundations*—An annual conference or conferences may establish a United Methodist Foundation. The purposes for establishing such a foundation may include:

1. Providing the services described in ¶ 2512.3 as designated by the donor or upon delegation from the conference board of trustees;

2. The promotion of planned-giving programs on behalf of local churches, conferences, and general Church boards and agencies;

3. Furnishing counsel and guidance to local churches with regard to promotion and management of permanent funds; and

4. Other responsibilities as requested by the annual conference. The United Methodist Foundation shall have an independent governing board as determined by the incorporating documents approved by the annual conference. The governing board will establish all policies and procedures upon which the foundation will operate. Due care will be exercised to maintain prudent organizational separation from beneficiary organizations while striving to maintain missional purpose and connection.

¶ 2514. *Jointly Owned Episcopal Residences*—When authorized by two-thirds of the annual conferences comprising an episcopal area, an episcopal residence for the resident bishop may be acquired, the title to which shall be held in trust by the trustees of the annual conference within which the residence is located.

Any such property so acquired and held shall not be sold or disposed of except with the consent of a majority of the conferences that participate in the ownership. Whenever there is a plan to sell an episcopal residence or to transfer an annual conference from one episcopal area to another, that plan shall include provision for safeguarding each conference's equity, if any, in an episcopal residence; except that an annual conference, by its own decision, may relinquish its claims to an equity interest in an episcopal residence.[7]

¶ **2515.** *Sale, Transfer, Lease, Mortgage, or Purchase of Annual Conference Property*—No annual conference real property shall be sold, transferred, or leased for a term that exceeds twenty years, or mortgaged or purchased without the consent of the annual conference or, *ad interim, (a)* the consent of the presiding bishop and of a majority of the district superintendents, and, in the case of discontinued or abandoned local church property or property to be purchased, the consent of a majority of the district board of church location and building (see ¶ 2549), and, in case of a discontinued Wesley Foundation or campus ministry property, the consent of the majority of the conference board of higher education and campus ministry, and the consent of the annual conference (see ¶ 634.4*d*); and *(b)* the bishop's determination that such transfer or encumbrance conforms to the *Discipline*. The bishop's written statement evidencing the satisfaction of this condition shall be affixed to or included in any instrument of transfer or encumbrance. Any required written instrument necessary to carry out the action so authorized shall be executed in the name of the conference corporation by any two of its officers or, where the conference is unincorporated, by any two officers of its board of trustees, and any written instrument so executed shall be binding and effective as the action of the conference.

¶ **2516.** *Camps, Conference Grounds, and Retreat Centers*—Title to annual conference or district camps, conference grounds, and retreat centers held in trust by an incorporated board or agency of an annual conference or district, or by an unincorporated board, commission, society, or similar body of the conference or district, can be mortgaged or sold and conveyed by such corporation or unincorporated body only after authorization by the annual or district conference to which such body is related.

---

7. See Judicial Council Decision 194.

¶ **2517.** *Responsibilities of Annual Conference Trustees Related to Health and Welfare Institutions.*

1. The annual conference shall designate a body that shall be responsible for establishing and maintaining the annual conference's relationship statements with related health and welfare organizations. If the annual conference does not designate a body for this purpose, the responsibility shall rest with the annual conference board of trustees. A related health and welfare organization is any organization that:

a) Provides health or welfare services;

b) Is located within the bounds of the annual conference; and

c) Either

(1) Seeks, or already has, a relationship or connection with an annual conference, regardless of whether the relationship or connection is formal or informal, official or unofficial, or does or does not involve any financial or legal commitments; or

(2) Markets, publicizes, or promotes itself as having a connection to the annual conference or to the denomination or uses the official United Methodist insignia or the term "United Methodist" in any way; provided, however, that health and welfare organizations that have a covenant relationship with the national office of the United Methodist Women may also seek a relationship or connection with an annual conference, pursuant to this section, but shall not be required to do so.

2. The body designated by the annual conference shall consult with the conference chancellor and the conference Health and Welfare Committee (or equivalent structure) in the development of relationship statements.

3. The body designated by the annual conference shall provide the General Council on Finance and Administration with current copies of all of the conference's relationship statements.

4. If the annual conference has a relationship with a related health and welfare organization, the legal and financial relationships between the annual conference and the health and welfare organization must be memorialized in a clearly stated document describing such relationships. This relationship statement shall:

a) Not purport to name as a party "The United Methodist Church" and/or any general agency of "The United Methodist Church";

b) Require the health and welfare organization to acquire approval from the General Council on Finance and Administration if the health and welfare organization wishes to use the official United Methodist insignia or the term "United Methodist" in its name, mission statement, publications, or promotional or marketing material;

c) Acknowledge that the annual conference shall not be legally responsible for the debts, contracts, or obligations, or for any other financial commitments of any character or description created, undertaken, or assumed by the health and welfare institution, absent the express consent of the annual conference;

d) Require the body designated by the annual conference and the health and welfare institution to review the relationship statement at least every four years; and

e) Comply with any further requirements adopted by the General Council on Finance and Administration, in collaboration with the United Methodist Association of Health and Welfare Ministries.

5. The body designated by the annual conference may encourage or require the health and welfare organization to:

a) Hold membership in the United Methodist Association of Health and Welfare Ministries;

b) Pursue accreditation in one of the industry-recognized, national accreditation bodies appropriate to faith-based organizations; or

c) Utilize the programmatic standards, self-study, and peer review appropriate to Church-related institutions and programs available to them through organizations that will promote excellence in Christian ministry and mission and enhance the quality of services offered.

6. If the body designated by the annual conference terminates, decides not to renew, or is unable, after reasonable efforts, to agree to, a relationship statement with a health and welfare organization, it shall report such termination, non-renewal, or inability to agree at the next session of the annual conference. This report shall then be published in the annual conference journal. The organization may then establish a relationship statement with the United Methodist Association consistent with the requirements of ¶ 2517.

Section V. District Property

¶ **2518.** *District Parsonages and Boards of Trustees*—1. A district parsonage for the district superintendent may be acquired when authorized by the charge conferences of two-thirds of the charges in the district or when authorized by a two-thirds vote of the district conference, subject to the advice and approval of the district board of church location and building as provided in ¶¶ 2519-2524.

2. Any district conference or district union that owns property or has employees may be incorporated in its own name if permitted by local law. Unless the district conference or district union is incorporated in its own name, each district's board of trustees shall be incorporated. The district board shall consist of not fewer than three nor more than nine members in accordance with ¶ 610.5, having the same qualifications provided for trustees of local churches (¶ 2525), who shall be nominated by the district superintendent in consultation with the district nominating committee, if one exists, and elected by the district conference. Where there is no district conference, they may be elected by the district board of stewards or by the annual conference on nomination of the district superintendent. They shall be elected for a term of one year and serve until their successors shall have been elected, and they shall report annually to the district conference or annual conference. Title to district property may be held in trust by the incorporated district conference or union, the incorporated district board of trustees, or the annual conference of which such district is a part, and such trustees shall report annually to the district or annual conference. Except as the laws of the state, territory, or country prescribe otherwise, district property held in trust by a district board of trustees may be mortgaged or sold and conveyed by them only by authority of the district conference or annual conference, or if such property is held in trust by the trustees of the annual conference, it may be mortgaged or sold and conveyed by such trustees only by authority of the annual conference. The district conference, or annual conference in the case of property held in trust by the trustees of the annual conference, may include in the resolution authorizing such proposed action a direction that any contract, deed, bill of sale, mortgage, or other necessary written instrument may be executed by and on behalf of the respective board of trustees by any two of its officers, who thereupon shall be duly authorized to carry out the direction of the district conference or annual conference; and any written instrument so executed shall be binding and effective as the action of the district conference or annual conference. The purchase price and main-

tenance cost of a district parsonage may be equitably distributed among the charges of the district by the district board of stewards. Where there is an incorporated district union (¶ 659.4), the board of directors of the district union shall have the same duties and responsibilities with respect to district property as are described here for the district board of trustees.

3. When district boundaries are changed by division, rearrangement, or consolidation so that a district parsonage purchased, owned, and maintained by one district is included within the bounds of another district, each such district shall be entitled to receive its just share of the then-reasonable value of the parsonage in which it has invested funds; and the amount of such value and just share shall be determined by a committee of three persons, appointed by the bishop of the area, who shall not be residents of any of the said districts. The committee shall hear claims of each district regarding its interest therein before making a decision. From any such determination, there is reserved unto each of the interested districts the right of appeal to the next succeeding annual conference. The same procedure shall be followed in determining equities of a district in any other property that may be included in another district by changes in district boundaries.

¶ **2519.** *Authorization and Establishment of District Boards of Church Location and Building*—There shall be in each district of an annual conference a district board of church location and building. The board shall consist of the district superintendent and a minimum of six and a maximum of nine additional persons nominated by the district superintendent in consultation with the district nominating committee, if one exists, and elected annually by the annual conference, provided that in a district of great geographical extent an additional board may be so elected. It is recommended that the membership include one-third clergy, one-third laymen, one-third laywomen, and, where possible, should be inclusive of gender, race, age, and people with disabilities. These persons shall be professing members of The United Methodist Church. The members of the board, excluding the district superintendent, shall be divided into three classes. One third shall be elected annually for a three-year term. A chairperson and a secretary shall be elected annually at the first meeting following annual conference. The board shall file a report of any actions taken with the charge conference of each local church involved, and the report so filed shall become a part of the minutes of the said conference or conferences. The board shall also make a written report to the district conference (or, if there is no district conference, to the district superintendent), and this report shall become a part of the records of that conference.

¶ **2520.** *Duties and Responsibilities of the District Boards of Church Location and Building*—1. *Local Church Building Sites and Plans*—The board of church location and building shall investigate all proposed local church building sites, ascertaining that such sites are properly located for the community to be served and adequate in size to provide space for future expansion and parking facilities. (See ¶¶ 259.1, 2544.2.)

2. If there is a district strategy committee for parish development or a metropolitan commission (¶ 633.5*j*) in the district, the board shall consider its recommendations in planning a strategy for continuing the service of The United Methodist Church in changing neighborhoods. If no parish development committee or commission is operative, the board shall study the duties assigned to each and seek ways to provide continuity of service in parishes where there is a change in the racial, ethnic, or cultural character of the residents, to the end that the resolutions of the General Conference involving such neighborhoods be given careful consideration. One member of the board shall also have membership on the strategy committee or on the commission.

3. The board of church location and building shall investigate all proposed local church or parsonage buildings to determine the best method to make the structure energy-efficient.

¶ **2521.** *Standards for the Approval of Building Proposals*—1. The District Board of Church Location and Building shall review the plans of any church in the district which proposes to construct or purchase a new church or educational building or a parsonage, or remodeling of such a building if the cost will exceed 25 percent of the value of the building. Such proposal shall include a statement of the need for the proposed facilities, preliminary architectural plans, cost estimate of the project, and a financial plan for defraying such costs. Before finally approving the building project, the board shall determine that the preliminary architectural design and financial plans have been evaluated and approved by proper authorities. Building plans shall provide for equal access to persons with disabilities as per ¶ 2544.4*b*(1), (2).

2. When the local church has secured final architectural plans and specifications and a reliable and detailed estimate of the cost

of the proposed undertaking as provided in ¶ 2544.7, the board shall require their submission for consideration and approval. The board shall study carefully the feasibility and financial soundness of the undertaking and ascertain whether the financial plan will provide funds necessary to ensure prompt payment of all proposed contractual obligations and provide for the full financial support of the program ministries, including annual conference and general Church benevolences. It shall report its conclusions to the Church and to the cabinet in writing.

3. A final decision of the board approving purchase, building, or remodeling shall automatically terminate after a period of one year where no action has been taken by the local church to carry out such decision.

¶ 2522. *Appeals of District Boards of Church Location and Building Decisions*—A decision of the board disapproving such purchase, building, or remodeling shall be final unless overruled by the annual conference, to which there is reserved unto the local church the right of appeal.

¶ 2523. *Application of Standards to the Acquisition of a District Parsonage*—The above provisions shall apply to the acquisition of a district parsonage.

¶ 2524. *Sale, Transfer, Lease, or Mortgage of District Property*—No district property shall be sold, transferred, or leased for a term that exceeds twenty years, or mortgaged, without: *(a)* the consent of the presiding district superintendent; and *(b)* the district superintendent's determination that such transfer or encumbrance conforms to the *Discipline*. The district superintendent's written statement evidencing the satisfaction of this condition shall be affixed to any instrument or transfer or encumbrance. Any required written instrument necessary to carry out the action so authorized shall be executed in the name of the corporation by any two of its officers, or any two officers of its board of trustees, and any written instrument so executed shall be binding and effective as the action of the corporation.

Section VI. Local Church Property

¶ 2525. *Local Church Board of Trustees' Qualifications*—In each pastoral charge consisting of one local church, there shall be a board of trustees, consisting of not fewer than three nor more than nine persons, and it is recommended that at least one-third be laywomen and that at least one-third be laymen. The trustees shall be of legal age as determined by law, and at least two-thirds shall be professing members of The United Methodist Church (see ¶¶ 258.1, .3; 2530). No pastor is a voting member of the board of trustees unless elected as a member.

¶ **2526.** *Local Church Board of Trustees' Election*—The members of the board of trustees shall be divided into three classes, and each class shall as nearly as possible consist of an equal number of members. At the charge conference, on recommendation by the committee on nominations and leadership development or from the floor, it shall elect, to take office at the beginning of the ensuing calendar year or at such other times as the charge or church conference may set, to serve for a term of three years or until their successors have been duly elected and qualified, the required number of trustees to succeed those of the class whose terms then expire; provided, however, that nothing herein shall be construed to prevent the election of a trustee to self-succession.[8] The charge conference may assign the responsibility for electing trustees to a church conference.

¶ **2527.** *Church Local Conference—Duties, Authority, and Membership*—1. In a pastoral charge consisting of two or more local churches, a church local conference, constituted and organized under the *Discipline* of The United Methodist Church in each local church therein, shall be vested with authority and power in matters relating to the real and personal property of the local church concerned. Such church local conference shall elect the board of trustees of such local church in number and manner described in ¶ 2526, and the duties of such trustees, duly elected, shall be the same as and identical with the duties described in ¶ 2528. The duties, authority, and power vested in the church local conference, insofar as they relate to the property, real and personal, of the local church concerned, are the same as and identical with the authority and power vested in the charge conference of a pastoral charge of one local church (¶ 2529); and the authority, power, and limitations therein set forth shall be applicable to the church local conference as fully and to the same extent as if incorporated herein. The effect of the provisions for a church local conference is to give to each local church in a charge of two or more churches, rather than to the pastoral charge conference, supervision over and control of its own property, subject to the

---

8. See Judicial Council Decision 130.

limitations prescribed in the *Discipline* with regard to local church property.

2. Whenever required under *The Book of Discipline of The United Methodist Church* for matters relating to real or personal property of the local church or to mergers of churches, a local church in a pastoral charge consisting of two or more local churches shall organize a church local conference. The membership of the church local conference shall consist of the persons specified for membership of the charge conference (¶ 246.2) so far as the officers and relationships exist within the local church, except that the pastor shall be a member of each church local conference. The provisions of ¶ 246.2-.10 relating to membership qualification and procedures of a charge conference shall be applicable to membership qualifications and procedures of a church local conference.

¶ **2528.** *Charge or Cooperative Parish Board of Trustees*—1. A pastoral charge composed of two or more churches, each having a local board of trustees, may have, in addition, a board of trustees for the charge as a whole. This board shall hold title to and manage the property belonging to the entire charge, such as parsonage, campground, burial ground, and such other property as may be committed to it. It shall receive and administer funds for the charge in conformity with the laws of the state, province, or country in which the property is located. This board shall consist of no fewer than three persons, at least two-thirds of whom shall be professing members of The United Methodist Church and of legal age as determined by law. These trustees shall be elected by the charge conference for three years or until their successors are elected.

2. A cooperative parish composed of two or more charges may have, in addition to its charge trustees and local church trustees, a board of trustees for the cooperative parish as a whole. This board shall hold title to and manage the property belonging to the cooperative parish in accordance with ¶¶ 2503, 2527, and 2528. These trustees shall be elected by the charge conference and/or church local conference related to the cooperative parish and shall be representative of each congregation that composes the cooperative parish.

3. The board of trustees of a charge shall provide for the security of its funds, keep an accurate record of its proceedings, and report to the charge conference to which it is amenable.

4. When two or more local churches compose a single pastoral charge having a parsonage and one or more thereof is separated

from such charge and established as a pastoral charge or united with another pastoral charge, each such local church shall be entitled to receive its just share of the then-reasonable value of the parsonage in which it has invested funds, with the exception that those churches departing from a circuit who had joined the circuit after the parsonage was acquired would have no claim on any value of the parsonage. The amount of such value and just share shall be determined by a committee of three persons, appointed by the district superintendent, who shall be members of The United Methodist Church but not of any of the interested local churches. Such committee shall hear all interested parties and shall take into account the investment of any church in any such property before arriving at a final determination. From any such determination there is reserved to each of the interested churches the right of appeal to the next succeeding annual conference, the decision of which shall be final and binding. Any sum received as or from such share shall not be applied to current expense or current budget.

¶ **2529.** *Charge Conference Authority*—In a pastoral charge consisting of one local church, the charge conference, constituted as set forth in ¶¶ 246-247, shall be vested with power and authority as hereinafter set forth in connection with the property, both real and personal, of the said local church. In fulfilling that duty, the charge conference may delegate certain duties and responsibilities to the board of trustees as described below. However, the board of trustees shall always be subject to the direction of the charge conference. The charge conference may:

1. *a*) If it so elects, direct the board of trustees to incorporate the local church, expressly subject, however, to the *Discipline* of The United Methodist Church (see ¶ 2506) and in accordance with the pertinent local laws and in such manner as will fully protect and exempt from any and all legal liability the individual officials and members, jointly and severally, of the local church and the charge, annual, jurisdictional, and general conferences of The United Methodist Church, and each of them, for and on account of the debts and other obligations of every kind and description of the local church.

   b) Regardless of whether the charge conference elects to incorporate the local church, the local church:

   (1) must be organized and operated in compliance with the *Discipline*;

(2) cannot act in a manner contrary to the purpose of The United Methodist Church, the annual conference, or the *Discipline*; and

(3) cannot sever its connectional relationship to The United Methodist Church without the consent of the annual conference.

c) The organizing documents (articles of incorporation, charter, bylaws, or equivalents) of a local church shall reflect its connectional relationship to The United Methodist Church. The adoption or modification of a local church's organizing documents must be approved, in writing, by its pastor and district superintendent. Specifically, local church organizing documents shall, at a minimum:

(1) require the local church to be organized and operated in compliance with the *Discipline*;

(2) prohibit the local church from acting in a manner contrary to the purpose of The United Methodist Church, the annual conference, or the *Discipline*;

(3) prohibit the local church from severing its connectional relationship to The United Methodist Church without the annual conference's consent;

(4) require the pastor and the district superintendent to approve, in writing, the adoption of, and changes to, the local church's organizing documents; and

(5) include language consistent with the Internal Revenue Code to protect the local church's tax-exempt status.

d) The failure of a local church's organizing documents to meet the requirements of ¶ 2529.1c(1)-(4) does not relieve the local church of its connectional responsibilities to The United Methodist Church, nor does it absolve its pastor and membership of the responsibility to operate the local church as a United Methodist church, in accordance with the *Discipline*. The organizing documents are deemed modified to the extent necessary to comply with ¶ 2529.1c(1)-(4) if any of the circumstances described in ¶ 2503.6a-c apply.

2. Direct the board of trustees with respect to the purchase, sale, mortgage, encumbrance, construction, repairing, remodeling, and maintenance of any and all property of the local church.

3. Direct the board of trustees with respect to the acceptance or rejection of any and all conveyances, grants, gifts, donations, legacies, bequests, or devises, absolute or in trust, for the use and

benefit of the local church, and to require the administration of any such trust in accordance with the terms and provisions thereof and with the local laws appertaining thereto. (See ¶ 2533.5.)

4. Direct the board of trustees to do any and all things necessary to exercise such other powers and duties relating to the property, real and personal, of the local church concerned as may be committed to it by the *Discipline*.

5. To recommend that consideration be given to placing such investable property with a United Methodist foundation serving such charge conference, to benefit the local church, charge conference or their successors, or in the absence of such a foundation, with the United Methodist Foundation.

¶ **2530.** *Local Church Board of Trustees' Organization and Membership*—The board of trustees shall organize as follows:

1. Within thirty days after the beginning of the ensuing calendar or conference year (whichever applies to the term of office), each board of trustees shall convene at a time and place designated by the chairperson, or by the vice chairperson in the event that the chairperson is not reelected a trustee or because of absence or disability is unable to act, for the purpose of electing officers of the said board for the ensuing year and transacting any other business properly brought before it.

2. The board of trustees shall elect from the membership thereof, to hold office for a term of one year or until their successors shall be elected, a chairperson, vice chairperson, secretary, and, if need requires, a treasurer; provided, however, that the chairperson and vice chairperson shall not be members of the same class; and provided further, that the offices of secretary and treasurer may be held by the same person; and provided further, that the chairperson shall be a professing member of the local church. The duties of each officer shall be the same as those generally connected with the office held and which are usually and commonly discharged by the holder thereof. The church local conference may, if it is necessary to conform to the local laws, substitute the designations *president* and *vice president* for and in place of *chairperson* and *vice chairperson*.

3. Where necessity requires, as a result of the incorporation of a local church, the corporation directors, in addition to electing officers as provided in § 2 above, shall ratify and confirm by appropriate action and, if necessary, elect as officers of the corporation the treasurer or treasurers, as the case may be, elected by

the charge conference in accordance with the provisions of the *Discipline*, whose duties and responsibilities shall be as therein set forth. If more than one account is maintained in the name of the corporation in any financial institution or institutions, each such account and the treasurer thereof shall be appropriately designated.

¶ **2531.** *Removal of Local Church Trustees; Vacancies*—1. Should a trustee withdraw from the membership of The United Methodist Church or be excluded therefrom, trusteeship therein shall automatically cease from the date of such withdrawal or exclusion.

2. Should a trustee of a local church or a director of an incorporated local church refuse to execute properly a legal instrument relating to any property of the church when directed so to do by the charge conference and when all legal requirements have been satisfied in reference to such execution, the said charge conference may by majority vote declare the trustee's or director's membership on the board of trustees or board of directors vacated.

3. Vacancies occurring in a board of trustees shall be filled by election for the unexpired term. Such election shall be held in the same manner as for trustees. A vacancy occurring ad interim may be filled until the next charge conference by the church council.

¶ **2532.** *Meetings of Local Church Boards of Trustees*—The board of trustees shall meet at the call of the pastor or of its chairperson at least annually at such times and places as shall be designated in a notice to each trustee and the pastor(s) at a reasonable time prior to the appointed time of the meeting. Waiver of notice may be used as a means to validate meetings legally where the usual notice is impracticable. A majority of the members of the board of trustees shall constitute a quorum.

¶ **2533.** *Board of Trustees' Powers and Limitations*—1. Subject to the direction of the charge conference, the board of trustees shall have the supervision, oversight, and care of all real property owned by the local church and of all property and equipment acquired directly by the local church or by any society, board, class, commission, or similar organization connected therewith, provided that the board of trustees shall not violate the rights of any local church organization elsewhere granted in the *Discipline;* provided further, that the board of trustees shall not prevent or interfere with the pastor in the use of any of the said property for religious services or other proper meetings or purposes recognized by the law, usages, and customs of The United Methodist

Church, or permit the use of said property for religious or other meetings without the consent of the pastor or, in the pastor's absence, the consent of the district superintendent; and provided further, that pews in The United Methodist Church shall always be free; and provided further, that the church local conference may assign certain of these duties to a building committee as set forth in ¶ 2544 or the chairperson of the parsonage committee, if one exists.

2. The board of trustees shall annually compare the existence and adequacy of the church's insurance coverages to an insurance schedule annually published by the General Council on Finance and Administration. The purpose of this review is to ensure that the church, its properties, and its personnel are properly protected against risks. The board shall include in its report to the charge conference (¶ 2550.7) the results of its review and recommendations needed to timely bring the church into compliance with the published schedule.[9]

3. When a pastor and/or a board of trustees are asked to grant permission to an outside organization to use church facilities, permission can be granted only when such use is consistent with the Social Principles (¶¶ 160-166) and ecumenical objectives.

4. The chairperson of the board of trustees or the chairperson of the parsonage committee, if one exists, the chairperson of the committee on pastor-parish relations, and the pastor shall make an annual review of the church-owned parsonage to ensure proper maintenance.

5. Subject to the direction of the charge conference as hereinbefore provided, the board of trustees shall receive and administer all bequests made to the local church; shall receive and administer all trusts; and shall invest all trust funds of the local church in conformity with laws of the country, state, or like political unit in which the local church is located. Nevertheless, upon notice to the board of trustees, the charge conference may delegate the power, duty, and authority to receive, administer, and invest bequests, trusts, and trust funds to the permanent endowment committee or to a local church foundation and shall do so in the case of bequests, trusts, or trust funds for which the donor has designated the committee or the local church foundation to receive, administer, or invest the same.

---

9. See Judicial Council Decisions 866, 1142.

The board of trustees is encouraged to invest in institutions, companies, corporations, or funds that make a positive contribution toward the realization of the goals outlined in the Social Principles of our Church. The board of trustees is to act as a socially responsible investor and to report annually to the charge conference regarding its carrying out of this responsibility. When such property is in the form of investable funds, the board of trustees shall consider placement for investment and administration with the United Methodist foundation serving that conference or, in the absence of such a foundation, with the United Methodist Church Foundation. A conscious effort shall be made to invest in a manner consistent with the Social Principles and the creation of an investment policy.

6. The board of trustees shall conduct or cause to be conducted an annual accessibility audit of their buildings, grounds, and facilities to discover and identify what physical, architectural, and communication barriers exist that impede the full participation of people with disabilities and shall make plans and determine priorities for the elimination of all such barriers. It is highly encouraged that members of the congregation or from the community who have disabilities, who are family members of persons with disabilities, and who are builders or architects or rehabilitation professionals be involved in conducting the audit. The Accessibility Audit for churches shall be used in filling out the annual church and/or charge conference reports.

¶ 2534. *Permanent Endowment and Planned Giving Ministry Committee*—A charge conference may establish a local church permanent endowment and planned giving ministry committee. The purposes for establishing such a committee include the responsibilities to:

1. Provide the services described in ¶ 2533.5 as designated by the donor or at the direction of the charge conference upon notice to the board of trustees. When such property is in the form of investable funds, the permanent endowment fund committee may consider placement for investment and administration with the United Methodist foundation serving that conference or, in the absence of such a foundation, with the United Methodist Church Foundation. A conscious effort shall be made to invest in a manner consistent with the Social Principles and the creation of an investment policy.

When the charge conference has designated the committee to provide the services described in ¶ 2533.5, the committee shall have the same investment and reporting duties as are imposed on the board of trustees in that paragraph.

2. The charge conference shall adopt guidelines for endowment and planned giving as developed by the permanent endowment and planned giving ministry committee. Subject to the direction and supervision of the charge conference, the committee shall fulfill its responsibilities in administering the planned-giving and/or permanent endowment fund.

Following each General Conference, the charge conference shall update any required changes in the planned-giving and/or permanent endowment fund documents.

3. Emphasize the need for adults of all ages to have a will and an estate plan and provide information on the preparation of these to the members of the congregation.

4. Stress the opportunities for church members and constituents to make provisions for giving through United Methodist churches, institutions, agencies, and causes by means of wills, annuities, trusts, life insurance, memorials, and various types of property.

5. Arrange for the dissemination of information that will be helpful in preretirement planning, including such considerations as establishing a living will, a living trust, and the need for each person to designate someone to serve as a responsible advocate should independent decision-making ability be lost.

6. Permanent endowment and planned giving ministry committee trustees are directed by the charge conference to follow the guidelines and actions initiated by the charge conference, overturn any transaction that the charge conference may deem excessive, and remove any trustee who does not carry out the directions of the charge conference. Careful attention will be given to the election of trustees to ensure that there is no conflict of interest. Following each General Conference, the permanent endowment document shall be brought into line with any changes in the *Discipline*.

7. Other responsibilities as determined by the charge conference.

8. Resources for these tasks may be secured from conference and/or area United Methodist foundations and development offices, the National Association of United Methodist Foundations, the General Board of Discipleship, the General Council on

Finance and Administration, and other appropriate sources for program assistance and direction.

¶ 2535. *Local Church Foundations*—After securing the written consent of the pastor and of the district superintendent, local churches may, by charge conference action, establish local church foundations whose trustees, directors, or governing body shall be elected by the charge conference. Such foundations shall be incorporated, organized, and function in compliance with state law and subject to the provisions of the *Discipline*. Any such foundation shall not violate the rights of any other local church organization and shall be subject to the direction of the charge conference. The charge conference may delegate to the foundation the power and authority to receive, invest, and administer in trust for the local church bequests, trusts, and trust funds upon notice to the board of trustees as provided in ¶ 2533.5, in which event the foundation shall have the same investment and reporting duties as are imposed on the board of trustees. No such delegation of authority shall be construed to be a violation of the rights of any other local church organization. Consideration shall be given to the placement of funds with the conference or area United Methodist foundation for administration and investment.

¶ 2536. *Unincorporated Local Church Property—Title and Purchase*—Unless otherwise required by local law (¶ 2506), title to all property now owned or hereafter acquired by an unincorporated local church, and any organization, board, commission, society, or similar body connected therewith, shall be held by and/or conveyed and transferred to its duly elected trustees, their successors and assigns, in trust for the use and benefit of such local church and of The United Methodist Church. The trustees shall be named as the board of trustees of the local church in the written instrument conveying or transferring title. Every instrument of conveyance of real estate shall contain the appropriate trust clause as set forth in the *Discipline* (¶ 2503).

¶ 2537. *Unincorporated Local Church Property—Notice and Authorization*—Prior to the purchase by an unincorporated local church of any real estate, a resolution authorizing such action shall be passed at a meeting of the charge conference by a majority vote of its members present and voting at a regular meeting or a special meeting of the charge conference called for that purpose; provided, however, that not less than ten days' notice of such meeting and the proposed action shall have been given from the pulpit and in the weekly bulletin, newsletter, or electronic notice of the church; and provided further, that written consent to such action shall be given by the pastor and the district superintendent. (See ¶ 2544.)

¶ **2538.** *Incorporated Local Church Property—Title and Purchase*—Unless otherwise required by local law (¶ 2506), the title to all property now owned or hereafter acquired by an incorporated local church, and any organization, board, commission, society, or similar body connected therewith, shall be held by and/or conveyed to the corporate body in its corporate name, in trust for the use and benefit of such local church and of The United Methodist Church. Every instrument of conveyance of real estate shall contain the appropriate trust clause as set forth in the *Discipline* (¶ 2503).

¶ **2539.** *Incorporated Local Church Property—Notice and Authorization*—Prior to the purchase by a local church corporation of any real estate, a resolution authorizing such action shall be passed by the charge conference in corporate session, or such other corporate body as the local laws may require, with the members thereof acting in their capacity as members of the corporate body, by a majority vote of those present and voting at any regular or special meeting called for that purpose, provided that not less than ten days' notice of such meeting and the proposed action shall have been given from the pulpit and in the weekly bulletin, newsletter, or electronic notice of the local church or other means if required or permitted by local law, and provided further, that written consent to such action shall be given by the pastor and the district superintendent, and provided further, that all such transactions shall have the approval of the charge conference.

¶ **2540.** *Unincorporated Local Church Property—Sale, Transfer, Lease, or Mortgage*—Any real property owned by or in which an unincorporated local church has any interest may be sold, transferred, leased for a term of thirty days or more (which shall include leases for less than thirty days if such a lease is consecutive with the same lessee), or mortgaged subject to the following procedure and conditions:

1. Notice of the proposed action and the date and time of the regular or special meeting of the charge conference at which it is to be considered shall be given at least ten days prior thereto from the pulpit of the church and in its weekly bulletin, newsletter, or electronic notice, or other means if required or permitted by local law.

2. A resolution authorizing the proposed action shall be passed by a majority vote of the charge conference members (in a pastoral charge consisting of two or more local churches, the church local conference; see ¶ 2527) present and voting at a special meeting called to consider such action.

3. The written consent of the pastor of the local church and the district superintendent to the proposed action shall be necessary and shall be affixed to or included in the instrument of sale, conveyance, transfer, lease, or mortgage. Prior to consenting to any proposed action required under this paragraph involving any United Methodist church property, the pastor, district superintendent, and the district board of church location and building shall ensure that: *(a)* a full investigation shall be made and an appropriate plan of action shall be developed for the future missional needs of the community; *(b)* the transfer or encumbrance shall conform to the *Discipline; (c)* the congregation, if no longer to continue as an organized local United Methodist Church, does not sell but may transfer title of its facilities to another United Methodist church or agency; and *(d)* the congregation, in case of relocation, first offers its property to a United Methodist congregation or agency at a price not to exceed fair market value. The district strategies or other missional strategies should include the ministries of both United Methodist congregations and the community where the existing facility is located. Certification by the district superintendent shall be conclusive evidence that the transfer or encumbrance conforms to the *Discipline.* The requirements of investigation and the development of a plan of action, however, shall not affect the merchantability of the title to the real estate or the legal effect of the instruments of sale or transfer.

4. Unless the charge conference directs otherwise, any contract, deed, bill of sale, mortgage, or other necessary written instrument needed to implement any resolution authorizing action regarding local church property may be executed by and on behalf of the local church by any two officers of the board of trustees, who thereupon shall be duly authorized to carry out the direction of the charge conference; and any written instrument so executed shall be binding and effective as the action of the local church.

¶ **2541.** *Incorporated Local Church Property—Sale, Transfer, Lease, or Mortgage*—Any real property owned by or in which an incorporated local church has any interest may be sold, transferred, leased for a term of thirty days or more (which shall include leases for less than thirty days if such a lease is consecutive with the same lessee), or mortgaged subject to the following procedure and conditions:

1. Notice of the proposed action and the date and time of the regular or special meeting of the members of the corporate body—i.e., members of the charge conference at which it is to be considered—shall be given at least ten days prior thereto from the pulpit of the church and in its weekly bulletin, newsletter, or electronic notice or other means if required or permitted by local law.

2. A resolution authorizing the proposed action shall be passed by a majority vote of the members of the corporate body present and voting at any regular or special meeting thereof called to consider such action and a majority vote of the members of the charge conference, if the corporate members are different than the charge conference members.

3. The written consent of the pastor of the local church and the district superintendent to the proposed action shall be necessary and shall be affixed to or included in the instrument of sale, conveyance, transfer, lease, or mortgage. Prior to consenting to any proposed action required under this paragraph involving any United Methodist church property, the pastor, the district superintendent, and the district board of church location and building shall ensure that—*(a)* a full investigation shall be made and an appropriate plan of action shall be developed for the future missional needs of the community; *(b)* the transfer or encumbrance shall conform to the *Discipline*; *(c)* the congregation, if no longer to continue as an organized United Methodist church, does not sell but may transfer title of its facilities to another United Methodist church or agency; and *(d)* the congregation, in case of relocation, first offers its property to a United Methodist congregation or agency at a price not to exceed fair market value. The district strategies or other missional strategies should include the ministries of both United Methodist congregations and the community where the existing facility is located. Certification by the district superintendent shall be conclusive evidence that the transfer or encumbrance conforms to the *Discipline*. The requirements of investigation and the development of a plan of action shall not affect the merchantability of the title to the real estate or the legal effect of the instruments of sale or transfer.

4. The resolution authorizing such proposed action shall direct and authorize the corporation's board of directors to take all necessary steps to carry out the action and to cause to be executed, as hereinafter provided, any necessary contract, deed, bill of sale, mortgage, or other written instrument.

5. The board of directors at any regular or special meeting shall take such action and adopt such resolutions as may be necessary or required by the local laws.

6. Any required contract, deed, bill of sale, mortgage, or other written instrument necessary to carry out the action so authorized shall be executed in the name of the corporation by any two of its officers, and any written instrument so executed shall be binding and effective as the action of the corporation.

¶ **2542.** *Disposition and Mortgage of Church Building or Parsonage*—Real property acquired by a conveyance subject to the trust clause may be sold in conformity with the provisions of the *Discipline* of The United Methodist Church when its use as a church building or parsonage, as the case may be, has been, or is intended to be, terminated; and when such real estate is sold or mortgaged in accordance with the provisions of the *Discipline* of The United Methodist Church, the written acknowledged consent of the proper district superintendent representing The United Methodist Church to the action taken shall constitute a release and discharge of the real property so sold and conveyed from the trust clause or clauses; or in the event of the execution of a mortgage, such consent of the district superintendent shall constitute a formal recognition of the priority of such mortgage lien and the subordination of the foregoing trust provisions thereof; and no bona fide purchaser or mortgagee relying upon the foregoing record shall be charged with any responsibility with respect to the disposition by such local church of the proceeds of any such sale or mortgage; but the board of trustees receiving such proceeds shall manage, control, disburse, and expend the same in conformity to the order and direction of the charge conference or church local conference, subject to the provisions of the *Discipline* of The United Methodist Church with respect thereto.

¶ **2543.** *Restriction on Proceeds of Mortgage or Sale*[10]—1. No real property on which a church building or parsonage is located shall be mortgaged to provide for the current budget or operating

---

10. See Judicial Council Decision 688.

expense of a local church. The principal proceeds of a sale of any such property shall not be used for the current budget or operating expense of a local church. Provided that provisions are made for the current and future missional needs of the congregation and the current and future housing needs of a pastor, the principal may be used for capital improvements beyond the regular operating budget when written approval is granted by the district superintendent and pastor. This provision shall apply alike to unincorporated and incorporated local churches.[11]

2. A local church, whether or not incorporated, on complying with the provisions of the *Discipline* may mortgage its unencumbered real property as security for a loan to be made to a conference board of global ministries or a city or district missionary society, provided that the proceeds of such loan shall be used only for aiding in the construction of a new church.

3. Exception to this restriction may be granted in specifically designated instances to allow use of equity and/or accumulated assets from the sale of property to provide for congregational redevelopment efforts including program and staff. Such exception may be granted by the annual conference, the bishop, and the cabinet upon request of the local church in consultation with congregation development staff where applicable. A clear and detailed three-to-five-year redevelopment plan that projects a self-supporting ministry must accompany the request.

¶ **2544.** *Planning and Financing Requirements for Local Church Buildings*—1. If any local church desires to:

    a) build a new church, a new educational building, or a new parsonage; or

    b) purchase a church, educational building, or parsonage; or

    c) remodel an existing church, an existing educational building, or an existing parsonage where the cost of the remodeling will exceed 25 percent of the value of the existing structure or require mortgage financing, then the local church shall first establish a study committee to:

        (1) analyze the needs of the church and community;

        (2) project the potential membership with average attendance;

        (3) write up the church's program of ministry (¶¶ 201-204); and

---

11. See Judicial Council Decision 399.

(4) develop an accessibility plan including chancel areas.

The information and findings obtained by the study committee shall:

(*a*) form the basis of a report to be presented to the charge conference (¶ 2544.4);

(*b*) be used by the building committee (¶ 2544.5); and

(*c*) become a part of the report to the district board of church location and building (¶¶ 2544.6, 2521.1).

2. After the study committee finishes its work, the local church shall secure the written consent of the pastor and the district superintendent to the building project, purchase proposal, or remodeling project.

3. In the case of a building project or purchase proposal, the local church shall secure the approval of the proposed site by the district board of church location and building as provided in the *Discipline* (¶ 2520.1).

4. The charge conference of the local church shall authorize the building project, purchase proposal, or remodeling project at a regular or called meeting. Notice of the meeting and the proposed action shall have been given for not less than ten days prior thereto from the pulpit of the church, and in its weekly bulletin, newsletter, or electronic notice or other means if required or permitted by local law.

a) After approving a building project or a remodeling project, the charge conference shall elect a building committee of not fewer than three members of the local church to serve in the development of the project as hereinafter set forth; provided that the charge conference may commit to its board of trustees the duties of the building committee.

b) After approving a purchase proposal, the charge conference shall be deemed to have authorized and directed the board of trustees to proceed with the purchase. In the case of the purchase of a parsonage, the board of trustees shall either:

(1) purchase a parsonage that has on the ground-floor level:

(*a*) one room that can be used as a bedroom by a person with a disability;

(*b*) one fully accessible bathroom; and

(*c*) fully accessible laundry facilities; or

(2) purchase a parsonage without the accessible features for persons with disabilities specified above and remodel it within one year's time, so that it does have those features.

5. The building committee shall:

a) use the information and findings of the study committee and any other relevant information to estimate carefully the building facilities needed, as the case may be, to house the church's program of worship, education, and fellowship or to provide for the present and future pastors and their families;

b) ascertain the cost of any property to be purchased; and

c) develop preliminary architectural plans that:

(1) comply with local building, fire, and accessibility codes;

(2) clearly outline the location on the site of all proposed present and future construction; and

(3) provide adequate facilities for parking, entrance, seating, rest rooms, and accessibility for persons with disabilities, but providing for such adequate facilities shall not apply in the case of a minor remodeling project;

d) provide on the ground-floor level of a newly constructed parsonage:

(1) one room that can be used as a bedroom by a person with a disability;

(2) a fully accessible bathroom; and

(3) fully accessible laundry facilities;

e) secure an estimate of the cost of the proposed construction;

f) develop a financial plan for defraying the total cost, including an estimate of the amount the membership can contribute in cash and pledges and the amount the local church can borrow if necessary.

6. The building committee shall submit to the district board of church location and building for its consideration and preliminary approval:

a) a statement of the need for the proposed facilities;

b) the preliminary architectural plans, including accessibility plans;

c) the preliminary cost estimate; and

d) the preliminary financial plan.

7. After preliminary approval by the district board of church location and building, the pastor, with the written consent of the

district superintendent, shall call a church conference, giving not less than ten days' notice (except as local laws may otherwise provide) of the meeting and the proposed action from the pulpit or in the weekly bulletin. At the church conference, the building committee shall present:

a) the preliminary architectural plans;
b) the preliminary cost estimate;
c) the preliminary financial plan; and
d) the building committee's recommendation.

A majority vote of the membership present and voting at the church conference shall be required to approve the preliminary architectural plans, cost estimate, and financial plan and the building committee's recommendation.

8. After approval by the church conference, the building committee shall develop detailed plans and specifications and secure a reliable and detailed estimate of cost, which shall be presented for approval to the charge conference and to the district board of church location and building.

9. After approval by the charge conference and district board of church location and building, the building committee may begin the building project or remodeling project. Written documentation substantiating the approvals of the charge conference and the district board of church location and building shall be lodged with the district superintendent and the secretary of the charge conference.

10. In metropolitan areas, the building committee shall ensure that adequate steps are taken to obtain the services of minority (nonwhite) and female skilled persons in the construction in proportion to the racial and ethnic balance in the area. In non-metropolitan areas, the building committee shall ensure that racial and ethnic persons are employed in the construction where available and in relation to the available workforce.

11. The local church shall acquire a fee simple title to the lot or lots on which any building is to be erected. The deed or conveyance shall be executed as provided in this chapter. It is recommended that contracts on property purchased by a local church be contingent upon the securing of a guaranteed title, and the property's meeting of basic environmental requirements of lending institutions and of local and state laws.

12. If a loan is needed, the local church shall comply with the provisions of ¶ 2540 or ¶ 2541.

13. The local church shall not enter into a building contract or, if using a plan for volunteer labor, incur obligations for materials until it has cash on hand, pledges payable during the construction period, and (if needed) a loan or written commitment therefore that will assure prompt payment of all contractual obligations and other accounts when due.

14. Neither the trustees nor any other members of a local church shall be required to guarantee personally any loan made to the church by any board created by or under the authority of the General Conference.

15. It is recommended that a local church not enter into a binding building contract without the contractor being properly bonded or furnishing other forms of security, such as an irrevocable letter of credit approved by the conference, district, or local church attorney.

¶ **2545.** *Consecration and Dedication of Local Church Buildings*— On acquisition or completion of any church-owned building, a service of consecration may be held. Before any church-owned building is formally dedicated, all indebtedness against the same shall be discharged.

¶ **2546.** *Merger of Local United Methodist Churches*—Two or more local churches, in order to more effectively fulfill their ministry (¶¶ 201-204), may merge and become a single church by pursuing the following procedure:

1. The merger must be proposed to the charge conference of each of the merging churches by a resolution stating the terms and conditions of the proposed merger.

2. The plan of the merger as proposed to the charge conference of each of the merging churches shall be approved by each of the charge conferences in order for the merger to be effected, except that for a charge conference that includes two or more local churches, the required approval shall be by the church local conference of each local church in accordance with the requirements of ¶ 2527.

3. The merger must be approved by the superintendent or superintendents of the district or districts in which the merging churches are located.

4. The requirements of any and all laws of the state or states in which the merging churches are located affecting or relating to the merger of such churches must be complied with, and in any case where there is a conflict between such laws and the pro-

cedure outlined in the *Discipline*, said laws shall prevail and the procedure outlined in the *Discipline* shall be modified to the extent necessary to eliminate such conflict.

5. All archives and records of churches involved in a merger shall become the responsibility of the successor church.

¶ **2547.** *Interdenominational Local Church Mergers*—One or more local United Methodist churches may merge with one or more churches of other denominations and become a single church by pursuing the following procedure:

1. Following appropriate dialogue, which shall include discussions with the United Methodist district superintendent of the district in which the merging churches are located and the corresponding officials of the other judicatories involved, a plan of merger reflecting the nature and ministry of the local church (¶¶ 201-204) shall be submitted to the charge conference of the local United Methodist church and must be approved by a resolution stating the terms and conditions and missional plans of the proposed merger, including the denominational connection of the merger church.

2. The plan of merger, as approved by the charge conference of the United Methodist church, in a charge conference including two or more local churches must be approved by the church local conference of each local church in accordance with the requirements of ¶ 2527.

3. The merger must be approved in writing by the superintendent of the district, a majority of the district superintendents, and the bishop of the area in which the merging churches are located.

4. The provisions of ¶ 2503 shall be included in the plan of merger where applicable.

5. The requirements of any and all laws of the state or states in which the merging churches are located affecting or relating to the merger of such churches must be complied with, and in any case where there is a conflict between such laws and the procedure outlined in the *Discipline*, said laws shall prevail and the procedure outlined in the *Discipline* shall be modified to the extent necessary to eliminate such conflict.

6. Where property is involved, the provisions of ¶ 2548 obtain.

¶ **2548.** *Deeding Church Property to Federated Churches or Other Evangelical Denominations*—1. With the consent of the presiding bishop and of a majority of the district superintendents and of the district board of church location and building and at the request of the charge conference or of a meeting of the membership of the church, where required by local law, and in accordance with the said law, the annual conference may instruct and direct the board of trustees of a local church to deed church property to a federated church.

2. With the consent of the presiding bishop and of a majority of the district superintendents and of the district board of church location and building and at the request of the charge conference or of a meeting of the membership of the local church, where required by local law, and in accordance with said law, the annual conference may instruct and direct the board of trustees of a local church to deed church property to one of the other denominations represented in the Pan-Methodist Commission or to another evangelical denomination under an allocation, exchange of property, or comity agreement, provided that such agreement shall have been committed to writing and signed and approved by the duly qualified and authorized representatives of both parties concerned.

¶ **2549.** *Disposition of Property of a Closed Local Church*— 1. Except as provided in ¶ 2549.3, the district superintendent may, pursuant to this paragraph, recommend the closure of a local church, upon a finding that:

a) The local church no longer serves the purpose for which it was organized or incorporated (¶¶ 201-204); or

b) The local church property is no longer used, kept, or maintained by its membership as a place of divine worship of The United Methodist Church.

2. *Procedure—a)* Prior to a recommendation to close a local church, the district superintendent shall:

(1) Guide the congregation in an assessment of its potential as outlined in ¶ 213, in consultation with the appropriate agency assigned the responsibility of the conference parish and community development strategy;

(2) Obtain and consider an opinion of legal counsel as to the existence of any reversion, possibility of reverter, right of reacquisition, or similar restrictions to the benefit of any party;

(3) Develop, in consultation with the appropriate district board of church location and building, a plan for the future use of all the real and personal, tangible and intangible property of the local church; and

(4) Develop a plan for the transfer of the membership of the local church (¶ 229).

b) Upon a recommendation by the district superintendent, and with the consent of the presiding bishop, a majority of the district superintendents, and the appropriate district board of church location and building, the annual conference may declare a local church closed. If the annual conference closes a local church, title to all the real and personal, tangible and intangible property of the local church shall immediately vest in the annual conference board of trustees, who shall hold said property in trust for the benefit of the annual conference.

c) The annual conference board of trustees may retain, sell, lease, or otherwise dispose of the property of a closed local church in accordance with the direction of the annual conference, if any. It shall be the duty of the annual conference board of trustees to remove, insofar as reasonably practicable or necessary, all Christian and United Methodist insignia and symbols from such property. In the event of loss, damage to, or destruction of such local church property, the annual conference board of trustees, as the duly and legally authorized representative of such local church, is authorized to make a claim for, and collect on, any applicable insurance policies. If the annual conference board of trustees sells or leases the property, consideration should be given to selling or leasing the property to one of the other denominations represented in the Commission on Pan-Methodist Cooperation and Union.

d) If the annual conference closes any local church, the failure to complete any of the prior steps will not invalidate such closure.

3. Ad Interim *Procedures*—a) At any time between sessions of annual conference, a local church may voluntarily transfer title to all its real and personal, tangible and intangible property to the annual conference board of trustees following the procedures set forth in ¶ 2540 or ¶ 2541. In such case, the annual conference board of trustees shall hold or dispose of such property in its sole discretion, subject to any standing rule of the annual conference. When it next meets, the annual conference shall decide whether to formally close the local church.

b) At any time between sessions of annual conference, if the presiding bishop, the majority of the district superintendents, and the appropriate district board of church location and building all consent, they may, in their sole discretion, declare that exigent circumstances exist that require immediate protection of the local church's property, for the benefit of the denomination. In such case, title to all the real and personal, tangible and intangible property of the local church shall immediately vest in the annual conference board of trustees who may hold or dispose of such property in its sole discretion, subject to any standing rule of the annual conference. Exigent circumstances include, but are not limited to, situations where a local church no longer serves the purpose for which it was organized or incorporated (¶¶ 201-204) or where the local church property is no longer used, kept, or maintained by its membership as a place of divine worship of The United Methodist Church. When it next meets, the annual conference shall decide whether to formally close the local church.

4. All the deeds, records, and other official and legal papers, including the contents of the cornerstone, of a closed local church shall be collected by the district superintendent and shall be deposited for permanent safekeeping with the annual conference commission on archives and history.

5. The annual conference board of trustees shall review all gifts held in trust, assets of any endowment funds, and assets of any foundation of the closed local church. The annual conference board of trustees shall dispose of the property in its discretion, unless otherwise directed by the annual conference or as required by law.

6. Any gift, legacy, devise, annuity, or other benefit that accrues to a closed local church shall become the property of the annual conference board of trustees. The annual conference board of trustees shall dispose of the property in its discretion, unless otherwise directed by the annual conference or as required by law.

7. If a local church in an urban center with more than 50,000 population is closed, any proceeds of the sale of its property must be used for new and/or existing ministries within urban transitional communities, as described in ¶ 212.

If a local church in a non-urban center is closed, any proceeds of the sale of its property may be used for new churches, new faith communities, new missional initiatives, relocating churches, churches building multi-campus facilities for the purpose of evangelistic church extension, or an organization that is a nonprofit and has values consistent with The United Methodist Church's values and is consistent with our Wesleyan heritage, theology, and United Methodist polity. In addition, the proceeds may be used to revitalize or enhance church ministry, or be given to an organization that is a vetted nonprofit and has values consistent with The United Methodist Church's values and is consistent with our Wesleyan heritage, theology, and United Methodist polity. In addition, the proceeds may be used to embrace or continue the work and vision of ministry with the poor in the community.[12]

¶ **2550.** *Board of Trustees Report to the Charge Conference*—The board of trustees shall annually make a written report to the charge conference, in which shall be included the following:

1. The legal description and the reasonable valuation of each parcel of real estate owned by the church;

2. The specific name of the grantee in each deed of conveyance of real estate to the local church;

3. An inventory and the reasonable valuation of all personal property owned by the local church;

4. The amount of income received from any income-producing property and a detailed list of expenditures in connection therewith;

5. The amount received during the year for building, rebuilding, remodeling, and improving real estate, and an itemized statement of expenditures;

6. Outstanding capital debts and how contracted;

7. A detailed statement of the insurance carried on each parcel of real estate, indicating whether restricted by co-insurance or other limiting conditions and whether adequate insurance is carried;

8. The name of the custodian of all legal papers of the local church, and where they are kept;

9. A detailed list of all trusts in which the local church is the beneficiary, specifying where and how the funds are invested, clarifying the manner in which these investments made a positive contribution toward the realization of the goals outlined in the Social Principles of the Church, and in what manner the income therefrom is expended or applied.

10. An evaluation of all church properties, including the chancel areas, to ensure accessibility to persons with disabilities; and when applicable, a plan and timeline for the development of accessible church properties.

---

12. See Judicial Council Decision 1202.

¶ 2551. *Covenant Relationships in Multi-Ethnic and Multi-Language Settings*—Ministry in The UMC tradition is about partnership and mission. In situations where a local church or churches share a building with a congregation or with another group performing ministries in different languages and/or with different racial and ethnic groups, it shall be in accordance with ¶¶ 202, 206, and 212. The district superintendent must consent to any such action before implementation. The district board of church location and building must be informed of such action.

1. If the congregations are United Methodist, the following shall apply:

a) By action of the charge conference(s) involved, a covenant relationship shall be mutually agreed upon in written form and shall include a statement of purpose for sharing the facility and shall state whether the agreement is seen as temporary, long-term, or permanent. The covenant of relationship may provide for mutual representation on such bodies as church council and other committees and work groups. The board of trustees of the church that holds title to the property may form a property committee composed of representatives of each congregation. The purpose of this arrangement is to enhance communication between the two or more congregations, to coordinate schedules and building usage, to involve the congregations in building maintenance and care under supervision of the board of trustees, and to coordinate cooperative programs.

b) The covenant relationship shall not require that a United Methodist congregation pay rent to another United Methodist church, or a United Methodist community of faith or a social ministry. The financial relationship established in the covenant is neither intended to generate profit nor to support the general budget (other than appropriate normal operating costs) of the receiving local church or any other entity involved in the sharing of the facilities.

c) Congregations that share the same facility and other properties are encouraged to organize and share intentionally in some mutual ministries to strengthen their relationships and their effectiveness when focusing on the same objectives. Cooperative programs may be developed that enhance the ministry of both congregations and their witness to the love of Jesus Christ in the community. Such programs may include joint bilingual worship services and Christian education programs, fellowship meals, and community outreach ministries.

d) Each congregation in a shared facility is strongly encouraged to accept an interdependent relationship in reference to use of the facility. Such a relationship affirms cooperatively planned and executed programs and activities as well as independently planned and executed programs and activities. Thus, scheduling programs and using the facility will be implemented in a manner that contributes to the positive growth of each congregation.

e) In situations where local congregations and/or ministries that share facilities cannot negotiate decisions that are supportive mutually by each congregation or ministry, the district superintendent shall consult with the leadership of each congregation and/or ministry prior to the implementing of any decision that may adversely affect the future of either congregation or ministry.

2. If a United Methodist church is sharing with a congregation of another denomination, the following should apply:

a) Prior to agreeing to share facilities with a congregation that is not United Methodist and is of a different ethnic or language background, the United Methodist pastor and the district superintendent shall first contact district and conference congregational development agencies and ethnic leadership to explore the possibilities of organizing as an ecumenical shared ministry or a new United Methodist congregation with that ethnic or language group.

b) If it is decided that the United Methodist congregation and the congregation of another denomination should share facilities, as a part of the covenant of mission, a property-use agreement shall be negotiated in writing in accordance with ¶ 2503; this agreement shall have the consent of the district superintendent and shall be approved by the United Methodist charge or church conference. Shared activities may be entered into to enhance the ministry of both congregations. A liaison committee to both congregations may be appointed to resolve conflicts, clear schedules, and plan cooperative activities.

3. Ninety-day notification of intent to terminate the covenant relationship shall be made to the district superintendent and to the other parties in the covenant relationship. This termination shall require the consent of the district superintendent following consultation with the parties involved.

4. The district committee on religion and race shall monitor all consultations and plans related to the transfer or use of property to ensure fairness and equity in situations involving two or more local congregations or ministries.

Section VII. Requirements—Trustees of Church Institutions

¶ 2552. *Standards and Requirements*—Trustees of schools, colleges, universities, hospitals, homes, orphanages, institutes, and other institutions owned or controlled by any annual, jurisdictional, or central conference or any agency of The United Methodist Church shall be at least twenty-one years of age. At all times, not less than three-fifths of them shall be members of a local church and/or members of an annual conference or the Council of Bishops of The United Methodist Church, and all must be nominated, confirmed, or elected by such conference or agency of the Church or by some body or officer thereof to which or to whom this power has been delegated by such conference or agency; provided that the number of trustees of any such institution owned or controlled by any annual conference or conferences required to be members of a local church and/or annual conference or the Council of Bishops of The United Methodist Church may be reduced to not less than the majority by a three-fourths vote of such annual conference or conferences; and provided further, that when an institution is owned and operated jointly with some other religious organization, said requirement that three-fifths of the trustees shall be members of a local church and/or annual conference or the Council of Bishops of The United Methodist Church shall apply only to the portion of the trustees selected by the United Methodist agency or annual, jurisdictional, or central conference. It is recognized that there are numerous educational, health-care, and charitable organizations that traditionally have been affiliated with The United Methodist Church and its predecessor denominations, which are neither owned nor controlled by any unit of the denomination.

Chapter Seven

JUDICIAL ADMINISTRATION

Section I. The Judicial Council

¶ **2601.** *Duties and Responsibilities of the Judicial Council*—The Judicial Council is the highest judicial body in The United Methodist Church. The Judicial Council shall have authority as specified in the Constitution, ¶¶ 55-57, and in ¶¶ 2609-2612.

¶ **2602.** *Members*—1. *Composition and Term*—The Judicial Council shall be composed of nine members and should reflect the diversity of The United Methodist Church, including racial, age, ethnic, gender, jurisdiction and central conferences, and congregational size. In the year 2000 and each sixteen years thereafter, there shall be elected three laypersons and two ordained clergy other than bishops. In 2004 and each eight years thereafter, there shall be elected two ordained clergy other than bishops and two laypersons. In 2008 and each sixteen years thereafter, there shall be three ordained clergy other than bishops and two laypersons. The laypersons shall be professing members of The United Methodist Church. Elections shall be held at each session of the General Conference for only the number of members whose terms expire at such session. A member's term of office shall be eight years. A member may serve a maximum of two consecutive eight-year terms, with a minimum of four years before reelection to the council.

2. *Nominations and Election*—Members of the council shall be nominated and elected in the manner following: At each quadrennial session of the General Conference, the Council of Bishops shall nominate by majority vote three times the number of ordained ministers and laypersons to be elected at such session of the General Conference. The number to be elected shall correspond to the number of members whose terms expire at the conclusion of such session. Each of the jurisdictions and the central conferences as a group shall be represented by at least one nominee, but it shall not be a requirement that each of the jurisdictions or the central conferences as a group be represented by an elected member.[1] At the same daily session at which the above nominations are announced, nominations of both ministers and laypersons

---

1. See Judicial Council Decision 540.

may be made from the floor, but at no other time. The names of all
nominees, identified with the conference to which each belongs,
and a biographical sketch that does not exceed one hundred
words shall be published by the *Daily Christian Advocate* at least
forty-eight hours prior to the time of election, which shall be set
by action of the General Conference at the session at which the
nominations are made; and from these nominations the General
Conference shall elect without discussion, by ballot and majority
vote, the necessary number of ministerial and lay members.

¶ 2603. *Alternates*—There shall be six alternates for the clergy
members and six alternates for the lay members, and their qualifications shall be the same as for membership on the Judicial Council. The term of the alternates shall be for four years.

The alternates shall be elected in the following manner: From
the clergy and lay nominees remaining on the ballot after the election of the necessary number of members of the Judicial Council
to be elected at sessions of the General Conference, the General
Conference shall by separate ballot, without discussion and by
majority vote, elect the number of clergy and lay alternates to be
chosen at such session of the General Conference.

¶ 2604. *Vacancies*—1. If a vacancy in the membership of the
council occurs during the interim between sessions of the General
Conference, a clergy vacancy shall be filled by the first-elected
clergy alternate and a lay vacancy by the first-elected lay alternate. The alternate filling such vacancy shall hold office as a member of the Judicial Council for the unexpired term of the member
whom the alternate succeeds. In the event of any vacancy, it shall
be the duty of the president and secretary of the council to notify
the alternate entitled to fill it.

2. In the event of an absence of one or more members of the
council during a session of the Judicial Council, such temporary
vacancy among the clergy members may be filled for that session
or the remainder thereof by the clergy alternates in order of election who can be present, and such temporary vacancy among the
lay members by the lay alternates in order of election who can
be present; but inability or failure to fill a vacancy does not affect
the validity or any action of the council so long as a quorum is
present.

¶ 2605. *Expiration of Term*—The term of office of the members
of the council and of the alternates shall expire upon the adjourn-

ment of the General Conference at which their successors are elected.

¶ **2606.** *Ineligibility of Members*—Members of the council shall be ineligible to serve as delegates to the General, jurisdictional, or central conference or to serve in any General, jurisdictional, or central conference board or agency.[2]

¶ **2607.** *Confidentiality and Ex Parte Communication*—1. The members of the Judicial Council will not permit discussion with them on matters pending before them or that may be referred to them for determination, save and except before the Judicial Council in session. Questions of procedure may be raised with the presiding officer or secretary of the Judicial Council. While strictly observing the intent of the preceding paragraph, a member of the council to whom a case has been assigned by the president may request that the secretary secure from persons and agencies concerned directly or indirectly with the case pertinent facts, briefs, and statements shall be sent promptly by the secretary of the council to other members of the council as is deemed necessary.[3]

2. Prior to the decision of a case in question, members of the Judicial Council shall not discuss with any party matters of substance pending in the judicial process unless all parties are privy to the discussion. Nor shall members of the Judicial Council or staff allow to be published or communicated, including electronic communications, to third parties any matters of substance pending in the judicial process.

The Judicial Council shall in all cases in which a decision or memorandum is issued set forth the specific provisions of the Constitution or the *Discipline* that provide the basis of the decision and the rationale that led to the conclusion.

¶ **2608.** *Organization and Procedure*—1. The Judicial Council shall provide its own method of organization and procedure, both with respect to hearings on appeals and petitions for declaratory decisions. All parties shall have the privilege of filing briefs and arguments and presenting evidence under such rules as the council may adopt from time to time; provided that at the time of filing, copies of such briefs are delivered to all parties of record. The complete wording in the document requesting an appeal, declaratory decision, or ruling on a question of law shall be posted on the

---

2. See Judicial Council Decision 196; and Decision 3, Interim Judicial Council.
3. See Judicial Council Decision 763.

Judicial Council website no less than thirty (30) days prior to the deadline for submitting briefs and arguments to allow for the filing of *amicus curiae* briefs. The council shall employ a part-time clerk to assist the council in all matters designated by the council as needed, but no more than an average 20 hours per week, and shall in consultation with the General Council on Finance and Administration provide an office for the clerk suitable to maintain records and conduct business as the council shall direct.

Funds for the operations of the clerk's office shall be appropriated by the General Conference. In selecting the location of the clerk's office, consideration shall be given to a location that provides visibility and reasonable accessibility to the church and parties. The council shall also give consideration to visibility and accessibility to the church and parties in selecting the places it holds sessions.

2. *Time and Place*—The council shall meet at the time and place of the meeting of the General Conference and shall continue in session until the adjournment of that body, and at least one other time in each calendar year and at such other times as it may deem appropriate, at such places as it may select from time to time. Seven members shall constitute a quorum except on questions of the constitutionality of acts of General Conference in which case a quorum shall be nine members or alternates duly seated according to the rules established by the Judicial Council. An affirmative vote of at least six members of the council shall be necessary to declare any act of the General Conference unconstitutional. On other matters, a majority vote of the entire council shall be sufficient. The council may decline to entertain an appeal or a petition for a declaratory decision in any instance in which it determines that it does not have jurisdiction to decide the matter.

¶ **2609.** *Jurisdiction and Powers*—1. The Judicial Council shall determine the constitutionality of any act of the General Conference upon an appeal by a majority of the Council of Bishops or one-fifth of the members of the General Conference.

2. The Judicial Council shall have jurisdiction to determine the constitutionality of any proposed legislation when such declaratory decision is requested by the General Conference or by the Council of Bishops.

3. The Judicial Council shall determine the constitutionality of any act of a jurisdictional or central conference upon an appeal

by a majority of the bishops of that jurisdictional or central conference or upon an appeal by one-fifth of the members of that jurisdictional or central conference.[4]

4. The Judicial Council shall hear and determine the legality of any action taken by any body created or authorized by the General Conference or any body created or authorized by a jurisdictional or central conference, upon appeal by one-third of the members thereof or upon request of the Council of Bishops or a majority of the bishops of the jurisdictional or central conference wherein the action was taken.

5. The Judicial Council shall hear and determine the legality of any action taken by any body created or authorized by a General Conference or any body created or authorized by the jurisdictional or central conference on a matter affecting an annual or a provisional annual conference, upon appeal by two-thirds of the members of the annual or provisional annual conference present and voting.

6. The Judicial Council shall pass upon and affirm, modify, or reverse the decisions of law made by bishops in central, district, annual, or jurisdictional conferences upon questions of law submitted to them in writing in the regular business of a session; and in order to facilitate such review, each bishop shall report annually in writing to the Judicial Council on forms provided by the council all the bishop's decisions of law. No such episcopal decision shall be authoritative, except in the case pending, until it has been passed upon by the Judicial Council, but thereafter it shall become the law of the Church to the extent that it is affirmed by the council. Normally, the bishop shall rule before the close of the annual conference session during which the question was submitted, but in no case later than thirty days after the close of the session. The annual conference secretary shall enter in the annual conference journal an exact statement of the question submitted and the ruling of the bishop.[5]

7. The Judicial Council shall hear and determine any appeal from a bishop's decision on a question of law made in a central, district, annual, or jurisdictional conference when said appeal has been made by one-fifth of that conference present and voting.

---

4. See Judicial Council Decision 338.
5. See Judicial Council Decisions 153, 747, 762, 763, 799, 1004, 1078, 1120, 1130, 1161, 1166, 1167, 1188.

8. The Judicial Council shall have power to review an opinion or decision of a committee on appeals of a jurisdictional or central conference if it should appear that such opinion or decision is at variance with the *Book of Discipline*, a prior decision of the Judicial Council, or an opinion or decision of a committee on appeals of another jurisdictional or central conference on a question of Church law. In the event the committee on appeals' decision appears to be at variance with the decision of another committee on appeals, then the following procedure should be followed:

a) Any party to the opinion or decision may appeal the case to the Judicial Council on the ground of such conflict of decisions; or

b) The committee on appeals rendering the last of such opinions or decisions may certify the case to, and file it with, the Judicial Council on the ground of such conflict of decisions; or

c) The attention of the president of the Judicial Council being directed to such conflict or alleged conflict of decisions, the president may issue an order directing the secretaries of the committees on appeals involved to certify a copy of a sufficient portion of the record to disclose the nature of the case and the entire opinion and decision of the committee on appeals in each case to the Judicial Council for its consideration at its next meeting.

The Judicial Council shall hear and determine the question of Church law involved but shall not pass upon the facts in either case further than is necessary to decide the question of Church law involved. After deciding the question of Church law, the Judicial Council shall cause its decision to be certified to each of the committees on appeals involved, and such committees on appeals shall take such action, if any, as may be necessary under the law as determined by the Judicial Council.

d) All opinions and decisions of jurisdictional and central conference committees on appeal shall be sent to the secretary of the Judicial Council within thirty days after a decision. These decisions shall be made available to those who are involved in trials and appeals when needed and for those preparing for trial or appeal, but not otherwise.

9. The Judicial Council shall have jurisdiction to hear and determine all appeals from decisions of the jurisdictional appeals committee.[6]

---

6. See Judicial Council decision 1276.

10. The Judicial Council shall have other duties and powers as may be conferred upon it by the General Conference.

11. All decisions of the Judicial Council shall be final. However, when the Judicial Council shall declare any act of the General Conference then in session unconstitutional, that decision shall be reported to that General Conference immediately. This legislation shall take effect immediately upon passage by the General Conference.

12. The Judicial Council shall not have the authority to grant or award compensation to cover or reimburse attorney fees to a party to an appeal in a matter of Church law.[7]

¶ **2610.** *Declaratory Decisions*—1. The Judicial Council, on petition as hereinafter provided, shall have jurisdiction to make a ruling in the nature of a declaratory decision as to the constitutionality, meaning, application, or effect of the *Discipline* or any portion thereof or of any act or legislation of a General Conference; and the decision of the Judicial Council thereon shall be as binding and effectual as a decision made by it on appeal.

2. The following bodies in The United Methodist Church are hereby authorized to make such petitions to the Judicial Council for declaratory decisions: *(a)* the General Conference; *(b)* the Council of Bishops; *(c)* any body created or authorized by the General Conference on matters relating to or affecting the work of such body; *(d)* a majority of the bishops assigned to any jurisdiction on matters relating to or affecting jurisdictions or the work therein; *(e)* a majority of the bishops assigned to any central conference on matters relating to or affecting the central conferences or the work therein; *(f)* any jurisdictional conference on matters relating to or affecting jurisdictions or jurisdictional conferences or the work therein; *(g)* any body created or authorized by the jurisdictional conference on matters relating to or affecting the work of such body; *(h)* any central conference on matters relating to or affecting central conference or the work therein; *(i)* any body authorized or created by a central conference on matters relating to or affecting the work of such body; and *(j)* any annual conference on matters relating to annual conferences or the work therein.

3. When a declaratory decision is sought, all persons or bodies who have or claim any interest that would be affected by the declaration shall be parties to the proceeding, and the petition shall

---

7. See Judicial Council Decision 1230.

name such parties. After receiving such request the secretary of the Judicial Council shall publish on the official United Methodist Internet pages a brief statement of the question involved. If the president of the council determines that other parties not named by the petition would be affected by such a decision, such additional parties shall also be added, and the petitioner or petitioners, upon direction of the secretary of the Judicial Council, shall then be required to serve all parties so joined with a copy of the petition within fifteen days after such direction by the secretary of the Judicial Council. In like manner, any interested party may, on the party's own motion, intervene and answer, plead, or interplead.

¶ **2611.** *Precedential Value*—The decisions of the Judicial Council of The Methodist Church heretofore issued shall have the same authority in The United Methodist Church as they had in The Methodist Church, persuasive as precedents, except where their basis has been changed by the terms of the Plan of Union or other revisions of Church law.

¶ **2612.** *Notification and Publication*—The decisions of the Judicial Council on questions of Church law, with a summary of the facts of the opinion, shall be filed with the secretary of the General Conference and with the bishop, chancellor, and secretary of each annual conference. Publication of decisions shall be as follows:

1. The decisions of the Judicial Council shall be posted on the official United Methodist Internet pages as soon as practicable, no later than ninety days following each meeting.

2. When the Judicial Council shall have declared unconstitutional any provision of the *Discipline*, the secretary of the Judicial Council shall notify the chairperson of the Committee on Correlation and Editorial Revision and the Editor of the *Discipline* which phrase or sentence was found to violate the Constitution so that it will not appear in the next edition. All such deletions also shall appear in the *Advance Daily Christian Advocate* or successor publication of the next General Conference for information purposes.

Section II. Investigations, Trials, and Appeals

FAIR PROCESS IN JUDICIAL PROCEEDINGS

¶ **2701.** *Preamble and Purpose*—The judicial proceedings and the rights set forth in this paragraph commence upon referral of a matter as a judicial complaint from the counsel for the Church to the committee on investigation. The judicial process terminates at the end of any appeal or right of appeal. The judicial process shall have as its purpose a just resolution of judicial complaints, in the hope that God's work of justice, reconciliation and healing may be realized in the body of Jesus Christ. The following procedures are presented for the protection of the rights of individuals guaranteed under Section III, Article IV, of our Constitution and for the protection of the Church. The presumption of innocence shall be maintained until the conclusion of the trial process. Special attention should be given to ensuring racial, ethnic, age, and gender diversity of boards, committees, and courts and the timely disposition of all matters.

1. *Rights of the Complainant (the person filing the complaint)*

   a) Right to Be Heard—In any judicial proceeding, the complainant shall have a right to be heard before any final action is taken.

   b) Right to Notice of Hearings—Notice of any hearing shall advise the complainant about proposed procedures, with sufficient detail to allow the complainant to prepare. Notice shall be given not less than twenty (20) days prior to the hearing. The complainant shall have the right to be present at any judicial process hearing.

   c) Right to Be Accompanied—The complainant shall have the right to be accompanied by another person to any interview or hearing to which they are subject. The person accompanying the complainant may be an attorney, but shall not have the right to voice. In no instance and under no circumstances shall the complainant be entitled to receive an award of compensation for or reimbursement of any expenses or fees associated with the complainant's use of an attorney.

   d) Right to Be Informed of Resolution—The complainant shall have the right to be informed of the disposition of the complaint of the judicial proceeding as part of a holistic process of healing. Church officials are encouraged, as may be permissible, to include rationale.

2. *Rights of the Respondent*

   a) Right to Be Heard—In any judicial proceeding, the respondent (the person to whom the procedure is being applied) shall have a right to be heard before any final action is taken.

b) Right to Notice of Hearings—Notice of any judicial process hearing shall advise the respondent of the reason for the proposed procedures, with sufficient detail to allow the respondent to prepare a response. Notice shall be given not less than twenty (20) days prior to the hearing. The respondent shall have the right to be present at any judicial process hearing.

c) Right to Be Accompanied—The respondent shall have a right to be accompanied by a clergyperson in full connection pursuant to ¶ 2706.2. The clergyperson accompanying the respondent shall have the right of advocacy. The respondent shall be entitled to choose one assistant counsel without voice who may be an attorney. In no instance and under no circumstances shall the respondent be entitled to receive an award of compensation for or reimbursement of any expenses or fees associated with the respondent's use of an attorney.

d) Right Against Double Jeopardy—No bill of charges shall be certified by any committee on investigation after an earlier bill of charges has been certified by a committee on investigation based on the same alleged occurrences.

e) Right of Access to Records—The respondent and the Church shall have access to all records relied upon in the determination of the outcome of the committee on investigation, trial court, or appeal committee or body.[8]

3. *Rights of the Church*

a) Right to Be Heard—In any judicial proceeding, the Church shall have the right to be heard before any final action is taken.

b) For other rights and responsibilities of the Church and counsel for the Church see ¶ 2706.

4. *Process and Procedure*

a) Failure to Appear or Respond—In the event that the respondent fails to appear for any judicial process hearing, refuses mail, refuses to communicate personally with the bishop or district superintendent, or otherwise fails to respond to requests from official judicial committees, such actions or inactions shall not be used as an excuse to avoid or delay any Church processes, and such processes may continue without the participation of such individual.

b) Communications—In any judicial proceeding, under no circumstances shall one party or counsel, in the absence of the other

---

8. See Judicial Council Decisions 691, 765.

party or counsel, discuss substantive matters with members of the pending hearing, trial, or appellate body while the case is pending. Questions of procedure may be raised and discussed ex parte, but only with the presiding officer or secretary of the hearing or appellate body.

c) Healing—As a part of the judicial process, the bishop and cabinet, in consultation with the presiding officer of the pending hearing, trial, or appellate body then sitting, shall provide for healing if there has been significant disruption to the congregation, the annual conference, or the context of ministry by the judicial matter. This may include a just resolution process for unresolved conflicts, support for victims, and reconciliation for all who are involved. This process may also include the sharing of information by the bishop or a cabinet member about the nature of the complaint without disclosing alleged facts underlying the complaint that might compromise the judicial process.

d) Immunity of Participants—In order to preserve the integrity of the Church's judicial process and ensure full participation in it at all times, the resident bishop, the cabinet, the presiding officer of the trial, trial officers, trial court, witnesses, counsels, assistant counsels, advocates, complainant, committee on investigation, and all others who participate in the Church's judicial process shall have immunity from prosecution of complaints brought against them related to their role in a particular judicial process, unless they have committed a chargeable offense in conscious and knowing bad faith. The complainant in any proceeding against any such person related to their role in a particular judicial process shall have the burden of proving, by clear and convincing evidence, that such person's actions constituted a chargeable offense committed knowingly in bad faith. The immunity set forth in this provision shall extend to civil court proceedings, to the fullest extent permissible by the civil laws.

5. *A Just Resolution in Judicial Proceedings*—A just resolution is one that focuses on repairing any harm to people and communities, achieving real accountability by making things right in so far as possible and bringing healing to all the parties. Special attention should be given to ensuring that cultural, racial, ethnic, age, and gender contexts are valued throughout the process in terms of their understandings of fairness, justice, and restoration. During the just resolution process, the parties may be assisted

by a trained, impartial third party facilitator(s) or mediator(s), in reaching an agreement satisfactory to all parties. Processes that seek a just resolution are encouraged at any time, including through the judicial proceedings. After the referral of a matter as a judicial complaint from counsel for the Church to the committee on investigation, if a process seeking a just resolution is used, the appropriate persons, including the counsel for the Church and the counsel for the respondent, should enter into a written agreement outlining such process, including any agreement on confidentiality. If resolution is achieved, a written statement of resolution, including terms and conditions, shall be signed by the same persons who signed the written agreement outlining the process, and they shall agree on any matters to be disclosed to third parties. If the resolution results in a change of ministerial status, the disclosure agreement shall not prevent the disciplinary disclosures required for possible readmission.

CHARGEABLE OFFENSES AND THE STATUTE OF LIMITATIONS

¶ **2702.** 1. A bishop, clergy member of an annual conference (¶ 370), local pastor,[9] clergy on honorable or administrative location, or diaconal minister may be tried when charged (subject to the statute of limitations in ¶ 2702.4)[10] with one or more of the following offenses: (a) immorality including but not limited to, not being celibate in singleness or not faithful in a heterosexual marriage;[11] (b) practices declared by The United Methodist Church to be incompatible with Christian teachings,[12] including but not limited to: being a self-avowed practicing homosexual; or conducting ceremonies which celebrate homosexual unions; or performing same-sex wedding ceremonies;[13] (c) crime; (d) disobedience to the order and discipline of The United Methodist Church; (e) dissemination of doctrines contrary to the established standards of doctrine of The United Methodist Church; (f) relationships and/or behavior that undermines the ministry of

---

9. See Judicial Council Decision 982.

10. The statute of limitations went into effect as law on a prospective basis starting on January 1, 1993. All alleged offenses that occurred prior to this date are time barred. See Judicial Council Decisions 691, 704, and 723.

11. The language beginning "including but not limited to . . . " first appeared in the 2004 *Book of Discipline*, effective January 1, 2005.

12. See Judicial Council Decisions 702, 984, 985, 1185.

13. The language beginning "including but not limited to . . . " first appeared in the 2004 *Book of Discipline*, effective January 1, 2005.

another pastor;[14] (g) child abuse;[15] (h) sexual abuse;[16] i) sexual misconduct[15] including the use or possession of pornography, (j) harassment, including, but not limited to racial and/or sexual harassment; (k) racial or gender discrimination; or (l) fiscal malfeasance.

2. A bishop, clergy member of an annual conference, or diaconal minister may be brought to trial when the appropriate body recommends involuntary termination.[17]

3. A professing member of a local church may be charged with the following offenses, and, if so, may choose a trial: *(a)* immorality; *(b)* crime; *(c)* disobedience to the order and discipline of The United Methodist Church; *(d)* dissemination of doctrines contrary to the established standards of doctrine of The United Methodist Church; *(e)* sexual abuse; *(f)* sexual misconduct;[18] *(g)* child abuse; *(h)* harassment, including, but not limited to racial and/or sexual harassment; *(i)* racial or gender discrimination; *(j)* relationships and/or behaviors that undermine the ministry of persons serving within an appointment; or (k) fiscal malfeasance.

4. *Statute of Limitations*—No judicial complaint or charge shall be considered for any alleged occurrence that shall not have been committed within six years immediately preceding the filing of the original complaint, except in the case of sexual or child abuse and in the case of immorality or crime, when the alleged occurrence(s) include allegations of sexual abuse or child abuse, there shall be no limitation (¶ 2704.1*a*).[15]

Time spent on leave of absence shall not be considered as part of the six years.

5. *Time of Offense*—A person shall not be charged with an offense that was not a chargeable offense at the time it is alleged to have been committed. Any charge filed shall be in the language of the *Book of Discipline* in effect at the time the offense is alleged to have occurred except in the case of immorality or crime, when the alleged occurrence(s) include allegations of sexual abuse or child abuse. Then it shall be in the language of the *Book of Discipline* in

---

14. See Judicial Council Decision 702.

15. This offense was first listed as a separate chargeable offense in the 1996 *Book of Discipline* effective April 27, 1996. See Judicial Council Decision 691.

16. See Judicial Council Decisions 736, 768

17. See Judicial Council Decision 767.

18. This offense was first listed as a separate chargeable offense in the 2000 *Book of Discipline*, effective January 1, 2001. See Judicial Council Decision 691.

effect at the time the charge was filed. Any charge must relate to an action listed as a chargeable offense in the *Discipline*.

PROCEDURES FOR REFERRAL AND INVESTIGATION OF A JUDICIAL COMPLAINT

¶ **2703.** *Composition of the Committee on Investigation*

1. *When respondent is a bishop*—There shall be a committee on investigation elected by each jurisdictional or central conference. Nominations shall be made by the College of Bishops in consultation with the jurisdictional episcopacy committee. Further nominations may be offered from the floor of the jurisdictional or central conference. The committee shall consist of seven clergy in full connection (with not more than one clergyperson from each annual conference, if possible), two lay observers, and six alternate members, five of whom shall be clergypersons in full connection (with not more than one clergyperson from each annual conference, if possible), and one of whom shall a layperson. If additional members or alternates are needed, they may be named by the College of Bishops. Committee members shall be in good standing and should be deemed of good character. The committee should reflect racial, ethnic, and gender diversity. The committee shall elect a chairperson and organize at the jurisdictional or central conference. Seven clergy or alternates seated as members of the committee shall constitute a quorum.

2. In each annual conference, there shall be a *committee on investigation* to consider judicial complaints against clergy members of the annual conference, clergy members on honorable location or administrative location from that annual conference, local pastors, and diaconal ministers. It shall consist of four clergy members in full connection, three professing members, three alternate clergy members in full connection, and six alternate lay members, three of whom shall be diaconal ministers if available within the bounds of the annual conference. The committee shall be nominated by the presiding bishop in consultation with the Board of Ordained Ministry (for clergy members) and the conference board of laity (for professing members) and elected quadrennially by the annual conference. If additional members or alternates are needed, the annual conference may elect members to serve for the remainder of the quadrennium. Committee members shall be in good standing and shall be deemed of good character. The committee should reflect racial, ethnic, and gender diversity. The

committee on investigation shall elect a chair and organize at the annual conference. None of the members or alternates shall be members of the Board of Ordained Ministry, the cabinet, or immediate family members of the above. Should a member of the committee on investigation have been a party to any of the prior proceedings in the case that finally comes before the committee, he or she shall be disqualified from sitting on the committee during its consideration of that case, and his or her place shall be taken by an alternate member. Seven members or alternates seated as members of the committee shall constitute a quorum.[19]

a) In cases of complaints against clergy members of the annual conference, clergy members on honorable location or administrative location from that annual conference, or local pastors, the committee shall consist of four clergy members and three professing members.

b) In cases of complaints against diaconal ministers, the committee shall consist of four clergy members and five professing members, two of whom shall be diaconal ministers if available within the bounds of the annual conference.

3. *When respondent is a layperson*—In all cases, the pastor or district superintendent should take pastoral steps to resolve any complaints. If such pastoral response does not result in resolution and a written complaint is made against a professing member for any of the offenses in ¶ 2702.3, the pastor in charge or co-pastors (¶ 205.1) of the local church, in consultation with the district superintendent and the district lay leader, may appoint a committee on investigation consisting of four professing members and three clergy in full connection (both clergy and professing members must come from other congregations, exclusive of the churches of the respondent or the complainant). Committee members shall be in good standing and should be deemed of good character. The committee should reflect racial, ethnic, and gender diversity. When the pastor in charge is (or co-pastors are) bringing the charge, the district superintendent, in consultation with the district lay leader, shall appoint the committee on investigation. Five members shall constitute a quorum.

¶ **2704.** *Referral of Original Complaint to Counsel for the Church, Who Shall Prepare Judicial Complaint and Supporting Material for Consideration by Committee on Investigation*

---

19. See Judicial Council Decision 1296.

1. *When respondent is a bishop*

a) *Judicial Complaint*—A complaint based on allegations that a bishop has committed one or more of the offenses listed in ¶ 2702 shall initially be served on the president and secretary of the College of Bishops. Upon receipt of the complaint the president of the College of Bishops shall forthwith deliver a copy of the complaint to the respondent bishop, notify active bishops of the existence and nature of the complaint, and refer the complaint to an elder in full connection within the same jurisdictional or central conference, who shall serve as counsel for the Church. By agreeing to serve, counsel for the Church signifies his or her willingness to uphold the requirements of Church law and the Discipline. Counsel for the Church shall represent the interests of the Church in pressing the claims of the person making the complaint. Counsel for the Church shall have the right to choose one assistant counsel without voice who may be an attorney. The counsel for the Church shall draft and sign the complaint as a judicial complaint, forward it to the jurisdictional or central conference committee on investigation (¶ 2703), and represent the Church in the judicial process. The fair process provisions in ¶ 2701 shall apply to this judicial process. The statute of limitations in ¶ 2702.4 should be considered prior to the referral of a judicial complaint.[20]

b) If a written complaint is made against a bishop for any of the offenses in ¶ 2702.1, the counsel for the Church, as appointed under ¶ 2704.1a, shall prepare, sign, and forward the judicial complaint and all documentary evidence under consideration to the chairperson of the committee on investigation, the person making the original complaint, and the bishop being charged (respondent). The respondent shall be given an opportunity to submit to the committee on investigation a written response to the judicial complaint within thirty days of receipt of the judicial complaint. The chairperson shall convene the committee on investigation within sixty days of receiving the judicial complaint.

c) If five or more members of the committee on investigation so recommend, the jurisdictional committee on the episcopacy may suspend the respondent pending the conclusion of the trial process.

---

20. The statute of limitations for bishops went into effect as law on a prospective basis on April 27, 1996. All alleged offenses that occurred prior to this date are time-barred. See Judicial Council Decisions 691, 704, and 761.

2. *When respondent is a clergy member of an annual conference, clergy on honorable or administrative location, or a local pastor*

a) *Judicial Complaint*—If the complaint is not dismissed pursuant to the provisions of ¶ 362 and if the bishop determines that the complaint is based on allegations of one or more offenses listed in ¶ 2702.1, the bishop shall refer the complaint to the counsel for the Church, who shall be appointed by the bishop. The counsel for the Church shall be a clergyperson in full connection and shall have the right to choose one assistant counsel without voice who may be an attorney. By agreeing to serve, counsel for the Church signifies his or her willingness to uphold the requirements of Church law and the *Discipline*. The counsel for the Church shall draft and sign a judicial complaint, attaching as exhibits all relevant written materials, including but not limited to information from the supervisory process and a suggested list of witnesses as deemed appropriate, forward the judicial complaint to the committee on investigation and represent the Church in the judicial process. The statute of limitations in ¶ 2702.4 should be considered prior to the referral of a judicial complaint.

b) If a written complaint is made against a clergyperson for any of the offenses in ¶ 2702.1, the bishop shall appoint a clergyperson in full connection as counsel for the Church (see ¶ 362.1e). Counsel for the Church shall prepare, sign, and refer the judicial complaint, with all relevant material, to the chairperson of the conference committee on investigation and represent the interests of the Church in pressing the claims of the person making the original complaint in any proceedings before the committee. A copy of the complaint and documentary evidence under consideration shall be sent to the respondent, the person making the original complaint, and the bishop. The respondent shall be given an opportunity to submit to the committee on investigation a written response to the judicial complaint within thirty days of receipt of the judicial complaint. The chairperson of the conference committee on investigation shall have sixty days to convene the committee on investigation after receiving the judicial complaint.

c) If five or more members of the committee on investigation so recommend, the bishop may suspend the person charged from all clergy responsibilities pending the outcome of the judicial process. The respondent retains all rights and privileges as stated in ¶ 334.

3. *When respondent is a diaconal minister*

a) If a written complaint is made against a diaconal minister for any of the offenses in ¶ 2702.1, the supervisory response should be initiated and a just resolution process may be used. (See ¶ 362.1c for a discussion of a just resolution.) If the supervisory process does not result in resolution, the respondent's district superintendent may appoint a clergyperson in full connection or diaconal minister as counsel for the Church. By agreeing to serve, counsel for the church signifies his or her willingness to uphold the requirements of Church law and the *Discipline*. Counsel for the Church shall prepare, sign, and refer the judicial complaint, with all relevant material, to the chairperson of the conference committee on investigation for diaconal ministers and represent the interests of the Church in pressing the claims of the person making the original complaint in any proceedings before the committee. A copy of the complaint and documentary evidence under consideration shall be sent to the respondent, the person making the original complaint, and the bishop. The respondent shall be given an opportunity to submit to the committee on investigation a written response to the judicial complaint within thirty days of receipt of the judicial complaint. The chairperson of the conference committee on investigation shall have sixty days to convene the committee on investigation after receiving the judicial complaint.

b) If at least two-thirds of the committee on investigation so recommend, the bishop may suspend the person charged from all professional responsibilities pending the conclusion of the trial process.

4. *When respondent is a layperson*

a) In all cases, the pastor or district superintendent should take pastoral steps to resolve any grievances or complaints. Such steps may include a just resolution process. See ¶ 362.1c for a discussion of a just resolution. If after such steps have been taken and have not resulted in a resolution and a written complaint is made against a layperson for any of the offenses in ¶ 2702.3, the pastor in charge or co-pastors (¶ 205.1) of the local church, in consultation with the district superintendent and the district lay leader, may appoint counsel for the Church, who shall be a United Methodist. By agreeing to serve, counsel for the Church signifies his or her willingness to uphold the requirements of Church law and the *Discipline*. Counsel for the Church shall prepare, sign, and refer

the judicial complaint, with all relevant material, to the chairperson of committee on investigation.

b) If five or more members of the committee so recommend, the pastor may suspend the charged professing member
from exercising any Church office pending conclusion of the trial
process.

c) All complaints against a professing member under
¶ 2702.3 shall be submitted in writing, signed by the person(s)
making the original complaint, and delivered to the pastor in
charge of the local church of which the respondent is a member,
and a copy shall be sent to the respondent.

d) The member shall be given an opportunity to submit to
the committee on investigation a written response to the judicial
complaint within thirty days of a receipt of the judicial complaint
and the appointing of the committee and before consideration of
the judicial complaint by the committee.

e) The district superintendent shall preside at all meetings of the committee, shall be given a copy of the judicial complaint and any response, and shall have the right to be present and
to speak at all meetings of the committee.

¶ **2705.** *The Form of the Judicial Complaint*—The judicial complaint shall be prepared and signed by counsel for the Church.
The complaint should explain to the committee on investigation the alleged events surrounding and relating to one or more
chargeable offense(s). All relevant documents and other exhibits
supporting the judicial complaint may be attached; and a true
copy of the complaint and reproducible documents and exhibits
shall be sent by counsel for the Church to the respondent and his
or her counsel at the same time as they are sent to the committee on investigation. The judicial complaint should include the
appropriate chargeable offense(s) based on the list in ¶ 2702 and
proposed specifications.

¶ **2706.** *Committee on Investigation—Procedures*

1. *Introduction*—The role of the committee on investigation is
to conduct an investigation into the allegations made in the judicial
complaint and to determine if reasonable grounds exist to bring
a bill of charges and specifications to trial. If so, it shall prepare,
sign and certify a bill of charges and specifications. The committee's duty is only to determine whether reasonable grounds exist
to support the charges. It is not the committee's duty to determine
guilt or innocence.

2. *Parties and Counsel*—The parties are the respondent and the Church.

a) *Counsel for the Church*—Counsel for the Church shall be appointed as provided in ¶ 2708.7. Counsel for the Church shall be entitled to choose one assistant counsel without voice who may be an attorney.

b) *Committee on Investigation*—The committee on investigation may have legal counsel present, who shall not be the conference chancellor, for the sole purpose of providing advice to the committee.

c) *When respondent is a bishop, a clergy member of an annual conference, clergy on honorable or administrative location, a local pastor, a clergyperson, or a diaconal minister*—A respondent who is a bishop, a clergyperson, or a diaconal minister shall be entitled to select a clergyperson in full connection to serve as respondent's counsel. A respondent shall be entitled to choose one assistant counsel without voice who may be an attorney. In no instance and under no circumstances shall the respondent be entitled to receive an award of compensation for or reimbursement of any expenses or fees associated with the respondent's use of an attorney.

d) *Investigation of a respondent who is a layperson*—A lay respondent shall be entitled to select a lay member or clergyperson to serve as respondent's counsel. A respondent shall be entitled to choose one assistant counsel without voice who may be an attorney. In no instance and under no circumstances shall the respondent be entitled to receive an award of compensation for or reimbursement of any expenses or fees associated with the respondent's use of an attorney.

3. *Preliminary Meeting*—Basic procedural decisions shall be made in a preliminary meeting. During this meeting, the respondent and the respondent's counsel, the person making the original complaint, and the counsel for the Church shall have the right to argue procedural points before a decision is made by the chair. All advance procedural decisions and such unanticipated decisions as may come in the course of the meeting of the committee on investigation shall be rendered in writing so as to be available for consideration in all further possible stages of the case.

4. *Hearing before the Committee on Investigation*

a) If possible, the respondent and the person(s) bringing the original complaint shall be brought face to face, but the inability to do this shall not invalidate an investigation. Notice of the hearings shall be given to all parties, and the person(s) bringing the original complaint and they all shall be permitted to be present during testimony, but not during deliberations. Proceedings in the investigation shall be informal. No oaths shall be taken. All procedural decisions shall be made by the chairperson.

b) Interview of witness prior to or outside of hearing—The chairperson shall have the power, whenever it is appropriate in the committee's own discretion, to appoint a member(s) of the committee to interview any witness(es), provided that all parties may be present (without voice) and that three days notice of the time and place of such interview shall have been given to all parties. The person(s) so appointed shall create a verbatim record of the interview and certify the record by signature for transmittal to the chairperson.

c) Examination of witnesses—The committee on investigation may call and question such persons or request such written information, including but not limited to materials from the supervisory process, as it deems necessary to establish whether or not there are reasonable grounds for formulating a charge or charges. The committee may receive from the counsels suggested lists of persons to be questioned, sources of written material or questions. There shall be no right of cross-examination by either the respondent or the person(s) bringing the original complaint.

d) Evidence—The committee should only consider testimony or evidence which is relevant and reliable. The chairperson or presiding officer, after consultation with counsel for both parties, shall rule on challenges to relevance and reliability. The introduction of any material relating to events barred by the statute of limitations (¶ 2702.4) as evidence, as preface to evidence, or as build-up for evidence in the procedures of the committee on investigation or the trial proceedings shall be permitted when the presiding officer, after consultation with counsel for both parties, rules that such material is relevant and reliable.

e) Verbatim transcript—There shall be a verbatim record of all proceedings of the committee on investigation, except when the committee meets in executive session. The term *executive session* shall mean the committee meeting alone or with its legal counsel. If the complaint is dismissed or returned to the bishop, no verbatim record need be transcribed and the record that exists will be sent to the conference secretary for retention.

5. *Bill of Charges and Specifications, Deliberations, Vote, and Referral*—A vote on each charge and each specification shall be taken separately. It is incumbent on each member of the committee to base his or her vote solely on whether reasonable grounds exist to support the charges. If there are members who are unwilling to uphold the *Discipline* for reasons of conscience or otherwise, such members must step aside in this matter and either alternate members or others who are willing to uphold the *Discipline* must be appointed to the Committee to enable it to complete its responsibility.[21]

    a) Bill of Charges and Specifications—A charge is one of the chargeable offenses listed in ¶ 2702. A charge shall not include more than one such chargeable offense. More than one charge against the same person may be presented and tried at the same time. Each charge must be written, with specifications that support the charge. Each charge must be accompanied by one or more specifications of fact. Each specification, standing alone, must allege a factual occurrence that, if found to be true, would support a finding of guilty on the related charge. The specifications should be as specific as possible with information such as date, place, and specific events alleged to have occurred.

    b) Finding of reasonable grounds by committee and referral of bill of charges and specifications for trial

    (1) *When respondent is a bishop*—A vote to adopt any charge or specification shall require five votes. Any bill of charges and specifications adopted shall be sent to the bishop charged, to the secretary of the jurisdictional or central conference, to the president and secretary of the College of Bishops, to counsel for the Church, and to the chairperson of the jurisdictional committee on the episcopacy.[22]

    (2) *When respondent is a clergyperson other than a bishop*—A vote to adopt any charge or specification shall require five votes. Any bill of charges and specifications adopted by the committee on investigations shall be sent by the chairperson within five days to the respondent, the person making the complaint, the secretary of the annual conference, the counsel for the Church, and the resident bishop.

    (3) *When respondent is a diaconal minister*—A vote to adopt any charge or specification shall require two votes. Any bill

---

21. See Judicial Council Decision 980.
22. See Judicial Council Decision 1275.

of charges and specifications adopted shall be sent to the respondent within five days, the secretary of the annual conference, the chairperson of the Board of Ordained Ministry, the respondent's district superintendent, counsel for the Church, and the resident bishop.

(4) *When respondent is a layperson*—A vote to adopt any charge or specification shall require five votes. Any bill of charges and specifications adopted by the committee shall be sent to the person charged, the recording secretary of the charge conference, counsel for the Church, the pastor(s), and the district superintendent.

c) Findings other than reasonable grounds by committee or other actions

(1) If the committee on investigation determines that there are no reasonable grounds for charges, it may dismiss the judicial complaint. When deemed appropriate, it may also refer matters of concern to the proper referring Church official (to the president or secretary of the College of Bishops in the case of bishop, to the resident bishop in the case of a clergyperson, or a diaconal minister, or to the pastor or co-pastors in the case of layperson) for administrative or other action. Notification of these actions, should be given to the respondent, the person making the original complaint, counsel for the Church and the proper referring Church officials.

(2) If the committee on investigation determines that the judicial complaint is not based upon chargeable offenses, or for other good cause, the committee may refer the complaint to the proper referring Church official (see ¶ 2706.5c[1] above) for administrative or other action. Such referral will not constitute a dismissal or double jeopardy under ¶ 2701.2d. Notification of these actions should be given to the respondent, the person making the original complaint, counsel for the Church and the proper referring Church officials.

(3) Upon recommendation of the counsel for the Church and the counsel for the respondent, the committee may refer the matter to the resident bishop as deemed appropriate for a process seeking a just resolution. The bishop shall institute such a process and may use the assistance of a trained, impartial third party facilitator(s) or mediator(s). Such referral will not constitute a dismissal or double jeopardy under ¶ 2701.2d. The appropriate persons, including the counsel for the Church and counsel for the

respondent, should enter into a written agreement outlining the process, including any agreements on confidentiality. If resolution is achieved, a written statement, affirming such resolution, including any terms and conditions, shall be signed by the same persons who signed the written agreement outlining the process, and they shall agree on any matters to be disclosed to third parties. If the resolution results in a change of ministerial status, the disclosure agreement shall not prevent the disciplinary disclosures required for readmission. The committee on investigation shall retain jurisdiction for the period of time stated for the implementation of the resolution agreement. The committee shall periodically monitor the progress of the completion of the terms and conditions of the resolution agreement, and shall certify when the terms and conditions of the agreement are completed. When the terms and conditions of the agreement are completed, the committee on investigation shall report its certification, and the status of the respondent as a result of completing the terms and conditions of the resolution agreement, to the resident bishop. If the process does not result in resolution, the matter shall be returned to the committee on investigation for further consideration. Also, decision(s) of a trial court that call for certification as to the completion of terms and conditions of the trial court's decision(s) after the end of a trial are to be assigned to the committee on investigation for monitoring and certification of completion of the decision. If the respondent fails to complete the terms and conditions of a trial court decision, the committee shall notify the presiding officer of the trial, who may reconvene the trial court for its further consideration.

6. *Special Investigations*—In the event that jurisdiction in a judicial proceeding is ended as a result of the death of, or surrender of credentials by, the respondent in cases where the chargeable offense includes those listed in ¶ 2702.1(h), (i), or (j), the committee on investigation may be convened at the request of the presiding bishop to make pastoral inquiry into the charges. The inquiry shall:

    (a) not be judicial in nature;

    (b) be empowered to receive witnesses and to consider evidence; and

    (c) make a report of the inquiry to the body where the respondent's membership was held, including recommendations if any.

7. *Records of the Committee on Investigation*—At the conclusion of the investigation process, all documents used by the committee on investigation, including transcriptions of its hearings, shall be sent to the secretary of the annual conference, the jurisdictional or central conference in the case of a bishop, who shall keep them in custody. Such documents are to be held in a confidential file and shall not be released except for the purposes of trial and then only to counsels for the Church and the respondent and to the presiding officer of the trial court who shall return them to the secretary of the annual, jurisdictional, or central conference following the conclusion of the trial and any appeal.

TRIALS

¶ **2707.** *Fundamental Principles for Trials*—Church trials are to be regarded as an expedient of last resort. Only after every reasonable effort has been made to correct any wrong and adjust any existing difficulty should steps be taken to institute a trial. No such trial as herein provided shall be construed to deprive the respondent or the Church of legal civil rights, except to the extent that immunity is provided as in ¶ 2701.4d. All trials shall be conducted according to the *Book of Discipline* in a consistent Christian manner by a properly constituted court after due investigation.

¶ **2708.** *General Organization and Pre-Trial Procedures*

1. *Officers of the Court*—Officers shall consist of a presiding officer (see ¶¶ 2712.2, 2713.2, 2714.2), who shall appoint a secretary and such other officers as deemed necessary. The presiding officer may have legal counsel, who shall not be the conference chancellor, at the expense of the annual conference holding the trial, for the sole purpose of advice to the presiding officer during the trial.

2. *Time and Place of Trial*—The official charged with convening the trial shall also fix the time and place for the trial and will notify the presiding officer, the respondent, counsel for the Church and the person making the original complaint. In all cases, sufficient time shall be allowed for these persons to appear at the given place and time and for the respondent to prepare for the trial. The presiding officer shall decide what constitutes "sufficient time," but in no case shall this time be less than twenty days.

3. *Pre-Trial Motions and Referrals*—All appeals of any procedural or substantive matters that have occurred prior to referral of the charges to trial must be appealed to the presiding officer

of the trial court before the convening of the trial. Otherwise, the right to appeal on such matters is forfeited. All objections to and motions regarding the regularity of the proceedings and the form and substance of charges and specifications must be made before the convening of the trial court. The presiding officer may determine all such preliminary objections and motions; in furtherance of truth and justice may permit amendments to the specifications or charges not changing the general nature of the same; and may dismiss all or any part of the bill of charges upon a finding by the presiding officer (1) that all or such part is without legal or factual basis or (2) that, even assuming the specifications to be true, they do not constitute a basis for a chargeable offense. The presiding officer may refer the matter as deemed appropriate for a process seeking a just resolution to the resident bishop upon consultation with the counsel for the Church and counsel for the respondent. The bishop shall institute such a process and may use the assistance of a trained, impartial third party facilitator(s) or mediator(s). Such referral will not constitute a dismissal or double jeopardy under ¶ 2701.2*d*. If a process seeking a just resolution is used, the appropriate persons, including the counsel for the Church and counsel for the respondent, should enter into a written agreement outlining such process, including any agreement on confidentiality. If resolution is achieved, a written statement, affirming such resolution, and any terms and condition, shall be signed by the same persons who signed the written agreement outlining the process, and they shall agree on all matters to be disclosed to third parties. Such a written statement shall be given to the presiding officer and the presiding officer shall take action consistent with the agreement. If no resolution results, the matter is returned to the presiding officer for further action.

4. *Change of Venue*—The respondent may request a change of venue. This shall be a written request to the presiding officer of the court within ten days of receipt of notice to appear for trial. The presiding officer shall rule upon the request after hearing arguments by the respondent and the Church. If the motion is approved, the presiding officer shall name the annual conference outside the episcopal area wherein the trial shall be held and shall notify the resident bishop of that conference, who shall convene the court. The cost of prosecution shall be borne by the conference where the case originated.

5. *Notice*

　　a) All notices required or provided for in relationship to investigations, trials, and appeals shall be in writing, signed by or on behalf of the person or body giving or required to give such notice, and shall be addressed to the person or body to whom it is required to be given. Such notices shall be served by delivering a copy thereof to the party or chief officer of the body to whom it is addressed in person or sent by other delivery system to the last-known residence or address of such party. Proof of notice shall be provided and becomes a part of the record of the case.

　　b) In all cases wherein it is provided that notice shall be given to a bishop or district superintendent and the charges are against that particular person, then such notice (in addition to being given to the accused) shall be given, in the case of a bishop, to another bishop within the same jurisdiction and, in the case of a district superintendent, to the bishop in charge.

　　6. *Trial Scheduling and Continuances*—If in any case the respondent, after due notice (twenty days) has been given, shall refuse or neglect to appear at the time and place set forth for the hearing, the trial may proceed in the respondent's absence. However, if in the sole discretion of the presiding officer there is good and sufficient reason for the absence of the respondent or another essential person, the presiding officer may reschedule the trial to a later date.

　　7. *Counsel*—In all cases, a respondent shall be entitled to appear and to select and be represented by counsel, a clergyperson in full connection of The United Methodist Church if the respondent is a bishop, a clergyperson, or a diaconal minister; and a lay or clergy member of The United Methodist Church if the respondent is a lay member. The respondent and the Church shall be entitled to have counsel heard in oral or written argument or both. The official charged with convening the court (see ¶¶ 2712.1, 2713.1, 2714.1) shall, within thirty days after receiving a copy of the charges and specifications, appoint counsel for the Church, if counsel has not been previously appointed. In the case of a trial of a bishop, clergyperson, or local pastor, counsel for the Church shall be a clergyperson in full connection (¶¶ 2704.2*a*, 2712.4) to represent the interests of the Church in pressing the claims of the person making the complaint.

　　No person who was a member of the cabinet, Board of Ordained Ministry, or committee on investigation who earlier considered the case now before the trial court shall be appointed counsel for the Church or serve as counsel for the respondent or any of the persons bringing complaints in a case. In all cases of trial where counsel has not been chosen by the respondent, counsel shall be appointed by the presiding officer. The counsel for the Church and for the respondent each shall be entitled to choose one assistant counsel, who may be an attorney, without voice. "Without voice" means without the ability to speak to or within the hearing of the trial court. In no instance and under no circumstances shall the respondent be entitled to receive an award of compensation for or reimbursement of any expenses or fees associated with the respondent's use of an attorney.

8. *Witnesses*—Notice to appear shall be given to such witnesses as either party may name and shall be issued in the name of the Church and be signed by the presiding officer of the trial. It shall be the duty of all clergy and lay members of The United Methodist Church to appear and testify when summoned. Refusal to appear or to answer questions ruled by the presiding officer to be relevant may be considered as disobedience to the order and discipline of The United Methodist Church except when refusal to answer is based on a good faith claim that answering might tend to incriminate the witness under state or federal criminal law or is based on a claim of confidential communication to a clergyperson under ¶ 341.5.

9. *Witness Qualifications*—A witness, to be qualified, need not be a member of The United Methodist Church.

10. *Commissioned Out-of-Court Testimony*—The presiding officer of any court before which a case may be pending shall have power, whenever the necessity of the parties or witnesses shall require, to appoint, on the application of either party, a commissioner or commissioners, either a clergy or a layperson or both, to examine the witnesses; provided that three days' notice of the time and place of taking such testimony shall have been given to the adverse party. The party making this request shall have the burden of showing good cause and shall bear the cost of such commissioned out-of-court testimony. Counsel for both parties shall be permitted to examine and cross-examine the witness or witnesses whose testimony is thus taken. The commissioners so appointed shall take such testimony in writing as may be offered by either party. The testimony properly certified by the signature of the commissioner or commissioners shall be transmit-

ted to the presiding officer of the court before which the case is pending.

11. *Amendments to Bill of Charges and Specifications*—After consultation with counsels, the presiding officer of the trial may make amendments to the bill of charges, or request that the committee on investigation make amendments to the bill of charges; provided that they do not change the nature of the charges and specifications and do not introduce new matter of which the respondent has not had due notice. When an amendment or amendments to a bill of charges is or are denied by the presiding officer, it or they shall not be introduced in the form of testimony in the trial. Charges or specifications previously considered and dropped by the committee on investigation shall not be introduced in the trial in the form of evidence or otherwise.

12. *Open or Closed Trials*—The deliberations of the trial court shall be closed. All other sessions of the trial shall be open. The presiding officer may, in extenuating circumstances, in his or her judgment on motion of counsel for either party or on the presiding officer's own motion, declare a particular session of the court to be closed. At all times, however, in the hearing portion of the trial, the presiding officer, the members of the trial court, the person(s) making the original complaint, the person representing the Church as well as counsel for the Church, the respondent, and counsel for the respondent shall have a right to be present.

13. *Combined Trials of Multiple Persons*—In cases in which a number of persons have allegedly engaged in the same offense at the same time and place, their trials may be combined into one trial for that same offense. The presiding officer shall make the determination on combination of trials.

¶ **2709.** *Trial Convening and Organization*

1. *Convening of the Trial*—The convenor shall notify the respondent in writing to appear at a fixed time and place no less than twenty days after service of such notice and within a reasonable time thereafter for selection of the members of the trial court.

2. *Trial Pool*—At the appointed time, in the presence of the respondent, counsel for the respondent, counsel for the Church, and the presiding officer, thirteen persons shall be selected as a trial court out of a pool of thirty-five or more persons selected according to ¶¶ 2712.3, 2713.3, and 2714.3. Special consideration should be given so that the pool includes persons representative of racial, ethnic, and gender diversity.

3. *Selection of the Trial Court*—No person shall serve as a member of the trial court who was a member of the cabinet, Board of Ordained Ministry, or committee on investigation who considered the case in the process of coming to trial court. The counsel for the Church and the respondent shall each have up to four peremptory challenges and challenges for cause without limit. If by reason of challenges for cause being sustained the number is reduced to below thirteen, additional appropriate persons shall be nominated in like manner as was the original panel to take the places of the numbers challenged, who likewise shall be subject to challenge for cause. This method of procedure shall be followed until a trial court of thirteen members and two alternate members has been selected.

4. *Alternates*—The two alternate members shall sit as observers of the trial. They shall replace members of the trial court who are not able to continue to serve, so that the trial court shall always consist of thirteen members, unless the respondent and counsel for the Church agree to a lesser number.

5. *Trial Court Questions*—The members of the trial court, including the alternate members, may, subject to the approval of the presiding officer of the court, ask questions on matters on which evidence has been presented.

¶ **2710.** *Trial Guidelines and Rules*

1. *Authority of Presiding Officer*—After the trial is convened the authority of the presiding officer shall include the right to set reasonable time limits, after consultation with counsel for the Church and counsel for the person charged, for the presentation of the case, provided such time is equal for both. The authority of the presiding officer shall be limited to ruling upon proper representation of the Church and the person charged, admissibility of evidence, recessing, adjourning, and reconvening sessions of the trial, charging the members of the trial court as to the Church law involved in the case at the beginning of the trial and just before they retire to make up their verdict, and such other authority as is normally vested in a civil court judge sitting with a jury, but he or she shall not have authority to pronounce any judgment in favor of or against the person charged other than such verdict as may be returned by the trial court, which body shall have the exclusive right to determine the innocence or guilt of the person charged.

2. *Order of Trial*—After selection of the trial court, each counsel may make an opening statement to inform the trial court of

what the evidence is expected to be. Evidence shall then be offered by questioning of witnesses and by documents shown to be reliable. Each counsel shall have opportunity to make closing arguments before the trial court begins deliberations. Deliberations of the trial court and receiving of the verdict shall follow.

3. *Oaths*—The administration of oaths shall not be required. At the beginning of the trial, the presiding officer shall remind all parties of the duties and responsibilities of Church membership (¶ 218) and/or the clergy covenant (¶¶ 304.2 and 330.5*c*[3]).

4. *Entering of the Plea*—At the beginning of the trial, the respondent shall be called upon by the presiding officer to plead to the charge, and the pleas shall be recorded. If the respondent pleads "guilty" to the charges preferred, no trial shall be necessary, but evidence may be taken with respect to the appropriate penalty, which shall thereupon be imposed. If the respondent pleads "not guilty" or if the respondent should neglect or refuse to plead, the plea of "not guilty" shall be entered, and the trial shall proceed. The respondent shall at all times during the trial, except as hereinafter provided, have the right to produce testimony and that of witnesses and to make defense.

5. *Recess and Trial Procedures*—The court may recess from time to time as convenience or necessity may require. During the time of recess, the members of the trial court shall be instructed that under no circumstance will they speak to one another or to others about the trial or observe media reports regarding the case. When, in consultation with counsel for both parties, the presiding officer finds it advisable, the members and reserves shall be sequestered. Threatening or tampering with the trial court or officers of the trial court shall be considered disobedience to the order and discipline of The United Methodist Church. The presiding officer shall remain and preside until the decision is rendered and the findings are completed and shall thereupon sign and certify them.

6. *Objections and Rulings*—Objections of any party to the proceedings shall be entered on the record. All rulings on pre-trial appeals, objections, and motions shall be entered on the record. All objections and motions from counsels during the proceedings of the trial shall be made in open session before the trial court and entered on the record along with the rulings of the presiding officer on all such objections and motions.

7. *Exclusion of Witnesses*—With the exception of the complainant and respondent, no witness to be examined shall be present

during the examination of another witness if the opposing party objects. Witnesses shall be examined first by the party producing them, then cross-examined by the opposite party and may be questioned by members of the trial court, with the approval of the presiding officer. The presiding officer of the court shall determine all questions of relevancy and competency of evidence.

8. *Recording of Proceedings*—A verbatim record of all proceedings of the trial shall be by stenograph or other appropriate means and reduced to writing and certified by the presiding officer or secretary. The record, including all exhibits, papers and evidence in the case, shall be the basis of any appeal that may be taken.

9. *Evidence*—The introduction of any material relating to events happening before the six-year statute of limitation period as evidence, as preface to evidence, or as build-up for evidence in the procedures of the trial proceedings may be permitted when the presiding officer, after consultation with counsel for both parties, rules that such material is relevant and reliable. Documentary evidence deemed by the presiding officer to be relevant and reliable may be in the physical possession of the trial court during deliberations.

10. *Instructions and Charges*—The presiding officer shall not deliver a charge reviewing or explaining the evidence or setting forth the merits of the case. The presiding officer shall express no opinion on the law or the facts while the court is deliberating. If requested by either party's counsel, the presiding officer shall instruct the trial court on Church law applicable to the case. Instructions may be given at the beginning of the trial, during the trial, before the trial court begins deliberations or a combination of any of these. If requested by the trial court, instructions may be given during deliberations. The presiding officer shall not review or explain the evidence or comment on the merits of the case.

¶ **2711.** *Power of the Trial Court*

1. *Instruction, Disqualification, Voting, and Verdicts*—The trial court shall have full power to try the respondent. The trial court shall be a continuing body until the final disposition of the charge. If any regular or alternate member of the trial court fails to attend any part of any session at which evidence is received or oral argument is made to the trial court by counsel, that person shall not thereafter be a member of the trial court, but the rest of the trial court may proceed to judgment.

2. *Votes*—It shall require a vote of at least nine members of the trial court to sustain the charge(s) and nine votes also shall be required for conviction. Fewer than nine votes for conviction shall be considered an acquittal. The burden of proof for a vote to convict shall be clear and convincing. The trial court shall present to the presiding officer a decision on each charge and each individual specification under each charge. Its findings shall be final, subject to appeal to the committee on appeals of the jurisdictional conference or the central conference, as the case may be.

3. *Penalties—If the Trial Results in Conviction.*—Further testimony may be heard and arguments by counsel presented regarding what the penalty should be. The trial court shall determine the penalty, which shall require a vote of at least seven members. The trial court shall have the power to remove the respondent from professing membership, terminate the conference membership, and revoke the credentials of conference membership, commissioning, ordination, or consecration of the respondent, suspend the respondent from the exercise of the functions of office, or to fix a lesser penalty. The penalty fixed by the trial court shall take effect immediately unless otherwise indicated by the trial court. Should any penalty fixed by a trial court be altered or reduced as a result of the appellate process, the respondent shall be restored and/ or compensated as appropriate, provided that in no instance and under no circumstances shall the respondent be entitled to receive an award of compensation for or reimbursement of any expenses or fees associated with the respondent's use of an attorney.[23]

¶ 2712. *Trial of a Bishop*

1. The president of the College of Bishops of the jurisdictional or central conference—or in case the person charged is the president, the secretary of the college—shall proceed to convene the court under the provisions of ¶ 2709.

2. The president of the College of Bishops (or in the case the person charged is the president, the secretary) may preside or designate another bishop to serve as presiding officer.

3. The trial shall be convened as provided in ¶ 2709 with the pool of thirty-five or more persons to consist of clergy in full connection named by the College of Bishops in approximately equal numbers from each episcopal area within the jurisdictional or central conference. Special consideration should be given so that the

---

23. See Judicial Council Decision 1201.

pool includes persons representative of racial, age, ethnic, and gender diversity.

4. Counsel for the Church shall be a bishop or another clergyperson in full connection.

5. The secretary of the court shall at the conclusion of the proceedings send all trial documents to the secretary of the jurisdictional or central conference, who shall keep them in custody. If an appeal is taken, the secretary shall forward the materials forthwith to the secretary of the Judicial Council. After the appeal has been heard, the records shall be returned to the secretary of the jurisdictional or central conference.

6. A bishop suspended from office shall have claim on the Episcopal Fund for salary, dwelling, pension, and other related benefits. A bishop removed from office shall have no claim upon the Episcopal Fund for salary, dwelling, pension and other related benefits from the date of such removal.

¶ **2713.** *Trial of a Clergy Member of an Annual Conference, Local Pastor, Clergy on Honorable or Administrative Location, or Diaconal Minister*

1. The resident bishop of the respondent shall proceed to convene the court under the provisions of ¶ 2709.

2. The resident bishop shall designate another bishop to be presiding officer.

3. *a)* The trial for a clergy member or a local pastor shall be convened as provided in ¶ 2709 with the pool of thirty-five or more persons to consist of clergy in full connection. If there are not enough persons in appropriate categories in an annual conference to complete the pool, additional persons may be appointed from other annual conferences. All appointments to the pool shall be made by the district superintendents. Special consideration should be given so that the pool includes persons representative of racial, age, ethnic, and gender diversity.

b) The trial for a diaconal minister shall be convened as provided in ¶ 2709 and shall consist of a pool of thirty-five or more persons who shall be diaconal ministers or, when necessary, members of the Church. Special consideration should be given so that the pool includes persons representative of racial, ethnic, and gender diversity.

4. Counsel for the Church shall be a clergyperson in full connection.

5. The secretary of the court shall at the conclusion of the proceedings send all trial documents to the secretary of the annual conference, who shall keep them in custody. Such documents are to be held in a confidential file and shall not be released for other than appeal or new trial purposes without a signed release from both the clergyperson charged and the presiding officer of the trial that tried the case. If an appeal is taken, the secretary shall forward the materials forthwith to the president of the court of appeals of the jurisdictional or central conference. If a president has not been elected, the secretary shall send the materials to such members of the court of appeals as the president of the College of Bishops shall designate. After the appeal has been heard, the records shall be returned to the secretary of the annual conference unless a further appeal on a question of law has been made to the Judicial Council, in which case the relevant documents shall be forwarded to the secretary of that body.[24]

¶ **2714.** *Trial of Lay Member of a Local Church*

1. The district superintendent of the person charged shall proceed to convene the court under the provisions of ¶ 2709.

2. The district superintendent may be the presiding officer or may designate another clergyperson in full connection to preside.

3. The trial shall be convened as provided in ¶ 2709, with the pool of thirty-five or more persons to consist of professing members of local churches other than the local church of the charged layperson within the same district. Appointments to the pool shall be made by the district superintendent, who may consult with the district lay leader. Special consideration should be given so that the pool includes persons representative of racial, age, ethnic, and gender diversity.

4. Counsel for the Church shall be a professing member or clergyperson of The United Methodist Church.

5. The person charged may request a change of venue. This shall be a written request to the officers of the court within ten days of receipt of notice to appear for trial. The presiding officer shall rule upon the request after hearing argument for the defense and the Church. If the motion is approved, the presiding officer shall name another district wherein the trial shall be held and shall notify the district superintendent, who shall convene the court. The thirty-five-member pool shall consist of professing

---

24. See Judicial Council Decisions 751, 1201, 1250.

members from that district. The cost of prosecution shall be borne by the annual conference.

6. If the trial court finds that the charges are proven by clear and convincing evidence, then it may impose such penalties as it may determine, including that the professing membership of the charged layperson in The United Methodist Church be terminated; provided that the trial court shall first consider other remedies that would fulfill the provisions of ¶ 221.

7. The appropriate officer of the trial shall, at the conclusion of the proceeding, deposit all trial documents with the secretary of the charge conference. If an appeal is taken, the secretary shall deliver all documents to the district superintendent. After the appeal has been heard, the records shall be returned to the custody of the secretary of the charge conference.

APPEALS

¶ 2715. *Appeal Procedures—General*

1. In all cases of appeal, the appellant shall within thirty days give written notice of appeal and at the same time shall furnish to the officer receiving such notice (¶¶ 2716.2, 2717.1, 2718.2) and to the counsel a written statement of the grounds of the appeal, and the hearing in the appellate body shall be limited to the grounds set forth in such statement.[25]

2. When any appellate body shall reverse in whole or in part the findings of a committee on investigation or trial court, or remand the case for a new hearing or trial, or change the penalty imposed by the trial court, it shall return to the convening officer a statement of the grounds of its action.

3. An appeal shall not be allowed in any case in which the respondent has failed or refused to be present in person or by counsel at the investigation and the trial. Appeals shall be heard by the proper appellate body unless it shall appear to the said body that the appellant has forfeited the right to appeal by misconduct, such as refusal to abide by the findings of the trial court; or by withdrawal from the Church; or by failure to appear in person or by counsel to prosecute the appeal; or, prior to the final decision on appeal from conviction, by resorting to suit in the civil courts against the complainant or any of the parties connected with the ecclesiastical court in which the appellant was tried.[26]

---

25. See Judicial Council Memorandum 826.
26. See Judicial Council Decision 3.

4. The right of appeal, when once forfeited by neglect or otherwise, cannot be revived by any subsequent appellate body.

5. The right to prosecute an appeal shall not be affected by the death of the person entitled to such right. Heirs or legal representatives may prosecute such appeal as the appellant would be entitled to do if living.

6. The records and documents of the trial, including the evidence, and these only, shall be used in the hearing of any appeal.

7. The appellate body shall determine two questions only: (*a*) Does the weight of the evidence sustain the charge or charges? (*b*) Were there such errors of Church law as to vitiate the verdict and/or the penalty? These questions shall be determined by the records of the trial and the argument of counsel for the Church and for the respondent. The appellate body shall in no case hear witnesses. It may have legal counsel present, who shall not be the conference chancellor for the conference from which the appeal is taken, for the sole purpose of providing advice to the appellate body.

8. In all cases where an appeal is made and admitted by the appellate committee, after the charges, findings, and evidence have been read and the arguments conclude, the parties shall withdraw, and the appellate committee shall consider and decide the case. It may reverse in whole or in part the findings of the committee on investigation or the trial court, or it may remand the case for a new trial to determine verdict and/or penalty. It may determine what penalty, not higher than that affixed at the hearing or trial, may be imposed. If it neither reverses in whole or in part the judgment of the trial court, nor remands the case for a new trial, nor modifies the penalty, that judgment shall stand. The appellate committee shall not reverse the judgment nor remand the case for a new hearing or trial on account of errors plainly not affecting the result. All decisions of the appellate committee shall require a majority vote.

9. In all cases, the right to present evidence shall be exhausted when the case has been heard once on its merits in the proper court, but questions of Church law may be carried on appeal, step by step, to the Judicial Council.

10. The Church shall have no right of appeal from findings of the trial court. In regard to cases where there is an investigation under ¶ 2702, but no trial is held, egregious errors of Church

law or administration may be appealed to the jurisdictional committee on appeals by counsel for the Church. The committee on investigation's decision not to certify a bill of charges does not alone constitute an egregious error of Church law or administration. When the committee on appeals shall find egregious errors of Church law or administration under this part, it may remand the case for a new hearing, in which event it shall return to the chair of the committee on investigation a statement of the grounds of its action. This is not to be double jeopardy.[27]

11. Questions of procedure may be raised with the presiding officer or secretary of the appellate body. Under no circumstances shall one party in the absence of the other party discuss substantive matters with members of any appellate body while the case is pending (cf. ¶¶ 2607, 2701.4).

12. In all matters of judicial administration, the rights, duties, and responsibilities of clergy members and diaconal ministers of missionary conferences and provisional annual conferences are the same as those in annual conferences, and the procedure is the same.

13. Contacts with members of any appellate body shall be limited to matters of procedure and shall be directed only to the presiding officer or secretary of the appellate body. Under no circumstances shall matters of substance be discussed.

¶ 2716. *Appeal of a Bishop, Clergy Member of an Annual Conference, Clergy on Honorable or Administrative Location, Local Pastor, or Diaconal Minister*

1. Each jurisdictional and central conference, upon nomination of the College of Bishops, shall elect a committee on appeals composed of four clergy, one diaconal minister, one full-time local pastor, and three laypersons who have been at least six years successively members of The United Methodist Church, and an equal number of corresponding alternates. This committee shall serve until its successors have been elected. No member shall participate in the hearing of an appeal who is a member of a conference in the episcopal area of the appellant. Any vacancy shall be filled by the College of Bishops.

The committee on appeals shall have full power to hear and determine appeals of bishops, clergy members, clergy members on honorable or administrative location, local pastors, and dia-

---

27. See Judicial Council Decision 985.

conal ministers from any annual conference, provisional or missionary conference within the jurisdiction or central conference. The committee shall elect its own president and secretary and shall adopt its own rules of procedure, and its decisions shall be final, except that an appeal may be taken to the Judicial Council only upon questions of law related to procedures of the jurisdictional committee on appeals, central conference committee on appeals, or under the provisions of ¶ 2609.8. A bishop designated by the College of Bishops shall convene the committee at the site of jurisdictional or central conference for the purpose of electing officers.

2. In case of conviction by a trial court, a bishop, clergy member, local pastor, clergy on honorable or administrative location, or diaconal minister shall have the right of appeal to the jurisdictional or central conference committee on appeals above constituted, provided that within thirty days after the conviction, the appellant shall notify the presiding bishop of the conference (or, when the appellant is a bishop, the president and secretary of the College of Bishops) and the presiding officer of the court in writing of the intention to appeal.

3. When notice of an appeal has been given to the presiding officer of the court, the presiding officer shall give notice of the same to the secretary of the committee on appeals of the jurisdictional or central conference and submit the documents in the case, or in case the documents have been sent to the secretary of the annual conference, instruct the secretary to send the documents to the president of the committee on appeals. The jurisdictional or central conference committee on appeals shall within thirty days give notice to the presiding bishop of the conference from which the appeal is taken (or to the president and secretary of the College of Bishops when the appellant is a bishop) and to the appellant of the time and place where the appeal will be heard. Such hearing shall occur within 180 days following receipt of notice to the committee on appeals. Both the annual conference, missionary conference, or provisional conference and the appellant may be represented by counsel as specified in ¶ 2708.7. The presiding bishop of the conference or, in the appeal of a bishop, the president or secretary of the College of Bishops, shall appoint counsel for the Church.

4. All necessary traveling and sustenance expense incurred by the committee on appeals, including any cost for legal coun-

sel retained to advise the committee, in the hearing of an appeal case coming from an annual conference and appearing before any jurisdictional or central conference committee on appeals, shall be paid out of the administrative fund of the central or jurisdictional conference in which the proceedings arise. The president of the committee on appeals shall approve all expenses. Expenses for counsel for the Church shall be paid by the annual conference. Such expenses for counsel for the respondent shall be paid by the respondent, unless in the interest of fairness, the committee on appeals orders the annual conference or jurisdictional conference to reimburse the respondent.

¶ 2717. *Appeal of a Lay Member*

1. A lay member convicted by a trial court shall have the right of appeal and shall serve written notice of appeal with the pastor and the district superintendent within thirty days of conviction.

2. The district superintendent shall, on receipt of notice of appeal, give written notice to all concerned of the time and place of the convening of a committee on appeals not less than ten nor more than thirty days after such notice has been delivered.

3. The committee on appeals shall be constituted in the following manner: The district superintendent shall appoint eleven professing members of United Methodist churches within the annual conference other than the appellant's local church, none of whom shall have been members of the trial court, and who hold office either as lay leader or lay member of the annual conference. At the convening of the committee on appeals, from seven to eleven of these shall be selected to serve on the committee. The counsel for the appellant and the counsel for the Church shall have the right to challenge for cause, and the decisions on the validity of such challenges shall be made by the presiding officer, who shall be the district superintendent.

4. The findings of the committee on appeals shall be certified by the district superintendent to the pastor of the church of which the accused is a member.

¶ 2718. *Other Appeals*

1. The order of appeals on questions of law shall be as follows: from the decision of the district superintendent presiding in the charge or district conference to the bishop presiding in the annual conference, and from the decision of the bishop presiding in the annual conference to the Judicial Council, and from a central conference to the Judicial Council.

2. When an appeal is taken on a question of law, written notice of the same shall be served on the secretary of the body in which the decision has been rendered. It shall be the secretary's duty to see that an exact statement of the question submitted and the ruling of the chair thereon shall be entered on the journal. The secretary shall then make and certify a copy of the question and ruling and transmit the same to the secretary of the body to which the appeal is taken. The secretary who thus receives said certified copy shall present the same in open conference and as soon as practicable lay it before the presiding officer for a ruling thereon, which ruling must be rendered before the final adjournment of that body, that said ruling together with the original question and ruling may be entered on the journal of that conference. The same course shall be followed in all subsequent appeals.

3. The order of appeals on questions of procedures in an administrative process shall be as follows: from the decision of the conference relations committee to the administrative review committee who has original jurisdiction over the administrative matter, and from the administrative review committee to the central conference or jurisdictional appeals committee in which the appellant holds membership, and from the jurisdictional appeals committee to the Judicial Council.

4. When an appeal is made on questions of procedure in an administrative process:

a) In all cases of appeal, the appellant shall within thirty days give written notice of appeal and at the same time furnish to the officer receiving such notice a written statement of the grounds of appeal, and the hearing in the appellate body shall be limited to the grounds set forth in such statement.

b) The appellant body shall return to the convening officer of the administrative hearing and to the appellant a written statement of the grounds of its action.

c) An appeal shall not be allowed in any case in which the respondent has failed or refused to be present in person or by counsel during the administrative hearing. Appeals shall be heard by the proper appellate body unless it shall appear to the said body that the appellant has forfeited the right to appeal by misconduct; by withdrawal from the Church; by failure to appear in person or by counsel to prosecute the appeal; or, prior to the final decision on appeal by resorting to suit in the civil courts against any of the parties connected with the ecclesiastical administrative process.

d) The right to appeal, when once forfeited by neglect or otherwise, cannot be revived by any subsequent appellate body.

e) The right to prosecute an appeal shall not be affected by the death of the person entitled to such right. Heirs of legal representatives may prosecute such appeal as the appellant would be entitled to do if living.

f) The records and documents of the administrative process, including any evidence, and these only, shall be used in the hearing of any appeal.

g) The appellate body shall determine one question only: Were there such errors of Church law as to vitiate the recommendation and/or action of the administrative body? This question shall be determined by the records of the administrative process and the arguments of the official representatives of all parties. The appellate body shall in no case hear witnesses. It may have legal counsel present for the sole purpose of providing advice to the appellate body.

h) If the appellate body determines that any error has occurred, it may recommend to the appropriate person or body that action be taken promptly to remedy the error, decide the error is harmless, or take other action. The appellate committee shall not reverse the judgment nor remand the case for a new hearing on account of error plainly not affecting the result. All decisions of the appellate committee shall require a majority vote.

i) In all cases, the right to present evidence shall be exhausted when the case has been heard once on its merits in the proper administrative hearing body, but questions on Church law may be carried on appeal, step by step, to the Judicial Council.

j) Questions of procedure may be raised with the presiding officer or secretary of the appellate body. Under no circumstances shall one party in the absence of the other party discuss substantive matters with members of any appellate body while the case is pending.

k) Contacts with members of any appellate body shall be limited to matters of procedure and shall be directed only to the presiding officer or secretary of the appellate body. Under no circumstance shall matters of substance be discussed.

MISCELLANEOUS PROVISIONS

¶ **2719.** 1. Any clergy members residing beyond the bounds of the conference in which membership is held shall be subject to the procedures of ¶¶ 2701-2718 exercised by the appropriate officers of the conference in which he or she is a member, unless the presiding bishops of the two annual conferences and the clergy member subject to the procedures agree that fairness will be better served by having the procedures carried out by the appropriate officers of the annual conference in which he or she is serving under appointment, or if retired, currently residing.

2. When a bishop, clergy member, local pastor, or diaconal minister is the respondent to a complaint under ¶ 362.1*e* and desires to withdraw from the Church, the jurisdictional or central conference in the case of a bishop, the annual conference in the case of a clergy member, or the district conference (where there is no district conference, the charge conference) in the case of a local pastor or diaconal minister will ask him or her to surrender his or her credentials and will remove his or her name from professing membership; in which case the record shall be "Withdrawn under complaints" or "withdrawn under charges," whichever is appropriate.

3. When a professing member of the Church is charged with an offense and desires to withdraw from the Church, the charge conference may permit such member to withdraw his or her name from the roll of professing members, in which case the record shall be "Withdrawn under complaints." If formal charges have been presented, such member may be permitted to withdraw, in which case the record shall be "Withdrawn under charges."

4. In all matters of judicial administration, the rights, duties, and responsibilities of clergy members, local pastors, clergy on honorable or administrative location, and diaconal ministers of missions, missionary conferences, and provisional annual conferences are the same as those in annual conferences, and the procedure is the same.

5. For procedural purposes, the judicial process shall be governed by the *Discipline* in effect on the date a complaint is forwarded to the counsel for the Church.

INDEX

The numbers, unless otherwise indicated, refer to paragraphs (¶) and to subparagraphs. Subparagraphs are indicated by the numerals and/or letters following the decimal points.

C

annual conference boundaries fixed by, ¶¶ 40 *Article IV*, 543.8

annual and provisional annual conference membership of, ¶¶ 29 *Article II*, 541

authorization, ¶ 540

bishops
in retired relation, ¶ 548
number of, ¶ 31.2 *Article IV*
term expiration, ¶ 411

boundaries, ¶¶ 28 *Article I*, 38 *Article II*

composition of, ¶ 541

historical recordkeeping, ¶ 572.1

language and translation, ¶ 543.17

lay delegate election to, ¶ 36 *Article V*

meetings of, ¶ 30 *Article III*

membership on general program boards, ¶ 705.4c

negotiation with Protestant bodies, ¶ 543.21

names, ¶ 540

numbers of, ¶ 28 *Article I*

organization of, ¶ 542

powers and duties of, ¶¶ 31 *Article*, 542.5, 543

presiding officer role, ¶ 542.4

property, ¶ 546

provisional conference becoming a central conference, ¶ 540.4

records and archives of, ¶ 545

rules of procedure for investigation and trial, ¶ 543.12

standards of character for lay members ¶543.9

territory divisions, ¶ 543.20

witness ministries, ¶ 547.5

women's work, committee on, ¶ 547.1

See also **Provisional Central Conferences;** *specific central conferences*

certificate of baptism. *See* **baptism**

certificate of honorable location. *See* **honorable location**

certified candidate for licensing or ordination. *See* **Board of Ordained Ministry, conference**

certified lay minister, ¶ 268

certified lay missioner, ¶¶ 237, 269

certified lay servant, ¶ 266

certified lay speaker, ¶ 267

chancellor of conference,
annual conference membership, ¶ 602.10
associate chancellor(s), ¶ 603.8
committee on investigation ¶ 2706.2b
nomination and election, ¶ 603.8

chaplains,
annual conference membership, ¶ 602.1e
continuing education, ¶ 1421.4a
military student candidate programs, ¶ 1421.5d

Chaplains Supplemental Pension Grant Fund, ¶ 1421.5o

charge conference, ¶ 12 *Article V*, 43 *Article I*, 246 - 251
authority and local laws, ¶ 2529
church council chairperson election, ¶ 251.3
church historian election, ¶ 247.5
church membership records, ¶ 231
church officer elections, ¶ 44 *Article II*
co-chairs ¶ 249.8
committee on records and history, ¶ 247.5b
duties of leaders and members, ¶ 251
election of leaders, ¶ 249
general provisions, ¶ 246
honorary members, ¶ 246.3
joint, ¶ 246.10
lay leader of, ¶ 251.1
meeting
fixing time and place, ¶ 246.4

consultation,
bishop assignment, ¶¶ 406, 407
General Council on Finance and
Administration service to
general agencies, ¶ 807.13
with Higher Education and
Ministry, General Board,
¶ 1418
superintendency appointment-
making, ¶ 426
of University Senate, ¶ 1418.3

consumerism, social principles,
¶ 163D

consumption, social principles,
¶ 163D

continuing education,
Board of Ordained Ministry
setting standards and guidelines, ¶ 334.2d, 635.2o
clergy, ¶¶ 258.2g5, 349.1, 350
church secretaries, ¶ 807.18
district superintendent,
¶ 669.4a,e
extension ministry, ¶ 337.3c3
General Board of Higher Education and Ministry responsibility for, ¶1421.4a
Ministerial Education Fund use,
¶ 816
spiritual growth leaves,
¶ 350.2&3
pastor-parish relations committee responsibilities,
¶¶ 258.2g(5)&(8)

**conveyances, conformance with
local law,** ¶ 2508

conviction, of crime,
candidacy, ¶ 310.2b(1)
license for pastoral ministry,
¶ 315.6a(1)
ordained clergy from other
denominations, ¶ 346.2
provisional membership,
¶ 324.12

cooperative ecumenical parish,
¶ 206.3c3

cooperative parish, ¶¶ 205.2, 206
appointment to, ¶ 428.5b
board of trustees, ¶ 2528

coordinators,
annual conference
Board of Discipleship, ¶ 630.1i
Board of Global Ministries,
¶ 633.4b
disaster response, annual
conference, ¶ 633.4b(22)
district
for witness ministries, ¶ 661
jurisdiction
United Methodist Men ministry coordinators, ¶ 537
youth ministries, ¶ 533
local church
age-level, family and specialized-ministries, ¶ 253
children's ministries, ¶ 256.2a
health-and-welfare ministries,
¶ 255(2)
small-group, ¶ 255(1)
specialized ministry groups,
¶¶ 253–257
youth ministries, ¶ 256.3a,
scouting, training for ¶ 2302.5a

corporate governance. *See* **legal
responsibilities and corporate
governance committee**

corporate responsibility, social
principles, ¶ 163I

corruption, social principles,
¶ 163L

Council of Bishops, ¶¶ 47 *Article
III*, 422
Act of Covenanting, ¶ 573.2
bishop assignment in another
jurisdiction, ¶ 49 *Article V*
central conferences episcopal
visit assignments, ¶¶ 542.3,
567
concordat agreements, ¶ 574.1
ecumenical relationships,
¶ 431.2
officer, ¶ 906.1c

Curriculum Resources Committee, ¶¶ 1121, 1123, 1124
membership, ¶ 1126.1
secretary participation in, ¶ 1126.1c
education responsibilities and standards, ¶ 1109
ethnic local church concerns, ¶ 1118
evangelism, ¶¶ 1111, 1112
fiduciary functions, ¶ 1101.3
financial support, ¶ 1106
foundation guidance, ¶ 1114.6
incorporation, ¶ 1104
laity ministry, ¶ 1116
members, ¶¶ 705.3a, 1101.4, 1105.1
central conference membership, ¶¶ 705.1c, 1105.1b
episcopal members, ¶ 1105.1c
jurisdictional members, ¶ 1105.1a
liaison representative, ¶ 1105.2
Ministries With Young People, Division, ¶¶ 1105.1d, 1205
nominations and election of members, ¶ 705
mission education program, ¶ 1110.2
Ministries With Young People, Division, ¶¶ 1201–1212
See also **Ministries With Young People, Division**
organization, ¶ 1105
personnel policy and practices committee, ¶ 805.4b
purpose, ¶ 1101
responsibilities, ¶ 1102
ritual of the United Methodist Church, ¶ 1113.4
spiritual formation responsibilities, ¶ 1115
stewardship responsibilities, ¶ 1114
United Methodist Publishing House, relationship with, ¶ 1124

Upper Room, financial relationship with, ¶ 1107
worship responsibilities, ¶ 1113

Discipline. *See **Book of Discipline***

discrimination,
gender chargeable offense, ¶ 2702.1k&3i
inclusiveness denying, ¶ 140
social principles, ¶ 162A-J
See also **racial discrimination**

dismissal, of members and employees authorized by General Conference, ¶ 711

disposal schedule, for records, ¶ 1711.3b

disposition of property of a closed church, ¶ 2549

distribution system, of United Methodist Publishing House, ¶ 1641

district board of church location and building, ¶¶ 2518-2524
appeals of decisions of, ¶ 2522
authorization and establishment of, ¶ 2519
district parsonage, ¶¶ 2518.1, 2523
duties and responsibilities, ¶ 2520
membership, ¶¶ 2518.2, 2519
role in assessment of local church potential, ¶ 213.3b
sale, transfer, lease or mortgage of district property, ¶ 2524
standards for approval of building proposals, ¶ 2521

district committee on lay servant ministries, ¶ 668

district committee on ordained ministry, ¶ 666
amenability, ¶ 666.1
candidacy, ¶¶ 659.3, 666.3-8
lay ministers, ¶ 666.11
local pastor, ¶ 666.6-10

clergy from other annual conferences and Methodist denominations, ¶ 346.1
clergy from other denominations, ¶ 346.2
cabinet priority, ¶ 211
connectional responsibilities,
¶ 210
covenanting, ¶ 209
definition, ¶ 208

editor. *See* **Church School Publications editor**

**editorial director, of general pub-
lishing,** ¶ 1628
See also **United Methodist Publishing House, book editor**

education,
social principles, ¶ 164E

elders, ¶¶ 32 *Article I,* 139, 332–344
admission requirements, ¶¶ 324,
335, 336
annual conference membership,
¶¶ 32 *Article I,* 304.4, 369.1,
602.1
annual conference voting rights,
¶¶ 334.1, 602.1a
appointment, ¶¶ 337–344
availability for appointment,
¶ 333.1
ecumenical shared ministries,
¶ 345
extension ministry appointments, ¶¶ 337.3, 343-344
itineracy, ¶ 338
limited itineracy, ¶ 338.2a
security of, ¶¶ 334.1, 337.1
support for, ¶ 342
to attend school, ¶¶ 338.4,
416.6
base compensation, ¶ 342.1
changes in conference relationship, ¶¶ 352–360
administrative location,
¶ 359.2
honorable location, ¶ 358
See also **honorable location**
involuntary leave, ¶¶ 354, 363

maternity or paternity leave,
¶ 355
medical leave, ¶¶ 356, 652
provisions for change, ¶ 352
retirement, ¶ 357
appointment, ¶ 357.6
charge conference member-
ship, ¶ 357.5
involuntary, ¶¶ 357.3, 363
mandatory, ¶ 357.1
return to effective relationship, ¶ 357.7
voluntary, ¶ 357.2
voluntary leave of absence,
¶ 353
family leave, ¶ 353.2b
personal leave. ¶ 353.2a
transitional leave, ¶ 353.2c
withdrawal, ¶ 360
between annual confer-
ences, ¶ 360.4
from ministerial office,
¶ 360.2
to unite with another de-
nomination, ¶ 360.1
withdrawal under complaint
or charges, ¶ 360.3
chargeable offenses, ¶ 2702.1
complaint procedures, ¶ 362
continuing education and spiritual growth, ¶¶ 334.2d, 350
definition of pastor, ¶ 339
evaluation, ¶ 349
executive (clergy) session
membership, ¶¶ 334.1, 369.5,
602.1a
from other denominations,
¶ 346.2
from other annual conferences
and other Methodist denominations, ¶ 346.1
General Conference legislative
power, ¶ 16.2 *Article IV*
ministry, authority and responsibilities, ¶¶ 332, 334, 340
orders, ¶¶ 305–309
changing orders, ¶¶ 309.2&3
elders, ¶ 306
membership, ¶ 309

annual conference funding,
¶ 614.1*c*
membership, ¶ 638.2
responsibility, ¶ 638.4

episcopal residences, jointly owned, ¶ 2514

episcopal supervision, ¶¶ 45
Article I – 54 Article X

equal opportunity employment policies, ¶ 807.12

Equitable Compensation, Commission on. *See* **annual conference agencies**

Equitable Compensation Fund,
¶¶ 342.1&2, 622
apportionment distribution,
¶ 621
budgeting for, ¶¶ 614.1*e*, 625.7
disbursal, ¶ 625.8
membership, ¶ 625.1
proportional payment and distribution, ¶ 622
purpose, ¶ 625.2
responsibilities, ¶ 625.3-13
short-term emergency subsidy grant, ¶ 624
utilization, ¶ 625.6

Equitable Compensation of The United Methodist Church, National Association of Ethnic Commissions on, ¶ 807.18

Ethnic In-Service Training Program, ¶¶ 263.3*c*, 824.4*b*

ethnic local church concerns,
¶ 1118
conference committee, ¶ 632

Ethnic Scholarship Program,
¶¶ 263.3*b*, 824.4*b*

Ethnicity rights, social principles,
¶ 162*A*

evaluation,
of bishops, ¶¶ 412, 524.3*a*

for continuing formation for full members and local pastors,
¶¶ 349-351
of deacons, ¶¶ 331.3, 349-351

Evangelical United Brethren Church,
Confession of Faith, ¶ 104

evangelism, General Board of Discipleship. *See* **Discipleship, General Board of**

evangelist, general, ¶ 1112.7

executive session. *See* **clergy session**

exhorters, ¶ 16.2 *Articles IV*

experience, ¶ 105

extension ministries. *See* **clergy**

F

fair process, ¶ 361
administrative hearings, ¶ 361.2
before administrative location,
¶¶ 359.2, 636
before involuntary leave of absence, ¶¶ 354.1, 353.11
before involuntary retirement,
¶¶ 353.11, 357.3
conference administrative review committee, ¶ 636
involuntary retirement,
¶¶ 357.3, 636
judicial proceedings, ¶ 2701
communications, ¶ 2701.4*b*
Discipline in effect on date complaint filed, ¶ 2719.5
double jeopardy, ¶ 2701.2*d*
failure to appear or respond,
¶ 2701.4*a*
healing, ¶ 2701.4*c*
hearing notice, ¶ 2701.1*b*
just resolution, ¶ 2701.5
immunity of participants,
¶ 2701.4*d*
process and procedure,
¶ 2701.4
record access, ¶ 2701.2*e*

rights of the church, ¶ 2701.3

rights of the complainant, ¶ 2701.1

rights of the respondent, ¶ 2701.2

right to be heard, ¶ 2701.1*a*&3*a*

provisional member right to, ¶ 327.6

recommendations for clergy involuntary status change, ¶ 363

unresolved issues related to request for medical leave, ¶ 356.4

fair trade, social principles, ¶¶ 162*Q,* 163*D*

Faith and Order, Committee, ¶¶ 443–450

funding, ¶ 450

membership, ¶ 447

organization, ¶ 448

purpose, ¶ 444

responsibilities, ¶ 445

staffing, ¶ 449

faith, good works and, ¶ 102

faithful ministry, ¶ 130

family, social principles, ¶ 161*B*

family farms, social principles, ¶ 163*H*

Family Life Committee, ¶ 1119.4

family ministries, ¶ 1119.4

family violence and abuse, social principles, ¶ 161*H*

federated church, ¶ 208*(a)*

deeding property to, ¶ 2548

Fellowship of Local Pastors ¶ 323

chair of, on Ordained Ministry Board, ¶ 635.1*a*

function, ¶ 323.1

General Board of Higher Education and Ministry

constituent contact through gatherings of, ¶ 1421.6

standards of ministry maintenance, ¶ 1421.4*h*

support and accountability, ¶ 1421.4*c*

membership requirement, ¶ 323

organization of, ¶ 323.2

fellowships, ¶ 703.12

finance, social principles, ¶ 163*J*

Finance and Administration, Conference Council, ¶¶ 611-619

administrative budget, ¶ 614.2

amenability, ¶ 612.6

apportionments, ¶ 615

apportionment distribution, ¶¶ 614.3, 621–622

apportionment formula, ¶ 613.3

other apportioned causes, ¶ 614.4

auditing, ¶ 617

bonding, ¶ 618

clergy support budgets, ¶ 614.1

conference benevolences budgets, ¶ 614.3

conference treasurer/director of administrative services, ¶ 619

Council on Finance and Administration authority over, ¶¶ 613.11, 619.3

election, ¶ 619

ex officio member of Council on Finance and Administration, ¶¶ 258.4, 612.2*c*

functions, ¶ 619.1

presence at Cabinet meetings, ¶ 619.2

responsibilities, ¶ 619.2

conflict of interest, ¶ 612.4

depository, ¶ 616

ex officio members, ¶ 612.2c

equitable compensation, ¶ 625.7

membership, ¶ 612.2

minimum clergy compensation recommendation, ¶ 625.7

officers, ¶ 612.3

"self-avowed practicing,"
¶¶ 304.3, 2702.1*b*
social principles, ¶ 161*G*

honorable location, ¶ 358
appointment *ad interim*, ¶ 358.2
Board of Ordained Ministry
recommendations, ¶ 635.2*l*
chargeable offense, ¶ 2702.1
judicial complaint against,
¶ 2704.2
membership in annual conference, ¶ 358.2
readmission, ¶¶ 365, 635.2*l*
retirement, ¶ 358.3

hospice care, social principles,
¶ 161*N*

housing allowance,
bishops on sabbatical leave,
¶ 410.3
local church, ¶¶ 247.19,
258.2*g(16)*, 627

housing for bishops. *See* **bishops**

housing for pastors. *See* **pastors**

Human Relations Day, ¶¶ 262,
263.1, 824.1, 1806.12

Human Relations Day Fund,
¶ 810.1

human rights, social principles,
¶ 164*A*

human sexuality, social principles, ¶ 161*G*

hymnals,
*Come, Let Us Worship: The
Korean-English United Method-
ist Hymnal*, ¶ 1113.3
*Mil Voces Para Celebrar: Himnario
Metodista*, ¶ 1113.3
United Methodist Hymnal,
¶¶ 630.4*b*, 1113.3

I

*Iglesia Metodista Autonóma Af-
filiada de Puerto Rico,*
¶ 705.4*f&g*

Iliff School of Theology, ¶ 1422.3

immigrant rights, social principles, ¶ 162*H*

**immunity from prosecution of
complaints,** ¶ 361.3

**immunity of participants, and
fair process in judicial proceedings,** ¶ 2701.4*d*

inclusiveness, ¶¶ 4 *Article IV*, 124,
140
annual conference membership,
¶¶ 605.3, 610.5
Archives and History, General
Commission, ¶ 1704.2
audit review committee, annual
conference, ¶ 617.4
board of church and society, annual conference, ¶ 629.2
Communication, General Commission, ¶ 1807.1*f*
Constitution, ¶ 4 *Article IV*
district conference, ¶ 659.1
district superintendents, ¶¶ 417,
419.1
election of bishops, ¶ 405.2*a*
episcopacy, conference committee, ¶ 637.3*f*
equitable compensation commission, ¶ 625.1
General Conference, ¶ 502.1*a*
local church tasks and, ¶¶ 243(6),
244.3
older-adult ministry council, annual conference, ¶ 651.2
pastor's responsibilities and,
¶ 340.2*c(4)*
religion and race, conference
commission annual confer-
ence, ¶¶ 643.3*b-d*
Status and Role of Women, General Commission, ¶¶ 2102,
2103.9
United Methodist Men, General
Commission, ¶ 2303.1*f*
young-adult ministry council,
annual conference, ¶ 650.2

information communication technology, social principles, ¶ 162*T*

information technology, in local church, ¶ 245

insignia of The United Methodist Church, ¶ 807.10

institutions,
annual conference auditing of funds, ¶ 617.2
definition of annual conference institutions, ¶ 614.3*c*
elder appointment to, ¶ 344.1*a(3)*
employment of ordained minister, ¶ 343.2
General Board of Higher Education oversight and responsibilities, ¶¶ 1404, 1405.16-19, 1410, 1412
General Conference responsibility, ¶ 16.14 *Article IV*
jurisdictional conference responsibility, ¶ 27.1 *Article V*
Ministerial Education Fund distribution to theological schools, ¶ 816.2*a*
nondiscrimination policies, ¶ 716
promotion of financial support for educational institutions, ¶ 1413.2&3
socially responsible investments, ¶ 717
submission of employment inclusiveness and nondiscrimination and purchase policies to General Council on Finance and Administration, ¶ 811.1
trustees of church institutions requirements, ¶ 2552
United Methodist Committee on Relief assist in clarification of relationships, ¶ 1315.1
United Methodist Higher Education Foundation, ¶ 1419
University Senate responsibilities, ¶¶ 1414-1418

interdenominational agencies,
Committee on Family Life and, ¶ 1119.4
Communication, General Commission and, ¶ 1806.4
Discipleship, General Board responsibility, ¶ 1102.8

Interdenominational Cooperation Fund, ¶ 814
annual conference treasurer's remittance of, ¶¶ 619.1*a(5)*, 808.1
Communication, General Commission marketing, ¶¶ 814.7, 1806.12
funding for, ¶¶ 432, 434.2*b&3b*, 806.1*b*
General Council on Finance and Administration support from, ¶ 805.6*a(2)*
as general fund, ¶¶ 810.1, 814

interdenominational local church mergers, ¶¶ 209, 2547, 2548

Interjurisdictional Committee on Episcopacy, ¶ 512

International Court of Justice, ¶ 165*D*

Internet, social principles, ¶ 162*T*

investigation, committee on, ¶¶ 2703, 2706
bill of charges and specifications, ¶ 2706.5
certification of trial decision(s), ¶ 2706.5*c(2)*
composition for a bishop, ¶ 2703.1
composition for clergy, ¶ 2703.2
composition for diaconal minister, ¶ 2703.3
composition for layperson, ¶ 2703.4
evidence, ¶ 2706.4*d*
hearing before, ¶ 2706.4
implementation of resolution agreement, ¶ 2706.5*c(2)*
introduction and role of, ¶ 2706.1

Program Council of The United Methodist Church, ¶ 902

Program of Religious Activities with Youth (P.R.A.Y.) program, ¶¶ 226.4&5, 256.4

property, ¶¶ 2501-2552
annual conference,
  auditing of church officers, ¶ 2511
  authority, ¶ 2512.3
  bonding of church officers, ¶ 2511
  camps, conference grounds, and retreat centers, ¶ 2516
  civil actions regarding, ¶ 2509
  compliance with law, ¶¶ 2506-2510
  conference trustees, ¶ 2512.1
  decisions *ad interim,* ¶ 2515
  deeds and conveyances conformity, ¶ 2508
  jointly owned episcopal residences, ¶ 2514
  meetings, ¶ 2512.2
  responsibilities related to health and welfare institutions, ¶ 2517
  sale, transfer, lease, mortgage, or purchase, ¶ 2515
  United Methodist Foundations, ¶ 2513
district, ¶¶ 2518-2524
  appeals, ¶ 2522
  audits and bonding of church officers, ¶ 2511
  authorization and establishment of district Boards of Church Location and Building, ¶ 2519
  boundaries of, and sales, parsonage, ¶ 2518.3
  building proposal approval, ¶ 2521
  duties and responsibilities of district Boards of Church Location and Building, ¶ 2520

financial obligations limitation, ¶ 2510
local church building sites and plans, ¶ 2520.1
local laws, ¶¶ 2506, 2508
parsonage and boards of trustees, ¶ 2518
Plan of Union, ¶ 2504
sale, transfer, lease, or mortgage, ¶ 2524
standards to acquisition, ¶ 2523
standards for approval of building proposals, ¶ 2521
trust clause requirement, ¶¶ 2501, 2503
local church, ¶¶ 2536–2551
  consecration and dedication of buildings, ¶ 2545
  deeding, to federated churches or other evangelical denominations, ¶ 2548
  disposition of building or parsonage, ¶ 2542
  disposition property of a closed church, ¶ 2549
  effect of union on property titles, ¶ 2504
  incorporated, ¶¶ 2538-2539, 2541
    notice and authorization, ¶ 2539
    sale, transfer, lease, and mortgage, ¶ 2541
    title and purchase, ¶ 2538
  mortgage of building or parsonage, ¶ 2542
  parsonage. *See* **parsonage**
  planning and finance requirements of, ¶ 2544
  proceeds of mortgage or sale restrictions, ¶ 2543
  shared facilities, ¶ 2551
  trust clause requirement, ¶¶ 2501, 2503
  unincorporated, ¶¶ 2536-2537, 2540
    notice and authorization, ¶ 2537

sale, transfer, lease, and
mortgage, ¶ 2540
title and purchase, ¶ 2536

property titles in Constitution,
¶¶ 7 *Article VII*, 2504

provisional annual conferences,
¶¶ 580-583
clergy members of, ¶ 581.1
definition, ¶ 580
elections to General and jurisdictional conferences, ¶ 582.4
financial support, ¶ 581.2
Global Ministries Board,
¶¶ 582.1, 583
location of annual meeting,
¶ 582.2
meeting, ¶ 582.2
organization, ¶ 582
progress of, ¶ 581.3
provisions, ¶ 581
superintendent, ¶ 582.1

provisional central conferences,
¶¶ 560-567
ad interim provisions, ¶ 563
ad interim provisions for conferences outside United States,
¶ 565
authorization, ¶ 560
episcopal supervision, ¶ 566
episcopal visitation of mission
fields, ¶ 567
lay membership, ¶ 564
organization, ¶ 561
powers of, ¶ 562

provisional membership, ¶¶ 324-
327
academic credentials and,
¶ 635.2a
annual conference membership,
¶¶ 32 *Article I*, 370
annual conference transfer and,
¶ 604.5&7
bishop appointment of, ¶¶ 326,
425.1
change in conference relationship, ¶ 352

involuntary leave of absence,
¶ 354
maternity or paternity leave,
¶ 355
medical leave, ¶ 356
See also **Board of Ordained
Ministry, conference** *and/
or* **clergy**
chargeable offenses, ¶ 2702.1
commissioning, ¶ 325
complaints ¶ 362.1
complaint procedures and,
¶ 362
discontinuance from, ¶ 327.6
district committee recommendation for, ¶ 666.9
eligibility and rights of, ¶ 327
local pastors, ¶¶ 315.1, 324.6
mission annual meeting and,
¶ 591.6
missionary conference and,
¶ 586.4g
qualifications and requirements
for election to, ¶ 324
readmission to, ¶ 364
responsibilities, ¶ 316.1
retirement restriction, ¶¶ 320.5,
327.7
service of, ¶ 326

public indebtedness, social principles, ¶ 163M

Publication, General Board,
¶ 1608

purgatory, ¶ 104 *Article XIV*

Q

quadrennium, ¶ 721.2

questions of law decisions,
appeals, ¶ 2718
bishop, ¶¶ 51 *Article VII*, 419.10,
542.4
Judicial Council, ¶¶ 2609.6&7

quorum,
Archives and History, General
Commission meetings, ¶ 1705
for charge conference, ¶ 246.6

salaries,
annual conference pastors,
¶ 604.13
associate members, ¶ 321.3
bishops, ¶ 818.4
leave of absence and, ¶ 410
recommendation responsibility for, ¶ 818.2(1)
under special assignment,
¶¶ 406.3, 408.1d
Church School Publications editor, ¶ 1634
clergy from other annual conferences or Methodist denominations, ¶ 346.1
clergy from other denominations, ¶ 346.2
clergy salary, local church obligation to pay, ¶ 624
deacon, ¶ 331.10b
nonsalaried positions,
¶ 331.6d&10d
Finance and Administration,
General Council and,
¶¶ 807.12, 818.2(1)
involuntary leave and, ¶ 354.6
local church, ¶ 252.4d
proportional payment, ¶ 639.4
pensions, ¶ 639.4a
suspension and, ¶¶ 362.1d,
2704.2c
theological school faculty and
staff, ¶ 816.2a
United Methodist Publishing
House corporate officers,
¶ 1623
voluntary leave and, ¶ 353.6

salvation, ¶¶ 102 *(p. 49)*, 104 *Article V (p. 66)*

sanctification, ¶¶ 102 *(p. 53)*, 104
(p. 72), Article XI (p. 75)

**Schools and Colleges of The
United Methodist Church, National Association of,** ¶ 1414.2

**schools of theology of United
Methodist Church,** ¶¶ 1422-
1423

in central conferences, ¶ 1422.4
Board of Ordained Ministry
recommendation to, ¶ 635.2a
deacon or elder candidates attending, ¶ 1422.2
education of ordination candidates, ¶ 1423
extension ministry appointments to, ¶ 344.1a(3)
globally, ¶ 1422.5
goals, ¶ 1422.1
in United States, ¶ 1422.3
mission education emphasis,
¶ 1314.3e
Native American Ministries
Sunday scholarships,
¶¶ 263.6c, 824.6

science and technology, social
principles, ¶ 160F

Scouting Ministries, ¶¶ 256.4,
2302.5b

Scripture, ¶ 105

seminaries,
certification, ¶ 1421.3b
United Methodist
Americans With Disabilities
Act, ¶ 140
candidates encouraged to attend, ¶ 310.2f,
General Board of Higher Education and Ministry,
¶ 1421.1e
jurisdictional boards of ordained ministry, ¶ 535
United Methodist Schools of
Theology in USA, ¶ 1422.3

servant leadership, ¶¶ 133-134,
138-139

servant ministry, ¶¶ 133-137

Service Loans, ¶¶ 816.1a&b

sexual abuse,
judicial complaint, ¶ 2702.1h
social principles, ¶ 161I

sexual assault, social principles,
¶ 161P